The Cloud Security Ecosystem

The Cloud Security Ecosystem
Technical, Legal, Business and Management Issues

Edited by

Ryan Ko

Kim-Kwang Raymond Choo

AMSTERDAM • BOSTON • HEIDELBERG • LONDON
NEW YORK • OXFORD • PARIS • SAN DIEGO
SAN FRANCISCO • SINGAPORE • SYDNEY • TOKYO

Syngress is an Imprint of Elsevier

SYNGRESS.

Acquiring Editor: Chris Katsaropoulos
Editorial Project Manager: Benjamin Rearick
Project Manager: Priya Kumaraguruparan
Designer: Matthew Limbert

Syngress is an imprint of Elsevier
225 Wyman Street, Waltham, MA 02451, USA

Library of Congress Cataloging-in-Publication Data
A catalog record for this book is available from the Library of Congress

British Library Cataloguing in Publication Data
A catalogue record for this book is available from the British Library

ISBN: 978-0-12-801595-7

For information on all Syngress publications
visit our website at http://store.elsevier.com/

Working together
to grow libraries in
developing countries

www.elsevier.com • www.bookaid.org

Soli Deo Gloria

Contents

Contributors xix
Foreword xxiii
Preface xxv
About the Authors xxvii
List of Reviewers.. xxxvii
Acknowledgments xxxix

CHAPTER 1   Cloud security ecosystem 1
   1 How It All Started—The Story of an Online Bookstore..............1
   2 Consolidation of Terminologies and Perspectives.......................2
      2.1 Perspective 1: Essential Characteristics...............................2
      2.2 Perspective 2: Layers and Scope..3
   3 The Achilles' Heel—Depending on a Trust Relationship.............4
      3.1 Case Study 1: Breach of Trust by a Public Cloud
          System Administrator..5
      3.2 Case Study 2: Liability of a Liquidated Cloud Business 5
      3.3 Gatekeepers—Governments Versus Technology Creators.....6
   4 Top Threats and Vulnerabilities of Cloud Security......................6
      4.1 Cloud Security Alliance's Top Threats to Cloud
          Computing Research..7
      4.2 Statistics of Common Vulnerabilities Faced by Cloud
          Service Providers...8
   5 Managing Cloud Security Risks with the Deming Cycle............10
   6 Plan—Threats, Risk, and Requirements Landscape....................11
   7 Do—Cloud Security Approaches and Challenges.......................12
   8 Check—Forensics and Incident Response 13
   9 Act—Governance and Auditing...13
  10 Summary...13
      References...14

PART 1 PLAN: THREATS, RISK, AND REQUIREMENTS LANDSCAPE

CHAPTER 2   Cybercrime in cloud: Risks and responses in Hong Kong, Singapore.................................17
   1 Introduction..17
      1.1 Definition of Cloud Computing 17
      1.2 Growth in Cloud Computing: Hong Kong and Singapore ... 18

2 Key factors shaping "Response": Hong Kong, Singapore 22
  2.1 Hong Kong...22
  2.2 Singapore 25
3 Discussion...28
  References..34

**CHAPTER 3 CATRA: Conceptual cloud attack taxonomy
and risk assessment framework** **37**

1 Introduction...37
2 Taxonomies: A literature survey 38
  2.1 Taxonomy Characteristics 38
  2.2 Attack Taxonomy Classifiers 38
  2.3 Attack Taxonomies...40
  2.4 Literature Gaps 47
3 Cloud attacks literature review...48
  3.1 Vulnerabilities and Threat Vectors 48
  3.2 Threat Actors 52
  3.3 Countermeasures...54
  3.4 Cloud Attack Targets...58
  3.5 Impact of Cloud Attacks 59
  3.6 Literature Gaps 59
4 Conceptual cloud attack taxonomy and risk assessment
  framework..59
  4.1 Source Dimension..60
  4.2 Vector Dimension..60
  4.3 Vulnerability Dimension 62
  4.4 Target Dimension..63
  4.5 Impact Dimension...63
  4.6 Defense Dimension...65
5 Example scenario: extortion by DDoS and account hijacking....66
  5.1 Parameters..66
  5.2 Risk Assessment Method 67
  5.3 Analysis..70
  5.4 Limitations 71
6 Conclusion and future work 71
  References..75

CHAPTER 4 Multitiered cloud security model **83**

1 Introduction...83
2 The Problem..83
3 Holistic approach 84
  3.1 Awareness...84

3.2 Classification 84
3.3 Technology 85
3.4 Policy and Regulation 85
3.5 Certification 85
3.6 Standards.. 85
4 Why Develop Cloud Security Standards and Guidelines........... 86
5 Related Work.. 86
6 Design considerations of multitiered cloud security 87
7 Benefits to Stakeholders.. 88
8 MTCS standards 89
9 Self-Disclosure.. 92
10 Certification Scheme 92
11 Status... 92
12 Deployment.. 94
13 Harmonization 94
14 Future Work.. 96
15 Conclusion 96
Acknowledgments 96
References.. 96

PART 2 DO: CLOUD SECURITY APPROACHES AND CHALLENGES

CHAPTER 5   A guide to homomorphic encryption 101
1 Introduction.. 101
2 Current industry work-arounds and their gaps 103
3 History and Related Work.. 104
4 Overview of partial homomorphic encryption schemes........... 105
4.1 Public Key Encryption 106
4.2 El Gamal 107
4.3 Paillier Cryptosystem 109
5 Fully homomorphic encryption 111
5.1 Lattices.. 111
5.2 Lattice Problems.. 112
5.3 Learning With Errors.. 113
5.4 Approximate Eigenvector Algorithm.............................. 114
6 Homomorphic Encryption in the Cloud............................... 122
7 Future of Homomorphic Encryption and Open Issues 122
8 Alternatives to homomorphic encryption............................. 123
9 Summary 125
References.. 125

CHAPTER 6 Protection through isolation: Virtues and pitfalls ... 129

    1 Introduction...129
    2 Hypervisors...130
        2.1 General Architectures...................................130
        2.2 Practical Realization....................................131
    3 Shared networking architecture.................................134
        3.1 Packet Scheduling.......................................135
        3.2 Traffic Shaping...136
    4 Isolation-based attack surface 138
    5 Inventory of known attacks.......................................140
    6 Protection strategies..142
    7 Conclusion 144
        References..145

CHAPTER 7 Protecting digital identity in the cloud...................149

    1 Introduction...149
    2 The rise of digital identity...151
        2.1 Composition and Functions of Digital Identity 153
    3 The rise of cloud computing 158
        3.1 The Impact of Cloud Computing and
            Cross-Border Data 159
    4 Protecting digital identity in the era of cloud computing..........166
    5 Conclusion 169

CHAPTER 8 Provenance for cloud data accountability...............171

    1 Introduction...171
        1.1 Background...171
        1.2 Provenance Reconstruction 172
    2 Related Work..174
    3 Data Provenance Model for Data Accountability....................176
        3.1 A Case for Provenance................................177
        3.2 Elements of the Data Provenance Model.............................178
        3.3 Rules for Data Provenance Model 179
    4 Reconstructing the Data Provenance 180
    5 Challenges..182
    6 Future Work and Concluding Remarks 182
        References..183

CHAPTER 9 Security as a service (SecaaS)—An overview........187

    1 Introduction...187
        1.1 History Repeating Itself...............................187
        1.2 The Growth of Cloud Computing Services 187

1.3 Defining Security as a Service 188
1.4 Motivation for This Chapter 188
2 Background 189
2.1 Security as a Service 189
2.2 Outsourcing Model 191
3 Traditional Security 191
3.1 On-Premise 192
3.2 Managed Security Services 192
4 SecaaS Categories of Service 193
4.1 System Security 194
4.2 Network Security 196
4.3 Web Security 197
4.4 Data Security 199
5 Gaps Identified After SecaaS Classification 200
5.1 Gaps in SecaaS Web Technologies 200
5.2 Lack Of True Risk Evaluation 200
5.3 Lack of a Data-centric Approach 200
5.4 No Real Classification for Mapping Legitimate
    Communicating Services 201
6 Future Work 201
7 Concluding Remarks 201
References 202

CHAPTER 10 Secure migration to the cloud—In and out **205**
1 Introduction 205
2 Who Are Cloud Consumer and CSP? 206
3 IT-Service of a small lawyer office migrates into the cloud 206
4 Requirements for cloud migration 208
4.1 Security Policy 209
4.2 Policy Development 209
4.3 Security and Privacy 210
4.4 Detecting and Preventing Sensitive Data Migration to
    the Cloud 210
4.5 Protecting Data Moving to the Cloud 211
4.6 Protecting Data in the Cloud 211
4.7 IT-Knowledge 211
4.8 Control and Visibility 211
4.9 Costs 212
4.10 Interoperability and Portability 212
4.11 Performance 212
5 Rollback Scenarios 214
5.1 Vendor Lock-In 214

6   Legal aspects...215

7   Challenges in cloud migration 218

     7.1 Latency...219

     7.2 Security 219

     7.3 Interoperability...220

     7.4 Internet Speed 221

     7.5 Cloud Integration 221

8   Migration phases...222

     8.1 Planning 224

     8.2 Contracts 224

     8.3 Migration 225

     8.4 Operation 226

     8.5 Termination...226

9   Auditing 227

10   Summary 228

     Abbreviations..228

     References...229

CHAPTER 11 Keeping users empowered in a cloudy Internet of Things **231**

1   Introduction...231

2   Problem Space Assumptions 232

     2.1 Physical Limitations of Smart Objects 233

     2.2 Security Objectives...234

     2.3 Authentication-Related Tasks 235

     2.4 Authorization-Related Tasks 236

     2.5 Implications of Device Constraints for Authenticated Authorization 237

3   Delegated Authenticated Authorization 238

     3.1 Constrained Level...238

     3.2 Principal Level...239

     3.3 Less-Constrained Level 239

     3.4 Authorization to Authorize: Choosing the Authorization Managers...240

4   Usage Example 245

5   Conclusion 246

     References...247

CHAPTER 12 Cloud as infrastructure for managing complex scalable business networks, privacy perspective ..**249**

1   Introduction...249

2   Knowledge management 250

2.1 Definitions and Concepts 250
2.2 Social Networks in Business Environment.......................251
2.3 Technology as KM Enabler 251
2.4 Security and Privacy in KM Context..............................252
3 Cloud computing overview 252
3.1 Cloud Computing Concepts 252
3.2 Knowledge as a Service 254
3.3 Privacy and Security Issue in Cloud Computing..............255
4 Strategies toward successful KM system..........................256
4.1 Modeling Knowledge Organizations and Groups..............256
4.2 Modeling Knowledge Activities and Allocations..............258
5 Modeling scalability and privacy 259
6 Concluding summary...264
References 266

**CHAPTER 13 Psychology and security: Utilizing psychological
and communication theories to promote safer
cloud security behaviors** **269**
1 Introduction...269
2 Communication Theories 270
2.1 CPM Theory 270
2.2 Hyperpersonal Communication 271
3 Cognitive psychology 271
4 Other relevant theories 274
4.1 Learning Theories...275
4.2 Protection Motivation Theory 275
5 Overcoming Inhibitions to Safer Security
Behaviors 276
6 Conclusion 279
Suggested Further Readings...279
References...280

PART 3 CHECK: FORENSICS AND INCIDENT RESPONSE

**CHAPTER 14 Conceptual evidence collection and analysis
methodology for Android devices** **285**
1 Introduction...285
2 Related Work..286
2.1 Background..286
2.2 Existing Literature 288
3 An Evidence Collection and Analysis Methodology
for Android Devices 289

3.1 Identify Device and Preserve Evidence 291
3.2 Collect Evidence..292
3.3 Examination and Analysis...296
3.4 Reporting and Presentation 304
4 Conclusion 304
References..306

CHAPTER 15 Mobile cloud forensics: An analysis of seven popular Android apps **309**
1 Introduction..309
2 Android cloud apps..309
2.1 Dropbox 309
2.2 Box...314
2.3 OneDrive..321
2.4 ownCloud...324
2.5 Evernote 327
2.6 OneNote 332
2.7 Universal Password Manager 336
2.8 Further App Analysis 337
2.9 Our Research Environment 342
3 Conclusion 344
References..345

CHAPTER 16 Recovering residual forensic data from smartphone interactions with cloud storage providers **347**
1 Introduction..347
2 Related work...349
3 Experiment design 353
4 Findings...357
4.1 Detailed Dropbox Findings 362
4.2 Detailed Box Findings..364
4.3 Detailed SugarSync Findings 366
4.4 Detailed Syncplicity Findings 367
5 Discussion 370
6 Conclusions and Future Work..376
Appendix A Metadata artifacts recovered dropbox service 377
Appendix B Metadata Artifacts Recovered Box Service 378
Appendix C Metadata Artifacts Recovered Syncplicity Service 379
References..379

CHAPTER 17 Integrating digital forensic practices in cloud incident handling: A conceptual Cloud Incident Handling Model **383**

1   Introduction 383
2   Background 384
   2.1   Cloud Computing Infrastructure 384
   2.2   Incident Handling in Cloud Computing 385
   2.3   Related Work 386
3   Cloud Incident Handling Model: A Snapshot 387
4   Case Study Simulation: ownCloud 389
   4.1   Preparation and Forensic Readiness 390
   4.2   Identification 391
   4.3   Assessment, Forensic Collection, and Analysis ... 392
   4.4   Action and Monitoring 393
   4.5   Recovery 394
   4.6   Evaluation and Forensic Presentation 394
5   Concluding Remarks 395
    References 398

CHAPTER 18 Cloud security and forensic readiness: The current state of an IaaS provider **401**

1   Introduction 401
2   Review of the private IaaS provider 403
   2.1   Overview of the Case Study Organization 404
   2.2   Security Analysis Methodology 405
   2.3   Cloud Vulnerabilities and Threat Assessment 414
   2.4   Digital Forensic Readiness Assessment 419
3   Conclusions 425
    References 426

CHAPTER 19 Ubuntu One investigation: Detecting evidences on client machines **429**

1   Introduction 429
2   Related Work 430
3   Methodology 431
4   Experiment Setup 431
5   Discussion and Analysis 434
   5.1   Windows Browser Based 434
   5.2   Windows App-Based 438

     5.3 Mac OS X App-Based 442

     5.4 iOS App-Based 443

  6 Conclusion 444

     References..445

PART 4 ACT: GOVERNANCE AND AUDITING

CHAPTER 20 Governance in the Cloud 449

  1 Why is governance important?..449

  2 What are the questions that boards should be asking?..............450

  3 Calculating ROI...453

  4 Auditing the cloud 455

     4.1 Planning and Scoping the Audit..455

     4.2 Governance and enterprise risk management 456

     4.3 Legal and electronic discovery 457

     4.4 Compliance and audit..458

     4.5 Portability and interoperability..459

     4.6 Operating in the cloud...460

     4.7 Identity and access management.......................................461

  5 Conclusion 461

CHAPTER 21 Computational trust methods for security quantification in the cloud ecosystem.....................463

  1 Introduction...463

  2 Computational Trust: Preliminaries 464

  3 State-of-the-art Approaches Tackling Cloud Security..............464

     3.1 Computational Trust Models and Mechanisms 465

     3.2 Trusted Computing Technologies 465

     3.3 Cloud Security Transparency Mechanisms.........................466

     3.4 Cloud Security Quantification Methods.............................466

  4 Computational Trust Methods for Quantifying Security
Capabilities 466

     4.1 Formal Analysis of Security Capabilities 467

     4.2 Evaluating Security Capablities 470

     4.3 Visually Communicating Multiple Security Capabilities...477

  5 Case Studies...479

     5.1 Case Study 1: Quantifying and Visually Communicating
Security Capabilities...479

     5.2 Case Study 2: Quantifying and Communicating
Security Capabilities in Presence of Multiple
Sources...485

  6   Conclusion 490
       Acknowledgment 491
       Appendix. Proof for Theorem 1 491
       References...492

CHAPTER 22 Tool-based risk assessment of cloud infrastructures as socio-technical systems 495

  1   Introduction...495
  2   Structure of a Typical Cloud Infrastructure Scenario...............496
       2.1 Levels of Abstraction 497
       2.2 Attacker Goals 497
       2.3 A Cloud Scenario 498
  3   The TRE$_S$PASS Project...499
  4   Modeling the Scenario for Analysis..500
       4.1 High-Level Model 503
       4.2 Middle-Level Model...503
       4.3 Low-Level Model 504
       4.4 Modeling Typical Network Components...........................505
       4.5 Modeling Actors 511
       4.6 Process Library 512
  5   Identifying Attacks 512
  6   Risk Assessment 514
       6.1 Model-Based Risk Assessment 514
       6.2 Attack-Based Risk Assessment 515
       6.3 Combined Risk Assessment 515
  7   Conclusion 516
       Acknowledgments 516
       Acknowledgment 516
       References...516

Index 519

Contributors

Vivek Agrawal
Norwegian Information Security Laboratory (NISLab), Gjøvik university College, Norway

Abdussalam Ali
Faculty of Engineering and IT, School of Systems, Management and Leadership, University of Technology, Sydney, Australia

Olaf Bergmann
Universität Bremen, Bremen, Germany

Carsten Bormann
Universität Bremen, Bremen, Germany

Kim-Kwang Raymond Choo
Information Assurance Research Group, School of Information Technology and Mathematical Sciences, University of South Australia, Adelaide, Australia

Ali Dehghantanha
School of Computing, Science and Engineering, University of Salford, Greater Manchester, UK

Baden Delamore
Cyber Security Lab, Department of Computer Science, University of Waikato, Hamilton, New Zealand

Quang Do
Information Assurance Research Group, University of South Australia, Adelaide, Australia

Marieta Georieva Ivanova
Technical University of Denmark, Kongens Lyngby, Denmark

Stefanie Gerdes
Universität Bremen, Bremen, Germany

William Bradley Glisson
School of Computing, University of South Alabama, Mobile, Alabama, USA

George Grispos
School of Computing Science, University of Glasgow, Glasgow, United Kingdom

Sascha Hauke
Telecooperation Lab, Technische Universität Darmstadt/CASED, Darmstadt, Germany

Igor Hawryszkiewycz
Faculty of Engineering and IT, School of Systems, Management and Leadership, University of Technology, Sydney, Australia

Geoff Holmes
Cyber Security Lab, Department of Computer Science, University of Waikato, Hamilton, New Zealand

Sai Honig
Waikato District Health Board, Hamilton, New Zealand

Nina Viktoria Juliadotter
Information Assurance Research Lab, University of South Australia, Adelaide, South Australia, Australia

Thomas Kemmerich
Norwegian Information Security Laboratory (NISLab), Gjøvik university College, Norway

Gráinne Kirwan
Institute of Art, Design and Technology, Dublin, Ireland

Ryan K. L. Ko
Cyber Security Lab, Department of Computer Science, University of Waikato, Hamilton, New Zealand

Yiu Chung Laurie Lau
Asia Pacific Association of Technology and Society, Hong Kong SAR

Hing-Yan Lee
Info-communications Development Authority of Singapore, Singapore

Sheikh Mahbub Habib
Telecooperation Lab, Technische Universität Darmstadt/CASED, Darmstadt, Germany

Ben Martini
Information Assurance Research Group, University of South Australia, Adelaide, Australia

Carsten Momsen
Leibniz University Hanover, Hanover, Germany

Max Mühlhäuser
Telecooperation Lab, Technische Universität Darmstadt/CASED, Darmstadt, Germany

Michael Nidd
IBM Research, Zürich, Switzerland

Christian W. Probst
Technical University of Denmark, Kongens Lyngby, Denmark

Nurul Hidayah Ab Rahman
Information Assurance Research Lab, University of South Australia, Adelaide, Australia, and Information Security Department, Faculty of Computer Science and Information Technology, University of Tun Hussein Onn Malaysia, Batu Pahat, Johor, Malaysia

Bill Rogers
Cyber Security Lab, Department of Computer Science, University of Waikato, Hamilton, New Zealand

Mohammad Shariati
School of Computing, Science and Engineering, University of Salford, Greater Manchester, UK

Tim Storer
School of Computing Science, University of Glasgow, Glasgow, United Kingdom

Clare Sullivan
School of Law, University of South Australia, Adelaide, Australia

Alan Y.S. Tan
Cyber Security Lab, Department of Computer Science, University of Waikato, Hamilton, New Zealand

Axel Tanner
IBM Research, Zürich, Switzerland

Yao-Sing Tao
Info-communications Development Authority of Singapore, Singapore

Johanna Ullrich
SBA Research, Vienna, Austria

Chaz Vidal
Information Assurance Research Group, School of Information Technology and Mathematical Sciences, University of South Australia, Adelaide, Australia

Florian Volk
Telecooperation Lab, Technische Universität Darmstadt/CASED, Darmstadt, Germany

Edgar R. Weippl
SBA Research, Vienna, Austria

Mark A. Will
Cyber Security Lab, Department of Computer Science, University of Waikato, Hamilton, New Zealand

Foreword

Cloud computing is touted to herald in a new generation for computing. It is the future of information technology (IT), a mature manifestation of the Internet and the Cyberspace. However, I beg to differ. I see cloud computing heralds the coming of the IT Security industry.

For many years, historically, IT Security professionals plying their trade often came from a defence or national security background. They were used to an environment of secrecy and normally to socialize in a closed group. They mixed poorly with other groups of the organization or even society and preferred to conduct their business under a veil of secrecy and more importantly, fear. Hence, their favourite tool had always been case studies after case studies of infamous hacking incidents telling you why it was important not to be one of the firms! Any colleague could be a 007 secret agent working for some purported rival firms that would steal your technology. A system of distrust and silos was created. The security guy is most likely the most hated and feared figure in the company! And the security guy has never been boardroom power puncher, and most likely not even part of the organization's executive team! In today's knowledge economy, it is common for information to be the main, if not, the only valuable asset for all organizations. So why is IT Security not in the corporate mainstream?

The reasons are not hard to comprehend. Firstly, IT has always been an expensive investment in any company, where its worth has never be adequately justified - which brings us to the security of these systems, related services and compliance requirements, which can be costly and take off a sizeable chunk off the IT budget. But these "security controls" have always been shrouded in secrecy, as it was the nature of security itself. Secondly, any presentation of what they do or function often ended up in a presentation overloaded with technical mambo jambo that only the Security team understands. As such, it is not hard to imagine that there are even more (unanswered) questions on the value of these IT Security purchases. This brings us to the third reason. Oddly, though we refer to IT Security with an "IT" and by its naming, assumes that it will be under the IT department, there is no consistency where the IT Security budget comes from. Sometimes it is from Finance, other times from Internal Audit. This situation is exacerbated with the various so-called "disciplines" that emerged over the years, and the seemingly unrelated regulatory requirements that come with it. We have seen IT Security, Data Privacy, Digital Forensics, IT Governance, Information Risk Management, IT Compliance, Cybersecurity, and even Homeland Security/Critical Infrastructure requirements that mangle up the entire space and makes definition almost impossible. Yet they are intricately related to each other. It all boils down to the internal "champions" who the department that "funds" such activities and thus the different references. In short, it is hard to find a champion within organisations consistently. You don't have that problem with Finance, Human Resource, Sales, Marketing, for example. Not even IT!

However, with the introduction of cloud computing and the concept of Compute-as-a-Unity, we have reinvented the wheel. Or shall I say we pressed the reset button for the industry. The security industry is positioning ourselves as the "watchers" of keepers of the keys of the data that applications run on top of the cloud infrastructure that we come to term as "services". In other words, IT Security is being positioned as a mainstream corporate services that have a direct impact, and therefore, demonstrate value to whatever business objectives that the company is set out to accomplish! So IT Security does not belong to any camp, whether IT, Finance, Audit, etc. and therefore the diasporas of whether it is called "Cybersecurity" or "IT Audit". Based on the Compute-as-a-Unity model, security becomes a part of whatever services that is provided, just like you would expect potable water from a tap or electricity when you flip that switch.

Thus, I was extremely happy when Ryan and Raymond shared their thoughts with me on this book covering the Cloud Security Ecosystem. I believe this is the book to read for a totally new perspective that will hope to bring forth a completely different perspective and therefore understanding of the nature of cloud computing and what makes it tick—Security!

Aloysius Cheang
Managing Director, Asia Pacific
Cloud Security Alliance

Preface

The vision for the book started as a discussion about the perennial multidisciplined, cross-border issues constantly faced by cloud security providers and cloud users.

When we started the process of inviting experts and calling for chapters, cloud computing was starting to become more of a utility than a novelty or a buzzword. The industry has since matured and cloud services are now a critical part of businesses—from start-ups to multinational corporations.

However, one thing remained unchanged—the concerns about the security, trust, and privacy of using cloud services. Varying levels of understanding and expectations of the cloud's security by different countries and institutions further complicate the widespread adoption of cloud services.

This book attempts to be a slight nudge toward improving the current understanding (and clarifying the confusion), and aims to report on the state-of-the-art advances and notable efforts around the world. One shining example is the Cloud Security Alliance's Cloud Controls Matrix (CCM) project—a simple but elegant alignment of government regulations from different countries against common cloud control requirements.

Our vision was to encompass as much wisdom and experience as possible, in a burgeoning field like cloud security. With the field being less than a decade old, it is challenging, if not impossible, for a single person to have multidisciplinary domain knowledge in the fast-paced cloud computing industry. This is why we chose the edited book path. Editing this book was a privileged experience for us, as we benefited from the various discussions and contributions from experts in different disciplines and countries.

HOW TO READ THIS BOOK

As expected of information security professionals, we have ordered the chapters in a Plan-Do-Check-Act (*cf.* Deming) manner:

- Plan: Threats, Risk, and Requirements Landscape
- Do: Cloud Security Approaches and Challenges
- Check: Forensics and Incident Response
- Act: Governance and Auditing

Sequentially, Chapters 2–4 form the "Plan" portion of the book. Having learned about the "Plan" components, we move to the "Do" chapters in Chapters 5–13. After that we "Check" with Chapters 14–19. Finally, we "Act" and improve the security posture and manage risks with Chapters 20–22.

It is our sincere hope that you will gain valuable insights from this book. If you have comments or suggestions, we are happy to hear and learn from you.

Ryan Ko and Kim-Kwang Raymond Choo
February 18, 2015

About the Authors

Nurul Hidayah Ab Rahman is a Ph.D. Scholar at the University of South Australia, Australia. She received the B.Sc. (Hons.) degree from Universiti Teknologi MARA, Malaysia, and M.Sc. degree from Universiti Teknologi, Malaysia, in 2006 and 2010, respectively. Since 2011, she has been with the Information Security Department, University of Tun Hussein Onn, Malaysia, where she is currently an Academician.

Her main areas of research interest are information security management and cloud computing security.

Abdussalam Ali is a Ph.D. Scholar at the University of Technology, Sydney, Australia. He has a Bachelor degree in computer engineering and a Master's degree in computer science.

Vivek Agrawal is a Ph.D. Scholar at Gjøvik University College, Norway. He received the M.S. degree in information and communication systems security from Royal Institute of Technology, Sweden, in 2013. He is currently working toward the Ph.D. degree in migration of risk analysis tool to cloud at University College Gjøvik, Norway. His general interests are in the field of information security. His specific interests include software engineering, network security, secure cloud computing, risk analysis methods, and tools.

Olaf Bergmann is a Lecturer in communication networks and Internet technology at Universität Bremen, Germany. He received his Doctorate in engineering (Dr.Ing.) in 2007 from Universität Bremen and holds a Master in commercial law since 2010. He has been involved in several national and international research projects in the areas of wireless and interpersonal multimedia communications. Olaf also has continuously participated in IETF standardization since 2000 and has coauthored several books on Web technologies. His current research focus is on architectures and communication protocols for constrained environments. Recently, he has initiated the open-source projects *libcoap* and *tinydtls* to leverage development of applications for the Internet of Things.

Carsten Bormann, Honorarprofessor for Internet technology at the Universität Bremen, Germany, is a board member of its Center for Computing and Communications Technology (TZI). His research interests are in protocol design and system architectures for networking. In the IETF, he led a number of efforts on making IP networking work on unusual devices, including ROHC and 6LoWPAN. Most recently, he initiated the IETF work on Constrained RESTful Environments and the CoAP (Constrained Application) Protocol and is cochairing the IETF CoRE WG. He has authored and coauthored 29 Internet RFCs, which are in turn cited 211 times in other RFCs.

Kim-Kwang Raymond Choo is a Fulbright Scholar and Senior Researcher at the University of South Australia, Australia. He is the coinventor of three provisional patents on digital forensics and mobile app security. His publications include a book published in Springer's *Advances in Information Security* book series, and a book published by Syngress/Elsevier (Forewords written by Australia's Chief Defence Scientist and Chair of the Electronic Evidence Specialist Advisory Group, Senior Managers of Australian and New Zealand Forensic Laboratories). He is currently the Editor of IEEE Cloud Computing Magazine's "Cloud and the Law" column, coeditor for Syngress/Elsevier's "Advanced Topics in Security, Privacy and Forensics" Book Series, and Research Director of Cloud Security Alliance Australia Chapter. He is also guest-editing an IEEE Cloud Computing Magazine Special Issue, IEEE Transactions on Cloud Computing Special Issue, Future Generation Computer Systems Special Issue, Journal of Computer and System Sciences Special Issue, Pervasive and Mobile Computing Special Issue, Digital Investigation Special Issue and ACM Transactions on Internet Technology Special Issue. In 2009, he was named one of 10 Emerging Leaders in the Innovation category of The Weekend Australian Magazine/Microsoft's Next 100 series. He is the recipient of the Highly Commended Award in the 2014 "Best Chapter in a Book" Category by Australia New Zealand Policing Advisory Agency (ANZPAA) National Institute of Forensic Science (NIFS), 2014 Academic Impact and Uptake Award (University of South Australia), 2010 Australian Capital Territory Pearcey Award, 2010 Consensus IT Professional Award, 2008 Australia Day Achievement Medallion, and the British Computer Society's Wilkes Award for the best (sole-authored) paper published in the 2007 volume of *The Computer Journal*.

Ali Dehghantanha is a Cyber Security Researcher and Lecturer at University of Salford—Manchester, UK. He has served for several years in variety of industrial and academic positions with leading players in Cyber-Security and E-Commerce. He has long history of working in different areas of computer security as security researcher, malware analyzer, penetration tester, security consultant, professional trainer, and university lecturer. As a security researcher, Ali is actively researching on latest trends in "Real-Time Malware Detection and Analysis in Mobile and Pervasive Systems," "0-Day Malware and Exploit Detection Techniques," and "Big-Data Forensics". He leads several academic research teams working on above-mentioned projects in University of Salford (UoS)—Greater Manchester.

Baden Delamore is a Masters student at the University of Waikato undertaking research with the Cyber Security Researchers of Waikato (CROW). Recipient of the Waikato University Masters Research Scholarship, he holds a Bachelor of information technology, two Diploma's in information and communication technology and a Postgraduate Diploma in computer science. Prior to his research, Baden developed applications for numerous software projects (e.g. Waikato Institute of Technology Sports Science Department, Internet Marketing solutions) currently in production today. His main research interests are software engineering and cyber security, in particular, the application of offensive and defensive security techniques. His Master's research thesis proposes an efficient and effect user-centric security assessment methodology of Web servers. He is a member of the IEEE.

Quang Do is a Ph.D. Scholar at the University of South Australia, Australia, and holds a Bachelor of computer science (First Class Honors). He is the recipient of the prestigious University of South Australia Vice Chancellor and President's Scholarship and is an active Android security researcher.

Stefanie Gerdes is a Research Scientist in computer science at the AG Rechnernetze at Universität Bremen in Germany. Her research focuses on information security, in particular, on the specific challenges of securing smart objects in the Internet of Things. Currently, she participates in standardization efforts in the Internet Engineering Task Force (IETF) concerning authentication and authorization in constrained environments (ACE).

William Bradley Glisson is currently an Associate Professor at the University of South Alabama, USA. He has a Ph.D. in computing science from the University of Glasgow, Scotland, 2008; Master of Science in information management from the University of Strathclyde, Scotland, 2001; Bachelor of Science in information systems & operations management from the University of North Carolina at Greensboro, 1999; and a Bachelor of Science in management from the University of North Carolina at Greensboro, 1993. Dr. Glisson has 10 years of industrial experience which includes working for U.S. and UK Global Fortune 500 financial institutions. Dr. Glisson has been the primary investigator on residual data research projects funded predominantly by industry. His area of research focuses on digital forensics, information assurance, software engineering, and applied computing science with a specific interest in the security and business implications of residual data. Previous to this appointment, he was the Director of the Computer Forensics M.Sc. program at the University of Glasgow for 5 years. He builds on previous administrative and teaching experiences to teach and improve digital forensic courses while researching relevant real-world digital forensic issues at the University of South Alabama.

George Grispos is a Doctoral Researcher at the University of Glasgow, Scotland. He is currently completing a Ph.D. in computing science which focuses on the business implications of information security incidents along with the subsequent management and handling of such incidents. Previously, George completed a Master of Science (M.Sc.) in computer forensics and e-discovery from the University of Glasgow, and a Bachelor of Science (B.Sc. Hons.) in computer networks from Middlesex University in London. In addition to security incident response, his research interests include: digital forensics, information security management, as well as examining the managerial and technical issues surrounding secure cloud computing services within organizations.

Sheikh Mahbub Habib is a Postdoctoral researcher at the Telecooperation Lab. and Coordinator of CASED Secure Services research area in Germany. Additionally, he is leading the Smart Security & Trust area as a part of the Telecooperation Lab. since September 2013. Sheikh obtained his doctoral degree from Technische Universität Darmstadt in 2013 for his work on computational trust mechanisms with focus on distributed service environments. His current research interests includes trust and reputation models, logical reasoning of trust, trust management techniques, trust enhanced security techniques, and their application in complex distributed systems.

Sascha Hauke is a Doctoral researcher and research assistant at the Center for Advanced Security Research Darmstadt (CASED) and the Telecooperation Group of TU Darmstadt, Germany. He is working on developing techniques for extending reputation-based trust models into advanced trust management solutions. He received the degree of Diplom-Informatiker (Dipl.-Inform.) from the Westfälische Wilhelms-Universität Münster (WWU), specializing in machine learning, soft computing, and linguistics. His current research interests include reputation-based trust management, the application of machine-learning techniques for prediction, and their application in service-oriented environments.

Igor Hawryszkiewycz is a Professor and the Head of the School of Systems, Management and Leadership at the University of Technology, Sydney, Australia. His current work is on developing design thinking environments to provide business solutions in complex environments by integrating processes, knowledge, and social networking, and Facilitating agility and evolution of business systems through collaboration. He has over 200 research publications and 5 books.

Geoff Holmes is currently Dean of the Faculty of Computing and Mathematical Sciences at the University of Waikato, New Zealand. He has been head of the machine-learning group and has been involved in several open source projects over the last 20 years. He has made contributions in machine learning across several branches of the subject and has been active in finding ways to reward researchers for their efforts to produce open-source software. In this regard, he acts as an action editor for the branch of JMLR dedicated to open-source software. He was part of the team that in 2005 won the SIGKDD Data Mining and Knowledge Discovery Service Award for Weka and regularly serves on senior PCs for KDD, ECMLPKDD, and Discovery Science. Since 2006 he has been working on the MOA project (Massive Online Analysis) making contributions to Big Data Analytics. He obtained B.Sc. and Ph.D. degrees in Mathematics from Southampton University, UK in 1986. After time as a research assistant in Cambridge University he joined Waikato in 1987, after moving up the ranks, he was promoted to Professor in 2008.

Sai K. Honig has more than 10 years of experience preparing and executing financial, operational, and IT audits as well as enterprise wide risk assessments. She is familiar with software life cycle development, Oracle ERP, PeopleSoft ERP, business continuity, and cloud implementations (SaaS). She has conducted postimplementations of cloud technologies (SaaS) and became interested in the governance processes that are needed between cloud provider and cloud consumer. She has focused these interests and skills by assisting Grameen Foundation as it prepares its internal audit and IT field processes. She has also served as expert reviewer for ISACA white papers focused on cloud governance. Currently, Sai is the Information Security Manager at the Waikato District Health Board headquartered in Hamilton, New Zealand, which provides hospital, health, and disability services to the more than 373,000 people.

Marieta Georgieva Ivanova is a Ph.D. Scholar at the Technical University of Denmark. The topic of her thesis is the development of socio-technical security models for risk assessment. Marieta earned her master degree from the Technical University of Denmark for work on cognitive systems.

Nina Viktoria Juliadotter is a Software Engineer with a research interest in cyber security and digital forensics. Her professional experience has focused on risk management and algorithmic trading environments, while also contributing to several open-source security projects. She is currently a Master student in cyber security at University of New South Wales Canberra.

Thomas Kemmerich is an Associate Professor at University College Gjøvik. He is teaching Network and Network Security. He is head of the local Cisco Academy Support Center and Study Program Director for the Bachelor of Information Security. He worked for many years as a consultant in his own company in the area of ISMS and ISO 27001 certification. He accompanied SMEs according their migration to cloud providers. He taught Information Security Management (ISMS) and Cloud Computing at the University College Dublin (UCD) and at a Baltic Summer School in Tartu and Vilnius. He organized an international Seminar at Schloss Dagstuhl with the topic of "Digital Evidence and Forensic Readiness" in 2014. His research work is in the fields of network security, Cloud Security, and forensic readiness.

Gráinne Kirwan is a Chartered Psychologist with the British Psychological Society and a lecturer in psychology in the Institute of Art, Design and Technology (IADT), Dun Laoghaire, Ireland. She instigated and led the development of the MSc in Cyberpsychology in IADT, as well as teaching on the undergraduate BSc (Hons) in Applied Psychology. Her specialisms include the interaction between psychology and technology, particularly in relation to online behavior and the psychological applications of virtual reality. She is particularly interested in aspects of health psychology and forensic psychology online She holds a Ph.D. in Criminology, an M.Sc. in Applied Forensic Psychology, a PgCert in Third Level Learning and Teaching and an MLitt in Psychology. She is a member of the editorial board of the international journal 'Cyberpsychology, Behavior and Social Networking', as well as a reviewer for several other journals, conferences and academic book publishers. She has coauthored two books with Dr. Andrew Power (IADT): *Cybercrime: The Psychology of Online Offenders* (Cambridge University Press, 2013) and *The Psychology of Cybercrime* (IGI Global, 2012) as well as coediting *Cyberpsychology and New Media* (Psychology Press, 2014).

Ryan K. L. Ko is a Senior Lecturer with the Computer Science department of the University of Waikato (UoW), New Zealand, and Asia Pacific Research Adviser in the Cloud Security Alliance (CSA). He leads the Cybersecurity Researchers of Waikato (CROW) and established NZ's first cyber security masters degree and cyber security lab. He is an international faculty member with the National Information Assurance Training and Education Center (NIATEC), Idaho State University. He was one of the subject matter experts who developed the CSA-(ISC)^2's international Certified Cloud Security Professional (CCSP) certification and examination. Prior to his academic career, he was a lead computer scientist with Hewlett-Packard Labs' Cloud and Security Lab. Recipient of the CSA Ron Knode Service Award, UoW Early Career Academic Excellence Award, and the 2014 Faculty Teaching Excellence Award, he is currently the science leader of the STRATUS project, a 6-year, NZD10.6 million MBIE-funded research aiming to create a new IT industry empowering users with capabilities to take control of their data in cloud environments. He serves as an associate editor for several academic journals, including Wiley's Security and Communication Networks, Australasian Journal of Information Systems and Elsevier's Computers and Electrical Engineering. He is also a committee member of the ISO/IEC JTC1/SC27 IT Security Techniques Working Group 4 technical committee.

Yiu Chung Laurie Lau is currently Chair of the Asia Pacific Association of Technology and Society (APATAS). He is an entrepreneur and philanthropist in Hong Kong with a Doctor of Philosophy from the Faculty of Humanities, Law and social sciences at the University of Glamorgan. He has wide experience in research on policing Internet-related crime, including O2O fraud, technology and society, Internet of Things. In addition, he frequently presents paper at International and Hong Kong Conferences. Laurie is actively involved in mentoring students at Wu Yee Sun College, and as Honorary Research Fellow of the Pearl Delta Social Research Centre at the Chinese University of Hong Kong.

Hing-Yan Lee is Director of National Cloud Computing Office at the Infocomm Development Authority of Singapore, where he oversees the national program in cloud computing. Prior to this, Hing-Yan was Deputy Director of National Grid Office at the Agency of Science, Technology and Research as well as Principal Scientist at Institute for Infocomm Research. He has held senior management and technical positions at Kent Ridge Digital Labs, Japan-Singapore AI Centre, Information Technology Institute and two high-tech start-ups. Hing-Yan is an Adjunct Associate Professor in National University of Singapore, member of School of Digital Media & IT advisory panel at Singapore Polytechnic, vice chair of SIG on Cloud Computing and Fellow (Singapore Computer Society), and member of Cloud Computing Standards Coordinating Task Force (IT Standards Committee). He has served on NatSteel Corporate R&D advisory panel, Singapore National Archives Board, Australia-Singapore Joint ICT Council, and cochair of National Infocomm Competency Framework technical committee on Cloud Computing. He graduated from the University of Illinois at Urbana-Champaign with Ph.D. and M.S. degrees in computer science. He also studied at Imperial College London where he obtained a B.Sc. (Eng.) with First Class Honors in Computing and M.Sc. in management science.

Ben Martini is a Postdoctoral Researcher at the University of South Australia. He is the coinventor of a provisional patent on cloud forensics filed in December 2014, and has published the first academic book on cloud storage forensics (Forewords written by

Australia's Chief Defense Scientist and Chair of the Electronic Evidence Specialist Advisory Group, Senior Managers of Australian and New Zealand Forensic Laboratories). He has spoken at a number of events and served on various conference program committees as well as serving as a reviewer for a number of conferences and journals.

Carsten Momsen is currently Professor for "Criminal Law, Criminal Procedural Law and White Collar Crimes" and head of the "Institute for Criminal Sciences" at Leibniz University Hannover, Germany (since 2010). Since 2013, he serves as dean of the law faculty of Leibniz University. From summer 2015, Carsten Momsen will hold a chair for "Criminal Law, Criminal Procedural Law and White Collar Crimes" at the Free University of Berlin (FU Berlin). Between 2004 and 2010, Prof. Momsen held the chair for "Criminal Law, White Collar Crimes and criminal procedure" at the University of Saarland. Prior to his career as a law professor, Prof. Momsen worked as a currency dealer. He teaches Criminal Law, Procedural Law and about organized crime and white-collar-crimes. His research includes digital evidence and digital forensics in criminal trials. He was a participant of the international Seminar at Schloss Dagstuhl with the topic "Digital Evidence and Forensic Readiness" in 2014.

Apart from his university career, Prof. Momsen also works part-time as a defense lawyer at the Bremen-based law firm Hannover & Partner.

Max Mühlhäuser is a Full Professor of Computer Science at Technische Universität Darmstadt, Germany, and head of the Telecooperation Lab Max is deputy speaker of a Nationally Funded Cooperative Research Center on the Future Internet and directorate member of CASED, a leading European IT Security Research Center. He received his Doctorate from the University of Karlsruhe and founded a Research Center for Digital Equipment (DEC) in 1986. Since 1989, he worked as either professor or visiting professor at universities in Germany, Austria, France, Canada, and the U.S. Max published over 450 articles, coauthored and edited books about ubiquitous computing, e-learning, and distributed multimedia software engineering. Together with a team of over 30 staff members and some 60 students, his lab works in three fields: (1) Big Networks (middleware, tools, and services for smart environments; sensor, P2P, and social networks; Internet of services and things; knowledge and media networks); (2) Novel Human Computer Interaction (interaction concepts for novel mobile devices, for interactive and collaborative surfaces, and for custom-designed and 3D printed objects; implicit and on-body interaction; voice, multi-modal and federated interaction; UI development and engineering methods); (3) dependable infrastructures (computational trust; resilient critical infrastructures; collaborative attack and intrusion detection; ubiquitous privacy).

Michael Nidd is a research staff member in the services group of the IBM Zurich Research Lab. Michael works primarily on the discovery and configuration management of network appliances in the data center, especially firewalls and load balancers. The primary application for this effort is the Transition and Transformation phase of outsourcing contracts. In 2001, he received his doctorate from the Swiss Federal Institute of Technology (EPFL) in Lausanne, with a thesis on service discovery in transient wireless ad-hoc networks. He earned his bachelor and master degrees from the University of Waterloo (Canada) in 1993 and 1995, respectively.

Christian W. Probst is an Associate Professor in the Department of Applied Mathematics and Computer Science at the Technical University of Denmark, where he works in the section for Language-Based Technologies. The motivation behind Christian's research is to realize systems with guaranteed properties. Important aspects of his work are questions related to safety and security properties, most notably insider threats. He is the creator of ExASyM, the extendable, analyzable system model, which supports the identification of insider threats in organizations. Christian has coorganized cross-disciplinary workshops on insider threats and has coedited a book on the topic. He holds a masters and a doctoral degree from the University of Saarbrücken, Germany.

Bill Rogers is a Senior Lecturer with the Computer Science department of the University of Waikato, New Zealand. He teaches a range of computer science subjects, ranging from architecture through most aspects of software development. His early research interests were in the programming language and compiler construction area. More recently, he has been interested in programming and evaluation of human-computer interfaces and the software architectures that support HCI programming.

Mohammad Shariati is an independent academic researcher currently undertaking research studies in area of Digital Forensic Investigation, especially with focus on cloud environment with collaboration other scholars in this field worldwide. He graduated from The University of Nottingham with Master of IT. In addition, He has over six years of experience as a Network Security Administrator served private and governmental sectors in Iran. Those valuable experiments along with his academic background which followed by relevant certificates (CEH and CHFI) in the Digital Forensic area allow him to have deep insights into different aspects of research study in this respect.

Tim Storer is a Lecturer in Software Engineering at the University of Glasgow. Scotland. His research interests concern the use of large scale data sets to understand and enhance software engineering and other socio-technical practices. Application domains include scientific programming, data evolution and management, software project management, software quality assurance planning, and digital forensics.

He also has interests in the dependability and reliability of software and socio-technical systems. This work has covered the application of computational trust models to large scale infrastructures and the design and implementation of electronic voting systems.

He received a Ph.D. in computer science from the University of St. Andrews, Scotland in 2007.

Clare Sullivan is a Cyber Lawyer and Lecturer at University of South Australia's School of Law. Dr Sullivan's research examines whether the digital identity that people use for transactions, especially in the context of e-government, is emerging as a new legal concept. Her research has implications for a number of legal areas particularly the emergent right to identity in this context and its relationship to the right to privacy, as well as the policy implications of the move to national and international e-citizenship and e-residency. Dr Sullivan's research has been published in leading peer-reviewed international computer law journals and book chapters. Dr Sullivan is the author of "Digital Identity," the leading international legal study of digital identity as an emergent legal concept and its implications for individuals, businesses and government. Dr Sullivan is a Fulbright scholar, an Endeavour scholar, and a consultant to the £1.85 million Super Identity Project, jointly funded by the UK government and the U.S. Department of Homeland Security under its Global Uncertainties program. In 2015, Dr Sullivan was invited to be a Fellow of the Institute for National Security and the Law, School of Law, Georgetown University, Washington DC.

Alan Yu Shyang Tan is currently a Ph.D. student with the Cyber Security Lab in the Faculty of Computing and Mathematical Science, University of Waikato, New Zealand. His research looks at enabling data security using the provenance of data in computer systems. His other research interests include Distributed Computing and Data Analytics. Prior to undertaking his Ph.D., Alan was with Hewlett Packard Labs, Singapore, as a research engineer. Some of his notable achievements during his time with HP Labs Singapore include an honorable mention and invitation to Techcon'12, an HP internal international technical conference, and one filed patent. Alan obtained his Master of engineering and Bachelor of computer science degrees from the Nanyang Technological University, Singapore.

Axel Tanner is a research staff member in the security group of the IBM Zurich Research Lab. Since 2002, he is active in research in areas of computer security and intrusion detection, services and systems management. Current interests include data integration to enable awareness of the overall state of an ICT environment, socio-technical risks in cloud environments, as well as secure digital identities. He joined IBM Research in 1993, first as part of the IT group of the lab, later serving as the manager of the IT department. Axel Tanner received his diploma in physics (1988) at the University of Heidelberg, Germany, and a Ph.D. in physics (1993) at the University of Zürich, Switzerland.

Yao-Sing Tao is Assistant Director at the National Cloud Computing Office of Infocomm Development Authority of Singapore. He is a deputy chair of the Working Group responsible for the development of Multi-Tiered Cloud Security (MTCS SS584:2013) standard and several cloud-technologies-related Guidelines. Prior to his current position, he was a VP in a local bank for more than 10 years and undertook bank-group wide projects including the design and implementation of security infrastructure, particularly in identity management and authentication services, both locally and regionally. He received his B.E. degree with First Class Honors at University of Singapore and a M.Sc. in engineering from University of Pennsylvania.

Johanna Ullrich is a Ph.D. Scholar at SBA Research, Vienna, Austria, the National Competence Center for Information Security. Recipient of three outstanding student awards, she achieved a Bachelor of electrical engineering and information technology in 2010, and a Master of automation engineering in 2013, both with distinction from Vienna University of Technology. For her master thesis on Header Compression of IPsec in Powerline Networks, she received the diploma prize of the city of Vienna. Her research interests include network security and cloud security, and in raising awareness for security and privacy in traditional engineering.

Chaz Vidal is a Master of Cyber Security and Forensic Computing research student and an Information Technologist at the University of South Australia. He manages hosted application and server platforms for the University and has been in the IT industry for the last 15 years working in various roles from and implementation of systems monitoring systems, supporting data center management software and managed IT services solutions designs. He has firsthand experience of the challenges and opportunities of cloud computing through his work in managing hosting environments for clients of various industries.

Florian Volk is a Doctoral researcher and research assistant at the Telecooperation Lab of Technische Universität Darmstadt and the Center of Advanced Security Research Darmstadt (CASED), Germany. He is working on trust decomposition, i.e., he is investigating the question how to distribute ratings for collaborative efforts among the participating collaborators. He received his M.Sc. in computer science with a focus on IT security from Technische Universität Darmstadt in 2011. His current research interests include reputation-based trust models, fairness, and the distribution of trust among collaborators that are seen as one indivisible unit by trustors.

Edgar R. Weippl is Research Director of SBA Research and associate professor at the Vienna University of Technology. His research focuses on applied concepts of IT-security; he organizes the ARES conference, and is on the editorial board of Elsevier's Computers & Security journal (COSE) and chair of SACMAT 2015, ESORICS 2015, and ACM CCS 2016.

Mark A. Will is currently a Ph.D. Scholar at The University of Waikato in the Faculty of Computing and Mathematical Sciences. Recipient of the University of Waikato Doctoral Scholarship, and the University of Waikato Top Achiever Doctoral Scholarship, Mark completed his Bachelor of Computing and Mathematical Sciences with First Class Honors at Waikato in 2013. His honors project, titled Low Latency Video Processing, looked into processing video in real-time on $\times 86$ processors using machine-specific instructions, and on a Zynq 7000 series chip, which houses a dual-core ARM and an FPGA on the same die. This project clinched the Best Project Award at the 2013 Computer Science Honours Conference. He is now a member of the CROW (Cyber Security Researchers of Waikato) lab and is currently researching on the performance of processing encrypted data. His research interests are hardware, low-level programming, and cyber security. He is a member of the IEEE and reviewer for academic journals such as Security and Communication Networks.

List of Reviewers

Nurul Hidayah Ab Rahman
University of South Australia, Australia

Jemal Abawajy
Deakin University, Australia

Abdullah Azfar
University of South Australia, Australia

Kim-Kwang Raymond Choo
University of South Australia, Australia

Ali Dehghantanha
University of Salford, UK

Sheikh Mahbub Habib
Technische University Darmstad, Germany

Rafiqul Islam
Charles Sturt University, Australia

Martin Gilje Jaatun
SINTEF, Norway

Grainne Kirwan
Institute of Art, Design and Technology, Ireland

Ryan Ko
University of Waikato, New Zealand

Yiu Chung Laurie Lau
Asia Pacific Association of Technology and Society, Hong Kong

Ivan Lee
University of South Australia, Australia

K K Lim
Singapore Cloud Forum, Singapore

Ben Martini
University of South Australia, Australia

Josef Pieprzyk
Queensland University of Technology, Australia

Darren Quick
University of South Australia, Australia

Rick Sarre
University of South Australia, Australia

Clare Sullivan
University of South Australia, Australia

Joseph C.M. Teo
Institute for Infocomm Research, A*Star, Singapore

Ian Welch
Victoria University of Wellington, New Zealand

Lena Wiese
University of Göttingen, Germany

Liang (Richard) Zhao
NSFocus, China

Acknowledgments

Writing and editing this book could not have been possible without a lot of comments, critique, contributions, and support from the cloud security research and practitioner communities. We would also like to thank Ben Rearick, Chris Katsaropoulos, and the Elsevier/Syngress editorial team for making sure that the publication stays in shape and on time.

We are indebted to Aloysius Cheang for penning the foreword in this book, and the book chapter authors and expert reviewers for selflessly contributing their wealth of experience and expertise that surpasses what a single author can offer.

We would like to thank our colleagues for their support and encouragement, and many of whose research results appear in this book.

- University of Waikato: Professor Geoff Holmes, Associate Professor Stephen Joe, Professor Ian Witten and Bill Rogers at the Faculty of Computing and Mathematical Sciences in the University of Waikato, and Mark Will, Baden Delamore and Alan Tan at the Cyber Security Researchers of Waikato (CROW);
- University of South Australia: Professor Andy Koronios, Dr Ben Martini, Nurul Hidayah Ab Rahman, Quang Do, Nina Juliadotter, and Chaz Vidal; and
- Cloud Security Alliance (CSA) Asia Pacific Region: staff and volunteer leadership.

Most importantly, we thank our families (Ryan: wife, Denise, and daughter, Angela; Raymond: wife, Jin Nie, and kids, Julian and Elissa) for their love and unwavering support.

Ryan Ko and Kim-Kwang Raymond Choo
18 February 2015

Cloud security ecosystem

1

Ryan K. L. Ko[a] and Kim-Kwang Raymond Choo[b]

University of Waikato, Hamilton, New Zealand[a]

Information Assurance Research Group, School of Information Technology and
Mathematical Sciences, University of South Australia, Adelaide, Australia[b]

Cloud computing (Ko, 2010) may be the most important information technology (IT) innovation of the twenty-first century, and it is now common to see individuals and organizations using online computing services that classify themselves as "cloud services." While cloud is becoming mainstream, several aspects of cloud security and privacy concerns are still in development or unaddressed.

1 HOW IT ALL STARTED—THE STORY OF AN ONLINE BOOKSTORE

It is not clear when the term "cloud computing" was first coined (Choo, 2010). However, cloud computing started to become prevalent in 2008 on the back of the USA presidential election, and some mentioned the success of the campaigns were hinged to the scale and elasticity brought forth by cloud computing.

To most cloud industry practitioners, the concept of cloud computing started from an online book shop—Amazon.com in 2003. That year, the world was still counting its losses from the Dotcom bubble burst, and the world's largest online bookstore was facing a critical economical decision-making problem—resource utilization versus capital investment.

Werner Vogels, then Amazon's Chief Technology Officer (CTO), said "From experience we knew that the cost of maintaining a reliable, scalable infrastructure in a traditional multi-datacentre model could be as high as 70%, both in time and effort, and requires significant investment of intellectual capital to sustain over a longer period of time."[1]

Hence, the company's goal was "to deliver services that could reduce that cost to 30% or less."[2] In other words, Amazon was trying to grow their infrastructure while finding out a method to offload the operational costs to others. While Amazon's

---

[1]Src: http://www.zdnet.com/how-amazon-exposed-its-guts-the-history-of-awss-ec2-3040155310/.
[2]Src: http://blog.b3k.us/2009/01/25/ec2-origins.html.

servers are up 24 hours a day, 7 days a week, there are constantly ups and downs in terms of demand for the utilization of the servers, at different time zones around the world. It would be great if the "wastage" of utilization can be offloaded to some other customers who may need it. When the folks in Asia are sleeping, wouldn't it be great that the related underutilized servers serving them can be sold for usage by the businesses in the Americas?

In the meantime, Chris Pinkham and Benjamin Black, another Amazon engineer, wrote a short paper outlining the ideas for Amazon's chief executive officer (CEO) Jeff Bezos, who liked it and followed up by asking for more details on a "virtual cloud-provisionable server."

However, Pinkham and his wife had a baby on the way and, after talking with other people at Amazon, left to set up a satellite development office in South Africa—Amazon's first in the region—where he and some other engineers, including Christopher Brown and Wiljem Van Biljon, worked on designing the Amazon EC2 service.

In 2006, the cloud services for computing (EC2), storage (S3), and outsourcing of tasks only achievable by humans (Mechanical Turk) were launched. The rest, as they say, is history.

Since that movement, several IT companies have "embraced" cloud computing. Google positioned themselves as a public cloud service provider. Microsoft quickly joined the fray by offering its Azure services. Startups such as Foursquare, DropBox, Quora, and many young IT companies were started quickly over the Amazon cloud services—without the need to invest in hardware up front.

Even the large IT companies (such as Oracle and SAP) that initially dismissed cloud computing as a "buzzword" has come to accept its business model and have entered the market to offer what is known as a "hybrid cloud." This brings us to the next and very necessary section (Section 2).

2 CONSOLIDATION OF TERMINOLOGIES AND PERSPECTIVES

As with many IT paradigms, cloud computing has its fair share of overlapping terminologies. If you are coming into this field as a professional or a student in the recent year(s), you would be heartened to know that the concept of cloud computing has consolidated to the following perspectives.

2.1 PERSPECTIVE 1: ESSENTIAL CHARACTERISTICS

Essentially, cloud computing offers the following characteristics as defined by NIST (NIST, 2011):

- *On-demand self-service*: Consumers are able to help themselves and decide which services to subscribe to, and how much to invest—all at the swipe of a credit card or using an online payment system. An IT department can now quickly purchase more resources on-demand to cater to sudden spikes in user load.

- *Ubiquitous network access*: Cloud services hinge on the Internet's infrastructure, and as such provide a ubiquitous availability of services as long as there is an Internet connection. An USA-based executive can perform his roles during business travel, accessing his company's online resources hosted in Ireland via the Internet connection in Singapore.
- *Resource pooling*: The combined computational power of large amounts of physical and virtual servers provides a cost-effective pooling of resources. Multitenancy solutions have enabled several organizations to share the same cloud computing resources without worrying about data spilling into each other's logical boundaries.
- *Rapid elasticity*: Cloud services leverage on technologies such as server and storage virtualization to rapidly meet the rise and fall of user load and service demand. A newly launched business expecting 10,000 customers will be able to handle an unexpected load of 1 million customers without worrying about the need to purchase or set up new servers in short notice. Elasticity also improves the utilization of the cloud resources.
- *Measured service with pay-per-use*: Given the above characteristics, it works for both service providers and consumers to have an easy-to-measure payment scheme mimicking the power utilities and cable television model—pay-per-use. At the appropriate price point, pay-per-use has the potential to alleviate the need for forecasting and planning of resources, and reduce wastage of overheads.

The eagle-eyed reader will observe that the above five points do not point to a new technology paradigm, but an Internet-empowered, high-utilization business concept that simply works.

It replaces the awkwardness of predecessor technologies, such as utility computing and grid computing, as it comes with an easy-to-implement and easy-to-understand business and revenue model. Cloud also reduces the expectations on businesses to forecast demand correctly—which like weather forecasting, is rarely achieved successfully.

Currently, most stakeholders reference the NIST Definition of Cloud Computing (NIST, 2011). Recently, ISO/IEC 17788 (Information technology—Cloud computing—Overview and vocabulary) started defining the cloud computing definitions, but the uptake of the fresh set of definitions remains to be seen.

2.2 PERSPECTIVE 2: LAYERS AND SCOPE

With the characteristics, many cloud services are often categories by their "layers" (NIST, 2011):

- *Applications of Software-as-a-Service (SaaS)*: Highly scalable software services such as e-mail software, accounting software, software engineering and deployment tools, and Web site creation tools. Examples include Outlook.com, Gmail, Salesforce.com, etc.

- *Applications of Platform-as-a-Service (PaaS)*: Elastic provision of integrated cross-platform software such as combinations of databases, software development environments with operating systems. An example would be Microsoft Azure.
- *Applications of Infrastructure-as-a-Service (IaaS)*: Elastic provision of computation (servers) and storage. An example would be Amazon Web Services' EC2.

This method of layering and naming has also given rise to the popularity of using "as-a-service" to describe cloud-delivered services, for example, security-as-a-service (SecaaS), which will be covered in Chapter 9.

Another way to look at cloud services would be to look at the scope. If a particular cloud service is run entirely on-premise, and within your own organization's physical boundaries, it is generally known as the private cloud (*note*: some vendors may have varying understandings depending on their sales pitch). If it is run entirely outside of your organization's physical boundaries, it will be generally referred to as a public cloud. If it is a mix of both public and private cloud, it is commonly referred to as a hybrid cloud.

At the time of writing, the hybrid cloud approach is the most common approach by both vendors and consumers mainly due to data sovereignty and data governance considerations. Roles of the cloud, such as the role of a so-called "cloud broker," are still under much debate and have not witnessed consolidation. Hence, it is not the interest of this book to discuss this, and we take a simple approach—cloud vendors/service providers versus cloud consumers/users.

It is important to note that regardless of public, private, or hybrid boundaries, the service consumer technically provides the data and mostly owns the data. However, that may change when they upload their data into the respective cloud services. For example, in some free social media sites, the copyright of user-uploaded pictures technically belongs to the social media site after the upload. Important issues such as legal implications for cloud service providers and users if the data is breached or users suffer an economic loss resulting from the provider's negligent act have also remained unanswered (Choo, 2014a, 2014b).

There will always be some percentage of a loss of control over how their data are managed or processed. In other words, we always have to depend on a trusted administrator or provider to handle the processing of our data.

This brings us to the crux of what this book is about—the complications caused by the dependency of a trust relationship between a service provider and a service consumer.

3 THE ACHILLES' HEEL—DEPENDING ON A TRUST RELATIONSHIP

The root of the perennial cloud security and privacy problem stems from the basis of a trust relationship.

By signing up for the use of a cloud service—whether it is private, public, or hybrid—we are explicitly placing our trust into the people running the services to observe the highest ethical principles. This may not always be the case.

3.1 CASE STUDY 1: BREACH OF TRUST BY A PUBLIC CLOUD SYSTEM ADMINISTRATOR

In 2010, Google fired its site reliability engineer, David Berksdale, for breaking Google's internal privacy policies (Chen, 2010). Berksdale was found to have misused his position to break into the Google's cloud e-mail service (Gmail) and Internet phone service (Google Voice) accounts of several children. Particularly, he spied on four teenagers for months before the company was notified of the abuses. Some of the abuses include the accessing of contact lists and chat transcripts. Notice that Google did not know about these abuses, and reportedly "it was unclear how widespread Barksdale's abuses were" (Chen, 2010).

In one of the incidents in Spring 2010, Barksdale tapped into the call logs of a 15-year-old boy's Google Voice after the boy refused to tell him the name of his new girlfriend. After accessing the boy's account to retrieve her name and phone number, Barksdale taunted the boy and threatened to call her.

These incidents not only highlight the dangers of "trusting" a third party but also reveal the lack of technical solutions, legal guidelines, and business management controls for preventing and identifying the risks. We also cannot be assured that there will not be other "Berksdales" in other cloud providers.

This book attempts to highlight, discuss, and address these types of issues in Chapters 2–4.

3.2 CASE STUDY 2: LIABILITY OF A LIQUIDATED CLOUD BUSINESS

In 2011, storage cloud company Iron Mountain announced its liquidation, shocking several of its customers. In a statement released by Gartner in 2011[3]:

> On 8 April 2011, Iron Mountain confirmed that it is sunsetting its public cloud storage business. The company said that the official end date for the service would be "no sooner than the first half of 2013," but said it stopped accepting any new customers as of 1 April 2011. Iron Mountain says it will continue to offer services to its current cloud storage customers, help them migrate to another provider or return the data. Virtual File Store customers that stay with Iron Mountain will be transferred to a higher-value offering, File System Archiving (FSA) in 2012. The new offering will be a hybrid that leverages policy-based archiving on site and in the cloud with indexing and classification capabilities. Archive Service Platform customers have no migration path and are being terminated or moved to an alternative service provider.

---

[3]http://www.theregister.co.uk/2011/04/11/iron_mountain_exits_public_storage_cloud/.

Many consumers who entrusted their data into Iron Mountain's storage servers have not previously planned alternative storage. This case also raised the awareness that even large cloud service providers can fold, and consumers should never take their availability for granted. What if public cloud giants such as Google, Amazon, or Microsoft fold? What will happen to the customers' massive amounts of data and our cloud-dependent lives?

If a company liquidates, what happens to the data stored in the cloud? Who can be held accountable for the state of affairs? What powers do cloud consumers have? These are the questions we will further explore in this book.

3.3 GATEKEEPERS—GOVERNMENTS VERSUS TECHNOLOGY CREATORS

In 2011, at the University of the West of England (UWE) in Bristol, UK, Ko attended an interesting symposium which placed legal professionals and computer scientists in the same room—to discuss about the upcoming technical and legal challenges of cloud computing.

At the symposium, the concept of the two "gatekeepers" of technology was proposed—technology creators and the governments. Due to its high concentration of high-tech startups and companies, many view Silicon Valley as the gatekeeper of sorts for several technological advances.

Why was this raised? This is because when one understands the gatekeepers' concept, we understand the state of the art of our cloud security ecosystem. At the time of writing, the technology creator gatekeepers are currently almost exhausting their capabilities to push the security agenda. Further, Choo (2014a,b) noted that a legitimate need exists for cooperation between the different gatekeepers, but there are also legitimate concerns about cloud service providers being compelled to scan or hand over user data of interest that reside in the cloud or to report on/monitor particular types of transactional data to government agencies without the user's knowledge or consent due to territorial jurisdiction by a foreign government. In addition, overseas cloud service providers might not be legally obliged to notify cloud users (i.e., the data owners) about such requests.

It is now time for the legal echelons and governments in the international community to take lead. For example, we are starting to see the gradual release of international standards and criteria for cloud security, and development of certified cloud security professionals (CCSP).

Most recently, we witnessed the launch of a new professional certification—the (ISC)2-CSA CCSP (which Ko is one of the pioneer group of subject matter experts developing the curriculum and exam).

4 TOP THREATS AND VULNERABILITIES OF CLOUD SECURITY

Given the above scenarios and context, it is timely to cover some of the top threats and vulnerabilities of cloud computing security. Understanding the top threats in this chapter sets the scene for all readers when they approach the remaining chapters.

4.1 CLOUD SECURITY ALLIANCE'S TOP THREATS TO CLOUD COMPUTING RESEARCH

In 2009 and 2010, the Cloud Security Alliance (CSA) published two relevant publications, namely, (1) Security Guidance for Critical Areas of Focus in Cloud Computing v2.16 (Cloud Security Alliance, 2009) and (2) Top Threats to Cloud Computing (Cloud Security Alliance, 2010). In the Top Threats article, seven threats were listed as the top threats to cloud computing (Table 1).

The CSA list is seminal in cloud security as it brought much-needed awareness to the flip side of cloud computing in 2009. For example, because of the low price and availability of cloud services, it is easy for a malicious attacker to use the cloud for nefarious uses. Some news articles have mentioned about the use of cheap cloud servers to crack Wi-Fi access points' passwords via sheer brute force.[4]

It is also interesting to note that all threats have elements of technical, legal, and management aspects involved. The focus has always been on the technologies but this view has to broaden to take a holistic ecosystem view for true risk management. It is not surprising and cyber security is no longer the preserve of any single country, entity, (industry) sector, or disciplinary field because of the nature and extent of an increasingly connected and sophisticated technological and user bases (Choo, 2014a,b). There is, therefore, a need to bring together perspectives and approaches from different disciplines and countries and investigate what we can do singularly and collaboratively to secure our cyber space and future.

However, while these pioneering CSA documents raised the awareness of the threats, the documents depended on initial expert opinion but were unable to gather ample empirical support for the justification of the top threats—which is extremely difficult to achieve without participation from all stakeholders. Empirical data enable the research and practitioner industry to focus on addressing the "true" reported top threats. While the Top Threats report highlighted the potential risks cloud users and service providers face, debates about whether opinion-based lists such as the CSA

Table 1 Overview of CSA Top Threats to Cloud Computing v1.0 (Cloud Security Alliance. 2010)

No.	CSA Top Threat
1	Abuse and nefarious use of cloud computing
2	Insecure interfaces and APIs
3	Malicious insiders
4	Shared technology issues
5	Data loss or leakage
6	Account or service hijacking
7	Unknown risk profile

---

[4]Src: http://www.theregister.co.uk/2011/01/11/amazon_cloud_wifi_cracking/.

top threats (and the latest version—the so-called Notorious Nine) stand to hold against the test of time.

For example, the CSA top threat "Shared technology issues" highlights the potential for a company A to look into company B's data while sharing the same cloud technologies via multitenancy software controls. At the time of writing, it is a common view among the cloud security research and practitioner communities that this is a relatively remote risk, and this has been the subject of various research initiatives.

4.2 STATISTICS OF COMMON VULNERABILITIES FACED BY CLOUD SERVICE PROVIDERS

This calls for the need for empirical data to study the "real" situation. Given cloud computing is still in its early stages, and the general reluctance for companies to release public data on cloud security-related outages, it is very difficult to achieve full empirical analysis on the top threats and vulnerabilities of cloud security.

The closest empirical study was perhaps the 2013 study conducted by Ko et al. (2012, 2013) of the Cyber Security Researchers of Waikato (CROW) at the University of Waikato in New Zealand, and Nanyang Technological University and Cloud Security Alliance's Asia Pacific region in Singapore. This study looked at 11,491 news articles on cloud computing-related outages from 39 news sources (e.g., CNet, TechTarget, CNN, etc.) between January 2008 and February 2012—effectively covering the "first 5 years" of cloud computing's boom in a best effort fashion. Through a strict definition and qualification process for what constitutes a "cloud outage" incident, 172 unique incidents were identified from the overlapping, duplicated news articles (*note*: this also shows the state of today's news dissemination). While it does not necessarily cover the entire cloud security ecosystem, it is the "best one can get" given the nature of security incident disclosures.

Of the 172 reported cloud vulnerability incidents, 129 (75%) declared the cause(s) while 43 (25%) incidents did not. It was observed that the top three cloud providers, Amazon, Google, and Microsoft, account for about 56% of all nontransparent incidents of cloud vulnerability. It was also reported that beginning in 2010, cloud providers became more transparent with their reports of cloud vulnerability incidents, most likely because Amazon became more open about the causes of their incidents. As is to be expected with the growth of cloud vulnerability, over the years, the number of cloud vulnerability incidents has risen (see Figure 1). In fact from 2009 to 2011, the number of cloud vulnerability incidents more than doubled—from 33 to 71, most likely due to the phenomenal growth in cloud services.

The statistics collected from actual news reports not only validated CSA's top threat categories but also empirically revealed five newly discovered categories of vulnerabilities in cloud security. Five new threat categories (*T8—Hardware Failure, T9—Natural Disasters, T10—Closure of Cloud Service, T11—Cloud-Related Malware, and T12—Inadequate Infrastructure Design and Planning*) are needed for a more accurate representation of cloud outage threats and vulnerabilities. The new CSA revised threat list encompassing reported outages is listed in Table 2.

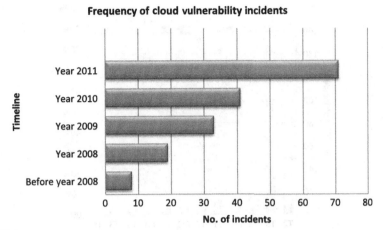

FIGURE 1

Frequency of cloud vulnerability incidents from 2008 to 2011 (Ko et al., 2012, 2013).

Table 2 Vulnerability Classification Derived from Reported Cloud Outages

No.	Top Cloud Vulnerability Classification Based on Outages Reported in the News (2008–2011)
T1	Abuse and Nefarious Use of Cloud Computing
T2	Insecure Interfaces and APIs
T3	Malicious Insiders
T4	Shared Technology Issues
T5	Data Loss or Leakage
T6	Account or Service Hijacking
T7	Unknown Risk Profile
T8	Hardware Failure
T9	Natural Disasters
T10	Closure of Cloud Service
T11	Cloud-Related Malware
T12	Inadequate Infrastructure Design and Planning

Figure 2 shows the frequency of occurrence of the existing seven CSA threats and five new threats proposed by the authors of the vulnerability statistics report. The three most frequent incidents are (Ko et al., 2012, 2013):

- CSA Threat 2 "*Insecure Interfaces & APIs*" with 51 incidents accounting for 29% of all threats;
- CSA Threat 5 "*Data Loss & Leakage*" with 43 incidents accounting for 25% of all threats reported;
- CSA Threat 8 "*Hardware Failure*" with 18 incidents accounts for 10% of all threats reported.

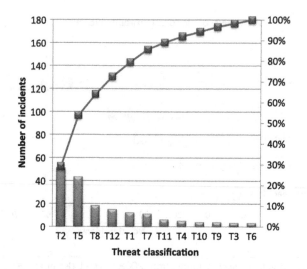

FIGURE 2

Pareto analysis of the number of incidents between 2008 to 2011 (Ko et al., 2012, 2013).

All other threats have 15 or fewer cloud vulnerability incidents each, accounting for 8.5% or less. A Pareto analysis reveals that the first three threats, CSA Threat 2, CSA Threat 5, and New Threat 8, account for 64% of all cloud vulnerability incidents, although collectively they make up only 25% of total threats (see Figure 2).

This study also reported that most vulnerabilities (except two, namely, Insecure Interfaces & APIs and Data Loss or Leakage) are decreasing by the year, showing an improvement and stability of cloud computing services. However, the top three culprits (Insecure Interfaces & APIs, Data Loss or Leakage, Hardware Failure) form about 60% of the incidents! If we can reduce them, the cloud security ecosystem will definitely be very reliable. The study also shows there are still lots of room for accountability to the users. Prominent cloud service providers with large market shares have to take the lead and show increased transparency.

It is our hope that readers and organizations using the cloud or developing cloud services take note of these top risks, so that they can identify and manage them in advance of a catastrophic event. This leads us to Section 5.

5 MANAGING CLOUD SECURITY RISKS WITH THE DEMING CYCLE

One way to manage the risks well is to adopt the Plan-Do-Check-Act (or Plan-Do-Check-Adjust) (PDCA) cycle, also known as the Deming Cycle as it was proposed by Dr. W. Edwards Deming. The Deming Cycle mimics the rigorous scientific method without being tied to the different departmental constraints of an organization. This is also the reason why we chose to structure our book according to the Deming Cycle—to integrate the technical, legal, and management aspects of the cloud security ecosystem.

No one can expect full security, but one can expect high assurance from doing their due diligence with the breadth and depth of a full Deming Cycle implementation.

The Deming Cycle has been adopted by the best practices in the security field, including the ISO/IEC 27001 standard, which recommends the PDCA cycles for every institution's Information Security Management System (ISMS)—a thorough set of policies concerned with information security management or IT-related risks, primarily found in the ISO 27000 series of standards.

In the context of the cloud security ecosystem, let us dive into the details of each step in the following sections.

6 PLAN—THREATS, RISK, AND REQUIREMENTS LANDSCAPE

This book is divided into four main parts, guided by the PDCA stages. We have chosen to organize the technical, business, and legal aspects of cloud security into these stages to remove the current siloed view of the cloud. It is our hope that the PDCA approach extends into the multidisciplinary field of cloud security.

Part 1 of this book focuses on providing an overview of the threats, risks, and requirements landscape in the global cloud computing industry.

Chapter 2 introduces us to the cyber crime landscape in two Asian economical superpowers—Singapore and Hong Kong. The factors shaping the response to these criminal threats are also discussed.

Chapter 3 introduces taxonomies of the cloud attacks and provides an insight into the threat vectors, targets, actors, countermeasures, and the impact of the attacks. After which, this chapter introduces a conceptual risk assessment framework and describes an example scenario of a distributed denial of service and account hijacking (one of the top threats of cloud computing mentioned earlier).

Chapter 4 introduces the Multitiered Cloud Security Model (MTCS), a world-leading government-led cloud service provider evaluation model implemented by the Singapore government as a standard SS 584. The SS 584 is the world's first cloud security standard that covers multiple tiers and can be applied by cloud service providers to meet differing cloud user needs for data sensitivity and business criticality. The model has three tiers ordered by data sensitivity and criticality. Tier 1 is designed for nonbusiness critical data and system, with baseline security controls to address security risks and threats in potentially low-impact information systems using cloud services (e.g., Web sites hosting public information). Tier 2 is for organizations running business critical data and systems through a set of more stringent security controls to address security risks and threats in potentially moderate impact information systems using cloud services to protect business and personal information (e.g., Confidential business data, e-mail, CRM—customer relation management systems). Tier 3 is designed for regulated organizations with specific requirements and more stringent security requirements. Industry-specific regulations may be applied in addition to these controls to supplement and address security risks and threats in high impact information systems using cloud services (e.g., highly confidential business data, financial records, medical records).

7 DO—CLOUD SECURITY APPROACHES AND CHALLENGES

After understanding the Plan stage of the Cloud Ecosystem, it is key to understand the current and emerging technologies to uphold the security and privacy of cloud consumers and service providers. The trust relationship discussed in Section 3 is neither sustainable nor long term. This calls for novel techniques which will empower better security and privacy for data owners in the cloud, covered in Part 2 of this book.

Chapter 5 presents an introduction to a much-talked about, but seldom understood holy grail of cloud security—homomorphic encryption. Intentionally written in plain English and with easy-to-follow examples, it provides an overview of the partial and fully homomorphic encryption techniques and discusses the open issues surrounding this area of cloud security.

Chapter 6 looks at the general pitfalls and advantages of protection via isolation techniques. The chapter introduces the isolation techniques in virtualization hypervisors and networking architectures, and provides an in-depth overview of the known attacks and protection strategies.

Chapter 7 then takes a legal perspective on the protection of digital identity in the cloud. It highlights the difficulties of identity protection given the nature of cloud computing handling cross-border data. The chapter also discusses the strategies recommended for the uphill task of protecting the digital identity in the era of cloud computing.

On the topic of cross-border data, Chapter 8 looks at another key question commonly asked of cloud data—provenance or "what has happened to the cloud data?" The chapter discusses about the use of provenance for data accountability and the challenges of conducting provenance reconstruction from environments which lack prior provenance tracking. A provenance-based model for cloud data accountability is also introduced in this chapter.

Chapter 9 covers the emerging security deliver model—Security-as-a-Service (SecaaS). It addresses the current lack of review of the SecaaS industry and identifies gaps after the SecaaS categories are classified. Chapter 10 talks about the technical, legal, and management issues of secure migration to and from the cloud.

Chapter 11 introduces readers to another emerging security challenge related to the cloud—the Internet of Things. Chapter 12 talks about knowledge management concepts to manage the scalability and privacy of business networks, while leveraging the capabilities of the cloud.

Chapter 13 takes a unique technical aspect—the utilization of psychological and communication theories to promote safer cloud security behaviors. Humans are always seen as the weakest links to an organization, and readers can learn from the communication theories and related psychological theories toward enhancing safer security behaviors.

8 CHECK—FORENSICS AND INCIDENT RESPONSE

Malicious cyber activities are no longer a matter of if but of when (Quick et al., 2014), and when such an incident is detected, we need to be able to respond and investigate—the focus of Part 3.

Chapter 14 presents an evidence collection and analysis methodology for Android devices. Chapter 15 demonstrates the utility of the methodology using seven popular Android apps (i.e., Dropbox, OneDrive, Box, ownCloud, Evernote, OneNote, and Universal Password Manger) as a case study. Various information were recovered and using the information obtained, the investigators could access the cloud service's servers as the user (and access their files) on the device for five of the six apps examined that communicated and authenticated with their servers. Similarly, findings from the forensic investigations undertaken in Chapters 16 and 19 contribute to an up-to-date understanding of cloud data artifacts that could be recovered from mobile and other computing devices.

Chapter 17 introduces a conceptual cloud incident handling model by integrating digital forensic practices in cloud incident handling and presents a case study implementation using the open-source OwnCloud solution.

Using a higher education organization as a case study, Chapter 18 reviews the cloud security and forensic readiness of the IaaS provider. Findings from the case study echoed several of the concerns identified in this and other chapters such as a lack of clarity with regard to the requirements for specific IaaS security, digital evidence collection, and digital investigation.

9 ACT—GOVERNANCE AND AUDITING

Part 4 focuses on long-term actions and adjustments for higher security postures of the cloud.

It starts from an IT auditor's point of view, with Chapter 20 introducing the steps for planning, scoping and executing the auditing of cloud service providers. Chapter 21 introduces a computational trust method for quantifying security capabilities, so that capabilities can be effectively communicated.

Chapter 22 introduces a tool-based risk assessment of cloud infrastructures as social-technical systems, using model-based, attack-based, and combined techniques.

10 SUMMARY

Cloud computing challenges the concept of boundaries. It is common for a consumer to use a cloud e-mail service offered by a company located in country A, while this service runs on infrastructure hosted by another company at country B located in another continent. Our vision is that cloud service providers should be data processors and not data owners (Ko et al., 2011).

This is the beginning of a new era where computing is increasingly expected to be hosted on the cloud. Hence, to embark on this book, we invited several experts in their own fields to contribute the several aspects of this. As expected by security professionals, we have organized our chapters into a Plan-Do-Check-Act cycle. We hope that you will enjoy reading the rest of this book. One thing for sure, the cloud is here to stay, and it is to our best interest that we secure it.

REFERENCES

Chen, A., 2010. GCreep: Google Engineer Stalked Teens, Spied on Chats (Updated), *Gawker. com*. Retrieved from http://gawker.com/5637234/gcreep-google-engineer-stalked-teens-spied-on-chats (4 September 2010).

Choo, K.-K.R., 2010. Cloud computing: challenges and future directions. Trends Iss. Crime Crim. Justice 400, 1–6.

Choo, K.-K.R., 2014a. A conceptual interdisciplinary plug-and-play cyber security framework. In: Harleen, K., Xiaohui, T. (Eds.), ICTs and the Millennium Development Goals—A United Nations Perspective. Springer, New York, USA, pp. 81–99.

Choo, K.-K.R., 2014b. Legal issues in the cloud. IEEE Cloud Comput. 1 (1), 94–96.

Cloud Security Alliance, 2009. Security Guidance for Critical Areas of Focus in Cloud Computing V2.16. Retrieved from https://cloudsecurityalliance.org/csaguide.pdf.

Cloud Security Alliance, 2010. Top Threats to Cloud Computing (V1.0). Retrieved from https://cloudsecurityalliance.org/topthreats/csathreats.v1.0.pdf.

Ko, R.K.L., 2010. Cloud computing in plain English. ACM Crossroads 16 (3), 5–6. http://dx. doi.org/10.1145/1734160.1734163.

Ko, R.K.L., Kirchberg, M., Lee, B.S., 2011. From system-centric to data-centric logging—accountability, trust & security in cloud computing. In: Paper Presented at the Defense Science Research Conference and Expo (DSR).

Ko, R.K.L., Lee, S.S.G., Rajan, V., 2012. Understanding cloud failures. IEEE Spectr. 49 (12), 84.

Ko, R.K.L., Lee, S.S.G., Rajan, V., 2013. Cloud computing vulnerability incidents: a statistical overview: Cloud Security Alliance Cloud Vulnerabilities Working Group.

NIST, 2011. The NIST Definition of Cloud Computing. Retrieved from http://csrc.nist.gov/publications/nistpubs/800-145/SP800-145.pdf.

Quick, D., Martini, B., Choo, K.-K.R., 2014. Cloud Storage Forensics. Syngress Publishing/Elsevier, Waltham, MA, USA.

Plan: Threats, risk, and requirements landscape

Cybercrime in cloud: Risks and responses in Hong Kong, Singapore

2

Yiu Chung Laurie Lau

Asia Pacific Association of Technology and Society, Hong Kong SAR

1 INTRODUCTION

1.1 DEFINITION OF CLOUD COMPUTING

Although the term "cloud computing" has already been used elsewhere in this publication, for ease of understanding, in this chapter I follow the model used by Quick et al. in their 2014 book, *Cloud Storage Forensics*. Basically, cloud computing comprises three models:

> *Cloud IaaS: This provides clients with access to storage space, bandwidth, and other fundamental computing services. It effectively expands the computing capability of the customer, allowing them to run their own software and applications using the cloud infrastructure;*
>
> *Cloud PaaS: This allows the customer to gain access to the computer platform or operating systems of the cloud instances (e.g. Windows and Linux) and an underlying database so that they can create or acquire applications;*
>
> *Cloud SaaS: This allows clients of the CSP to utilize software and applications running on the cloud infrastructure. The applications are accessed via remote computers and mobile devices using the appropriate cloud interface software. The consumer's device acts like a portal to the software and data stored in the cloud.*

However, describing cloud computing crime in simple terms has been a challenge ever since the early days of the Internetwork revolution. A variety of terms are used when explaining the criminality associated with the popularity and commercialization of information communication technology (ICT), including "new technology crime," "online crime," "cybercrime," and "Internet crime." These terms tend to be used interchangeably, which makes it difficult to provide universal definitions. ICT is constantly evolving along with the associated criminality, including cloud computing crime. In addition, certain types of online activities considered to be

"Internet" or "cloud computing" crime in some countries are not considered as such in others. For example, in most Western common law countries, if a female posts topless beach holiday "selfies" on Facebook via a smart mobile phone to share among friends, the act would be considered a harmless private activity. In many Muslim countries, and certainly those in the Middle East, however, the act would be considered a criminal offense; the woman would be subject to criminal prosecution in court and the act would be punishable by public lashing. Both polity and invested interests are at play, and the novelty of the "risk" or "threat" posed by new forms of technology-associated crimes can be used to support a larger share of government funding.

Cloud computing crime has become a broad term that embraces all forms of digital crime such as television and film piracy and location-based smart mobile phone crime. The growth and development of cloud computing crime has largely been a consequence of the expansion of cloud computing environments capable of facilitating criminality. Thus, for the purposes of this chapter, "cloud computing crime" is any criminality committed with the aid of recognized cloud computing models, including the smart mobile phone operation system model.

1.2 GROWTH IN CLOUD COMPUTING: HONG KONG AND SINGAPORE

In recent years, places such as Hong Kong, Singapore, and other parts of Asia have witnessed noticeable growth in cloud computing. The popularity of smaller mobile computing devices such as smart phones, which have resulted from advancements in Internet technologies, has been combined with the nature of cloud computing, which provides faster, easier access to files in remote locations, to allow users to access and update files on the move. Although cloud computing technologies offer efficiency in terms of users' hardware requirements and access barriers, they also create challenges for both law enforcement authorities and individuals alike. One such issue is the policing of computer-related crime, which involves gathering evidence from, storing data in, the cloud, and then prosecuting the perpetrator. Scholars have drawn attention to some of these issues, but the socio-legal perspective treated here has not received much attention in the literature to date. Policing priority is typically set by country or place individually according to their needs. Factors affecting policing include the economy, legal traditions, police structure and organization, cultural factors, and political structure. The protection of these factors and their perceived importance is different in each jurisdiction and under each government in power, and thus policing varies accordingly.

This phenomenon is also true for policing the Internetwork, as the development and level of Information Technology (IT) access and infrastructures differ in different parts of the world. For instance, in accordance with the United Nation International Telecommunication Union (UNITU) report on the digital divide in 2012,[1] IT

---

[1] See United Nation Telecommunication Union Report (2012).

disparities in terms of access to information and communication technology are pronounced between the developed Western economies such as those of America, Canada, and Western European countries (this group includes a few advanced economies in Asia such as those of Japan, South Korea, Singapore, and Hong Kong), and the less-developed economies such as those of Northern Africa, Latin America, Pacific Ocean Islands, and some parts of South Eastern Asia. The level of policing for the Internetwork is also different, as each country prompts different government perceptions of its level of technology risk or economic threat. These perceptions are largely dependent on the level of technology each country relies on to generate wealth, and sometimes on how much a given government sees technology as a threat to its political structure and systems. Thus, technology policing is prioritized differently from country to country.

However, the same UNITU 2012 report stressed that the digital divide had closed significantly between developed and developing nations, particularly in South East Asia and numerous African countries due to the increase in portable devices such as smart phones and the decrease in their cost. As International Telecommunication Union (ITU) director Brahima Sanou[2] said:

> The surge in numbers of mobile-broadband subscriptions in developing countries has brought the Internet to a multitude of new users. Despite the downward trend, prices remain relatively high in many low-income countries. For mobile broadband to replicate the mobile-cellular miracle and bring more people from developing countries online, 3G network coverage has to be extended and prices have to go down even further. ... Mobile-cellular subscriptions registered continuous double-digit growth in developing country markets, for a global total of six billion mobile subscriptions by end 2011 ... noting that China and India each account for around one billion subscriptions. Mobile broadband continues to be the ICT service displaying the sharpest growth rates. Over the past year, growth in mobile-broadband services continued at 40 per cent globally and 78 per cent in developing countries. There are now twice as many mobile-broadband subscriptions as fixed-broadband subscriptions worldwide.

The increased ownership of smart phones in these countries has not only narrowed the gap between them and traditional fixed-location devices such as desktop computers, but also shifted the information and communication technology landscape. The technique of virtualization in cloud computing has created an economy of scale, such that services are only provided when there is consumer demand. This allows service providers to reduce their materials and service costs. On one hand, almost all smart phone devices now allow users to constantly connect with the Internetwork on the go; anytime, anywhere. On the other hand, to enhance the user's smart mobile phone experience, service providers must design their services based on users' needs. This can result in compromised safe-guards and security, which in turn create opportunities

---

[2]United Nation Telecommunication Union Report (2012).

for criminal activity, and authorities have yet to catch up to these technologies, especially when perpetrators can be located overseas or in different police jurisdictions.

The increase in mobile smart phone use has also been rapid and significant in Singapore and Hong Kong. To put it in perspective, according to the Nielsen smart phone report in 2013,[3] both Hong Kong and Singapore were ranked at the top for smart phone penetration rate in the Asia Pacific region, with more than 87% of their populations owning smart mobile phones. As Sagar Phadke, Director of Nielsen's Telecom and Technology Practice in Southeast Asia, North Asia, and the Pacific said:

> *The growth in connected device ownership across Asia Pacific has been staggering in recent years. While this growth is expected to begin levelling out, consumers' use of connected devices will continue to evolve and expand, presenting vast opportunities for organisations to engage with consumers on an almost ubiquitous platform. It is becoming more critical than ever for companies to develop sophisticated mobile strategies designed to leverage changing connected device behaviours and develop ongoing consumer engagement.[4]*

There has been an ample and growing opportunity for smart phone commerce in fields such as mobile banking, games and videos, and advertising in the Asia Pacific region, particularly in Hong Kong and Singapore. However, the rapid increase in smart phone use and penetration has greatly increased the potential for corresponding growth in smart mobile phone crime. For example, according to a 2011 KPMG International report on cybercrime, cybercriminals are moving beyond desktop computers to target smart mobile phones and other mobile devices. The report stated that in the previous 2 years, digital crimes specifically targeting mobile devices had risen 46%.[5] Although the actual level of smart mobile phone crime is not known, and what is known is probably just the tip of the iceberg, the potential for problems is sobering. What follows are examples of smart phone crime in Hong Kong and Singapore.

In Hong Kong, a local Chinese newspaper reported that during the 2014 World Cup, the Hong Kong Police noticed that betting on illegal football matches through mobile phone apps increased.[6] Mobile apps have also been used to sell counterfeit goods in Hong Kong. In a joint operation between Customs and Excise and the police in April 2014 in the Tsim Sha Tsui area, 7 people were arrested and 1156 items of suspected counterfeit goods valued at HK$270,000[7] were seized. In July 2014, a similar operation was mounted by the Hong Kong authorities and 42 people (7 of whom were younger than 22) were arrested and goods valued at about HK$340,000 were seized.[8] According to Hong Kong authorities, in the first 6 months

---

[3]Cited Media Research Asia (2013).
[4]Media Research Asia (2013).
[5]See KPMG International (2011).
[6]See Sing Tao Daily Newspaper (2014).
[7]See Press Release (2014a).
[8]See Press Release (2014b).

of 2014 the number of people arrested who are younger than 22 has risen by 67% compared to the same period in 2013. In these cases, most of the young offenders participated in the sale of suspected counterfeit goods on Internet platforms via mobile phones, through auction sites or social networks, during their leisure time. Other types of crime have been committed using smart mobile phones. In January 2014, according to Paul Gordon, Sai Kung divisional commander, thieves used surveillance cameras to monitor their targets instead of doing their own reconnaissance:

> *A device will be fixed outside a house and linked to their [smart]-mobile phones, to monitor when it is left unattended. Then they will take the chance to break in. The device was low-tech and could be bought cheaply in the Sham Shui Po electronics market. But it was the first time police had seen it used in this kind of crime.*[9]

In Singapore, for example, according to a report released by WebSynergies,[10] there have been a million Singaporean cybercrime victims. The report estimated a total of US$1 billion lost through cybercrime over the period of a year. Smart mobile phones have become the tool of choice for cybercriminals in Singapore, as viruses can migrate from Personal Computers (PCs) to mobile devices. The incidence of related petty crimes such as smart phone snatching has also risen. In another example from Singapore, Channel News Asia[11] interviewed an Inspector of the Singapore Police. During the live interview, conducted on April 23, 2014, the Inspector described a smart mobile phone crime case involving a woman in her late 40s who was an accountant by profession. She allegedly befriended a male who claimed to be a pilot for Singapore Airline. They met and chatted on Whatsapp[12] through their smart phones for some time, and ultimately agreed to meet face-to-face in a café near the Singapore International Airport. The supposed pilot told the woman that he had been in a hurry to get out of his flat and had forgotten to bring enough Euros with him. He asked the woman if she would transfer 2000 Singapore dollars to a certain bank account under his name, so that when he landed in Germany the next day he could withdraw the cash from an ATM. He promised to repay her in a week's time, when he returned. The woman agreed and transferred the money via her smart phone. For some time, she did not hear from the man and could not contact him on Whatsapp. After 4 months she reported him to the police. The man was eventually arrested wearing a pilot's uniform near the international airport, in a sting operation mounted by the police after a few more women fell victim to his scam and reported him.

---

[9]See Mok and Lo (2014).
[10]See WebSynergies.
[11]The Researcher has watched this program on April 23, 2014, at 10 p.m., live at home and took note for the case.
[12]WhatsApp is a live chat application use on smart mobile phone, in August 2014, tweeted by WhatsApp CEO Jan Koum, which revealed more than 600 millions of registered active users globally.

We only know about these cloud computing-enabled smart mobile phone crimes because they were in the public domain, but the true level of such crime remains unclear. The lack of reports on cloud computing crime is probably related to the fact that cloud computing is a relatively new concept for law enforcement authorities. The term was only coined in the late 2000s. Victims of cloud computing crime might not even realize their status as such, or they may choose not to report it, as the police are sometimes unable to recognize it as such and instead record it as traditional street crime. Even when the police recognize and record an event as cloud computing crime, they may have difficulty following up, especially if the servers and data involved are located overseas or in multiple jurisdictions. As Quick et al. explain, "the key component of cloud computing is multi-tenancy capability, which is referred to as a shared pool of resources . . . individual files may be distributed across multiple disks and storage systems across multiple jurisdictions."[13] Securing and preserving a chain of evidence for prosecution in court involves significant police resources, and even if the culprit is deported to face justice, the case may not pass the prosecution's test of public interest and the perpetrator could escape justice.

2 KEY FACTORS SHAPING "RESPONSE": HONG KONG, SINGAPORE

2.1 HONG KONG

2.1.1 Economy

Hong Kong, founded by the British for trade purposes, was a British colony for over 150 years before it was restored to the People's Republic of China (PRC) on July 31, 1997. As an entrepot[14] and capitalist enclave without natural resources, Hong Kong's economy has largely been dependent on international and interregional trade. In the intermittent period between the 1950s and the early 1980s, Hong Kong was labeled a sweat-shop for the world's light manufactured goods, but with the open-door policy introduced by Communist China in 1978, Hong Kong industrialization came to an abrupt end in the early 1980s. Almost all of the manufacturing factories were moved northward across the border to Shenzhen City or beyond in mainland China, due to cheaper wages and land. By this time, Hong Kong was beginning to establish itself as a financial center and professional services hub, largely serving the booming mainland China economy supported by the open-door policy and the growth of the Asian economy. By the beginning of the twenty-first century, Hong Kong had become well established as the fourth largest global financial and banking center in the region. Over 90% of Hong Kong's Gross Domestic Product (GDP) is generated from nonmanufacturing-related industries, including banking, financial and professional services, and retail.

---

[13]See Quick et al. (2014, p. 5).
[14]Entrepot is a term use to describe a place where merchandise can be imported and exported without paying duties or tax, therefore the profit is being maximize.

Without other industries to generate wealth for Hong Kong, what is left is its status as an international financial center and its professional service-based industry, both of which are highly dependent on modern ICT to operate from, protect, and maintain the integrity of Hong Kong's ICT infrastructure.

2.1.2 Cultural factors

To its advantage, culturally, Hong Kong has been very receptive to newer technologies. The rapid adoption rate of smart mobile phones is one example. This is partially due to the fact that most new technology is manufactured in Asia, and thus the closest source of production is relatively cheap to purchase. Hong Kong's per capita income is also relatively high (at US$38,124 in 2013), and that wealth and purchasing power means the general population can afford to buy newly marketed technology rapidly, and as such they have become increasingly technologically savvy. For example, Hong Kong was one of only a few places on the globe to launch Apple's iPhone 6 in August 2014.

2.1.3 Political structure

Hong Kong's political structure reflects its legacy as a British colony. Characterized as a semiauthoritarian city state, Hong Kong did not become a democracy after its return to the PRC in 1997. Although there is currently an ongoing debate in Hong Kong over the democratic election (supposedly one man, one vote) of the Chief Executive of the Hong Kong Government Special Administrative Region in 2017, things remain uncertain because Beijing is wary about democracy in Hong Kong out of a fear that it might become a base for subversion to undermine the communist party rule in mainland China.

Hong Kong's governmental decision making is semiauthoritarian and top-down in nature, and the selection of the Chief Executive (formerly Governor) is tightly controlled from Beijing. Only 1200 members of a select committee are allowed to vote in the Chief Executive election, and a great majority of them are pro-Beijing merchants and professionals. The first Chief Executive was a well-known shipping tycoon, and the man who currently holds the office is also a well-known professional-turned-merchant. The Hong Kong Executive Councilors (the executive branch of government policy decision-making body, who act as a cabinet to the government) are largely appointed from a pool of merchants and professionals. Government policy does not answer to the public, and the general population does not vote the government into power. Policy answers only to Hong Kong's tycoons the small number of select committee members and the political master in Beijing. Ultimately, government policy's priority is to protect and reflect the interests of the ruling elite and their supporters, rather than those of the general public, because the latter does not vote.

Since Hong Kong's reintegration with China in 1997, there have been fears that some of the former's core values are being threatened, such as the erosion of rule of law due to the ways in which things are done in mainland China (corruption, nepotism, gangsterism, and the use of power and connections to avoid the law). Some events have been cause for concern in Hong Kong. For example, Beijing interpreted the Basic Law (the mini constitutional law of Hong Kong) in the late 1990s and early 2000s, but the major clash between Beijing and Hong Kong over the rule of law occurred in 2003, when Beijing instructed Hong Kong's government to introduce Article 23 into the Basic Law to regulate subversion. Article 23 is similar to the national security laws in many Western countries, but the very idea of such a law was new to postcolonial Hong Kong, and given the Chinese Communist Party and the Chinese government's track record, it sent chills down the spines of many in Hong Kong. The legislative process for Article 23 triggered a mass public outcry, with over half a million people protesting in the streets against the legislation. Eventually, Hong Kong's government put the National Security Bill on hold indefinitely, temporarily shielding the rule of law in Hong Kong from being "mainlandized."

However, the "mainlandization" of Hong Kong has accelerated, especially since 2003, after a series of crises including the Asian financial crisis in 1997 and the avian flu and severe acute respiratory syndrome outbreaks. These crises prompted Hong Kong to actively seek help from the mainland and push for greater economic integration. The Closer Economic Partnership Arrangement between mainland China and Hong Kong is a case in point. Politically, it is in Beijing's interest to help Hong Kong, as it would be seen as a failure for Beijing if Hong Kong failed only a few years after reintegration. These factors have helped to accelerate the pace of Hong Kong's integration with the mainland, both politically and economically.

2.1.4 Criminal justice and legal systems

Hong Kong's police force, as an arm of the government established in the early 1840s, is directly funded by the government. The Commissioner of Police is appointed by and answers directly to the Chief Executive. The police force as a whole is directly accountable to the government officials at the Security Bureau. The Commissioner of Police, government officials, and the Chief Executive can be called before the Legislative Council to explain their decisions on issues relating to policing, but because Hong Kong is not a democratic society, the priorities for policing in Hong Kong are not set by election manifesto. Thus, policing priorities are more likely to reflect the interests of the officials at the highest level of government than those of the general public.

As a former British colony, Hong Kong is founded on common law. The main piece of legislation on computer-related crime is the Computer Crimes Ordinance of 1993. According to a report released by the Hong Kong interdepartment working group on computer-related crime, the Computer Crimes Ordinance was instituted by amending existing laws and creating some new offenses to broaden the coverage of the extant legislation. Hong Kong's computer-related crime legislation is sufficiently flexible to cover both the physical and the virtual worlds.[15]

---

[15]See Inter-department Working Group on Computer Related Crime Report (2000, pp. 5–8).

2.2 SINGAPORE

2.2.1 Economy

Like Hong Kong, Singapore was also part of the British Empire. However, unlike Hong Kong, Singapore gained independence from Malaysia in the late 1960s as a fully sovereign nation. Singapore's economy is also different from that of Hong Kong. It comprises manufacturing (including hi-tech manufacturing and R&D), biotechnology, pharmaceuticals, electronics, technology and telecommunications, import and export, oil refinery, shipping and transport (South East Asian hub), financial and banking services and professional services, and retail. Almost 50% of Singapore's export trades are interregional: Malaysia (12.2%), Hong Kong (10.9%), mainland China (10.7%), Indonesia (10.5%), and Japan (5.5%). Hence, Singapore economy is diverse.

As an independent nation, Singapore's clear advantage over Hong Kong is that she does not answer to a political master and is free to decide her own economic policy. One benefit of this is Singapore's technological policy. From early on in its independence, Singapore's government has exploited technology as leverage for economic development.[16] As a result, Singapore's economy has improved by adopting technology as its bedrock to upgrade industries across the economy.[17] Meanwhile, Singapore's government has directly nurtured new technology-based industries, especially in the economy's indigenous sectors such as IT, biotechnology, microelectronics, robotics and artificial intelligence, lasers/optics, and communications technology. The establishment of Infocomm Development Authority (IDA) of Singapore is a case in point. As Connie Carter put it:

> *Few can doubt that Singapore is a successful example of a growth-oriented, interventionist, capitalist state ... For four decades the Singapore government resolutely promoted economic development by: providing free market access to certain things; establishing and maintaining efficient infrastructure; orchestrating and investing in key export-led sectors of the economy; disciplining and educating the work force; and creating an ideology and delivering social justice and tangible benefits that secure the acquiescence of the people to the activities of the state and its elite bureaucrats.*[18]

Singapore's technological economy policy not only directly rewards indigenous sectors for innovation and high-tech adoption, but Singaporean society at large also benefits from this technology-focused economy policy by being receptive to newer technology and becoming early adopters of high-tech products. The high penetration rate of the latest smart mobile phone is such an example.

---

[16]Loh (1998, p. 46).
[17]*Ibid.*, p. 47.
[18]Carter (2002, pp. 1–2).

Unlike Hong Kong, Singapore is not dependent on a single industry to generate wealth. Despite being capitalist and unlike Hong Kong, whose government is not directly involved in the economy, the Singaporean government is deeply involved in the economy.[19] In Singapore, the domestic economy is largely dominated by two sovereign wealth funds: Temasek Holdings and GIC Private Limited (formerly known as Government of Singapore Investment Corporation, GIC). They are used to manage the country's reserves. Initially, the state's role was oriented more toward managing industries for economic development, but in recent decades the objectives of Singapore's sovereign wealth funds have shifted to a commercial basis. As a result, in recent years, government-linked corporations (GLCs) have played an increasingly substantial role in Singapore's domestic economy. The top six Singapore-listed GLCs account for about 17% of total capitalization of the Singapore Exchange. These fully and partially state-owned enterprises operate on a commercial basis and are granted no competitive advantage over privately owned enterprises. State ownership is prominent in strategic sectors of the economy, including telecommunications, media, public transportation, defense, ports, airport operations and banking, shipping, airlines, infrastructure, and real estate.

For example, IDA is the Singaporean government's invisible hand—a statutory board of the Singapore government under the Ministry of Communications and Information. It was formed in 1999 when the government merged the National Computer Board and Telecommunication Authority of Singapore to facilitate the convergence of IT and telephony. With an annual budget of more than S$34 million, the IDA is responsible for the development and growth of the infocomm sector in Singapore, and it functions as the country's infocomm industry champion, the national infocomm master planner and developer, and the Government Chief Information Officer. The IDA's most recent project has been Intelligent Nation 2015, a 10-year master plan. Singapore is aiming to be the first nation in Asia to be considered an IT-related "Smart Nation." In 2014, Singapore has achieved a number of top benchmarks, including having the most digitized government (with 98% of government services online and in the cloud and more that 60% of Singapore's Information Technology and Communication (ITC) in the cloud) and being the most networked country in the world (with 97% of the school-age population reporting access to a computer at home and 87% of households reporting access to broadband).[20]

2.2.2 Cultural factors

Like Hong Kong, Singapore is also very receptive to newer technology, and its population is technologically savvy. The British Broadcasting Corporation (BBC) has profiled Singapore as ". . . a hi-tech, wealthy city-state in south-east Asia."[21] Singapore's per capita income is also relatively high (at US$55,182 in 2013). With this

---

[19]Trocki (2006, p. 166).
[20]See IDA.
[21]See BBC News.

kind of wealth and purchasing power, the latest technological products are easily afforded by the general population. However, unlike Hong Kong, Singapore is recognized by its government as a multiracial society with different ethnicities (Chinese is the majority at almost 70%, with the rest of the population comprising those of Malay and Indian heritage). Singapore's government has managed its society carefully, through social engineering of ethnicity and by providing subsidy housing (today over 90% of the population is housed through the government housing scheme) and socially engineering education, particularly that with an English language base. This has transformed Singapore from a society once characterized by sharp contrast between ethnic groups who spoke different dialects and were separated by a large wealth gap into an affluent, English-speaking, middle-class industrialized metropolis. This has made Singapore culturally different from many of its neighbors in South East Asia, with the former being more in tune with technological development around the world because English is the common language used in commerce and in top scientific publications. Thus, Singapore has had an easy time acquiring newer technological knowledge and upgrading their skills.

2.2.3 Political structure

In theory, unlike Hong Kong, Singapore is a democratic nation state with a parliament based on the Westminster model. The government is voted into office via a one man–one vote election process. Every 5 years there are free and fair elections. The majority party or coalition gets to choose the prime minister, who then selects his/her cabinet of ministers. However, in practice, there is a similarity between Hong Kong and Singapore. As Vadaketh explains, "Singapore has been governed as an authoritarian state. One party, the People Action Party (PAP), dominates parliament."[22] Democracy in Singapore, however, is "Singapore style" or "Asian democracy" whereby political power is in the hands of few Singaporean elites. This "elite governance" or, more importantly the PAP, has been active since 1955 for almost 60 years. Decision making is largely a top-down process because there is little-to-no opposition in the parliament. As Low said, "the PAP government has viewed the economy and society as machines,"[23] and since PAP came to power, its legitimacy has largely been gained through a strategy of social pacification and the institution of repression and redistribution.[24] However, in recent years the PAP suffered a setback in the popularity vote at the 2011 general election, only receiving 60.1%, which was down 15% from the general election in 2001. PAP is facing the call for legitimacy in the government. Nonetheless, with more than 60% of the popular vote, PAP is still firmly in power.

Policymaking is largely pursuing economic growth, and anything else is a secondary consideration for the PAP government, as they believe that economic growth would benefit most segments of society.

---

[22]Vadaketh (2014, p. 189).
[23]Low (2014, p. 174).
[24]See Dezalay and Garth (2010, p. 141).

2.2.4 Criminal justice and legal systems

Like Hong Kong, Singapore was a British colony, and thus it has a common law tradition and a court system similar to that of Hong Kong, with a Court of Appeals at the top (equivalent to the Court of Final Appeal in Hong Kong, since July 1, 1997), then the High Court and the subordinate courts such as District, Magistrates', etc. However, the foundation of Singapore's penal code is different from that of Hong Kong's, as the former was taken from India's penal code in its exact entirety[25] and gradually developed a local flavor. Another difference is the Syariah Court,[26] which Hong Kong does not possess. One of the important first local pieces of legislation was the Criminal Procedure Ordinance of 1870, which was subsequently revised in 1900. Over time, various criminal laws were enacted. One of the most relevant to IT was the Computer Misuse Act, amended in 1998. Although Singapore's Computer Misuse Act followed the English act, one noteworthy difference from the Hong Kong Computer Crime Ordinance is that the offense created by the Singapore Act has extraterritorial effects, as Chan and Phang explain:

> *Provided either the accused person was in Singapore at the time or if the computer, program or data was in Singapore at the time. This is in recognition of the widespread reliance on computer technology all over the world and its vulnerability to manipulation either from within our shores or abroad.*[27]

As a former British colony, Singapore's criminal justice system is a punitive regime with no jury at court trial and punishment based on hard labor. The prison system is designed to be as degrading as possible, and public caning is not a rare punishment for wrongdoers. Although Singapore's prison system has been reformed in recent years with the introduction of concepts such as restorative justice, rehabilitation, education and training, the police, courts, and other regulatory agencies still take a hard line on crimes by "nipping them the bud" as a deterrent to others.

3 DISCUSSION

According to the Bitglass[28] Cloud Adoption Report published in August 2014, over 60% of businesses are still hesitant to transfer their data to the cloud due to security risk concerns that are largely about the cloud core architect of leveraging on virtualization. For example, Dropbox for Android smart phones uses cloud technology, and each time

---

[25]See Chan and Phang (2005, p. 245).

[26]The Singapore Syariah Court was established in 1955 by the government as an institution in settling disputes between divorcing Muslim couple and related matters, such as maintenance, mut'ah-consolatory gift payable to the ex-wife upon divorce, custody care control and access to children, and matrimonial property (see Syariah Court Singapore).

[27]Chan and Phang (2005, p. 256).

[28]See Bitglass, 2014.

data are delivered over the Internetwork through different telecommunication channels, the data are virtualized, leaving the user unaware of which servers are involved or which host is delivering and its location, because the cloud only delivers a minimum volume of data stored for any given client.

Businesses that worry about data integrity and that fear losing their sensitive data have questioned whether their data are protected from outsiders and from other tenants sharing the same cloud data center. Small business is especially vulnerable to this, as Australian Institute of Criminology research[29] in 2013 (Hutchings et al., 2013) shows that small business is vulnerable to side channel attack or cross-guest virtual machine breaches, because in cloud, resources are shared with different tenants at the same cloud data center. As a result, tenants might crossing the shared virtual machine segment and accessing the data of other tenants using shared physical resources. More importantly, the same research has identified that small business is more vulnerable because they operate in highly financially constrained environment when compared with larger "global multinational" business, yet they are induced by the promise of cloud computing to save on their ICT overhead. As Hutchings et al. said "However, in adopting cloud computing, it is this distinct operating environment that also renders small businesses vulnerable to criminal and security threats [once attack happened some small businesses might not able to recover from it and the business could possibly come to abruptly end]."[30] Nevertheless, nearly 90% of the businesses in Hong Kong and in Singapore are regarded as small businesses employing less than 20 people. Interestingly, users also wonder whether the data are protected from the cloud provider. Cloud computing is largely modeled on the demand for access to a shared pool of configurable computing resources such as networks, servers, storage, applications, and services. All such resource sharing is to ensure fast provision and saving on costs. For example, US researchers were able to hack into Gmail accounts with a 92% success rate by exploiting a weakness in smart mobile phone memory. The same research also found that once a smart mobile phone memory has been exploited, there is a great risk of collateral damage to other mobile apps on the same smart phone. As Zhiyun Qian said:

> *The assumption has always been that these apps can't interfere with [each] other easily, but such assumption was wrong, one app can in fact significantly impact another and result in harmful consequences for the user.*[31]

Although in theory Hong Kong and Singapore are exposed to similar risks and threats in the cloud, their level of readiness depends on how they perceive risk, as each individual jurisdiction interprets and responds to risk differently according to their unique policing needs. For example, Hong Kong would react strongly if its economy was threatened, particularly banking, financial, and professional services, because

---

[29]See Hutchings et al. (2013, p. 4).
[30]Hutchings et al. (2013, p. 7).
[31]See BBC News (2014).

they represent the only industries by which wealth is generated. Hong Kong's reputation as an international financial center is dependent on the integrity of its ICT. Thus, the Hong Kong police keep a watchful eye on the IT infrastructure to maintain foreign investor confident in Hong Kong, which creates employment and facilitates the payment of government taxes. Furthermore, as a part of China since 1997, Hong Kong must consider internal national politics, such as the growing threat of the separatist terrorism group from the Xinjiang region.

In June 2014, Hong Kong's government proposed to upgrade its Technology Crime Division (TCD) to the Cyber Security and Technology Crime Bureau. They tabled a proposal to the Legislative Council and explained the rationale behind the upgrade:

> *With increasing reliance on information and communication technology infrastructures and rising popularity of the Internet, local reports of technology crime have increased sharply by 18 times since 2002, i.e. from 272 cases in 2002 to 5 133 in 2013. The respective financial loss has also increased by almost 20 times from $45 million to $917 million over the past five years from 2009 to 2013. To enhance the Police's capability in combating technology crime, the establishment of TCD has increased from 26 posts in 2002 to the current establishment with 98 posts. Nevertheless, the current setup of TCD, with limited manpower and as a division within the CCB, is not able to meet the challenges of the increasingly sophisticated technology crimes and cyber security threats, not to mention the constant support provided by TCD to other formations of the Police in various cases, such as death inquest and locating missing persons. Today, Hong Kong has one of the highest concentrations of Wi-Fi hotspots in the world, and 97% of households are able to access to broadband services. With a high mobile phone penetration rate of 237% which is expected to grow further, individuals, corporates, and critical infrastructure are prone to technology crimes and cyber security threats.*[32]

Subsequently, a more dedicated police formation "organization and structure" is needed to tackle the fast growing technology crime trend, including smart mobile phone crime:

> *... to tackle the fast growing technology crime trend have become one of the operational priorities of the HKPF. Given the rapid advancement in information technology and the transnational nature of technology crime, there is a pressing need to strengthen the overall capability of the HKPF in combating technology crime and cyber security incidents.*[33]

Hong Kong's police have carefully explained their strategies to the Legislative Councilors, to take effect once the new technology crime bureau is established in early 2015:

---

[32]See LC Paper No. CB(2)1621/13-14(05) (2014, p. 1).
[33]*Ibid.*, p. 1.

Dedicated attention and strategic planning to tackle the fast growing technology crime trend have become one of the operational priorities of the HKPF. Given the rapid advancement in information technology and the transnational nature of technology crime, there is a pressing need to strengthen the overall capability of the HKPF in combating technology crime and cyber security incidents. With the establishment of a new bureau dedicated to the prevention and detection of technology crime and protection of cyber security, the HKPF's capability in combating technology crime and handling cyber security incidents will be greatly enhanced through the formulation of long-term objectives and strategies and expanded and dedicated efforts in the following areas –

i) *detecting syndicated and highly sophisticated technology crimes and conducting proactive intelligence-led investigation; providing assistance to critical infrastructure in conducting timely cyber threat audits and analysis in preventing and detecting cyber attacks against them;*

ii) *enhancing incident response capability to major cyber security incidents or massive cyber attacks;*

iii) *strengthening thematic researches on cyber crime trend and mode of operation, vulnerabilities of computer systems and development of malware;*

iv) *strengthening partnership with local stakeholders and overseas law enforcement agencies in information exchange and sharing of best practices to counter prevalent technology crime and cyber threats; and*

v) *developing new training programmes on cyber security and technology crimes.*[34]

Hong Kong's government recognizes the need to upgrade the police and equip them to face the ever-evolving technological landscape, with its ubiquitous mobile electronic devices such as smart mobile phones and tablets. Furthermore, after being reintegrated with China for more than 14 years, Hong Kong is far closer to China than ever before, economically and politically. The threat of terrorism from inside mainland China and especially from the Xinjiang region has increased, and this terrorist group is known to be quite IT savvy, often using social media to disseminate information and communicate with like-minded group members around the globe. They were said to have downloaded a video clip onto their smart mobile phones via the cloud and then watched it before carrying out their bombing attack inside mainland China. Therefore, the Hong Kong government must consider this type of threat. The increase in Muslim militant extremists represents an interregional, if not a global threat, and such militants are also known to use the electronic highway and smart mobile phones to carry out attacks and spreading ideological campaign material among themselves and other affiliated groups in Asia.

Like Hong Kong, Singapore is an important international financial center, yet its economy is more diverse, with a mixture of industries such as manufacturing,

---

[34]*Ibid.*, p. 2.

oil refinery, shipping, and biotechnology. Singapore is a democratic and a sovereign state with self-determination, even though its democratic process is regarded as a "controlled" democracy because the PAP has been in power since the first day of independence from Malaysia more than 50 years ago, with little or no opposition in parliament. On August 18, 2014, in a Singapore National Day speech broadcast live on Channel News Asia, Prime Minister Lee Hsien Leong said, "Keep Singapore special in Asia" by transforming it into "a smart nation." He introduced the Singapore Smart Nation Plan and provided detailed examples of a brand new housing community to be built in Jurong Lake District. The community will feature sensor boxes connected to fiber-optic lines deployed across the community and, eventually the entire country, at street lights, or bus stops. The sensor boxes can be designed to detect air pollutants, heavy rainfall, or traffic jams, or to report how full rubbish bins are, paired with cameras that can detect litter and remind litterbugs to pick up their trash. Singapore has already laid the groundwork for the Smart Nation plan. For example, fiber Internet is available to most households in the country, with super-fast 1 Gbps service costing as little as US$50 per month.

One of the key features of the proposed smart cities is the use of sensor boxes to set up wireless hotspots for a heterogeneous network, allowing smart phones and mobile devices to switch seamlessly between mobile data and Wi-Fi. Singapore has also set aside spectrum to create new super Wi-Fi networks with greater range and coverage but a lower power requirement compared to standard Wi-Fi. The network will also be used to transmit Smart Nation data via the cloud.

Singapore is controlled from the top-down; it is an authoritarian society. The government is trying to harness the power of technology to increase the economy's productivity and efficiency. Therefore, if the PAP responds and wants to increase the resources provided to the Singapore police to further increase their ability to fight the growing threat of technology-related crime, doing so will be relatively easier than it would be in many other democratic societies in Western developed economies. Singaporean voters may not necessarily agree with the PAP's decisions regarding finite public resources being transferred from other more pressing social needs, as when they voted to form the government. However, the PAP's manifesto may not mention anything about resources being earmarked for fighting technology-related crime, rather they may prefer to say that they will tackle traditional street crime and other forms of crime important to Singaporean voters.

Even if both Hong Kong and Singapore have the resources to respond to the potential risk of surging smart mobile phone crime, cloud computing-related crime is relatively new, and what worked in the past for less mobile devices such as personal computers may not work for the constant connectivity inherent in mobile devices. In the cloud, the configuration is usually a many-to-many network. To maximize the computing efficiency, virtualization is adopted, and thus data storage is located in host machine severs located in a many different places or countries. As Gray explains:

Cloud technology offers wonderful potential for users in terms of convenience, ease of obtaining updates etc. However, it presents significant legal challenges. Our laws, largely based on notions of territoriality, struggle to respond to technology in which lines on maps are largely irrelevant[35]

Therefore, providing the financial resources is an important first step for law enforcement agencies to build up their policing capabilities in the cloud. Other important elements are also required, such as knowledge of the cloud and the skills to find and collect electronic evidence in a live flow of data on a distribution network in the cloud, especially in a virtual machine. For example, in cloud data environments, it is often not possible to access the physical media that stores a customer's data, because cloud data are likely to be stored overseas and outside the investigating officer's jurisdiction. As Hooper et al. noted:

Even if the data is stored within jurisdiction, data distribution technologies [in cloud] may split a user's data across a number (potentially thousands) of storage devices within the cloud computing environment. LEAs would need to rely upon the cloud technology and the cloud service provider to gain access to the data that is stored by a customer and this can introduce issues with chain-of-custody best practices.[36]

Another problem facing the investigating officer is the preservation of the cloud data evidence. The integrity of the data is important, so potential data evidence cannot be modified. However, when exporting cloud data evidence for examination by the investigating officer, there is a high chance of modification, as Hooper et al. explain:

Preserved (to ensure that the potential evidence is not modified) function which many cloud computing environments do not currently support. Consequently, this could result in accidental modification of data as it is exported from the cloud computing environment for LEA [Law Enforcement Agency] use or intentional destruction of data by the suspect. Once the LEA has secured access to the cloud computing data, the format of the data is still not guaranteed and most of the prevalent digital forensic analysis tools have not yet been updated to decode the major cloud computing data export formats. While many IaaS data exports will likely mimic the data format that is currently supported as virtual machines, SaaS instances are more likely to use proprietary data formats and as such are unlikely to be supported by current tools[37]

Finally, even if the police in Singapore and Hong Kong do increase their policing capabilities in smart mobile phone and cloud-related crime, the legal limitations

---

[35]Gray (2013, p. 1).
[36]See Hooper et al. (2013, p. 156).
[37]*Ibid.*

remain a key factor in whether the perpetrator faces justice for the crime they have committed. Even though Singapore has enacted an extraterritorial law, because each country has enacted their own law according to their own socio-politic, socio-economic, cultural and legal traditions, and regulatory regimes, policing priorities differ by jurisdiction. There has been good progress on harmonizing the laws in recent years (INTERPOL 24/7 mutual legal assistant, Council of Europe Convention on Cybercrime, etc.), but the task remains problematic due to jurisdictional issues. Both Hong Kong and Singapore will have trouble bringing an overseas perpetrator from their country of domicile to face justice for committing a cloud computing crime in Hong Kong or Singapore.

In short, it is clear from this chapter that lots of catching up need to be done for Hong Kong and Singapore in order to beef-up their policing capability on cloud. At the domestic level, both governments in Hong Kong and in Singapore must provide sufficient financial support to the policing agencies to enable them to fight the emerging crime such as cloud and smart mobile phone crimes. Fighting technology-related crimes is an "arms race" which needs both money and human resources. More importantly, the government must provide training opportunities and education (including general public education to increase public awareness on emerging technologies crimes like cloud and smart mobile phone crimes and learning to cooperate with the private sector or businesses to reduce crime) for the law enforcement officers to upgrade their skills and knowledge on cloud which eventually help increase the success rate in bringing the perpetrator to face justice and punish them in court—as a deterrent to others not to commit the same offense. However, at the international level, it seems there is little that Hong Kong and Singapore can do to alter the current situation, except to participate actively within the international bodies and convention on technology-related crime, and to learn from other jurisdictions around the world on what they are doing and, at the same time, tap into latest information on cloud computing crime to get a head start in fighting the emerging technology-related crime for themselves in the region.

REFERENCES

BBC News. Gmail smartphone app hacked by researchers, August 22, 2014.

BBC News. Available: http://www.bbc.com/news/world-asia-15961759 (accessed September 13, 2014).

Bitglass. Available: http://www.bitglass.com/ (accessed August 27, 2014.).

Carter, C., 2002. Eyes on the Prize: Law and Economic Development in Singapore. Kluwer Law International, The Hague.

Chan, W.C., Phang, A.B.L., 2005. The development of criminal law and criminal justice. In: Tan, K.Y.L. (Ed.), Essays in Singapore Legal History. Marshall Cavendish, Singapore.

Dezalay, Y., Garth, G.B., 2010. Asian Legal Revivals. The University of Chicago Press, Chicago.

Gray, A., 2013. Conflict of laws and the cloud. Comput. Law Security Rev. 29, 58–65.

Hooper, C., Martini, B., Choo, R.K.K., 2013. Cloud computing and its implications for cybercrime investigations in Australia. Comput. Law Security Rev. 29, 152–163.

Hutchings, A., Smith, R.G., James, L., 2013. Cloud computing for small business: criminal and security threats and prevention measures. In: Trends and Issues in Crime and Criminal Justice, vol. 456. Australian Institute of Criminology, Canberra, Australia. May.

IDA. Available: http://www.ida.gov.sg/~/media/Files/About%20Us/Corporate%20Publications/Corporate%20Brochures/Smart%20Nation%20Infographic.pdf (accessed September 6, 2014).

Inter-department Working Group on Computer Related Crime Report, 2000. Hong Kong Government, Hong Kong, September.

KPMG International, 2011. Cyber Crime—A Growing Challenge for Governments. Available: https://www.kpmg.com/Global/en/IssuesAndInsights/ArticlesPublications/Documents/cyber-crime.pdf, accessed July 15, 2014.

LC Paper No. CB(2)1621/13-14(05), 2014. Legislative Council Panel on Security Creation of a permanent Chief Superintendent of Police post of the Cyber Security and Technology Crime Bureau. Hong Kong Police Force, Hong Kong, June 3.

Loh, L., 1998. Technological policy and national competitiveness. In: Mun Heng, T., Kong Yam, T. (Eds.), Competitiveness of the Singapore Economy. Singapore University Press, Singapore.

Low, D., 2014. What went wrong for the PAP in 2011. In: Low, D., Vadaketh, S.T. (Eds.), Hard Choices: Challenging the Singapore Consensus. NUS Press, Singapore.

Media Research Asia, 2013. Available: http://www.mediaresearchasia.com/view.php?type=press&id=3184 (accessed July 9, 2014).

Mok, D., Lo, C., 2014. Lockup or lose it, residents warned. South China Morning Post Newspaper, January 30.

Press Release, United Nation International Telecommunication Union Report, 2012. Available: http://www.un.org/apps/news/story.asp?NewsID=43265&Cr=digital+divide&Cr1#.U7tFmf2KCM9.

Press Release, 2014a. Information Service Department, Hong Kong SAR Government, April 2.

Press Release, 2014b. Information Service Department, Hong Kong SAR Government, July 3.

Quick, D., Martini, B., Choo, K.K.R. (Eds.), 2014. Cloud Storage Forensics. Syngress, Waltham.

Sing Tao Daily Newspaper, 2014. Midnight World Cup Favours Illegal Bookmakers Drawing New Blood, June 10.

Syariah Court Lengkok Bahru, Singapore. Available: http://app.syariahcourt.gov.sg/syariah/front-end/SYCHome_E.aspx.

Trocki, C.A., 2006. Singapore: Wealth, Power and the Culture of Control. Routledge, London.

Vadaketh, S.T., 2014. The future of democracy in Singapore. In: Low, D., Vadaketh, S.T. (Eds.), Hard Choices: Challenging the Singapore Consensus. NUS Press, Singapore.

WebSynergies. Available: http://blog.websynergies.biz/?p=996 (accessed 27.07.14.).

CATRA: Conceptual cloud attack taxonomy and risk assessment framework

3

Nina Viktoria Juliadotter, Kim-Kwang Raymond Choo

*Information Assurance Research Group, School of Information Technology and
Mathematical Sciences, University of South Australia, Adelaide, Australia*

1 INTRODUCTION

Cloud services are attractive to businesses as they are cost effective and offer flexibility, but adoption is hindered by concerns about security (Kotadia, 2014). Criminals also consider cloud services attractive as an attack on this target can yield large amounts of valuable data, or be a vector for extortion as the account is held hostage (Paganini, 2014; Raiu and Emm, 2014).

The first step toward increased security is to know and name the elements of the attack, and a taxonomy is useful for this purpose as it provides a basis for a common and consistent language. For example, you need to be able to distinguish between a virus and a worm, as they have different vectors, propagation mechanisms, and impacts (Hansman and Hunt, 2005). Another benefit is that it assists greatly in developing defenses against new types of attacks if the past attacks are known and classified (Igure and Williams, 2008).

The next step in the process of managing attacks on cloud services is to assess and quantify the risk. By utilizing the dimensions of the attack taxonomy as parameters in a risk assessment framework, areas of concern can be identified and treated with risk management techniques.

As most of the technologies underpinning cloud services are shared with other types of networked computer systems, so are the characteristics of attacks. In order to understand these, a literature review of taxonomies of more general cyber attacks has been conducted. In addition, the specifics of attacks on cloud services have been investigated.

This chapter is organized as follows. Section 2 discusses the characteristics of taxonomies in general and those of attacks in particular, and then presents a comprehensive review of computer-related attack taxonomies published between January 2003 and April 2014. Following this, the gap in the literature with regard to cloud attack taxonomies is identified. Section 3 investigates the different aspects of attacks against cloud services. Section 4 proposes a conceptual cloud attack taxonomy and risk assessment framework (CATRA). We demonstrate the utility of CATRA with an example scenario in Section 5. Section 6 concludes this chapter and outlines future work.

2 TAXONOMIES: A LITERATURE SURVEY
2.1 TAXONOMY CHARACTERISTICS

Taxonomies had been widely studied in the computer systems and network security literature (Amoroso, 1994; Bishop, 1999; Howard, 1997; Krsul, 1998; Lindqvist and Jonsson, 1997). Lough (2001), for example, summarizes the properties of a computer systems and network security taxonomy, which are further refined by Hansman and Hunt (2005) and Simmons et al. (2009):

- Accepted
- Comprehensible/exhaustive
- Complete
- Deterministic
- Mutually exclusive
- Repeatable
- Terms well defined/Terminology complying with established security terminology
- Unambiguous
- Useful

However, not all published taxonomies have all the above properties. For example, the taxonomy of Killourhy et al. (2004) uses only mutual exclusivity, exhaustivity, and replicability. The necessity of the criteria for mutual exclusivity has also been debated (Hansman and Hunt, 2005). Igure and Williams (2008) argue that a nonmutually exclusive taxonomy would provide a greater vulnerability coverage.

In this chapter, we would also argue that *purposeful* is an important criteria. The purpose of the taxonomy has an impact on the level of detail that is suitable, and taxonomies need to vary in their scope, purpose, depth, and breadth. The appropriate number of levels in a taxonomy is dependent on its scope and purpose. For example, a taxonomy for operational purposes such as choosing or developing network security tools (see Hoque et al. (2014) for an excellent example) requires attention to details, and a taxonomy targeted for managerial and policy makers would need to be high level (and abstract). We have also found that taxonomies without a clearly stated purpose are less useful and comprehensible.

2.2 ATTACK TAXONOMY CLASSIFIERS

ISO/IEC (2014, p.1) defines an attack as an "attempt to destroy, expose, alter, disable, steal or gain unauthorized access to or make unauthorized use of an asset," where the asset in our context is the cloud service, its applications and data. An attack taxonomy is a framework for describing the characteristics of attacks and the classifiers chosen are fundamental to achieving a taxonomy with the above properties.

The creators of taxonomies put varying emphasis on the scientific underpinnings of the classification system used and use different means of classifying the objects. Researchers such as Dagon et al. (2007), Mirkovic and Reiher (2004), Pothamsetty and Akyol (2004), Simmons et al. (2009), and Specht and Lee (2004) use "characteristics," "discriminators," "classes," "categories," and "factors" without justifying their choice or provide an underlying theoretical foundation, and organized their taxonomies using tree structures. Kjaerland (2006), on the other hand, use "facets," which is a formal method of classification based on facet theory (Borg, 1995). Hansman and Hunt (2005) give an insight into their process of choosing the means of classification. Their first attempt was in the form of tree structures, but this was found to result in a complex taxonomy that did not handle blended attacks well. Lists were also attempted, until they settled on dimensions.

In a comprehensive survey of taxonomies of vulnerabilities in computer systems, Igure and Williams (2008) conclude that the basic dimensions for attack classification are impact, target, source, and vulnerability. Based on our survey, we concur with this finding but have also identified an additional dimension: the vector of attack. The attack vector is the method or point of attack whereas vulnerability is the flaw of the system that is exploited in the attack (via the attack vector). For example, the vulnerability of "insufficient input validation" would allow the successful execution of the attack vector "SQL injection."

Both Hansman and Hunt (2005) and Weaver et al. (2003) also use "payload," albeit not as the first dimension. Other deviations can be derived back to the basic five categories, namely, impact, target, source, vulnerability, and vector. For example, Kjaerland (2006)'s facet "Method of Operation" can be synonymized with vector. In attempting to classify Weaver et al. (2003)'s "Target Discovery" into one of the four basic categories, we discover that there is no consensus on how to classify attack preparation. Hansman and Hunt (2005) and Kjaerland (2006) allocate this to the vector dimension as it is, in fact, enabling the attack. However, Simmons et al. (2009) argue that discovery such as scanning is not an attack vector but rather has an (informational) impact. In contrast, Weaver et al. (2003)'s "Propagation carriers and distribution mechanisms" and "Activation" would be part of the vector category and "Motivations and attackers" can be equated with the source category.

On the topic of attack preparation, it is interesting to note that attack activities can be classified by stage, namely, preattack (information gathering/target discovery/vulnerability assessment), attack launch, and postattack (removing evidence such as log entries) (Hoque et al., 2014). The countermeasures applied to each stage of attack can be categorized the same way, namely, preattack (security assessment, patching, prevention, and detection setup), attack launch (preventing, detecting, mitigating, stopping), and postattack (digital forensics) (Hoque et al., 2014; Specht and Lee, 2004).

2.3 ATTACK TAXONOMIES

Cloud services are built on the same technologies as other networked computer systems and therefore suffer the same security problems as any computer system or network (Chen et al., 2010; Choo, 2010; Gruschka and Jensen, 2010; Quick et al., 2014). For example, Chow et al. (2009) observed that due to the implementation of cloud services, some traditional attack surfaces are even heightened, and Choo (2010) noted cloud-specific vulnerabilities.

Although the body of work with regard to taxonomies of cloud attacks is limited, analyzing attacks against connected computer and network systems (e.g., grid computing) will inform the classification of cloud attacks due to the overlapping infrastructure. Therefore, in this chapter, we surveyed attack taxonomies in the areas of computer, network, cyber, and cloud attacks published between 2003 and 2014 to assist us in developing a conceptual cloud attack taxonomy. An overview of the taxonomies reviewed is available in Table 1.

2.3.1 Cyber attack taxonomies

Although the taxonomy by Hansman and Hunt (2005) does not explicitly refer to cyber attacks, the taxonomy is designed to cover all dimensions of an attack, namely, vector, target, vulnerability, and payload, as well as details such as operating system, version number, and patch level.

Kjaerland (2006) analyzed a large number of intrusions reported to Computer Emergency Response Teams with the goal of criminal profiling of the cyber attackers. The taxonomy is based on the facets of attack impact, method of operation, source sector, and target sector (based on global top level domains such as .com and . gov). These facets are analyzed with respect to statistical relationships using facet theory and multidimensional scaling, which are commonly used for profiling of crimes.

Simmons et al. (2009) critique Kjaerland (2006)'s work and suggest that the latter should be more detailed in the methods of operation so that the attack inception could have been more easily identified. The goal of the cyber attack taxonomy by Simmons et al. (2009) is to identify and defend against cyber attacks, and it is envisioned that the taxonomy can be used in a game theoretic defense system with automatic vulnerability identification and defense capability. The major classifiers are attack vector, operational impact, defense, information impact, and target. The taxonomy aims to be more thorough than its predecessors of Lough (2001), and Hansman and Hunt (2005) in that it can provide defense strategies and describe variations. However, a limitation of this taxonomy is that it does not differentiate between vulnerabilities and attack vectors. For example, "Misconfiguration" is listed as an attack vector and the operational impact as "Installed Malware: Worm: Network aware." We, however, argue that misconfiguration is a vulnerability that can be exploited by an attacker (e.g., using malware such as a worm) and the operational impact would be violation of data confidentiality, integrity, availability, and/or authentication.

Table 1 Survey of Attack Taxonomies 2003-2014

Taxonomy	Scope	Purpose	Depth	Breadth
General cyber, computer, network attacks				
Hansman and Hunt (2005)	Computer and network attacks	Categorize and classify computer and network attacks for the benefit of information bodies such as CERT	Three to six levels deep depending on dimension, down to distinct "DoS attacks" such as "ICMP flooding"	Covers vectors, targets, vulnerabilities, and payloads of attacks on computers and networks
Hoque et al. (2014)	Tools for network attacks and defense	Provide a comprehensive taxonomy for further network security research	Up to six levels deep, down to distinct "application layer attack" "server attacks" such as "SQL injection" using the tool "RefRef"	Covers attack launching, information gathering, and network monitoring tools classified by vector
Kjaerland (2006)	Cyber attacks	Improve the understanding of the motivation of cyber attackers	Two levels deep down to "impact" such as "disrupt"	Covers impact, method of operation, source sectors, and target sectors of cyber attacks
Simmons et al. (2009)	Cyber attacks	Aid the network administrator mitigate and remediate vulnerabilities in order to avoid or alleviate the impact of the attack	Up to six levels deep, for example, "operational impact" of "installed malware" "worm" of type "mass mailing"	Covers attack vector, operational impact, defense, informational impact, and target
Venter and Eloff (2003)	Information technology security technologies	Provide information for organizations; stimulate new research	Three levels deep to description of "proactive" "network level" measures such as "Virtual Private Networks"	Covers proactive and reactive countermeasures classified by target type (host, network, application)
Specific attack targets				
East et al. (2009)	DNP3	Facilitate risk analysis and mitigation strategies	Four levels deep, for example, "common attacks," "passive network reconnaissance," "interception of master data"	Covers targets, threats and impacts

(Continued)

Table 1 Survey of Attack Taxonomies 2003-2014—cont'd

Taxonomy	Scope	Purpose	Depth	Breadth
Kotapati et al. (2005)	3G networks	To assist in identifying security threats, vulnerabilities and attacks	Two levels deep	Covers physical access to the network, attack categories and attack means
Mokhov et al. (2008)	Linux vulnerabilities and solutions	Present results of a case study of software vulnerabilities	One level deep, two taxonomies	Covers 12 types of errors
Yue et al. (2009)	P2P attacks	Provide an understanding of the attacks in order to help build and organize defense mechanisms	Up to three levels deep, for example, "application," "decoy," "index poisoning"	Covers identity management, routing and application
Specific attack vectors and vulnerabilities				
Dagon et al. (2007)	Botnet structures	To aid in the process of selecting responses and remediation strategies	Two levels deep, for example, "efficiency," "network diameter"	Covers effectiveness, efficiency, and robustness
Mirkovic and Reiher (2004)	DDoS Attack and defenses	Provide a basis for further research by classifying and linking attack and defense strategies	Up to three levels deep down to "semi-automatic" "host scanning strategy" of "random"	Covers degree of automation, exploited weakness, source address validity, attack rate dynamics, possibility of characterization, persistence of agent set, victim type, impact
Pothamsetty and Akyol (2004)	Protocol vulnerabilities and countermeasures	Help network protocol engineers to not repeat past errors	Up to two levels deep, for example, the vulnerability of "Non-Robust Protocol Message Parsing" with the subcategory "inability to handle packet size variations"	Covers vulnerabilities and countermeasure in the form of test techniques, the resulting test metrics, and engineering best practices
Rutkowska (2006a)	Stealth malware	Unclear	One level deep	Covers four different classes of malware

Specht and Lee (2004)	DDoS Attacks and countermeasures	Assist in the development of countermeasures of both known and future attacks	Up to four levels deep, down to the "bandwidth depletion" through a "flood attack" using the "UDP" port that uses a "random port"	Attack taxonomy covers both bandwidth depletion and resource depletion, classified by vulnerability exploited. Countermeasure taxonomy covers detection and neutralization of handlers, detection, and prevention of secondary victims and potential attackers, mitigation and deflecting of attacks, and postattack forensics
Vorobiev and Han (2006)	Web Services attacks	Provide a common vocabulary for IDS vendors	Up to four levels deep, for example, an "XML attack" that is a "parsing attack" of type "DOM attack" that uses "extremely complicated but legal XML"	Ontology that covers eight types of attacks based on vulnerabilities and vectors
Weaver et al. (2003)	Worm attacks	Provide an understanding of the threat worms pose in order to develop defenses	Two levels deep, for example, the "attacker's motivation" of "political protest"	Covers target discovery, carrier mechanisms, activation, payloads, and attacker motivation
Welch and Lathrop (2003)	Wireless network attacks and countermeasures	Provide an understanding of the risks for the network designer in order to be able to mitigate these	Two levels deep, down to for example attack on "integrity" by means of "session hijacking"	Covers attacks and countermeasures against the integrity and confidentiality of wireless networks classified by vulnerability
Cloud taxonomies with security				
Gruschka and Jensen (2010)	Cloud attacks	Anticipate classes of vulnerabilities in cloud computing	One level: attack surface	Vulnerabilities only

(Continued)

Table 1 Survey of Attack Taxonomies 2003-2014—cont'd

Taxonomy	Scope	Purpose	Depth	Breadth
Hoefer and Karagiannis (2010)	Cloud services	Assist in comparison between cloud services for the benefit of potential users and developers	Seven levels deep: Main service category, License type, Intended user group, Payment system, Formal agreements, Security measures, Standardization efforts	Covers IaaS, PaaS, and SaaS
Prodan and Ostermann (2009)	IaaS and Web hosting providers	To identify a common terminology, architectural and functional similarities, as well as gaps for future research	Up to five levels deep, for example, business model-pricing-data-traffic-outgoing	Covers service type, resource deployment, hardware, runtime tuning, security, business model, middleware, and performance
Rimal et al. (2010)	Cloud services	To create a better understanding of the categories of applications that could benefit from cloudification	Two levels deep, for example, "security," "encryption/decryption"	Covers architecture, virtualization management, core services, security, data governance, and management services
Srinivasan et al. (2012)	Cloud security challenges	Provide assistance to providers to enhance security and to enable users to evaluate the providers security	Two levels deep, for example, "architectural and technological aspects": "logical storage segregation and multi-tenancy security issues"	Covers architectural and technological aspects as well as process and regulatory-related aspects

2.3.2 Countermeasures taxonomies

Killourhy et al. (2004) broadly categorize taxonomies into attack-centric (the goal of the attack, such as privilege escalation) and defense centric (classifying the attacks according to similarities in defense). Their research suggests that defense-centric taxonomies are more effective at predicting attacks than attack-centric taxonomies.

While the majority of the taxonomies reviewed by Killourhy et al. (2004) are attack-centric, the taxonomy by Venter and Eloff (2003) could be said to be defense centric as it is entirely dedicated to information security technologies. They classify the countermeasures into two categories: proactive measures to avoid a security breach and reactive measures once an attack has been detected. The second level of classification is the target: network, host, or application level. Proactive network level security measures include Virtual Private Networks (VPNs), security protocols and cryptography, whereas the reactive measures include access control, firewalls, and passwords. This is a high-level taxonomy that does not go into specifics on the mitigation strategies for the various cyber attacks.

While the concepts discussed in these taxonomies are relevant to cloud computing, there is no cloud-specific technical taxonomy and as Choo (2014, p.90) noted "Understanding the different approaches is important, as there will most certainly be variations in the way we respond to different types of malicious cyber activities perpetrated by different threat actors" in different contexts.

2.3.3 Network attack and countermeasure tools taxonomy

Hoque et al. (2014) present a comprehensive taxonomy of network security tools, where practical application of specific tools for different attack categories is outlined. The tools covered in the taxonomy are, perhaps, illustrative of the current network security situation where there are more offensive than defensive tools (46 attack tools but only 27 defense tools discussed by Hoque et al. (2014)).

2.3.4 Distributed denial of service taxonomies

Distributed denial of service (DDoS) attacks against cloud providers are a serious threat due to the high impact of availability disruptions, with consequences such as loss of business, loss of reputation, and possible ransom demands by the attackers (Chonka et al., 2011).

Specht and Lee (2004) present three taxonomies in the DDoS space, namely, attacks, attack tools, and countermeasures. The attack taxonomy uses impact as its main classifier, where the impact of the attack is either resource depletion or bandwidth depletion. The tools used in orchestrating a DDoS give an insight into how the attack is performed. Specht and Lee (2004) classify the tools into agent setup, attack network communication, and targets. Comparing this with the tool taxonomy by Hoque et al. (2014), the agent setup is similar to the preattack tool category, and the attack network communication in Specht and Lee (2004) can be seen as the vector of the attack in Hoque et al. (2014). The countermeasure taxonomy can also be seen in parallel to those of Hoque et al. (2014) and Venter and Eloff (2003), as the former effectively classifies the defense mechanisms by stage of the attack: detect/prevent, mitigate/stop and deflect, and finally postattack forensics.

While Mirkovic and Reiher (2004) include impact as one of the classes, their focus is on the attack and defense strategies of DDoS. It is a comprehensive taxonomy which includes classifications of scanning strategies, propagation mechanisms, spoofing techniques, and attack rate dynamics. Their defense mechanisms taxonomy differentiates between preventative and reactive strategies (similar to that of Venter and Eloff (2003)).

Douligeris and Mitrokotsa (2004) classify DDoS attacks based on the degree of automation, the vulnerability that was exploited, the attack rate dynamics, and whether the impact is disruptive or degrading. The vulnerabilities enumerated are UDP/ICMP flooding attacks, Smurf and Fraggle amplification attacks, protocol exploit attacks, and malformed packet attacks.

2.3.5 Protocol vulnerability taxonomies

Some of the vulnerabilities exploited in a DDoS attack are found in network protocols (Peng et al., 2007). Errors in network protocol engineering are being repeated and the resulting vulnerabilities had been exploited in different types of attacks (Pothamsetty and Akyol, 2004). Pothamsetty and Akyol (2004) developed a taxonomy for these vulnerabilities along with the corresponding engineering countermeasures. It is a low-level and practical taxonomy, which should prove useful to protocol designers and developers, complete with testing techniques. Network protocol vulnerabilities are also particularly relevant to cloud services given their dependence on the network protocols used in communications between the provider and the user.

One popular network protocol that has been shown to be susceptible to attacks is the Wireless Local Area Network protocol 802.11 (Borisov et al., 2001). Welch and Lathrop (2003) analyzed the threats and classified them in a taxonomy based on confidentiality and integrity (availability is outside their scope). They cover all well-known wireless attacks such as session hijacking and replay, in order to help network designers mitigate these threats. Insecure wireless networks are a vector for attacks on cloud services, for example, by session hijacking where an attacker gains authenticated but unauthorized access to the cloud service account.

Yue et al. (2009) propose a taxonomy of P2P attacks in which they identify attack chains, where an occurrence of one attack creates a condition for a subsequent attack. They focus on the vulnerabilities and vectors of the attack. Attack chains are also relevant in the context of cloud attacks. For example, cross-VM attacks are made up of two steps, namely, placement and extraction (Ristenpart et al., 2009). Another example in the cloud context is where attackers abuse free cloud services to create a botnet (Ragan and Salazar, 2014).

The taxonomy of attacks against the Distributed Network Protocol (DNP3) in East et al. (2009) is another example of classifying attack vectors (threat categories) in network protocols. The dimensions used are interception, interruption, modification and fabrication, which are then mapped onto the targeted assets.

2.3.6 Botnets and malware taxonomies

While the taxonomies reviewed so far focus on the impact, vulnerability or target of the attack, Weaver et al. (2003) focus on a particular attack vector, namely, malware worms. Their work lays out how worms find and select their target, how they propagate and distribute, and their activation mechanisms and payloads. The taxonomy by Rutkowska (2006a) focuses on the broader malware family, and how malware interacts with the target machine's operating system. As explained by Hwang et al. (2009) and others, malware containment is one of essential proactive measures to secure cloud platforms.

2.3.7 Web service attacks

Some might argue that Service Oriented Architecture, typically implemented through Web Services, is a prerequisite for cloud computing (Baun et al., 2011, p. 5; Sosinsky, 2011, p. 271). Popular cloud service providers such as Amazon Elastic Compute Cloud (EC2) use Web Services to provide compute and storage infrastructure services (Gruschka and Iacono, 2009). Vorobiev and Han (2006) classified Web Service attacks into five "attack zones," namely, Application, Simple Object Access Protocol (SOAP) attacks, XML, Discovery, and Semantic attacks. The zones all then further defined according to technical vectors such as SQL injection and replay attacks. Their classification is solely based on attack vectors and vulnerabilities, and appears to be a practical ontology.

2.3.8 Cloud security and attack taxonomies

The taxonomy by Gruschka and Jensen (2010) examines cloud attacks from the perspective of communication channels between the cloud service provider, user, and cloud service instance. They model cloud attack scenarios based on whether the attack belongs in the group service-to-user, user-to-service, cloud-to-service, service-to-cloud, cloud-to-user, or user-to-cloud. While they do give some examples, there is no further classification scheme.

Srinivasan et al. (2012) developed a taxonomy of cloud security challenges and divided the vulnerabilities into two categories, namely, architectural and technological aspects, and process and regulatory-related aspects. They list one particularly dangerous attack, namely, that of the insider. As Subashini and Kavitha (2011) pointed out, external criminals pose the greatest threat but generally have the least impact, whereas internal attackers pose the least threat but may result in significant damage to the organization (e.g., the case involving the US Defense Contractor, Edward Snowden, Savage and Shane, 2013). The taxonomy also covers vulnerabilities such as logical storage segregation and multi-tenancy security issues, identity management issues, and insecure application programming interfaces as particular cloud computing vulnerabilities.

2.4 LITERATURE GAPS

Table 1 summarizes the taxonomies examined in this survey. General information system attacks are well understood and studied. As cloud computing is relatively new, it is not surprising that there is only one published taxonomy specifically dealing with cloud attacks (Gruschka and Jensen, 2010). The taxonomy, however, lacks breadth as well as depth. It only covers vulnerabilities at a very high level and does not include clear sublevels or consider other factors such as impact, target, source, or countermeasures. This echoes the observations of researchers such as Hoefer and Karagiannis (2010) who highlighted the need for more work in this area. This is one of our research motivations, and in the next section, we describe the various cloud attack aspects and mitigation strategies before presenting our conceptual CATRA in Section 4.

3 CLOUD ATTACKS LITERATURE REVIEW

Cloud services are particularly vulnerable to threats which compromise their availability and confidentiality, such as DDoS attacks and data breaches (Subashini and Kavitha, 2011). In addition, they introduce new vectors of attack (e.g., cross-VM attacks and malware targeting the hypervisor) but may also be less exposed to some traditional threats as cloud service providers such as Amazon WebServices use strong network traffic encryption techniques (Choo, 2010; Subashini and Kavitha, 2011). While there is no evidence that the threat agents are any different from those in cyber attacks where the target is not a cloud service, the motivation of the attackers may differ from traditional cyber attacks based on the potential vector, vulnerability, and impact. For example, there are concerns about cloud service providers who have been compelled to scan or search data of interest to "national security" and to report on, or monitor, particular types of transactional data. Foreign intelligence services and industrial spies may also gain clandestine entry to cloud services in order to collect information relevant to their national or corporate interests (Choo, 2010).

The underlying technologies in cloud services and client applications may have specific vulnerabilities and attack vectors, and "traditional" countermeasures may not be fit-for-purpose. For example, potential cloud attack vectors include vulnerabilities in the host OS, guest OS client's application or data, the cloud service account, and co-located virtual machines (VMs) (Martini and Choo, 2014; Ristenpart et al., 2009).

3.1 VULNERABILITIES AND THREAT VECTORS

The attack vector and the vulnerability it exploits are closely coupled and really two sides of the same coin. However, vectors are typically technical in nature whereas a vulnerability may also be related to lack of policy or poorly trained staff.

3.1.1 People, process, and physical vulnerabilities

People are generally regarded as the weakest link for security as insiders can bypass technical security barriers (Choo et al., 2007; Modi et al., 2013; Popovic and Hocenski, 2010). Insider threats could be perpetrated by a number of means. A cloud-related example is to obtain credentials to a victim's cloud service account via means such as phishing and social engineering with the aims of hijacking the account and gaining unauthorized access to the stored data (Foozy et al., 2011; Khorshed et al., 2012).

All security measures to mitigate attacks should be based on a systematic approach, using an effective cyber security policy (Choo, 2010). Policies should be developed, documented, and implemented based on assessment of requirements, and then maintained to maintain relevance (Popovic and Hocenski, 2010). Failure to understand security threats is a vulnerability in itself.

While cloud security often focuses on logical vulnerabilities in software, the cloud environment is different from traditional corporate IT infrastructure in that it resides outside of the organization, and may not even in the same jurisdiction (Hooper et al., 2013). However, the provider's data center is located somewhere in the world and is vulnerable to natural and intentional disasters as well as physical intrusions.

3.1.2 Technical vulnerabilities and vectors
3.1.2.1 Distributed denial of service
Cloud services, having service delivery over the Internet as its core service, are particularly vulnerable to DoS attacks where the cloud network's bandwidth, processing power, and storage capacities are targeted (Chonka et al., 2011). Due to the elastic nature of cloud computing, where additional capacity is added when needed, a DoS attack targeting one server also has the potential of flooding the entire cloud system by the targeted provider (Zunnurhain and Vrbsky, 2010). On the other hand, being the large network that cloud providers typically are, cloud services typically have a much larger bandwidth than traditional networks (Paganini, 2013b). However, cloud service providers are not immune from DDoS attacks. For example, the popular Git revision control system, hosted on Amazon's EC2, was reportedly down for a total of 19 h due to a DDoS attack (Metz, 2009).

3.1.2.2 Cross-VM attacks
The co-location of VMs on the same physical server creates a new vulnerability and enables an attack vector that is somewhat unique to cloud computing. Ristenpart et al. (2009), for example, demonstrated how cross-VM attacks can take place by exploiting hypervisor vulnerabilities where side channels are utilized to gain access to a co-located VM.

3.1.2.3 The malware vector and virtualization vulnerabilities
Malware can also be coded to target cloud services by changing or blocking certain functionality. For example, malware can be coded to redirect valid requests to a malicious service (Modi et al., 2013) and Hardware-based Virtual Machine (HVM) rootkits (malware targeting hypervisor) can silently and invisibly take complete control over a host (Choo, 2010). Examples of HVM rootkits include SubVirt (King and Chen, 2006), Blue Pill (Rutkowska, 2006b), and DKSM (Bahram et al., 2010).

They operate by inserting a malicious hypervisor and convert the host OS to a guest on-the-fly (Modi et al., 2013).

3.1.2.4 Phishing

Phishing, where an attacker presents a fake Web page to gain a legitimate user's credentials (Jensen et al., 2009), targeting cloud service user is another potential attack vector. For example, cloud service users who are victims of phishing could have their data stolen or be required to pay for service hijacked by cyber criminals (Somorovsky et al., 2011), such as be part of a botnet to conduct DDoS attacks, spamming, and other criminal activities (Modi et al., 2013).

3.1.2.5 Web services

Cloud services often use Web Services and, therefore, vulnerabilities in the underlying Web Services could be exploited to target a particular cloud service. For example, SOAP messages can be manipulated in what is referred to as an XML Signature Element Wrapping attack, where the body of the message is replaced with malicious code in stealth (Gruschka and Iacono, 2009). Another example of a SOAP manipulation attack is the Coercive Parsing Attack, which manipulates the Web Service request to use a continuous sequence of open tags, which exhausts the CPU on the Web server (Chonka et al., 2011). An ontology of Web Service attacks is available in Vorobiev and Han (2006).

3.1.2.6 Browser

SaaS can be accessed using (a mobile app or) a Web browser, which means they are vulnerable to any weaknesses in Web browser and Web application security (Jensen et al., 2011; Subashini and Kavitha, 2011). The following top 10 security risks in Web applications identified by Open Web Application Security Project (2013a) could also affect SaaS users:

1. Injection flaws such as SQL, OS, and LDAP: Malicious parameters are sent as part of a command or query to the backend server to access data without authorization.
2. Broken authentication and session management: Session IDs or authentication credentials are being reused by authorized users.
3. Cross-site scripting: Client-side scripts are injected in order to, for example, bypass access controls or redirect users to malicious sites.
4. Insecure direct object references: References to backend objects are exposed at the frontend, allowing an attacker to manipulate these in order to gain unauthorized access to data.
5. Security misconfiguration: Security configuration of any part of the application or server is not done in accordance with best practices and standards, such as changing default passwords.
6. Sensitive data exposure: Sensitive data such as credit cards and passwords can be stolen and misused if not protected with encryption on the server and during transactions.

7. Missing function level access control: Allow users without appropriate authority to access, for example, administrative functions.
8. Cross-site request forgery: An attacker embeds a forged request into an authenticated user's request, which is interpreted as a legitimate request.
9. Using components with known vulnerabilities: Components used to build a Web application usually run with full privileges, and vulnerabilities in these components can be exploited by an attacker.
10. Nonvalidated redirects and forwards: Attackers redirect users from legitimate to malicious Web sites.

3.1.2.7 Management console
The cloud service account is managed through the management console in a Web browser, which is convenient but can also be a weakness. By providing a registered e-mail address and valid password to the Amazon Web Services dashboard, for example, a user or attacker can download authentication credentials and hijack the account (Jansen, 2011).

In 2014, a hosting service had their EC2 account held hostage by an attacker who gained access to their management console. When the ransom was not paid, most of the data (including backup data) and machine configurations were reportedly deleted (Paganini, 2014).

3.1.2.8 Cryptography
Cryptography is one of the core technologies in securing cloud services. Similar to other underlying services and infrastructure, vulnerability(ies) in the cryptographic algorithm or its implementation could be exploited to violate the confidentiality and integrity of cloud service users (Grobauer et al., 2011), such as in the case of the HeartBleed bug (where various affected cloud service providers had to quickly patch their systems, Sullivan, 2014).

3.1.2.9 Network protocols
Cloud services are networked over the Internet and use standard network protocols such as IP, TCP, and HTTP and are, therefore, susceptible to attacks which exploit their vulnerabilities, such as man-in-the-middle attacks (Grobauer et al., 2011; Modi et al., 2013).

3.1.2.10 Expanded network attack surface
One of the key benefits of cloud computing, namely, its inherent 24/7 access-anywhere feature, also increases its vulnerability as it is not only the cloud service that needs to be protected but also clients of all sorts. This effectively means that the attack surface is expanded, where a cloud service can be compromised by attacking or stealing a client device (Chow et al., 2009). For example, it has been demonstrated that the username and passwords of popular public and private cloud storage services could potentially be forensically recovered if the users had used mobile apps or

browsers to access these services on the devices (Dykstra and Sherman, 2013; Hale, 2013; Martini and Choo, 2013; Quick and Choo, 2013a–c, 2014).

3.2 THREAT ACTORS

Threat actors can be broadly categorized into script kiddies motivated by curiosity, more advanced hackers with financial motivations and those utilized by criminal organizations for data theft, extortion, or Bitcoin theft (Choo, 2014; Kjaerland, 2000; Paganini, 2013a, 2014). In addition, there are state-sponsored groups involved in espionage and propaganda, and nonaffiliated hacktivist groups raising awareness of their political beliefs (Crane, 2005; Leyden, 2013; Olson, 2012). Table 2 presents an example of how threat actors can exploit potential attack vectors to target cloud services. The categories of threat actors are then discussed in further detail.

3.2.1 Financially motivated

Cloud-based businesses are particularly sensitive to disruptions to their operations and this weakness can be exploited by attackers. For example, source code hosting service Code Spaces became victims of a DDoS attack, rendering their service unavailable to their clients. The attackers made extortion demands in order to stop the DDoS and also gained access to Code Spaces EC2 control panel. When the ransom was not paid, the attackers deleted all data, including backups, resulting in the victim's bankruptcy (Paganini, 2014).

With the rising interest in crypto-currencies like Bitcoin, new ways of making money illegally by attacking cloud services are emerging. For example, using the

Table 2 Threat Actors

Threat Actors (Individuals and/or Organized Crime Groups)	Exploiting Vulnerabilities in One or More of the Following Potential Attack Vectors		
	Technologies (e.g., Using Malware and Embed Vulnerabilities or Malicious Code in Technologies During Manufacturing and/or Supply Chain)	People (e.g., Social Engineering)	Processes (e.g., Policies and Procedures)
Criminally motivated Issue/ideologically motivated Financially motivated State sponsored/ affiliated Others (e.g., curiosity and fame seeking)	The aim is to disrupt one or more combinations of the following security (CIAA) notions: • Data *confidentiality* • Data *integrity* • Data *availability* • Data *authentication* (data origin authentication or entity authentication)		

computing power of compromised cloud accounts for mining purposes, direct theft of Bitcoins, or attacking the virtual currency scheme for speculation purposes.

Cloud services hold a huge amount of valuable data, making such services a tempting target for attackers. Web site account credentials and other personal data are being stolen and sold at market places in what is known as the "darknet," sites only accessible through anonymizing services (Finkle, 2014). For example, 360 million stolen credentials were found at a black market like this, and a Russian crime gang reportedly stole over a billion username and password combinations (Perlroth and Gelles, 2014).

3.2.2 Ideologically motivated

Hacktivist group Anonymous comprises individuals who may not know each other in real life but get together to conduct an attack against a target based on a common belief. Example incidents include DDoS attacks Church of Scientology, US Copyright Office, PayPal, Mastercard, Visa, and Web sites of individuals (Olson, 2012).

The Syrian Electronic Army (SEA) is another ideologically motivated organized crime group, and the group is reportedly controlled by the Assad regime in Syria (Leyden, 2013). The SEA was allegedly involved in pro-Assad defacement attacks on news outlets, universities, and social media, as well as other types of attacks such as hijacking Twitter accounts to spread false information, stolen large amounts of data relating to phone numbers and VoIP users, and DDoS attacks against a range of targets (Chalbi, 2014).

3.2.3 State and corporate backed

As organizations move their data into the cloud, so does the focus of corporate and political espionage. As noted by Choo (2014), countries such as China and Russia were often singled out as the originating country of corporate and political espionage. However, cyber warfare is global and typically involves various nation-states (Choo, 2010; Information Warfare Monitor and Shadowserver Foundation, 2010). Theft of national secrets and intellectual property is a threat to national security and stability to the economy, in addition to the enormous costs to the individual corporations (O'Hara, 2010).

3.2.4 Insiders

While external criminals pose the greatest threat, statistically they have the least impact, whereas insiders are rare but far more effective (Subashini and Kavitha, 2011). Kaspersky Lab (2013), for example, reported that "hackers are increasingly targeting cloud service employees, seeing them as the weakest link in the security chain." Cloud services offer an attractive target for any attacker due to the concentration of data and utility in one (logical) convenient place (Subashini and Kavitha, 2011). For example, cloud servers could be compromised, say by a malicious insider, to push malicious or potentially unwanted applications to their users managed by the affected servers. For example, in recent work, O'Malley and Choo (2014) presented a method that a corrupt insider could use to facilitate (inaudible) data exfiltration from an air-gapped system without using any modified hardware. Such techniques could easily be used to exfiltrate data from cloud servers.

3.2.5 Script kiddies

Other threat actors include so-called script kiddies who are motivated by curiosity (Kjaerland, 2006). They are generally distinguished by a relatively low level of skill and often perform unsophisticated attacks which are easily detected by an IDS. However, with the increase in easy-to-use hacking toolkits such as Kali Linux, poorly protected cloud services are still at risk of attack by this threat actor (Offensive Security, 2014).

3.3 COUNTERMEASURES

The chain of events during attack is central to determining defense strategies. The risk mitigation strategy should be both proactive (e.g., with the aims of preventing or reducing security incidents) and reactive (e.g., detect and investigate security breaches in order to contain, minimize the damage, and/or recover and restore services and data) (Sherwood et al., 2005). The division of responsibility for cloud attack countermeasures and examples of proactive and reactive measures are discussed below.

3.3.1 Responsibility

The division of responsibility for the security of IaaS services varies between providers. On Amazon, for example, the provider is responsible for anything up to the hypervisor, such as physical and virtualization, while the user is responsible for OS, applications, and data. When PaaS is used, developers build their own applications and deploy to the cloud platform. The security of the application is then the responsibility of the user, but anything below the application level has to be protected by the provider. For example, the provider must secure the network against intrusion and the data against unauthorized access (Subashini and Kavitha, 2011).

In SaaS, the user has to rely on the provider for security measures. Subashini and Kavitha (2011) provide an in-depth discussion about the security aspects of the SaaS application development and deployment process, in which they list data security, network security, data locality, data integrity, data segregation, data access, and authentication and authorization as key security elements (see Figure 1).

3.3.2 Prevention

Prevention is better than cure, and rather than adopting a "detect-and-response" approach, it is important to identify and act upon mitigation and preventative strategies (e.g., security policies for both provider and users). Mitigation and preventative strategies should be designed to address risks associated with the potential threat vectors, such as people, process, and technology. For example, the threat of insider attacks and phishing can be reduced by having ongoing employee security awareness training (Ross et al., 2005) and conducting employee due diligence.

Applications	Applications	Applications
Application support	Application support	Application support
Basic services	Basic services	Basic services
OS	OS	OS
Virtualization	Virtualization	Virtualization
Data centre	Data centre	Data centre
SaaS	**PaaS**	**IaaS**

Provider responsibility	User responsibility

FIGURE 1

User/provider security responsibility.

Adapted from Subashini and Kavitha (2011).

3.3.2.1 People, process, and physical vulnerabilities

All security measures to mitigate attacks should be based on a systematic approach, using an effective cyber security policy (Choo, 2010). Policies should be developed, documented, and implemented based on assessment of requirements, and then maintained to maintain relevance (Popovic and Hocenski, 2010). Failure to understand security threats is in itself a vulnerability.

3.3.2.2 Cross-VM attacks

Ristenpart et al. (2009) posited that the only effective method to avoid cross-VM attacks is to only have one VM on each physical machine. This, however, is unlikely to be financially viable for most public cloud service providers. Therefore, to reduce the risk when co-locating, Ristenpart et al. (2009) recommend that cloud service providers obfuscate the internal structure of their services and the placement policy. In addition, blinding techniques such as cache wiping can be deployed to reduce the risk of side-channel vulnerabilities being exploited.

3.3.2.3 Web services and applications

Well established Web application design principles, guidelines, and practices apply equally to applications deployed in the cloud (Krutz and Vines, 2010). However, it is helpful to understand the vulnerabilities in technologies common in cloud computing, such as Web Services, to build more secure software and focus testing efforts more appropriately. One related work is that of Mainka et al. (2012) who developed a penetration testing tool "WS-Attacker" for Web Services in order to combat Web Services specific attacks. Their work also features a plugin architecture for attacks to be simulated.

3.3.2.4 Management console

Like any resource protected by authentication with a username and password, enforcing a strong password policy will impede a brute-force attack (Kelley et al., 2012). Some cloud services offer the option of a multi-factor authentication as an extra level of security (Todorov and Ozkan, 2013, p. 16). LaBarge and McGuire (2013) analyzed the security of the OpenStack cloud platform by performing penetration testing with session hijacking and credential theft in focus. They were able to hijack the session and access the victim's dashboard and other unauthorized areas. Consequently, unencrypted credentials were stolen from the disk. They then recommended that cloud users only connect to their dashboard over HTTPS and that all files with sensitive data are encrypted.

3.3.2.5 Cryptography and network protocols

As emphasized in Section 3.3.2.4, using a secure protocol such as Transport Layer Security or connecting through a secure VPN is essential when connecting to a password-protected URL. In addition, sensitive data need to be protected by encryption and a policy regarding key strength and key management defined and implemented (Krutz and Vines, 2010, p. 256). Merely obscuring data using, for example, XOR, Base64, or Uuencode is easy for an attacker to reverse engineer, and it is recommended that proper encryption tool such as TrueCrypt or PGP be utilized (Gregg, 2014).

3.3.3 Detection

3.3.3.1 Cloud intrusion detection systems

Intrusion Detection/Prevention Systems (IDPS) are commonly used in traditional enterprise systems but face a number of challenges in the cloud environment. One issue is the separation of responsibility between the provider and user and the practicality of who and how the IDS should be administered by (Roschke et al., 2009). Patel et al. (2013) identify that the characteristics of cloud computing systems (elasticity, reliability, QoS, agility, adaptability, and availability) render traditional IDPS inefficient and incompatible with cloud systems. They propose a set of requirements for a cloud IDPS, involving ability to handle large-scale, dynamic multi-tiered autonomous computing and data processing environments; to quickly adapt to new attacks as well as new configurations and deployments; and be scalable.

Nevertheless, Roschke et al. (2009) and Lee et al. (2011) assert that cloud users can and should use IDPS to detect attacks on their services and providers to detect attacks on their infrastructure. It is stressed that the IDPS should be separated from the system it is monitoring. For example, cloud users should deploy their IDPS on a different VM as the IDPS can otherwise be compromised and not function properly.

3.3.3.2 HVM malware

A key challenge of HVM attacks is that they are extremely difficult to detect (King and Chen, 2006). Desnos et al. (2011) point out that common malware detection techniques using memory fingerprints or pattern matching of signatures are ineffective against HVM attacks. The creator of the Blue Pill HVM, Joanna Rutkowska, reflects that the only remotely possible detection method would be through timing analysis (Rutkowska, 2006b). This was further investigated by Desnos et al. (2011) who through experiments demonstrated that instruction execution times were significantly higher when a HVM rootkit was present, which would be a means for detection. There are some ideas on how to prevent HVM malware but there is no known efficient solution to mitigate HVM malware (Desnos et al., 2011; Rutkowska, 2006b).

3.3.3.3 Phishing

Fette et al. (2007) use machine learning to detect and filter out phishing e-mails as well as Web sites. From the user's perspective, it is important to make sure the employees with access to the cloud account use a Web browser that can detect and actively warn the user of phishing Web sites (Egelman et al., 2008). If the browser does not have sufficient built-in support, there are also plugins and extensions available for installation (Chou et al., 2004). Dhamija and Tygar (2005) emphasize that it is generally very difficult for users alone to distinguish phishing e-mails and Web sites from legitimate ones and propose a technique where a legitimate Web site can be easily identified.

3.3.4 Containment, recovery, and restoration

3.3.4.1 DDoS defense mechanisms

In the taxonomy on DDoS defense mechanisms by Mirkovic and Reiher (2004), the attack response attack strategies were classified into those using agent identification, rate-limiting, filtering, and reconfiguration. Based on our review of the current literature on DDoS defense for cloud environments, current research efforts appear to focus on agent identification and filtering techniques. For example, Chonka et al. (2011) developed a technique for defending against DDoS attacks in the cloud that use what they call Cloud Track Back (CTB) and Cloud Protector. The foundations for these are to identify the true source of the attack by using a deterministic packet marking algorithm and then filter the incoming messages based on a trained back propagation neural network. The efficiency of the CTB was subsequently tested by Joshi et al. (2012) who found that it successfully traced back 75-81% of traffic.

Another packet filtering method for defense against DDoS attacks in the cloud environment is that of Chen et al. (2011). Their idea is to build a profile of the characteristics of a normal packet and use this to determine which packets are DDoS packets.

3.3.4.2 Backups

The SaaS user needs to ensure that the chosen cloud service provider regularly backup all sensitive enterprise data, to facilitate a quick recovery in the case of an attack on the data (Subashini and Kavitha, 2011). The additional data copy is another attack surface; thus, it is essential that backups are encrypted and stored in a securely configured system.

3.3.4.3 Utilizing virtualization

Cloud services have an advantage over traditional enterprise systems in that they are virtualized. If the VM image is managed with recovery in mind, they can be stopped, replaced, and resumed quite easily (Roschke et al., 2009).

3.3.4.4 Expanded network attack surface

The prevalence of employees connecting to the corporate cloud using their own devices is likely to increase as cloud adoption rise and "bring your own device" (BYOD) is already common (Cisco, 2012). Miller et al. (2012) suggest that organizations implement the principle of least privilege and partition the data so that each employee only have access to the information needed to perform their duties. This would limit the damage an attacker could do if they obtained an authorized and authenticated user's device. In a recent work, for example, Do et al. (2015) presented a mobile data exfiltration technique designed to exploit various exfiltration mediums and support numerous methods of code injection (entry points) with a view to covertly exfiltrate data from Android devices. Two proof-of-concepts were implemented to demonstrate the feasibility of exfiltrating data via SMS and inaudible audio transmission using standard Android devices.

3.4 CLOUD ATTACK TARGETS

Our survey of attack taxonomies suggests that the targets of attacks traditional systems (e.g., servers) are typically network, host/OS, and application. Attacks targeting cloud services are, however, slightly different due to the architecture of cloud services. Cloud service providers are particularly sensitive to DDoS attacks and their data center may be the "preferred" target of unauthorized access or physical attacks due to the amount of data stored on these sites. Other attack targets include the physical machine's OS (the host OS) and hypervisor (e.g., which can be the target of HVM malware and cross-VM attacks). The hypervisor manages the execution of a number of guest OS, which may be used by users as a whole or in part. As the resources required varies depending on their needs and delivery model chosen (SaaS, PaaS, IaaS), it is important to understand that the account itself may also be a target of an attack. The data stored by the user may also be the target in, for example, the case of data theft. Malware have also been known to attack applications provided by SaaS. For example, SalesForce.com, a cloud-based CRM provider, was recently attacked by Zeus Trojan (Khandelwal, 2014a).

3.5 IMPACT OF CLOUD ATTACKS

Attacks against cloud infrastructure have the potential to have a much greater impact than those against single tenanted architectures, due to the large number of users and the fact that many of them are co-located (Joshi et al., 2012; Peake, 2012). Code Spaces, a source code repository hosted on Amazon, was recently attacked (Paganini, 2014). The initial impact on their business was disruptions to the availability of the services. Subsequently, most of the data belonging to their users were lost, which resulted in Code Spaces filing for bankruptcy. There is also the likelihood of lawsuits from users who lost their data stored on the services.

There is an emerging trend of utilizing cloud services for data and applications not only for business but also for parts of SCADA systems, electronic voting systems, and resources used by schools (Copeland, 2013; Khandelwal, 2014b; Wilhoit, 2013). Recently in 2014, a large-scale DDoS attack targeted Hong Kong's online democracy poll Web site, which was set up to promote the upcoming elections (Pauli, 2014). The Web site was hosted on Amazon, Cloudflare, and UDOmain, and was attacked by a huge botnet at three hundred gigabits per second.

The benefits of cloud computing are not only financial. For example, in addition to cost savings and convenience when using cloud storage and other cloud services, the latter would enable students to get access to learning resources they may not otherwise have. Sugata Mitra, a Professor of educational technology, explained that "By most measures they (i.e., students in schools using cloud services) were learning more and more quickly, and doing it mostly on their own. It just requires broadband, collaboration and encouragement" (Copeland, 2013). However, a successful attack against the system will disrupt the students' learning.

Understandably, some critical infrastructure sectors such as those using industrial control systems have been reluctant to adopt cloud services due to security concerns and the far reaching impact on the society should an attack be conducted successfully against the underlying cloud services supporting the sector.

3.6 LITERATURE GAPS

Although cloud infrastructure is built on traditional technologies and, therefore, can be said to be susceptible to the same type of attacks as traditional systems; the cloud environment does have its distinguishing characteristics, such as elasticity, abstract deployment, and multi-tenancy (Peake, 2012). Most of the discussions pre-date cloud and there is no cloud-specific attack taxonomy and risk assessment framework—the gap that this research aims to fill.

4 CONCEPTUAL CLOUD ATTACK TAXONOMY AND RISK ASSESSMENT FRAMEWORK

We now present a taxonomy of attacks against cloud services. The dimensions of attacks are *source, vector, vulnerability, target, impact,* and *defense.* These dimensions lend themselves naturally to the attack risk scenario, where "threat actors" (the source) exploit "vulnerabilities and threat vectors" against "cloud attack targets." Successful attacks can result in significant "impacts." To mitigate existing "vulnerabilities and threat vectors" and minimize "impacts," we need effective "countermeasures" (defense strategies and mechanisms). To understand and assess the risks of an attack on data and applications in the cloud, we follow the taxonomy left-to-right to create scenarios. Figure 2 illustrates the top two levels of the taxonomy.

The dimensions are discussed and illustrated in more detail below. The levels of the taxonomy are color coded as shown in Figure 3.

4.1 SOURCE DIMENSION

The first dimension is the source of the attack, or the threat agent. It is vital to understand who the attackers are, their motivations for the attack, the skills they possess and what opportunities they have to perform the attack. See Figure 4 for an illustration of the source dimension.

The agent may be classified based on the context, such as whether they are a script kiddie or an organized crime gang (Kjaerland, 2000, 2006). Motivation or type of reward can be simple curiosity, political and ideological motives, and financially driven motives such as selling data or extortion (Paganini, 2014; Weaver et al., 2003). To gain an understanding of the level of risk this threat poses, we also need to classify their skills levels (OWASP, 2013b).

4.2 VECTOR DIMENSION

The second dimension is the vector of the attack, which is the method of operation for the attack, or by what means the attack was carried out. The success of an attack is partly dependent on a combination of factors such as the skills and resources of the

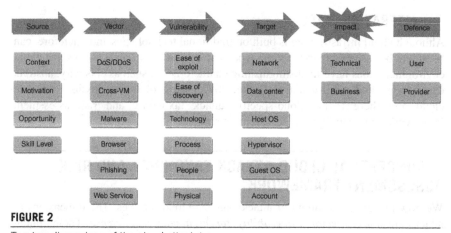

FIGURE 2

Top two dimensions of the cloud attack taxonomy.

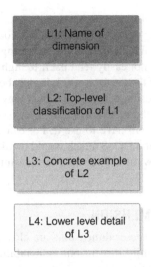

FIGURE 3

Legend of taxonomy levels color coding.

FIGURE 4

Source dimension.

attacker, presence of vulnerabilities, and absence of capable defense mechanisms. Attack vectors range from sending e-mails to cloud account holders in the hope that they will be deceived to reveal their credentials, to renting a botnet, and performing a DDoS. This dimension does not easily lend itself to higher classification other than the actual technical aspect of the vector itself. It is also the most volatile and hard-to-grasp dimension as vectors change as fast as technology.

In addition to the technical dimension of the attack vector, one must also consider the opportunity the attacker will have to use it. For example, a SQL injection on a small scale may be trivial but a DDoS attack would require significantly more computing resources (e.g., bandwidth). The vector dimension is illustrated in Figure 5.

4.3 **VULNERABILITY DIMENSION**

While the vulnerability and vector dimensions are closely coupled and sometimes difficult to distinguish, the third dimension, vulnerability, refers to the weakness of the system that can be exploited to conduct an attack. A vulnerability can also be thought of as an entry point for the attack. The broad categories are technology, process, people, and physical vulnerabilities (Choo, 2014; Subashini and Kavitha, 2011). Sources of technical vulnerabilities include *software* bug, weakness in network *protocol*, and *configuration* problem in a network service (Peng et al., 2007; Simmons et al., 2009; Viega and McGraw, 2002). The risk rating of the technical vulnerability depends on how easy it is to discover and exploit the vulnerability (OWASP, 2013b).

As pointed out by Choo (2010) and Srinivasan et al. (2012), cyber security requires adequate and efficient security processes, procedures, and policies. See Figure 6 for an illustration of the vulnerability dimension.

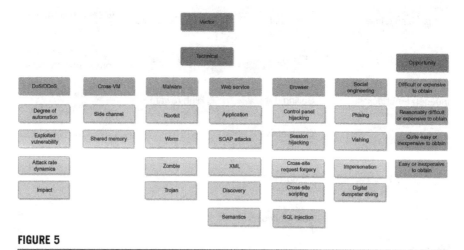

FIGURE 5

Vector dimension.

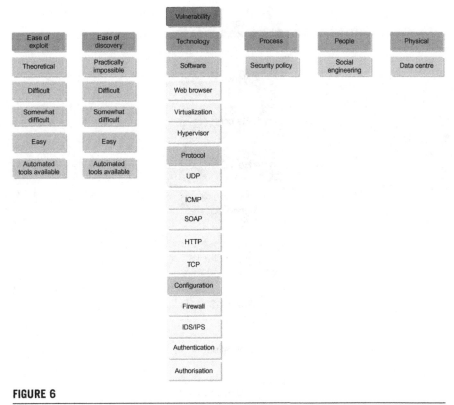

FIGURE 6

Vulnerability dimension.

4.4 TARGET DIMENSION

The target of the attack can be thought of as different physical and logical levels, depending on the attacker's goal and vulnerability exploited. These include the data center where the provider is hosting the service and its network connection, the physical server's OS; the hypervisor; and the guest OS. On the guest OS, the target may be the data or an application (Subashini and Kavitha, 2011). The target of a cloud attack may also be the account in the case of extortion (Figure 7).

4.5 IMPACT DIMENSION

The impact dimension has three subdimensions, namely, technical impacts, impacts on society, and business impacts depending on the nature of the attack, motivations of the attacker, and the type of organization targeted.

The technical impacts are separated into *availability*, *integrity*, and *confidentiality*, based on Welch and Lathrop (2003). An attack is an action or a set of actions with the goal of compromising any of these and it is important to ascertain what type of

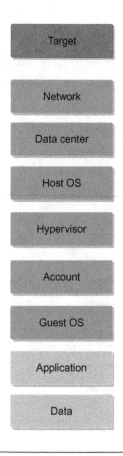

FIGURE 7

Target dimension.

damage has been done (Venter and Eloff, 2003). The next level down is inspired by Simmons et al. (2009)'s "Informational Impact": *disrupt*, *distort*, *destruct*, *disclosure* and *discovery*. The availability of a cloud service can be disrupted by a denial of service attack and the cloud account holder's access to the management console may be hijacked. The impact is a loss of data integrity if it is distorted (changed) or destructed (deleted). If there is a disclosure or discovery of information, the confidentiality is compromised (Kjaerland, 2006). Preattack activities such as scanning, sniffing, and mapping to find out information about the potential target are part of the discovery.

The technical impact of an attack naturally has an impact on the business or society (Saripalli and Walters, 2010). To fully comprehend the risk of an attack against a business organization's cloud services, the business impact for different scenarios must be analyzed and estimated. This also assists in directing security efforts and gaining buy-in from senior management. The dimensions relevant here can be unique to individual businesses, but the four common considerations of financial damage, reputation damage, noncompliance, and privacy violation are a good start (OWASP, 2013b).

Considering the current trend of moving everything from school resources to elections to SCADA system components into the cloud, the impact of cloud attacks on our society must also be considered (Copeland, 2013; Khandelwal, 2014b; Wilhoit, 2013). The impact dimension is illustrated in Figure 8.

4.6 DEFENSE DIMENSION

The defense strategies and mechanisms are closely coupled with the vulnerabilities that would be exploited and the vector used for this purpose. The purpose of the defense mechanism is to remove the weakness that makes that asset or system vulnerable and thereby block the attack vector. In addition, the defense mechanisms must consider the chronological order of the attack, starting with prevention, then moving on to detection, containment, notification, and finally recovering and restoring (Sherwood et al., 2005).

The defense dimension is illustrated in Figure 9. The responsibility of the respective defense mechanisms may be shared between the user and provider and depends on the delivery model (SaaS, PaaS, or IaaS). It is not a coincidence that the Containment and Recovery dimensions lack detail. The specifics of these procedures depend

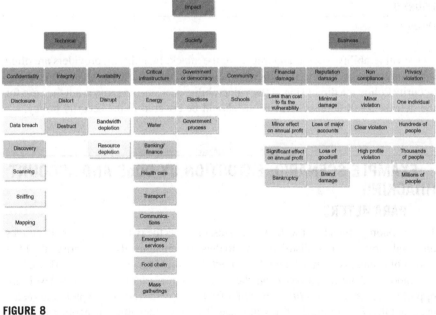

FIGURE 8

Impact dimension.

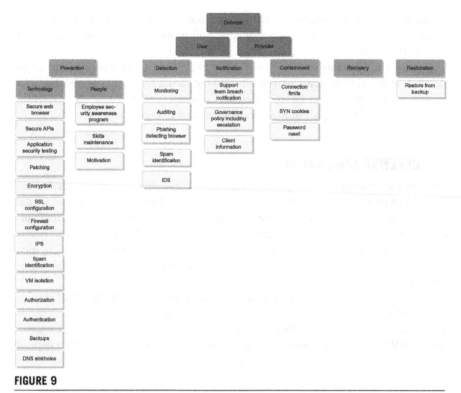

FIGURE 9

Defense dimension.

on the vulnerability, vector, and impact of the attack. In addition, providers are often reluctant to publicize details of their strategies (see Metz, 2009). Although Process-Security Policy is a dimension in the vulnerability section, the same is not the case for the defense as all defense dimensions should be covered in the security policy.

5 EXAMPLE SCENARIO: EXTORTION BY DDoS AND ACCOUNT HIJACKING

5.1 PARAMETERS

This taxonomy lends itself well to risk assessment, as the risk associated with attacks on cloud services can be distilled down to these dimensions. Risk comprises the likelihood of a successful attack and the *impact* this would have (OWASP, 2013b). The likelihood is determined based on the *attack source*'s motivation, skill level and opportunity; the *vulnerability*'s level of difficulty in discovery and exploit; the *vector* used and the *defense* mechanisms in place. The risk of an attack is applied to a particular *target*, in this case, specifically, to a provider and, more particularly, to the host OS, guest OS, hypervisor, or the physical machine.

5.2 RISK ASSESSMENT METHOD

To give an example of how we can classify an attack and assess its risk, we use our taxonomy together with a simple risk assessment formula adapted from the OWASP risk-rating methodology (OWASP, 2013b). Each parameter is rated from 1 (low risk of attack) to 9 (high risk of attack) and the risk rating is then estimated by calculating the overall likelihood and overall impact of a given attack. Any defense parameter would have a low value if there is a strong defense and a high value is there is a low defense, so opposite from the other dimensions. Table 3 contains the risk ratings associated with the attack taxonomy.

Table 3 Risk-Rating Reference

Likelihood		Rating
Source		
Context	(State backed; organized crime; script kiddie; hacker; terrorist; insider)	
Motivation	(Curiosity; political; financial)	
Skill level	Some technical skills	3
	Advanced computer user	4
	Network and programming skills	6
	Security penetration skills	9
Reward potential	Low or no reward	1
	Worthwhile reward	4
	Sizable reward	6
	High reward	9
Vector		
Technical	(DDoS; cross-VM; malware; Web Service; browser; social engineering)	
Opportunity	Difficult or expensive to obtain	1
	Reasonably difficult or expensive to obtain	3
	Quite easy or inexpensive to obtain	6
	Easy or inexpensive to obtain	9
Vulnerability		
Technology	(software; protocol; configuration)	
Process		
People		
Physical		
Ease of exploit	Theoretical	1
	Difficult	3
	Easy	6
	Automated tools available	9

(Continued)

Table 3 Risk-Rating Reference—cont'd

Likelihood		Rating
Ease of discovery	Practically impossible	1
	Difficult	3
	Easy	6
	Automated tools available	9
Target	(Network; data center; host OS; hypervisor; account; guest OS]	
Defense		
Prevention	State-of-the-art technical prevention mechanisms in place	1
	Pretty good technical prevention mechanisms in place	3
	Some technical prevention mechanisms in place	6
	No technical prevention mechanisms in place	9
	Staff are exceptionally competent and well motivated	1
	Staff are reasonably competent and well motivated	3
	Staff have some security awareness but needs improvement	6
	There are severe competency gaps and/or low morale	9
Detection	State-of-the-art monitoring and audit mechanisms in place	1
	Pretty good monitoring and audit mechanisms in place	3
	Some monitoring and audit mechanisms in place	6
	No monitoring or auditing mechanisms in place	9
Notification	State-of-the-art notification procedures in place	1
	Pretty good notification procedures in place	3
	Some notification procedures in place	6
	No notification procedures in place	9
Containment	State-of-the-art containment procedures in place	1
	Pretty good containment procedures in place	3
	Some containment procedures in place	6
	No containment procedures in place	9
Recovery	State-of-the-art recovery procedures in place	1
	Pretty good recovery procedures in place	3
	Some recovery procedures in place	6
	No recovery procedures in place	9
Restoration	State-of-the-art restoration procedures in place	1
	Pretty good restoration procedures in place	3
	Some restoration procedures in place	6
	No restoration procedures in place	9

Table 3 Risk-Rating Reference—cont'd

Likelihood		Rating
Impact		
Technical impact		
Confidentiality	Minimal nonsensitive data disclosed/discovered	2
	Minimal critical data disclosed/discovered	6
	Extensive nonsensitive data disclosed/discovered	6
	Extensive critical data disclosed/discovered	7
	All data disclosed/discovered	9
Integrity	Minimal slightly corrupt data or minimal amount of data deleted	1
	Minimal seriously corrupt data	3
	Extensive slightly corrupt data or extensive amount of data deleted	5
	Extensive seriously corrupt data	7
	All data totally corrupt or deleted	9
Availability	Minimal secondary services disrupted	1
	Minimal primary services disrupted	5
	Extensive secondary services disrupted	5
	Extensive primary services disrupted	7
	All services completely lost	9
Financial impact		
Financial damage	Less than the cost to fix the vulnerability	1
	Minor effect on annual profit	3
	Significant effect on annual profit	7
	Bankruptcy	9
Reputation damage	Minimal	1
	Loss of major accounts	4
	Loss of goodwill	5
	Brand damage	9
Noncompliance	Minor violation	2
	Clear violation	5
	High profile violation	7
Privacy violation	One individual	3
	Hundreds of people	5
	Thousands of people	7
	Millions of people	9

The likelihood and impact levels are calculated by selecting the best estimated rating and averaging them. The risk of the attack is then estimated by calculating the average of the likelihood and impact levels. A risk severity of 0-3 is considered low, 3-6 medium, and 6-9 is high.

5.3 ANALYSIS

Our scenario is based on the recent cloud attack that forced source code hosting service Code Spaces out of business (Paganini, 2014). They were victim of a targeted DDoS attack, followed by extortion demands after the attackers gained access to their Amazon EC2 control panel. Although it is too late to assess the risk for Code Spaces, such attacks could happen again. This is a scenario where there is one source and one target of the attack, but the vectors, vulnerabilities, defenses, and impacts of the attack are two.

5.3.1 Source

We assume that this attack was performed by a sophisticated attacker or attackers (e.g., an organized cyber crime group) motivated by a financial gain (due to the extortion demands). The potential reward can be considered worthwhile as it is reasonable for the attackers to assume that the victim (the code hosting and collaboration platform) would be keen to recover from the attack, but they could not expect a high reward as there is nothing indicating that this is a highly profitable business.

5.3.2 Vectors

There were two vectors used, namely, DDoS and control panel hijacking, both of which would require costs and technical expertise.

5.3.3 Vulnerabilities

As we do not know what vulnerability was exploited in the attack, we will just assume that it was a UDP flood attack, where a botnet was used to send large amounts of IP traffic to the victim's system. In a statement by Code Spaces, they are adamant that their employees were not involved in the account hijacking. Therefore, we assume that the vulnerability was weak authentication where credentials were possible to guess or brute force or a vulnerability in their system that resulted in the leakage of credentials.

5.3.4 Defenses

It is reasonable to assume that there were security mechanisms in place and that the staff were reasonably competent and well motivated to do a good job. We also assume that the provider had in place monitoring and notification procedures for DDoS attacks, but that neither the provider nor the user had any detection or notification mechanisms for account hijacking. The provider probably had containment, recovery and/or restoration mechanisms in the event of a DDoS attack, and so did the user. The cloud service user had some containment, recovery, and restoration procedures in place for the account hijacking. When the breach was discovered by the users, they managed to regain control of their account. However, the attacker was prepared for this event and already created a number of backup logins which were then used instead.

5.3.5 Targets

The DDoS attack was directed at Code Spaces servers, which means that the target would have been the guest OS in this case. The target of the account hijacking attack was the cloud service account.

5.3.6 Impacts

This attack had an impact on all of confidentiality, integrity, and availability of services and data. Initially, a DDoS attack restricted the availability of the service and data. While the attacker had control of the account, Code Spaces key asset, the code repositories were accessed and deleted, including offsite backups, causing a loss of confidentiality and integrity.

The initial DDoS attack had a limited business impact, but the account hijacking and subsequent deletion of their data had significant financial and reputation impacts. This is likely to result in legal implications for the cloud service provider (e.g., law suits by affected users).

5.3.7 Risk rating

To quantify this attack risk, the ratings tables for this two-attack are shown in Tables 4 and 5. Both scenarios are given a risk rating of "Medium," one in the lower range and the other in the upper range.

5.4 LIMITATIONS

We acknowledge that estimates for risk assessments are notoriously difficult to get right. However, this issue is not in the scope of this research as we assume that the risks factors are researched and provided by relevant and qualified staff. In addition, "black swan" events, unlikely events that are only easily explainable in retrospect, are not susceptible by expert advice and, therefore, outside the scope of this risk assessment framework (Taleb, 2010).

6 CONCLUSION AND FUTURE WORK

In this chapter, we presented our taxonomy of attacks on cloud computing services that is comprehensive yet extensible, useful, and purposeful. The taxonomy classifies cloud attacks based on source, vectors, vulnerabilities, targets, impacts, and defenses and can easily be utilized for risk assessment by providers and consumers of cloud computing services. The classification scheme draws from an array of existing

Table 4 Risk Rating of the DDoS Scenario

Likelihood		Rating
Source		
Motivation	Financial	
Context	Organized crime group	
Skill level	Security penetration skills	9
Reward potential	Possible reward	4
Vector		
Technical	Semi-automatic DDoS flood attack with a variable attack rate with a degrading impact	
Opportunity	Difficult or expensive to obtain	2
Vulnerability		
Technology	UDP and network device configuration	
Process	No evidence of process issue	
People	No evidence of people issue	
Physical	No physical vulnerabilities	
Ease of exploit	Difficult	3
Ease of discovery	Easy	8
Defense by user		
Technical prevention	Some technical prevention mechanisms in place	6
Human prevention	Staff are reasonably competent and well motivated	3
Detection	Pretty good monitoring and audit mechanisms in place	3
Notification	Pretty good notification procedures in place	3
Containment	Some containment procedures in place	6
Recovery	Some recovery procedures in place	6
Restoration	Some restoration procedures in place	6
Defense by provider		
Technical prevention	Some technical prevention mechanisms in place	6
Human prevention	Staff are reasonably competent and well motivated	3
Detection	Pretty good monitoring and audit mechanisms in place	3
Notification	Pretty good notification procedures in place	3
Containment	Some containment procedures in place	6
Recovery	Some recovery procedures in place	6
Restoration	Some restoration procedures in place	6

Table 4 Risk Rating of the DDoS Scenario—cont'd

Likelihood		Rating
Total likelihood		4.84
Target	Guest OS and network	
Impact		
Technical impact		
Confidentiality	No sensitive data disclosed	0
Integrity	No data corrupt	0
Availability	All services completely lost	9
Business impact		
Financial damage	Minor effect on annual profit	3
Reputation damage	Loss of major accounts	4
Noncompliance	Clear violation	4
Privacy violation	No privacy violation	0
Total impact rating		2.86
Total risk rating		3.85

Table 5 Risk Rating of the Account Hijacking Scenario

Likelihood		Rating
Source		
Motivation	Financial	
Context	Organized crime group	
Skill level	Security penetration skills	9
Reward potential	Possible reward	4
Vector		
Technical	Account hijacking using the cloud service control panel	
Opportunity	Difficult or expensive to obtain	2
Vulnerability		
Technology	Weak authentication	
Process	Lack of security policy regarding authentication strength	
People	Lack of awareness of importance of strong authentication	
Physical	No physical vulnerabilities	

(Continued)

Table 5 Risk Rating of the Account Hijacking Scenario—cont'd

Likelihood		Rating
Ease of exploit	Difficult	3
Ease of discovery	Easy	8
Defense by user		
Technical prevention	Some technical prevention mechanisms in place	6
Human prevention	Staff are reasonably competent and well motivated	3
Detection	No monitoring or auditing mechanisms in place	9
Notification	No monitoring or auditing mechanisms in place	9
Containment	Some containment procedures in place	6
Recovery	Some recovery procedures in place	6
Restoration	Some restoration procedures in place	6
Defense by provider		
Technical prevention	Some technical prevention mechanisms in place	6
Human prevention	Staff are reasonably competent and well motivated	3
Detection	No monitoring or auditing mechanisms in place	1
Notification	No monitoring or auditing mechanisms in place	1
Containment	Some containment procedures in place	6
Recovery	Some recovery procedures in place	6
Restoration	Some restoration procedures in place	6
Total likelihood rating		5.26
Target	Account	
Impact		
Technical impact		
Confidentiality	Extensive critical data disclosed	7
Integrity	Almost all data deleted	8
Availability	All services completely lost	9
Business impact		
Financial damage	Bankruptcy	9
Reputation damage	Brand damage	9
Noncompliance	Clear violation	6
Privacy violation	No indication of privacy violation	0
Total impact rating		6.86
Total risk rating		6.06

taxonomies of attacks on computer and networks as well as the unique security challenges present in the cloud.

As cloud services increase in popularity, so do organizations' dependence on them and the likelihood of attack. Future work includes validating and refining CATRA using real case studies.

REFERENCES

Amoroso, E.G., 1994. Fundamentals of Computer Security Technology. Prentice-Hall, Inc., Upper Saddle River, NJ.

Bahram, S., Jiang, X., Wang, Z., Grace, M., Li, J., Srinivasan, D., Rhee, J., Xu, D., 2010. Dksm: Subverting virtual machine introspection for fun and profit. In: 29th IEEE Symposium on Reliable Distributed Systems, 2010, pp. 82–91.

Baun, C., Kunze, M., Nimis, J., Tai, S., 2011. Cloud Computing: Web-Based Dynamic IT Services. Springer, Heidelberg, Germany.

Bishop, M., 1999. Vulnerabilities analysis. In: Proceedings of the Recent Advances in intrusion Detection, pp. 125–136.

Borg, I., 1995. Facet Theory. SAGE Publications, Inc., Thousand Oaks.

Borisov, N., Goldberg, I., Wagner, D., 2001. Intercepting mobile communications: The insecurity of 802.11. In: MobiCom '01 Proceedings of the 7th annual international conference on Mobile computing and networking, pp. 180–189. [see http://dl.acm.org/citation.cfm?id=381695].

Chalbi, M., 2014. Syrian Electronic Army's War on the Web: Interactive Timeline. The Guardian (viewed October 21, 2014). http://www.theguardian.com/world/interactive/2013/sep/03/syrian-electronic-army-war-web-timeline.

Chen, Y., Paxson, V., Katz, R.H., 2010. What's new about cloud computing security. Berkeley report no. UCB/EECS-2010-5 January, vol. 20, no. 2010, pp. 2010–2015, University of California.

Chen, Q., Lin, W., Dou, W., Yu, S., 2011. CBF: A packet filtering method for DDoS attack defense in cloud environment. In: IEEE Ninth International Conference on Dependable, Autonomic and Secure Computing (DASC), pp. 427–434.

Chonka, A., Xiang, Y., Zhou, W., Bonti, A., 2011. Cloud security defence to protect cloud computing against HTTP-DoS and XML-DoS attacks. J. Netw. Comput. Appl. 34 (4), 1097–1107.

Choo, K.K.R., 2010. Cloud computing: challenges and future directions. Trends Iss. Crime Crim. Justice 400, 1–6.

Choo, K.-K.R., 2014. A Conceptual Interdisciplinary Plug-and-Play Cyber Security Framework. ICTs and the Millennium Development Goals. Springer, NY, USA, pp. 81–99.

Choo, K.K.R., Smith, R.G., McCusker, R., American Institute of Criminology, 2007. In: Future directions in technology-enabled crime: 2007-09. In: Research and Public Policy Series, vol. 78.

Chou, N., Ledesma, R., Teraguchi, Y., Mitchell, J.C., 2004. Client-side defense against web-based identity theft. In: NDSS Symposium, San Diego, CA, USA.

Chow, R., Golle, P., Jakobsson, M., Shi, E., Staddon, J., Masuoka, R., Molina, J., 2009. Controlling data in the cloud: outsourcing computation without outsourcing control. In: Proceedings of the 2009 ACM Workshop on Cloud Computing Security, pp. 85–90.

Cisco, 2012. Cisco Study: IT Saying Yes to BYOD (viewed May 16, 2012). http://newsroom.cisco.com/release/854754/Cisco-Study-IT-Saying-Yes-To-BYOD.

Copeland, M.V., 2013. A school in the cloud and the future of learning. Wired. http://www.wired.com/2013/02/a-school-in-the-cloud-and-the-future-of-learning/.

Crane, A., 2005. In the company of spies: When competitive intelligence gathering becomes industrial espionage. Bus. Horiz. 48 (3), 233–240.

Dagon, D., Gu, G., Lee, C.P., Lee, W., 2007. A taxonomy of botnet structures. In: Twenty-Third Annual Computer Security Applications Conference (ACSAC 2007), Miami, Florida, USA, pp. 325–339.

Desnos, A., Filiol, É., Lefou, I., 2011. Detecting (and creating!) a HVM rootkit (aka BluePill-like). J. Comput. Virol. 7 (1), 23–49.

Dhamija, R., Tygar, J.D., 2005. The battle against phishing: Dynamic security skins. In: Proceedings of the 2005 Symposium on Usable Privacy and Security, pp. 77–88.

Do, Q., Martini, B., Choo, K.-K.R., 2015. Exfiltrating data from android devices. Comput. Secur. 48, 74–91

Douligeris, C., Mitrokotsa, A., 2004. DDoS attacks and defense mechanisms: classification and state-of-the-art. Comput. Netw. 44 (5), 643–666.

Dykstra, J., Sherman, A.T., 2013. Design and implementation of FROST: Digital forensic tools for the OpenStack cloud computing platform. Digit. Investig. 10, S87–S95.

East, S., Butts, J., Papa, M., Shenoi, S., 2009. A taxonomy of attacks on the DNP3 protocol. Critical Infrastructure Protection III. Springer, NY, USA, pp. 67–81.

Egelman, S., Cranor, L.F., Hong, J., 2008. You've been warned: an empirical study of the effectiveness of web browser phishing warnings. In: Proceedings of the SIGCHI Conference on Human Factors in Computing Systems, pp. 1065–1074.

Fette, I., Sadeh, N., Tomasic, A., 2007. Learning to detect phishing emails. In: Proceedings of the 16th International Conference on World Wide Web, pp. 649–656.

Finkle, J., 2014. 360 Million Newly Stolen Credentials on Black Market: Cybersecurity Firm (viewed October 21, 2014). http://www.reuters.com/article/2014/02/25/us-cybercrime-databreach-idUSBREA1O20S20140225.

Foozy, C., Ahmad, R., Abdollah, M., Yusof, R., Zaki, M., 2011. Generic Taxonomy of Social Engineering Attack. In: Malaysian Technical Universities International Conference on Engineering & Technology, pp. 527–533.

Gregg, M., 2014. Certified Ethical Hacker (CEH) Cert Guide. Pearson Education, Inc., Indianapolis, IN.

Grobauer, B., Walloschek, T., Stocker, E., 2011. Understanding cloud computing vulnerabilities. IEEE Secur. Priv. 9 (2), 50–57.

Gruschka, N., Iacono, L.L., 2009. Vulnerable cloud: Soap message security validation revisited. In: IEEE International Conference on Web Services, 2009 (ICWS 2009), pp. 625–631.

Gruschka, N., Jensen, M., 2010. Attack surfaces: A taxonomy for attacks on cloud services. In: IEEE 3rd International Conference on Cloud Computing (CLOUD), 2010, pp. 276–279.

Hale, J.S., 2013. Amazon Cloud Drive forensic analysis. Digit. Investig. 10 (3), 259–265.

Hansman, S., Hunt, R., 2005. A taxonomy of network and computer attacks. Comput. Secur. 24 (1, 2), 31–43.

Hoefer, C.N., Karagiannis, G., 2010. Taxonomy of cloud computing services. In: GLOBECOM Workshops (GC Wkshps), 2010 IEEE, pp. 1345–1350.

Hooper, C., Martini, B., Choo, K.-K.R., 2013. Cloud computing and its implications for cybercrime investigations in Australia. Comput. Law Secur. Rev. 29 (2), 152–163.

Hoque, N., Bhuyan, M.H., Baishya, R.C., Bhattacharyya, D., Kalita, J.K., 2014. Network attacks: Taxonomy, tools and systems. J. Netw. Comput. Appl. 40, 307–324.

Howard, JD, 1997. An analysis of security incidents on the Internet 1989-1995, DTIC Document.

Hwang, K., Kulkareni, S., Hu, Y., 2009. Cloud security with virtualized defense and reputation-based trust mangement. In: Eighth IEEE International Conference on Dependable, Autonomic and Secure Computing, 2009 (DASC'09), pp. 717–722.

Igure, V., Williams, R., 2008. Taxonomies of attacks and vulnerabilities in computer systems. IEEE Commun. Surveys Tuts. 10 (1), 6–19.

ISO/IEC 27000:2014. Information technology—Security techniques—Information security management systems—Overview and vocabulary, Switzerland.

Jansen, W.A., 2011. Cloud hooks: Security and privacy issues in cloud computing. In: 44th Hawaii International Conference on System Sciences (HICSS), 2011, pp. 1–10.

Jensen, M., Schwenk, J., Gruschka, N., Iacono, L.L., 2009. On technical security issues in cloud computing. In: IEEE International Conference on Cloud Computing, 2009 (CLOUD'09), pp. 109–116.

Jensen, M., Schwenk, J., Bohli, J.-M., Gruschka, N., Iacono, L.L., 2011. Security prospects through cloud computing by adopting multiple clouds. In: IEEE International Conference on Cloud Computing (CLOUD), 2011, pp. 565–572.

Joshi, B., Vijayan, A.S., Joshi, B.K., 2012. Securing cloud computing environment against DDoS attacks. In: International Conference on Computer Communication and Informatics (ICCCI), 2012, pp. 1–5.

Kelley, P.G., Komanduri, S., Mazurek, M.L., Shay, R., Vidas, T., Bauer, L., Christin, N., Cranor, L.F., Lopez, J., 2012. Guess again (and again and again): Measuring password strength by simulating password-cracking algorithms. In: IEEE Symposium on Security and Privacy (SP), 2012, pp. 523–537.

Khandelwal, S., 2014a. Largest DDoS attack hit Hong Kong democracy voting website. The Hacker News. (viewed July 4, 2014). http://thehackernews.com/2014/06/largest-ddos-attack-hit-hong-kong.html.

Khandelwal, S., 2014b. ZeuS Trojan Variant Targets Salesforce Accounts and SaaS Applications. (viewed July 3, 2014). http://thehackernews.com/2014/02/Salesforce-malware-attack-zeus-trojan.html.

Khorshed, M.T., Ali, A., Wasimi, S.A., 2012. A survey on gaps, threat remediation challenges and some thoughts for proactive attack detection in cloud computing. Futur. Gener. Comput. Syst. 28 (6), 833–851.

Killourhy, K.S., Maxion, R.A., Tan, K.M., 2004. A defense-centric taxonomy based on attack manifestations. In: International Conference on Dependable Systems and Networks, 2004, pp. 102–111.

King, S.T., Chen, P.M., 2006. SubVirt: Implementing malware with virtual machines. In: IEEE Symposium on Security and Privacy, 2006, pp. 14–327.

Kjaerland, M., 2000. Electronic Civil Disobedience: A Differentiation Between 'Hacktivists' Based on Target and Message of Web Site Hacks (Master thesis). Department of Psychology, University of Liverpool.

Kjaerland, M., 2006. A taxonomy and comparison of computer security incidents from the commercial and government sectors. Comput. Secur. 25 (7, 10), 522–538.

Kotadia, M., 2014. Public cloud adoption stalling in US. itnews. (viewed June 16, 2014). http://www.itnews.com.au/News/375532,%20public-cloud-adoption-stalling-in-us-research-finds.aspxt.

Kotapati, K., Liu, P., Sun, Y., LaPorta, T.F., 2005. A taxonomy of cyber attacks on 3G networks. Intelligence and Security Informatics. Springer, Lecture Notes in Computer Science 3498, pp. 631–633.

Krsul, I.V., 1998. Software Vulnerability Analysis (Doctoral thesis). Department of Computer Science, Purdue University.

Krutz, R.L., Vines, R.D., 2010. Cloud Security: A Comprehensive Guide to Secure Cloud Computing. John Wiley & Sons, Indiana, USA.

LaBarge, R., McGuire, T., 2013. Cloud penetration testing, arXiv, http://arxiv.org/ftp/arxiv/papers/1301/1301.1912.pdf.

Lee, J.-H., Park, M.-W., Eom, J.-H., Chung, T.-M., 2011. Multi-level intrusion detection system and log management in cloud computing. In: 13th International Conference on Advanced Communication Technology (ICACT), 2011, pp. 552–555.

Leyden, J., 2013. Syrian Electroinic Army no longer just Twitter feed jackers... and that's bad news. The Register. (viewed October 21, 2014). http://www.theregister.co.uk/2013/08/01/sea_analysis/.

Lindqvist, U., Jonsson, E., 1997. How to systematically classify computer security intrusions. In: Proceedings of the 1997 IEEE Symposium on Security and Privacy, pp. 154–163.

Lough, D.L., 2001. A Taxonomy of Computer Attacks with Applications to Wireless Networks (Doctoral thesis). Faculty of Computer Engneering, Virginia Polytechnic Institute and State University.

Mainka, C., Somorovsky, J., Schwenk, J., 2012. Penetration testing tool for web services security. In: IEEE Eighth World Congress on Services (SERVICES), 2012, pp. 163–170.

Martini, B., Choo, K.-K.R., 2013. Cloud storage forensics: ownCloud as a case study. Digit. Investig. 10 (4), 287–299.

Martini, B., Choo, K.-K.R., 2014. Remote Programmatic vCloud Forensics. In: Proceedings of 13th IEEE International Conference on Trust, Security and Privacy in Computing and Communications (TrustCom 2014), Beijing, China.

Metz, C., 2009. DDoS attack rains down on Amazon cloud. The Register. (viewed June 10, 2014). http://www.theregister.co.uk/2009/10/05/amazon_bitbucket_outage/.

Miller, K.W., Voas, J., Hurlburt, G.F., 2012. BYOD: security and privacy considerations. IT Professional 14 (5), 0053–0055.

Mirkovic, J., Reiher, P., 2004. A taxonomy of DDoS attack and DDoS defense mechanisms. Comput. Commun. Rev. 34 (2), 39–53.

Modi, C., Patel, D., Borisaniya, B., Patel, A., Rajarajan, M., 2013. A survey on security issues and solutions at different layers of Cloud computing. J. Supercomput. 63 (2), 561–592.

Mokhov, S.A., Laverdière, M.-A., Benredjem, D., 2008. Taxonomy of linux kernel vulnerability solutions. Innovative Techniques in Instruction Technology, E-learning, E-assessment, and Education. Springer, NY, USA, pp. 485–493. http://www.springer.com/gp/book/9781402087387.

O'Malley, S.J., Choo, K.-K.R., 2014. Bridging the Air Gap: Inaudible Data Exfiltration by Insiders. In: 20th Americas Conference on Information Systems (AMCIS 2014), pp. 7–10.

Offensive Security, 2014. Kali Linux (viewed October 21, 2014). http://www.kali.org/.

O'Hara, G., 2010. Cyber-Espionage: A Growing Threat to the American Economy. Comm-Law Conspectus 19, 241.

Olson, P., 2012. We Are Anonymous: Inside the Hacker World of Lulzsec, Anonymous, and the Global Cyber Insurgency. Little, Brown and Company, New York, NY.

OWASP, 2013a. 2013 Top 10 List, Open Web Application Security Project (viewed June 26, 2014). https://www.owasp.org/index.php/Top_10_2013-Top_10.

OWASP, 2013b. OWASP Risk Rating Methodology, Open Web Application Security Project (viewed June 26, 2014). https://www.owasp.org/index.php/OWASP_Risk_Rating_Methodology.

Paganini, P., 2013a. How to Profit Illegally from Bitcoin … Cybercrime and Much More. Infosec Institute. (viewed June 23, 2014). http://resources.infosecinstitute.com/how-to-profit-illegally-from-bitcoin-cybercrime-and-much-more/.

Paganini, P., 2013b. DDoS mitigation—choosing a cloud-based solution. Security Affairs (viewed July 4, 2013). http://securityaffairs.co/wordpress/15097/security/choosing-a-cloud-based-ddos-mitigation-solution.html.

Paganini, P., 2014. Hosting service Code Spaces goes out of business due a cyber attack. Security Affairs (viewed June 21, 2014). http://securityaffairs.co/wordpress/25912/cyber-crime/code-spaces-out-of-business.html.

Patel, A., Taghavi, M., Bakhtiyari, K., Celestino JúNior, J., 2013. An intrusion detection and prevention system in cloud computing: A systematic review. J. Netw. Comput. Appl. 36 (1), 25–41.

Pauli, D., 2014. Most sophisticated DDoS' ever strikes Hong Kong democracy poll. The Register. (viewed June 24, 2014). http://www.theregister.co.uk/2014/06/23/most_sophisticated_ddos_strikes_hk_democracy_poll/.

Peake, C., 2012. Security in the cloud: Understanding the risks of cloud-as-a-service. In: IEEE Conference on Technologies Homeland Security (HST), 2012, pp. 336–340.

Peng, T., Leckie, C., Ramamohanarao, K., 2007. Survey of network-based defense mechanisms countering the DoS and DDoS problems. ACM. Comput. Surv. 39(1), Article No. 3.

Perlroth, N., Gelles, D., 2014. Russian hackers amass over a billion internet passwords. New York Times (viewed October 21, 2014). http://www.nytimes.com/2014/08/06/technology/russian-gang-said-to-amass-more-than-a-billion-stolen-internet-credentials.html.

Popovic, K., Hocenski, Z., 2010. Cloud computing security issues and challenges. In: Proceedings of the 33rd International Convention MIPRO, 2010, pp. 344–349.

Pothamsetty, V., Akyol, B.A., 2004. A vulnerability taxonomy for network protocols: corresponding engineering best practice countermeasures. In: The Seventh IASTED International Conference on Communication, Internet, and Information Technology, pp. 168–175.

Prodan, R., Ostermann, S., 2009. A survey and taxonomy of infrastructure as a service and web hosting cloud providers'. In: 10th IEEE/ACM International Conference on Grid Computing, 2009, pp. 17–25.

Quick, D., Choo, K.-K.R., 2013a. Digital droplets: Microsoft SkyDrive forensic data remnants. Futur. Gener. Comput. Syst. 29 (6), 1378–1394.

Quick, D., Choo, K.-K.R., 2013b. Dropbox analysis: Data remnants on user machines. Digit. Investig. 10 (1), 3–18.

Quick, D., Choo, K.-K.R., 2013c. Forensic collection of cloud storage data: Does the act of collection result in changes to the data or its metadata? Digit. Investig. 10 (3), 266–277.

Quick, D., Choo, K.-K.R., 2014. Google Drive: Forensic analysis of data remnants. J. Netw. Comput. Appl. 40, 179–193.

Quick, D., Martini, B., Choo, R., 2014. Cloud Storage Forensics. Syngress, Rockland, MA.

Ragan, R., Salazar, O., 2014. CloudBots: Harvesting Crypto Coins Like a Botnet Farmer. Black Hat, Las Vegas, CA.

Raiu, C., Emm, D., 2014. The top stories of 2013. Kaspersky Security Bulletin (viewed June 23, 2014). http://report.kaspersky.com/.

Rimal, B.P., Choi, E., Lumb, I., 2010. A taxonomy, survey, and issues of cloud computing ecosystems. Cloud Computing. Springer, NY, USA, pp. 21-46.

Ristenpart, T., Tromer, E., Shacham, H., Savage, S., 2009. Hey, you, get off of my cloud: exploring information leakage in third-party compute clouds. In: Proceedings of the 16th ACM Conference on Computer and Communications Security, pp. 199–212.

Roschke, S., Cheng, F., Meinel, C., 2009. Intrusion detection in the cloud. In: Eighth IEEE International Conference on Dependable, Autonomic and Secure Computing, 2009 (DASC'09), pp. 729–734.

Ross, R., Katzke, S., Johnson, A., Swanson, M., Stoneburner, G., Rogers, G., Lee, A., 2005. Recommended security controls for federal information systems. In: NIST Special Publication, vol. 800. p. 53.

Rutkowska, J., 2006a. Introducing stealth malware taxonomy. COSEINC Advanced Malware Labs, Singapore, pp. 1–9. http://virii.es/I/Introducing%20Stealth%20Malware%20Taxonomy.pdf.

Rutkowska, J., 2006b. Subverting Vista™ Kernel for Fun and Profit. Black Hat Briefings, Las Vegas, CA.

Saripalli, P., Walters, B., 2010. Quirc: A quantitative impact and risk assessment framework for cloud security. In: IEEE 3rd International Conference on Cloud Computing (CLOUD), 2010, pp. 280–288.

Savage, C., Shane, S., 2013. Secret court rebuked N.S.A. on surveillance. New York Times (viewed August 21, 2014). http://www.nytimes.com/2013/08/22/us/2011-ruling-found-an-nsa-program-unconstitutional.html.

Shadows in the Cloud: Investigating Cyber Espionage 2.0 (viewed October 21, 2014). http://shadows-in-the-cloud.net.

Sherwood, J., Clark, A., Lynas, D., 2005. Enterprise Security Architecture: A Business-Driven Approach. Taylor & Francis Ltd, Lawrence.

Simmons, C., Ellis, C., Shiva, S., Dasgupta, D., Wu, Q., 2009. AVOIDIT: a cyber attack taxonomy. Technical report CS-09-003, University of Memphis.

Somorovsky, J., Heiderich, M., Jensen, M., Schwenk, J., Gruschka, N., Lo Iacono, L., 2011. All your clouds are belong to us: security analysis of cloud management interfaces. In: Proceedings of the 3rd ACM Workshop on Cloud Computing Security Workshop, pp. 3–14.

Sosinsky, B., 2011. Cloud Computing Bible. Wiley Pub, Chichester/Indianapolis, IN.

Specht, S.M., Lee, R.B., 2004. Distributed Denial of Service: Taxonomies of Attacks, Tools, and Countermeasures. In: ISCA PDCS, pp. 543–550.

Srinivasan, M.K., Sarukesi, K., Rodrigues, P., Manoj, M.S., Revathy, P., 2012. State-of-the-art cloud computing security taxonomies: a classification of security challenges in the present cloud computing environment. In: Proceedings of the International Conference on Advances in Computing, Communications and Informatics, pp. 470–476.

Subashini, S., Kavitha, V., 2011. A survey on security issues in service delivery models of cloud computing. J. Netw. Comput. Appl. 34 (1), 1–11.

Sullivan, N., 2014. The Heartbleed Aftermath: all CloudFlare certificates revoked and reissued. *CloudFlare Blog*, blog posting, viewed. http://blog.cloudflare.com/the-heartbleed-aftermath-all-cloudflare-certificates-revoked-and-reissued.

Taleb, N.N., 2010. The Black Swan: The Impact of the Highly Improbable Fragility. Random House LLC, New York, NY.

Todorov, D., Ozkan, Y., 2013. AWS Security Best Practices (viewed October 16, 2014). http://media.amazonwebservices.com/AWS_Security_Best_Practices.pdf.

Venter, H.S., Eloff, J.H.P., 2003. A taxonomy for information security technologies. Comput. Secur. 22 (4, 5), 299–307.

Viega, J., McGraw, G., 2002. Building secure software. Addison-Wesley.

Vorobiev, A., Han, J., 2006. Security attack ontology for web services. In: Second International Conference on Semantics, Knowledge and Grid, 2006 (SKG'06), article 42.

Weaver, N., Paxson, V., Staniford, S., Cunningham, R., 2003. A taxonomy of computer worms. In: Proceedings of the 2003 ACM workshop on Rapid malcode, pp. 11–18.

Welch, D., Lathrop, S., 2003. Wireless security threat taxonomy. In: Information Assurance Workshop, 2003. IEEE Systems, Man and Cybernetics Society, pp. 76–83.

Wilhoit, K., 2013. SCADA in the Cloud: A Security Conundrum?, vol. 29. (viewed July 4, 2014). http://www.trendmicro.com/cloud-content/us/pdfs/security-intelligence/white-papers/wp-scada-in-the-cloud.pdf.

Yue, X., Qiu, X., Ji, Y., Zhang, C., 2009. P2P attack taxonomy and relationship analysis. In: 11th International Conference on Advanced Communication Technology, 2009 (ICACT 2009), pp. 1207–1210.

Zunnurhain, K., Vrbsky, S., 2010. Security attacks and solutions in clouds. In: Proceedings of the 1st International Conference on Cloud, Computing, pp. 145–156.

Multitiered cloud security model

4

Hing-Yan Lee, Yao-Sing Tao

Info-communications Development Authority of Singapore, Singapore

1 INTRODUCTION

This chapter highlights the impediments to cloud adoption arising from cloud security and describes the establishment of a framework to address the adoption issue in general and the design of a multi-tiered cloud security model to help users to better appreciate the security provisioning by cloud service providers (CSPs).

Cloud computing shifts much of the control over data and operations from the user organization to CSPs, much in the same way organizations entrust their Information Technology (IT) operations (or part of) to outsourcing companies. In addition to the usual challenges in delivering secure IT services, cloud computing presents an elevated level of risk in outsourcing to a third party as the computing environment becomes more complex and dynamic to manage.

Cloud computing has introduced key enabling technologies such as hypervisors and virtual machines to create a very agile and dynamic computing environment. These technologies however, also bring about a host of challenges and risks. Additionally, the massive sharing of infrastructure and computing resources in a multi-tenanted environment, especially with users spanning different organizations and security needs, creates a "shared virtual environment" where users/organizations are no longer clearly divided by physical server racks and separate networks. New users in cloud computing can be easily changed or created by initializing online additional virtual machines and networks. Inside a cloud, it is difficult to physically locate where the data is stored and how it is segregated. This lack of visibility, and thus ability to audit and verify, pose a number of security and compliance issues.

2 THE PROBLEM

According to IDC (IDC, 2009), cloud security is the Number One concern cited by IT managers when they consider cloud deployments. Another study (Launchpad, 2009) conducted by Launchpad Europe, a company that helps emerging firms with global business expansion, found that nearly half of organizations say they have no plans to use any cloud computing technologies in the next year, citing security concerns as the primary reason.

Every industry has its own unique characteristics and concern. The tolerance level of security risk differs from sector to sector. For example, the banking community is extremely concerned with the risk exposure of their customer information stored in cloud. They may take a more cautious step and a longer time to move their mission critical banking applications to the cloud.

Other industries may feel that the benefits outweigh the potential risk and may be more forthcoming in adopting cloud. CSPs today provision security to a much better degree that small- or medium-sized enterprises (SMEs) could not achieve by themselves. In the past, the cost and complexity to ensure such security meant that it used to be only accessible to large enterprises. Also many corporate-grade applications (e.g., CRM) are available to these SMEs. Thus, the security challenge of cloud computing needs to be viewed in this perspective, relative to what we have now and matching of provisions by the CSPs to users' needs. The crux of issue in cloud adoption is therefore, devising a security framework that provides visibility and clarity of security provisions of the CSPs to facilitate matching with users' needs.

3 HOLISTIC APPROACH

Security (or its lack thereof) is not an insurmountable obstacle to cloud computing adoption. It is important to understand that the concern of cloud security arises from various sources, ranging from a lack of understanding to unavailability of common standards for assessment. We therefore need to take a multi-pronged holistic approach in the framework to tackle adoption issues relating to cloud security, as depicted in Figure 1.

3.1 AWARENESS

One reason people are paranoid about security arises from a lack of understanding of what cloud computing is. Increasing awareness education will enable potential users to have a better knowledge of cloud and its security implications.

3.2 CLASSIFICATION

Users must undertake their own necessary risk assessment and definition of security needs in using cloud services. This process of classification of data and applications will ensure their security needs will accordingly be matched with the security provisions offered by CSPs. For example, while the financial services industry (FSI) is disinclined to use public cloud, not every FSI application faces the same level of risks. Hence it is possible for banks to have web hosting of nonsensitive information using a public CSP.

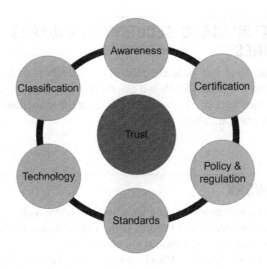

FIGURE 1

Holistic approach to cloud security.

3.3 TECHNOLOGY

Cloud-related technologies bring about an entire new dimension of technical risks and challenges. Some of these risks can be addressed through research.

3.4 POLICY AND REGULATION

Adoption of cloud computing is a matter of trust building among all the stakeholders, namely, CSPs, cloud users, auditors, and regulators. An appropriate policy and regulatory framework to govern the use and provisioning of cloud services and a scheme that helps CSPs to get certified independently are needed to be put in place. The necessary policy and regulation to get the CSPs certified may be achieved through industry self-regulation or made mandatory.

3.5 CERTIFICATION

To provide transparency and visibility of security measures adopted by CSPs, it is important that the security provisions implemented by CSPs can be independently certified by competent auditors.

3.6 STANDARDS

There are several initiatives undertaken worldwide to address cloud security issues, noticeably in US and Europe. Please see Section 6 for details.

Subsequent sections will focus on the design, development, and deployment, including certification of a cloud security standard.

4 WHY DEVELOP CLOUD SECURITY STANDARDS AND GUIDELINES

Today, there are no cloud standards and guidelines currently available that have been widely accepted and adopted by CSPs and cloud users. A survey of current initiatives in cloud security (see Section 5) reveals that none of the guidelines can be directly adopted without significant changes.

5 RELATED WORK

There are several initiatives undertaken worldwide to address cloud security issues, noticeably in the United States and Europe. In the United States and Europe, industry players are working together to tackle these challenges.

The Cloud Security Alliance (CSA) security guidelines are high-level recommendations and are not auditable standards. CSA's Governance, Risk Management and Compliance (GRC) Stack guidelines provide a set of questions and requirements which is difficult for users to evaluate and assess the detailed responses for adequacy of the security provisions by CSPs (CSA, 2010).

In Europe, ENISA, a 24-member strong consortium of service providers, vendors, government organizations, and consultants together define common assurance metrics to allow businesses to compare the security standards of CSPs. These guidelines provide a set of questions and requirements that the users can ask CSPs to assure themselves that they are sufficiently protecting the information entrusted to them. The guidelines and assurance metrics document does not provide a standard response format for the CSPs, so detailed responses are in a free-text format which makes it difficult for users to evaluate and assess the adequacy of the security provisions by CSPs (ENISA, 2009a,b).

The FedRAMP (Federal Risk and Authorization Management Program) was established to provide a standard approach to assessing and authorizing cloud services. Based on an elaborate Federal Information Security Management Act (FISMA) framework, FedRAMP is however, specifically designed for use by the US federal government. It is not a national standard for all industries and sectors of economy (FedRAMP, 2014).

SAS70 was created by the American Institute of Certified Public Accountants in 1992. It was originally intended to review the controls in service providers for material effect on the annual financial statements. SAS70 is narrow in scope and not a comprehensive security framework when compared with ISO27001 (ISO/IEC, 27001:2005). The rise of cloud computing pushes CSPs to adapt the report to auditing controls in cloud service provisioning. As the security requirements and controls are self-defined by CSPs, the onus is on the cloud user to determine if these self-defined controls are adequate to meet his security needs (SAS70, 1992).

However, the current ISO27001 (ISO/IEC, 27001:2005) is not cloud specific. It establishes a generic Information Security Management System. The Japanese Industrial Standards Committee has proposed to ISO/IEC to establish guidelines for the use of cloud computing services. This new initiative (ISO/IEC JTC1/SC 27) would take at least another 3 years or so to develop into an international standard or technical report.

The above notwithstanding, it is important to establish necessary cloud standards and guidelines to guide the security provisioning by CSPs, as a step toward addressing a major impediment in cloud adoption. While the CSA GRC stack, ENISA and FISMA/FedRAMP standards and guidelines are not readily suitable for use, they serve as good references and inputs to our own standards development work.

6 DESIGN CONSIDERATIONS OF MULTITIERED CLOUD SECURITY

As the tolerance level of security risk differs from sector to sector, one solution to address such immediate security issues arising from cloud computing is to provide a multi-tiered model satisfying security needs of different cloud user groups; it may take a form similar to the well-known tiered service model in data center offerings (Uptime, 2013). This multi-tiered model covers users (including SMEs) with basic requirements to one that needs high confidentiality and high availability such as FSI. The tiered model must be able cover and differentiate between CSPs offering significant customization/private cloud and utility providers merging more features and capabilities with a less flexible model/public cloud.

These guidelines highlight the key security areas and associated controls to be addressed arising from the new cloud computing environment. These controls are defined to address or mitigate the new or elevated risks identified.

Some of the key design considerations are:

(a) Different levels of control that correspond to different levels of security requirements will have to be specified for each tier. Each higher cloud security tier builds upon lower tier, either with additional security requirements or more stringent controls and/or audit checks.

(b) To manage the scope and avoid duplication of work, such guidelines do not replace but complement and leverage on existing noncloud-specific security standards. Indeed the MTCS uses ISO27001:2005 as its foundation. It is important to provide CSPs a familiar basis to embark upon to attain MTCS certification.

(c) To consider riding on existing relevant standards and guidelines by including these as part of the control requirements, we need to consider the impact of direct dependencies which we are unable to influence or control. After careful evaluation, the decision was to make MTCS as self-contained as possible; this standard will include both implementation guides and necessary audit procedures.

(d) Other relevant standards, guidelines, and reference documents considered include Technical Reference 30 (TR30, 2012), Technical Reference 31 (TR31, 2012), CSA Cloud Computing Matrix (CSA, 2010), Payment Card Industry Data Security Standard (PCI, 2010), European Union Agency for Network & Information Security guidelines (ENISA, 2009a,b), National Institute of Standards & Technology SP 800 series (NIST, 2007–2013), and Technology Risk Management from Monetary Authority of Singapore (MAS, 2013).

(e) The number of tiers should not be so many that a cloud user would have difficulty understanding. The purpose of each tier should be intuitive to the cloud user. The eventual decision to have three tiers is arrived at after taking into account the focus group feedback received from cloud users and CSPs.

(f) The three tiers are so designed to cover different security needs of various cloud users; from baseline requirements of general SMEs through needs of most enterprises (protection of sensitive business information) to stringent demand of the regulated industries (high availability/reliability and resiliency plus better customers isolation and data segregation).

(g) While cloud service models like Infrastructure-as-a-Service (IaaS), Platform-as-a-Service (PaaS), and Software-as-a-Service (SaaS) have been defined (for example, by the National Institute of Standards & Technology (NIST, 2011), their implementations vary greatly across CSPs. Thus CSPs may scope out only different security controls that are applicable and relevant to their implementation of the service model. As such, we avoid associating specific security controls with each service model.

(h) Arising from the above point on not associating cloud service model with prespecified security controls is the issue of how each service model can be certified, given that each may be delivered by a distinct and separate commercial entity. For example, a straightforward solution is to require a PaaS (or an SaaS) seeking MTCS certification at Level x to be hosted on an IaaS that is already MTCS certified at Level y and ensuring that the $y \geq x$.

7 BENEFITS TO STAKEHOLDERS

The benefits of MTCS to the four major stakeholders in cloud computing are as follows.

- *CSPs*: It helps CSPs to better meet the security needs of specific segments of cloud users. Adherence to such industry best practices removes doubts, uncertainties, and thus builds trust with the users. This not only cuts down the client engagement time and sales cycle but also minimizes or avoids future disputes with cloud users as the mismatch of security needs surfaces much later.

- *Cloud users*: Currently, it is a time-consuming exercise for the cloud users to carry out proper due diligence to source for the right CSP with appropriate security provisions. Many cloud users or companies may not even have the necessary technical expertise to carry out such an evaluation adequately. Cloud users, given such a yardstick, are able to validate controls and thus have assurance that their applications and data are protected. It also facilitates comparison of the security provisions of CSPs making it easier to identify the right CSP and resulting in faster cloud deployment.
- *Auditors and regulators*: These major stakeholders are able to use the guidelines to interpret security requirements consistently when auditing CSPs/users. Otherwise, the audit results may vary subject to the interpretation by different auditors/regulators and unnecessary disputes with the CSPs and/or cloud users. This saves time and effort in auditing and achieves compliance faster.

8 MTCS STANDARDS

The MTCS standards are built upon the international standard, ISO27001:2005 as its base. Many of the controls are being interpreted under the cloud computing environment and new cloud related/specific controls are then added as necessary. The standards are meant to be general and applicable to all sectors and industries even though it is designed to have multiple security levels. Those sector-specific controls such as use of special hardware or equipment or specific sectorial practices are being excluded. For the standards to be adopted in specific sectors or industries, additional industry specific standards and controls would have to be applied as depicted in Figure 2.

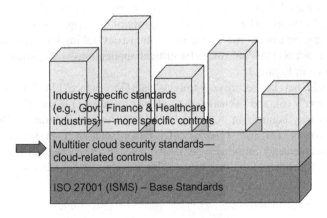

Industry-specific standards (e.g., Govt, Finance & Healthcare industries) —more specific controls

Multitier cloud security standards— cloud-related controls

ISO 27001 (ISMS) – Base Standards

FIGURE 2

MTCS relative to ISO 27001 and sector-specific requirements.

Level	Overview	Security Control Focus	Typical User	Typical Usage
1	Designed to be low cost with a minimum of required controls	Baseline security controls – "security 101"	SMEs	• Hosting Web site • Test & Development • Simulation • Noncritical biz apps
2	Address the needs of most organizations that are concerned about data security	A set of more stringent security controls required to address security risks & threats to data	Enterprises	• The majority of cloud usages. • More critical biz apps
3	Designed for regulated organizations with specific requirements & are willing to pay for more stringent security requirements	Additional set of security controls are necessary to supplement & address security risks & threats in high-impact information systems using cloud services	Regulated Industries	• Hosting applications & systems with sensitive information & regulated systems

FIGURE 3

MTCS tiers and typical users/usage.

The design of tiers in MTCS standards is based on feedback from numerous focus groups comprising CSPs and cloud users from industry. It is structured according to usage types, sensitivity of data, and types of applications being hosted. The base tier, Level 1, has minimal controls, designed to host nonbusiness critical applications and nonsensitive data. Level 2 is focused on data protection, catered for more critical business applications and data, covering majority of the usages. The top tier is most stringent, oriented toward use by regulated industries, taking the common security requirements across such industries for critical applications with sensitive information as shown in Figure 3.

Level 2 adds new key security controls in "Data Governance" (24),[1] "Cloud Services Administration" (16), and "Tenancy & Customer Isolation" (16), while Level 3 adds new key security controls in "Operations" (16), "Business Continuity Planning & Disaster Recovery" (7), and "Tenancy & Customer Isolation" (11) (Figure 4).

While multitenancy introduces additional risks to cloud users, cloud computing risks overlap with other IT delivery models. These include risks associated with access,

---

[1]The number in the brackets refers to the number of security controls in each of the control areas.

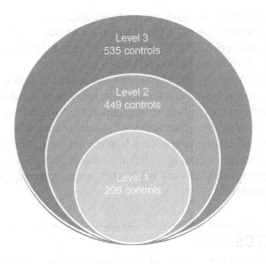

FIGURE 4

Key differences of MTCS levels.

infrastructure, operations and governance. This standard breaks those risks into six categories as outlined in Figure 5. They are broadly grouped into two as follows:

- The core information security
- The cloud-specific information security

"Cloud Governance" covers generic issues ranging from management of information security, incidents, risks, and information assets but interpreted under cloud environment. "Cloud Infrastructure Security" specifies requirements of the underlying cloud

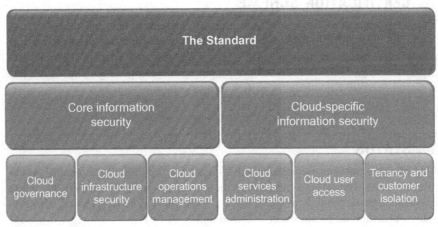

FIGURE 5

Structure of MTCS standards.

infrastructure to ensure proper tracking, configuration, testing, monitoring, systems and services management, while "Cloud Operations Management" entails environment security, secured operations, management of changes to cloud infrastructure, and prevention of disruption to cloud services.

"Cloud Services Administration" ensures enforcement of policies, standards and procedures relating to creation, maintenance, and removal of privilege accounts used for managing cloud services and supporting networks. "Cloud User Access," on the other hand, looks into securing user accounts to restrict access and safeguards user credentials to prevent unauthorized access. Last but not least, "Tenancy & Customer Isolation" dwells into issues dealing with multitenancy, data segregation, supporting infrastructure segmentation, network protection, virtualization risks (TR30, 2012), and storage area network.

9 SELF-DISCLOSURE

A unique feature of MTCS is its spirit of building trust through transparency. Besides security, a self-disclosure requirement on their service-oriented parameters has been introduced. CSPs are required, as part of the certification process, to complete a self-disclosure form (see Section 5 and Annex A of MTCS, 2013) on key characteristics of their services such as legal and compliance, data control, performance, service elasticity, and support. Such disclosure enables potential cloud services buyers to better understand the differences among CSPs and evaluate more holistically how those service parameters may impact their needs beyond security requirements. See Figure 6 for a listing of the service parameters.

10 CERTIFICATION SCHEME

The certification of a CSP is valid for 3 years. A yearly surveillance audit needs to be conducted by qualified assessors for MTCS certification. Such assessors are existing accredited certification bodies for ISO27001, with at least 3 years of relevant audit experience (e.g., ISO27001) and cloud computing knowledge (e.g., CSA Certificate of Cloud Security Knowledge) certified in near future.

11 STATUS

All CSP applicants must complete self-disclosure and prepare Statement of Applicability (SoA). They must agree to have their certification, SoA, and self-disclosure information made publicly available on a CSP Registry. The registry will also provide information on performance and availability of CSPs.

The development of MTCS started in 2011 under the auspices of the Singapore IT Standards Committee (ITSC) by a working group comprising representatives from

Criteria	Measures / disclosure requirements
1. Right to audit	Ability to conduct own reviews (e.g., site assessment, penetration test) & costs
2. Compliance	List of compliance statuses
3. Data ownership	Data ownership limitations
4. Data retention	Periods for user data, user log data, and infrastructure log data
5. Data sovereignty	Data locations, capability to restrict geographies, and DR locations
6. Information nondisclosure	What if any information may be disclosed
7. Availability	Mean time between failures; service availability
8. BCP / DR	Recovery point objective; Recovery time objective
9. Liability	Limits in-case of incidents/failure to meet service commitment
10. Change Management	Comms plan and procedures for managing changes
11. On-demand self-service*	Users can unilaterally provision computing capabilities as needed automatically without requiring human interaction with CSPs
12. Incident & problem management	Support provided (e.g., notification, cooperation with outside parties)
13. Billing (Measured service)*	Metrics & accuracy
14. Data portability	Mechanisms supported including media and format upon termination
15. Access to CSP's network*	Methods to access the provider (e.g., Internet IPV4/6, site-to-site VPN, frame relay)
16. User management	Options for integrating with customer IDM, 2-factor solutions
17. Lifecycle	Notice & choice for changes
18. Security configuration enforcement checks	Mechanism to enforce check on security configuration
19. Multitenancy*	Tenancy options
20. Capacity elasticity*	Peak load handling capabilities for capacity
21. Network resiliency & elasticity	Peak load handling capabilities for network
22. Storage redundancy & elasticity	Peak load handling capabilities for storage

*Five essential characteristics of Cloud Computing as defined by NIST

FIGURE 6

CSP self-disclosure for greater transparency.

industry. After 18 months of development, MTCS was approved as a Singapore Standard by ITSC Council in August 2013, following two rounds of 2-month public comments on the draft standards that elicited more than 350 comments from both local and foreign CSPs and users.

12 DEPLOYMENT

The standards are now in active deployment phase since its official launch in November 2013. One way to deploy MTCS is to find a "lead user" such as the public sector or more "cloud ready" enterprises to pave the ways for its adoption. These early adopters will lead and demonstrate to other sectors that are more cautious and risk averse, especially those sectors that are regulated such as healthcare and financial. The regulated sectors can be in the next phase when exemplary deployments are established and environment is conducive and ready.

As of April 2014, MTCS certification has been made a mandatory requirement for the public cloud services bulk tender that seeks to qualify IaaS, PaaS, and SaaS on a shortlist for procurement by government agencies in Singapore. Hitherto, more than 10 IaaS, PaaS, and SaaS have been MTCS certified.

13 HARMONIZATION

To enhance recognition of MTCS beyond Singapore, we have embarked on cross-certification (or harmonization) of MTCS with other international frameworks such as ISO27001 and CSA's Open Certification Framework (OCF)[2]. This minimizes the effort needed for CSPs certified to those international standards to gain MTCS certification and vice versa. It also benefits MTCS-certified CSPs with regional business to be recognized globally.

For each direction (represented by an arrow in Figure 7), a set of three documents have been developed; these are (a) Gap Analysis report; (b) Implementation Guide; and (c) Audit Checklist. Hence, four sets of such documents exist for the following:

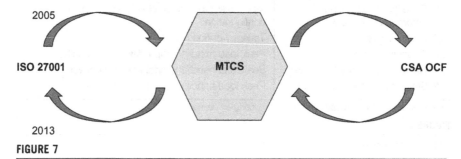

FIGURE 7

Harmonization of MTCS with international frameworks.

---

[2]CSA OCF comprises the Security, Trust, and Assurance Registry (STAR) self-assessment, third-party assessment/certification and high-assurance specification that are continuously monitored. The harmonization effort discussed here is with respect to the third-party assessment/certification-based specified set of criteria as outlined in the Cloud Control Matrix (CCM).

(a) ISO27001:2005 to MTCS
(b) MTCS to ISO27001:2013
(c) CSA OCF to MTCS
(d) MTCS to CSA OCF

As an example, a systematic three-step approach is taken to map detailed requirements in ISO27001:2005 to corresponding requirements in MTCS.

(a) Mapping of control areas
(b) Mapping of specific requirements in each control area
(c) Mapping details of each requirement

The table in Figure 8 provides a summary of the gaps analysis of the mapping from ISO27001:2005 to MTCS. As MTCS control requirements are more specific and detailed, the percentage of matched MTCS clauses is only around 40% (referring to the number of matched MTCS clauses at Level 2 which is 179 out of a total of 449). As one progresses from the low to high tiers, the percentage of matched MTCS clauses from Level 1 to Level 3 drops from 45% to 37%.

Understandably, the key gaps are found in the areas of cloud-specific controls such as "Tenancy & Customer Isolation," "Cloud Service Administration," and "Cloud User Access" besides other core controls like "Data Governance," "Infrastructure Security," and "Operations Management."

In the reverse direction, the table in Figure 9 provides a summary of gaps analysis of the mapping from MTCS to ISO27001:2013. The 2013 edition of the ISO27001 was published in September 2013, at about the same time as MTCS SS584:2013. As expected, the MTCS gaps with ISO27001:2013 are minimal around 10% (with reference to the number of gaps at Level 2 which is 26 out of 254). The gaps are found mainly in the area of "Performance Evaluation" of ISMS which is the new emphasis in the 2013 edition.

MTCS Level	MTCS Clauses	"MATCHED"		"GAPS"	
		Total	%	Total	%
1	296	134	45	162	55
2	449	179	40	270	60
3	535	196	37	339	63

FIGURE 8

Mapping of ISO27001:2005 to MTCS.

MTCS Level	Total ISO Clauses	"MATCHED"		"GAPS"	
		Total	%	Total	%
1	254	220	87	34	13
2	254	228	90	26	10
3	254	230	91	24	9

FIGURE 9

Mapping of MTCS to ISO27001:2013.

14 FUTURE WORK

Besides harmonizing MTCS with other international frameworks, alignment of MTCS standards with various regulated industries (such as healthcare and financial sectors) is in the plan for next phase of deployment.

15 CONCLUSION

MTCS standards are the world's first cloud security standards that feature multiple tiers. It is aimed at spurring the adoption of cloud computing across industries by providing greater clarity on the level of security offered by different CSPs. The standards are supplemented with a self-disclosure requirement on service-oriented information that is normally included in Service Level Agreement, giving potential cloud buyers a comprehensive tool to compare and evaluate the cloud service offerings across multiple CSPs beyond just cloud security.

ACKNOWLEDGMENTS

The effort reported here has benefited from the contributions of many talented individuals from the industry who comprised the MTCS Working Group; they are Meng-Chow Kang, Alan Sinclair Dawson, Gregory Boleslaw Malewski, Kwok-Yan Lam, Onn-Chee Wong, John Yong, and Hector Goh. We also thank Buaey-Qui Ho and Pei-Wee Kong of the ITSC Secretariat. The effort also received critical comments from Anthony Ma, Aaron Thor, Siow-Fah Lim, and Lek-Heng Ngoh.

REFERENCES

CSA, 2010. Cloud Control Matrix V1.0. CSA, USA, November.
ENISA, 2009a. Cloud Computing: Information Assurance Framework. ENISA, Greece, November.

ENISA, 2009b. Cloud Computing: Benefits, Risks and Recommendations for Information Security. ENISA, Greece, November.

FedRAMP, 2014. FedRAMP Security Assessment Framework V2.0. FedRAMP, USA, June.

IDC, 2009. IT Cloud Services Survey: Top Benefits and Challenges. IDC, USA, December 15.

ISO/IEC 27001:2005, 2005. Information Technology—Security Techniques—Information Security Management Systems—Requirements, ISO, September.

ISO/IEC 27001:2013, 2013. Information Technology—Security Techniques—Information Security Management Systems—Requirements, ISO, September.

ISO/IEC JTC 1/SC 27, 2010, Proposal for a new WG1 on "Information security management guidelines for the use of cloud computing services based on ISO/IEC 27002", ISO, September.

Launchpad, 2009. Europe IT Security Index 2009. Launchpad Europe, UK, December.

MAS, 2013. Technology Risk Management Guidelines. Monetary Authority of Singapore, Singapore, June.

MTCS, 2013. Specification for Multi-Tiered Cloud Computing Security, Singapore Standard 584:2013, SPRING, Singapore.

NIST, 2007–2013. NIST Special Publication 800 Computer Security Series, NIST, USA.

NIST, 2011. The NIST Definition of Cloud Computing, SP-800-145, NIST, USA, October.

PCI, 2010. Payment Card Industry Data Security Standard, Version 2.0, PCI Security Standards Council LLC, USA, October.

SAS70, 1992. Statement of Auditing Standards, No. 70, AICPA, April.

SSAE16, 2010. Statement on Standards for Attestation Engagement No. 16, AICPA, April.

TR30, 2012. Virtualization Security for Servers, Technical Reference 30:2012, SPRING Singapore.

TR31, 2012. Guidelines for Cloud Security and Service Level Agreement for End Users, Technical Reference 31:2012, SPRING Singapore.

Uptime, 2013. Tier Standard: Operational Sustainability. Uptime Institute, USA, April.

Do: Cloud security approaches and challenges

A guide to homomorphic encryption

Mark A. Will, Ryan K. L. Ko

Cyber Security Lab, Department of Computer Science, University of Waikato, Hamilton,
New Zealand

1 INTRODUCTION

In cloud computing, fully homomorphic encryption (FHE) is commonly touted as the "holy grail" (Gentry, 2009a; Micciancio, 2010; Van Dijk and Juels, 2010) of cloud security. While many know this potential, few actually understands how FHE works and why it is not yet a practical solution despite its promises. Homomorphic encryption schemes allow users' data to be protected anytime it is sent to the cloud, while keeping some of the useful properties of cloud services like searching for strings within files. This is because it can allow operations and functions to be preformed over encrypted data, meaning that the data is never unencrypted outside the users' environment. It prevents malicious employees of cloud service providers from accessing private data. A report (Chen, 2010) of an employee at Google in 2010 described a former engineer abusing his privileges to view private information. He used this information to stalk teenage girls and spy on their chat sessions. Many employees of cloud services have the required privileges to view our data, and we need to prevent such incidents from happening again.

There are two flavors of homomorphic encryption: *partially* and *fully*. Partially Homomorphic Encryption (PHE) is where only a single operation can be performed on cipher text, for example, addition or multiplication. Schemes for PHE exist and are usable today, with two being described in Section 4. However, many cloud services require more functionality than just addition or multiplication. This is where FHE, also known as the "holy grail" of encryption, can start to play a huge role in securing cloud services. FHE can support multipliable operations (currently addition and multiplication), allowing more computation to be performed over encrypted data.

Looking at an example, Alice runs an accounting firm, which stores all of her customers balances on the cloud. By utilizing the cloud, it means that she does not have to manage the underlying infrastructure of the cloud. Instead it is managed by a third-party cloud service provider. The problem Alice faces is that in order to keep her customers accounts secure, she encrypts them when they are in the database/ storage. This prevents a malicious outsider gaining direct access to the information, while also stopping the cloud service employees from being able to see the data.

But when she needs to make a change to an account balance, she has to either transfer the encrypted account back to the her trusted environment, or decrypt the account data in the cloud, update the account, then encrypt it again before storage. This creates a risk where the data has to be decrypted at a point before it can be used. Because homomorphic encryption can process data while encrypted, Alice can simply apply changes to the encrypted account balance by sending encrypted data to the cloud and have the account updated without it ever being in decrypted form (i.e., plaintext). This allows Alices' cloud accounting firm to keep its customers secure, while having the added benefits of using the cloud.

There is however a catch with this example. The performance of FHE is currently quite inefficient, where simple operations can take anywhere from seconds to hours depending on security parameters (Gentry and Halevi, 2011). Therefore, homomorphic encryption is currently a balancing act between utility, protection, and performance. FHE has good protection and utility, but poor performance. Where PHE has good performance and protection, but is very limited in its utility. This is illustrated in Figure 1, where the perfect solution would be in the center of the Venn diagram.

This chapter will give an in-depth overview of homomorphic encryption, and why it is so important for the cloud. We start with why homomorphic encryption is needed in the cloud, and some basic background information on the history of homomorphic encryption. In Section 4, we will describe and provide examples of two PHE schemes, El Gamal and Paillier. This leads into FHE where the Approximate Eigenvector Algorithm will be given, with details of how it works, the mathematical properties, and an example. From Section 6, some examples of homomorphic encryption in use today will be shown, followed by the some thoughts about the future of homomorphic encryption. For businesses requiring the protection of their data, homomorphic encryption is not the only answer available today, and Section 8 will give another methodology for storing encrypted data in the cloud.

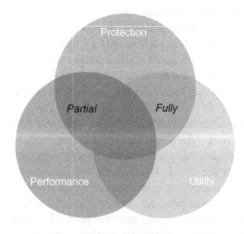

FIGURE 1

Protection versus utility versus performance for homomorphic encryption

2 CURRENT INDUSTRY WORK-AROUNDS AND THEIR GAPS

The cloud is built upon many technologies and ideas, but none more important than trust. As uses of cloud services, we have to trust that the providers will not misuse our data and information, but on top of that, we have to trust that their security defences will prevent malicious users from gaining access it as well.

Dropbox is one of the most widely used cloud storage services today, producing equivalent to one-third of the traffic that YouTube produces (Drago et al., 2012). On a help page titled *How secure is Dropbox?* (Dropbox Inc, 2014), is some useful information on how Dropbox is trying to protect its users. Analyzing a couple of these points: *Dropbox uses modern encryption methods to both transfer and store your data* (Secure Sockets Layer and AES-256 bit encryption) and *Dropbox employees are prohibited from viewing the content of files you store in your account* (Dropbox Inc, 2014). It is clear that even though your data is encrypted when stored, it is still possible for someone other than you to view the data in the unencrypted form. Be it a rogue Dropbox employee or a malicious attacker.

Then there are cloud storage services such as Mega Limited (Mega ltd, 2014), which provide privacy and protection by only having the end users device encrypt and decrypt their data. This ensures that only the user can access the unencrypted data, even if the service is compromised. This does however come with a cost, because only you can view your files. Therefore, it is difficult for Mega to provide advanced features such as searching for strings within files or sharing files with others. These features are still possible to implement, for example, having the client build and use a search index which can be encrypted and stored in the cloud, or for sharing files, encrypt with a different key allowing the user to give it to whomever needs access.

The problem is that Dropbox can perform the same tasks automatically, faster, and more efficiently. So the trade-off between utility, protection, and performance is a key problem for cloud service providers. This is where homomorphic encryption can play such a huge role in the cloud, because it can help combine the features of both Dropbox and Mega. Allowing the creation of more secure and trustworthy cloud services, by bridging the gap between utility and protection. Note that the algorithms for how homomorphic encryption will be able to actually search files is still unknown. However it could be done in a similar manner as encryption gateways described in Section 8 or using another encrypted search technique (Li et al., 2014; Kuzu et al., 2012; Li et al., 2010; Wang et al., 2014). But once FHE becomes more practical, these algorithms will start to be developed.

Even though homomorphic encryption cannot currently easily support searching, it is ideal for computing mathematical functions on encrypted data. For example, computing statistics, such as the mean or average value in a large dataset. Other application groups that can benefit are banking and data mining. So, therefore, homomorphic encryption is very important for the cloud, and once it matures, it will be widely used.

3 HISTORY AND RELATED WORK

To the best of our knowledge, the idea of using homomorphic encryption for protecting data has been around for decades, with Rivest et al. proposing special encryption functions called "privacy homomorphisms" in 1978 (Rivest et al., 1978b). The authors discuss the use of hardware to process data securely, with the data only ever decrypted on a physically secure processor. This way, any time the data leaves the processor (i.e. to memory) it is encrypted, similar to the AEGIS chip we see today (Suh et al., 2003, 2005). However, the issue with these types of chips is that because it is custom hardware, costly to implement, and still requires a decryption key for the data. Rivest el al. then mention a solution where the data is not decrypted, but standard hardware can still process the data correctly, and the concept of homomorphic encryption was born. They present some proof-of-concept examples that are not practical for use, but importantly show that this idea of processing encrypted data is possible, finishing off with two open questions:

- Does this approach have enough utility to make it worthwhile in practice? (Rivest et al., 1978b)
- For what algebraic systems U does a useful privacy homomorphism exist? (Rivest et al., 1978b)

In the same year, the RSA encryption scheme was made public by the same two authors of Rivest et al. (1978b), Rivest and Adleman, with the addition of Shamir (Note: RSA actually stands for the initials of the authors) (Rivest et al., 1978a). The original paper has no mention of homomorphic encryption; however, it was later proved that RSA does support multiplication over encrypted data (Denning, 1982). This is due to the mathematical properties of RSA, where by raising a message to e in modulo n, allows the two encrypted messages to be multiplied correctly once the e's are removed at the decryption stage. Therefore, PHE has been conceptually supported for some time now.

In 1985, Blakley et al. proposed a database encryption scheme which supports computing some statistical operations over encrypted data stored in the database. Even though the paper does not specifically mention homomorphism, this is a step in showing that homomorphic encryption can be worthwhile in practice. In 1987 Ahituv et al. (1987) provides some more example algorithms that can support homomorphic operations, however have very weak security. In the following year Brickell and Yacobi (1988) evaluated the security of the first proposed homomorphic algorithms in Rivest et al. (1978b) and proposed an additive homomorphic algorithm where there was a maximum number of additions that could occur before it would break.

It was not until 1996 that we saw the first homomorphic algorithm to support both addition and multiplication (Ferrer, 1996). Domingo-Ferrer provided a needed breakthrough in the field, and later showed in 2002 that the proposed scheme was secure against known clear-text attacks; however, the scheme was broken a year later by Wagner (2003).

Table 1 Historic Overview of Homomorphic Encryption

2013	Homomorphic encryption from learning with errors: Conceptually simpler, asymptotically faster, attribute-based (Gentry et al., 2013)
2010	Fully homomorphic encryption over the integers (Van Dijk et al., 2010)
2009	A fully homomorphic encryption scheme (Gentry, 2009a)
	Fully homomorphic encryption using ideal lattices (Gentry, 2009b)
2008	A new approach for algebraically homomorphic encryption (Armknecht and Sadeghi, 2008)
2002	A provably secure additive and multiplicative privacy homomorphism (Domingo-Ferrer, 2002)
1996	A new privacy homomorphism and applications (Ferrer, 1996)
1988	On privacy homomorphisms (Brickell and Yacobi, 1988)
1987	Processing encrypted data (Ahituv et al., 1987)
1985	A database encryption scheme that allows the computation of statistics using encrypted data (Blakley and Meadows, 1985)
1982	Signature protocols for RSA and Other Public-Key Cryptosystems (Denning, 1982)
1978	On data banks and privacy homomorphisms (Rivest et al., 1978b)

The problem up until this point was developing a scheme that was secure, without losing its homomorphic properties, able to support the repeating of operations many times, or being incredibly inefficient. Armknecht et al. proposed a solution which supported arbitrary number of additions and a fixed number of multiplications (Armknecht and Sadeghi, 2008), while remaining secure under a known decoding problem.

However, the real breakthrough occurred in 2009 when Gentry proposed a scheme that could support an arbitrary number of additions and multiplications and based the security on the hardness of lattice problems (Gentry, 2009a). Since then, Gentry has been involved in many different schemes (Gentry, 2009b; Van Dijk et al., 2010; Gentry et al., 2013) for FHE, gradually improving the schemes, but still to this day are not efficient enough to be used in the real world. The brief history given in this section is summarised in Table 1.

4 OVERVIEW OF PARTIAL HOMOMORPHIC ENCRYPTION SCHEMES

Algorithms supporting the idea of homomorphic encryption have been around for quite some time, as discussed by Section 3. In this section, two PHE schemes, ElGamal (1985) and Paillier (1999), will be covered. These were chosen so that an addition and a multiplication scheme were shown. This section will first introduce the idea of public key encryption, since both of these schemes fall into that category. Before describing El Gamal and Paillier in detail, examples of addition and multiplication are included.

4.1 PUBLIC KEY ENCRYPTION

Diffie and Hellman (1976) introduced the concept of public key encryption, also known as asymmetric cryptography in 1976. Like FHE today, practical implementations of public key encryption were limited. However they are now widely used, including the El Gamal and Paillier schemes. Both of these schemes use a large prime number for a modulus operation, which is a security parameter. It is important to note however that even though these schemes can provide homomorphic operations, because of the nature of modulus operation, if the input or output values are greater than the modulus, results may not be as expected.

Looking at an example of public key encryption, Alice, Bob and Claire are good friends who send each other online chat messages at night after school. However, Alice and Bob would like to throw Claire a surprise birthday party. The problem is that neither Alice or Bob can figure out how to remove Claire from the chat session. But they do not want Claire to be able to see their conversion because it will ruin the surprise. One solution to this problem is for them both to create a private and public key, known as public key encryption. Then they can send their public key to everyone in the chat session. This allows Bob to encrypt a secret message to Alice using her public key, before broadcasting it in the chat session. Only Alice will be able to decrypt and read the message, meaning Claire is unable to read any messages about her surprise party.

However looking at the bigger picture, it also prevents malicious users from reading the messages as well. For example, the chat services' administrators can only see the public key and encrypted messages. The same applies for any user sniffing the network, and finally this means that even if the chat service gets compromised, Alice and Bobs chat history is safe. This is not to say that the encrypted chat is 100% guaranteed to be safe and secure, but it adds another layer of protection to their data.

Therefore, public key encryption proves a means to encrypt data that only the holder of the private key can read. Anyone can gain access to the public key, which is used to encrypt the data. But ideally, only one person/system has the private key to decrypt the data. Everyone using the Internet would have experienced public key encryption, but probably without knowledge. For example, Hypertext Transfer Protocol Secure (HTTPS) sets up a secure tunnel using public key encryption within a browser. The client sends data to the server using the servers public key, and the server sends data back to the client using the clients public key. The setup of the keys is a bit more complicated than the example before, but it all happens in the background.

When designing and setting up a cloud service, it is important to consider how public key encryption will play a role in making the service more secure. Providing secure channels for authentication is a must today, and HTTPS is a viable solution. However, there are other ways to make the service more secure, like the use of PHE. Some real-world examples of homomorphic encryption will be covered in Section 6, but now El Gamal and Paillier's scheme will be described to show how simple it is to implement PHE.

4.2 EL GAMAL

The security strength of El Gamal is based on the hardness of solving discrete logarithms, which was first proposed in 1985 by ElGamal (1985). Conceptually, El Gamal supports homomorphic multiplication operations on encrypted data. The key generation algorithm is given in Algorithm 1.

Algorithm 1 EL GAMAL KEY GENERATION ALGORITHM

1: Select a large prime p
2: Select a primitive value α in modulo p
3: Randomly select d so that $2 \leq d \leq p-2$
4: Calculate $\beta = \alpha^d \bmod p$
5: Public Key $= (p, \alpha, \beta)$
6: Private Key $= d$

Now that the keys are generated, the algorithms to encrypt $E(x)$ and decrypt $D(x)$ are given in Algorithms 2 and 3, respectively.

Algorithm 2 EL GAMAL ENCRYPTION ALGORITHM

Encrypt an Integer message M where M is less than the large prime p

1: Select a random integer k (which must remain private)
2: Calculate $r = \alpha^k \bmod p$
3: Calculate $t = \beta^k \times M \bmod p$
4: Discard k
5: Encrypted Message $= (r,t)$

Line 2 in Algorithm 2 allows us to hide k, so that it can be removed from t when we are decrypting the message. We discard k so that it remains a secret and cannot be leaked. This is necessary because the strength of this algorithm is based upon solving for k is hard. Therefore, if a malicious user gains access to k, they can decrypt the message without the private key.

Algorithm 3 EL GAMAL DECRYPTION ALGORITHM

Decrypt a message (r, t) to find M

1: Calculate $M = t \times r^{-d} \bmod p$

It is important to understand the proof of encryption and decryption as it shows how the public and private keys cancel each other out, leaving the original message. This allows an appreciation of the mathematics behind El Gamal. Even though to implement an encryption algorithm does not require knowledge of how they work, security holes found are often in the implementation, and not the algorithm itself.

Proof:

1: $M = t \times r^{-d} \mod p$
2: $M = \beta^k \times M \times (\alpha^k)^{-d} \mod p$
3: $M = (\alpha^d)^k \times M \times (\alpha^k)^{-d} \mod p$
4: $M = M \times (\alpha^{dk} \times \alpha^{-dk}) \mod p$
5: $M = M \times 1 \mod p$

Because the algorithm only uses multiplication operations on the message value, it is quite easy to see how it supports homomorphic multiplication operations. Given a and b, we want to show that encrypting them, multiplying, then decrypting gives $a \times b$.

$$D(E(a) \times E(b)) \mod p = t_a \times t_b \times (r_a \times r_b)^{-d} \mod p$$

First, when the r values are multiplied, because the k values are random, then adding them still gives a random k.

$$\Rightarrow r = r_a \times r_b \mod p$$
$$r = \alpha^{k_a} \times \alpha^{k_b} \mod p$$
$$r = \alpha^{k_a + k_b} \mod p$$
$$r = \alpha^k \mod p$$

The multiplication of the t values also involves random ks, which can be combined in the same manner. This leaves the a and b values multiplied together, along with β^k.

$$\Rightarrow t = t_a \times t_b \mod p$$
$$t = (\beta^{k_a} \times M_a) \times (\beta^{k_b} \times M_b) \mod p$$
$$t = \beta^{k_a + k_b} \times M_a \times M_b \mod p$$
$$t = \beta^k \times M_a \times M_b \mod p$$

Now by substituting the t and r values into the decryption equation, the αs cancel themselves out, resulting in the decrypted value equaling $a \times b$.

$$\Rightarrow D(c) = (\beta^k \times M_a \times M_b) \times (\alpha^k)^{-d} \mod p$$
$$D(c) = (\alpha^d)^k \times M_a \times M_b \times (\alpha^k)^{-d} \mod p$$
$$D(c) = M_a \times M_b \times (\alpha^{dk} \times \alpha^{-dk}) \mod p$$
$$\therefore D(c) = a \times b \mod p$$

To this point, the mathematics show that El Gamal supports homomorphic multiplications. However to conclude, an example of El Gamal in operation will be shown.

Given 6 and 5, we want to solve $E(6) \times E(5)$ where $p=47$, $\alpha=7$, $d=35$, and $\beta=7^{35}$ mod $47 = 17$. Also this example will show that addition is not supported.

Encrypt 6

$$
\begin{aligned}
k &= 41 \\
r &= 7^{41} \mod 47 \\
&= 42 \mod 47 \\
t &= 17^{41} \times 6 \mod 47 \\
&= 14 \mod 47 \\
E(6) &= (42, 14)
\end{aligned}
$$

Encrypt 5

$$
\begin{aligned}
k &= 29 \\
r &= 7^{29} \mod 47 \\
&= 8 \mod 47 \\
t &= 17^{29} \times 5 \mod 47 \\
&= 23 \mod 47 \\
E(5) &= (8, 23)
\end{aligned}
$$

Calculate $E(6) \times E(5)$

$$
\begin{aligned}
&= E(6) \times E(5) \\
&= (42 \times 8, 14 \times 23) \\
&= (7, 40)
\end{aligned}
$$

Calculate $E(6) + E(5)$

$$
\begin{aligned}
&= E(6) + E(5) \\
&= (42 + 8, 14 + 23) \\
&= (3, 37)
\end{aligned}
$$

Decrypt (7,40)

$$
\begin{aligned}
&= 7^{-35} \times 40 \mod 47 \\
&= 30 \mod 47
\end{aligned}
$$

Decrypt (3,37)

$$
\begin{aligned}
&= 3^{-35} \times 37 \mod 47 \\
&= 7 \mod 47
\end{aligned}
$$

4.3 PAILLIER CRYPTOSYSTEM

Proposed in 1999 by Paillier (1999), the Paillier cryptosystem is based on the problem that computing nth residue classes is computationally intensive. The nature of the algorithm allows for homomorphic addition operations to produce the current answer once decrypted. The key generation for Paillier Cryptosystem given in Algorithm 4, is a bit more complicated than El Gamal.

Algorithm 4 PAILLIER CRYPTOSYSTEM KEY GENERATION ALGORITHM

1: Select two large prime numbers p and q where $gcd\ (pq, (p-1)(q-1)) = 1$
2: Calculate $n = pq$
3: Calculate $\lambda = lcm(p-1, q-1)$
4: Select g as a random integer where $g \in \mathbb{Z}_{n^2}^*$
5: Define $L(x) = \frac{x-1}{n}$
6: Ensure n divides the order of g by checking the existence of the following modular multiplicative inverse
7: $u = (L(g^{\lambda} \mod n^2))^{-1} \mod n$
8: Public Key $= (n, g)$
9: Private Key $= (\lambda, u)$

To encrypt a message, the message is used as the exponent for g, then a random value is raised to the other public key value n, as shown in Algorithm 5. This produces a cipher value in modulo n^2. Decryption is again a simple equation, like El Gamal, and is given in Algorithm 6. Note that the definition for $L(x)$ was given with key generation.

Algorithm 5 PAILLIER CRYPTOSYSTEM ENCRYPTION ALGORITHM

Encrypt a message M where $M \in \mathbb{Z}_n$

1: Select r as a random integer where $r \in \mathbb{Z}_{n^2}^*$
2: Calculate $c = g^m \times r^n \bmod n^2$

Algorithm 6 PAILLIER CRYPTOSYSTEM DECRYPTION ALGORITHM

Decrypt a message c where $c \in \mathbb{Z}_{n^2}^*$

1: Calculate $m = L(c^\lambda \bmod n^2) \times u \bmod n$

The proof of the encryption and decryption will be now given to show how the public and private key values cancel each other out. This is important because it will help to show why the Paillier Cryptosystem can support homomorphic addition operations.

PROOF:

1: $m = L(c^\lambda \bmod n^2) \times u \bmod n$

2: $m = L(c^\lambda \bmod n^2) \times (L(g^\lambda \bmod n^2))^{-1} \bmod n$

3: $m = \dfrac{L\left(c^\lambda \bmod n^2\right)}{L\left(g^\lambda \bmod n^2\right)} \bmod n$

4: $m = \dfrac{\lambda[c]1+n}{\lambda[g]1+n} \bmod n$ *(By Lemma 10 in Paillier (1999)*

5: $m = \dfrac{[c]1+n}{[g]1+n} \bmod n$

6: $m = [c]_g \bmod n$

7: $m = m \bmod n$ *(Because $c = g^{[c]_g} \times r^n \bmod n^2$ ((Paillier, 1999))*

If an addition operation is desired to be computed on the encrypted data, it is actually a multiplication operation that needs to be used. This is because the message is encrypted as an exponent. Therefore to add exponents, a multiplication operation needs to be computed on two values of the same base, which in this case is g. Note that because the r_0 and r_1 values are random, they can be combined to form another random value r.

$$D(E(a) \times E(b)) = a + b$$
$$\Rightarrow \quad c = c_a \times c_b \bmod n^2$$
$$c = g^a \times r_0^n \times g^b \times r_1^n \bmod n^2$$
$$c = g^{a+b} \times r_0^n \times r_1^n \bmod n^2$$
$$c = g^{a+b} \times r^n \bmod n^2$$
$$\therefore \quad D(c) = a + b$$

5 FULLY HOMOMORPHIC ENCRYPTION

There are many schemes being introduced today that claim to support FHE (Armknecht and Sadeghi, 2008; Gentry, 2009a,b; Van Dijk et al., 2010; Brakerski and Vaikuntanathan, 2011; Gentry et al., 2013; Brakerski and Vaikuntanathan, 2014). In this chapter, we will focus on just one which uses the Learning With Errors (LWE) problem for FHE as described by Gentry et al. (2013). They call their method the *approximate eigenvector* method, which allows homomorphic addition and multiplication computation. This is achieved by using matrix addition and multiplication operations and without the need for bootstrapping user keys.

This section will cover some of the ideas that the approximate eigenvector algorithm is based upon. Lattices are a key building block and are explained first, before the problems that help make this algorithm hard to break are covered. Finally, the algorithm will be described, including a small example of homomorphic encryption.

5.1 LATTICES

In order to understand why lattices are useful for FHE, we must first understand the basic properties of a lattice.

Definition 1 *A lattice is made up of a set of points $p_0...p_n$ in d-dimensional space, which forms independent linear vectors $v_0...v_n$ (also known as the basis vectors), forming a geometrical pattern.*

It is important to note that the same lattice can be formed from different basis vectors; therefore, it is said that a lattice is made up of an unique set of vectors which are the closed to the origin.

Any point that is the result of combining these vectors is known as a lattice point, and the region that can be translated by a lattice point while repeating the pattern is known as the fundamental region. The fundamental region is used to calculate the determinate of a lattice, which is the volume of the fundamental parallelepiped and represents the reciprocal of the density. Looking at the example in Figure 2, we are given the basis vectors v_0 and v_1, and combining these vectors together in many different ways gives a grid pattern of lattice points. The fundamental region is shown in red (dark gray in the print version), and with this simple 2D example it is easy to see how to repeat the fundamental region to continue the pattern.

Now imagine adding a basis vector v_2 which is on the z-axis, making the lattice three dimensions as shown in Figure 3. The square fundamental region is replaced with a cubic one. As humans, lattices beyond three dimensions can be difficult to picture, but larger dimensions are simple for a computer to compute over as the input it receives is a matrix. In August 2010, IBM held a competition (IBM, 2010) for contestants to break FHE keys. The "toy" challenge used for testing had a dimension of 512, and the hardest problem had 32,768 dimensions. This shows that the number of dimensions is directly related to the strength of the key.

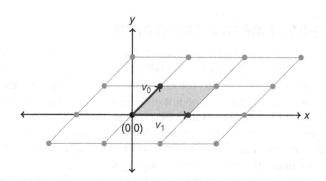

FIGURE 2

Basic 2D lattice.

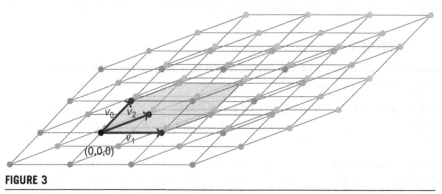

FIGURE 3

Basic 3D lattice using the 2D lattice in Figure 2.

5.2 LATTICE PROBLEMS

A couple of hard lattice problems which cryptography can be built upon is the Closest Vector Problem (CVP) and Shortest Vector Problem (SVP).

Definition 2 *Given a point P and the lattice M, the Closest Vector Problem asks us to find the nearest lattice point L in M.*

In Figure 4, it is easy to see the closest lattice point in pictorial form. However because a computer is only given a matrix, and the dimensions are much larger, it makes finding the closest lattice point much more computationally intensive.

Definition 3 *Given the lattice M, the Shortest Vector Problem as us to find the smallest non-zero vector V in M.*

Non zero is important because every lattice technically has a zero vector. In Figure 4, this is simply v_0 because the example lattice is only showing the basis vectors. However, if larger vectors are given, there may exist a smaller vector which can make up the fundamental region. Note that CVP is actually a generalization of

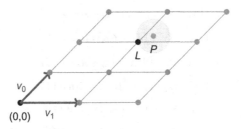

FIGURE 4

Finding the nearest lattice point.

SVP, because if you are given an oracle (function) for CVP, it is possible to find the shortest vector by querying the oracle (Micciancio and Goldwasser, 2002; Goldreich et al., 1999). Therefore because CVP is a NP-Hard problem, so is SVP (van Emde-Boas, 1981; Micciancio, 2001).

5.3 LEARNING WITH ERRORS

The LWE problem was introduction by Regev (2010) and is widely used for a range of cryptographic functions, such as public key encryption (Peikert, 2009). This is because it claims to be as hard as worst-case lattice problems (Regev, 2010), implying that any functions built upon LWE are secure. This was briefly discussed in Section 5.2. It is also currently assumed that worst-case lattice problems are even secure against the likes of quantum computers.

Definition 4 *The LWE problem asks us to recover a secret $x \in \mathbb{Z}_q^n$ given a sequence of approximate random linear equations on x (Regev, 2010).*

Relating this back to lattices, the definition means distinguishing vectors that are created from a set of noisy (contains some error) linear equations between uniformly random vectors. Looking at an example from Regev (2010), we are given the set of linear equations shown in Figure 5 where in this case each equation has an error of approximately ± 1, then all we have to do is solve for x. But by introducing the error it makes solving x more difficult. If you were to try and solve the set of equations using Gaussian elimination (row reduction), for example, the errors would accumulate making the result invalid.

Given $2^{O(n \log n)}$ equations we can deduce the secret x in $2^{O(n \log n)}$ time but this approach is based more around luck than sense. A simpler technique is the Maximum Likelihood algorithm, which only requires $O(n)$ equations and computes the only value for x that can satisfy the equations. This is achieved with brute force by computing all possible values, resulting in a run time of $2^{O(n \log n)}$ (Regev, 2010). Currently, the best, known algorithm for solving LWE is by Blum et al. and requires $2^{O(n)}$ equations and time (Blum et al., 2003), which relates to the fact that the best algorithms for solving lattice problems need $2^{O(n)}$ time (Ajtai et al., 2001; Micciancio and Voulgaris, 2013).

Therefore, homomorphic schemes built on the LWE problem need to keep the errors relatively small otherwise results can become invalid. For example, Figure 6 shows a lattice point L, and the point P which has some error added so that

$$14x_1 + 15x_2 + 5x_3 + 2x_4 \approx 8(\mathrm{mod}\ 17)$$

$$13x_1 + 14x_2 + 14x_3 + 6x_4 \approx 16(\mathrm{mod}\ 17)$$

$$6x_1 + 10x_2 + 13x_3 + 1x_4 \approx 3(\mathrm{mod}\ 17)$$

$$10x_1 + 4x_2 + 12x_3 + 16x_4 \approx 12(\mathrm{mod}\ 17)$$

$$9x_1 + 5x_2 + 9x_3 + 6x_4 \approx 9(\mathrm{mod}\ 17)$$

$$3x_1 + 6x_2 + 4x_3 + 5x_4 \approx 16(\mathrm{mod}\ 17)$$

$$\vdots$$

$$6x_1 + 7x_2 + 16x_3 + 2x_4 \approx 3(\mathrm{mod}\ 17)$$

FIGURE 5

Example set of linear equations (Regev, 2010).

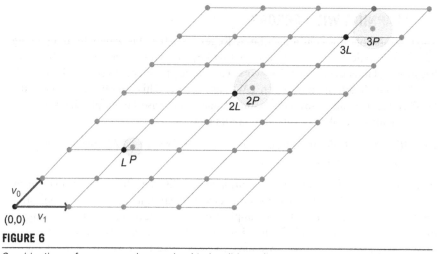

FIGURE 6

Combinations of errors or noise can lead to invalid results.

by solving CVP, L will be the result. If P is doubled, $2L$ is still the closest lattice point, however by adding P again giving $3P$, the closest lattice point is not $3L$, but instead $3L + v_0$; therefore, the result is now invalid. Managing this error is one of the key challenges to homomorphic encryption in general and is a contributing factor to the performance limitations of current FHE schemes, such as the Approximate Eigenvector algorithm.

5.4 APPROXIMATE EIGENVECTOR ALGORITHM

The Approximate Eigenvector scheme for FHE was proposed by Gentry et al. (2013) in 2013, which uses the LWE problem previously described in Section 5.3. This scheme allows for addition and multiplication homomorphic operations to be computed the same as matrix addition and multiplication operations, for most cases. Gentry et al. claim this makes the scheme asymptotically faster and easier to understand (Gentry et al., 2013), which is why we chose it for this chapter. The formal definition of an eigenvector is given below, where T is a square matrix and λ is a scale. Essentially for $\vec{v}$ to be classified as an eigenvector for the matrix T, the result must be equivalent to multiplying $\vec{v}$ by some scale factor. In this scheme, $\vec{v}$ is an approximate eigenvector, not a perfect one.

Definition 5 A vector $\vec{v}$ is an eigenvector (also known as a characteristic vector, proper vector, or latent vector) if $T(\vec{v}) = \lambda \vec{v}$ for some scale λ (Marcus, 1988).

To make this a leveled scheme (i.e. it will work up to a certain depth), the error must be controlled. As seen in Figure 6, controlling the size of the error is extremely important, so that the decrypted value will be correct. This is achieved by flattening the cipher matrix so that it contains values in $\{0,1\}$. Flattening uses bit decomposition operations, which does not affect dot product operations on the matrices. This allows homomorphic operations still be computed correctly, while keeping the errors small.

We will now cover the scheme, starting with the security parameters and function definitions. Before giving the key generation, encryption and decryption algorithms. We will then prove that the scheme does in fact support homomorphic addition and multiplication operations, which will be followed by an example.

SECURITY PARAMETERS

q = modulus
n = lattice dimension
χ = error distribution
$m = O(n \log q)$
$\ell = \lfloor \log_2 q \rfloor + 1$
$N = (n+1) \times \ell$

DEFINITIONS

Define $BitDecomp(a)$ = Each coefficient of a decomposed into bits = $(a_{0,bit(0)},...,a_{0,bit(l-1)},...,a_{k-1,bit(0)},...,a_{k-1,bit(l-1)}) \in \{0,1\}^N$

Define $BitDecomp^{-1}(b \in \mathbb{Z}_q^N)$ = revert b back to a if $b = BitDecomp(a)$ i.e., $b \in \{0,1\}$, else $b \in \mathbb{Z}_q^k$ therefore multiple the coefficients by powers of 2. = $(\sum_j 2^j b_{0,j} \bmod q,...,\sum_j 2^j b_{k-1,j} \bmod q)$

Define $Flatten(b \in \mathbb{Z}_q^N) = BitDecomp(BitDecomp^{-1}(b))$ Define $Powersof2(s) = (s_0 2^0, s_0 2^1, s_0 2^2,...,s_0 2^{l-1},...,s_{k-1} 2^0, s_{k-1} 2^1, s_{k-1} 2^2,...,s_{k-1} 2^{l-1}) I_N$ denotes the N-dimensional identity matrix.

Key Generation

Given the security parameters, the secret key generation is shown in Algorithm 7, where $\vec{s}$ is the secret key. The vector $\vec{t}$ is randomly generated with integer values in modulo q (no values are larger than q) and has the length n. The length is the same as the number of lattice dimensions so that a dot product can be computed over the lattice matrix. The secret key $\vec{s}$ has one more value than $\vec{t}$ (i.e., $n+1$), which appends

1 to the front of $\vec{t}$ multiplied by -1. Vector $\vec{v}$ is the result of the *Powersof2* function defined earlier.

Algorithm 7 APPROXIMATE EIGENVECTOR SECRET KEY GENERATION

1: Randomly generate $\vec{t} \leftarrow \mathbb{Z}_q^n$
2: Calculate $\vec{s} = (1, -t_1, \ldots, -t_n) \in \mathbb{Z}_q^{n+1}$
3: Calculate $\vec{v} = Powersof2(\vec{s})$

Once the secret key is generated, we can generate the public key matrix A, as shown in Algorithm 8. We start by randomly generate a matrix B with integer values in modulo q, with the size $n \times m$. Now we must generate an error vector $\vec{e}$ of size m using the error distribution χ. To link together the public and secret key, the vector $\vec{b}$ must be calculated using random vector $\vec{t}$ from the secret key generation step, with some error added. Finally, the public key matrix A can be created by joining together the vector $\vec{b}$ and the matrix B, such that the first column of A is the $\vec{b}$, with the remaining columns being B. This will be easier to understand in the example given in Section 5.4.1.

Algorithm 8 APPROXIMATE EIGENVECTOR PUBLIC KEY GENERATION

1: Randomly generate matrix $B \leftarrow \mathbb{Z}_q^{m \times n}$
2: Generate $\vec{e} \leftarrow \chi^m$
3: Calculate $\vec{b} = B \cdot \vec{t} + \vec{e}$
4: Generate matrix A to have $(n+1)$ columns, where the first column is $\vec{b}$, and the remaining columns are that of matrix B.

5.4.1 Encryption and Decryption

Now that the public and secret keys can be generated, we will show how they can be used to encrypt and decrypt data. The algorithm for encrypting an integer u in modulo q is given in Algorithm 9. In order to make cipher values different even if the input message u is the same, first we must generate a random matrix R. The matrix R is then multiplied (dot product) by the public key matrix A before applying the bit decomposition function. This result will vary each time which helps hide the message. The message u is multiplied by an identity matrix I of size $N \times N$ (u is diagonally added to a square matrix of zeros), before being added to the result of the bit decomposition function. The message u becomes the scale value λ in the eigenvector definition shown earlier.

Algorithm 9 APPROXIMATE EIGENVECTOR ENCRYPTION

To encrypt a message u where $u \in \mathbb{Z}_q$

1: Randomly generate a uniform matrix $R \in \{0,1\}^{N \times m}$
2: Calculate cipher matrix $C = Flatten(u \cdot I_N + BitDecomp(R \cdot A)) \in \mathbb{Z}_q^{N \times N}$

Decrypting a cipher matrix can be achieved using a couple of different techniques, depending on the value chosen for q. If q is a power of 2, then the *MPDec* function can be used for decryption. Otherwise the standard *Decrypt* function will have to be used. First, we will describe the standard *Decrypt* function given in Algorithm 10, where C is the encrypted cipher matrix. Once a value for i has been chosen which meets the conditions shown, compute the inner product (scalar product) of the ith row in matrix C, and $\vec{v}$. Now the message u can be recovered.

Algorithm 10 APPROXIMATE EIGENVECTOR DECRYPTION

1: Set i where $i < \ell$ and $q/4 < 2^i < q/2$
2: Compute $x_i \leftarrow \langle C_i, \vec{v} \rangle$ where C_i is the $i-th$ row
3: Then message $u = x_i/2^i$

The description of the *MPDec* function shown in Algorithm 11 is better shown in Section 5.4.1 and in Micciancio and Peikert (2012). However to summarize, we can recover the least significant bit of the message u from the $\ell - 2$ column of the cipher matrix C. Then process the columns back to the 0th column, which will contain the most significant bit. Whether the bit should be high or low, given the column C_i, and the current result will now be described. Note that the result should be initialized to 0 when computing $C_{\ell-2}$.

Algorithm 11 APPROXIMATE EIGENVECTOR MPDEC

1: $x = C_i \cdot \vec{v} - (result \times (1 \ll i))$
2: if x is closer to $q/2$ than q or 0, then the bit is high, else low
3: $result += bit \ll (\ell - 2 - i)$

Proof for Homomorphic Addition and Multiplication

Now that the algorithm has been described, we will now prove that homomorphic addition and multiplication operations are supported.

Given:

$$C_n \cdot \vec{v} = u_n \cdot \vec{v} + \vec{e_n} \qquad \text{(where } \vec{e} \text{ is small)}$$

Addition:

$$
\begin{aligned}
(C_1 + C_2) \cdot \vec{v} &= (C_1 \cdot \vec{v}) + (C_2 \cdot \vec{v}) \\
&= (u_1 \cdot \vec{v} + \vec{e_1}) + (u_2 \cdot \vec{v} + \vec{e_2}) \\
&= (u_1 + u_2) \cdot \vec{v} + \vec{e_1} + \vec{e_2} \\
&= (u_1 + u_2) \cdot \vec{v} + \vec{e} \qquad \text{(where } \vec{e} \text{ is small)}
\end{aligned}
$$

Multiplication:

$$
\begin{aligned}
(C_1 \cdot C_2) \cdot \vec{v} &= C_1 \cdot (u_2 \cdot \vec{v} + \vec{e_2}) \\
&= (C_1 \cdot \vec{v}) \cdot u_2 + (C_1 \cdot \vec{e_2}) \\
&= (u_1 \cdot \vec{v} + \vec{e_1}) \cdot u_2 + (C_1 \cdot \vec{e_2}) \\
&= u_1 \cdot u_2 \cdot \vec{v} + (u_2 \cdot \vec{e_1}) + (C_1 \cdot \vec{e_2}) \\
&= u_1 \cdot u_2 \cdot \vec{v} + \vec{e} \qquad \text{(where } \vec{e} \text{ is small)}
\end{aligned}
$$

Example

To help make this algorithm easier to understand, a simple example will now be explained for the addition of 5 and 20. Due to the large sizes of the matrices that are generated, they will be shown in a compressed form. The following parameters have been chosen for this example in order to keep the sizes of the vectors and matrices small.

$$q = 65,536 \quad n = 3 \quad \chi = 8 \quad m = 48 \quad \ell = 17 \quad N = 68$$

Now we need to generate the secret key. First, $\vec{t}$ is randomly generated with values in modulo q. The secret key vector can then be created, be simpling joining 1 and the negative values of $\vec{t}$. For example, $\vec{t} = 4754$, becomes -4754, then find the modulus in q, $-4754 + 65,536$ which results in 60,782.

$$\vec{t} = [4754 \ 38,896 \ 47,731]$$
$$\vec{sk} = [1 \ 60,782 \ 26,640 \ 17,805]$$

Calculating $\vec{v}$ involves computing the *Powersof2* function on $\vec{sk}$. The first 17 values are powers of 2 from 2^0 to 2^{16}, because they are multiplied by $\rightarrow sk_0$ which is 1. Note that these are the modulus values in q, hence $1 \times 2^{16} = 0$. Now we do the same but instead multiply 2^0 to 2^{16} by $\rightarrow sk_1$. Therefore, the next value is $2^0 \times 60,782 = 60,782$, followed by $2^1 \times 60,782 = 121,564 = 56,028 \ (mod \ q)$.

$\vec{v} = [1 \ 2 \ 4 \ 8 \ 16 \ 32 \ 64 \ 128 \ 256 \ 512 \ 1024 \ 2048 \ 4096 \ 8192 \ 16384 \ 32768 \ 0, 60782 \ 56028 \ 46520 \ 27504 \ 55008 \ 44480 \ 23424 \ 46848 \ 28160 \ 56320 \ 47104 \ 28672 \ 57344 \ 49152 \ 32768 \ 0 \ 0, \ 26640 \ 53280 \ 41024 \ 16512 \ 33024 \ 512 \ 1024 \ 2048 \ 4096 \ 8192 \ 16384 \ 32768 \ 0 \ 0 \ 0 \ 0 \ 0, \ 17805 \ 35610 \ 5684 \ 11368 \ 22736 \ 45472 \ 25408 \ 50816 \ 36096 \ 6656 \ 13312 \ 26624 \ 53248 \ 40960 \ 16384 \ 32768 \ 0]$

The public key now needs to be generated. We randomly generate the matrix B and vector $\vec{e}$.

$$B = \begin{bmatrix} 24159 & 15679 & \dots & 19457 & 1520 \\ 60227 & 16241 & \dots & 21388 & 55398 \\ 40328 & 9895 & \dots & 36960 & 6044 \end{bmatrix}$$

$\vec{e} = [14 \ 65532 \ 1 \ 65529 \ 65531 \ 65528 \ 3 \ 5 \ 65526 \ 10 \ 1 \ 65533 \ 5 \ 11 \ 11 \ 65531 \ 9 \ 65521 \ 65532 \ 65530 \ 65520 \ 14 \ 65535 \ 65534 \ 4 \ 0 \ 65514 \ 6 \ 6 \ 65531 \ 0 \ 6 \ 6 \ 7 \ 7 \ 1 \ 6 \ 4 \ 65529 \ 65527 \ 65535 \ 7 \ 1 \ 3 \ 4 \ 65528 \ 2 \ 5]$

Compute the vector $\vec{b}$.

$$\vec{b} = [4754 \ 38896 \ 47731] \cdot \begin{bmatrix} 24159 & 15679 & \dots & 19457 & 1520 \\ 60227 & 16241 & \dots & 21388 & 55398 \\ 40328 & 9895 & \dots & 36960 & 6044 \end{bmatrix} + [14 \ 65532 \ \dots \ 2 \ 5]$$

$$= [10276 \ 12255 \ \dots \ 60660 \ 40328]$$

Now we can join the vector $\vec{b}$ with the matrix B, to form the matrix A.

$$A = \begin{bmatrix} 10276 & 12255 & \ldots & 60660 & 40328 \\ 24159 & 15679 & \ldots & 19457 & 1520 \\ 60227 & 16241 & \ldots & 21388 & 55398 \\ 40328 & 9895 & \ldots & 36960 & 6044 \end{bmatrix}$$

That concludes the key generation, so we can start encrypting an integer value. The encryption process for 20 will be shown now, and the cipher matrix for 5 will be given. So first we randomly generate the matrix R. It is important to note that the random matrix R will be different for the encryption of 20 and 5. Then we multiple this random matrix by the public key (matrix A).

$$R = \begin{bmatrix} 0 & 0 & \ldots & 0 & 0 \\ 0 & 0 & \ldots & 1 & 0 \\ \ldots & & \ldots & & \ldots \\ 0 & 1 & \ldots & 1 & 0 \\ 0 & 0 & \ldots & 1 & 1 \end{bmatrix} \qquad A \cdot R = \begin{bmatrix} 23482 & 31088 & \ldots & 507 & 48622 \\ 39624 & 49556 & \ldots & 36113 & 62689 \\ 62379 & 56720 & \ldots & 38675 & 355 \\ 42466 & 276 & \ldots & 20430 & 31877 \end{bmatrix}$$

Because we want values in $\{0,1\}$ to keep errors small, we must now bit decompose $A \cdot R$. If we take the first value 23,482, converted to a 17 bit value it becomes 00101101110111010_2. This is then put into a matrix vertically, from the least significant bit. Only the values 23,482, 31,088, 507 and 48,622 are shown. We must also calculate the identity matrix and multiply it by the value u we are encrypting, which is 20.

$$BitDecomp(A \cdot R) = \begin{bmatrix} 0 & 0 & \ldots & 1 & 0 \\ 1 & 0 & \ldots & 1 & 1 \\ 0 & 0 & \ldots & 0 & 1 \\ 1 & 0 & \ldots & 1 & 1 \\ 1 & 1 & \ldots & 1 & 0 \\ 1 & 1 & \ldots & 1 & 1 \\ 0 & 1 & \ldots & 1 & 1 \\ 1 & 0 & \ldots & 1 & 1 \\ 1 & 1 & \ldots & 1 & 1 \\ 1 & 0 & \ldots & 0 & 0 \\ 0 & 0 & \ldots & 0 & 1 \\ 1 & 1 & \ldots & 0 & 1 \\ 1 & 1 & \ldots & 0 & 1 \\ 0 & 1 & \ldots & 0 & 1 \\ 1 & 1 & \ldots & 0 & 0 \\ 0 & 0 & \ldots & 0 & 1 \\ 0 & 0 & \ldots & 0 & 0 \\ \ldots & & \ldots & & \ldots \end{bmatrix} \qquad u \cdot I_N = \begin{bmatrix} 20 & 0 & \ldots & 0 & 0 \\ 0 & 20 & \ldots & 0 & 0 \\ \ldots & & \ldots & & \ldots \\ 0 & 0 & \ldots & 20 & 0 \\ 0 & 0 & \ldots & 0 & 20 \end{bmatrix}$$

These two matrices now have to be added together. Note that in the example, only the top 17 rows are shown, hence only two additions of 20 appear.

$$u \cdot I_N + BitDecomp(A \cdot R) = \begin{bmatrix} 20 & 0 & \ldots & 1 & 0 \\ 1 & 20 & \ldots & 1 & 1 \\ 0 & 0 & \ldots & 0 & 1 \\ 1 & 0 & \ldots & 1 & 1 \\ 1 & 1 & \ldots & 1 & 0 \\ 1 & 1 & \ldots & 1 & 1 \\ 0 & 1 & \ldots & 1 & 1 \\ 1 & 0 & \ldots & 1 & 1 \\ 1 & 1 & \ldots & 1 & 1 \\ 1 & 0 & \ldots & 0 & 0 \\ 0 & 0 & \ldots & 0 & 1 \\ 1 & 1 & \ldots & 0 & 1 \\ 1 & 1 & \ldots & 0 & 1 \\ 0 & 1 & \ldots & 0 & 1 \\ 1 & 1 & \ldots & 0 & 0 \\ 0 & 0 & \ldots & 0 & 1 \\ 0 & 0 & \ldots & 0 & 0 \\ \ldots & & \ldots & & \ldots \end{bmatrix}$$

After the addition, we must get the values small again. This involves using the *Flatten* function, which performs an inverse bit decomposition, then a regular bit decomposition. Taking the values in the 0th column [20, 1, 0, 1, 1, 1, 0, 1, 1, 1, 0, 1, 1, 0, 1, 0, 0], performing an inverse bit decomposition becomes the value $0010110111011010_2 + 20$, resulting in 23,502. This value is then represented in bits from least to most significant bits 0111001111011010100 and stored in the cipher matrix vertically. Note than when undecomposing column 1, the 20 is added as $20 \ll 1$. The final cipher matrix is given as $E(20)$, and the cipher matrix for 5 is also given.

$$E(20) = \begin{bmatrix} 0 & 0 & \ldots & 1 & 0 \\ 1 & 0 & \ldots & 1 & 1 \\ 1 & 0 & \ldots & 0 & 1 \\ 1 & 1 & \ldots & 1 & 1 \\ 0 & 1 & \ldots & 1 & 0 \\ 0 & 0 & \ldots & 1 & 1 \\ 1 & 0 & \ldots & 1 & 1 \\ 1 & 1 & \ldots & 1 & 1 \\ 1 & 1 & \ldots & 1 & 1 \\ 1 & 0 & \ldots & 0 & 0 \\ 0 & 0 & \ldots & 0 & 1 \\ 1 & 1 & \ldots & 0 & 1 \\ 1 & 1 & \ldots & 0 & 1 \\ 0 & 1 & \ldots & 0 & 1 \\ 1 & 1 & \ldots & 0 & 0 \\ 0 & 0 & \ldots & 0 & 1 \\ 0 & 0 & \ldots & 0 & 0 \\ \ldots & & \ldots & & \ldots \end{bmatrix} \quad E(5) = \begin{bmatrix} 1 & 1 & \ldots & 0 & 0 \\ 0 & 1 & \ldots & 0 & 0 \\ 1 & 1 & \ldots & 0 & 1 \\ 0 & 0 & \ldots & 1 & 1 \\ 1 & 1 & \ldots & 1 & 0 \\ 1 & 0 & \ldots & 0 & 1 \\ 0 & 1 & \ldots & 1 & 1 \\ 1 & 1 & \ldots & 1 & 1 \\ 1 & 0 & \ldots & 0 & 1 \\ 1 & 0 & \ldots & 1 & 0 \\ 0 & 1 & \ldots & 1 & 1 \\ 0 & 0 & \ldots & 1 & 0 \\ 0 & 1 & \ldots & 0 & 1 \\ 1 & 0 & \ldots & 1 & 0 \\ 1 & 0 & \ldots & 1 & 0 \\ 1 & 0 & \ldots & 1 & 1 \\ 0 & 0 & \ldots & 0 & 0 \\ \ldots & & \ldots & & \ldots \end{bmatrix}$$

With the encryption done, we can now perform the addition of the two cipher matrices. This is just a simple matrix addition operation. Note that if many operations are required, the result matrix will need to be flattened. If multiplication is performed on two cipher matrices. The result matrix will also need to be flattened. In this example, we do not require a flatten operation because the values are still small.

$$E(20)+E(5) = \begin{bmatrix} 1 & 1 & \dots & 1 & 0 \\ 1 & 1 & \dots & 1 & 1 \\ 2 & 1 & \dots & 0 & 2 \\ 1 & 1 & \dots & 2 & 2 \\ 1 & 2 & \dots & 2 & 0 \\ 1 & 0 & \dots & 1 & 2 \\ 1 & 1 & \dots & 2 & 2 \\ 2 & 2 & \dots & 2 & 2 \\ 2 & 1 & \dots & 1 & 2 \\ 2 & 0 & \dots & 1 & 0 \\ 0 & 1 & \dots & 1 & 2 \\ 1 & 1 & \dots & 1 & 1 \\ 1 & 2 & \dots & 0 & 2 \\ 1 & 1 & \dots & 1 & 1 \\ 2 & 1 & \dots & 1 & 0 \\ 1 & 0 & \dots & 1 & 2 \\ 0 & 0 & \dots & 0 & 0 \\ \dots & & \dots & & \dots \end{bmatrix}$$

Because the q in this example is a power of 2, we can use the *MPDec* function to decrypt. Using *MPDec* allows us to start at column 15 and work back to column 0 to give the 16-bit answer. Column 15 contains the value for the 0th bit, and column 0 has the value for the 15th bit.

$$
\begin{aligned}
result &= 0 \\
x &= \vec{v} \cdot C_{15} - (result \times (1 \ll 15)) \\
&= 32802 - 0 \\
bit &= min(32802, 65536 - 32802) >= abs(32802 - (65536 \gg 1)) \\
&= 1 \\
result &= result + (bit \ll (15 - 15)) \\
result &= 1 \\
x &= \vec{v} \cdot C_{14} - (result \times (1 \ll 14)) \\
&= 16430 - 16384 \\
bit &= min(46, 65536 - 46) >= abs(46 - (65536 \gg 1)) \\
&= 0 \\
result &= result + (bit \ll (15 - 14)) \\
result &= 1 \\
&\dots \\
x &= \vec{v} \cdot C_{12} - (result \times (1 \ll 12)) \\
&= 36849 - 4096 \\
bit &= min(32753, 65536 - 32753) >= abs(32753 - (65536 \gg 1)) \\
&= 1 \\
result &= result + (bit \ll (15 - 12)) \\
result &= 9
\end{aligned}
$$

$$
\begin{aligned}
x &= \vec{v} \cdot C_{11} - (result \times (1 \ll 11)) \\
&= 51252 - 18432 \\
bit &= min(32820, 65536 - 32820) >= abs(32820 - (65536 \gg 1)) \\
&= 1 \\
result &= result + (bit \ll (15 - 11)) \\
result &= 25
\end{aligned}
$$

6 HOMOMORPHIC ENCRYPTION IN THE CLOUD

Today real-world applications of FHE in the cloud are nigh-on impossible to find, due to the severe performance limitations of currently proposed schemes making them unattractive for cloud services to employ. Research for practical implementations of FHE are currently pursued by organizations such as IBM Research and Microsoft. But also by universities across the global, for example, Stanford and The University of Waikato (CROW, 2014). Until schemes are made practical, we will not see them in services exposed to the public. On the other hand, PHE has enabled some cloud services and systems to reap benefits. Some examples are:

- *CryptDB* (Popa et al., 2011) is a database privacy layer that explored the use of FHE for performing queries over encrypted data but opted do use a selection of techniques to perform different types of queries. For basic addition operations over integers, the Paillier cryptosystem (Paillier, 1999) was implemented, which offers PHE. When using Paillier, to perform the addition of two values x and y, the encrypted values are multiplied together, which when decrypted, is the equivalent of adding the unencrypted values together.
- *Helios* (Adida, 2008) is a cloud-based open-audit voting system, which as off version 2.0 uses homomorphic encryption to tally the votes (Adida et al., 2009). This allows all the votes to be submitted and tallied in an encrypted form, then only once the final votes have been cast and added to the tallies, is the result decrypted. The PHE scheme used is a variant of El Gamal, which was described in Section 4.2, Exponential El Gamal.
- Porticor (2014a), which was founded in 2010, is to the best of our knowledge one of the first commercial implementations of homomorphic encryption, which provides a secure cloud key management platform using PHE. The company states that FHE *isn't yet feasible for a real-world system* (Porticor, 2014b), and that by only supporting a few computational operations *you benefit from fast, reliable performance for your business-critical applications* (Porticor, 2014b) while keeping the keys secure.

7 FUTURE OF HOMOMORPHIC ENCRYPTION AND OPEN ISSUES

Homomorphic encryption in the cloud is still relatively young and is only being adopted at a slow rate. Even though FHE is currently not plausible to implement for real-world scenarios, there is no reason why PHE cannot offer cloud providers an extra level of security right now. Then in time migrate to FHE when schemes offer better performance. The cloud requires an increased level of security, and homomorphic encryption is a viable answer. Some cloud solutions have already realized this, like the samples in Section 6, but in the near future this will be more common across a far more diverse group of cloud applications and services.

As discussed throughout this chapter, there are still some problems with homomorphic encryption which will impact its future. For example, FHE can support more than a single operation. However, an open issue is that FHE also has limitations on supporting a wide range of operations/functions, even though this is the very definition of FHE. This is because two operations could be used to cancel each other out and make the security pointless. Supporting subtractions by an unencrypted value and comparing the encrypted value with zero would be one case. Because a malicious user can just subtract 1 until the encrypted value is zero, giving the answer. This leads to another issue, currently FHE is thought of as the perfect solution; however, it needs to be considered on an application by application basis. A one size fits all solution is not going to be as secure as a scheme which is designed for the application in mind. And finally, by having homomorphic encryption protect user information/data, it stops cloud services from learning information about them. This can stop targeted ads, selling anonymous user data and many other ways cloud services make money even though there is no cost to the end user. The issue is that even though users want to be more secure online, will they be willing to pay for the cloud service, or will they prefer the free, unsecured service instead? These are just some of the current issues that homomorphic encryption faces as it tries to become the future of security in the cloud.

8 ALTERNATIVES TO HOMOMORPHIC ENCRYPTION

Cloud adoption by businesses handling sensitive data is slow because they cannot afford their data to be leaked. Be it their private cooperate data, or their customers data. This could be to protect their image, or because they are contractible obliged to keep the data confidential. While homomorphic encryption is a viable answer, there are other solutions which target this problem, and for some businesses could be a perfect fit for their business model or infrastructure.

A model widely adopted for securing cloud data is to provide a gateway between the cooperate network and the cloud (Salehi et al., 2014), which encrypts data before it leaves the network, and decrypts data from the cloud. This is similar to the Mega cloud service (Mega ltd, 2014) described early, however it is designed for enterprise, where Mega is intended more for personal use. That is not to say Mega cannot be used for enterprise, in fact it is perfect for small businesses, but the gateway solution is more powerful and flexible.

The general idea of using an encryption gateway is shown in Figure 7. This shows two computers within the company, used by Alice and Bob, that are

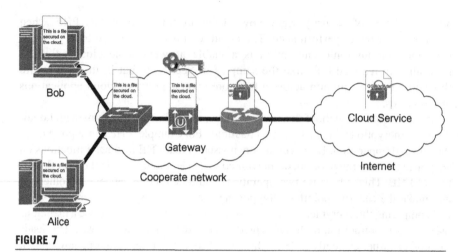

FIGURE 7

Encryption gateway

connected to the companies internal network. Then any traffic leaving the internal network exists through what is known as the border router. However, there is a gateway that any data heading for the cloud service must go through. For example, Bob creates a files and wants to save it to the cloud. When the file is being saved, before it goes out onto the Internet, it must go through the gateway appliance. This gateway encrypts the file and forwards it to the cloud service via the border router. Then Alice wants to view this file, so she requests it from the cloud service. The encrypted file then goes back through the gateway appliance and is decrypted before reaching Alice. This guarantees that files are always encrypted before leaving the internal network to be stored on the cloud service. It also means that the company manages its own keys, unlike services like Dropbox. Alice and Bob are not affected by the encryption gateway, yet the companies data remains secure.

Encryption gateways can do more than just encrypting and decrypting data. RESeED (Salehi et al., 2014) allows searching over encrypted files in the cloud using regular expressions, by creating an index from the unencrypted files before they are encrypted and saved to the cloud. This device still has some limitations, such as the keys cannot be recovered off the device. So if the device has a fault and stops working, the encrypted data stored in the cloud is not recoverable. CipherCloud (2014) is another example of an encryption gateway, which supports cloud services such as Amazon Web Services, Gmail, and Office 365. These encryption gateway devices can be implemented into networks now, unlike solutions involving homomorphic encryption which are still years away from full-scale use.

9 SUMMARY

This chapter has given an in-depth overview of homomorphic encryption schemes. It has provided proofs to show that the schemes can support homomorphic operations, while also providing examples to help make the mathematics and algorithms easier to understand. Homomorphic encryption will become more essential for cloud services as the performance of the schemes improves, allowing for more secure and trust worthy applications. Some cloud services are already benefiting from homomorphic encryption, and hopefully many more will follow.

REFERENCES

Adida, B., 2008. Helios: web-based open-audit voting. In: Usenix Security Symposium, 17, pp. 335–348.

Adida, B., De Marneffe, O., Pereira, O., Quisquater, J.J., 2009. Electing a university president using open-audit voting: analysis of real-world use of Helios. In: Proceedings of the 2009 Conference on Electronic Voting Technology/Workshop on Trustworthy Elections. USENIX Association, p. 10.

Ahituv, N., Lapid, Y., Neumann, S., 1987. Processing encrypted data. Commun. ACM 30 (9), 777–780.

Ajtai, M., Kumar, R., Sivakumar, D., 2001. A sieve algorithm for the shortest lattice vector problem. In: Proceedings of the Thirty-Third Annual ACM Symposium on Theory of Computing. ACM, New York, pp. 601–610.

Armknecht, F., Sadeghi, A.R., 2008. A new approach for algebraically homomorphic encryption. IACR Cryptol. ePrint Arch. 2008, 422.

Blakley, G., Meadows, C., 1985. A database encryption scheme which allows the computation of statistics using encrypted data. In: IEEE Symposium on Security and Privacy, 2012. IEEE Computer Society, p. 116.

Blum, A., Kalai, A., Wasserman, H., 2003. Noise-tolerant learning, the parity problem, and the statistical query model. J. ACM 50, 506–519.

Brakerski, Z., Vaikuntanathan, V., 2011. Fully homomorphic encryption from ring-LWE and security for key dependent messages. In: Advances in Cryptology—CRYPTO 2011, Springer, Berlin, pp. 505–524.

Brakerski, Z., Vaikuntanathan, V., 2014. Efficient fully homomorphic encryption from (standard) LWE. SIAM J. Comput. 43, 831–871.

Brickell, E.F., Yacobi, Y., 1988. On privacy homomorphisms. In: Advances in Cryptology—EUROCRYPT'87. Springer, Berlin, pp. 117–125.

Chen, A., 2010. Google Engineer Stalked Teens, Spied on Chats, Published on Gawker, September 2010. [Online] http://gawker.com/5637234/gcreep-google-engineer-stalked-teens-spied-on-chats (accessed 26/08/14).

CipherCloud, 2014. [Online] http://www.ciphercloud.com (accessed 20/10/2014).

Cyber Security Researchers of Waikato (CROW), 2014. [Online] https://crow.org.nz (accessed 14/12/14).

Denning, D.E., 1982. Signature Protocols for RSA and Other Public-Key Cryptosystems.

Diffie, W., Hellman, M.E., 1976. New directions in cryptography. IEEE Trans. Inform. Theory 22, 644–654.

Domingo-Ferrer, J., 2002. A provably secure additive and multiplicative privacy homomorphism. In: Information Security, Springer, Berlin, pp. 471–483.

Drago, I., Mellia, M., Munafo, M.M., Sperotto, A., Sadre, R., Pras, A., 2012. Inside dropbox: understanding personal cloud storage services. In: Proceedings of the 2012 ACM Conference on Internet Measurement Conference. ACM, New York, pp. 481–494.

Dropbox Inc, 2014. Dropbox Help, [Online] https://www.dropbox.com/help/27 (accessed 10/08/2014).

ElGamal, T., 1985. A public key cryptosystem and a signature scheme based on discrete logarithms. In: Advances in Cryptology. Springer, Berlin, pp. 10–18.

Ferrer, J.D.i., 1996. A new privacy homomorphism and applications. Inform. Process. Lett. 60, 277–282.

Gentry, C., 2009a. A fully homomorphic encryption scheme. Ph.D. thesis. Stanford University.

Gentry, C., 2009b. Fully homomorphic encryption using ideal lattices. In: Proceedings of the 41st Annual ACM Symposium on Symposium on Theory of Computing—STOC\'09. ACM Press, New York, p. 169.

Gentry, C., Halevi, S., 2011. Implementing gentry's fully-homomorphic encryption scheme. In: Advances in Cryptology—EUROCRYPT 2011, Springer, Berlin, pp. 129–148.

Gentry, C., Sahai, A., Waters, B., 2013. Homomorphic encryption from learning with errors: conceptually-simpler, asymptotically-faster, attribute-based. In: Advances in Cryptology—CRYPTO 2013, Springer, Berlin, pp. 75–92.

Goldreich, O., Micciancio, D., Safra, S., Seifert, J.-P., 1999. Approximating shortest lattice vectors is not harder than approximating closest lattice vectors. Inform. Process. Lett. 71, 55–61.

IBM Public Challenges for Fully Homomorphic Encryption, [Online] http://researcher.watson.ibm.com/researcher/view_group.php?id=1548 (accessed 14/10/14).

Kuzu, M., Islam, M.S., Kantarcioglu, M., 2012. Efficient similarity search over encrypted data. In: IEEE 28th International Conference on Data Engineering (ICDE), 2012. IEEE, Piscataway, NJ, pp. 1156–1167.

Li, J., Wang, Q., Wang, C., Cao, N., Ren, K., Lou, W., 2010. Fuzzy keyword search over encrypted data in cloud computing. In: Proceedings of the 29th Conference on Information Communications. IEEE Press, Piscataway, NJ, pp. 441–445.

Li, R., Xu, Z., Kang, W., Yow, K.C., Xu, C.Z., 2014. Efficient multi-keyword ranked query over encrypted data in cloud computing. Future Gener. Comput. Syst. 30, 179–190.

Mega ltd, 2014. Mega, [Online] https://mega.co.nz (accessed 10/08/2014).

Marcus, M., 1988. Introduction to Linear Algebra. Courier Dover Publications, Berlin.

Micciancio, D., 2001. The shortest vector in a lattice is hard to approximate to within some constant. SIAM J. Comput. 30, 2008–2035.

Micciancio, D., 2010. A first glimpse of cryptography's holy grail. Commun. ACM 53, 96.

Micciancio, D., Goldwasser, S., 2002. Complexity of Lattice Problems: A Cryptographic Perspective. Springer, Berlin, 671.

Micciancio, D., Peikert, C., 2012. Trapdoors for lattices: simpler, tighter, faster, smaller. In: Advances in Cryptology—EUROCRYPT 2012, Springer, Berlin, pp. 700–718.

Micciancio, D., Voulgaris, P., 2013. A deterministic single exponential time algorithm for most lattice problems based on Voronoi cell computations. SIAM J. Comput. 42, 1364–1391.

Paillier, P., 1999. Public-key cryptosystems based on composite degree residuosity classes. In: Advances in Cryptology—EUROCRYPT'99. Springer, Berlin, pp. 223–238.

Peikert, c., 2009. Public-key cryptosystems from the worst-case shortest vector problem. In: Proceedings of the Forty-First Annual ACM Symposium on Theory of Computing. ACM, New York, pp. 333–342.

Popa, R.A., Zeldovich, N., Balakrishnan, H., 2011. CryptDB: A Practical Encrypted Relational DBMS.

Porticor, 2014a. [Online] http://www.porticor.com (accessed 06/08/14).

Porticor—Homomorphic Encryption, 2014b. [Online] http://www.porticor.com/homomorphic-encryption/ (accessed 06/08/14).

Regev, O., 2010. The learning with errors problem (invited survey). In: IEEE 25th Annual Conference on Computational Complexity (CCC), 2010. IEEE, New York, pp. 191–204.

Rivest, R., Shamir, A., Adleman, L., 1978. A method for obtaining digital signatures and public-key cryptosystems. Commun. ACM 21, 120–126.

Rivest, R.L., Adleman, L., Dertouzos, M.L., 1978. On data banks and privacy homomorphisms. In: Foundation of Secure Computation. Academic Press, New York, pp. 169–179.

Salehi, M.A., Caldwell, T., Fernandez, A., Mickiewicz, E., Rozier, E.W., Zonouz, S., Redberg, D., 2014. Reseed: regular expression search over encrypted data in the cloud. Proceedings of the 7th IEEE International Conference on Cloud Computing (CLOUD'14).

Suh, G.E., Clarke, D., Gassend, B., Van Dijk, M., Devadas, S., 2003. Aegis: architecture for tamper-evident and tamper-resistant processing. In: Proceedings of the 17th Annual International Conference on Supercomputing. ACM, New York, pp. 160–171.

Suh, G.E., O'Donnell, C.W., Devadas, S., 2005. Aegis: a single-chip secure processor, Information Security Technical Report 10, pp. 63–73.

van Emde-Boas, P., 1981. Another NP-Complete Partition Problem and the Complexity of Computing Short Vectors in a Lattice. University of Amsterdam, Amsterdam.

Van Dijk, M., Gentry, C., Halevi, S., Vaikuntanathan, V., 2010. Fully homomorphic encryption over the integers. In: Advances in Cryptology—EUROCRYPT 2010, Springer, Berlin, pp. 24–43.

Van Dijk, M., Juels, A., 2010. On the impossibility of cryptography alone for privacy-preserving cloud computing. In: HotSec'10, pp. 1–8.

Wagner, D., 2003. Cryptanalysis of an algebraic privacy homomorphism. In: Information Security, Springer, Berlin, pp. 234–239.

Wang, B., Yu, S., Lou, W., Hou, Y.T., 2014. Privacy-preserving multi-keyword fuzzy search over encrypted data in the cloud. In: IEEE INFOCOM.

Protection through isolation: Virtues and pitfalls

Johanna Ullrich, Edgar R. Weippl

SBA Research, Vienna, Austria

1 INTRODUCTION

Cloud computing has emerged from a combination of various technologies (primarily virtualization, increased networking capabilities, and large storage devices) and has led to significant cost reductions based on economy-of-scale effects. Beyond hardware, noncomputational resources such as maintenance staff or air conditioning are also shared, leading to multitenancy being a key feature of cloud computing. However, sharing's negative impacts on security among coresiding parties are often glossed over in discussions of cloud computing. This is of particular interest on public clouds because your neighbor is unknown to you. As it is generally easy to subscribe to cloud services, malicious parties are also able to settle within the cloud. Once there, they may seek to exploit other users from their privileged starting position, targeting the collection of private information using covert channels or taking over their neighbors via hypervisor exploits. The main mitigation strategy against these hazards is distinct isolation between instances, provided by the hypervisor, although the quality of isolation is far from being absolutely reliable and varies significantly. Although it is the cloud provider's responsibility to protect its customers from each other, it is also highly important for the latter to know of the drawbacks of isolation across various hypervisors in order to deal accordingly with the given environment.

In the case of cloud computing, networking capabilities will inevitably provide access to nodes with the appropriate basics for most hosted applications. Sharing usually one network interface card among a number of virtual hosts causes distinct limitations, e.g., the inability to send at the same time, delays due to the intermediate hypervisor or interference with inherent protocol features. While this may play only a minor role in inferring the existence of virtualization, it becomes a serious issue in case certain parameters can be influenced by other parties to determine coresidency of virtual instances, deanonymize internal addresses or gain secret information. The latter case unquestionably raises serious security and privacy risks. As the prohibition of network access is impractical due to its importance, network isolation plays a major role in instance isolation generally.

The Cloud Security Ecosystem

This chapter investigates the topic of instance isolation in clouds and illustrates the matter in detail through the example of networking. In a first step, we investigate the mechanisms which are intended to provide proper isolation among coresiding instances and familiarize ourselves with the overview and specifics of general hypervisor architecture through the example of the open-source implementations Xen and KVM.

We focus on how hypervisors handle sharing of the networking resources among a number of virtual instances and discuss inherent challenges such as network scheduling to determine which node's packets are allowed to send at a certain point in time, or traffic shaping to restrict an instance to a certain bandwidth. Then, we identify potential attack surfaces and emphasize a discussion on how shared networking can be exploited. This is accompanied by an inventory of currently known attacks analyzing the exploited attack vectors.

Although full isolation seems to be utterly impossible considering the vast attack surface and the need for networking, we develop strategies for mitigation of isolation-based threats and discuss their limitations. Finally, we draw conclusions on the most important aspects of cloud computing and highlight inevitable challenges for cloud security research.

2 HYPERVISORS

Hypervisors, or also virtual machine monitors (VMMs), are pieces of software that enable multiple operating systems to run on a single physical machine. Although a key enabler for today's success of cloud computing, virtualization has been an issue in computer science for at least four decades (e.g., Goldberg, 1974). Here, we discuss different hypervisor architectures and present the architecture of common implementations before focusing on their networking behavior.

2.1 GENERAL ARCHITECTURES

A hypervisor provides an efficient, isolated duplicate of the physical machines for virtual machines. Popek and Goldberg (1974) claimed that all sensitive instructions, i.e., those changing resource availability or configuration, must be privileged instructions in order to build an effective hypervisor for a certain system. In such an environment, all sensitive instructions cross the hypervisor, which is able to control the virtual machines appropriately.

This concept is today known as *full virtualization* and has the advantage that the host-operating system does not have to be adapted to work with the hypervisor, i.e., it is unaware of its virtualized environment. Obviously, a number of systems are far from perfect and require a number of additional actions in order to be virtualizable, leading to the technologies of *paravirtualization, binary translation, and hardware-assisted virtualization* (Pearce et al., 2013).

Paravirtualization encompasses changes to the system in order to redirect these nonprivileged, but sensitive, instructions over the hypervisor to regain full control on the resources. Therefore, the host-operating system has to undergo various modifications to work with the hypervisor, and the host is aware that it is virtualized. Applications running atop the altered OS do not have to be changed. Undoubtedly, these modifications require more work to implement, but on the other hand may provide better performance than full virtualization which often intervenes (Rose, 2004; Crosby and Brown, 2006). The best-known hypervisor of this type is Xen (Xen Project, n.d.).

Hardware-assisted virtualization is achieved by means of additional functionality included into the CPU, specifically an additional execution mode called guest mode, which is dedicated to the virtual instances (Drepper, 2008; Adams and Agesen, 2006). However, this type of virtualization requires certain hardware, in contrast to paravirtualization, which is in general able to run on any system. The latter also eases migration of paravirtualized machines. A popular representative for this virtualization type is the *Kernel-based Virtual Machine (KVM)* infrastructure (KVM, n.d.). Combinations of the two techniques are commonly referred to as *hybrid virtualization*.

Binary translation is a software virtualization and includes the use of an interpreter. It translates binary code to another binary, but excluding nontrapping instructions. This means that the input contains a full instruction set, but the output is a subset thereof and contains the innocuous instructions only (Adams and Agesen, 2006). This technology is also the closest to emulation, where the functionality of a device is simulated and all instructions are intercepted. The performance is dependent on the instructions to translate. VMware is an example of virtualization using binary translation (VMware, n.d.).

Hypervisors can also be distinguished by their relation to the host-operating system. In the case where the hypervisor fully replaces the operating system, it is called a bare-metal or Type I hypervisor, and where a host-operating system is still necessary, the hypervisor is hosted, or of Type II. Classifying the aforementioned hypervisors: *Xen* and *KVM* are both bare-metal—VMware ESX also, but its Workstation equivalent is hosted. Most workstation hypervisors are hosted as they are typically used for testing or training purposes.

2.2 PRACTICAL REALIZATION

Table 1 provides an overview on leading public cloud providers and their preferred hypervisor. Three specific hypervisors are frequently used: *KVM, Xen*, and *VMware vCloud*, and so we will focus on these when discussing implemented architectures. KVM and Xen are both open-source products and full insight into their behavior is provided; due to this, they have been extensively studied in the scientific literature, especially *Xen*. Their counterpart *vCloud* is a proprietary product. We would have to rely on its documentation, and therefore, exclude it from in-depth investigation.

Xen is the market's old bull. Although being the typical representative for paravirtualization, it is nowadays also capable of hardware-assisted virtualization. Being

Table 1 Leading cloud providers and hypervisors

Hypervisor	Cloud providers
Azure Hypervisor	Microsoft Azure
KVM	Google Compute Engine, IBM SmartCloud, Digital Ocean
vCloud	Bluelock, Terremark, Savvis, EarthLinkCloud, CSC
Xen	Rackspace Open Cloud, Amazon EC2, GoGrid

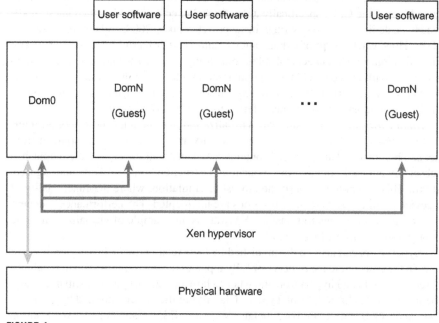

FIGURE 1

Architecture of the *Xen* hypervisor, drawn by the author.

a bare-metal hypervisor it resides directly above the hardware as depicted in Figure 1. The hypervisor itself performs only basic operations, such as CPU scheduling or memory management. More complex decisions are transferred to *Domain0*, a privileged virtual machine with rights to access physical I/O and interact with the other virtual instances. *Domain0* runs a *Linux* kernel running the physical drivers and provides their virtual representations. The guests run in their own domains, *DomainN*, and access I/O devices like disk by means of *Domain0*'s abstractions. This approach has the advantage that physical drivers have to be available only for the OS used in *Domain0*. (Barharm et al., 2003; Pratt et al., 2005)

The host and guest notify each other by means of *hypercalls* and *events*. *Hypercalls* are comparable to system calls and allow the domain to perform privileged instructions by trapping into the hypervisor. Communication in the opposite direction is done by asynchronous *events*: Pending events are indicated in bit masks before calling the host via callback. Data transfer is performed with descriptor rings which refer to data buffers. These kinds of ring buffers are filled by domains and the hypervisor in a producer-consumer manner. (Barharm et al., 2003)

As mentioned in the previous chapter, paravirtualization requires modification of the guest-operating system. A variety of *Linux* and *BSD* distributions are supported as they require few changes; however, for Windows, it is recommended to use hardware-assisted mode (DomU Support, 2014).

KVM is short for *Kernel-based Virtual Machine Monitor*. Being developed later than *Xen*, it relies heavily on CPU virtualization features. Beyond *kernel* and *execution* mode, these CPUs provide an additional mode—*guest* mode. In this mode, system software is able to trap certain sensitive instructions guaranteeing the fulfillment of Popek's requirements.

As depicted in Figure 2, the hypervisor itself is a *Linux* kernel module and provides a device node *(/dev/kvm)*. It enables the creation of new virtual machines, running and interrupting virtual CPUs, as well as memory allocation and register

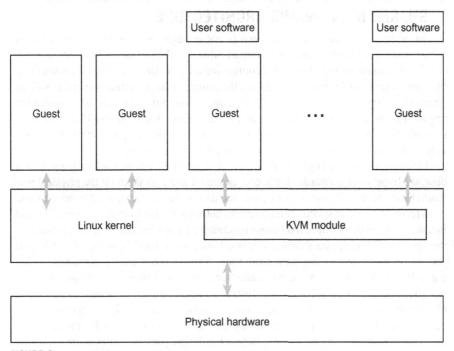

FIGURE 2

Architecture of the *KVM* Hypervisor, drawn by the author.

access. During the hypervisor's development, reusability of existing Linux technology was important, e.g., CPU scheduling, networking or memory management. This way, KVM is able to profit from the collective experience included in the operating systems and benefit from future improvements. Virtual machines are ordinary Linux processes having their own memory and are scheduled onto the CPU as is every other process. (Kivity et al., 2007; Redhat, 2008)

For I/O, two mechanisms are available: programmed I/O (PIO) traps privileged CPU instructions for I/O of the virtualization extension, whereas memory-mapped I/O (MMIO) means using the same instruction for device access as for memory access. All accesses lead to a switch from guest to kernel mode, but finally I/O processing is executed in guest mode by means of a device model. Communication from the guest to the host is possible via virtual interrupts, trigged by the hypervisor after an ordinary hardware interrupt from a device (Kivity et al., 2007).

KVM has been included into the 2.6 kernel and is thus available in practically all *Linux* distributions. Unlike *Xen*, the plain hardware-assisted alternative does not require changes to guest-operating systems. However, today there are also paravirtualized device drivers available for I/O interfaces for performance improvement as the PIO and MMIO require mode switching (Kivity et al., 2007).

---

3 SHARED NETWORKING ARCHITECTURE

A virtual network interface on its own is not enough. Successful communication requires also a network—plugging a virtual cable into the virtual interface. Numerous possibilities exist: an internal virtual connection only, a virtual network equipment on the data layer (virtual bridge or switch) or the transport layer (virtual router), as well as Network Address Translation. The first is unusual for cloud services as the nodes are required to be accessible from the outside. In public clouds, it would not even be possible to access your instances for management issues despite paying for them. However, it is more commonly used on workstation hypervisors.

Despite the variety of options, the majority of tutorials recommend bridging. In this case, the hypervisor forwards all packets unaltered and puts them on the physical network. From the guest's point of view, they seem to be directly connected to the network.

Irrespective of the specific architecture, network traffic from a number of virtual instances has to be multiplexed before reaching the physical network, and this raises the question of adequate sharing. On one hand, an instance's share of bandwidth should be more or less constant over time. On the other hand, interactive tasks, e.g., a Web server, are less affected by a reduced bandwidth than scarce responsiveness due to latencies. While private clouds might be able to adapt to certain needs, public cloud providers targeting a diverse mass of customers cannot. Thus, hypervisors in general target a balance between throughput and responsiveness by means of an adequate packet-scheduling policy. Beyond ordering packets ready to be sent onto the physical wire, traffic shaping is a second important aspect regarding cloud networking. A physical node is shared among instances which do not necessarily have to be of the same performance, which may, for example, vary based on purpose or the owner's financial investment, and instances' bandwidth is limited by means of traffic shaping. We will discuss the two issues network scheduling and traffic shaping in-depth.

3.1 PACKET SCHEDULING

A scheduling algorithm decides in which order packets of various guests are processed and is thus an important part of hypervisor performance. A number of different CPU scheduling algorithms exist to support a variety of applications. Some hypervisors additionally implement specific packet schedulers. As a consequence, the hypervisor architectures may lead to varying packet sequences.

With KVM which aims to minimize changes to ordinary Linux, virtual instances are scheduled on the CPU like is any other process, e.g., a server daemon or your text processor. Irrespectively, the kernel is asked to run these instances in guest mode—the certain kernel mode that has been added for virtualization support.

Guest mode is exited and kernel mode entered if an I/O instruction or external signals occurs. The I/O itself is then handled in user mode. Afterwards, user mode again asks the kernel mode for further execution in guest mode. This is also depicted in Figure 3. Frequent mode switches, however, are time consuming and lead to negative impacts on performance. (Kivity et al., 2007) In conclusion, the chosen CPU scheduler directly impacts the order of packets being sent in *KVM*.

In contrast, *Xen* hypervisor uses dedicated packet scheduling in addition to CPU scheduling due to its standalone architecture (Figure 4). Every virtual instance contains a *netfront* device which represents its virtualized network interface and is further connected to its counterpart in privileged *Domain0*. Interfaces with pending packets to be sent are registered in *netback*'s *TX* queue. At a regular interval, a kernel thread handles these packets in round-robbing style. It takes the first pending device, processes a single pending packet, and then inserts the device again at the queue's end if further packets are available. The number of processed packets per round is limited in dependence of the page size. The processed packets are forwarded to a single queue and are processed for the time of two jiffies.

Receiving packets is less complex: The *netback* driver holds an *RX* queue containing all packets addressed to virtual instances. They are processed according to the first-input-first-output principle and delivered to the adequate device. The number of maximum processed packet per round is limited to the same page-size-related number as for sending. Forwarding is handled by the same kernel thread mentioned above. Per round, the thread handles packet receiving prior sending (Xi et al., 2013; Fraser, 2005).

The *XEN* scheduler is simple and vastly fair among instances, but does not allow to prioritize traffic over others due to its single queue ton the packets' way to the physical network. The packet-wise quantum for round-robin, however, targets to maintain high bandwidth for large data transmission and short latency for responsive tasks. CPU scheduling still affects packet ordering, e.g., due to inserting interfaces into the *netback RX* queue, but effects are minor in comparison to the dedicated packet scheduler.

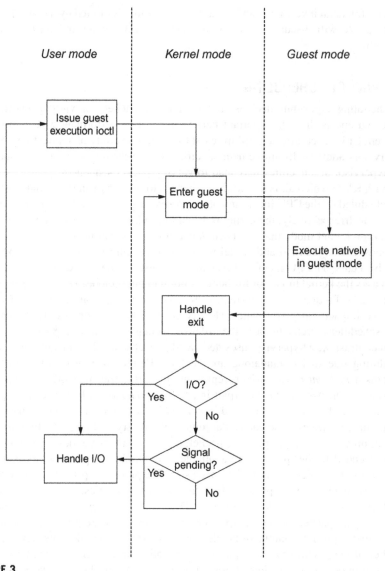

FIGURE 3

KVM guest execution loop, a cut-out from Kivity et al. (2007).

3.2 TRAFFIC SHAPING

Traffic shaping throttles an instance's throughput, potentially even in the case of idling resources. Hypervisors use various schedulers; however, credit-based token-bucket schedulers appear to dominate. Thereby, every instance receives a

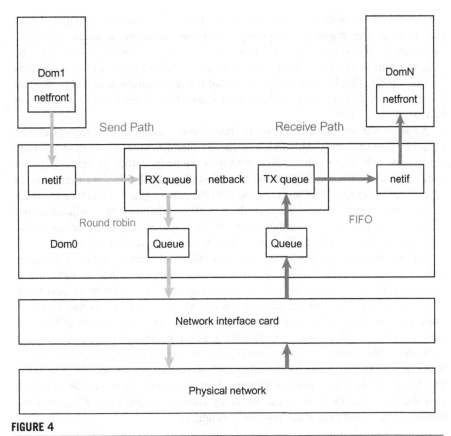

FIGURE 4

Xen networking architecture, drawn by the author.

certain amount of tokens which can be spent for traffic at a regular interval. The implementations vary in details, e.g., regarding bucket size or the time interval.

Xen allows the definition of a maximum bandwidth which allows a burst of adequate size, bandwidth multiplied by time interval, per time interval. Traffic shaping is part of the *netback* driver's *net_tx_action* function. For *netfront* interfaces with a pending packet, credit-based scheduling is applied. If enough credits are available anyway, the packet's size is subtracted, processed, and sent. Alternatively, if credits are not sufficient, it is checked whether enough time has passed to add further credits. If it is time for further credits to be added, the replenish timeout is set to the current time and the packet is passed on as above. The provided credits are equivalent to the above-mentioned burst size. Otherwise, a callback for replenish after timeout is set, and the packet has to wait. Token-bucket-based traffic shaping is, however, applied only to outgoing traffic; incoming traffic is unlimited (Fraser, 2005).

By default, this time interval is 50 ms but can be modified (Redhat, n.d.), although this is unlikely to be done in the wild. In general, the smaller the chunks, the smaller the latencies are and the smoother the traffic is. However, smaller chunks can increase the required computing effort due to more frequent callbacks. Furthermore, the netback driver ensures that bursts are able to transmit jumbo packets of up to 128 kB because the interface may seize up due to lacking credits (Fraser, 2005). This leads to a dependence of the factual minimum bandwidth and the time interval. For example, the default interval of 50 ms leads to a minimum bandwidth of 2.5 kB/s.

KVM-virtualized instance traffic is shaped using the kernel's *Traffic Control*, e.g., via (libvirt, n.d.). Although the kernel module provides various shaping algorithms, only hierarchical token bucket is common, which is emphasized by configuration tools solely supporting this option. In general, this algorithm provides each instance the requested service limited to the rate assigned to it (Devera, 2002). In comparison to *Xen*, inbound as well as outbound bandwidth is adjustable per virtual interface. Both traffic directions are defined by the three parameters *average*, *peak* and *burst*. Outgoing traffic can further be parameterized through *floor*.

It is unlikely that all coresident instances utilize all their resources at the same time and send data packets on the network as fast as they can. Idle bandwidth is lent out to neighbors, which are now able to send at higher rates, though the resource is of course returned to the borrower as soon as required. Borrowing in this way improves resource utilization while maintaining fairness. The *peak* parameter defines the maximum borrowed amount by ceiling the maximum data rate.

Many network connections are bursty, i.e., short periods of heavy traffic stagger with idleness. If guaranteed bandwidth is shifted to times of demand, the instance is able to send at the maximum rate, response time decreases and more interactivity is provided. *Burst* parameter limits the data being transferred at *peak* rate. *Floor* has been introduced later and guarantees minimal throughput.

4 ISOLATION-BASED ATTACK SURFACE

All network traffics of coresiding instances have to cross the underlying hypervisor before reaching the network interface card and being released to the network. As a result sharing a single network interface card among a number of hosts inevitably means distinct limitations. First, packets of different hosts will never appear on the network at the same point in time because the physical network interface is only able to put one packet at once onto the network. Second, routing packets through the hypervisor means time delays and lengthens the round-trip time in comparison to interacting with plain physical nodes. The additional time for outgoing as well as incoming packets is spent passing data to the hypervisor, queuing or delays caused by traffic shaping due to lacking credits. Finally, there is an additional chance for packets to be lost. Buffers in hypervisors, like everywhere else, are limited to a certain size. Packets beyond the capacity will be dropped, causing an increased need for packet retransmission or other measures of robustness.

As fair use of physical bandwidth among strangers seems unlikely, certain bandwidth per instance is guaranteed. The latter is limited to a certain value and controlled by means of traffic shaping. Being a part of the hypervisor and, thus, the responsibility of the cloud provider, the customer is not able to choose an appropriate technology, e.g., fitting best to his/her application.

Increased round-trip times and packet loss as well as limited bandwidth seem unremarkable at first. They may indicate that the respective host is virtualized but they become a more apparent issue if these parameters can be influenced from the outside. For example, if a coresident host is able to increase the neighbor's round-trip time, or the number of retransmissions due to packet loss, the latter's throughput is negatively affected. Isolation should prevent this.

However, isolation performance is not perfect, as shown in various publications, for example, Adamczyk and Chydzinski (2011) investigated the Xen hypervisor networking isolation. Measuring the impact of two virtual instances on each other has shown various interdependencies. In general, the higher the rate limits and thus assigned bandwidth to the instances, the more the actual achieved rate fluctuates, being on average slightly below the parameterized value. It is even possible that one instance is assigned the total bandwidth for a short period of time despite the neighbor also wanting to transmit. The authors further have shown that a chatty neighbor seizes more bandwidth than its calm counterpart.

Pu et al. (2010) measure the interference of CPU- and I/O-intensive instances on the same physical node, also on a *Xen* hypervisor. The results show that a certain workload combination allows the highest combined throughput, while others lead to significantly worse performance. While the authors target to optimize performance, an adversary might also utilize this to decrease performance.

Similarly, Hwang et al. (2013) combined networking with other resource-intensive instances on four hypervisors, including *KVM* and the *Xen*. Claiming that a Web server is a popular setup on a cloud instance, they measure the HTTP response time while stressing the components CPU, memory, or disk, respectively, by coresident instances. The decline in responsiveness for KVM is comparably small, *Xen* especially suffers from coresident memory use and network access.

In fact, *Xen* contains a boost mechanism to support latency-critical applications. It preempts other virtual machines and schedules latency-critical ones; however, it works only in the case where the neighbor runs full CPU usage and increases latency for networking. Xu et al. (2013) presented a solution to mitigate these increased round-trip times experienced in presence of neighbors with high CPU load. Up to now, this mitigation strategies deployment is scarce and the inert hypervisor issue might be exploited by malicious coresidents.

The discussed measurement setups all represent highly idealized clouds. In production cloud environments, the number of instances per physical node tends to be higher and the network is shared among a cluster of servers. As a consequence, the question arises whether it is feasible to exploit these issues in the wild, since attackers have to deal with a noisy environment and adjust their measurements accordingly. Anticipating the answer given in the following chapter, attacks are also feasible in production environments. Various works have shown that the isolation can be circumvented for address deanonymization, coresidence checking, communication via covert channels, load measuring, and increase of instance performance without paying. In conclusion, attacks exploiting improper isolation are feasible.

5 INVENTORY OF KNOWN ATTACKS

Here, we present attacker models applicable to the cloud and describe currently known attack techniques. We address the five network-based cloud vulnerabilities of *address deanonymization*, *coresidence detection*, *covert channels and side channels*, and *performance attacks* (Table 2).

Cloud instances in a data center are internally connected to each other by means of a local network using private addresses, whereas access from outside the cloud uses public addresses. From an adversary's point of view, launching an attack inside the cloud is definitely of more interest, e.g., due to higher available bandwidth and decreased latency, and is easily achieved by renting an instance, especially in public clouds. However, to target a certain victim the adversary must infer the other's internal address from their public one, commonly referred to as *address deanonymization*. Herzberg et al. (2013) propose the use of two instances, a prober and a

Table 2 Inventory of network-based attacks in clouds

References	Description	Vulnerability type
Herzberg et al. (2013)	Additional latencies by packet flooding	Address deanonymization
Ristenpart et al. (2009)	Request to DNS from internal network	Address deanonymization
Bates et al. (2012)	Additional latencies by packet flooding	Coresidence detection
Herzberg et al. (2013)	Additional latencies by packet flooding	Coresidence detection
Ristenpart et al. (2009)	Investigate provider's placement strategy	Coresidence detection
Bates et al. (2012)	Additional latencies by packet flooding	Covert channel
Bates et al. (2012)	Load measurement based on connection's throughput	Side channel
Farley et al. (2012) and Ou et al. (2012)	Performance differences due to heterogeneous hardware	Performance attack
Varadarajan et al. (2012)	Tricking neighbor into another resource's limit	Performance attack

malicious client, controlled by the adversary. The prober sweeps through the publicly announced address range and sends packet bursts to each instance. The benign client connects to a legitimate service on the victim. In case the prober hits the same instance as the client is connected to, the time to download a certain file increases and allows the correlation of private to public addresses. Some clouds allow even simpler address deanonymization by DNS querying the same autogenerated domain name from inside and outside the cloud. However, a number of similar simple attack vectors have been closed in reaction to publications like presented by Ristenpart et al. (2009) in the past and it is likely that the same will happen to DNS querying.

Multitenancy is, as already stated a few times, one of the major aspects of cloud computing and thus the main reason to introduce isolation among neighbors. Nevertheless, hypervisor exploits are still found every now and again (e. g., US-CERT, 2007; US-CERT, 2010), and these require prior coresidence of the victim and the attacker on the same physical machine. The process of checking the coresidence of an instance to another owned by oneself is referred to as *coresidence detection*.

Early works relied on measuring round-trip times, number of hops *en route* or matching *Domain0* addresses (Ristenpart et al., 2009). Assuming that these native timing channels are disabled, a better representation of contemporary cloud computing, Bates et al. (2012) propose a means of detection again using a flooder and a malicious client. The first floods the network, while the second is connected to victim via a benign service, e.g., a Web server. If the flooder is coresident with the victim, its large amount of sent packets negatively impacts the neighbor's access to the resource. This is measured by the packet arrival rate on the client.

Herzberg et al. (2013) propose a reversed approach but one that requires at least three nodes under the attacker's controls. The flooder again saturates the network but targets another of the attacker's instances, while another client maintains a benign connection to the victim. If the flooded instance is coresident with the victim, the mass of packets again impacts the benign connection. In this work, the additional latency of a file download is measured.

Beyond network-based coresidency detection, a variety of alternatives exists which target the exploitation of other shared resources (e.g., Ristenpart et al., 2009; Zhang et al., 2011; Wu et al., 2012). Gaining insight into a cloud provider's placement strategy to assign virtual instances to physical nodes, the attacker is able to improve their own strategy to place an instance next to a targeted node (e.g., Ristenpart et al., 2009).

Covert channels are communication channels which are not permitted for information exchange as they contain the risk of revealing secret information, e.g., private keys. Coresidency of virtual instances, therefore, adds new alternatives for attackers. In this case, the sender is coresident with another instance which provides a publicly available service, e.g., a Web server. The receiver connects to this server and measures the packet rate. The sender modulates this packet rates by flooding the network (Bates et al., 2012).

Besides extracting the key, attackers may also be interested in the victim's load, e.g., to infer economic background. Therefore, a client maintains a connection to the

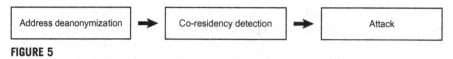

FIGURE 5

Sequence of a cloud-based attack, drawn by the author.

victim as well as to the coresiding host under its control. Network congestion or other coresident nodes impact both connections the same way. Only additional loads for the victim change the ratio of the connections' throughput. Obviously, the load on the coresiding attacker instance also changes the ratio, but since it is under the control of the attacker they can take steps to prevent this (Bates et al., 2012).

In general, the more a cloud customers pays, the more performance is provided. Instances of the same size and thus of the same cost can differ in their performance caused by hardware differences through data center expansion, contention, and coresiding instances. Customers may seek to maximize their performance for free and therefore choose the best performing from a number of launched instances, or decide based on a stochastic model (Farley et al., 2012; Ou et al., 2012). While this approach is legal considering cloud computing, malicious customers might aim to maximize their performance at their neighbors' expense. Applications frequently face a single bottleneck resource. While waiting for this specific resource, the calls for other resources also decrease making it more accessible to other instances. By leading a neighbor into another's resource limit, an attacker is able to free the required resource, increase its own performance and perform resource-freeing attacks (Varadarajan et al., 2012). These attacks however require that the victim provides a publicly available service, providing a means to influence resource use. Their feasibility has been verified by freeing the cache by tricking the neighbor into its CPU use limits. The victim's behavior was triggered by accessing dynamic content of its publicly available Web server, which uses CPU more heavily in contrast to processing static content.

All these scenarios, however, are not independent of each other, as a cloud-based attack typically requires a sequence of steps as depicted in Figure 5. Once a victim is spotted, *address deanonymization* allows shifting the attack to being launched from within the cloud. Afterwards, targeted placement of a malicious instance next to a victim can be checked by means of *coresidency detection* technologies before the final attack, e.g., a covert channel or load measuring, is started.

6 PROTECTION STRATEGIES

Malicious cloud users are able to cause serious harm to cloud providers and other customers. The described attacks exploit the fact that sharing a physical node's networking capability means one instance's performance is dependent on its neighbor's behavior. Outgoing packets from instances have to be multiplexed before being sent onto the physical network, because a network interface card is only able to send one packet at a certain point in time. Likewise, only one packet at a time can be received, and these packets have to be demultiplexed to the respective guest instance.

Tackling the root cause of the issue and providing each virtual instance its own path to the physical network, i.e., its own physical network interface, would sufficiently mitigate the presented attacks. However, this approach contradicts the cloud-computing principles of resource sharing and flexibility, and so alternative mitigation methods are highly important. Nevertheless, the majority of mitigation strategies aim to tackle the problem in the hypervisor as the single guest instances are not aware of this issue.

Specifically, three types of mitigations are feasible. First, *randomization* prohibits deterministically inferring neighbor behavior. Second, adjusting *bandwidth assignment* hinders the influence of neighbor demands. Third, *add-on mitigation* as changes or supplements to today's infrastructure (Table 3).

Regarding randomization, two alternatives are available: Keller et al. (2011) propose random scheduling to prevent cache side channels. Instead of randomizing the scheduler, it is also possible to prevent accurate measurement. Vattikonda et al. (2011) claim that cache side channels require a timer resolution of tens of nanoseconds. The elimination of this resolution does not disrupt applications whilst preventing the side channels attacks, and adopts a solution already known from the *VAX* security kernel to the *Xen* hypervisor (Hu, 1992). However, randomization has up to now only been investigated for cache side channels. Nevertheless, Bates et al. (2012) advise randomly scheduling outgoing packets in order to hinder attacks. Fuzzy timing is infeasible for network side channels as a lower time resolution is sufficient. Eliminating this coarse solution would presumably also break ordinary benign applications. In general, the impact of randomizing solutions must be investigated carefully, because dependent on their time resolution they are able to seriously interfere with networking, e.g., TCP retransmission. Furthermore, they require a change of sensitive hypervisor code.

A reasoned parameterization of bandwidth limits per instance prevents heavy dependence on each other (Bates et al., 2012). By preventing overprovision, i.e., assigning in total less bandwidth to virtual instances than physical bandwidth available, it is guaranteed that every guest gets its quota. Further, borrowing bandwidth

Table 3 Inventory of potential countermeasures

Randomization	Bandwidth assignment	Add-on mitigation
Random scheduling (Keller et al., 2011; Bates et al., 2012)	Prevention on overprovisioning (Bates et al., 2012)	Rate limiting (Herzberg et al., 2013)
Reduction of timer resolution (Hu, 1992; Vattikonda et al., 2011)	Stringent time-division multiplexing	Blocking of internal traffic (Herzberg et al., 2013)

from other, currently idle nodes should be prevented, which removes an attacker's motivation to influence others to gain resources. However, this means less efficient resource use and less revenue for the provider who aims to minimize idle resources.

The radical opposite to randomized scheduling is stringent time-division multiplexing, which also enables mitigating isolation-based vulnerabilities. Time slices are assigned to virtual instances and its packets are only sent within these slices. This prevents the instances influencing each other and includes rate limiting and a maximum bandwidth automatically. While the implementation seems straightforward, questions arise when considering handling incoming packets as well as global synchronization.

Herzberg et al. (2013) additionally propose add-on mitigation strategies which do not involve changes in the hypervisor algorithms. Although they have the advantage of being easily applicable, they nevertheless bear the risk of not fully mitigating the issue. First, a number of attacks, such as address deanonymization and coresidency checking, require flooding. Sending a high number of packets can be prevented by the implementation of rate limiting, but must be careful not to negatively impact benign traffic. Some cloud providers already have a process for spam prevention which could be adopted: Only a limited number of mails are allowed to be sent from a cloud instance unless an unlimited quota is manually requested via a Web form. This request includes an explanatory statement which is checked by the provider. This approach could be adopted for benign applications which conflict with rate limiting. A further alternative is blocking internal communication between nodes of different accounts, a means of indirect rate limiting. The attacker has to use public addresses, the traffic is routed outside and back inside to the cloud network. Additionally, this way address deanonymization becomes futile.

The above-mentioned mitigation strategies help to prevent attacks where multiplexing one resource among various virtual instances plays a role, i.e., address deanonymization, coresidency checking, covert channels and load measuring. In contrast, resource-freeing attacks aim to redirect the neighbor to another resource, and so changing the networking scheduler would not mitigate the issue. Therefore, Varadarajan et al. (2012) propose smarter scheduling. The hypervisor could monitor the virtual instances and schedule them in order to prevent conflicts.

7 CONCLUSION

We have seen that isolation is one of the main mitigation strategies to protect instances against each other on single physical hosts. Looking at today's best-known open-source hypervisors provides an insight of how isolation is achieved: *Xen* is representative of paravirtulization, providing abstractions of devices to its instances using *Domain0*, while *KVM* is a full-virtualized hypervisor requiring specific hardware support and heavily reusing *Linux* code. Looking at networking in more detail, has revealed that scheduling and traffic shaping contribute to isolation.

However, today's hypervisors are still vulnerable to a number of attacks which exploit improper isolation, e. g., address deanonymization, coresidency detection, covert channels and resource-freeing attacks. These attacks exploit the fact that, in order to maintain performance, virtual instances share physical resources and are thus not fully independent of each other.

This leads to a general conclusion that there is a tradeoff between security and performance. Security aims to uncouple instances through isolation, but isolation comes at a cost. To guarantee a certain amount of resources to every instance, scheduling cannot be as seamless as it could be and has to dedicate quotas to certain instances. Idle resources cannot be lent out to others. Overprovision is frowned upon as the guarantees cannot be fulfilled in the worst-case scenario.

While isolation is a strong means of mitigation, it also challenges a number of the main principles of cloud computing. Cloud computing looks to maximize resource use and isolation comes always at a cost, leaving fewer resources for the actual desired computation. This leads to the conclusion that the scope of isolation is also dependent on its operational use. Low security applications might be satisfied with today's state-of-the-art and prefer cheaper prices. Those with high security needs will have to accept the costs to maintain their standards.

After years of increased attention, it is unlikely that cloud computing is just a passing trend and it seems certain to become a standard technology in the future. Nevertheless, challenges for the future remain and research is ever more necessary in contributing to hypervisor security. Besides analyzing hypervisors for further vulnerabilities, security in clouds has to be tackled with a holistic approach. Further, it has to be determined which amount of isolation is adequate for certain security levels. Last but not least, cloud customers still only have limited options to verify their cloud security. It is neither possible to verify easily whether a cloud provider acts compliantly, nor test an infrastructure's security in a comprehensive manner. Up to now, security seems to be taking a back seat to reducing costs.

REFERENCES

Adamczyk, B., Chydzinski, A., 2011. On the performance isolation across virtual network adapters in Xen. In: Cloud Computing 2011, the Second International Conference on Cloud Computing, GRIDs, and Virtualization, pp. 222–227.

Adams, K., Agesen, O., 2006. A comparison of software and hardware techniques for x86 virtualization. In: Proceedings of the 12th International Conference on Architectural Support for Programming Languages and Operating Systems, pp. 2–13.

Barharm, P., Dragovic, B., Fraser, K., Hand, S., Harris, T., Ho, A., Neugebauer, R., Pratt, I., Warfield, A., 2003. Xen and the art of virtualization. ACM SIGOPS Operat. Syst. Rev. 37 (5), 164–177.

Bates, A., Mood, B., Pletcher, J., Pruse, H., Valafor, M., Butler, K., 2012. Detecting co-residency with active traffic analysis techniques. In: Proceedings of the 2012 ACM Workshop on Cloud Computing Security, pp. 1–12.

Crosby, S., Brown, D., 2006. The virtualization reality. Queue 4 (10), 34–41.

Devera, M., 2002. HTB Linux queuing discipline manual—user guide, Available at: http://luxik.cdi.cz/~devik/qos/htb/manual/userg.htm [Accessed 21 July 2014].

DomU Support for Xen, 2014. Available at: http://wiki.xen.org/wiki/DomU_Support_for_Xen [Accessed 7 August 2014].

Drepper, U., 2008. The cost of virtualization. Queue 6 (1), 28–35.

Farley, B., Juels, A., Varadarajan, V., Ristenpart, T., Bowers, K.D., Swift, M., 2012. More for your money: exploiting performance heterogeneity in public clouds. In: Proceedings of the 3rd Symposium on Cloud Computing, pp. 20:1–20:14.

Fraser, K.A., 2005. Back-end driver for virtual network devices, Available at http://www.takatan.net/lxr/source/drivers/xen/netback/netback.c [Accessed 7th May 2014].

Goldberg, R.P., 1974. Survey of virtual machine research. IEEE Comput. 7 (3), 34–45.

Herzberg, A., Shulman, H., Ullrich, J., Weippl, E., 2013. Cloudoscopy: services discovery and topology mapping. In: Proceedings of the 2013 ACM Workshop on Cloud Computing Security, pp. 113–122.

Hu, W.-M., 1992. Reducing timing channels with fuzzy time. J. Comput. Secur. 1 (3), 233–254.

Hwang, J., Zhen, S., Wu, F., Wood, T., 2013. A component-based performance comparison of four hypervisors. In: 2013 IFIP/IEEE International Symposium on Integrated Network Management, pp. 269–276.

Keller, E., Szefer, J., Rexford, J., Lee, R.B., 2011. Eliminating the hypervisor attack surface for a more secure cloud. In: Proceedings of the 18th ACM conference on Computer and Communication Security (CCS), pp. 401–412.

Kivity, A., Kamay, Y., Laor, D., Lublin, U., Liguori, A., 2007. KVM: the Linux virtual machine monitor. In: Linux Symposium, pp. 225–230.

KVM, Kernel Based Virtual Machine, Available at: http://linux-kvm.org [Accessed 6 August 2014].

libvirt, Virtualization API. Domain XML format, Available at: http://libvirt.org/formatdomain.html [Accessed 4 August 2014].

Ou, Z., Zhuang, H., Nurminen, J.K., Ylä-Jääski, A., Hui, P., 2012. Exploiting hardware heterogeneity within the same instance type of amazon EC2. In: 4th USENIX Workshop on Hot Topics in Cloud Computing (Hot Cloud).

Pearce, M., Zeadally, S., Hunt, R., 2013. Virtualization: issues, security threats, and solutions. ACM Comput. Surv. 45 (2), 17.

Popek, G., Goldberg, R., 1974. Formal requirements for virtualizable third generation architecture. Commun. ACM 17 (7), 412–421.

Pratt, I., Fraser, K., Hand, S., Limpach, C., Warfield, A., 2005. Xen 3.0 and the art of virtualization. In: Linux Symposiump. 65.

Pu, X., Liu, L., Mei, Y., Sivathanu, S., Koh, Y., Pu, C., 2010. Understanding performance interference of I/O workload in virtualized cloud environments. In: 2010 IEEE 3rd International Conference on Cloud Computing (CLOUD), pp. 51–58.

Redhat, 2008. KVM—Kernel Based Virtual Machine, Whitepaper.

Redhat. Limit network bandwidth for a Xen guest, Available at: https://access.redhat.com/documentation/en-US/Red_Hat_Enterprise_Linux/5/html/Virtualization/sect-Virtualization-Tips_and_tricks-Limit_network_bandwidth_for_a_Xen_guest.html [Accessed 5 May 2014].

Ristenpart, T., Tromer, E., Shacham, H., Savage, S., 2009. Hey, you, get off of my cloud: exploring information leakage in third-party compute clouds. In: Proceedings of the 16th ACM conference on Computer and Communication Security (CCS), pp. 199–212.

Rose, R., 2004. Survey of system virtualization techniques, Available at: http://www.robertwrose.com/vita/rose-virtualization.pdf [Accessed 6 August 2014].

US-CERT, 2007. System Vulnerability Summary for CVE-2007-4993, Available at: http://web.nvd.nist.gov/view/vuln/detail?vulnId=CVE-2007-4993 [Accessed 28 August 2014].

US-CERT, 2010. System Vulnerability Summary for CVE-2010-2240, Available at: http://web.nvd.nist.gov/view/vuln/detail?vulnId=CVE-2010-2240 [Accessed 28 August 2014].

Varadarajan, V., Kooburat, T., Farley, B., Ristenpart, T., Swift, M., 2012. Resource-freeing attacks: improve your cloud performance (at your neighbor's expense). In: Proceedings of the 2012 ACM Conference on Computer and Communications Security, pp. 281–292.

Vattikonda, B.C., Das, S., Shacham, H., 2011. Eliminating fine grained timers in Xen. In: Proceedings of the 2011 ACM Workshop on Cloud Computing Security, pp. 41–46.

VMware, Available at: http://vmware.com [Accessed 6 August 2014].

Wu, Z., Xu, Z., Wang, H., 2012. Whispers in the hyper-space: high-speed covert channel attacks in the clouds. In: Usenix Security Symposium, pp. 159–173.

Xen, Available at: http://xenproject.org [Accessed 6 August 2014].

Xi, S., Li, C., Lu, C., Gill, C., 2013. Prioritizing local inter-domain communication in Xen. In: IEEE/ACM 21st International Symposium on Quality of Service (IWQoS), pp. 1–10.

Xu, Y., Musgrave, Z., Noble, B., Bailey, M., 2013. Bobtail: avoiding long tails in the cloud. In: 10th Usenix Symposium on Networked Systems Design and Implementation (NSDI), pp. 329–341.

Zhang, Y., Juels, A., Oprea, A., Reiter, M.K., 2011. Homealone: co-residency detection in the cloud via side-channel analysis. In: Proceedings of the 2011 IEEE Symposium on Security and Privacy, pp. 313–328.

Protecting digital identity in the cloud

7

Clare Sullivan
School of Law, University of South Australia, Adelaide, Australia

1 INTRODUCTION

Technological advances have created a whole new environment for interaction. As dealings previously conducted in person are replaced by dealings without personal interaction, the requirement to provide digital identity for transactions has increased. Now digital identity is poised to assume an even greater role as governments around the world fully digitalize government services and transactions.

This is revolutionizing service delivery and the way in which government interacts and transacts with its citizens. While there are many efficiency and cost benefits, there are also significant ramifications. One of the most important ramifications is the emerging importance of digital identity.

Historically, identity has been a rather nebulous notion, especially at common law.[1] For contractual purposes, for example, identity has largely been in the background as the law focused on issues such as whether there was the necessary meeting of the minds, informed consent, and arms-length dealing. This focus, which mainly developed in response to commercial practice in the nineteenth century and early twentieth century, has led to uncertainty about the role of identity in commercial dealings.[2] Now identity, in the form of digital identity, has emerged from the shadows. While a concept of digital identity for transactions has been emergent for many years for private transactions using credit and debit cards, for example, the full implications of digital identity are now becoming apparent as governments

---

[1]Identity rights are generally more developed in civil law jurisdictions like France and under German and Dutch doctrine which has influenced other civil law systems such as in South Africa. Identity is recognized as an interest in personality under civil law. See, for example, in South Africa, Neethling, J., Potgeiter, J., Visser, P., 2005. Neethling's Law of Personality, 36.

[2]As one commentator observes in relation to identity, "much legal doctrine obscures the salience of identity qua identity, though when confronted directly with the issue, the law does give substance to the importance of identity." See Brookes, R.R.W., 2006. Incorporating race. Columbia Law Rev. 106, 2023–2097.

move services and transactions[3] online[4] This chapter analyzes the functions and nature of digital identity in this context, considers its vulnerability to error, and the consequences, particularly for individuals. May need to define what is digital identity in the first place.

Digital identity is an identity which is composed of information[5] stored and transmitted in digital form. Digital identity is all the information digitally recorded about an individual, i.e., a natural person that is accessible under the particular scheme. Digital identity consists of two components. The first component is a small set of defined, static information which must be presented for a transaction. Invariably, this transaction identity consists of an individual's full name, gender, date of birth, and a piece of identifying information which is typically a numerical identifier and/or a signature. The second component is a larger collection of more detailed "other information" which sits behind transaction identity in the database. This other information is updated on an on-going basis to record transaction history and can be used to profile an individual.

In many ways, transaction identity is the most important part of this digital identity because of its transactional functions which are described later in this chapter and because it is most susceptible to system error. In this chapter, system error is used in its widest sense to describe any malfunction whereby an otherwise authentic and valid digital identity is not recognized by the system.[6] This may be a spontaneous malfunction or one induced by fraud, or the malfunction may be the result of all or part of an individual's digital identity that is being used by another person. In most instances, the latter will involve dishonesty but not always.[7]

As explained in this chapter, the nature and functions of the part of digital identity required for transactions, i.e., transaction identity, mean that impact of system error on an innocent individual can be profound. This is because transaction identity directly implicates the individual linked to that identity on record, irrespective of whether or not that person actually used the digital identity to transact. Transactional rights and duties, including those arising under contract, attach to the digital identity through transaction identity. If there is subsequent default, the transacting entity will, as a matter of practicality, and arguably law,[8] look to the person linked to that identity under the scheme.

The transaction will also form part of the other information which comprises digital identity. As mentioned earlier, this other information profiles an individual. It can

---

[3]A transaction in this context is any dealing for which an individual is required to use digital identity. A transaction may be between an individual and a government department or agency or with a private sector entity if that is permitted under the scheme, and can range from an enquiry to a contract.

[4]Digital identity is all the information digitally recorded about an individual—i.e., a natural person—that is accessible under the particular scheme. "Information" includes "data."

[5]"Information" includes "data."

[6]This may be caused by spontaneous system failure or the malfunction may be caused by malware.

[7]The other person may use an individual's identity accidentally such as by inadvertently keying-in incorrect information, for example, though these instances would be comparatively rare.

[8]For a detailed discussion of the legal nature of transaction identity, see Sullivan, C., 2009. Digital identity—the 'legal person'? Comput. Law Secur. Rev. 25 (2), 227.

be used for both commercial and law enforcement purposes. Just as a transacting entity will look to the person linked to the identity under the scheme, so too will law enforcement authorities. As is discussed below, system error can result in a spurious record and that record can affect an individual's ability to transact under the scheme and it can have serious and long-term impact, affecting reputation and legal and commercial standing. This is more than just a remote possibility. It is a direct consequence of the architecture of the types of the scheme.

By requiring that an individual have a digital identity to transact, obviating the need for personal interaction and by automating transactions, these schemes establish a revolutionary means of transacting. They herald a new era of digital citizenship but in doing so that fundamentally change the balance of responsibility and accountability between government and citizens. Individuals, the most vulnerable sector with comparably less access to resources and information, are most affected when the system does not operate as intended.

Section 2 examines this digital identity, its functions, and its implications especially for individuals in the context of cloud computing as governments increase their use of, and reliance on, the cloud.

This development highlights the need for more effective regulation of cross-border data so the following sections of the chapter examine this emerging issue, particularly whether the focus should be on regulating cross-border data disclosure, rather than data transfer. Internationally, cross-border data protection, including the new proposal for the European Union (EU), continues to regulate cross-border data transfer, whereas the new Australia approach now regulates cross-border data disclosure. Sections 3 and 4 examine the international approach which in this respect is also supported by the United States and Asia Pacific Economic Cooperation (APEC), and compares it to the Australian regime in its ability to protect the integrity of an individual's digital identity.

May need to streamline and bring into sharper focus what is it that you want to explore and want to write about—too many themes in the introduction.

2 THE RISE OF DIGITAL IDENTITY

A specific digital identity is now emerging as governments around the world[9] move their services and transactions online. This digital identity is the primary means by which a natural person can access these services which range from social security benefits and health care to tax filing.[10] Example of what kind of information stored is important to illustrate the concept.

---

[9]The new scheme being rolled out in India is the most recent example of a comprehensive scheme. See IGovernment. India plans multi-purpose national ID card for citizens. igovernment.in, August 24, 2013.

[10]This chapter focuses on the consequences for individuals, i.e., natural persons.

Of the countries which are incrementally implementing these schemes, Australia is notable for its candor. The Australian government has now unequivocally stated that Australia is moving to what it calls "digital citizenship."[11] In a Discussion e-Paper released in 2011, the Australian Government acknowledges the importance of digital identity and the significant implications in the event of it being compromised:

> *In an era where our online identity is central to accessing information and services, ensuring the integrity of that identity is increasingly important. The loss or compromise of our online identity can have wide-ranging implications, including financial loss, emotional distress and reputational damage[12]*

Significantly, the paper also states that:

> *... there would be value in revisiting the distribution of responsibility among individuals, businesses and governments...Developing a common understanding of a model of accountable and responsible digital citizenship—a digital social contract—may need to be part of the debate about Australia's digital future.[13]*

In many countries, digital identity will soon be the primary means of access as government services are progressively moved online and into a digital format. There is a general requirement to use digital identity to access government services.[14] What is the linkage for this paragraph to the below?

The digital identity schemes used by governments around the world are necessarily based on the premise of one person: one digital identity. This alone is a major change, especially for common law jurisdictions in which identity traditionally has not been recognized as a distinct legal concept. How about electronic transactions in countries like Singapore under the common law? In fact, the government e-service has been ranked ahead of United States—read the Electronic Transactions Act (ETA) of Singapore to see how they handle as we are a common law country. Historically, there has been no general requirement for one legal identity. One person: one identity

---

[11]*Ibid.* The scheme is now well underway, its foundations being laid primarily through Medicare, the national health care scheme which covers all registered Australians and eligible residents. In June 2010, e.g., the Coalition supported the Labor government's proposal to compulsorily assign (with some minor exceptions) a 16-digit individual identifier to every Australian resident on the Medicare database on July 1, 2010. In relation to this Australian Individual Healthcare Identifier (IHI) which has been assigned to Australians, see the Office of the Privacy Commissioner, privacy.gov.au, September 11, 2010.

[12]*Ibid*,10.

[13]*Ibid.*

[14]While it may seem that it is still possible for an individual to transact outside the new digital system, that is generally not the case. For example, during the current transition phase, a paper tax return can still be lodged in Australia rather than using the e-filing portal. However, this is illusory. All data must now be entered into, and processed by, the digital system. If a paper tax return is filed, the information on the document is scanned into, and processed by, the digital system.

has also not been an essential commercial requirement. It has not been a requirement of private schemes like Visa credit and debit card transactions,[15] for example. For a government scheme, however, it is essential. Digitalization of government services and transactions is driven by the need to reduce costs and to increase efficiency in service delivery but most importantly, by the need to reduce fraud. A government scheme requires uniqueness and exclusivity. Consequently, an individual can legitimately have only one digital identity under this type of scheme.

The digital identity used for government services will likely set the standard for transactions with the private sector. That has been the experience internationally in the advanced digital economy of Estonia for example, and it is an outcome which is probably inevitable from a practical point of view.[16] In effect, it means that the digital identity for government transactions is the primary means by which the individual is recognized and can enter into commercial transactions. This transition is well underway in the United States, the United Kingdom, Australia, and many Asian countries but is most advanced in Europe, with Estonia the leading example of a country in which most commercial transactions require digital identity.

2.1 COMPOSITION AND FUNCTIONS OF DIGITAL IDENTITY

Digital identity in this context has specific composition and transactional functions which make its accuracy and integrity critical.

A feature of all schemes which require digital identity for transactions is that they consist of two sets of information—a small set of defined information which must be presented for a transaction, i.e., transaction identity; and the larger collection of more detailed "other information" which is updated on an on-going basis. This architecture can be depicted diagrammatically in Figure 1).

These two sets of information collectively comprise digital identity, but they are different in composition and function.

Because of its nature and functionality transaction identity is the most important part of digital identity and it is also most vulnerable to system error as defined in this chapter. Transaction identity is comparatively static, with much of the information being established at birth.[17] It typically consists of full name, gender, date of birth,

---

[15]An individual may have more than one credit card with more than one transaction identity. A simple example of this is an individual who has a credit card for personal use in the name John Smith which is billed to his home address and another card even from the same credit card company for business transactions in the name of Dr. J. M. Smith billed to his work address and to which is a different customer number and PIN is assigned.

[16]This is a feature of similar schemes in other countries. It is a stated feature of the new national identity scheme being rolled out in India and it was a feature of the scheme planned for the United Kingdom which was extensively documented. See for example, United Kingdom Information Commissioner. The Identity Cards Bill–The Information Commissioner's Concerns (June 2005), ico.gov.uk, May 10, 2006.

[17]Other than in exceptional cases such as gender reassignment, for example, the information which is most commonly subject to change is surname, mainly for women in the event of marriage.

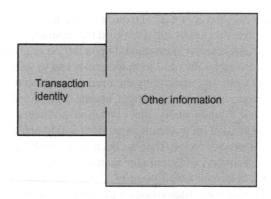

FIGURE 1

The relationship between transaction identity and the other information, which collectively make up digital identity under the scheme.

and at least one piece of what is referred to as "identifying information" which is most often a signature or numerical identifier.[18] The information which comprises transaction identity is largely public and is not of a nature which naturally seems to attract privacy protection.[19] Most significantly, transaction identity is not just information. As discussed below, it is functional.

The information which constitutes transaction identity is fundamentally different from the larger body of other information which sits behind it. That larger body of information tells a story about a person and that is its sole purpose. It is also dynamic. It is augmented on an on-going basis. Even information which at first sight seems largely administrative adds to the profile. This is also information which is not generally in the public domain. It is generally considered to be personal information which is typically protected by privacy and data protection regulation in most jurisdictions, including Australia, United Kingdom, United States of America, and in the EU. Why is this passage relevant? Access to the other information is primarily via transaction identity. The system is designed so that transaction identity is the access point and transaction identity has a gate-keeper role. Transaction identity links digital identity to an individual through the identifying information (Figure 2).[20]

These digital identity schemes depend on two processes—first, authentication of identity, and second, verification of identity. Both processes are founded on the integrity of transaction identity.

---

[18]In some schemes such as those in Europe and Asia, identifying information also includes biometrics, as well as a head and shoulders photograph. However, even in these schemes, biometrics is not currently required for most transactions.

[19]While being in the public domain does not necessary preclude privacy protection, the information must be of an intimate nature to attract protection. The information which constitutes transaction identity is generally not intimate in that sense.

[20]This is clear from scheme documentation. See, for example, Australian Government, Submission to the Senate Enquiry on the Human Services (Enhanced Service Delivery) Bill 2007, 33 and 36.

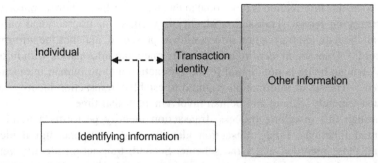

FIGURE 2

The relationship between an individual and digital identity.

The information collected when an individual is registered under the scheme is used to authenticate identity in the sense that it is used to prove authenticity. The identifying information is used to link an individual to the registered digital identity. Typically, the identifying information is a number,[21] a handwritten signature, and sometimes also a head and shoulders photo. Some schemes include biometrics as part of the identifying information. The biometrics[22] typically used are 10 fingerprints, two iris scans, and a face scan.[23] The identifying information is regarded as being associated inseparably with that individual. Once authenticated, the identity is recorded in the system.

Transaction identity, the defined, limited set of information which determines identity for transactional purposes, is then used to verify transactions.[24] Invariably, full name, gender, date of birth, and a piece of identifying information will be required to transact. Not all the recorded information need to be used for every transaction. A feature of the scheme is that the information varies, to an extent, depending on the requirements of the transacting entity. The identifying information most commonly required is a signature and/or a numerical identifier.

---

[21]In Australia, a 16-digit numerical identifier was assigned to every Australian resident on the Medicare database on July 1, 2010. See the Office of the Privacy Commissioner, privacy.gov.au, September 11, 2013.

[22]Depending on the nature and value of the dealing, not all or even any of these biometrics may be required for a transaction. For high level, high-value transactions, biometrics may be required as part of transaction identity but the primary role of the identifying information is to link an individual to transaction identity.

[23]Photograph is distinguished from a face scan. A face scan is a biometric. In schemes that use a face scan, the scan is not used to verify identity for all transactions. Many transactions only involve matching the appearance of the person with the photograph.

[24]Note that this is the way these terms, i.e., authentication and verification, are typically defined for the purposes of a national digital identity scheme. It is the approach used for the new Indian scheme, for example. Authentication and verification are often misused in describing the functions of transaction identity.

As a set, this information is functional in that it enables the system to transact with the identity on record. Transaction identity is verified for transactional purposes when all the required transaction information as presented, matches the information on record.[25] Transaction identity is verified by matching information with information. A human being is not central to the transaction and no human interaction is required.[26] The set of information required to establish transaction identity can be provided remotely without any human involvement at that time.

Through this matching process, transaction identity performs a number of sequential functions. First, transaction identity singles out one digital identity from all those recorded under the scheme. Second, transaction identity verifies that identity by determining whether there is a match between all the transaction identity information as presented, with that on record.[27] These two steps enable the system to recognize and then transact with that digital identity as depicted in Figure 3.

Under the scheme, there is an important distinction between identification[28] and identity. Identification is just one part of the two processes used to establish identity for a transaction. Although in some respects transaction identity may seem to replicate the traditional function of identity credentials, there is an important difference in the role played by human beings and information. Unlike traditional identity

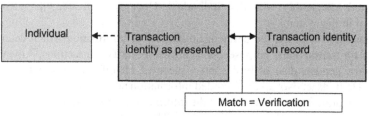

FIGURE 3

To enable transactions under the scheme, the transaction identity presented must match the identity on record.

---

[25]"Verify" as used in these schemes accords with its definition in the Merriam Webster Dictionary: "to establish the truth, accuracy, or reality of <verify the claim>."

[26]The set of information required to establish transaction identity can be provided remotely without any human involvement at that time.

[27]Such as name, date, and place of birth as well as with signature, photograph, and biometrics but bear in mind that not all transactions require all the identifying information. Routine transactions may only require matching photo or signature. Many low-value transactions such as those using the new Paywave technology do not require a signature or photo check.

[28]Note that separately, the information which comprises transaction identity is of limited use in identifying an individual. For example, unless it is especially unusual, name alone will not single out an individual from a population, nor will name, gender, and date of birth usually be all that is required to identify a person.

papers, the information which comprises transaction identity plays the critical role in the transaction, not the individual.[29] Digital identity does not merely support a claim to identity. Digital identity, specifically transaction identity, is the actor in the transaction. This function distinguishes transaction identity.[30]

Although the assumption is that there is a reaching behind transaction identity to deal with a person, the system does not actually operate in that way. The primary role of the identifying information is to link the registered digital identity to a person. The individual who is assumed to be represented by that identity is connected to transaction identity by the identifying information. However, this link is relatively tenuous.

A human being is not central to, or necessary, for the transaction. Transaction identity enables the transaction. The interaction is machine to machine, based on matching datasets. As a matter of fact, if not law,[31] the transaction is with the digital identity, not a person. If all the transaction identity information as presented, matches the information on record, then the system automatically authorizes dealings with that digital identity as depicted in Figure 4.

Within the scheme parameters, the system can "act and will for itself"[32] to recognize the defined set of information which comprises transaction identity and

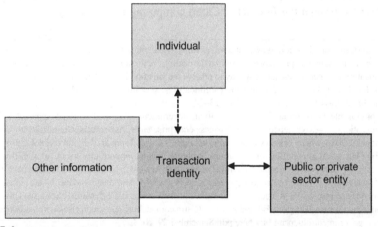

FIGURE 4

The transaction is actually with the transaction identity, not the individual.

---

[29]The information may be presented remotely and even automatically using computer programming, without any active involvement by an individual at the time of a transaction, though of course some human involvement is required at some stage.

[30]It distinguishes transaction identity from passports, particularly biometric passports, which are now very close to transaction identity in content, though not yet in functionality for commercial transactions.

[31]See, n 8 above.

[32]Derham, D.,1958. Theories of Legal Personality. In: Webb, L.C., (Ed.), Legal Personality and Political Pluralism, vol. 1, 14.

then transact with that identity.[33] This has significant consequences for the government as scheme administrator, for public and private sector entities using the scheme but the individual bears the most direct and significant consequences. This is because transaction identity directly implicates the individual linked to the digital identity by the identifying information,[34] and why it is important to protect the integrity of digital identity, especially now that governments are increasingly using cloud computing for their e-services and transactions. How is this link to the below passage?—sudden introduction of cloud computing?

3 THE RISE OF CLOUD COMPUTING

The cloud is now an integral part of next-generation government in many countries.[35] The widespread use of cloud computing by government and businesses has prompted the EC to describe cloud computing as providing large scale computing services as a service to the data economy in the same way as power plants supply the manufacturing industry."[36]

In essence, cloud computing is Internet-based computing. Services such as servers, storage, and applications are delivered to an organization's computers and devices through the Internet.[37] Cloud computing is commonly used to refer to

---

[33]The significance of this becomes evident when an otherwise legitimate digital identity is not recognized by the system. In this situation, protocol requires that the dealings be authorized with the individual, not with the digital identity. In other words, the only way to resolve the situation is to go outside the scheme.

[34]For a detailed analysis of the contractual implications, see Sullivan, C, 2012. Digital identity and mistake. Int. J. Law Inform. Technol. 20, 223–241.

[35]See, for example, in Australia, Telstra Corporation. Government: Integrated National Approach to Secure Communications. www.telstra.com.au/business-enterprise/enterprise-solutions/industries/government, September 29, 2013, where Telstra Corporation explains, "The rapid spread of digital technology and cloud computing has given government organizations an unprecedented opportunity for creating citizen-based online services, while both raising the standard of service delivery and reducing its costs. Telstra calls it "Connected Government," where government agencies at every level—federal, state, and local—are learning to be more flexible and responsive in meeting changing social and demographic dynamics. See also, Telstra Corporation. Government Blueprint Brochure. www.telstra.com.au/business-enterprise/download/document/enterprise-government-blueprint-brochure.pdf, September 29, 2013.

[36]European Commission. Communication from the Commission to the European Committee, Parliament, the Council, the European Economic and Social Committee, and the Committee of the Regions: Towards a thriving data-driven economy, SWD (2014) 214 final, 2.

[37]The generally accepted official definition of cloud computing is that of the National Institute of Standards and Technology (NIST), an agency of the US Department of Commerce published in September 2011. After, in its own words, "years in the works and 15 drafts," the final NIST definition is: "Cloud computing is a model for enabling ubiquitous, convenient, on-demand network access to a shared pool of configurable computing resources that can be rapidly provisioned and released with minimal management effort or service provider interaction," See National Institute of Standards and Technology. The NIST Definition of Cloud Computing. www.nist.gov/itl/csd/cloud-102511.cfm, September 24, 2013. See also the definition used by the Article 29 Working Party on the Protection of individuals with regard to the Processing of Personal Data: "[C]loud computing consists of a set of technologies and service models that focus on the Internet-based use and delivery of IT applications, processing capability, storage and memory space." See Article 29 Data Protection Working Party, "*Opinion 05/2012 on Cloud Computing*," 4.

network-based services which to the user, give the appearance of being provided by a hardware server but instead the server is simulated by software.[38] Cloud computing does away with the constraints and costs of the traditional computing environment and because of its flexibility and cost effectiveness, cloud computing has been embraced by government and businesses.

Cloud computing, by its nature, presents a significant risk to the integrity of digital identity. In its opinion on Cloud Computing adopted on 1 July 2012, the Article 29 Working Party on the Protection of individuals with regard to the Processing of Personal Data (Article 29 Working Party) highlights the range of cloud computing services[39]:

> *There is a wide gamut of services offered by cloud providers ranging from virtual processing systems (which replace and/or work alongside conventional servers under the direct control of the controller) to services supporting application development and advanced hosting, up to web-based software solutions that can replace applications conventionally installed on the personal computers of end-users. This includes text processing applications, agendas and calendars, filing systems for online document storage and outsourced email solutions.[40]*

The likelihood that the same digital identity will be used for government and private sector dealings increases the probability that it will be stored and/or processed in the cloud.

3.1 THE IMPACT OF CLOUD COMPUTING AND CROSS-BORDER DATA

Cloud computing has made data storage and access cost effective and as a consequence, it has changed the nature of cross-border data. As observed by Viviane Reding, Vice-President of the EC, EU Justice Commissioner,

> *Our world is no longer defined by physical borders. Data races from Barcelona to Bangalore. It is processed in Dublin, stored in California and accessed in Milan. In the digital age, the transfer of data to third countries has become an important part of daily life. And this affects both businesses and citizens.[41]*

---

[38]The Cloud is an enabler. Mobile IT, social IT, and big data, for example, are all cloud based.

[39]The Article 29 Working Party is an independent advisory body on data protection and privacy, set up under Article 29 of the *Data Protection Directive 95/46/EC*. It is composed of representatives from the national data protection authorities of the EU Member States, the European Data Protection Supervisor, and the EC. Its tasks are described in Article 30 of Directive 95/46/EC and Article 15 of Directive 2002/58/EC.

[40]Article 29 Data Protection Working Party Opinion 05/2012 on Cloud Computing, 4.

[41]Viviane Reding, Vice-President of the EC, EU Justice Commissioner Binding Corporate Rules: unleashing the potential of the digital single market and cloud computing, IAPP Europe Data Protection Congress Paris, 29 November 2011.

Data does not have to be stored or processed in another country or transferred across a national border in the traditional sense to be cross-border data. This is an important development considering the functions of transaction identity and the consequences of system error. While cloud computing has many benefits, it has inherent risks. On 1 July 2012, the Article 29 Working Party in its opinion on Cloud Computing[42] stated that,

> Despite the acknowledged benefits of cloud computing in both economic and societal terms, ... the wide scale deployment of cloud computing services can trigger a number of data protection risks, mainly a lack of control over personal data as well as insufficient information with regard to how, where and by whom the data is being processed/sub-processed. These risks need to be carefully assessed by public bodies and private enterprises when they are considering engaging the services of a cloud provider[43]

The opinion lists the specific risks of personal data processing using cloud computing, in two broad categories: control and lack of transparency,

> Lack of control
> By committing personal data to the systems managed by a cloud provider, cloud clients may no longer be in exclusive control of this data and cannot deploy the technical and organizational measures necessary to ensure the availability, integrity, confidentiality, transparency, isolation, intervenability and portability of the data.
> Lack of information on processing (transparency)
> Insufficient information about a cloud service's processing operations poses a risk to controllers as well as to data subjects because they might not be aware of potential threats and risks and thus cannot take measures they deem appropriate [44]

These risks can undermine the integrity and functionality of digital identity. A digital identity scheme is characterized by the enduring nature of the identity information required for transactions and its unique association with that individual. The transacting entity will, as a matter of practicality, if not law, look to the person linked to that identity.

The challenge then faced by that individual can have two aspects. Difficulty can arise in that individual establishing that "I am who I say I am" and in establishing "I am not who the record says I am." This is so if the set of information which constitutes transaction identity is used by another person or if the transaction identity information is misrecorded, misread, or incorrectly linked as a result of system malfunction or fraud. Another person's signature, for example, may be being linked with the full name, gender, and date of birth of individual A. In this situation, individual A will be on record as entering into the transaction. The person identified as

---

[42]Above n 40, 8.
[43]Above n 40, 2.
[44]*Ibid.*

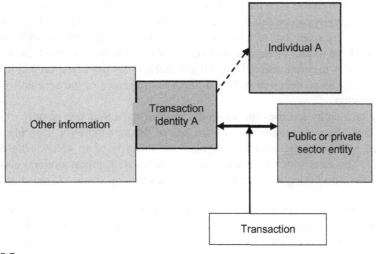

FIGURE 5

The transaction is with transaction identity A and that identity is linked to individual A.

doing the transaction is individual A and written records of the dealing will also refer to individual A as depicted in Figure 5.

This scenario illustrates the practical and legal implications for an innocent individual. Individual A must establish that he/she did not enter into the transaction and this can present significant difficulty. Considering that transactions can be conducted from anywhere in the world, 24 h a day, individual A may not be able to establish that he or she did not enter into this transaction. Individual A may not even become aware of the transaction until much later, such as when an item appears on an account or overdue notice.

The impact on the innocent individual is immediate though, even if he/she is not immediately aware of it. The other information, which makes up digital identity, records transactions on an on-going basis. That information is used to monitor and establish the basis on which an individual can continue to transact under the scheme. Protection protocols programmed into the system can cause considerable harm to an innocent individual. If wrong-doing is suspected or there are suspicions that the digital identity has been compromised, the system can automatically suspend transactions with transaction identity A. Not being able to transact under the system goes beyond frustration and inconvenience. In a world where digital identity is required for everything from employment applications and tax filing, to welfare payments and health care, being unable to use the system, even temporarily, can have major consequences.

There can be even more serious implications. The other information which makes up digital identity can also be used to profile an individual for other purposes. If, for example, transaction identity A is used by individual B to order material which can be used for bomb making or to download bomb-making instructions, that activity can be detected through routine monitoring. It could lead to individual A being suspected of terrorist activity. The consequences for individual A can range from impact on reputation, to criminal charges, both of which can be very difficult for A to refute and defend. This scenario is far from fanciful and it is not just an unfortunate occurrence. It is a direct consequence of the scheme's design and operation.

Digital identity schemes operate on the premise that transaction identity will only be used by the person on record. Regardless of whether the error is accidental or induced by misuse, the error compromises the integrity of an individual's digital identity. The ease with which data can now be moved, processed, and accessed around the world using the cloud, heightens the concern, as the EC noted in 2013:

> *The rapid pace of technological change and globalisation have profoundly transformed the scale and way personal data is collected, accessed, used and transferred. There are several good reasons for reviewing and improving the current rules, which were adopted in 1995: the increasingly globalised nature of data flows, the fact that personal information is collected, transferred and exchanged in huge quantities, across continents and around the globe in milliseconds and the arrival of cloud computing. In particular, cloud computing—where individuals access computer resources remotely, rather than owning them locally—poses new challenges for data protection authorities, as data can and does move from one jurisdiction to another, including outside the EU, in an instant. In order to ensure a continuity of data protection, the rules need to be brought in line with technological developments[45]*

Cross-border data is currently regulated in the European Union (EU) under the Data Protection Directive 95/46 EU of the European Parliament and of the European Council of 24 October 1995 (Directive). The Directive protects EU citizens in relation to processing of their personal data and the movement of that data,[46] and covers the use of cloud computing services.[47]

Article 25.1 of the Directive prohibits the transfer of personal data to a third county (i.e., a country or territory outside the European Economic Area (EEA)) unless that third country provides an adequate level of protection for the rights and freedoms of data subjects in relation to the processing of personal data. An organization is prohibited from transferring data about EU citizens, whether they

---

[45]EC. How Will the EU's Reform Adapt Data Protection Rules to New Technological Developments? 1 ec.europa.eu/justice/data-protection/document/review2012/factsheets/8_en.pdf, September 29, 2013.

[46]The reference to data is of no consequence because the definitions under the Directive and the Australian Privacy Act include both data and information.

[47]This is confirmed by the Article 29 Working Party in its opinion on cloud computing. In that opinion, the Article 29 Working Party also confirmed that the e-privacy Directive 2002/58/EC (as revised by 2009/136/EC) also applies to the processing of personal data in connection with the provision of publicly available electronic communications services in public communications networks (telecom operators) and is relevant if those services are provided by means of a cloud solution. See above n 40, 6.

are employees, customers, or other contacts, unless there is compliance with Article 25. This means that organizations are prohibited from sending personal information outside the EEA except where adequate protections have been put in place, or where the destination country has been pre-approved as having adequate data protection.

Data transfers to third countries can occur in many circumstances, such as where an EU-based business relocates functions to subsidiaries outside the EEA, establishes an offshore shared service center which processes HR or payroll data, for example, hosts offshore and/or processes data as part of an outsourcing agreement with a third-party supplier or uses cloud computing. The onus is on the data controller to ensure that there is compliance with the 8th data protection principle in relation to any cross-border data transfer of personal data.

In January 2012, the EC proposed "comprehensive reform of the EU's 1995 data protection rules to strengthen online privacy rights and boost Europe's digital economy through a global standard[48]:

". . ..the Commission is proposing a system which will ensure a level of protection for data transferred out of the EU similar to that within the EU. This will include clear rules defining when EU law is applicable to companies or organisations established outside the EU, in particular by clarifying that whenever the organisation's activities are related to the offering of goods or services to EU individuals or to the monitoring of their behaviour, EU rules will apply. The Commission is proposing a streamlined procedure for so-called "adequacy decisions" that will allow the free flow of information between the EU and non-EU countries. An adequacy decision is an acknowledgement that a given non-EU country ensures an adequate level of data protection through its domestic law or international commitments. Such adequacy decisions will be taken at European level on the basis of explicit criteria which will also apply to police cooperation and criminal justice.

Businesses operating globally will benefit from clear and explicit rules for making use of binding corporate rules, as well as from the fact that prior authorisation will no longer be needed for transfers covered by binding corporate rules or standard contractual clauses. The proposal will promote effective international cooperation for data protection enforcement between the Commission, European data protection authorities and authorities outside the EU, through investigative assistance, information exchange and complaint referral. Lastly, by promoting global standards, the Commission's proposals will ensure continued European leadership in protecting data flows around the world."[49]

---

[48]EC. Commission Proposes a Comprehensive Reform of the Data Protection Rules, Brussels, January 25, 2012. ec.europa.eu/justice/newsroom/data-protection/news/120125_en.htm, September 29, 2013. See also, EC. Proposal for a Regulation of the European Parliament and of the Council on the Protection of Individuals with Regard to the Processing of Personal Data and on the Free Movement of Such Data (General Data Protection Regulation) (25 January 2012). ec.europa.eu/justice/data-protection/document/review2012/com_2012_11_en.pdf, September 29, 2013.
[49]EC. How will the EU's Data Protection Reform Simplify the Existing Rules?. ec.europa.eu/justice/data-protection/index_en.htm, September 29, 2013.

The key changes proposed by the Commission are:

- "Clear rules on when EU law applies to data controllers outside the EU, in particular, by specifying that whenever controller's activities are related to the offering of goods or services to EU individuals, or to the monitoring of their behavior, EU rules will apply.
- Streamlined adequacy decisions that allow free flow of information between the EU and non-member countries taken at European level on the basis of explicit criteria, and which will also apply to police cooperation and criminal justice.
- Making legitimate transfers easier and less burdensome by reinforcing and simplifying other rules on international transfers, in particular by:
    Streamlining and extending the use of tools such as 'binding corporate rules',[50] so that they can be used to also cover data processors and within 'groups of companies', thus better reflecting the multiplicity of actors involved in data processing activities especially in the framework of cloud computing."[51]

In effect, the proposed regulation will establish a single European law for data protection, replacing the current inconsistent patchwork of national laws. The hope is that increased harmonization will be achieved by having a single set of rules applicable across the EU and a "one-stop-shop" enforcement system, whereby a single data protection authority is responsible for an organization operating in several countries. The example given by the Commission is of a chain of shops which "has its head office in France and franchised shops in 14 other EU countries. Each shop collects data relating to clients and transfers it to the head office in France for further processing. Under current rules, France's data protection laws would apply to the processing done by head office, but individual shops would still have to report to their national data protection authority, to confirm they were processing data in accordance with national laws in the country where they were located."[52] The responsible authority will be the data protection authority in the organization's home base. Each business will be answerable to only one data protection authority, and both businesses and consumers will have a single point of contact.

---

[50]The EC explains, "Binding corporate rules are one tool that can be used to adequately protect personal data when it is transferred or processed outside the EU. Businesses can adopt these rules voluntarily and they can be used for transfers of data between companies that are part of the same corporate group. Currently, in order to be approved, binding corporate rules must be verified by at least three data protection authorities" See, EC. "How Will the EU's Data Protection Reform Make International Cooperation Easier?. ec.europa.eu/justice/data-protection/index_en.htm, September 29, 2013. The current major data transfer schemes are the EU's Binding Corporate Rules framework (BCR) and the Asia Pacific Economic Cooperation's (APEC's) Cross Border Privacy Rules System (CBPR) which are under review and following similar approach to that proposed by the EC.
[51]*Ibid.*
[52]See, above n 48.

Most importantly, under this proposal, companies based outside the EU will have to abide the same rules as European companies. The stated objective is to protect EU citizens' data throughout the world:

> When the EU cooperates with non-member countries, the Commission's proposals will make sure that citizens' data is protected throughout the world, and not only within the EU. This will help to improve international trust in the protection of individuals' personal data, wherever the data is located. This will in turn promote growth opportunities for EU businesses. EU data protection standards have to apply independently of the location where the data relating to EU individuals is processed. At the same time, data transferred outside the EU should be protected. Businesses committed to a high level of data protection should be provided with simple tools to ease legitimate transfers. Third party cooperation on these new proposals will help to ensure that Europeans' personal information is safe wherever it is in the world.[53]

European regulators will have strong enforcement powers. Data protection authorities will be able to fine companies who do not comply up to 2% of their global annual turnover.

On March 12, 2014, this reform was strongly endorsed by the European Parliament. This is a significant development which indicates that this reform will proceed to a Regulation of general application to members of the European Union.[54]

The EC proposal is therefore the most important international development in terms of its international application and its influence. Similar cross-border data protection proposals have also been advanced by the United States and by APEC. While there are presently some differences in approach that are likely to be resolved soon, there is broad international agreement on the need to harmonize the major data protection regimes, especially as they apply to cross-border data[55] and for a new global standard.

The key point, however, is that by framing regulation in terms of transfer, all these proposals fail to address full the impact of cloud computing and the risks it entails, especially to digital identity. Transaction identity is required for processing transactions so it is disclosed when dealing with overseas call centers, for example, even if it is not actually transferred across a border. Yet the notion of physical borders and transfers still pervades these proposals for reform.

---

[53]*Ibid.*

[54]With 621 votes in favor, 10 against and 22 abstentions for the Regulation; and 371 votes in favor, 276 against and 30 abstentions for the Directive, providing an important signal of support in the legislative process. See, Progress on EU Data Protection Reform Now Irreversible Following European Parliament Vote, Strasbourg, March 12, 2014.

[55]This point has been made by the United States' Federal Trade Commission: "[e]fforts underway around the world to re-examine current approaches to protecting consumer privacy indicate an interest in convergence on overarching principles and a desire to develop greater interoperability." See FTC Report. *Protecting consumer privacy in an era of rapid change*, March 2012, 10.

The notable exception is Australia which in the 2013 reforms to the Privacy Act 1988 (Cth) (Privacy Act) moved from regulating transfer of cross-border data to regulating disclosure.

What is the relevance of EU in this whole scheme?

4 PROTECTING DIGITAL IDENTITY IN THE ERA OF CLOUD COMPUTING

In 2012, the Privacy Amendment (Enhancing Privacy Protection) Act 2012 (Cth) (Reform Act) was passed by the Australian federal Parliament. The Reform Act was the culmination of a comprehensive privacy law reform process which began almost 20 years after the Privacy Act was first introduced in 1988.[56] Most of the changes came into operation on 12 March 2014.[57]

Until the enactment of the Reform Act, the Australian Privacy Commissioner's role was largely one of monitoring and conciliation, with some power to investigate and take action in respect of clear breach of the Privacy Act. Under the new regime, Australia has moved to a stronger regulatory scheme with greater powers given to the Commissioner. Most significant, however, is Australia's new approach in regulating cross-border disclosure.

The Reform Act continues to permit the collection, use, and disclosure of personal information with consent but creates a new set of "Australian Privacy Principles" (APPs) that apply to both government agencies and private sector entities.[58] The APPs echo the earlier privacy principles in many respects but are structured differently, stepping through the data-handling process from the stage of planning the collection of personal information, collecting the information, using and handling it, and finally

---

[56]On January 31, 2006, the Australian Law Reform Commission (ALRC) received Terms of Reference from the Australian Attorney-General for an inquiry into the extent to which the Privacy Act 1988 (Cth) and related laws continue to provide an effective framework for the protection of privacy in Australia. The changes made by the Reform Act implement the Australian Government's first-stage response to the ALRC's Report 108: *For Your Information: Australian Privacy Law and Practice*. Some notable reforms recommended by the ALRC have not yet been enacted. These recommendations include proposals to remove certain exceptions such as the small business exception, make data breach notification mandatory, and to introduce a statutory cause of action for interference with an individual's privacy. However, the Government has expressed an intention to deal with these in a second stage of reforms.

[57]The Privacy Amendment (Enhancing Privacy Protection) Act 2012 was passed by federal Parliament on 29 November 29, 2012 and received royal assent on December 12, 2012. The majority of the amendments take effect in March 2014, though a handful of provisions apply from the date of royal assent, i.e., December 12, 2012.

[58]Previously, there were two sets of principles, one for government and the other for business, though they were very similar. This reflected the Act's evolution. Initially, the legislation applied only to government. The Act was later amended to apply to the private sector. The Act now defines "entity" to mean: "(a) an agency; or (b) an organization; or (c) a small business operator." See section 6(1) Privacy Act.

disposing of it. Generally, the APPs have a greater emphasis on open and transparent management of personal information.

A number of APPs introduce significant change,[59] the most notable of which is the new APP 8 which with section 16C regulates cross-border disclosure of information. APP 8.1 introduces a new accountability approach to cross-border disclosure of personal information which fundamentally changes the previous liability regime regulating transfer of personal information to recipients outside Australia. The main reason for the change seems to be to deal with temporary transfers such as those often used for e-mail routing which were the discussed in the report of the Australian Law Reform Commission which prompted reform of the Privacy Act.[60] However, the change to disclosure is a major reform which has far reaching implications, especially now that the cloud is now an integral part of next-generation government.[61] The Senate Report notes that the use of the term disclosure creates more clarity than transfer:

> *the ordinary meaning of disclosure is to allow information to be seen rather than the implication of 'transfer' of a cross-border movement of information. This means that a disclosure will occur when an overseas recipient accesses information, whether or not the personal information that is accessed is stored in Australia or elsewhere.[62]*

---

[59]Significant amendments which can be relevant to the other information which comprises digital identity are made to the credit reporting scheme through new rules that regulate information disclosed to and by credit reporting bodies, credit providers, and other information recipients. The new rules for credit reporting bodies and credit providers balance the protection afforded to the individual and the credit provider's access to reliable credit information about an individual. Disclosure of repayment history is permitted in certain instances from the date of assent. The disclosure of this historical data allows the credit reporting system to play a more meaningful role in assessing an individual's credit worthiness from commencement. Civil penalties replace the majority of the criminal offences with respect to noncompliance with the new rules, however, criminal offence provisions still apply with respect to false and misleading information. Civil penalties of up to $1.1 million can be sought by the Commissioner for breaches of credit reporting requirements.

[60]ALRC. Review of Australian Privacy Law, DP 72 (2007), Question 28–1. The impact of the Internet on privacy is discussed in Chapters 9 and 11.

[61] Telstra Corporation. *Government: Integrated National Approach to Secure Communications*. www. telstra.com.au/business-enterprise/enterprise-solutions/industries/government, September 29, 2013 where Telstra Corporation explains, "The rapid spread of digital technology and cloud computing has given government organizations an unprecedented opportunity for creating citizen-based online services, while both raising the standard of service delivery and reducing its costs. . . . .Telstra calls it "Connected Government," where government agencies at every level—federal, state, and local— are learning to be more flexible and responsive in meeting changing social and demographic dynamics. See also, Telstra Corporation. Government Blueprint Brochure. www.telstra.com.au/business-enter prise/download/document/enterprise-government-blueprint-brochure.pdf, September 29, 2013.

[62]*Senate Finance and Public Administration Committees, Parliament* of Australia, Senate, *Exposure Drafts of Australian Privacy Amendment Legislation Report Part 1–Australian Privacy Principles* (2011), http://www.aph.gov.au/~/media/wopapub/senate/committee/fapa_ctte/completed_inquiries/ 2010-13/priv_exp_drafts/report_part1/report.ashx, para 11.47, October 17, 2012.

By regulating disclosure,[63] rather than transfer, the scope of APP 8 is broadened both in the activities it covers and the entities to which it applies. Increasing use of technology-related services which involve immediate exchange of information through global telecommunications networks and cloud computing means that most entities are more likely to be involved in disclosure of personal information to overseas recipients. Under APP 8, an entity may disclose personal information to an overseas recipient, provided it takes such steps as are reasonable in the circumstances to ensure that the overseas recipient does not breach the APPs in relation to that information. However, even where the entity does so, the entity will, in certain circumstances, be deemed to be liable for any subsequent breaches of the Privacy Act committed by the overseas recipient. The only way an entity can escape the effect of this deeming provision is to rely on one of the relatively narrow exceptions now specified in the Act which in summary, are where there is:

1. Reasonable belief by the entity that:
    (i) the recipient of the information is subject to a law, or binding scheme, that has the effect of protecting the information in a way that, overall, is at least substantially similar to the way in which the APPs protect the information; and
    (ii) there are mechanisms that the individual can access to enforce the protection of that law or binding scheme
    or
2. Consent by the Individual
   The individual consents to disclosure of the information after being expressly informed by the entity that if the individual consents to the disclosure of the information, the requirement to take reasonable steps will not apply to that disclosure.
   or
3. Information disclosure compelled by law
    • where the cross-border disclosure is required or authorized by or under an Australian law, or a court/tribunal order (APP 8.2(c))
    • where an organization reasonably believes that the disclosure is necessary to lessen or prevent a serious threat to the life, health or safety of any individual, or to public health or safety (APP 8.2(d), s16A item 1)
    • where an organization reasonably believes that the disclosure is necessary to take action in relation to the suspicion of unlawful activity or misconduct of a serious nature that relates to the organization's functions or activities (APP 8.2(d), s 16A item 2)

---

[63]Disclosure lies at the heart of the right to privacy. This is so in relation to the right to privacy under the *European Convention for the Protection of Human Rights and Fundamental Freedoms*, opened for signature November 4, 1950) 213 UNTS 221, which is the basis for privacy protection in Europe and which is influencing the development of privacy in Australia, and it is also so for the right to privacy under US law.

- where an organization reasonably believes that the disclosure is necessary to assist any entity, body, or person to locate a person who has been reported as missing (APP 8.2(d), s 16A item 3).

The new APP 8 has a number of significant ramifications for Australian organizations. APP 8 applies to all offshore outsourcing including offshore call centers, offshore data hosting, and/or processing services, and cloud computing generally where there is access to information. Deemed liability under APP 8 and the new penalties and powers of the Commissioner significantly increase the risk of liability. Where entities are unable to rely on the consent or reasonable belief exceptions, they can potentially be held liable for serious or repeated breaches of privacy by the overseas recipient. Entities covered by the Act[64] which handle personal information must ensure that their privacy policies and procedures comply with the new privacy principles.

Any disclosure of personal information must comply. There are no "saving provisions" for disclosures made under existing contracts. Entities will have to check that their existing and planned offshoring arrangements and cloud computing contracts comply with the new requirements. In effect this means that entities have to manage the risk they face through a combination of technical measures and provisions in their contracts with the overseas entities.

Most significantly, by regulating cross-border disclosure, APP 8 applies to offshoring arrangements which were established on the basis of no transfer of personal information. Even if the information remains in Australia, APP 8 applies provided there is disclosure to a party offshore. This is an important step in increasing protection of all the information which comprises digital identity but especially for increasing protection for transaction identity.

5 CONCLUSION

Digital identity schemes are now part of life in many countries and are set to become the norm as more governments digitalize services and transactions. What sets this type of scheme apart is the impact of system error on the individual. This is because the digital identity required for transactions is now the primary means by which a person is able to operate in this new virtual world.

The scheme is also characterized by the enduring nature of the identity information required for transactions and its unique association with an individual. These two essential features result in practical and legal issues for that individual when system does not correctly recognize the identity or when it permits the identity to

---

[64]The Act applies to individuals, bodies corporate, partnerships, unincorporated associations, and trusts. There is an exemption for small business. See section 6 C Privacy Act. A business is a small business at a time (the test time) in a financial year (the current year) if its annual turnover for the previous financial year is $3,000,000 or less. See section 6 D Privacy Act.

be misused by another person. Regardless of whether it is spontaneous or is induced, the error compromises the integrity of an individual's digital identity.

Offshore storage, hosting, and processing, especially in the cloud, increases the risk of compromise. The EU, United States, and regional bodies are working to address the challenges presented by technology and all seek to address the shortcomings of the present piecemeal approach. There are clear benefits for individuals and organizations in streamlining compliance. The EC's view is that "new simpler, clearer and stronger rules will make it easier for citizens to protect their data online. They will also cut costs for business considerably, providing EU companies with an advantage in global competition, as they will be able to offer their customers assurances of strong data protection whilst operating in a simpler regulatory environment."[65] There is, however, an important distinction between data transfer and disclosure which has been overlooked in the proposals of the EU, United States, and APEC.

With the advent of cloud computing there may not be a transfer of data across a border but there can be disclosure. In recognizing that disclosure is the now key issue, the Australian approach is a preferable model. APP 8 provides much needed additional protection to an individual's personal information in a contemporary environment which is characterized by the growing significance of digital identity and the increasing use of cloud computing. In line with the Australian government's statement about developing a model of accountable and responsible digital citizenship, APP 8 clearly signals that it is important for both government and private sector entities to be aware of when and how personal information is disclosed. APP8 requires that the entity obtain individual consent after having clearly and unambiguously set out how at the information is or may be disclosed. In the absence of that consent, the entity must ensure that information is protected to the same standard as it would be in Australia.

This level of specificity is necessary to alert individuals to their rights, and in the case of government and private sector entities, to make them fully aware of their data-handling responsibilities. This awareness of rights and responsibilities is more important than ever, at a time when an individual's ability to transact increasingly depends on the integrity and functionality of digital identity.

The whole essay seems to be a description of various schemes without any unifying focus—pretty confusing about what the author is trying to say—lack of indepth treatment or analysis and not quite sure what is the problem the author is trying to solve or described. More of a survey—overview.

---

[65]EC.   ec.europa.eu/justice/data-protection/document/international-transfers/adequacy/index_en. htm#h2-14, September 29, 2013.

Provenance for cloud data accountability

8

Alan Y.S. Tan, Ryan K. L. Ko, Geoff Holmes, Bill Rogers

Cyber Security Lab, Department of Computer Science, University of Waikato, Hamilton,
New Zealand

1 INTRODUCTION

1.1 BACKGROUND

While cloud computing has been proposed for some years, surveys (Attunity, 2013; Linthicum, 2013) have shown that the adoption of cloud by businesses is only starting to increase in recent years.

Issues related to data accountability and cloud security such as the vulnerabilities identified in the cloud, the confidentiality, integrity, privacy, and control of data have been the inhibitors of cloud adoption by businesses (North Bridge, 2013). Even with security losing its position as the primary inhibitor for cloud adoption (North Bridge, 2013), accountability-related issues such as data regulatory compliance and privacy of data are still concerns for businesses when considering moving their businesses to cloud services. These issues are primarily made difficult due to the lack of transparency in cloud environments (Chow et al., 2009).

Government regulations which safeguard sensitive data, such as the Health Insurance Portability and Accountability Act (HIPAA) in the United States (U.S. Department of Health and Human Services, 1996) and the Data Protection Act (DPA) in the United Kingdom (Directorate General Health and Consumers, 2010), mandate companies dealing with sensitive data to comply with regulations laid out in the policies. These regulations often require companies to place measures to assure the confidentiality and accountability of data. However, none of the current cloud providers provide tools or features that guarantee customers accountability and control over their data in the cloud. This lack of means to enable data accountability in the cloud needs to be addressed.

Data Provenance—the information about actions performed on data and related entities involved (Tan et al., 2013), directly addresses the data accountability issue. Recent data provenance research has resulted in various tools that can be deployed into the cloud. Provenance collection tools such as Progger (Ko and Will, 2014), S2Logger (Suen et al., 2013), Flogger (Ko et al., 2011a), SPADE (Gehani and Tariq, 2012), Lipstick (Amsterdamer et al., 2011), and Burrito (Guo and Seltzer,

2012) serve to capture and record provenance at various levels of granularity within cloud environments. The resulting provenance logs, a collection of captured data provenance, can then be analyzed in data audits to find out whether a data breach or policy violation has taken place.

However, as with any data-generating tools, these provenance collecting tools incur time and storage overheads (Carata et al., 2014). In input/output (I/O) intensive environments, the cost can be exceptionally high. For example, Muniswamy-Reddy et al. (2006) reports PASS, their implementation of an active provenance collector, incurred a time overhead ranging from 230% to 10% under different I/O loads and a storage overhead of around 33%. While 33% may seem a small figure, provenance logs will only continue to grow over time. Hence, overheads incurred through active provenance collection should not be overlooked.

Another disadvantage of provenance collecting tools is the need to deploy them on the target infrastructure and before any data are processed. Should the data be moved from a system with the tools deployed to another system without the collection tools, or data were accessed before the tool was deployed, the problem of missing data provenance arises. This is analogous to crime scenes which could have benefited from closed-circuit television (CCTV) cameras installed.

These gaps show that we should not solely rely on the use of active provenance collection tools to generate the data provenance required for cloud data accountability. The associated overhead costs also imply the use of these tools may not be a long-term solution. For a more robust and efficient solution, we look at the notion of reconstructing the required data provenance.

1.2 PROVENANCE RECONSTRUCTION

Provenance reconstruction looks at piecing back the provenance by mining readily available information sources from the relevant environment (Groth et al., 2012). In our context, we are interested in reconstructing the provenance of data stored in the cloud using information that is readily available in the cloud environment.

The following are some advantages of using provenance reconstruction as opposed to active provenance collection.

- *Reduced reliance on active provenance collection tools*: With the data provenance being reconstructed, we can reduce or remove the need for using active provenance collection tools to actively track data. This reduces the storage overhead significantly. However, a certain degree of computational overhead is still required for reconstructing the provenance.
- *Increase system portability of tools*: Active provenance collection tools such as Progger (Ko and Will, 2014) and PASS (Muniswamy-Reddy et al., 2006) usually require modifying the target system (e.g., the operating system hosting the cloud environment). Such modifications are considered intrusive and reduce the portability of the tools across different systems due to architecture and implementation differences. By contrast, provenance reconstruction usually only

requires interacting with data files that already exist on the system. Since no modifications to the system are required, it results in a tool that is more portable compared to active provenance collection tools.

- *Reduced complexity in analysis*: Active provenance collection tools usually collect data provenance indistinguishably. As a result, analysts have to shuffle through large amounts of data (Ko and Will, 2014; Chen et al., 2012a), making the analysis laborious and complex. Even with the aid of graph manipulation (Jankun-Kelly, 2008; Chen et al., 2012b) and provenance querying tools (Biton et al., 2008), it takes time and effort for the analyst to identify which portion of the provenance to focus on due to the amount of noise (e.g., provenance of other unrelated data or activities). In contrast, provenance reconstruction rebuilds only the provenance of the data of interest. This removes the need for analysts to determine which part of the provenance graph to prune, hence reducing the complexity of provenance analysis.

As we can see, some of the listed advantages address directly the gaps identified in active provenance collection tools (e.g., overhead costs). Due to these advantages, we see provenance reconstruction as a complementary or replacement solution for active provenance collection tools.

In this chapter, we discuss the notion of using provenance reconstruction for generating the required data provenance for enabling cloud data accountability and how it can be achieved. Our assumption is that pieces of information that can form the data provenance when pieced together, can be mined from information sources found within the cloud environment. Some examples of such information sources are metadata of the data files or system log files.

However, simply extracting the pieces of information from information sources is insufficient for cloud data accountability. We need to be able to piece them together in a manner such that the result can describe what has happened to the data. As such, a data model is required to facilitate the identification or categorization of the *role* of each extracted piece of information and how these pieces can be fitted together. This is much like solving a jigsaw puzzle where we have to identify the image and shape of each piece in order for us to know how they can be fitted together to form the final picture.

We will discuss the types of *role* the data model should describe in Section 3 and the list of rules that govern the behavior of the *role* in the model in Section 3.3. We can think of the *role* as the image on the jigsaw puzzle piece and the rules as the shape of that puzzle piece. We then show how the list of *roles* and the list of rules defined in the two sections can aid the reconstruction of provenance in a cloud environment in Section 4. We then identify a list of challenges and future work in Sections 5 and 6, respectively.

However, before discussing the data model, we first look at applications of provenance reconstruction and understand how they differ with the situation in our context, in Section 2.

2 RELATED WORK

In this section, we look at some past applications of provenance reconstruction and discuss whether the methods used are applicable in the context of reconstructing data provenance in a cloud environment. We also take a look at some of the attributes that were used in those proposed methodologies. Our aim is to understand what type of attributes would help in enabling cloud data accountability.

Paraphrasing Weitzner et al. (2008), accountability refers to being able to hold individuals or institutes accountable for misuse under a given set of rules. In this case, our focus is cloud data accountability. The attributes should allow us to attribute actions to individuals or entities and understand when, if any, did a violation occur.

Content similarity analysis is probably one of the most common methodologies used for provenance reconstruction. To understand how content of files changes over time (e.g., evolution of files) (Deolalikar and Laffitte, 2009; Magliacane, 2012; Nies et al., 2012) the analysis attempts to relate files by measuring the similarity distance between content of files. The files are then linked based on the computed similarity scores and ordered based on timestamps (e.g., date of creation or date of last modification). The assumption is that files that are derived from another file would bear a high similarity in terms of content.

Content similarity analysis would not be applicable in our context simply because file relationship is not our primary focus. We are interested in information such as what actions were executed, by whom and when was the action executed, with respect to the data. In terms of attributes, Deolalikar and Laffitte (2009), Magliacane (2012), and Nies et al. (2012) focused on inter-file similarity and timestamp. While timestamp enables us to determine the time period of an event, looking at file similarity may not necessarily tell us whether a violation has occurred or who is liable in the event of a rule violation.

Having said that, the workflow proposed by Magliacane (2012) is very much applicable to our case. Her proposed workflow splits the reconstruction process into *preprocessing*, *hypothesis generation*, *hypothesis pruning* and *aggregation and ranking*, as shown in Figure 1. Algorithms that calculate similarity scores (Lux and Chatzichristofis, 2008; Bendersky and Croft, 2009) were used in the hypothesis generation phase to determine how each file can be linked together to form potential provenance chains. Non-relevant and inconsistent provenance chains were then pruned away based on a set of defined domain-specific rules in the hypothesis pruning phase. Finally, the remaining provenance chains were aggregated and assigned a confidence value based on the semantic type of data in the aggregation and ranking phase. This workflow can be adapted to match our objectives. The extraction of information from various information sources can be done in the preprocessing phase. In the hypothesis generation phase, the pieces of extracted information can be pieced together in a logical manner to form potential provenance chains that describe the history of the relevant data. We discuss this in more detail in Section 4.

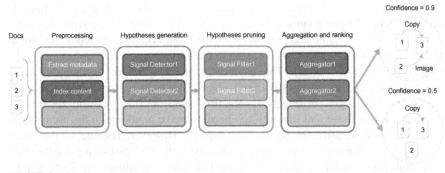

FIGURE 1

Workflow proposed by Magliacane (2012).

Zhao et al. (2011) showed how missing provenance of a dataset can be inferred from other similar datasets that has a complete provenance. This was based on their observation that data items linked by special semantic "connections" (i.e., datasets that would be treated by the same process) would have similar provenance. In a workflow or process driven environment, such observations would be valid as one would expect to apply the same workflow on datasets with the similar property (e.g., in a biology experimental lab, gene data would be analyzed using similar workflows). However, in a cloud environment, even the same dataset can undergo different "treatment" from different users. For example, a clerk can be entering data and updating an excel sheet in the cloud, which would then be read by the clerk's manager. Actions that will be executed on the data are purely based on the intent of each individual. As such, we cannot expect a user to perform the same action on every file of the same type. Hence, inferring data provenance from other datasets is not likely to produce favorable results in our context.

Much like the content similarity methodology, Zhao et al.'s proposed system relies on semantic similarity between datasets to determine which dataset's provenance can be used for inference. However, as discussed earlier, attributes that look at similarity scoring may not be useful for determining who should be liable in the event of a violation of rules that governs the data.

Huq et al. tries to infer the data provenance from the scripting grammar used in a given script (Huq et al., 2013). By analyzing the syntax used in a given script (e.g., a Python script), the proposed system can extract out the control-flow, data-flow and executed operations from the script. A workflow provenance is then built based on the analyzed grammar. However, the proposed system requires the script to be available for analysis. Intuitively, such a system would not be applicable on a dataset as datasets usually do not contain information on actions that were executed on it.

Provenance reconstruction is also used to help reduce the need for human involvement in the provenance capturing process. Active monitoring strategies such as source code annotation and process execution monitoring, were used to monitor a process's interaction with its environment in the Earth System Science Server (ES3) project (Frew et al., 2008). The captured interactions were decomposed into object references and linkages between objects before being used to reconstruct the provenance graphs. In doing so, scientists using the ES3 platform are free to use their own software and libraries and need not have to adhere to the use of specially modified libraries for provenance capture. However, because of the need to actively monitor each process during execution, the ES3 platform possesses the disadvantages of active provenance collection tools mentioned in Section 1.1. This is in contrast to our goal of using information that is readily available in the cloud environment (e.g., system logs that are gathered by the system or file's metadata).

Information such as the universally unique identifier (UUID) for provenance-relevant objects (files or processes) and operations executed (e.g., file accesses) were captured during the monitoring of processes in ES3. This information allows analysts of the resulting provenance graph to trace back which files were used and the actions that were executed on them. An analyst would be able to determine whether a process has accessed a file it should not and as such this information is desirable in our context.

Our discussion on related work has thus far shown that methods used to reconstruct provenance are not applicable in our context. This is because our focus is on deriving the historical events of the data rather than its relationship with other files. It is more likely that information sources such as system log files or the file's metadata contain events that are related to the data of interest. However, using the jigsaw puzzle analogy, we need a data model to systematically determine how each piece of information can be fitted together. Performing an exhaustive matching (e.g., permutation of n pieces of information) would result in a huge search space. Interestingly, the use of a data model to aid provenance reconstruction has been absent in the methodologies reviewed thus far. We shall look at describing such a data model in detail in the following sections.

3 DATA PROVENANCE MODEL FOR DATA ACCOUNTABILITY

In this section, we discuss what information should the data provenance contain for it to be useful for data accountability. This would help us identify what *role* should the model be able to categorize.

In Section 2, we identified time and attributes that would allow us to reference an object (e.g., UUID) and operations as desirable attributes. However, these three classes of attributes only tell us the when, what, and how of a violation. More information is required for us to find out who should be held responsible (Ko et al., 2011b; Ko, 2014). To further understand what is required for data accountability, we look at a privacy breach incident case study.

3.1 A CASE FOR PROVENANCE

In 2010, David Barksdale, Google's ex-Site Reliability Engineer (SRE), was fired for breaching Google service users' privacy (Protalinski, 2010). Barksdale abused the data access rights given to him for performing his role as an SRE. He tapped into call logs, extracted information such as names and phone numbers of users and used this information for stalking and spying on teenagers. Barksdale's activities went unnoticed by the company until complaints were filed. If not for the complaints, the extent of violation that Barksdale had undertaken might not have been uncovered.

We have to ask ourselves two questions: "Why did Barksdale's activities go unnoticed by the company?" and "Were there any other victims that were not discovered?." One likely possibility is that Google does not monitor or maintain data access records of their SREs. One can imagine with such records, a review process would easily uncover the answers to both questions. Such data access records should at least contain the following information:

- *Entities*—Users or processes that have come into contact with the dataset. Information of entities involved can help investigators narrow down the investigation scope to only datasets which Barksdale looked at.
- *Time*—Timestamps that indicate the time period and duration in which Barksdale accessed the dataset can help correlate incidents to data accesses or vice versa.
- *Operations performed*—When correlated with entity and timestamp, knowing the type of operation performed on the dataset (e.g., read, write, transfer of data from a file) by Barksdale allows investigators to trace how Barksdale was able to obtain information required to commit the said offences.
- *Context*—Contextual information such as the owner of the dataset and whether this dataset has a phone record between two individuals is useful for investigators in attempting to understand what kind of information or the likely victims that can result through unauthorized access of the said dataset.

With this list of information, investigators would be able to trace and find out who are the violators and determine the extent of damage caused by such malicious insiders. With reference to our discussion of attributes in Section 2, the addition of entities would enable us to trace back to the individual responsible for a violation. While the above list is not an exhaustive one, we argue this is the minimal information required for any investigator to find out when did a violation happen, who did it, what objects are involved and how did the violation occur (operations executed).

Barksdale's case is only one example of how data provenance can aid forensic investigations in the cloud. Investigators or auditors can easily assess whether the data stored in the cloud has violated any regulations governing the data (e.g., the data have to stay within the country's jurisdiction) by analyzing the provenance of the dataset. Should a violation be identified, other information such as timestamps and entities can help attribute the violation to individual user accounts.

In the following sections, we look at a model for data provenance. The model defines the types of information data provenance should contain such that it can be used for enabling cloud data accountability.

3.2 ELEMENTS OF THE DATA PROVENANCE MODEL

In Section 1.2, we used the term *role* as a unit for information types. However, we see the list of information types discussed in this section as the basic building blocks of any data provenance chain for cloud data accountability. Hence, we shall use the term *element* in place of *role*.

With reference to our discussion on the case study of David Barksdale, we formulate our data provenance model to consist of the following elements, *Artifact*, *Entity*, *Actions*, *Time*, and *Context*. These elements are used to represent various components within a computer system. The rationale for having this list of elements is so that we can categorize different information mined from log files or other types of information sources found within a computer system. We then discuss how these elements can be pieced together in Section 3.3.

3.2.1 Artifact

Artifact generally refers to objects that are immutable on their own. An example of an artifact within a computer system is a data file. While artifacts cannot change state on their own, other elements can change the state of an artifact. One such scenario is when a user writes to a file through a program. The artifact element helps to identify which data file is involved within the data provenance. This piece of information is useful when the provenance record contains more than one affected artifact (e.g., copying of content from one file to another).

3.2.2 Entity

An entity refers to user, process, or even an application within a computer system. Entities are generally what starts an action within the system. We classify process and application under entity, even though they have to be started by a user, because both of them are capable of running other actions once started (e.g., background process). In terms of data accountability, entity is the element to look for when determining the ones responsible for a malicious action.

3.2.3 Actions

Actions can range from atomic operations such as system calls executed by the kernel to compound operations like functions within system libraries or user application programming interfaces (APIs). Knowing the action that was executed helps in understanding the relationship between two artifacts and how an artifact reaches its current state.

3.2.4 Context

Context within a computer system covers details that ranges from metadata of a file that includes file names, description of a file; to file descriptors that are used by the kernel in system calls. The context element can help in establishing the importance of the artifact the investigator is looking at (e.g., a description that indicates the file contains classified information) or even help determine how different system calls should be linked together (e.g., how different read system calls should be linked to different write system calls at the kernel level).

3.2.5 *Time*

The coverage of the time element is intuitive. Other elements such as artifact and actions should have a timestamp value associated to it. These timestamps can indicate varying pieces of information crucial for investigators in piecing the provenance back together in the correct order. Some examples of timestamps are time of creation, time of access, and time of execution.

Once information mined from log files and other information sources are categorized, we can start piecing the various elements together to form the complete provenance picture of the data. To aid the reconstruction process, we define a set of rules that would help guide the reconstruction process, based on certain assumptions.

3.3 RULES FOR DATA PROVENANCE MODEL

In this section, we list the assumptions made on how elements in the model should behave and define a set of actions that governs the behavior of these elements. The objective is to be able to piece together elements mined from different information sources to form logical chains of provenance that can possibly describe how the data reaches its current state. These chains of provenance form the search space for the original provenance of the target dataset.

Assumption 1. An action has to be executed by an entity

In the context of a computer system, a function cannot start execution by itself and a system call cannot be executed without invocation by the kernel or a process. The command to execute has to originate either from a user or a process that is already executing. Hence, when there is an action element, it should always have an accompanying entity that is responsible for its execution.

Assumption 2. A user is able to run processes

The result of this assumption is that entities can be said to start another entity in the model. One possible scenario would be a user (with valid user ID) is able to start processes (with process ID) within its privilege. As such, entities can be linked directly to another entity. Once a process is started, it is considered as an entity by itself with attribution to a valid user.

Assumption 3. Artifacts are immutable. Their state can only be changed by an action

Artifacts such as files within a computer system are assumed to be unable to change their own state. This includes modifying its own content or other file's content. State transition on an artifact is only possible through a direct action being executed on the artifact itself. Together with Assumption 1, we say that there will always be a relative action and its associated user that can be attributed for the artifact's arrival at its current state. One example of such a scenario is when a file is created by a user using an editor. The user and the action of creating the file will be the cause of how the file came into existence on the file system.

While we explicitly listed three assumptions here, we did not include other more intuitive assumptions. Some of these assumptions include actions should be ordered based on the timestamp tagged to them and actions with timestamp older than an artifact's creation timestamp (if any) should not be associated with the artifact.

While there exists other provenance models such as the Open Provenance Model (OPM) (Moreau et al., 2011) and the PROV Data Model (PROV-DM) (Moreau et al., 2013), the objectives of those models differ from our presented model. OPM and PROV-DM seek to define a common format to describe provenance from different sources for inter-operability between tools that produce and consume provenance. These models also aim to describe provenance used in fields of research such as databases and the semantic Web. This resulted in an extensive set of vocabulary being developed for describing various components of those models (Zhao, 2010; Hartig and Zhao, 2012). While this helps in cross domain applications of provenance, it causes the vocabulary to become complex and heavy-weight as concepts from different fields have to be incorporated into the model.

OPM and PROV-DM models also assume that the provenance being described is of the same granularity (e.g., components of a workflow provenance of an application are all generated at the application level). In our case, we are looking to use information extracted from different information sources to piece together the data provenance. It is likely that these information sources (e.g., system log file generated by the system or a file's metadata or network log files) are generated by different logging mechanisms residing at different granularity levels in a cloud system. Hence the model must be aware that each information piece may be of different granularity and be still able to relate them together. We discuss this in more detail in Section 5.

4 RECONSTRUCTING THE DATA PROVENANCE

Having described the model and the rules governing the elements' behavior in Sections 3 and 3.3, we show how the model can be used in the provenance reconstruction process. Figure 2 illustrates the overview of our provenance reconstruction workflow.

The whole process starts when a user (e.g., investigator) issues a query to retrieve the data provenance of a certain file. The element miner then crawls relevant information based on user's inputs and categorizes the information according to the defined elements in the model.

The elements mined are then passed on to the reconstruction algorithm. Here, AI planning techniques, such as those described in Groth et al. (2012) or other forms of heuristics can be applied on the elements to reconstruct potential provenance chains that represents how the data can possibly reach its current state.

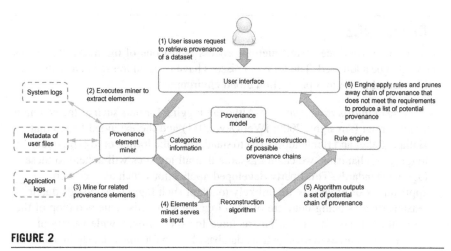

FIGURE 2

Overview of the workflow used for provenance reconstruction.

Once the algorithm generates the output list of provenances, the next step is to prune away those that are logically incorrect. This is achieved through the rule engine. The rule engine will apply a set of rules on each of the generated provenance chains from the previous step to ensure that the provenance elements are joined in a manner that satisfy all rules. Those provenance chains that are joined in a manner that does not satisfy the set of rules are considered as non-logical provenance chains and pruned away. The set of rules can be divided into two sets, model specific and domain specific. Model-specific rules dictate the behavior of the provenance elements. Examples of model-specific rules are those mentioned in Section 3.3. Domain-specific rules are rules inserted by users (e.g., system forensic analysts) for reasons such as to narrow down the provenance chains to look at. Examples of domain-specific rules could be, "remove provenance chains that involve network communications." Domain specific-rules should be specified with care as over-strict rules may result in pruning away relevant provenance chains from the search space.

From Figure 2, we can see that the model plays two crucial roles in the reconstruction process. The first is in the mining of elements from the various information sources. Without the model to help categorize the information mined, the reconstruction algorithm would have no clue on what these information represent. By knowing the nature of the mined information, the reconstruction algorithm would be able to have a basic knowledge on how each of these separate information can be pieced together to form the provenance chain.

The second role of the model is to help reduce the provenance chain search space generated by the reconstruction algorithm. The reduction is achieved by pruning away provenance chains that are consider non-logical. This is done in conjunction with the rule engine and is explained in the previous paragraphs above.

5 CHALLENGES

Guiding the provenance reconstruction process is just one of the many challenges that need to be addressed. The following issues have to be addressed before the concept is ready for use in a production cloud environment:

- *Parsing of information sources*—Although logging formats such as the common event format (Arcsight, 2009; iWebDev, 2011) and the extended log format Hallam-Baker and Behlendorf exist to standardize the format of logs produced by logging mechanisms, we cannot assume that all log files will adhere to these logging standards. Third party developed applications such as user web applications or programs are unlikely to adopt such logging standards due to reasons such as being unaware of such logging standards. This is on top of the possibility of having semi or unstructured log files or even wide variety of information sources that range from database logs to file meta-data to image files. Therefore, the miner has to be designed in a modular and robust manner such that users can easily incorporate in new heuristics for the mining to be done. Having a modular miner also allows incorporating new logging standards or adapting to different types of information sources with minimal changes.
- *Difference in granularity*—The granularity of logs produced by different applications or logging mechanisms can differ. One simple example is the comparison between a user application's log and a system log such as dmesg (Linux system log). In the user application's log, one can expect information such as functions called, input and output parameters and even program errors caused by user inputs. In a system log, information such as the devices that were invoked or system calls resulting from the function call by a user's application are being logged instead. The challenge here is given the difference in granularity, how can one link elements together such that they form the provenance chain that describes the history of the data.

6 FUTURE WORK AND CONCLUDING REMARKS

In this chapter, we introduced the concept of provenance reconstruction as an alternative solution for active provenance collection tools in generating the data provenance for enabling cloud data provenance. We then focused our discussion on the data provenance model, a crucial component in our provenance reconstruction workflow. The data model consists of a list of provenance elements (Section 3.2) for categorizing information extracted from various information sources and a set of rules (Section 3.3) which define the behavior of these elements. We explained how the rules could be used for pruning away non-logical provenance chains generated by the provenance reconstruction algorithm in Section 4. We also illustrated and briefly explained how the model is incorporated into the provenance reconstruction workflow.

We are currently working on implementing the data model discussed in this chapter. This is but the first step toward having a working prototype for generating data provenance using provenance reconstruction in a cloud environment. However, the challenges mentioned in Section 5 have to be addressed first in order for the model to be robust and agnostic to the range of information sources within a cloud environment.

After the extracted information are modeled into provenance elements, the next step is to piece them together to form possible provenance chains that describe the historical events of the data. We plan to look into the area of artificial intelligence planning (AI planning) for deriving an algorithm for construction of provenance chains. By modeling each element as a service, AI planning used in automatic web service composition (Oh et al., 2006) could be adapted for generating the required provenance chains.

Our vision is to create a robust and platform independent tool that can generate the required provenance for cloud data accountability. Provenance reconstruction techniques provide the means for creating such a tool. Provenance reconstruction-based tools would not only help cloud providers provide the necessary guarantees to businesses looking to move their services and infrastructure to the cloud, but also increase users' confidence in cloud technologies and services.

REFERENCES

Amsterdamer, Y., Davidson, S.B., Deutch, D., Milo, T., Stoyanovich, J., Tannen, V., 2011. Putting Lipstick on Pig: Enabling Database-style Workflow Provenance. In: Proceedings of the VLDB Endowment (PVLDB), pp. 346–357.

Arcsight, 2009. Common Event Format, Retrieved 03/09/2014 from mita-tac.wikispaces http://mita-tac.wikispaces.com/file/view/CEF+White+Paper+071709.pdf.

Attunity, 2013. Cloud adoption rates reaching 75 percent in 2013, Retrieved: 14/08/2014 from Attunity: http://www.attunity.com/learning/articles/cloud-adoption-rates-reaching-75-percent-2013.

Bendersky, M., Croft, W.B., 2009. Finding Text Reuse on the Web. In: Proceedings of the Second ACM International Conference on Web Search and Data Mining. ACM, New York, NY, USA, pp. 262–271.

Biton, O., Cohen-Boulakia, S., B.Davidson, S., Hara, C.S., 2008. Querying and managing provenance through user views in scientific workflows. In: Proceedings of the 2008 IEEE 24th International Conference on Data Engineering (ICDE'08), pp. 1072–1081.

Carata, L., Akoush, S., Balakrishnan, N., Bytheway, T., Sohan, R., Seltzer, M., Hopper, A., 2014. A Primer on Provenance. Communications of the ACM 57, 52–60.

Chen, P., Plale, B., Aktas, M.S., 2012a. Temporal Representation for Scientific Data Provenance. In: IEEE 8t International Conference on E-Science (e-Science), pp. 1–8.

Chen, P., Plale, B., Cheah, Y., Ghoshal, D., Jensen, S., Luo, Y., 2012. Visualization of network data provenance. In: High Performance Computing (HiPC), 2012 19th International Conference on, pp. 1–9.

Chow, R., Golle, P., Jakobsson, M., Shi, E., Staddon, J., Masuoka, R., Molina, J., 2009. Controlling Data in the Cloud: Outsourcing Computation Without Outsourcing Control.

In: Proceedings of the 2009 ACM Workshop on Cloud Computing Security. ACM, New York, NY, USA, pp. 85–90.

Deolalikar, V., Laffitte, H., 2009. Provenance as data mining: combining file system metadata with content analysis. In: Proceeding of First Workshop on Theory and Practice of Provenance (TAPP'09).

Directorate General Health and Consumers, 2010. Data protection in the EU, Retrieve: 24/08/2014 from European Commission Public Health, http://ec.europa.eu/health/data_collection/data_protection/in_eu/index_en.htm.

Frew, J., Metzger, D., Slaughter, P., 2008. Automatic Capture and Reconstruction of Computational Provenance. Journal of Concurrency and Computation: Practice and Experience - The First Provenance Challenge 20, 485–496.

Gehani, A., Tariq, D., 2012. SPADE: Support for Provenance Auditing in Distributed Environments. In: Narasimhan, P., Triantafillou, P. (Eds.), Middleware 2012. In: volume 7662 of Lecture Notes in Computer Science, Springer Berlin Heidelberg, pp. 101–120.

Groth, P., Gil, Y., Magliacane, S., 2012. Automatic metadata annotation through reconstructing provenance. In: Third International Workshop on the role of Semantic Web in Provenance Management (ESWC).

Guo, P.J., Seltzer, M., 2012. Burrito: Wrapping Your Lab Notebook in Computational Infrastructure. In: USENIX Workshop on the Theory and Practice of Provenance (TaPP).

Hallam-Baker, P.M., Behlendorf, B., Extended Log File Format (working draft). Retrieved 03/09/2014 from W3C http://www.w3.org/TR/WD-logfile.html.

Hartig, O., Zhao, J., 2012. Provenance Vocabulary Core Ontology Specification, Retrieved 03/09/2014 from Open Provenance Model http://trdf.sourceforge.net/provenance/ns.html.

Huq, M.R., Apers, P.M.G., Wombacher, A., 2013. ProvenanceCurious: A Tool to Infer Data Provenance from Scripts. In: Proceedings of the 16th International Conference on Extending Database Technology (EDBT), pp. 765–768.

iWebDev, 2011. Common Event Format (CEF), Retrieved 03/09/2014 from iWebDev's Blog http://www.iwebdev.it/blog/?tag=common-event-format.

Jankun-Kelly, T.J., 2008. Using Visualization Process Graphs to Improve Visualization Exploration. Springer-Verlag Berlin, Heidelberg.

Ko, R.K., 2014. Data Accountability in Cloud Systems, 211–238.

Ko, R.K.L., Jagadpramana, P., Lee, B.S., 2011a. Flogger: A File-centric Logger for Monitoring File Access and Transfers with Cloud Computing Environments. In: 3rd IEEE International Workshop on Security in e-Science and e-Research (ISSR'11), in conjunction with IEEE TrustCom'11, pp. 765–771.

Ko, R.K.L., Lee, B.S., Pearson, S., 2011b. Towards Achieving Accountability, Auditability and Trust in Cloud Computing. In: Advances in Computing and Communication.

Ko, R.K.L., Will, M.A., 2014. Progger: A Efficient, Tamper-Evident Kernel-Space Logger for Cloud Data Provenance Tracking. In: Proceedings of the 7th IEEE International Conference on Cloud Computing (CLOUD'14), Anchorage, Alaska, USA.

Linthicum, D., 2013. Cloud adoption's tipping point has arrived, Retrieved, 14/08.2014 from InfoWorld: http://www.infoworld.com/d/cloud-computing/cloud-adoptions-tipping-point-has-arrived-221335.

Lux, M., Chatzichristofis, S.A., 2008. Lire: Lucene Image Retrieval: An Extensible Java CBIR Library. In: Proceedings of the 16th ACM International Conference on Multimedia. ACM, New York, NY, USA, pp. 1085–1088.

Magliacane, S., 2012. Reconstructing Provenance. The Semantic Web - ISWC, 399–406.

Moreau, L., Clifford, B., Freire, J., Futrelle, J., Gil, Y., Groth, P., Kwasnikowska, N., Miles, S., Missier, P., Myers, J., Plale, B., Simmhan, Y., Stephan, E., den Bussche, J.V., 2011. The Open Provenance Model core specification (v1.1). Future Generation Computer Systems 27, 743–756.

Moreau, L., Missier, P., Belhajjame, K., B'Far, R., Cheney, J., Coppens, S., Cresswell, S., Gil, Y., Grotha, P., Klyne, G., Lebo, aTimothy, McCusker, J., Miles, S., Myers, J., Sahoo, S.S., Tilmes, C., 2013. PROV-DM: The PROV Data Model, Retrieved: 04/09/2014 from W3C Recommendations.

Muniswamy-Reddy, K.K., A.Holland, D., Braun, U., Seltzer, M., 2006. Provenance-aware Storage Systems. In: Proceedings of the Conference on USENIX'06 Annual Technical Conference (ATEC'06), p. 4.

Nies, T.D., Coppens, S., Deursen, D.V., Mannens, E., de Walle, R.V., 2012. Automatic Discovery of High-Level Provenance using Semantic Similarity. In: Proceedings of the 4th International Conference on Provenance and Annotation of Data and Processes (IPAW), pp. 97–110.

North Bridge, 2013. 2013 Future of Cloud Computing Survey Reveals Business Driving Cloud Adoption in Everything as a Service Era; IT Investing Heavily to Catch up and Support Consumers Graduating from BYOD to BYOC, Retrieved: 14/08/2014 from Business Wire: http://www.businesswire.com/news/home/20130619005581/en/2013-Future-Cloud-Computing-Survey-Reveals-Business\#.U-wqSWPCuVo.

Oh, S.C., Lee, D., Kumara, S.R.T., 2006. A Comparative Illustration of AI Planning-based Web Services Composition. SIGecom Exch. 5, 1–10.

Protalinski, E., 2010. Google Fired Employees for Breaching User Privacy, Retrieved, 03/09/2014 from Techspot: http://www.techspot.com/news/40280-google-fired-employees-for-breaching-user-privacy.html.

Suen, C.H., Ko, R.K.L., Tan, Y.S., Jagadpramana, P., Lee, B.S., 2013. S2Logger: End-to-End Data Tracking Mechanism for Cloud Data Provenance. In: Proceedings of 12th IEEE International Conference on Trust, Security and Privacy in Computing and Communications (TrustCom'13), pp. 594–602.

Tan, Y.S., Ko, R.K.L., Holmes, G., 2013. Security and Data Accountability in Distributed Systems: A Provenance Survey. In: Proceedings of the 15th IEEE International Conference on High Performance Computing and Communications (HPCC'13).

U.S. Department of Health and Human Services, 1996, Health Insurance Portability and Accountability Act of 1996, Retrieved: 24/08/2014 from U.S. Department of Health and Human Services, http://www.hhs.gov/ocr/privacy/hipaa/administrative/statute/hipaastatutepdf.pdf.

Weitzner, D.J., Abelson, H., Berners-Lee, T., Feigenbaum, J., Hendler, J., Sussman, G.J., 2008, Information Accountability. Communications of the ACM - Organic User Interfaces, vol. 51, 82–87.

Zhao, J., 2010. Open Provenance Model Vocabulary Specification, Retrieved 03/09/2014 from Open Provenance Model http://open-biomed.sourceforge.net/opmv/ns.html.

Zhao, J., Gomadam, K., Prasanna, V., 2011. Predicting Missing Provenance Using Semantic Associations in Reservoir Engineering. In: Proceedings of the 2011 IEEE Fifth International Conference on Semantic Computing. IEEE Computer Society, Washington, DC, USA, pp. 141–148.

CHAPTER

Security as a service (SecaaS)—An overview

9

Baden Delamore, Ryan K. L. Ko

*Cyber Security Lab, Department of Computer Science, University of Waikato,
Hamilton, New Zealand*

1 INTRODUCTION

1.1 HISTORY REPEATING ITSELF

The inception of cloud computing with respect to information technology (IT) represents a significant change in the way we process, store, and utilize data. This change has similarities with the way businesses used power at the turn of the century. In the late 1890s, every factory or business had in its basement a smoke belching, fuel consuming power generator that was tended to by gray boiler suited men who serviced it and kept it running as best as they could. This was fine when things worked nicely. But when they did not, more often than not, the machines ground to a halt, the lights went out and nothing could be done.

In the early 1900s, the Chicago-based Edison power company developed the turbine power station which could generate and distribute large-scale power to business. This provided cheaper, more reliable, and cleaner power than any factory or business base generator without many of the headaches. And by 1920 most businesses had made the switch to the grid. Business now access power simply by plugging into the wall.

Today we take virtually unlimited power for granted, and we cannot imagine it any other way. At the time of writing, a similar revolution is happening in IT called *Cloud Computing*. Enterprises no longer have to buy, build, and manage costly computer facilities on-site. Just as businesses learned that power provided by a specialized power company improved reliability and quality, cloud computing has been proven to be more secure, more reliable, more scalable, and ultimately more affordable than traditional on-site IT. This is why most new business applications are now deployed in the cloud.

1.2 THE GROWTH OF CLOUD COMPUTING SERVICES

Since its introduction to the mass market, cloud computing has seen a phenomenal level of growth all over the world (Ko, 2010). It represents one of the most significant shifts in IT many of us are likely to see in our lifetimes-reaching the point where the point where computing as a utility has so much innovation potential one cannot yet imagine. Many factors such as:

- *Less maintenance:* Hardware, applications, and bandwidth are managed by the provider.
- *Continuous availability:* Public cloud services are available where you are located.
- *Scalability:* Pay online for the applications and data storage you need.
- *Elasticity:* Private clouds can be scaled to meet your changing IT systems demands.

have influenced the transition from traditional on-site management to the cloud (NIST, 2014). Despite this rapid transition to the cloud, the deployment of cloud-based security services forms important challenges that need to be addressed. Hence, an extensive overview of security as a service (SecaaS) is presented in this chapter.

1.3 DEFINING SECURITY AS A SERVICE

At its core, SecaaS is a business model in which a security service provider integrates their security services into a corporate infrastructure, typically on a subscription basis delivered from the cloud without requiring on-premises hardware. This approach is one that is more cost effective as it does not require an individual or corporation to purchase, deploy or maintain their own infrastructure. Rather, ather businesses only need to subscribe to the service to reap SecaaS benefits.

1.4 MOTIVATION FOR THIS CHAPTER

SecaaS represents a new model for the deployment, management, and utilization of security services based on cloud computing principles. Although SecaaS is often considered an emerging trend in IT, the literature around it is sparse. This fact, coupled with an expected proliferation of cloud-based services over the coming years, demands that an overview of such a model is timely. Moreover, there exists a growing interest from business' for the adoption of this model. In fact, a press release in 2013 from Gartner, a research and IT consulting company, anticipated growth over the next 2 years for cloud security services to increase by nearly 40% (Gartner, 2013).

This is exciting times for business, academia, and corporate organizations who wish to protect their intellectual property and data from traditional threats, without major overhead to the day-to-day running of their operations. As we will soon discuss in this chapter there are a myriad of benefits for shifting to cloud-based security services, but with that said, there exists skepticism around the adoption of it.

This chapter aims to demystify cloud-based security services and provide a compelling discussion with regards to traditional on-premise, managed security services (MSS) and cloud-based security models.

2 BACKGROUND

This section aims to explain the background for SecaaS. This extends to the adoption of SecaaS which is defined in Section 1.3. Subsequently, an overview of related work regarding the adoption of similar technological innovations is provided in Section 2.1.

2.1 SECURITY AS A SERVICE

As mentioned, SecaaS is a business model that facilitates outsourcing of security management, engagements, and technologies to a trusted third party (cloud security service providers). It is further defined as a service-orientated approach and consequently the evolution of traditional security landscapes (Senk, 2013a; Hafner et al., 2009; Senk, 2013b). It combines managed services and security intelligence for the purpose of integrating security with traditional business processes in a cloud environment, and is arguably a cost-effective and more efficient solution with respect to previous security models.

In order to classify SecaaS, an extensive market-oriented taxonomy was undertaken by *Kark* which pertains to outsourced security services, specifically MSS (Kark et al., 2014). The results from the taxonomy provided Senk et al. with a sound foundation for their classification of SecaaS (see Table 1). His classification scheme was later validated by a survey of existing SecaaS offerings.

In an empirical study conducted in cooperation with the German Federal Association for IT, it was discovered that statistically, there were three main drivers for the adoption of SecaaS (Senk, 2013b):

- *Perceived ease of adoption:* Degree to which the adopter believes that the SecaaS adoption is effortless, both technically and organizationally speaking;
- *Perceived usefulness:* Degree to which the adopter believes that the adoption increases its performance—this includes cost and quality-related benefits;
- *Trust:* Degree to which the adopter believes that the adoption is free of risks, which includes mainly security-related but also social and strategic risks.

The authors for that study also noted the majority of existing SecaaS products cover *Endpoint Security* or *Content Security* applications (Senk, 2013b). Furthermore, they outline compliance deficiency with respect to Cloud and SaaS design principles in existing systems, in particular inflexible pricing models that restrict the potential value of existent SecaaS systems (Senk, 2013b).

According to the SecaaS model (Senk, 2013a), the delivery of security services differs clearly from traditional on-premise deployments and MSS provisioning (see Figure 1). *On-premise security systems* are deployed, operated, and maintained on the client's side and requires the allocation of trained IT and human resource capacities. MSS are described as services that are outsourced to another company which involve prior negotiation of Service Level Agreements (SLA) (Deshpande, 2005). Therefore, it is the MSS who is responsible for the management and operation of

Table 1 Classification of SecaaS Applications

Application type	Description
Application security	Secure operation of software applications (e.g., application firewalls, code analyzers)
Compliance and IT Security management (ITSM)	Support of the client organizations compliance and IT security management (e.g., automatic compliance checks, benchmarking)
Content security	Protection of content data from intended attacks and undesired events (e.g., e-mail encryption, filtering of network traffic)
Endpoint security	Protection of servers or client computers in networks (e.g., malware protection, host-based intrusion detection)
Identity and access management	Identification of users, provisioning of user identity attributes and assignment of necessary privileges (e.g., single sign-on, multi-factor authentication)
Devices management	Remote management of client-sided security systems (e.g., intrusion detection and prevention systems)
Security information and event management (SIEM)	Specific security-related functions for monitoring complex IT systems (e.g., archiving and analysis of log-data, forensic analysis)
Vulnerability and threat management (VTM)	Detection of threats apart of eminent internal security incidents (e.g., patch management, notifications on current attacks)

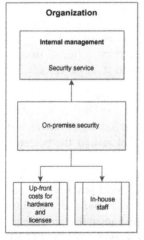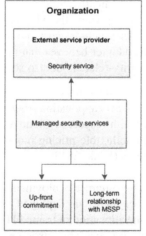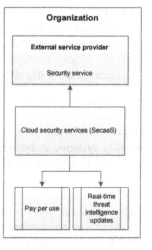

FIGURE 1

Security service delivery models.

systems. Further, it is often required that dedicated hardware and systems are deployed within the client organization, and due to the initial effort required, clients are bound by up-front commitments and long-term relationships with providers.

Traditional MSS provisioning follows the *Application Service Provider* (ASP) model (Senk, 2013b; Quirchmayr et al., 2006). In contrast, SecaaS solutions are fully operated and maintained by the cloud service provider. Thus, it is not necessary for clients to require dedicated hardware or software. Rather, services are provided to clients by means of a virtualized multi-tenant architecture that ensures the highest degree of capacity utilization. This makes the service usage highly cost-effective to the client and enables fine-grained pay-per-use models.

2.2 OUTSOURCING MODEL

The SecaaS model draws similar motivations from typical outsourcing situations. Just like manufacturing and transportation outsourcing commonly found in supply chains, security is an integral component to be considered by every business even though they may not have the resources or capability to execute it to the highest level. Outsourcing models for security assessment enables companies to achieve the following: (Bill Lakenan, 2001; Quin, 1999)

- *Economies of scale:* From the SecaaS provider point of view, an important objective of outsourcing is to reduce operational costs through the aggregation of service contracts from many different customers. The SecaaS provider would be able to disseminate the benefits of their latest developments around security and protection, and pass them on to their customers (regardless of the number of customers).
- *Risk pooling:* SecaaS also allows the customers to transfer the requirements for constant knowledge updating of security risks and mitigation to the SecaaS companies. This means that the latest developments and vulnerability mitigation techniques are implicitly shared between many of the customers while there is a higher-level overview of the trends developing.
- *Reduced capital investment:* The costs of hiring security resources are greatly reduced through SecaaS services since the customers' system administrators just need to ensure that the systems are regularly inspected by the SecaaS services—maximizing productivity.
- *Focus on core competency:* By carefully outsourcing security requirements to SecaaS suppliers, the customer can focus on its core strength without compromising on security capabilities.
- *Increased flexibility:* With SecaaS outsourcing models, customers can also better react to changes and developments in the rapidly developing security industry.

3 TRADITIONAL SECURITY

In this section we expand on our coverage of traditional security services (on-premise and MSS) with respect to the SecaaS model.

3.1 ON-PREMISE

On-premise security refers to the hardware and software solutions that protect businesses data from outside and inside threats. Such solutions require the hardware that houses the security infrastructure to be maintained and updated on-site. The upside of approach is that all the specialized hardware and software are managed by the businesses own internal IT department and thus does not rely on any external service providers. It is worthy to note that there are drawbacks to this solution, some of which are covered in Table 2.

Our comparison between cloud-based and on-premises solutions illustrates the differences in terms of cost, control, security, and the likes. While maintaining hardware on-site is regarded as less risky, the associated costs for hardware and software are significantly higher than the "pay as you go" approach that SecaaS offers. This is exacerbated by the fact that the price of hardware is to be covered up front and the ongoing cost of maintaining, upgrading, and servicing the hardware. Moreover, it is likely that on-premise training for staff is likely to be a recurring cost.

3.2 MANAGED SECURITY SERVICES

MSS are characterized in that a dedicated security service instance is set up for a client organization by an external service provider. This approach involves the prior negotiation of individual SLA (Senk, 2013a; Deshpande, 2005). Such a service, in the past, has been provided by a range of different entities. For example, startups, established companies, telecommunication and computer companies, ASPs

Table 2 On-Premises versus SecaaS

	SecaaS	On-premises
Cost	Pay as you go, per user, per month, etc.	Up-front capital costs for hardware, software licensing, lab space, air conditioning, etc.
Customization	Customizable and scalable services	Somewhat customizable depending on software vendor
Hardware	Hardware and software owned reside at provider site	Customer must provide hardware and system platforms to run apps
Security	Access to SecaaS apps is via Internet	Less risky because of on-premises location
Mobile access	Accessible via browsers running on mobile devices	Limited access to business applications via browsers running on mobile devices
Integration	Limited integration, even though this is an important requirement	Integration with existing software is commonplace
Control	SecaaS provider controls systems and is entrusted with customer data	Control of systems and data

and consulting firms are examples of businesses who have been involved in providing MSS for their customers. Listed below are some of the services that MSS provide that are discussed in the literature (Deshpande, 2005).

- *Perimeter management and network boundary protection:* This service usually includes installation and maintenance of virtual private networks (VPNs), IDSs / IPSs, and firewalls.
- *Managed security monitoring (MSM):* MSM is more focused on the monitoring of the client's network. It deals with interpreting whether data passing through the network is malicious or benign and deals with incident response measures.
- *Vulnerability assessment/penetration testing:* This service deals with identifying flaws within a company's services (e.g., web, mail, network, etc.) that could lead to exploitation by adversaries.

Although MSS covers a range of security services, there are trade-offs between this model and SecaaS. For example, consider a firewall under the MSS scheme which is outsourced to an MSSP (managed security service provider). The client who subscribes to the service need not worry about log inspection, rather it is the responsibility of the MSSP to collect, store, and review the logs and take the necessary mitigation steps. With the SecaaS model, given the same scenario, only the delivery model is outsourced—the mechanics of the collection and storage tasks including the software and hardware that enable it—but it is the clients personnel or staff that are responsible for the firewall security. Therefore, the role of log inspection, report generation is maintained by the client. This general definition is the same for any security task, whether it is e-mail security, vulnerability assessment, network intrusion, SIEM, and so forth.

4 SecaaS CATEGORIES OF SERVICE

Based on our observations of the literature for categories of service regarding SecaaS, we have identified two main viewpoints around this topic. The first comes from Senk et al. in their paper Adoption of SecaaS (Senk, 2013a), and the second is the *Cloud Security Alliance* in their paper *Defined Categories of Service* (Cloud Security Alliance, 2011a). The CSA working group is perhaps best known for its extensive research around the adoption of cloud computing, and its guidelines for best practices within cloud environments. In their paper, the CSA notes that the following service categories were identified as most significant to experienced industry consumers and security professionals (Cloud Security Alliance, 2011a): identity and access management (IAM); data loss prevention (DLP); Web security; email security; security assessments; intrusion management; security information and event management (SIEM); encryption; business continuity and disaster recovery; network security. For the purposes of this section, we have classified the above into the four classes described by the CSA, namely protective; detective; preventive, and reactive. These are given in Table 3.

Table 3 SecaaS Categories by Class

Category	Domain	Protective	Preventative	Detective	Reactive
1	Identity and access management	X	X		
2	Data loss prevention		X		
3	Web security	X		X	X
4	Email security	X		X	X
5	Security assessment			X	
6	Intrusion management	X		X	X
7	Security information and event management			X	
8	Encryption	X			
9	Business continuity and disaster recovery	X		X	
10	Network security	X		X	X

For organizations to achieve a robust security posture, all of the aforementioned classes must be addressed. Where security is paramount, it is important for organizations to be able to cover the entire class scope for events that can occur. From security assessments, to intrusion detection/prevention and monitoring of ones files and event logs, it is essential to have a security posture in place that addresses these. It is simply not enough to have measures that address security after the fact where an adversary has succeeded in infiltrating ones organization. As such, in the following subsections, we will be addressing those categories for which protective, detective, and reactive measures can be deployed via the SecaaS model. In the authors opinion, for brevity, we can condense the aforementioned categories into four subsections. These are as follows: system security, data security, Web security and network security (see Table 4).

4.1 SYSTEM SECURITY

System security assessments are third-party or internal audits (by an independent department of an organization) of on premise or cloud-based systems (Cloud Security Alliance, 2011c). Typically, the core functionalities for cloud-based security assessments described in the literature are as follows:

- *Governance:* Process by which policies are set and decision making is executed.
- *Risk management:* Process for ensuring that important business processes and behaviors remain within the tolerances associated with those policies and decisions.

Table 4 Defined Categories of Service by Class

Category	Domain	Data	Web	System	Network
1	Identity and access management			X	
2	Data loss prevention	X			
3	Web security	X	X	X	
4	Email security	X		X	
5	Security assessment	X	X	X	X
6	Intrusion management				X
7	Security information and event management	X		X	X
8	Encryption	X			
9	Business continuity and disaster recovery	X			
10	Network security	X		X	X

- *Compliance:* Process of adherence to policies and decisions. Policies can be derived from internal directives, procedures, and requirements, or external laws, regulations, standard and agreements.
- *Technical compliance audits:* Automated auditing of configuration settings in devices, operating systems, databases, and applications.
- *Application security assessments:* Automated auditing of custom applications.
- *Vulnerability assessments:* Automated probing of network devices, computers and applications for known vulnerabilities and configuration issues.
- *Penetration testing:* Exploitation of vulnerabilities and configuration issues to gain access to an environment, network, or computer.
- *Security/risk rating:* Assessment of the overall security/vulnerability status of the systems being tested. This is usually based on the OWASP risk rating methodology (OWASP, 2014b).

Following the above functionalities, cloud providers can address concerns that relate to both traditional security assessment methods and cloud-related concerns. For example, the lack of continuous monitoring is a problem that can be mitigated some-what entirely by outsourcing services such as intrusion detection/prevention systems (IDS/IPS) and WAFs (Web application firewall) to a provider. This ensures continuous availability and real-time protection from outside threats. Indeed it is possible to implement such solutions without using cloud infrastructure and services, but doing so requires more hardware and software resources, staffing and cost overhead. Web application security assessments can also be carried out using the SecaaS model. Traditional approaches include black-box testing where the Web application is tested from the vantage point of an outside attacker without prior knowledge of its architecture and source code. The Web SecaaS providers toolkit should address the most common areas of deficiencies outlined by OWASP (2014b) which include: cross-site scripting flaws (XSS), structured query language (SQL) injection flaws, file inclusion issues, direct object references, directory traversal, information leakage, and session management.

Where clients have multiple sites or domains to manage, it may be advantageous for them to assess and monitor their Web applications from a single location. In doing so, it is possible to schedule active scanning during off-peak times, while keeping a threat database up to date in a single location. Leveraging the cloud, vulnerability assessment can be carried out across an internal network systematically. In some cases, it may be desirable to install agent software on devices that require endpoint and service protection. Vulnerability assessment, in this context, may take the form of network sweeping for open ports, in combination with identifying outdated services. Where required, the assessment process might also encompass exploitation of mal-configured software, in order to gain access to the machine or an environment. It is important to note that cloud security assessment tools should support common standards and industry best practices. For example, CVE (2014) for vulnerability assessments, OWASP top 10 (OWASP, 2014a) for Web application security assessment, NIST/CIS/FDCC/SANS (NIST, 2014; CIS, 2014; FDCC, 2014; SANS, 2014) guidelines and controls for compliance assessment.

4.2 NETWORK SECURITY

Network security, as defined by the CSA consists of security services that allocate access, distribute, monitor, and protect the underlying resource services (Cloud Security Alliance, 2011b). It addresses risks relating to the use of, and access to, enterprise networks. In a cloud environment, network security is likely to be a double prong approach comprising physical and virtual devices. Typically, the core functionalities for cloud-based network security described in the literature are as follows:

- *Security gateways:* This includes firewalls, WAF, SOA/API, VPN.
- *Integrity monitoring:* For example, IDS, IPS, Server Tier firewall, file integrity monitoring, DLP, anti-virus and anti-spam.
- *Secure services:* For example, DNS (domain name system) and/or DNSSEC, DHCP, NTP, RAS, OAuth, SNMP, and management network segmentation and security.
- *Traffic monitoring:* This includes monitoring network traffic and flows.
- *Denial of service protection:* For example, identifying anomalous network flows.

The above is a necessary list for network security but by no means a sufficient one. The authors would like to encourage interested readers to take a look at the CSA paper for network security deployment guidelines (Cloud Security Alliance, 2011b). In addition to the core functionalities described in the literature, there are several key network security services that are applicable to the SecaaS model that we will be addressing in this section. These are given in no particular order: *network service scanning, network intrusion detection, real-time configuration and alerts.*

4.2.1 Service scanning

Network service scanning is designed to probe a server or host for open ports that map to a particular service (Lyon, 2009). Not unlike traditional port scanning, cloud services provide similar functionality as traditional scanners which allow administrators to monitor services running on internal clients, with the additional benefits of the cloud delivery model. Network administrators ought to be equipped with the necessary tools to carry out these tasks. These tasks should include the ability to analyze networks and subnets for newly added machines, and the ability to recognize unauthorized services running on physical and virtual devices.

4.2.2 Intrusion detection

Network intrusion detection (IDS) and prevention (IPS) systems are systems that attempt to discover unauthorized access to an enterprise network by analyzing traffic on the network for signs of malicious activity. They are usually placed at ingress and egress points of the network to detect for anomalous traffic. These systems do this by combining signature and statistical anomaly detection and heuristic behavioral analysis (Cloud Security Alliance, 2011b). To differentiate the two, an IDS provides logging functionality and alerts to attacks, whereas an IPS takes preventative action and responds to attacks. Within a cloud providers network, the client should define specific locations to be monitored by the IDS/IPS, and agree to service and performance levels along with rules and policy management.

4.2.3 Real-time configuration and alerts

Real-time configuration and alerting are features that follow the SIEM category of service. The CSA defines SIEM as a system that accepts (via push or pull mechanisms) log and event information. This information is then correlated and analyzed to provide real-time reporting and alerting on incidents/events that may require intervention (Cloud Security Alliance, 2011d). Needless to say, SIEM deployed via the cloud provides a number of benefits that include powerful user interfaces, proactive alerting, reporting and analysis which make it easier for organizations to achieve compliance.

4.3 WEB SECURITY

Web security is defined by the CSA as real-time protection offered either on-premise through software/appliance installation or via the cloud by proxying or redirecting web traffic to the cloud provider (Cloud Security Alliance, 2011e). This provides an added layer of protection on top of things like anti-virus to prevent malware from entering the organization via activities such as web browsing. Policy rules can also be enforced by this extra layer of security. For example, an administrator may set a rule such that only particular departments can access parts of the web, whereas other departments may have different web policy rules as required. Web SecaaS, in contrast to traditional security services, utilizes the cloud computing model. Following this model, users of cloud security services can take advantage of its offerings regardless of geographic location (remote and on-premise). Proposed cloud web security solutions should aim to achieve the following goals: *reduce cost and complexity*; *provide real-time protection* and *provide web filtering*; *provide granular web application controls*. In the following subsections, we will be breaking down the aforementioned goals and examining how they can be realized.

4.3.1 Reduce cost and complexity

The inherent nature of cloud computing follows the pay-per-use business model. What this means in the context of SecaaS is that an enterprise pays only for the services and resources it uses, as it uses them (ISACA, 2013). By moving services and maintenance workloads to a cloud platform, the enterprise has the ability to instantly increase or decrease resources, depending on the immediate needs of a particular workload. With SecaaS, very limited, if any, up-front capital investment is required for hardware and software, ongoing software licenses are eliminated, the need for complex technologies is limited and services can be delivered and accessed regardless of geographic location. As a result, there are fewer servers running security applications and thus yielding a smaller data center footprint. To an enterprise, this translates to direct savings on real estate, power and cooling and indirect savings on facilities maintenance (Microsoft, 2014).

4.3.2 Provide real-time protection

Following the cloud computing model, the CSA's Web security implementation guidance paper (Cloud Security Alliance, 2011e) recognizes two capabilities which must be apart of a cloud web security solution. These are as follows: *A scalable threat assessment infrastructure:* Providers should have the ability to collect, classify, and correlate large quantities of security intelligence data from which zero-hour threats can be recognized. *A comprehensive centralized management interface:* The benefits of such a management interface will result in greater efficiencies, visibility, control, and management over combined web, data, and email security technologies from which unified content analysis and management can be delivered.

4.3.3 Web filtering

Routing traffic through a SecaaS proxy server allows for cleaning of web traffic (web content filtering) while keeping delays to a minimum (Getov, 2012). With the SecaaS model, the service receives and forwards both incoming and outgoing traffic (see Figure 2). Such an approach has several uses—URL filtering, HTTP header information screening and page content analysis. Moreover, the authors would suggest specific pattern matching analysis on content that passes through the web security service. One should be able to configure through the web interface, a simple string or regular expression match for content sensitive data, for example credit card and social security numbers.

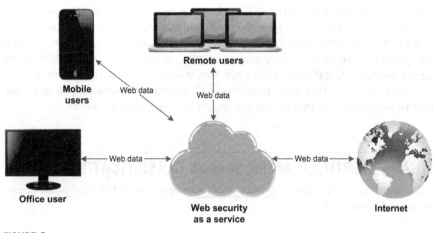

FIGURE 2

Overview of Web security architecture.

4.3.4 Granular Web application controls

Gone are the days of static HTML Web pages whereby information was delivered to the user exactly as stored. Nowadays, applications rely heavily on dynamic Web pages which are generated by Web applications. Instead of merely reading information from Web pages, users are invited to comment on published articles, create a user account or profile and thus increasing participation. This is what referred to as Web 2.0—coined by DiNucci (1999). This poses a significant challenge to traditional Web application controls wishing to impose high granularity. As a result, Web SecaaS providers are forced to adapt to these new Web technologies and provide a means for dealing with such dynamic content. For example, it may not be advantageous to block these sites entirely, rather it would be desirable for the provider to have policy control over content to be restricted (e.g., gaming, posting, viewing video, etc). This granular control over content passing through the proxy is simple to deploy, but at the same time, a powerful feature that highly configurable.

4.4 DATA SECURITY

Data security, in the context of a cloud service, the authors define it as the measures put in place to track, analyze and protect information on a system, medium, and in transit. This definition encompasses data that resides on physical and virtual devices, portable devices and data that are sent across a network. Although cloud computing promises lower costs, rapid scaling, easier maintenance and service availability anywhere, anytime, a key challenge is how to build confidence in how cloud can handle user data in a secure manner (Song et al., 2012). A recent Microsoft survey found that a majority of both public and business leaders are excited about the possibilities of cloud computing. Ninety percentage of them, however, are worried about availability, privacy and security of their data as it rests in the cloud (Dwork, 2009). The survey by Microsoft highlights the need for a transparent data-centric approach. To achieve these goals, control of data must be passed back to cloud end users rather than providers. To address the concerns relating to data trust and privacy, users require assurance that their data have not been passed on to a third party or susceptible to prying eyes. Therefore, protection of data that resides on disk or in transit must be adequately secured or encrypted with keys in the users possession.

5 GAPS IDENTIFIED AFTER SecaaS CLASSIFICATION

Following the classification of SecaaS, it became apparent that the following issues remain to be resolved.

5.1 GAPS IN SecaaS WEB TECHNOLOGIES

There are a numerous Web technologies and frameworks that enable developers to build and configure feature rich Web applications. But in the context of SecaaS and Web integration, there are no real guidelines for the development of such an application. One must first consider which Web technologies and frameworks conform with the implementation guidelines outlined by the CSA, before any decision is made to implement a cloud security service.

5.2 LACK OF TRUE RISK EVALUATION

Though some vendors claim that their products and services eliminate false positives entirely, to our best knowledge, this is largely unsubstantiated. This highlights the need for assessment techniques to be able to provide to its users a proof of concept for the vulnerabilities and flaws that it claims to detect. Such assessment techniques will demonstrate to users how, when, and where abouts in their services do the vulnerabilities reside. In doing so, true risk potential can be realized and appropriate action taken.

5.3 LACK OF A DATA-CENTRIC APPROACH

While two classifications of SecaaS have been proposed in the past, and standards for transmitting data across networks have been addressed, there is a need to address data, its integrity and provenance from a cloud-based perspective. Such an approach will enable users to track what has happened to their data across the physical and virtual infrastructure on which cloud services are built. In doing so, a relationship built on trust and transparency between the user and provider can be realized. Moreover, users ought to be able to track files and directories on their internal network and establish whether tampering has occurred.

5.4 **NO REAL CLASSIFICATION FOR MAPPING LEGITIMATE COMMUNICATING SERVICES**

Applications such as intrusion detection/prevention systems and firewalls allow network administrators to monitor inbound and outbound traffic on a network (Roesch, 1999), however, there is a need to distinguish applications that communicate over common whitelisted ports such as 80 and 443. This is due to the ever-changing complexity of malware that tend to "phone home" and transfer data over these ports (which are usually whitelisted by the firewall rulesets). Such a classification needs to differentiate between benign applications, for example, browsers and cloud services/agents, and malicious ones. It is worthy to note that this is not a cloud security specific problem, and many on-premise security solutions are still grappling with this.

6 **FUTURE WORK**

Recent studies have shown that security is regarded as the top concern for adopting cloud security services (Senk, 2013a; Al-Harthy and Al-Badi, 2014). And there are, of course, several key areas needed to be addressed for SecaaS to reach its full potential. Future work should aim at addressing the critical gaps outlined in this chapter, namely, *data-centricity*; *web technologies for SecaaS*; *differentiating malicious and benign services*; and *true risk evaluation*.

The fact that *trust* and *perceived usefulness* have been identified as the main barriers to the adoption of SecaaS (Senk, 2013b), future work on the topic ought to focus on areas in which usefulness and trust can be increased.

7 **CONCLUDING REMARKS**

The proliferation of cloud computing has changed the way we manage our IT infrastructure and services over the Internet. It has paved the way for a new approach to the security of our infrastructure, our data and our applications. SecaaS promises to deliver the scope, scale, and sophistication of tools required to protect information, while substantially decreasing the costs and resources associated with information security. In this chapter, we have described how SecaaS can be used as a tool to protect our data, while being a cost effective, elastic, flexible, and agile asset to enterprise. Furthermore, we have compared and contrasted the SecaaS model with respect to traditional on-premise and MSS, and provided a compelling discussion for moving such services to the cloud. Our observations note that while literature around cloud security services are sparse, future predictions by Gartner and Forrester show that growth for such services is expected to increase substantially. This chapter aimed to address this gap and made sense of this burgeoning field in cloud security.

REFERENCES

Al-Harthy, L.Y., Al-Badi, A.H., 2014. To cloudify or not to cloudify. Int. J. Social Manage. Econ. Bus. Eng. 8, 2402–2410.

Bill Lakenan, E.F., Boyd, D., 2001. Why Cisco Fell: Outsourcing and Its Perils. Booz & Company, New York.

CIS, 2014. Center for Internet Security, Retrieved 17/08/2014 from http://www.cisecurity.org/.

Cloud Security Alliance, 2011a. Defined Categories of Service, Retrieved 11/08/2014 from https://cloudsecurityalliance.org/wp-content/uploads/2011/09/SecaaS_V1_0.pdf.

Cloud Security Alliance, 2011b. Network Security Implementation Guidance, Retrieved 11/08/2014 from https://downloads.cloudsecurityalliance.org/initiatives/secaas/SecaaS_Cat_10_Network_Security_Implementation_Guidance.pdf.

Cloud Security Alliance, 2011c. Security Assessments Implementation Guideance, Retrieved 11/08/2014 from https://downloads.cloudsecurityalliance.org/initiatives/secaas/SecaaS_Cat_5_Security_Assessments_Implementation_Guidance.pdf.

Cloud Security Alliance, 2011d. SIEM Implementation Guidance, Retrieved 11/08/2014 from https://downloads.cloudsecurityalliance.org/initiatives/secaas/SecaaS_Cat_7_SIEM_Implementation_Guidance.pdf.

Cloud Security Alliance, 2011e. Web Security Implementation Guidance, Retrieved 11/08/2014 from https://downloads.cloudsecurityalliance.org/initiatives/secaas/SecaaS_Cat_3_Web_Security_Implementation_Guidance.pdf.

CVE, 2014. Common Vulnerabilities and Exposures, Retrieved 11/08/2014 from https://cve.mitre.org/.

DiNucci, D., 1999. Fragmented Future, Retrieved 25/08/2014 from http://www.darcyd.com/fragmented_future.pdf.

Deshpande, D., 2005. Managed security services: an emerging solution to security. In: Proceedings of the 2nd Annual Conference on Information Security Curriculum Development. ACM, New York, NY, pp. 107–111.

Dwork, C., 2009. The differential privacy frontier (extended abstract). In: Proceedings of the 6th Theory of Cryptography Conference on Theory of Cryptography. Springer-Verlag, Berlin, pp. 496–502.

FDCC, 2014. Federal Desktop Core Configuration, Retrieved 17/08/2014 from http://fdcccompliance.com/.

Gartner Press Release—Cloud Based Security Services, 2013. Retrieved 15/08/2014, from http://www.gartner.com/newsroom/id/2616115.

Getov, V., 2012. Security as a service in smart clouds—opportunities and concerns. In: Computer Software and Applications Conference (COMPSAC), 2012 IEEE 36th Annual, pp. 373–379.

Hafner, M., Memon, M., Breu, R., 2009. SeAAS—a reference architecture for security services in SOA. j-jucs 15, 2916–2936.

ISACA, 2013. Security as a Service—Business Benefits with Security, Governance and Assurance Perspectives, 3.

Kark, K., Penn, J., Whiteley, R., Coit, L., 2014. Market Overview: Managed Security Services, Retrieved 16/08/2014 from http://www.forrester.com/Market+Overview+Managed+Security+Services/.

Ko, R.K.L., 2010. Cloud computing in plain English. Crossroads 16, 5–6.

Lyon, G.F., 2009. Nmap Network Scanning: The Official Nmap Project Guide to Network Discovery and Security Scanning. Insecure, USA.

Microsoft, 2014. Get Cloud Empowered. See How the Cloud can Transform Your Business, Retrieved 20/08/2014 from www.microsoft.com/global/el-gr/cloud/RenderingAssets/Hero/results/MyCloudPowerBrief_7607.pdf.

NIST, 2014. National Institute of Standards and Technology, Retrieved 17/08/2014 from http://www.nist.gov/.

OWASP, 2014a. OWASP—Open Web Application Security Project Top 10, Retrieved 11/08/2014 from https://www.owasp.org/index.php/.

OWASP, 2014b. OWASP Risk Rating Methodology, Retrieved 11/08/2014 from https://www.owasp.org/index.php/OWASP_Risk_Rating_Methodology.

Quin, J.B., 1999. Strategic outsourcing: leveraging knowledge capabilities. Sloan Manage. Rev. 40, 4.

Quirchmayr, G., Karyda, M., Mitrou, E., 2006. A framework for outsourcing IS/IT security services. Inform. Manage. Comput. Secur. 14, 403–416.

Roesch, M., 1999. Snort—Lightweight Intrusion Detection for Networks. In: Proceedings of the 13th USENIX Conference on System Administration. USENIX Association, Berkeley, CA, pp. 229–238.

SANS, 2014. SANS Critical Security Controls—Guidelines, Retrieved 17/08/2014 from http://www.sans.org/critical-security-controls/guidelines.

Senk, C., 2013a. Adoption of security as a service. J. Internet Serv. Appl. 4.

Senk, C., 2013b. Future of cloud-based services for multi-factor authentication: results of a Delphi study. In: Yousif, M., Schubert, L. (Eds.), In: Cloud Computing. Lecture Notes of the Institute for Computer Sciences, Social Informatics and Telecommunications Engineering, 112, Springer International Publishing, Berlin, pp. 134–144.

Song, D., Shi, E., Fischer, I., Shankar, U., 2012. Cloud data protection for the masses. Computer 45, 39–45.

Secure migration to the cloud—In and out

10

Thomas Kemmerich[a], Vivek Agrawal[a], Carsten Momsen[b]

Norwegian Information Security Laboratory (NISLab), Gjøvik university College, Norway[a]
Leibniz University Hanover, Hanover, Germany[b]

1 INTRODUCTION

The decision of outsourcing the internal IT-Processes and IT-Services is mostly based on economic considerations today. Very often, the strategic and innovative role of "IT" for the cloud customer will be overseen. Taking this into account and considering the high dependency of more or less all companies according to their IT-Services, the migration of the local IT-Services to a Cloud Service Provider (CSP) has to be planned and realized very carefully. A rollback or change of the CSP is essential not to be locked-in to the chosen CSP or the need of large investments in money and manpower to change the current situation. It is important to detect and avoid the lock-in issue in any typical cloud-based service scenario. The Cloud Customer instead of the CSP should be interested to set up an IT-Service environment that could be very flexible developed and moved. This includes the avoidance of lock-in effects, which are often hidden details, and services of CSPs.

Proposed in this chapter is the description of factors that has to be concretely considered before and during the decision to move the IT-Services to a CSP along with the measures that have to be setup to be flexible in changing the conditions of delivering the IT-Services. This chapter also offers a discussion on the legal requirements of outsourcing IT-Processes since there are many obstacles and problems occurring using a CSP that are not visible at a glance. The legal consideration is mainly based on German and European legal systems in order to give a comprehensive overview. In practice, the local conditions and local legal systems and requirements have to be taken into consideration. This chapter also gives a brief overview on the requirement and challenges of cloud migration. Furthermore, this chapter concentrates on the cloud migration of small and medium enterprises (SMEs). For big companies and corporates, some other rules and boundary conditions are valid. Therefore, a separate consideration is necessary and the according measures will be in some fields different from these for SMEs.

2 WHO ARE CLOUD CONSUMER AND CSP?

A cloud consumer or cloud customer is the entity that maintains a business relationship with, and uses services from, CSPs (Armour et al., 2012). A cloud consumer selects a set of service according to its need and sets up service contracts with the CSP. The cloud consumer is charged for the services being provided. Consumers use SLAs to mention its requirements to the CSP. A cloud consumer can use application/service for business process operations (SaaS); develop, tests, deploys, and manages application hosted in a cloud environment (PaaS); create/installs, manages, and monitors services for IT infrastructure operations (IaaS) (Hogan et al., 2011).

A CSP is the entity responsible for making a service available to cloud consumers (Armour et al., 2012). It is the responsibility of the CSP to acquire and manage the computing infrastructure required for providing the cloud services to the cloud consumers. The role of a CSP is to install, manage, maintain, and support the software application on a cloud infrastructure (SaaS); to provide development, deployment, and administration tools (PaaS); manage physical processing, storage, networking, and the hosting environment (IaaS) (Hogan et al., 2011).

3 IT-SERVICE OF A SMALL LAWYER OFFICE MIGRATES INTO THE CLOUD

In this chapter, the motivation and realization of a small law office to move almost all its IT-Services and IT-Application to a CSP is described as an example. The following sections will refer to this scenario at various points to make the discussion simpler. The term "consumer," "cloud consumer," and "law office" will be used interchangeably.

During the separation process from a big law office to a small, four people, law office the question raised up, how to organize the IT-Services in a way, which is efficient and economically arguable. A business process analysis and a clear risk assessment were the kernels of this process.

The first and most important obstacle was the complete lack of IT-Knowledge of the lawyer combined with a common view of private usage of IT. Here appears an important aspect of serving information processing in SMEs. A private developed, auto-didactic experienced knowledge of IT comes into a professional environment where confidentiality, integrity, and availability play an important role, especially for lawyers and service-oriented business dealing with private data.

The primary IT-Applications the law office is using are (see Figure 1):

- Customer database → Processing
- Communication services (e-mail, . . .)
- Telephone services
- Office applications (word processing, etc.)
- Internet access
- Access to databases of relevant laws and cases

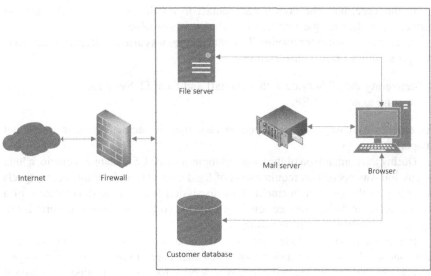

FIGURE 1

An overview of the law office.

- Access to court applications
- Storage of files (containing mostly confidential and/private data)

Before starting the migration, an evaluation of the required information processing was fulfilled. The evaluation starts with the business process of the lawyer. This results in the appraisal, which business process needs what kind of IT-Support. The next step was the mapping of the business processes to the IT-Applications. Based on this information, the planning was possible to determine the required IT-Systems and the essential services for installation and management of the IT-Systems and IT-Applications. It was important at this stage to clearly define the required amount of services for IT-Systems and IT-Applications. Three scenarios were considered:

- Complete transferring of all IT-Services and IT-Applications to the CSP (this means a total terminal-based application—no relevant IT-Services locally)
- Essential IT-Applications will be served locally and the rest will be transferred to the CSP (relevant IT-Power at the end-devices must be provided locally)
- Local delivering of IT-Services using an external IT-Service Provider (relevant IT-Power at the end-devices must be provided locally)

Independently from the technological aspects, a simplified risk analysis based on International Organization for Standardization (ISO) 27001 was done using the methodology of BSI Base Protection (BSI-Standard100-3, 2008) for all scenarios.

In this case, here the lawyer had contact to a CSP, who offered this kind of services. An offer for the first two scenarios was available.

A separate scenario for leaving the cloud service was also developed. There were two possibilities under consideration:

- delivering the IT-Service with own staff and local IT-Systems,
- moving to another CSP.

An emergency case was considered in case that the actual provider would not cooperate.

During the comparison of the three solutions and the CSP change scenario, a long discussion was opened on requirements of legal contracts and the different impacts according to the risk management. This discussion leads to the development of a legal contract including service-level agreements, conditions for service provisioning, costs, penalties, and responsibilities.

Before migration, a detailed test using the cloud environment in real work cases was conducted, and an evaluation took place after the test together with the lawyer. Several processes were adapted and a local service for one application was planned and established.

The new cloud environment was set up before the lawyer and his employees moved to a new office. In other cases, if the business goes on during the cloud migration process, a dedicated migration scenario has to be developed, tested, and fulfilled. This includes also a roll-back scenario at each point of the migration phase.

A Security Policy was developed and verified with the lawyer. The business process analysis was relatively simple but the discussion about the risk analysis was complex. Since data are mostly sensitive (case data, confidential information from the clients, etc.), a strong protection is essential. During the discussion of potential loss of reputation and, therefore, a public loss of trust, cryptographic measures to protect the integrity, and confidentiality were implemented.

A yearly audit of the cloud environment and service provisioning (local, at the law office) by an independent expert/auditor shall take place to check the functionality and security and propose measures to improve the services, security, or identify possibilities for savings.

4 REQUIREMENTS FOR CLOUD MIGRATION

Cloud computing is becoming a well-known solution to offer IT-Services and IT-Applications. However, it is necessary to assess all requirements before migrating to the cloud solution. There are essential factors and aspects related to the planning of the cloud migration. In this section, an overview of the most essential requirements is discussed.

4.1 SECURITY POLICY

The information security policy describes how information security has to be developed in an organization, for which purpose and with which resources and structures. A security policy describes information security objectives and strategies of an organization. The basic purpose of a security policy is to protect people and information, set the rules for expected behaviors by users, define, and authorize the consequences of violation (Canavan, 2006). There are many standards available to keep the information secure and establish security policy. ISO/IEC 27001 (ISO/IEC27001:2005, 2005), ISO/IEC 27002 (ISO/IEC27002:2005, 2005), ISO 13335 (ISO/IEC13335–1:2004, 2004), ISO 17799 (ISO/IEC17799:2005, 2005) are the best-known standards for providing requirements for an Information Security Management System (ISMS). A security policy for the law office is developed according to the BSI standard 100-1 (BSI-Standard100-1, 2008). The information security policy contains statements on the following issues:

- Information security objectives of the institution (e.g., a public agency or private company),
- relationship between the information security objectives and the business objectives or functions of the institution,
- aspired level of information security,
- guiding statements on how the aspired level of information security should be achieved,
- guiding statements whether and by what means the level of information security should be verified,
- the policy is approved by the management and made public in the company.

4.2 POLICY DEVELOPMENT

BSI-Standards 100-1, 100-2 (BSI-Standard100-2, 2008) and SANS institute (Institute, 2008; Canavan, 2006) describe the details of creation of a policy for information security. It is important that as many departments as possible should be involved in the development of a security policy. The security policy must be designed in such a way that all organizational units can be represented with its contents. The general composition of the policy development team varies according to the policy being developed and it is the task of an organization to decide which departments and hierarchical levels will be participated in the policy development. BSI standard 100-1 suggested a life cycle of a policy for information security. This model is known as PDCA cycle as it is based on four phases, i.e., (P)lan, (D)o, (C)heck, (A)ct. The life cycle starts with the *Planning and Conception* (P) phase to develop a strategy for handling risks in an organization, *Implementation* (D) phase to implement the plan for the security concept and safeguards, *Performance* (C) review and monitoring phase to monitor the performance of safeguards and security operations during operation, *Optimization and Improvement* (A) phase to correct any defects and improve the safeguards.

4.3 SECURITY AND PRIVACY

The loss of confidentiality, integrity, or availability of data of law office can have a negative impact on the business of the company. The company has an access to court application and database of sensitive information of its customers. Similarly, any breach in the information privacy is also an important concern. Privacy refers to an individual's ability to control how his or her information is collected, used, and disclosed. CSPs must protect consumer's assets from internal and external threats, maintain the privacy of the data, remain available and reliable, and perform consistently. A system must ensure that subjects cannot manipulate the protected data unnoticed or in an unauthorized way. CSPs store data on a virtual hard drive, which must be protected against unauthorized manipulation. A minute must be reliably assigned to the sender, and it can be proved that this information has not been changed since it was created or distributed. The Cloud Security Alliance has developed a useful model of information life cycle management, with phases of Create, Store, Use, Share, Archive, and Destroy, data (see Figure 2). The life cycle is shown in a linear progression but once the data is created, it can bounce between phases, and may not pass through all stages (Simmonds et al., 2011). There are many scenarios where security and privacy requirements play an active role in the context of moving a technology to the cloud.

4.4 DETECTING AND PREVENTING SENSITIVE DATA MIGRATION TO THE CLOUD

Many organizations face the problem with the management of sensitive data. They reported the migration of sensitive data to the cloud services by an individual or business unit without the approval or even notification. Data needs to be pulled out from

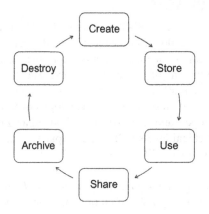

FIGURE 2

Data lifecycle.

Adapted from Cloud Security Alliance Guidance Version 3.0 (2011),
https://cloudsecurityalliance.org/guidance/csaguide.v3.0.pdf.

its existing repository before moving to the cloud. The law office must adopt database activity monitoring to detect any extraction of data or replication from a database.

4.5 PROTECTING DATA MOVING TO THE CLOUD

It is important to protect data in transit. Data can be moved from a traditional infrastructure to a CSP; data can be moved between CSPs and between instances or components within a given cloud. Data that a customer wants to upload into a cloud must be protected in transit; similarly, data that a customer wants to download from a cloud must be protected in transit.

4.6 PROTECTING DATA IN THE CLOUD

Data should be accessed only by entities that have been authorized by the concerned customer for specific access rights. CSP must enforce a mechanism to protect against access attempts by unauthorized entities or access in unauthorized modes while preserving the availability for authorized customers.

4.7 IT-KNOWLEDGE

The decision to move IT-Processes to a CSP implies by the stakeholders often to save costs for expensive, often less productive IT-Staff. However, it will be mostly forgotten that qualified IT-Knowledge is also necessary for planning and maintenance of a running business processes supported by the (outsourced) IT-Services. The law office needs to stress on the point that migration of computing and communication services into the cloud give the IT-Staff the opportunity to do strategic work in the direction of tactical and strategic business support. In most companies, IT is a strategic factor and mostly, maintenance effort and user support prevents IT-Staff from strategic development for improving the real business of the company (IT as an enabling factor).

4.8 CONTROL AND VISIBILITY

This requirement relates to the fact that cloud consumers have very limited visibility into the provider's policy, incident alert, audit information, and security measures. CSPs are reluctant to share this information to avoid any attack on their policies and avoiding disclosing internals. It is important for the law office to monitor their workloads, keep track of any security related incident, compliance, or privacy breach, and general the status of the systems. A workload is an encapsulation of one or more of the following: application processes, data, configuration information, and state. CSP can provide distinct and effective services but consumer must not be locked-in to the provider. Cloud consumers must be able to monitor the cloud operations so that they can replicate these operations elsewhere.

Consumers have very limited control over the security policies enforced by the CSPs. A proper set of control over the information is necessary while moving IT components to the cloud. It raises an important question on the maintenance of the control by the cloud consumers over their workloads even though they may not know the protection mechanisms and the locations of workload. It is essential for the cloud customer to define in their security policy the requirements for controlling the correct application of the policy rules by the CSP.

4.9 COSTS

Customers must assess payment and pricing models regarding the decision to migrate to cloud environment and a particular CSP. The decision to migrate to cloud must be considered only when it would be cost effective. The payment opportunities include the possible payment method (e.g., credit card or bank transfer), the time of payment (prepaid or postpaid) and which level of granularity is priced (e.g., storage capacity of 1 MB, 100 MB, or 1 GB steps, CPU utilization, or network transfer volume/throughput) (Repschläger et al., 2012). Service charging defines how the service is charged (volume based, time-based, account based) and the available booking concept, e.g., pay per use, a subscription fee, market-based prices (spot pricing). Figure 3 shows the cost using the cloud cost estimator of DimensionData (DimensionData, n.d.). Customers need to pay only what they use. DimensionData allows consumers to customize CPU (up to 16) and RAM (up to 128 GB) for each server on the fly.

4.10 INTEROPERABILITY AND PORTABILITY

This requirement ensures the ability to move data or services from one CSP to another, or rollback to traditional computing. It also defines the ease of ability to which application components are moved and reused regardless of provider, platform, OS, infrastructure, location, storage, the format of data, e.g., how proprietary virtual images (AMI) of Amazon are transferable to a Microsoft Azure platform (Repschläger et al., 2012). A lack of interoperability and portability can lead to being locked-in to a particular CSP. There must be adequate flexibility in the contract and renewal of contract between the law office and the CSP. The cloud computing community has not yet defined a universal set of standards, resulting in a significant risk of vendor lock-in. When a customer migrates workload from one CSP to another, it requires extracting the data from the existing cloud environment and uploading data into another cloud environment. The requirement of interoperability is necessary to ensure that any program that performing CRUD operations (create, retrieve, update, delete) on the migrated data in the original CSP continues to work with the new CSP.

4.11 PERFORMANCE

Performance includes more extensive concepts such as reliability, energy efficiency, and scalability. The time required retrieving the data in cloud when it faces any error or failure will be effective on the cloud performance. CSP and cloud customer must agree on a proper network bandwidth to initiate the cloud service. The performance

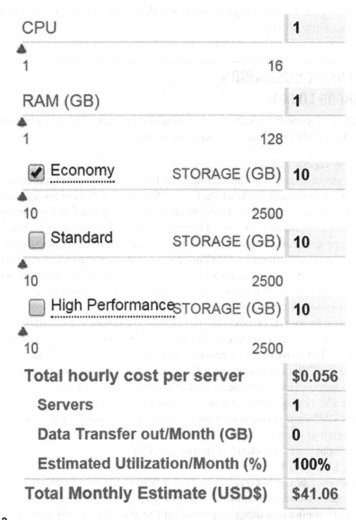

CPU		**1**
▲		
1	16	
RAM (GB)		**1**
▲		
1	128	
☑ Economy	STORAGE (GB)	**10**
▲		
10	2500	
☐ Standard	STORAGE (GB)	**10**
▲		
10	2500	
☐ High Performance	STORAGE (GB)	**10**
▲		
10	2500	
Total hourly cost per server		**$0.056**
Servers		**1**
Data Transfer out/Month (GB)		**0**
Estimated Utilization/Month (%)		**100%**
Total Monthly Estimate (USD$)		**$41.06**

FIGURE 3

Dimension data public cloud pricing.

can be degraded if the bandwidth is too low to provide service to the customer. Organizations usually discover issues with the communication bandwidth shortly after adopting cloud services (InformationWeek, 2008). Customer must assess the communication bandwidth requirements and evaluate the performance of the applications/services before migrating to cloud (Kim et al., 2009). Customers must also discuss the possible location of data centers and their distances from their location, as it is an important factor to affect the performance. Users who are at a long distance from CSPs may experience high latency and delays (Ravanmehr and Khanghahi, 2013; Borko Furht, 2010).

5 ROLLBACK SCENARIOS

5.1 VENDOR LOCK-IN

The concern of vendor lock-in is often described as the "Hotel-California" syndrome. You can check-in but you can never leave.

a. What is vendor lock-in?

In the given scenario in this chapter, the law office adopts cloud computing in order to outsource its workload to a CSP. The CSP provides services in terms of processing and/or storing the data, providing platform or infrastructure to develop application, maintain database, etc. CSP configures and optimizes the given application according to own standards, protocols, and policy. This creates a risk of vendor lock-in and makes customer dependent on the current vendor. Lock-in occurs when a cloud consumer cannot move, or it costs a significant amount of money or time to do it. Cloud consumer may want to move to another CSP or to move to its own infrastructure.

Robert Jenkins, CTO of Cloud Sigma, says in an article published on GigaOm,[1] "It's not just privacy and security. It's also—if I change my mind or it doesn't work out, how do I move on?" There may be many reasons for the cloud consumer to change the CSP or rollback to the On-premise technology. For instance:

- an unacceptable increase in cost at contract renewal time,
- the ability to get the same service at a cheaper price,
- the CSP shuts down one or more services being used without acceptable migration plans,
- a dispute between cloud customer and CSP,
- a CSP ceases business operations.

The absence of cloud computing standards has also led to vendor lock-in, where each cloud vendor offers a proprietary cloud. When a cloud consumer writes its application using a specific API of the CSP, it will be extremely difficult for him to move to another CSP, offering a different platform.

b. How to avoid lock-in?

"When you put a lot of your resources, a lot of your data in the cloud, you want to know that you can move all that away to another CSP, or even bring that back on premises, if that's the exit strategy," says Thomas Erl, CEO of Arcitura Education Inc. (McKendrick, 2011).

The law office must ensure during the planning phase of cloud migration that the architecture of the IT-Business can run on multiple cloud platforms and the data can be migrated from one CSP to another. Cloud Foundry[2]

---

[1]http://gigaom.com/2013/02/26/fear-of-lock-in-dampens-cloud-adoption/.

platform, which is Apache 2.0-licensed, is the industry's Open PaaS and provides a choice of clouds, frameworks, and application services. Some PaaS has limited offerings in terms of language and framework support that restrict the cloud consumer to deploy its technology to a single cloud.

There have been a major research and development efforts invested into methods, tools, and standards to avoid the problem of vendor lock-in. Open-source platform is designed to avoid the problem of lock-in. For instance, TM Forum Cloud Services Initiative is an approach to increase cloud computing adoption such as common terminology, transparent movement among CSPs, security issues, and benchmarking.

c. Steps to avoid lock-in

It is indeed a challenging task to figure out whether a vendor is trustworthy or trying to lock you in. However, there are certain steps that the law office can follow as a consumer to avoid lock-in.

i. Read the Service level agreement (SLA) of the CSP carefully. Check the definition of services, performance measurement, data handling, disaster recovery, termination of agreement. Accept the SLA only if it meets your need. The management team or the team responsible for the analysis of the SLA must consult IT-Team and the legal department.

ii. Ask the CSP before the planning phase about their policies of data moving. How the CSP supports toward moving the services to another CSP?

iii. Select the architecture of the selected technology such that it can be executed on multiple cloud platforms and can be easily moved from one cloud to another.

iv. Ask your CSP to give you detailed information about their architecture so that you can investigate the technical boundary conditions. If you are going to move large section of business functionality to a CSP then demand specific architecture diagrams and get it reviewed by the system architect.

v. Ask the CSP if it is possible for you to maintain same image of the data On-premise or to export data in raw format.

vi. Check with the provider if they use any standards to ensure transparent movement among CSPs.

vii. Check with the provider if they need your application to be rewritten in their proprietary language or they are comfortable with the favorable languages for cloud application, e.g., C++, Java, Python.

---

6 LEGAL ASPECTS

When it comes to the transfer of the IT-Systems and IT-Applications of a company into a cloud, there are many specifics according to civil law that need to be considered. These contain primarily legal issues in copyright, IT contract law, industrial property law, competition and antitrust law, data protection law, domain

---

[2]http://cloudfoundry.org/about/index.html.

procurement law, the applicability of the respective local law, and last but not least the liability. The questions that been highlighted at this point should be in respect of the contractual relationship and the liability between the CSP and the cloud customer. The following aspects should be understood as a general legal paradigm. References to German law are given only to point out particular aspects of interest under European law.

The question arising at first is the one concerning the contract type between the CSP and the cloud customer. This will mostly be a mixed contract type, which will be containing aspects of lease resp. loan agreements, as well as elements of contracts for services or employment (Splittgerber/Rockstroh, 2011). As far as the transformation of a system or an upgrade of that system, which the provider owes, goes, the legal assessment is measured, for example, in Germany according to the law concerning work and services. Other countries prioritize aspects of the sales or leasing agreement. The data transport, however, is generally done on the basis of the service contract law. When it comes to the availability of the data in a particular place at a particular time, the liability also falls under the rules of the service contract law. The assignment of storage capacity in a datacenter against remuneration, however, is usually subject to the law of tenancy. Even if no item as such is left, the leave of the software must be classed with that (Hanseatisches Oberlandesgericht Hamburg, Urt. v. 15. 12. 2011, 4 U 85/11). Regarding the rent it has to be noted that the rental object has to be kept, by the landlord, in a suitable condition for use. In the case of cloud services, whose content constitutes the continuous/permanent availability and retrievability would be tantamount to a guarantee. A provider must, therefore, bear in mind that his description of services in the "Terms and Conditions" also provides realistic system availability.

On this basis, it has to be assessed which rights and obligations emerge for the respective contract partner. Essentially it deals with ensuring data security. On the one hand, this may mean that the CSP has to protect the data of the cloud user from outsiders and must not misuse it himself. On the other hand, this may bring up the question for the cloud user, on which condition he is allowed to transfer data to a cloud. This is particularly relevant in sectors where confidential information (law firms, doctors, pharmacies) is affected.

This raises the question of who owns all the data within a cloud. First, the "ownership" of data from a legal point of view cannot be justified, insofar as data are - under the relevant law—not treated as items. However, data can be protected from accessing or the exploitation by third parties under different legal conditions. Primarily copyright, data protection law and criminal law protect the right on data. In principle, the right over data vests with the one who has the power of disposition regarding the data (e.g., §§ 87a/b Urheberrechtsgesetz (Germany)). There is no mandatory link between the originator of the data or the person on whose IT-System the data is stored and who has the power of disposition of the data. If the person authorized for the data has lawfully stored the data on the external IT-System (cloud), he becomes the beneficiary of the data. This also applies in relation to the operator of the (relevant) cloud. Therefore, it will be essential for a breach of the Copyright Act, whether the access to foreign databases has intruded database rights by illegitimate methods.

In addition, the producer of a database usually has the exclusive right to reproduce the database as a whole or at least a crucial part of the database, to distribute and to reproduce it publicly. However the CSP, as such, is the owner of the data, so that he does not intervene in the data inventory illegally, but on the basis of a contract. As soon as private files (not personal data) are sent to a third person or company for storing in a cloud, only the official agreement between the CSP and the cloud customer applies. Therefore, this agreement asks to regulate the legal relations between the two parties in detail and by taking into account the foreseeable conflict scenarios.

In this regard, at least in Germany, the data protection law does not help, because it usually requires the existence of private, data concerning a person (in Germany: § 1 Bundesdatenschutzgesetz (BDSG). In the act of outsourcing the data from a law office into the cloud (i.e., data of legal entities) this protection does not apply (Splittgerber/Rockstroh, 2011).

The question of data protection probably becomes relevant when it comes to the transfer of client data into the cloud. The loss or nonscheduled publication could trigger a liability of the firm in relation to the clients and other parties. It is important that the firm outsources the data and IT-Infrastructure to the cloud and undertakes an ordered-data processing (Nägele/Jacobs, 2010; Weichert, 2010). Therefore, the cloud user of such a cloud must be convinced before the start of the data processing by a CSP, which he complies with the technical and organizational measures. This means that the user must carry out a check (pre-control). This control can already be carried out within the scope of the supplier selection and must be completed no later than the beginning of the data processing. Even when in practice, the client must not perform this control Himself. The client should still be able to demonstrate by submission of appropriate certifications (e.g., ISO 27001/IT-Risk Management) from the CSP's compliance with data protection legislation. The same applies to the expressly by law required control in the course of the duration (current control) any duration or current control, as required by the local law. Furthermore, the German law prescribes explicitly that henceforth the pre- and the current control must be documented in writing. In Germany, therefore, all the rights and obligations of the data protection law do not apply toward the CSP, but the law firm. You must draft the cloud contract in writing and therefore necessarily regulate the following in it: subject and duration of the order, the nature, the scope and the purpose of the collection, processing, use of data, the possibility of cancelation and rectification of data, and the personal controlling rights of the client. The cloud customer is, therefore, liable for privacy violations.

But even this "pre-control" and the agreement of cancelation-conditions and corrections do not fully ensure the protection of data. For reasons of operational safety, the operator shall regularly backup copies of the files. Deleting a file will, therefore, not bring the necessary security. The obligations of the CSP are to be defined once again. The question arising for cloud users is whether the CSP is liable if he has fallen victim to a hacker attack and the data of the cloud user is affected. For claiming (civil) damages, it is crucial, in regard of hacked cloud data, to find out, whether the seller can be held responsible for the breach of the duty of care (culpability). This is the case, if the provider does not comply with recognized safety standards, and it has been the reason the hacking attack was possible in the first place (Splittgerber/Rockstroh, 2011).

Another relevant requirement for the contract is confidentiality. The cloud often contains company and business secrets or other confidential information. Therefore, in case of a breach of confidentiality there are often contractual penalties (Splittgerber/Rockstroh, 2011).

However, the essential question for the legal assessment is, which data protection law is applicable after all. For example, if data is collected anywhere in the EU (outside of Germany) but processed or used in Germany by a CSP, the "provisions of the German Data Protection Law do not apply (in Germany: § 1 "Bundesdatenschutzgesetz" (BDSG)). The idea behind this is that we assume that all Member States of the European Union would have a high level of data protection. In addition, it aims to help European companies to function easily and operate in other Member States without having to know all data protection regulations. The situation is different if the company has a subsidiary in Germany (Dammann, 2011). Then, the BSD is applicable, provided that the collection, processing, and storage are done domestically.

The territoriality principle applies for non-European companies. This is also relevant in terms of copyrights regarding the possible usage of the provided software by the CSP. In this way, it may come to licensing problems, when the cloud user uses the client software and therefore—due to the intermediate storage—duplicates (Splittgerber/Rockstroh, 2011). As a general rule: local law applies. According to Article 4 (paragraph 1 lit. c), the European Data Protection Directive (Directive 95/46/EC, 1995) finds it sufficient that the company "relies on means" that are located in the Member State. This leads to the conclusion that already uploading files through the cloud user in Germany to a non-European Server leads to the applicability of German law.

Finally, it should be said, however, that in terms of cloud contracts a clear agreement on the applicable law is recommended. This is also generally permitted under Article 3 Rome I (Regulation (EC) No. 593/2008 European Parliament and Council, 17.6.2008 (Rome I), 7.7.2008, L 177, 6). Since computerized litigation between foreign contractors often takes months and years, it should also be considered whether regulations in relation to the voluntary jurisdiction (arbitration) are useful.

7 CHALLENGES IN CLOUD MIGRATION

Although cloud computing seems like a trivial solution for many IT problems, there are many barriers in migrating to the cloud. A business unit will not surely move to the cloud solution if it imposes serious cost or slows down the business operation.

This section discusses several aspects related to cloud migration. Each and every aspect is important for a business unit before moving to the cloud.

7.1 LATENCY

Latency is becoming a major challenge for the cloud customer. It represents loss of availability and slows down network performance. Users access a cloud service through a network that introduces latency into every communication. Cloud latency is a bit different from the concept of latency known before the ubiquitous Internet. The latency is the time that packets use to travel from source to destination. In the case of cloud computing, the endpoints are not static. The geographical location of the user can be anywhere. Similarly, the cloud applications can be located anywhere. It is important to know the location of the ultimate end users and the networks that connect them to the destination networks (van der Zwet and Storm, n.d.).

According to White Paper published by Internap.com (Internap, 2013), every 0.1 s in latency reduces sales by 1% of Amazon.com. According to Equation Research sanctioned by Gomez, 78% of the site visitors have gone to a competitor's site due to poor performance during peak hours. CSPs like Amazon, Google, and Microsoft offer no better than 99.95% availability as Service Level Agreements. This signifies that the cloud service will remain down for an average time of 21.6 min per month. This can prevent enterprises from adopting IT-Services through a CSP.

7.2 SECURITY

Security is a major concern in the adoption of cloud computing services. Most customers are unwilling to place their sensitive corporate data in the cloud as the CSPs, or other competitive customers of the same CSP could compromise the data. Customers feel the lack of transparency as they are not aware of how, why, and where their sensitive data is processed. A customer can access cloud computing services anywhere with Internet. On the connection between the CSP and cloud customer, the data may be compromised if they are not secured. A survey conducted on 800 IT-Professionals across four countries by Intel in 2012 states that 57% of the respondents accepted that they are unwilling to move their workload and data into the cloud due to security and compliance issues (Intel, 2012).

Organizations do often not have control or knowledge of the location of the data storage in the cloud. Cloud customers have very limited control over the security policies enforced by the CSPs on their behalf. In traditional IT-Environments, IT-Infrastructure is present behind the firewall of an organization. Virtualized and nonvirtualized servers serve only a fixed line of business. IT-Professionals can select advanced security tools that give them a high degree of control over the security and compliance issues related to the organization. In the case of cloud infrastructure, servers are virtualized and shared across several lines of business or even across multiple organizations. It is important to connect multiple cloud data centers to gain efficiencies. For instance, IT-Professional may want to link a public cloud data center based in UK with their private cloud-based one in Germany. If there is not an advanced tool available to secure the connection among the distant infrastructure, local IT-Staff loses a degree of control and visibility into workload and data.

7.3 INTEROPERABILITY

Interoperability is still a big challenge in cloud migration. The cloud computing community does not have a universal set of standards now. Cloud interoperability might force the user to be dependent on a single CSP and causes vendor lock-in. Once an organization has selected a CSP, it is often extremely difficult to move to another CSP. It mostly incurs huge cost to change providers. It ceases the negotiation power toward the increment of service cost and service discontinuation.

The common practice to enable interoperability is the use of open standards. There are many cloud standardization projects. These projects focus on standardizing cloud computing solution such as workloads, authentication, and data access. The cloud standards coordination Wiki maintains a list of some projects (Standards, n.d.). Table 1 lists some of the projects related to standards for cloud computing interoperability (Hogan et al., 2011). The table titled "Cloud Standardization Effort" from the report "The Role of Standards in Cloud-Computing Interoperability" (http://www.sei.cmu.edu/reports/12tn012.pdf) (c) 2012 Carnegie Mellon University is used with special permission from its Software Engineering Institute.

Table 1 A List of Projects/Standards to Ensure Interoperability in Cloud Computing

CloudAudit, also known as Automated Audit, Assertion, Assessment, and Assurance API (A6)	Open, extensible, and secure interface, namespace, and methodology for cloud computing providers and their authorized consumers to automate the audit, assertion, assessment, and assurance of their environments. As of October 2010, CloudAudit is part of the Cloud Security Alliance
IEEE P2301, Draft Guide for Cloud Portability and Interoperability Profiles (CPIP), IEEE	Standards-based options for application interfaces, portability interfaces, management interfaces, interoperability interfaces, file formats, and operation conventions
IEEE P2302, Draft Standard for Intercloud Interoperability and Federation (SIIF), IEEE	This standard creates an economy among CSPs that is transparent to users and applications, which provides for a dynamic infrastructure that can support evolving business models
TM Forum Cloud Services Initiative	Approaches to increase cloud computing adoption such as common terminology, transparent movement among CSPs, security issues, and benchmarking

7.4 INTERNET SPEED

Cloud computing needs mostly a public network connection to access cloud data and applications with any computing device. To access cloud data, an Internet connection is used in the most cases. In a traditional noncloud environment, the server and client devices are connected by an internal high-speed network infrastructure. In cloud computing environment, all the access to data is done using an Internet connection. Internet speeds are on average 20 times slower than local network speeds. The download speed is in often (ADSL) not identical to upload speeds, i.e., pushing information from the cloud user device to the cloud server is slower than pulling information from the cloud to the device. Internet Service Provider (ISP) does not guarantee the Internet speed and performance. Internet bandwidth is typically shared by all users in the local office (TrinusTech, n.d.). The solution to mitigate this problem is to use an enterprise-class Internet connection (symmetric) that has better fault tolerance and repair service than a consumer-class connection. The main disadvantage of this solution is the high price of enterprise-class connection.

7.5 CLOUD INTEGRATION

The integration of "traditional" On-premise systems with a cloud infrastructure is still a huge problem. KPMG International's 2012 global CSPs survey (KPMG, 2012) found that the integration with existing architecture is the second biggest challenges/concerns (41%) about adopting cloud services (see Figure 4). The issue of integration takes into account the ability to connect with both source and target

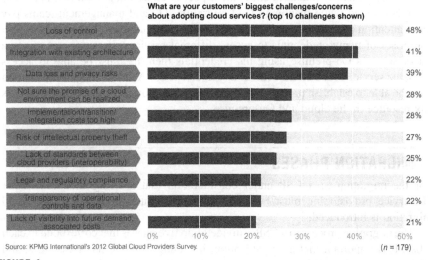

What are your customers' biggest challenges/concerns about adopting cloud services? (top 10 challenges shown)

Challenge	%
Loss of control	48%
Integration with existing architecture	41%
Data loss and privacy risks	39%
Not sure the promise of a cloud environment can be realized	28%
Implementation/transition/integration costs too high	28%
Risk of intellectual property theft	27%
Lack of standards between cloud providers (interoperability)	25%
Legal and regulatory compliance	22%
Transparency of operational controls and data	22%
Lack of visibility into future demand/associated costs	21%

Source: KPMG International's 2012 Global Cloud Providers Survey.   (*n* = 179)

FIGURE 4

What are the biggest challenges/concerns about adopting cloud services?

Used with permission of KPMG.

systems. In order to execute a smooth integration, data must be extracted from the source system, resolve all the technical and semantics differences and publish the data to the target system. In order to achieve the complete benefit of cloud computing, it is important to plan and execute integration for data, application, network, and identity:

Data—Data integration addresses the requirement to synchronize data that resides in two or more systems so that both systems always contain timely and meaningful data (SalesForce, 2014). InformaticaCloud (Cloud, n.d.) provides a solution for cloud data integration for SaaS and IaaS by integrating data between cloud-based and On-premise systems.

Application—Application integration addresses the requirement to connect business applications at a functional level. Application integration involves generation of an event in one application and triggering some activities in another application. The widely adopted application integration scenario is described by Kolluru and Mantha (2013):

- On-premise application to cloud application integration
- Cloud application to On-premise application integration
- Cloud to cloud application integration.

Network—Network integration ensures smooth and reliable communication between the On-premise and cloud server. Small size businesses often set up a Virtual private network (VPN) that connects the individual machine to the cloud network. VPN connection allows a user to access any application or database on the cloud server by using encrypted point-to-point communication.

Identity—Identity management is the aspect of cloud integration that is usually left unaddressed while planning cloud migration. IT- and management-teams pay great attention toward the integration of functionality and data. A business system comprises of many credentials to access different services. If a user can access a set of services On-premise using his credentials then, he must be able to access the same service in the cloud without any interruption. A cloud integration solution must be able to establish proper authentication and authorizing mechanism to access any resource in the cloud and On-premise.

8 MIGRATION PHASES

For the migration to a CSP under consideration that a remigration to another IT-Service provisioning must be possible, a Five-Phase-Model of secure cloud migration is introduced.

The migration process to a CSP is divided into five phases that correspond to each other. It is important that an organization, intending to move its IT-Services, and IT-Processes to a CSP is aware of all phases and develops and tests a strategy to get in each step of the phases during the whole process of migration and operation. It is also essential for an organization to think about cloud migration to develop a scenario to leave the CSP without any losses of IT-Services and data and with a predictable amount of investment and manpower. Applying the Five-Phase-Model of secure cloud migration will ensure this.

The five phases of cloud migration are:

1. Planning
2. Contracts
3. Migration
4. Operation
5. Termination

These five phases will not follow straightward each other. It depends on the success whether the next phase can be entered or not. Under every circumstance, it is necessary to develop the light gray (left in Figure 5) and gray strategy (right in Figure 5) to leave the CSP. The way back to an internal IT-Service is the safest backup, because the customer can define all SLAs and remigration conditions. But all assumed advantages of using a CSP would be lost. The gray strategy offers, on the one hand, the possibility to negotiate regularly new condition with the actual CSP. On the other hand, it is a clear strategy available to move to another CSP if

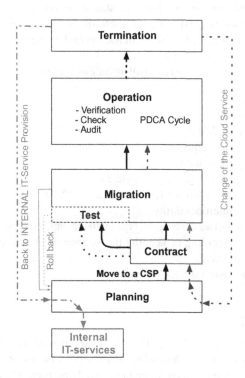

FIGURE 5

Five-Phase-Model of secure migration to a Cloud Service Provider.

the required service, the service quality, the maintenance, or the economical conditions are not sufficient anymore. In the following section, the single phases are described according to Figure 5. This subchapter gives an overview, which subtasks during each step of the Five-Phase-Model have to be fulfilled. A detailed description of all subtasks during the migration process is not scope of this chapter because the design of the subtasks depends strongly on the required IT-Services, the kind of data which shall be processed and which legal requirements have to be applied.

8.1 PLANNING

The planning phase is the most important phase because the prerequisites for all following phases and the accompanying procedures will be defined during the planning phase. Mistakes or uncertainties during this phase can affect the whole migration and operation. Especially an eventually necessary termination process could be massively disturbed or is not possible without enormous costs and may be with loss of reputation for the cloud customer.

The business analysis and the constitutive security analysis are the fundaments for all further decisions and concepts. So it is recommended to develop these two concepts very carefully and complete. From the practical experience, a comprehensive business analysis will often also give starting-points for an improvement of detailed or entire processes. So at the example of the lawyer office, we were able to detect optimization potentials in some of the internal workflows as well as in communication procedures with courts.

The subtasks of the planning phase shall include as a minimum the following points:

- Business analysis
- Security analysis
- Definition of required SLAs
- Definition of security requirements
- Definition of required cloud services
- Definition of required cloud deployment model
- Definition of the CSP (call for tender or scan the Internet)
- Requirements for interoperability
  - Virtualization software (vendor, type, version, upgrade cycle, ...)
  - Flexibility in upgrading or keeping the version level in accordance also to other cloud customers
- Definition of the basic rollback scenario

8.2 CONTRACTS

Based on the strategy and the cloud policy, the contracts with the CSP as well as with the ISPs have to be negotiated. Depending on the legal situation in the country of the cloud customer, the contracts have to be negotiated and regularly adopted if necessary. Basic guidelines are described in Section 5. Because network connectivity is the basis of the successful access to the cloud services, it is essential that the ISP (mostly the CSP will be accessed via Internet) will offer the required service quality and availability. All contractual defined service levels with the CSP cannot be provisioned if the network is not available in the required condition. This often causes complex disputes.

Furthermore, it is important to describe the termination processes in the contract that includes the secure and complete erasure of all customer data and process information (including backups). The CSP has to ensure that no data can be retrieved in any way from any media after termination of the cloud service. Nondisclosure agreements also for the time after service provisioning are essential and have to be part of the contract with the CSP.

Essential subtasks for the contract design are:

- Definition of the form of the contracts (especially in international services)
- Ensure that all related law areas are involved and covered
- Description of the location, where the service are allowed to be provided (processing and storage of data)
- Definition of indicators of service provisioning and other relevant requirements (measurability and auditing)
- Definition of required certifications, quality of the certifications, and cycles to renew the certifications
- Definition of the framework for auditing processes
- Definition of Service Level Agreements and how to ensure the provisioning of the defined services (this includes the conditions and terms of termination)
- Definition of technical forms and software versions
- Definition of termination of the cloud service.

8.3 MIGRATION

The migration phase is the most complex phase. On the basis of the former conducted business and security analysis the implementation and Migration Security Concept (MSC) has to be developed. The migration starts with a realistic test scenario, which is executed by employees of the cloud customer with real applications, but mostly as a simulation and not in real service. During this subphase, the decision to keep staying in the former situation or to migrate has to be made and necessary changes in the concept of service provisioning by the CSP can be done. During each stage of the migration phase, a rollback to the beginning must be possible.

Relevant aspects for the migration phase are:

- Implementation of the IT-Processes and IT-Services according to the business processes analysis
- Definition of the IT-Service concept
- Definition of the security concept for the migration phase (MSC) and the operation phase
- Definition of the migration concept, this includes:

- Test-concept, description, requirements, documentation, evaluation of the test
- Concept for change over (parallel service provision, consistency of services and data, rollback scenario)
- Secure transfer of the data and processes to the CSP
- Definition of a checklist for the migration process, as a basis for a necessary start of the rollback scenario
- Definition of responsibilities during the whole migration process from definition of concepts—testing—transfer—takeover, etc.

8.4 OPERATION

The operations phase is a more or less steady-state situation where the cloud customer mostly has to take care that the quality of the IT-Service provision is sufficient. Measures described in ISO 9000 (Quality Management) and ISO 27000 (Information Security Management) families have to be applied to guaranty the required service quality. Independent audits have to be done to guarantee the defined service quality.

Relevant aspects for the operation phase are:

- Definition of the IT-Service operation
  - What services are available?
  - How to access the services?
  - Authentication and authorization requirements and how are they realized
  - Service provisioning (e.g., based on ITIL)
- Security concept (based on ISO 27001)—follows from the planning phase
- Qualification concept for administrators and users
- Definition of the concrete auditing concept
- Emergency Handbook and test-procedure for the emergency case
- Auditing concept (see also Chapter 8)

8.5 TERMINATION

The termination phase is necessary under the consideration that the rollback to internal IT-Service provisioning or the change of the CSP usually is not under consideration by a cloud customer in long-term planning. Often economic reasons or insufficient service provisioning leads to a decision to change the IT-Service provisioning that might lead to leaving the actual CSP. An intensive preparation makes a change of the CSP safer and more secure.

Relevant aspects for the termination phase are:

- Termination plan
  - Definition, who shall provide the IT-Services
  - Ensure how to get access to all data and business processes during the whole termination process (documented guideline)
  - New contract with another CSP or an internal IT-Service Provider

- Time schedule of the termination and remigration process
- SLAs for the remigration
- Definition how to secure the processes and the data
  - Secure permanent access to the data during the termination process
  - Secure data in transit
  - Ensure secure and sustainable erasure of customer data
- Termination of the contract with the existing CSP
- Penalty rules if the CSP does not fulfill the SLAs (part of the contract)
- Definition of an emergency scenario for the case that the CSP does not cooperate
- Nondisclosure agreement for a time after service provisioning of the former CSP

9 AUDITING

A regular audit process must be introduced to ensure the service quality, the level of IT-Security, and the compliance using cloud services. In Cloud Computing there is a minimum of two organizations involved, the cloud customer and the CSP. Often one or more ISPs are the third or fourth party in the ensemble taking an essential part according to the quality of the service provisioning from the view of the cloud customer. The cloud customer considers the IT-Services provided by the CSP as a support for the own, entire business process. The underlying additional services of the ISPs also have to be taken into consideration concerning the service quality.

For a successful audit, the service provisioning and policies of the cloud customer, the ISPs and the CSP have to be audited. While the internal processes of the cloud customer can be audited by himself relatively easy, the ISPs and the CSP usually do not allow the cloud customer to audit there internal systems and policies. Both service providers offer their services for several customers on the same platform. So it is not possible to audit only the services, systems, applications, and policies according to one customer without getting information about other customers of the service providers (CSP, ISP). Additionally, the ISPs as well as the CSPs usually are not willing to give third parties a view into their internal system service policies.

A complete audit of the entire service provisioning system requires to know and to prove the quality management systems and the ISMS of the cloud customer and all involved service providers. Since the ISPs and CSPs do not let the cloud customer audit their internal systems, the only possibility to guarantee a limited level of quality is (a certification according to ISO 9000 and ISO 27000) that has to be delivered by the service provider.

If the cloud customer has to fulfill additional documentation and certification requirements, it should be negotiated and fixed by a contract that additional, external audits by an independent auditor have to take place. The independent auditor has to certify that certain conditions will be realized, e.g., storage of customer data outside of the national border is prevented. In the ISMS, the fulfillment of those requirements has to be documented. Voluntary certification by independent organization like governmental privacy protection centers or similar will improve the trust of the cloud customer. Since there is no legal force to publish all procedures and protection and documentation measures an entire secure cloud service cannot be guaranteed. Some customers cooperate in a common cluster and setup or charge their own CSP who acts as a community cloud. But this is especially for SMSs like the considered lawyer office not possible.

It is additionally to prove whether the cloud customer has to document certificates like ISO 9000, ISO 27000, or others to their customers. Under this circumstance, the decisions to move IT-Services to the cloud have to be planed very careful.

10 SUMMARY

Moving internal IT-Systems and IT-Applications to a CSP implies several requirements and should be planned very carefully. Especially, lock-in effects can become very cost intensive and lead to business problems if the lock-in effects are not detected in advance, before the migration process of IT-Services to the CSP has been started. The requirements for the migration to the cloud are security and privacy issues as well as the fact that parts of the control of the IT-Provisioning will not longer be in the hand of the cloud customer. An important aspect is that a sufficient IT-Know-How must be kept at the cloud customer, which has to be taken into account considering the economical advantages of the cloud migration (IT-Staff can not be completely substituted).

Because of the lock-in effects after migration, sufficient measures to avoid this locking-in have to be undertaken. An important part of the migration to the cloud is the legal part. The legal aspect is different according to the country and the kind of business of the cloud customer. The relevant considerations of legal requirements and contract development are described for the German legal system. For other legislation, this has to be adopted.

The challenges for using a CSP are security, network access, interoperability, and preserving IT-Know-How. An overview of the most important challenges is given and is described how to take care to deal with these challenges. In the end, a detailed Five-Phase-Model for the sustainable migration to the cloud based on planning—contracts—migration—operation—termination is described. Depending on the requirements and the economical and legal situation of a cloud customer, this model gives references what kind of aspects have to be considered while moving internal IT-Services to a CSP.

ABBREVIATIONS

ADSL Asymmetric Digital Subscriber Line (commonly used Internet access technology)
BDSG Bundes Datenschutz Gesetz

BGB German Civil Law (Bürgerliches Gesetzbuch)
BSI Bundesamt für Sicherheit in der Informationstechnik https://www.bsi.bund.de/EN/Home/home_node.html
CSP Cloud Service Provider
ISMS Information Security Management System
ISO International Organization for Standardization
ISP Internet Service Provider
MSC Migration Security Concept
SANS SANS Institute, SysAdmin, Audit, Networking, and Security, www.SANS.org
SME Small and medium enterprise
UrhG Urheberrechtsgesetz (Germany)
VPN Virtual private network

REFERENCES

Armour, W.W., Bukhari, N., Butler, W., 2012. NIST Cloud Computing Security Reference Architecture. NIST Cloud Computing Security Working Group, USA.

Borko Furht, A.E., 2010. Handbook of Cloud Computing. Springer, USA.

BSI-Standard100-1, 2008. Information Security Management Systems (ISMS). Bundesamt für Sicherheit in der Informationstechnik (BSI), Bonn.

BSI-Standard100-2, 2008. IT-Grundschutz Methodology. Bundesamt für Sicherheit in der Informationstechnik (BSI), Bonn.

BSI-Standard100-3, 2008. Risk Analysis Based on IT-Grundschutz. Bundesamt für Sicherheit in der Informationstechnik, Bonn.https://www.bsi.bund.de/DE/Themen/ITGrundschutz/ITGrundschutzInternational/itgrundschutzinternational_node.html.

Canavan, S., 2006. Information Security Policy—A Development Guide for Large and Small Companies. SANS.

Cloud, I., n.d. Cloud Data Integration: As Flexible and Agile as Your Cloud Applications (online). Available at: http://www.informaticacloud.com/cloud-data-integration, http://www.informaticacloud.com/cloud-data-integration, (accessed August 11, 2014).

Dammann, 2011. Simitis, Kommentar Zum BDSG, 7. Aufl. 2011, §1, Rn. 203.

DimensionData, n.d. Dimension Data Public Cloud Pricing (Compute Optimized), see more at: http://cloud.dimensiondata.com/saas-solutions/services/public-cloud/pricing#sthash.BTtvQf97.dpuf (online). Available at: http://cloud.dimensiondata.com/saas-solutions/services/public-cloud/pricing, http://cloud.dimensiondata.com/saas-solutions/services/public-cloud/pricing (accessed August 5, 2014).

Directive 95/46/EC of the European Parliament and of the Council of 24 October 1995 on the protection of individuals with regard to the processing of personal data and on the free movement of such data. Official Journal L 281, no. 23/11 (1995): 0031-0050.

Hogan, M.D., Liu, F., Sokol, A.W., Jin, T., 2011. NIST Cloud Computing Standrads Roadmap: Special Publication 500–291. NIST, Gaithersburg.

InformationWeek, 2008. How to Plug into the Cloud. informationweek.com.

Institute, 2008. Security Policy for the Use of Handheld Devices in Corporate Environments. SANS, USA.

Intel, 2012. What's Holding Back the Cloud? Intel Survey on Increasing IT Professionals' Confidence in Cloud Security. Intel, USA.

Internap, 2013. Latency: The Achilles Heel of Cloud Computing. Internap, Atlanta, USA.

ISO/IEC13335–1:2004. Information technology—Security techniques—Management of information and communications technology security.

ISO/IEC17799:2005. Information technology—Security techniques—Code of practice for information security management.

ISO/IEC27001:2005. Information security—Security techniques—Information security management systems—Requirements.

ISO/IEC27002:2005. Information security—Security techniques—Code of practice for information security management.

Kim, W., Dong Kim, S., Lee, E., Lee, S., 2009. Adoption Issues for Cloud Computing. ACM, New York, NY.

Kolluru, N.V.S., Mantha, N., 2013. Cloud integration 2014: strategy to connect applications to cloud. In: 2013 Annual IEEE India Conference (INDICON).

KPMG, 2012. Breaking Through the Cloud Adoption Barriers: KPMG Cloud Providers Survey. KPMG.

McKendrick, J., 2011. Cloud Computing's Vendor Lock-In Problem: Why the Industry is Taking a Step Backward (online). Available at: http://www.forbes.com/sites/joemckendrick/2011/11/20/cloud-computings-vendor-lock-in-problem-why-the-industry-is-taking-a-step-backwards/, http://www.forbes.com/sites/joemckendrick/2011/11/20/cloud-computings-vendor-lock-in-problem-why-the-industry-is-taking-a-step-backwards/ (accessed August 24, 2014).

Nägele/Jacobs, 2010. Rechtsfragen des Cloud Computing, Journal of Copyright and Media Law, ISSN: 0177–6762, Issue 4, Germany.

Ravanmehr, R., Khanghahi, N., 2013. Cloud Computing Performance Evaluation: Issues and Challenges. AIRCCSE, Taiwan.

Repschläger, J., Zarnekow, R., Wind, S., Klaus, T., 2012. Cloud Requirement Framework: Requirements and Evaluation Criteria to Adopt Cloud solutions. TU Berlin, Berlin.

SalesForce, 2014. Integration Patterns and Practice. SalesForce, USA.

Simmonds, P., Rezek, C., Reed, A., 2011. Security Guidance for Critical Areas of Focus in Cloud Computing V3.0. Cloud Security Alliance, USA.

Splittgerber/Rockstroh, 2011. Sicher durch die Cloud navigieren – Vertragsgestaltung beim Cloud Computing, Germany, BB 2179–2185.

Standards, C., n.d. Cloud Standards Wiki (online). Available at: http://cloud-standards.org/, http://cloud-standards.org/ (accessed 10 August 10, 2014).

TrinusTech, n.d. Cloud Computing—Storm or Silver Lining? (online). Available at: http://www.trinustech.com/cloud-computing-storm-or-silver-lining-pt-2/, http://www.trinustech.com/cloud-computing-storm-or-silver-lining-pt-2/ (accessed August 10, 2014].

van der Zwet, J.F., Strom, D., n.d. Truth and Lies About Latency in the Cloud. Interxion.

Weichert, 2010. Cloud Computing und Datenschutz, *Datenschutz und Datensicherheit - DuD* 34 (10), 679–687.

Keeping users empowered in a cloudy Internet of Things

11

Stefanie Gerdes[a], Carsten Bormann[a], Olaf Bergmann[a]

Universität Bremen, Bremen, Germany[a]

1 INTRODUCTION

In the beginning of electronic data processing, the abilities of devices were very limited: They could only fulfill a single task at a time. Since these early days, the capabilities of the devices increased rapidly, which eventually led to Gordon Moore's observation that "the complexity for minimum component costs has increased at a rate of roughly a factor of two per year," a rate which he expected to remain constant for at least 10 years ("Moore's Law," Moore, 1965). This prediction turned out to be more or less accurate since. As expected, the processing power increased while the size of the devices shrunk.

Nowadays more and more small devices with limited capabilities are being developed, such as temperature regulating devices, weather stations, or intelligent light switches. Interestingly, these devices often can again fulfill only single simple tasks. As they have limited processing capabilities, but are able to interact with their environment, they are also called "smart objects." They are developed to be integrated into the environment of their users with the purpose to, unseen and autonomously, make life easier for their users. To achieve that, smart objects are interconnected using Internet protocols, thus forming an *Internet of Things*. Thereby, "things" can interact with each other and their users and support a whole new range of applications. These devices need to be small and cost efficient to fulfill their purpose and thus are influenced by Moore's Law in a different way: Instead of increasing their processing abilities, further development is focused on making them cheaper and smaller.

These constrained devices are expected to be integrated in all aspects of every day life and thus will be entrusted with vast amounts of personal data. Without appropriate security, attackers might gain control over things relevant to our lives.

Owners of smart objects want to keep control over their data and devices. An important part of empowering owners is to make sure that they are in control of the authorization policies that define how an entity is allowed to access their data.

Since the devices can be connected to the Internet, storing authorization policies in the cloud is an evident solution. Cloud-based approaches pose attractions such as limited initial investment, sustained operation (outsourcing of maintenance), pretty web-based user interfaces, and the promise of easy and seamless integration.

However, the benefit of the cloud has limitations where access control is concerned (Bormann et al., 2014): Since cloud devices are not under the owner's direct control, a successful attack on the cloud might yield control over the access to users' data when the users cannot keep some security functions under tight reins.

This chapter discusses the functions that enable the establishment, and evolution over time, of security relationships between constrained devices. We examine alternatives for the allocation of these functions to local vs. cloud-based systems, with the objective of ensuring that the devices' owners have the option to maintain exclusive control over the access to their data.

2 PROBLEM SPACE ASSUMPTIONS

Smart objects have limited system resources such as processing power, memory, non-volatile storage, and transmission capacity. They are frequently powered from primary batteries and often lack user interfaces and displays. Due to these limitations, security mechanisms common in the Internet are not easily applicable. Cryptographic mechanisms are time and energy consuming and smart objects cannot store a large number of keys for secure data communication. Establishing security relationships is especially challenging: How can two devices that do not previously know each other establish a secure connection? How can a smart object determine if and how it is allowed to interact with another device and which data may be disclosed?

Owners will want to keep control over their data and decide about access authorizations. This is not easily achieved for small devices that do not even provide a keyboard or display and are so limited in terms of processing power and storage space that they are hardly able to enforce the owner's security policies. Some of the security-related tasks will need to be delegated to less-constrained devices which thus help with the authentication and authorization of peers.

In this chapter, we assume a web-of-things approach to communication: constrained devices operate like clients accessing and servers offering web resources (Bormann et al., 2012). Our communication scenario can then be summarized with these simple statements: A client (C) wants to access an item of interest, a resource (R) on a resource server (RS). C and RS may both be smart objects and thus have limited abilities. A priori, C and RS do not necessarily know each other and have no security relationship.

The owners of the devices want to be able to define authorization policies for their data on the devices. Only authorized users must be able to access. Configuring authorization policies must be simple for the owners. Once configured, the devices must interact with as little user interaction as possible. Day-to-day communication between the devices cannot require the presence of the owners, not even the presence of a specific device the owners would need to carry with them at all times.

2.1 PHYSICAL LIMITATIONS OF SMART OBJECTS

Although smart, the devices considered here are still objects, i.e., physical entities with a clear function, unlike general-purpose computers such as laptops or smart-phones. Their capabilities and user interfaces therefore are specifically tailored to their particular purpose, resulting in low cost and potentially small physical dimensions. To cover the needs of a specific user, a large number of smart objects may need to be deployed, leading to severe constraints on the cost of each one of them.

Tight cost constraints cause manufacturers of smart objects to restrict the hardware components on a device to the bare minimum that is needed to fulfill the desired functionality. These so-called *constrained devices* have significantly less processing power and storage than a common smartphone or modern notebook computer, and often lack a full-fledged user interface. While the limited processor speed just slows down program execution, the restricted memory sizes seriously affect the system design. For example, a basic Texas Instruments CC2538 chip is equipped with 128 KiB flash memory and 16 KiB RAM (Texas Instruments, Inc., 2013; this chip is one of the more modern ones available for Internet-connected smart objects). A simple UDP-based example application[1] built for this platform requires around 13,600 bytes of RAM, leaving less than 2800 bytes for security-related data. The security library tinydtls[2] needs around 1900 bytes in its smallest reasonable configuration for Contiki, not including any keying material. As the library requires another 750 bytes buffer space when public key cryptography using elliptic curves is enabled only 150 bytes—roughly the equivalent of two public keys—RAM are left.

Energy may be a limiting factor as well, especially when the device is powered from a primary battery, limiting the average power available over, say, a two-year battery lifetime to the order of hundreds of microwatts. Margi et al. (2010) show for a common embedded development board with an MSP430 microcontroller and a CC2420 radio transceiver that the transmission of a 12 byte block over a wireless interface costs more than 10 times the energy of encrypting it. This makes network operations one of the most energy-consuming tasks for smart objects besides calculations and powering dynamic memory. Power can also be saved by slowing down the system clock rate, and taking parts or the entire device into sleep mode for most of the time. Both methods lead to increased communication latency and thus reaction times.

The latter must be taken into consideration specifically for network protocols as it affects the time required for state convergence, i.e., the delay until all communication partners have received all the data needed. For security, this is particularly challenging as the receiver of a message must be able to tell whether or not it is fresh to prevent replay of intercepted messages. A common notion of elapsed time hence is

---

[1]Using the Contiki operating system: https://github.com/contiki-os/contiki/tree/master/examples/udp-ipv6.
[2]https://tinydtls.sourceforge.net.

crucial for the communicating parties but not all embedded devices are equipped with a sufficiently accurate battery-buffered real-time clock. In this case, sender and receiver must be able to synchronize their clocks over the network.

Besides these constraints on system resources, smart objects often have limited means of direct interaction with human users. Their user interfaces usually differ significantly from the displays and (virtual) keyboards or pointing devices we are familiar with from our mobile phones or laptop computers. For instance, a temperature sensor might have not more than a small LED light to indicate its operational status. The number of states that can be visualized in this way are very limited: on/off to indicate whether or not the device is active, and possibly flashing to signal that it is trying to establish a network connection. Actuators such as light switches or electronic locks may be restricted to a simple button to toggle their state, sometimes without any state indicator on the device itself.

2.2 SECURITY OBJECTIVES

An essential mechanism for enabling users to keep control over their data is *authorization*. This term refers to the process of giving permissions to an entity, such as a person, a device, or a piece of software. Authorization mechanisms enable users to decide who is authorized to access their data/devices, and how (e.g., read it, change it). For enforcing the authorization, it must be possible to distinguish authorized from unauthorized users. This is achieved by using an authentication mechanism.

Authentication is the process of validating that an entity actually has certain attributes it claims to have. In the physical world, examples for an attribute of a person are her name, her age, or her membership in an organization. Authentication attributes may be suitable to uniquely identify an individual entity, but this is not necessarily the case. To be authorized to buy a beer one only needs to be of age, an attribute shared with many other people. Users opening a bank account need to be uniquely identifiable as they are held responsible for it.

Authentication and authorization are closely related. The authorization mechanism must use the attributes provided by the authentication mechanism to determine whether a person is authorized: The authorization information that needs to be applied must be obtainable making use of the authentication attributes. We use the term *Authenticated Authorization* to refer to a synthesis of mechanisms for authentication and authorization. If one of the mechanisms or the interaction between them fails, the security they aim to provide is no longer assured.

Authenticated authorization is needed to achieve multiple security objectives. Security objectives specify how data need to be protected. The importance of a security objective depends on the use case where the mechanism is applied.

To illustrate the security objectives, we introduce the following use case: John has developed insulin-dependent diabetes and therefore has to check periodically the amount of blood glucose and administer a related charge of insulin whenever the glucose concentration exceeds a certain level. The insulin pump used for this can be placed on John's body and controlled electronically. (Those devices are quite common today, cf. Zisser, 2010; Horsley, 2011.)

John's latest acquisition is an automated blood glucose meter that can act autonomously and communicate its measurements to the insulin pump to relieve the device owner from manual checking of the sugar level, calculation of the correct insulin dose, and triggering the actual injection.[3] Both devices use wireless communication to avoid cables hanging around the user's body and to eliminate feedback loops between the glucose meter and the insulin injection.

Moreover, John wants to be able to monitor his health status and possibly change the device configuration from his smartphone or laptop computer whenever he likes to, and grant a medical practitioner access to his devices during consultation. Changing pricks and injection needles should be as easy as possible. For current systems where the sensor pads and infusion pumps are replaced, removal of old devices from John's personal network, and integration of the exchange units should work without complex manual reconfiguration.

This scenario opens up a full range of important security-related questions as John not only wants his insulin-level to be properly controlled but also keep sensitive information hidden from others.

Measurements and control data should be kept *confidential*. For example, the blood sugar values must be accessible only by entities that John has authorized, such as his insulin pump, monitoring applications, and possibly John's physician.

The data that is interchanged between the devices also must be *integrity* protected, i.e., they can only be manipulated by authorized entities. The autonomic insulin pump needs to make sure that the blood sugar values it uses to determine the amount of needed insulin stem from an authorized source, e.g., from John's blood sugar measurement device or a replacement device that is used instead.

In some cases, it is important that the entity which is responsible for an action can be identified. The respective security objective is called *accountability*. If it is also necessary to prove this to a third party, *non-repudiation* is needed. For example, if the insulin pump is underdosing the insulin resulting in medical problems for John, it might be necessary to find out (and prove) who is responsible for this. Accountability and non-repudiation require the authentication mechanism to uniquely identify an entity.

Another security objective that needs to be considered is *availability*: Authorized entities must not be kept from accessing data. For example, the insulin pump must be able to access the measured values of the blood sugar measurement device to determine the amount of needed insulin. Thus, the availability of this data must be ensured.

2.3 AUTHENTICATION-RELATED TASKS

To meet the security objectives, various tasks must be performed by different actors. As an example for authentication in the physical world, imagine buying an alcoholic drink: Here, the law mandates the seller to ask the customer to prove that she has the required age. The customer hence presents her identity card to the seller who needs to check the listed birth date and if the photo on the card matches the person in front of

---

[3]An example for such a combined system is discussed in O'Grady et al. (2012).

him. Moreover, it is in the responsibility of the seller to verify that the shown document is a proper identity card issued by the government.

This brief example illustrates the three important properties that an *authentication token* such as the identity card or an entrance ticket must provide:

1. *The attribute(s) needed for the authentication purpose*: This could be the age as in the previous example, or just the fact that a guest holds an entrance ticket. The only requirement on the attribute set is that it has to be meaningful for the purpose of the authentication and that the issuing party and the party that uses the authentication token for authentication have some common understanding of the meaning of the token. If the authentication is conducted for authorization, the attributes are required to determine the respective permissions.
2. *A verifier*: This is something to make the attributes attachable to the bearer such as the photo that is printed on the identity card.
3. *An endorsement*: The evidence that the issuer of the authentication token has validated the attributes listed therein and that the attached verifier is correct. For example, an identity card might have a stamp or holographical picture as endorsement. The essential feature is that only the government agency that has issued the card can generate this stamp or holography.

With this terminology, the steps performed by the seller and customer can be generalized as the following authentication-related tasks:

(1) *Attribute binding*: The attribute intended to be verifiable must be bound to a verifier, e.g., a cryptographic credential. To achieve this, an attribute binding authority checks if an entity actually has the attributes it claims to have and then binds it to a verifier. The authority must provide some kind of endorsement information which enables other entities to validate the binding.
(2) *Verifier validation*: The entity that wants to authenticate an entity checks the attribute-verifier-binding using the endorsement of the attribute binding authority.
(3) *Authentication*: The verifier is used for authenticating an entity or the source of a data item.

2.4 AUTHORIZATION-RELATED TASKS

The process of not selling alcoholic drinks to minors is the implementation of a specific policy. The government has set this policy as well as the rules to enforce it: A customer is authorized to buy a beer if she has a certain age. Sellers must therefore validate the customer's age by inspecting the identity card and make sure that the card holder is the same person that is about to buy the drink.

The latter is the aspect of authentication that has been discussed in Section 2.3. Defining and enforcing the policy requires the following authorization-related tasks:

(4) *Configuration of authorization information*: The authorization authority must configure the information that governs authorization. This can be achieved by uploading the access rules defined by the owner of a device to an authorization

server in a network. For the liquor store example, configuration of authorization information is the enactment and publication of the law that prohibits selling alcohol to people below a certain age.

(5) *Obtaining authorization information*: Authorization information must be made available to the entity which enforces the authorization. A device may need to retrieve authorization information from the authorization server before it can validate incoming requests. Shop owners must keep track of legislation activities that may effect their business, and instruct their employees to enforce applicable laws.

(6) *Authorization validation*: The authorization of an entity with certain attributes must be checked by mapping the attributes (which must be validated by authentication) to the authorization information.

(7) *Authorization enforcement*: According to the result of the authorization validation the access to a resource is granted or denied.

2.5 IMPLICATIONS OF DEVICE CONSTRAINTS FOR AUTHENTICATED AUTHORIZATION

In our medical device use case, some of the tasks for authentication and authorization must be fulfilled by the constrained devices, i.e., the blood glucose meter and the insulin pump. One of the most obvious limitations is the basic user interface exposed by these devices: For instance, the glucose meter might have only a power button and a status LED.

For complex interactions between a human and the device, more powerful user interfaces are necessary. In previous decades, this was accomplished using a wired point-to-point connection between a computer and the device's serial port or USB interface. Security in this case was achieved by physically restricting the access to the device or at least the respective socket. For smart objects, this is different by design as they use Internet protocols and thus communicate over a—potentially public—data network where it may traverse several insecure network segments, especially when transmitting data over the air through wireless links.

When applied properly, cryptography can be used to secure the communication of smart objects. Because of the devices' constraints, care must be taken which cryptographic primitives are actually used. Otherwise, the overhead from employing security measures might outweigh the gains from using smart objects.

For constrained devices, the selection of a viable security mechanism needs to consider power consumption, code size, and memory footprint. All three have in common that resources must be set aside that will no longer be available for the actual application.

Memory constraints make it difficult to store the authentication keys of all potential communication partners on a device. Instead, the device must obtain the keying material on demand. Although this could in theory be done using public key cryptography and certificates that bind the public keys to certain attributes, the need to parse large data structures and to store root certificates locally to enable validation of entire certificate chains makes this approach less viable in practice.

In addition to the scarce memory for storing large numbers of keys or root certificates, more energy is consumed by a node when additional messages for certificate validation have to be transmitted. The code size will increase due to the need to parse complex data structures. Depending on the capabilities of the device, the energy expended in such a validation may be significant.

As an alternative to public key cryptography, mechanisms using symmetric keys offer an option for scalable lightweight security. While public key cryptography works with pairs of asymmetric keys where one part can (and must) be disclosed, a symmetric key represents a secret that is shared only between communication parties. The immediate benefit of using symmetric keys is the smaller code size for cryptographic operations, less memory required for key storage, and smaller messages. However, as symmetric keys are shared between the communicating peers, care must be taken to avoid disclosure to non-authorized parties.

When applied to the diabetes use case, these observations imply that only the glucose meter and the insulin pump should know the key that is used to secure their communication. As their user interfaces are too restricted to enter a shared secret manually, the devices must obtain the secret on demand over a secure channel. This process may be facilitated by a less-constrained device that is under the user's control, e.g., a personal smartphone.

3 DELEGATED AUTHENTICATED AUTHORIZATION

Because of the limitations described in the previous section, achieving security objectives on constrained devices is not easy to accomplish, especially without the need for the user to conduct complicated tasks.

To save system resources, constrained devices should perform as little tasks as possible. To achieve this, parts of the authentication and authorization can be delegated to less-constrained devices which may or may not be cloud services. However, some tasks must be performed by the constrained devices themselves to achieve the desired security objectives.

To better understand which tasks a device needs to perform, we introduce the concept of *actors*. An actor is a logical functional entity which performs a number of tasks. Several actors may share a device or even a piece of software.

Actors that are involved in the authenticated authorization belong to one of three levels: constrained, less-constrained, or principal level. Note that an actor might be assigned to a level exhibiting more constraints than its actual realization may later have; the model is designed to *allow* the device implementing the actor to have those constraints, not to *require* them.

3.1 CONSTRAINED LEVEL

Actors on the constrained level may have only very limited system resources. They should be required to perform as little tasks as possible but must perform some security-related tasks to ensure the security of the data.

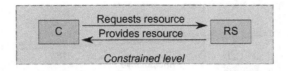

FIGURE 1

Constrained level.

The constrained level comprises the Resource Server (RS) and the client (C). RS hosts a piece of information, a web resource (R). C requests access to R (Figure 1), e.g., to read a value stored in R or to write a new value into R. C and RS want to communicate directly with each other and thus need means for secure communication.

C and RS must perform the following tasks to enforce the security policies of their owners:

- *Authentication of received information*: A device that receives a message has to authenticate its source.
- *Validation and enforcement of authorization as configured by the owner*: A device in possession of the owner's data has to enforce the owner's authorization policies. Specifically, received information is only acted upon after validating that the message is authorized, that its contents was protected as required, and that any response can be properly protected.

3.2 PRINCIPAL LEVEL

Actors on the principal level are the owners of the constrained level actors described above. They represent individuals or companies located in the physical world that own the devices and/or the data on them. The client owner (CO) is in charge of C and decides if RS is an authorized source for R. The resource owner (RO) owns RS and defines access policies for R. An actual device might host several RS' from different resource owners. Figure 2 depicts the relationship between the constrained level actors and their principal.

Actors on the principal level must perform the following task:

- Configuration of authorization policies for their respective constrained level actors. This includes the authorization to perform tasks on the less-constrained level for them.

3.3 LESS-CONSTRAINED LEVEL

To reduce the requirements on the actors of the constrained level, they can delegate some security-related tasks to *less-constrained devices*, the Authorization Managers. These act as a link between the constrained level actors and their respective principals. In particular, less-constrained actors can obtain security policies from the principals, interpret them to generate simplified rules, bind them to a verifier, and

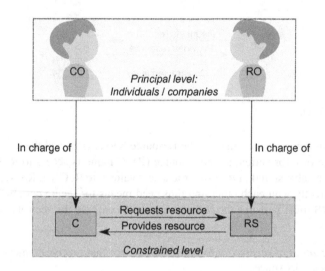

FIGURE 2

Constrained and principal levels.

provide them to the constrained level actors. Less-constrained devices may be able to use more elaborate user interfaces toward their principals than devices at the constrained level.

The relationship between the actors on all three levels is depicted in Figure 3. The Client Authorization Manager (CAM) is controlled by CO and acts as a less-constrained level actor for C, the Server Authorization Manager (SAM) poses as the link between RS and RO.

The tasks of the less-constrained level actors are the following:

• Obtain the authorization information provided by the principal.
• Potentially simplify it for use by the constrained level.
• Identify the authorization information that applies for the current request.
• Bind the authorization information to a verifier and thereby endorse that the entity in possession of the verifier is authorized as stated in the authorization information.
• Provide the verifier to the constrained devices.

3.4 AUTHORIZATION TO AUTHORIZE: CHOOSING THE AUTHORIZATION MANAGERS

The model described above requires the Authorization Managers to be available whenever a client initiates communication with an unknown RS. This limits the choice of devices that can be used as less-constrained level actors.

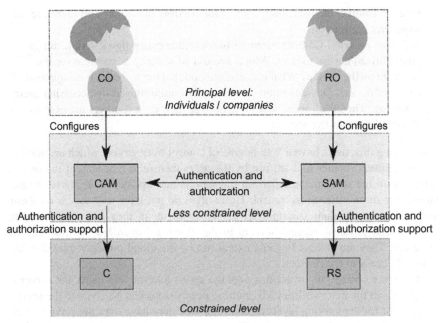

FIGURE 3

Architecture overview.

An evident solution for this problem is to outsource the tasks CAM and SAM are performing to a service in the cloud which is always available and can be used by C and RS as long as those can connect to the Internet.

Users have only limited control over servers in the cloud. These are run by enterprises that pursue their own interests which may conflict with the user's wishes (Chen et al., 2010). In particular, users do not control the access to data on cloud servers if they completely rely on the cloud providers for the protection of the data. Without precaution, access to data in the cloud is granted as the cloud provider sees fit. This is exacerbated by legal uncertainties and anomalies some jurisdictions exhibit with respect to the protection of data held in the cloud (Kerr and Nojeim, 2012; Mather et al., 2009, p. 33).

3.4.1 Estimating the amount of control

To deal with the potential insecurity of Authorization Managers it must be possible for users, i.e., the data owners, to limit the permissions these servers are allowed to grant: Their ability to grant permissions should depend on the amount of control the user has over the server. To estimate this amount of control, several factors have to be considered:

- *Administration*: Administrators may have permissions to access data directly or to install software that can be used to access data. If people other than the user control the server, the user loses control over the data stored there. To estimate the level of control, the user must know who controls the server and therefore has superuser permissions.

- *Software security*: Compromised software and security flaws may result in unauthorized access to data. Which amount of security is possible for the software on the device? What is the likelihood that the software is compromised?
- *Physical access*: Devices often can be easily compromised by accessing their hardware. Therefore, users lose control over their data if others are able to physically access the servers.

Considering this, users have a high degree of control over servers which are stationary in the users' homes and are run by the users themselves, at least if the user is careful with the software installed on the servers and updates it regularly. Smartphones are more difficult to control; Users often do not have root access on them, and as users carry their smartphones around with them, they are more prone to unauthorized physical access. Servers in the cloud are even less controllable by the users: They are at least to some extent run by the cloud provider who also has physical access to the devices.

The more control the owner has over the server and the less likely the server is compromised the more abilities for granting permissions can be given to the server. To account for the varying levels of control a user may have over the servers, multiple Authorization Managers with different permissions to grant access can be used.

3.4.2 Delegated key management

To prevent the Authorization Managers from abusing their power, organizational regulations are not sufficient. To safeguard the owners' control over their data, a technical solution must be used. A basic design principle for cryptographic mechanisms that continues to be valid today is Kerckhoffs's principle. It states that the security of a cryptographic mechanism must only depend on the confidentiality of the key (Kerckhoffs, 1883, p. 12). As long as the cryptographic mechanism is not broken, owners can therefore control the access to their data by a careful usage of encryption and safeguarding the respective keying material.

Each Authorization Manager shares a separate key with its respective constrained device. To restrict the authorization to authorize, the respective permissions are bound to the key. Because of the low storage capabilities of constrained devices, only a small number of keys can be held simultaneously. Therefore, the number of less-constrained devices that can act as an Authorization Manager for a single constrained device must be restricted.

The Authorization Managers and their keys can be put into a hierarchical order. On the lowest level, CAM and SAM can only grant very basic access permissions. We call the corresponding key *External Key* (EK), the SAM in possession of an EK *External Server Authorization Manager* (ESAM) and the corresponding CAM *External Client Authorization Manager* (ECAM). With an EK, no new permissions can be configured but the freshness of existing permissions can be validated and mapped to an access request. ECAM and ESAM must only be able to grant permissions they have themselves and they are not able to assign new Authorization Managers to a constrained device.

The *Owner Key* (OK) has all permissions EK has. Moreover, with an OK new access permissions can be created. Additionally, a device in possession of that key can assign a new Authorization Manager to their constrained device. These Authorization Managers are called *Owner Client Authorization Manager* (OCAM) and *Owner Server Authorization Manager* (OSAM), respectively.

Figure 4 depicts the relationship between the actors and the keys they are sharing.

As described above, the owner has different amounts of control over different types of devices. Therefore, the OK should be stored on a device the owner has a high amount of control over, e.g., a server in the user's home. Servers in the cloud should not know the OK. For more flexibility, the OK can be encrypted and stored in the cloud. The owner downloads the encrypted key to a more controllable device such as a smartphone when needed and decrypts it using a passphrase. The EK can be given to devices the owner has only very little control over, such as servers in the cloud. Thus, cloud servers can make simple authorization decisions on their own without further user interaction.

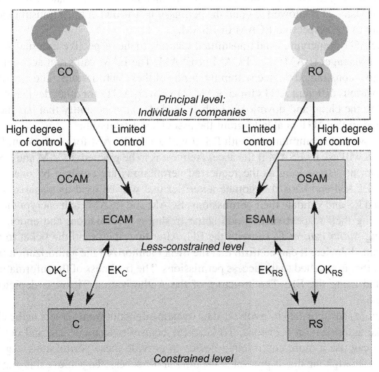

FIGURE 4

Key Management with External Authorization Managers.

FIGURE 5

Authorization granting ticket.

3.4.3 Implementation

The two types of keys described above are used in different ways. The OK is the only key that needs to be preconfigured on the device. The owner configures sets of access permissions that an Authorization Manager is allowed to grant. The EK is generated and added to the access permissions. To ensure the confidentiality of the EK, it is encrypted making use of the OK. The owner endorses the binding of these permission sets to the EK using the OK, thus creating an *Authorization Granting Ticket* (AGT) (see Figure 5). This enables the constrained device to validate if the Authorization Manager is allowed to grant the permission. The owner must transmit the EK securely to the respective ECAM or ESAM.

The AGT is encrypted and transmitted securely to the respective External Authorization Manager (EAM), i.e., ECAM or ESAM. The EAM can grant access to the respective constrained device within the limits of these permissions. The owner can create various different AGTs for an EAM. Moreover, AGTs for other devices can be stored in the cloud and downloaded when needed. Only the entity that has the EK specified in the AGT is able to grant the associated permissions.

If C wants to communicate with RS, it will ask its ECAM for permission. Likewise, RS will ask its ESAM if the access request is to be granted. ECAM and ESAM can grant access as long as the requested permissions are covered by one of the AGTs. ECAM and ESAM negotiate a verifier that will be used as a shared secret by C and RS and validate their permissions. ECAM and ESAM each encrypt the verifier using their respective EK, add some freshness information, and endorse the resulting *Authorization Ticket* with the EK. After that, they send the ticket to their constrained device. It can confirm that the owner authorized the authorization using the OK that is attached to the access permissions. The freshness of the information is validated using the EK. The structure of the Authorization Ticket is depicted in Figure 6.

If more sensitive data is involved, data owners might not want servers in the cloud to make authorization decisions. To keep the control over their data and devices, owners can use a more controllable device to provide these permissions, e.g., the owner's smartphone that is present at the time of the access. To achieve this, the sensitive permissions can also be stored in the cloud, but the respective EK is not made available to the cloud servers. Instead, the key is additionally stored in the cloud after

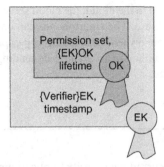

FIGURE 6

Authorization ticket.

being encrypted. The EK and associated permissions can be downloaded to the smartphone when needed. The owner types a passphrase to unlock the EK which is then used to provide endorsement information for the set of permissions.

4 USAGE EXAMPLE

This section describes how the approach described above works by means of a usage scenario.

Eric has bought a new smart sports watch to improve his training. It has an application that helps him keep track of his workout routine and is able to show various information measured by sensors such as the heart rate, the mileage, number of steps, and so on. He meets his friend Carol on the street who has smart running shoes. They contain sensors that can measure details about her training such as the number of steps she makes and her speed. Both the watch and the sensor controller in the shoes are constrained devices. Eric and Carol are curious if Eric's watch works with Carol's shoes.

Eric's watch has a display but only very limited means for interaction. Carol's shoes do not have any user interfaces or control buttons. Eric uses his smartphone to contact the cloud server where he earlier stored access permissions for his watch and downloads the permissions and the respective encrypted EK. Carol already has preconfigured access permissions on her smartphone and can use them to grant Eric's watch access to her shoes. Eric and Carol let their smartphones use near field communication (NFC) to negotiate the verifier for the communication between the constrained devices. Both friends type in their respective passphrase to unlock their EK, thus enabling their smartphones to bind the verifier to the permissions. The resulting Authorization Tickets are transmitted to the constrained devices, thus enabling them to validate each other's authorization and to securely communicate with each other.

The important characteristic of this exchange is that the authorization is done by the smartphones and cannot be performed by the cloud server. Although both the EK and the permissions are stored in the cloud, the cloud server cannot use them without the knowledge of the passphrase. The smartphones can only use preconfigured permissions and only after their owners provided the passphrase to decrypt the EK. Thus, the authorization to authorize is granted depending on the level of control the user has over that device.

5 CONCLUSION

In this chapter, we have discussed the security implications of interconnecting smart objects to participate in the Internet of Things and demonstrated how these devices can be associated with less-constrained devices to fulfill the security requirements.

We explained the dependencies between authentication and authorization which motivates the need for a carefully modeled composition of mechanisms that we call authenticated authorization.

Because of their limitations concerning storage space, network communication, processing power and energy consumption, constrained devices benefit from offloading complex tasks to less-constrained devices. However, when delegating tasks to other entities, care must be taken not to violate the application's security objectives. To precisely investigate the impact of delegating tasks related to authentication and authorization, we have developed a model that describes the actors and tasks for performing authenticated authorization for constrained devices.

To allow for dynamic interaction of constrained devices, the usage of cloud services is beneficial. They provide a vast amount of system resources and global accessibility. By delegating security-related tasks to external servers, constrained device owners risk losing the control over their data and devices. We suggested that the level of control a user has over a device can be estimated, thus providing means to calculate the risk that the data can be accessed without the user's consent.

To mitigate the risk induced by the lack of control, the ability of cloud servers to grant access authorizations needs to be restricted. Most importantly, external servers must not be enabled to generate valid authorization tickets without the owner's consent or to obtain the secrets used for authentication and authorization. We introduced a mechanism for granting a limited authorization to authorize to a server and to securely store authorization information on an untrusted device.

The resulting security model considers the limitations of constrained devices by outsourcing the more complex security tasks to less-constrained devices. Thus, the constrained devices only need to deal with simple security tasks such as validating an endorsement of the owner. Moreover, only a single key, the owner key, must be permanently stored on the constrained device. All other keys can be obtained during operation. This approach enables the owners of constrained devices to keep the control over their devices and data while still providing an easy to use mechanism for a dynamic authenticated authorization for constrained devices.

REFERENCES

Bormann, C., Castellani, A.P., Shelby, Z., 2012. CoAP: An application protocol for billions of tiny Internet nodes. IEEE Internet Comput. 16, 62–67.

Bormann, C., Gerdes, S., Bergmann, O., 2014. Clearing off the Cloud over the Internet of Things, W3C/IAB Workshop on Strengthening the Internet Against Pervasive Monitoring (STRINT). Position Paper.

Chen, Y., Paxson, V., Katz, R.H., 2010. What's new about cloud computing security, Technical Report UCB/EECS-2010-5.

Horsley, W., 2011. OmniPod® continuous subcutaneus insulin infusion pump system, Technical Report.

Kerckhoffs, A., 1883. La cryptographie militaire. J. Sci. Militaires 9, 5–38.

Kerr, O., Nojeim, G., 2012. The Data Question: Should the Third-Party Records Doctrine Be Revisited? ABA J. http://www.abajournal.com/magazine/article/the_data_question_should_the_third-party_records_doctrine_be_revisited/.

Margi, C., de Oliveira, B.T., de Sousa, G.T., Simplicio, M.A., Barreto, P.S., Carvalho, T.C.M., Naslund, M., Gold, R., 2010. Impact of operating systems on wireless sensor networks (security) applications and testbeds. In: Proceedings of 19th International Conference on Computer Communications and Networks (ICCCN), 2010. IEEE, New York, pp. 1–6.

Mather, T., Kumaraswamy, S., Latif, S., 2009. Cloud Security and Privacy: An Enterprise Perspective on Risks and Compliance. O'Reilly Media, Inc., Sebastopol.

Moore, G.E., 1965. Cramming more components onto integrated circuits. Electronics 38, 114–117.

O'Grady, M.J., Retterath, A.J., Keenan, D.B., Kurtz, N., Cantwell, M., Spital, G., Kremliovsky, M.N., Roy, A., Davis, E.A., Jones, T.W., Trang, T.L., 2012. The use of an automated, portable glucose control system for overnight glucose control in adolescents and young adults with type 1 diabetes. Diabetes Care 35, 2182–2187.

Texas Instruments, Inc., 2013. A Powerful System-On-Chip for 2.4-GHz IEEE 802.15.4, 6LoWPAN and ZigBee Applications. Technical specification SWRS096A.

Zisser, H.C., 2010. The OmniPod Insulin Management System: the latest innovation in insulin pump therapy. Diabetes Ther. 1, 10–24.

Cloud as infrastructure for managing complex scalable business networks, privacy perspective

12

Abdussalam Ali, Igor Hawryszkiewycz

*Faculty of Engineering and IT, School of Systems, Management and Leadership,
University of Technology, Sydney, Australia*

1 INTRODUCTION

In this chapter, we present strategies for designing and implementing a model to support KM as considering the privacy issue. These strategies are based on a current research that deals with implementing a model to support KM in complex business networks. Cloud computing infrastructure technology has been suggested as the infrastructure to implement this model. Also, we show the requirements of privacy and how it can be supported in the model. That is based on the fact that knowledge is a private asset in nature either it is owned by individuals, groups, or firms.

The advantages of cloud technology include scalability, availability, and its low cost. That extends its use in small and medium businesses in addition to enterprises. The scalability feature in cloud allows businesses to scale their activities without concern with hardware and storage. On the other hand, this technology has its concerns and risks which businesses should take into consideration when they use it. The top of that, of course, is the security and privacy issue.

To present our approach of modeling, we have structured this chapter as following:

In Section 1, we define knowledge and knowledge management (KM) based on a number of literatures. KM processes and systems are highlighted as well. In this section, the privacy and security have been presented in context of KM. We also investigate technology as a main success factor for supporting KM processes.

In Section 2, we present the cloud technology and declare why we have chosen this technology as infrastructure to implement our model. The concept of cloud computing has been presented in terms of its definition, types, and components. In this section, the scalability feature is explored and privacy issue is investigated as well. Concepts and approaches of knowledge and KM as a service (KaaS and KMaaS) are explored and explained in this section as well.

In Section 3, we present our principal ideas toward designing a model to support KM. In this section, we present how to model KM activities. Also, we present how people and social networks have been modeled in terms of groups and organizations based on living systems theory (LST) concepts. The privacy and how it can be supported is considered in the model. A scenario is presented to show how these strategies may be applied in reality.

2 KNOWLEDGE MANAGEMENT
2.1 DEFINITIONS AND CONCEPTS

KM in this chapter refers to processes and mechanisms of creating and sharing knowledge. KM can be defined as "the systematic and organizationally specified process for acquiring, organising and communicating knowledge of employees so that other employees may make use of it to be more effective and productive in their work" (Hahn and Subramani, 2000). There is extensive literature on KM processes including Fernandez and Sabherwal (2010), Awad and Ghaziri (2004), Dakilir (2011). Based on those literatures, these processes as shown in Figure 1 include:

- *Discovering*: The process of finding where the knowledge resides.
- *Gathering*: Knowledge gathering is alternatively used to explain the capturing. Fernandez and Sabherwal (2010) define capturing as the process of obtaining knowledge from the tacit (individuals) and explicit (such as manuals) sources.
- *Filtering*: The process of minimizing the knowledge gathered by rejecting the redundancy. That can be done by individuals or software agents (Dakilir, 2011).
- *Organizing*: The process of rearranging and composing the knowledge so that it can be easily retrieved and used to take decisions (Awad and Ghaziri, 2004).
- *Sharing*: It is the way of transferring knowledge between individuals and groups (Awad and Ghaziri, 2004). Fernandez and Sabherwal (2010) define knowledge sharing as "the process through which explicit or tacit knowledge is communicated to other individuals."

In our model, we consider these processes as the *functions* to be implemented by people to create and share knowledge. Later in section 4, we show how we model what is called *knowledge activities* according to these functions.

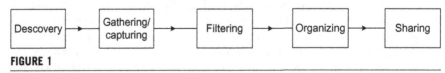

FIGURE 1

Knowledge management processes.

2.2 SOCIAL NETWORKS IN BUSINESS ENVIRONMENT

Social interaction has been mentioned by many authors as one of the factors for successful KM systems.

Businesses and organizations in the era of globalization become more dependent on each other. That is interpreted into collaboration where exchange of knowledge is a key factor to participate and collaborate. This collaboration is an interaction between individuals either within the business itself or between businesses. This interaction happens through what is called social networks. In the context of business, these networks are the business networks (Qureshi, 2006).

Networks support the organization to access knowledge, resources, technologies, and markets. Researchers argue that the most important benefit of social networks is approaching new sources of knowledge (Chatti, 2012). These social interactions should be supported in these environments (Fischer and Ostwald, 2001).

In our research, we propose a model to manage gathering, creating, organizing, and sharing the knowledge between business networks within the complex business networks environment. The research sees knowledge sharing as predominantly a socio-technical issue. From the point view of privacy, we show what strategies for controlling privacy between these networks.

2.3 TECHNOLOGY AS KM ENABLER

Technology in KM should be considered as a tool to support people to implement knowledge processes and activities. However, technology should not be a replacement to human factor.

Many literatures and researches consider technology as a critical success factor in supporting KM systems. These papers include Wong (2005), Moffett et al. (2003), Luo and Lee (2013), Alazmi and Zairi (2003), Davenport et al. (1998), and Rasmussen and Nielsen (2011).

Many authors also report that the approaches followed to use technology as KM driver is not adequate. That is because KM systems are treated in the same way as information systems in terms of design and implementation. Nunes et al. (2006) observe from the interviews that ICT presence and implementation does not mean that knowledge is shared effectively throughout the firm. Fischer and Ostwald (2001) report that technology alone is not adequate to solve the issue of KM.

Limitations of the technology in supporting KM can be summarized as following:

1. Technology does not serve more than the storage of information (Currie and Maire, 2004; Nunes et al., 2006; Birkinshaw, 2001).
2. Limitation to knowledge types. IT systems operate as storages for explicit knowledge more than tacit type (Nunes et al., 2006; Birkinshaw, 2001)
3. Overlooking the "social interaction" phenomena when introducing IT for KM. Considering this sort of limitation is crucial as the social interaction is a main mechanism in knowledge sharing and transferring activities (Birkinshaw, 2001).

Our approach in designing the model is considering technology as a supporter and enabler to the KM. Technology is to be employed to manage and support the social interaction between individuals and groups in business networks rather than substitute them.

2.4 SECURITY AND PRIVACY IN KM CONTEXT

Knowledge as an intellectual asset must be protected. Business secrets should be highly protected for not to be captured by the other competitors. In this case, an access control mechanisms should be implemented to provide this sort of protection (Bertino et al., 2006). These mechanisms suppose to control the access of knowledge when sharing and transferring processes take place. Knowledge creator or owner specifies who should be permitted to access this knowledge (Bertino et al., 2006; Muniraman et al., 2007).

Control access procedures should be easy and user friendly. As mentioned by Muniraman et al. (2007) that the system should not have much restrictions so users do not refuse to use the system. In other words, there should be a balance between privacy and accessibility. Knowledge is to be accessed only by authorized people, and those authorized are supposed to access knowledge easily when they need it.

It is known that knowledge is either in explicit or tacit form. Also, and as mentioned previously, that tacit knowledge presents the most of knowledge. In context of information systems, usually security and privacy techniques and procedures focus on how to control accessing the information storage artifacts. Tacit component of knowledge should be considered in designing privacy and security procedures and policies. Policies in organization must be implemented to control accessing knowledge and experts, and what kind of knowledge should be transferred and to whom.

As our choice for the infrastructure in implementing our model is the cloud technology, in Section 3 we present cloud computing overview and explain the issue of privacy and security. Then, we present the idea of our model and what are the strategies to be followed to implement privacy procedures and policies.

3 CLOUD COMPUTING OVERVIEW

3.1 CLOUD COMPUTING CONCEPTS

The idea behind cloud computing is that the local computer does not deal with running the applications. Instead, the powerful remotely accessed computers and servers are dealing with this job (Strickland, 2008).

Marston et al. (2011) define cloud computing as "an information technology service model where computing services, both hardware and software, are delivered on-demand to customers over a network in a self-service fashion, independent of device and location."

Accessing of cloud computers, network, and services is done through interface software that runs in the local computer. The simple example of that is the Web browser. Cloud computing is not a new idea as it has been implemented through remotely accessed applications such as Yahoo, Gmail, and Hotmail. Simply the cloud computing architecture can be defined through two parts, the front end and the back end. The front end represents the client that accesses the cloud via interface software, and the back end represents the cloud where the servers, data centers, and powerful computing machines reside. Here, the virtualization can be implemented to reduce the need of hardware machines (Strickland, 2008).

Features of cloud computing (Strickland, 2008) can be summarized as follows:

1. *Accessibility*: accessing applications anytime from any place.
2. *On demand self-service*: refers to the availability of service along time.
3. *Scalability*: it is the ability to quickly and automatically to scale out or to scale in.
4. *Cost reduction*: reducing hardware needs in client side, either for computing or storage. That reduces onsite infrastructure costs.

Three main layers of services represent cloud computing technology. These layers are (Furht, 2010) as follows:

1. *Infrastructure as a Service (IaaS)*: This refers to the hardware component of cloud. It includes the virtualized computers and the storage accessed by them. These computers should have a guaranteed processing power.
2. *Platform as a Service (PaaS)*: This layer is considered as development environment for developers. It contains the operating system and may contain Integrated Development Environment.
3. *Software as a Service (SaaS)*: It is shown as the top layer. It represents those services accessed remotely by the users to utilize and to make use of the platform and infrastructure.

The aim of our model is to implement services on cloud to support KM activities between business networks. These services are supposed to use cloud as infrastructure and to be implemented as SaaS on this infrastructure.

There are three types of cloud computing that can be described as follows (Furht, 2010):

1. *Public cloud*: Cloud computing resources are accessed through the Internet. It is called an external cloud as well.
2. *Private cloud*: It is also called internal cloud. It is the cloud computing on private network. In this type, the customer is provided with the full control on data and security.
3. *Hybrid cloud*: This type combines the public and private clouds.

Figure 2 illustrates the three types of cloud computing as derived from Furht (2010).

In terms of privacy and security, businesses have the choice to run their services either on public cloud, private cloud, or using both. That depends on the nature of business and the level of knowledge and information sensitivity within the firm.

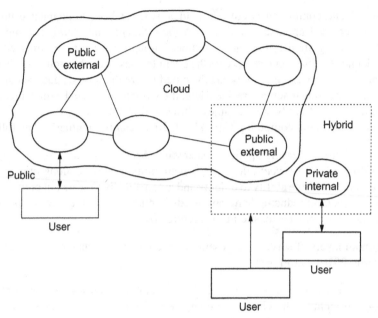

FIGURE 2

Public, private, and hybrid cloud computing (Furht, 2010).

3.2 KNOWLEDGE AS A SERVICE

Based on the concept of services layers, KaaS and KMaaS have been emerged. The research about these concepts addresses how to benefit from the cloud technology to support KM.

Shouhuai and Weining (2005) present their framework to illustrate the KaaS paradigm as in Figure 3. The framework shows the main participants in KaaS. They are the data owners, service providers, and knowledge consumers. Data owners are provided with data produced through their transactions. Knowledge consumers

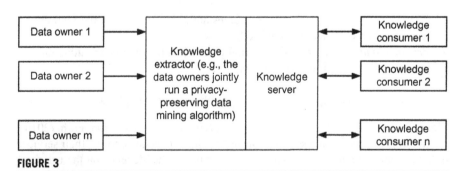

FIGURE 3

A framework of KaaS (Shouhuai and Weining, 2005).

extract knowledge from these datasets through services provided by the service provider. These services are provided by implemented algorithms to support knowledge extraction. In this framework, the Kaas can be described as the knowledge extracted from the owner's datasets by consumers through services upon the request of the consumer.

Lai et al. (2012) describe KaaS as the service provided by cloud to support the interprocess among the members in the collaborative knowledge network. In this research, authors derived another definition for KaaS. This definition states that KaaS is "the process in which a knowledge service provider, via a knowledge server, answers information requests submitted by some knowledge consumers."

The study of Lai et al. (2012) introduces a KaaS model that supports medical services in China. The model is to build services via cloud to facilitate knowledge flow between the hospitals and Bio-ART center. Bio-ART center is an advanced radiology center that forward the treatments and reports to the hospitals. Hospitals may forward these tests and results to external consultants to give their opinions about these tests and treatments back to hospitals and Bio-ART. This knowledge flow is provided through cloud services to share the knowledge among the network.

Although these models have been suggested for KaaS, but it is still information storage oriented. These models treat knowledge from the aspect of query and retrieve as in information systems and databases.

3.3 PRIVACY AND SECURITY ISSUE IN CLOUD COMPUTING

Privacy is one of the human rights. Controlling information owned by people is one type of privacy (Muniraman et al., 2007). Types of information need to be protected as mentioned by Muniraman et al. (2007) include:

- *Personal identifiable information*: Refers to the personal information used to identify people such as their names, addresses, and birth dates.
- *Sensitive information*: Any information considered as private. Example of that includes information about religion, race, and surveillance camera videos and images.
- *Usage data*: The information about habits and devices used through a computer. That includes the information about habits and interests observed through the history of Internet usage, for example.

Privacy and security is one of the main challenges in cloud computing environment. Understanding this issue is an important step to implement privacy and security solutions for cloud services and applications when needed (Chatti, 2012; Muniraman et al., 2007).

Pearson (2009) list the key privacy requirements for privacy solutions in cloud. These requirements are:

1. *Transparency*: Anyone who wants to collect information about users should tell what he wants to collect. Also, users should be told about what this

information is to be used for. At the same time, they should be given the choice if they want this information to be used by others or not.

2. *Minimization*: Only the needed information is collected and shared.
3. *Accessibility*: Users or clients must be given access to their information to check its accuracy.
4. *Security provision*: Security should be implemented to safeguard unauthorized access of users from accessing the private information.
5. *Limitation of usage*: Information should only be limited to the purpose of use.

From the aspect of KM and KM systems, one of the main private assets is the knowledge itself, either if it is tacit or explicit, is owned by an individual, business, or organization. That is in addition to the other information about users, groups, and relationships between them.

In designing such systems, privacy and security mechanisms and policy should be well defined and implemented. In the last section, we provide more explanation about how to support privacy and security in our model based on a real scenario.

4 STRATEGIES TOWARD SUCCESSFUL KM SYSTEM

In this section, we present some strategies that support modeling and design toward successful KM systems. These strategies are based on the previous discussions about the KM processes, technology, and privacy issue.

These strategies are part of a research that aims to implement services on cloud to support KM in complex business environments.

Our approach includes strategies to model the following:

1. Knowledge organizations and groups.
2. KM activities and allocations.
3. Scalability and privacy.

While we are going through these strategies, we suggest a scenario to apply these strategies. That is to help understand how these approaches may apply in reality. The scenario is titled as "Children Hospital and Bags Factory Scenario."

The story of the scenario is as in Box 1.

4.1 MODELING KNOWLEDGE ORGANIZATIONS AND GROUPS

One important aspect here is to define groups that manage knowledge activities and take responsibility for assigning them to roles and maintaining privacy.

In our model, we introduce what is called knowledge groups and knowledge organizations based on LST (Miller, 1971; Miller, 1972) concepts. By definition of LST, the group is a set of individuals and organization is a set of groups.

As shown in Figure 4, the member of a group is any individual (user) that is assigned to one role or more within the group. This individual can be assigned to

Box 1 CHILDREN HOSPITAL AND BAGS FACTORY SCENARIO:

The scenario that we will show here is for two firms who agreed to collaborate for new innovative product. The scenario describes the collaboration process between a children hospital and bags factory to produce adjustable back bags for children to avoid back pains.

Collaborative process passes through many stages of activities. These activities can be described as:

1. Initiating the idea from the hospital management.
2. Negotiating the idea between the hospital and factory.
3. Establishing the collaborative team between the two firms for innovation.

Collaborative team, established by the two firms, follows design thinking activities (Tschimmel, 2012) to end up with the final prototype of the production. These activities are empathize, define, ideate, prototype, and test.

These activities start with the idea initiation and end with testing the prototype including knowledge processes. Members involved in each activity rely on the knowledge captured, created, and shared between them to take decisions and actions.

In this chapter, we will only take a snapshot of this long process to explain how the strategies are applied and how privacy solutions are addressed. Our snapshot will be taken in the empathize activity.

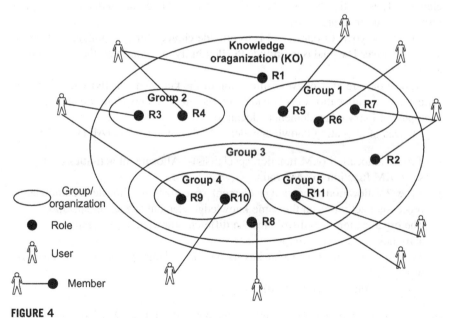

FIGURE 4

Organization, groups, and members in the model.

different roles in different groups. The role here is a number of tasks and responsibilities implemented by an individual(s) in the group.

We also here introduce what is called knowledge organization (KO). This organization contains the groups, groups of groups. The boundary of KO is defined by the knowledge requirements related to a specific knowledge project. For example, gathering for the market and subject material to establish a new course subject in a college or faculty. Figure 4 illustrates the concept of organization, group, and member in our model context.

4.2 MODELING KNOWLEDGE ACTIVITIES AND ALLOCATIONS

Based on knowledge functions presented in Section 1, our idea of modeling KM activities is presented in Ali et al. (2014). KM activity by our definition is applying what is called the *knowledge function* on the *knowledge element*. Formally, there may be any number of knowledge elements, for example, sales, purchases, proposals, and so on. So we might define a knowledge element as $K(sale)$ or $K(purchase)$.

Knowledge functions are the KM processes defined in Section 1 which include discovery, capturing, filtering, ..., etc. Each knowledge element is supposed to go through all the functions by default.

We use the notation $discover(K(sale))$, $capture(K(sale))$, $discover(K(purchase))$. We call these as *KM activities*.

A KM activity is a knowledge processing function applied to a knowledge element. These activities are allocated to what is called *knowledge organizations and groups* defined previously.

One of the goals of our model is to provide choices for changing allocations as systems evolve. The goal is to provide the flexibility to reconfigure the requirements as needed.

Allocations are at two levels, allocation of the knowledge activity to the group, followed by the allocation of action tasks to roles in the group. Here, we illustrate two examples of knowledge elements allocation.

Choices of allocating knowledge elements that are possible (Ali et al., 2014):

- Type 1 Allocation (KM function specialists)—Allocate all activities of the same KM function to one group.
- Type 2 Allocation (knowledge element specialists)—Allocate all knowledge processing activities on the same knowledge element to one organization. The organization then distributes the different knowledge processing activities to different groups.
- Type 3—Each functional unit has its own knowledge processing organization or group.
- Type 4—Totally open (hybrid).

In Figure 5, we illustrate an example of the network of Type 2 Allocation.

The organization is defined as a number of groups. Each group in the specific organization implements one or more of KM processes.

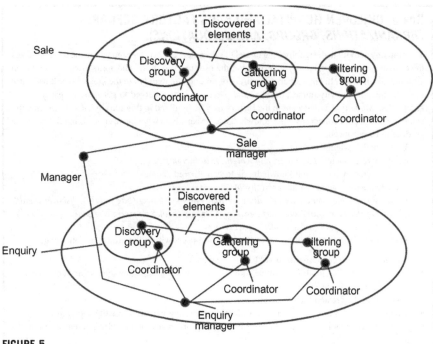

FIGURE 5

Type 2 allocation.

In the organization level, a coordinator role has been suggested to coordinate between the groups in the same organization for collaboration and knowledge sharing. The other main task of the coordinator is to manage these groups by creating and resigning them.

The services to be implemented on cloud should provide the following functions in terms of allocations:

- Creating and resigning organizations, groups, roles, and user accounts.
- Allocating groups to organizations.
- Allocating roles to groups.
- Allocating KM activities to roles and groups.

Privacy approaches should control who joins these groups and organizations, who accesses knowledge created by specific group or individual, and who can share it with others (Box 2).

5 MODELING SCALABILITY AND PRIVACY

1. The ability for flexible growth and shrink (scalability) is one of the main features of our model. Groups and suborganizations can be created within the KO in hierarchical manner. At the same time, any member in the KO can create his own KO.

Box 2 CHILDREN HOSPITAL AND BAGS FACTORY SCENARIO (*ORGANIZATIONS, GROUPS, AND ALLOCATIONS*):

The empathy activity in design thinking model (Tschimmel, 2012) is the step where the designer takes the dimensions of the product by investigating the user or even those who somehow have a relation with the user himself. In our scenario, the users of product are mainly are the kids who will use these bags. In empathy activity nurses, doctors, and parents can be involved to get more empathy knowledge. Marketing department in the factory may be involved in this activity as well. In empathy activity, the designer collects as much knowledge as he can about what the user needs in relation to the product to be produced.

To define knowledge activities:

Knowledge elements: *bag color, bag weight, health concerns*

These are the elements that knowledge is to be gathered about.

Knowledge management functions: *discover, create, organize*

Knowledge management activities: *discover (bag color), discover (bag weight), discover (health concerns), create (bag color), create (bag weight), create (health concerns), organize (bag color), organize (bag weight), organize (health concerns)*.

These activities are to be assigned to the roles and users within the groups as following:

- Empathy Knowledge Organization "EKO" is created.
- This organization contains two groups: empathy knowledge group "Empathy-k" and collaborative team group "C-Team."
- Roles are to be created into these groups.
- Emapathy-K roles are kid, nurse, carer, doctor, marketing person, Empathy-k-organizer.
- "Emapthy-K-organizer" role in "Emapthy-k" group organizes the knowledge created in this group.
- C-Team group roles: team-member, Empathy-k-organizer
- The "team-member" role task is to make sense about the knowledge created in "Empathy-k" group.
- "Empathy-k-organizer" in C-Team group organizes knowledge created by team members in this group.
- Hospital and factory managers assigned to admin role in the knowledge organization "EKO." That allows them to manage and modify the organization as needed.

Figure 6 shows how the activities are assigned to groups, roles, and users.

---

2. Taking KO inside the business as a reference point, two kinds of scalability can be identified as shown in Figure 7:

   a. *In-KO scalability*: That means the groups and suborganizations can be created within the KO itself due to organization requirements. Example of that if it is decided to establish new group for new knowledge requirement.

   b. *Out-KO scalability*: That is the ability of the KO members to create other KOs when required. Example of that is when a member in a KO creates his own KO to gather and share knowledge.

3. Taking the business as a reference point, two kinds of scalability can be identified as well:

   a. *In-Business scaling*: That is the business can create as many KOs as required.

   b. *Out-Business scaling*: The business can join/create as many KOs as it needs for collaborating with other businesses, groups, or individuals outside the business itself.

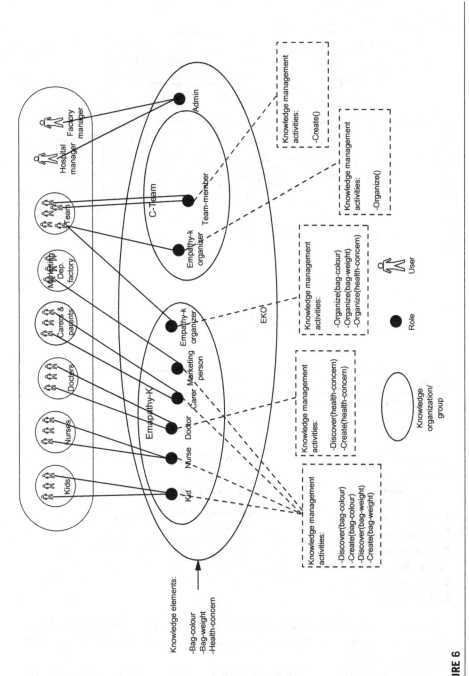

FIGURE 6

Allocations within empathy activity in hospital-factory scenario.

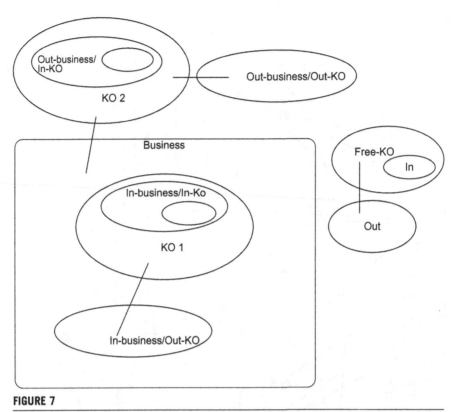

FIGURE 7

Scalability of knowledge organizations and groups.

Another kind of KOs is what we call Free-KO which can be created out of the business.

By combining the previous kinds, we get the following options of scalability:

1. In-Business/In-KO
2. In-Business/Out-KO
3. Out-Business/In-KO
4. Out-Business/Out-KO
5. In-Free-KO
6. Out-Free-KO

The model also gives the option for any individual or group to establish their KOs out of business environment. The two options of In-KO and Out-KO scaling can be applied here as well.

The scalability is considered as one of motivations toward designing robust privacy strategies and mechanisms. Adding more knowledge organizations and groups

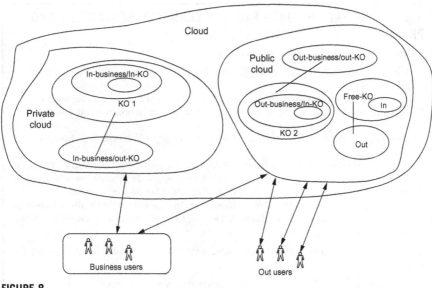

FIGURE 8

Public and private cloud to support privacy in the scalable knowledge networks.

to the business environment requires an effective way to control who access what and manage what.

Recalling the concepts of cloud computing, private and public cloud concepts can be implemented to control privacy of knowledge. For example, knowledge organizations that scaled within the business can be created within a private cloud. Those organizations are accessed by outside users and businesses can be implemented in the public cloud. Figure 8 illustrates this approach.

As mentioned previously, implementing privacy mechanisms is an important requirement for effective knowledge supporting systems. The level of importance increases when using cloud computing as an infrastructure.

These mechanisms should manage different levels of security and privacy. These levels include user level, group level, knowledge organization level, and business level. As the cloud stores information about businesses and individuals, there should be clear agreements with cloud providers to protect such information.

Services are accessed by users from their devices (through Web browser for example). As we see cloud stores the data structures of organizations, groups, roles, and users. In addition it stores the knowledge created by users. A control access layer should be implemented to manage accessibility. By this way, users only perform the operations that they are allowed and access only the knowledge permitted.

In Box 3, we explain how cloud concepts have been employed to implement our model by considering scalability and privacy.

> **Box 3 HOSPITAL AND BAGS FACTORY SCENARIO (SCALABILITY AND PRIVACY)**
>
> In Figure 9, the cloud environment has been added.
>
> 1. Referring to the IaaS and SaaS concepts, cloud should offer the storage and computing capabilities.
> 2. In the SaaS layer, two types of services are defined, KM services and access control service.
> 3. IaaS provides the mass storage for knowledge created, privacy information and knowledge organizations, and groups' data structures.
> 4. This data structure is created either on public, private cloud, or both depend on business requirements.
> 5. In the case of public cloud, accessibility will be decided against the public privacy information.
> 6. In the case of private cloud, accessibility will be decided against the private privacy information.
> 7. The decision of accessibility is decided by the "Access Control Service" sublayer.
> 8. Knowledge sets are classified based on the knowledge elements defined. The feedback knowledge set created by C-Team group members is a knowledge created by making sense of knowledge created in the Empathy-k group.
>
> Based on roles created, access control should achieve the following regarding the privacy and security:
>
> 1. Users with roles "kid," "nurse," "doctor," "marketing person," and "carer" access only the knowledge they create.
> 2. Accessing the knowledge created by each other is only by giving them permission from the "admin."
> 3. User with "Empathy-k-organizer" role in "Empathy-k group" organizes knowledge that created within this group.
> 4. As "Empathy-k-organizer" role is in the C-Team as well, it is not necessary that the user assigned to it accesses the knowledge of the organizer role in the other group. Roles in different groups may have the same name but not necessary that they have the same responsibilities. The user with "Empathy-k-organizer" in C-Team may only organize the knowledge created by other team members.
> 5. Admin role in the organization has the highest privileges and authorities over the other users.
> 6. Admins may provide authorities to the other users within the hierarchy.
> 7. Access control database should store access control information about users and roles to use it for controlling the access of knowledge.
>
> This information can be modified as the system scales.

6 CONCLUDING SUMMARY

In this chapter, we have presented some strategies that can be followed for implementing successful KM systems by highlighting the privacy issue. This presentation was in high level. The further research is to define the semantics and services and implementing them on cloud environment. In the chapter, we presented the concepts of KM and cloud computing technology. We have reflected these concepts on our modeling approaches. We have addressed the issue of the KM systems as they have shortcomings in supporting social interactions as a main mechanism to create and

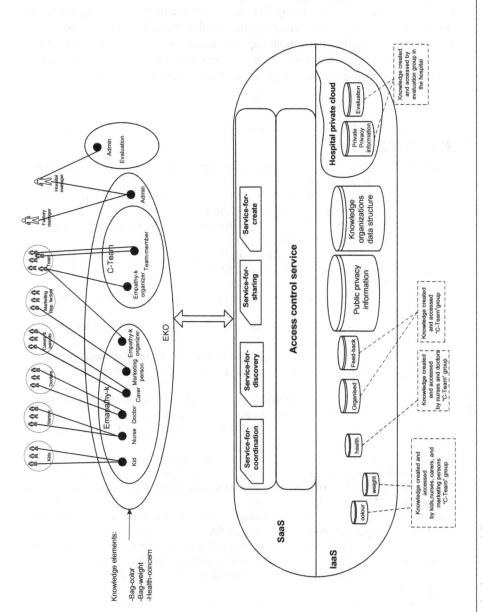

FIGURE 9

Scalability and privacy modeling.

share the knowledge. That encouraged us to investigate the business networks as one of the ways to do so. Our approach is to model these networks by what is called knowledge organization and groups. These groups contain roles and responsibilities that assigned to users. The privacy issue and scalability feature have been modeled as well. We have explained these modeling approaches by a scenario to help the reader understand them. However, these ideas may open new doors and research topics for those who are thinking toward implementing such systems.

REFERENCES

Alazmi, M., Zairi, M., 2003. Knowledge management critical success factors. Total Qual. Manag. Bus. Excell. 14, 199–204.

Ali, A., Hawryszkiewycz, I., Chen, J., 2014. Services for knowledge sharing in dynamic business networks. In: Australasian Software Engineering Conference, Sydney.

Awad, E.M., Ghaziri, H.M., 2004. Working smarter, not harder. In: Knowledge Management. Pearson Education, Inc., New Jersey.

Bertino, E., Khan, L.R., Sandhu, R., Thuraisingham, B., 2006. Secure knowledge management: Confidentiality, trust, and privacy. IEEE Trans. Syst. Man Cybern. Syst. Hum. 36, 429–438.

Birkinshaw, J., 2001. Why is knowledge management so difficult? Bus. Strateg. Rev. 12, 11–18.

Chatti, M., 2012. Knowledge management: a personal knowledge network perspective. J. Knowl. Manag. 16, 829–844.

Currie, G., Maire, K., 2004. The limits of a technological fix to knowledge management: epistemological, political and cultural issues in the case of intranet implementation. Manag. Learn. 35, 9–29.

Dakilir, K., 2011. The knowledge management cycle. In: Knowledge Management in Theory and Practice, second ed. Massachusetts Institute of Technology, London.

Davenport, T.H., De Long, D.W., Beers, M.C., 1998. Successful knowledge management projects. Sloan Manage. Rev. 39, 43–57.

Fernandez, I., Sabherwal, R., 2010. Knowledge management solutions: processes and systems. In: Knowledge Management, Systems and Processes. M.E. Sharpe, Inc., New York.

Fischer, G., Ostwald, J., 2001. Knowledge management: problems, promises, realities, and challenges. IEEE Intell. Syst. 16, 60–72.

Furht, B., 2010. Cloud computing fundamentals. In: Furht, B., Escalante, A. (Eds.), Handbook of Cloud Computing. Springer, New York, USA.

Hahn, J., Subramani, M.R., 2000. A framework of knowledge management systems: issues and challenges for theory and practice. In: Proceedings of the Twenty First International Conference on Information Systems. Association for Information Systems, Brisbane, Queensland, Australia.

Lai, I.K.W., Tam, S.K.T., Chan, M.F.S., 2012. Knowledge cloud system for network collaboration: a case study in medical service industry in China. Expert Syst. Appl. 39, 12205–12212.

Luo, S.-H., Lee, G.-G., 2013. Key factors for knowledge management implementation. Soc. Behav. Personal. 41, 463–476.

Marston, S., Li, Z., Bandyopadhyay, S., Zhang, J., Ghalsasi, A., 2011. Cloud computing—the business perspective. Decis. Support. Syst. 51, 176–189.

Miller, J.G., 1971. Living systems: the group. Behav. Sci. 16, 302–398.

Miller, J.G., 1972. Living systems—organization. Behav. Sci. 17, 1–182.

Moffett, S., McAdam, R., Parkinson, S., 2003. Technology and people factors in knowledge management: an empirical analysis. Total Qual. Manag. Bus. Excell. 14, 215–224.

Muniraman, C., Damodaran, M., Ryan, A., 2007. Security and privacy issues in a knowledge management system. In: 6th Annual Security Conference, 2007, Las Vegas, NV.

Nunes, M.B., Annansingh, F., Eaglestone, B., Wakefield, R., 2006. Knowledge management issues in knowledge-intensive SMEs. J. Doc. 62, 101–119.

Pearson, S., 2009. Taking account of privacy when designing cloud computing services. Proceedings of the 2009 ICSE Workshop on Software Engineering Challenges of Cloud Computing, IEEE Computer Society: 44–52.

Qureshi, S., 2006. Collaboration for knowledge networking in development. Inf. Technol. Dev. 12, 87–89.

Rasmussen, P., Nielsen, P., 2011. Knowledge management in the firm: concepts and issues. Int. J. Manpow. 32, 479–493.

Shouhuai, X., Weining, Z., 2005. Knowledge as a service and knowledge breaching. In: IEEE International Conference on Services Computing, July 11–15, 2005, vol. 1. pp. 87–94.

Strickland, J., 2008. How Cloud Computing Works (Online). Available:http://computer. howstuffworks.com/cloudce_la-computing/cloud-computing.htm, (Accessed September 14, 2011).

Tschimmel, K., 2012. Design thinking as an effective toolkit for innovation. In: Proceedings of the XXIII ISPIM Conference: Action for Innovation: Innovating from Experience, 2012, Barcelona.

Wong, K.Y., 2005. Critical success factors for implementing knowledge management in small and medium enterprises. Ind. Manag. Data Syst. 105, 261–279.

Psychology and security: Utilizing psychological and communication theories to promote safer cloud security behaviors

13

Gráinne Kirwan

Institute of Art, Design and Technology, Dublin, Ireland

1 INTRODUCTION

The managing director is confident that he has taken all of the security measures that he needs to in order to protect his company's cloud based data—his IT manager has tested the system, the software and hardware are the best that money can buy, and employees are given excellent training in data protection. On the day that a security breach is uncovered, he is perplexed and horrified, and he begins an investigation into why the breach occurred. Eventually, he discovers that one of his management team has used the same password for their company file access as they do for an online dating account. When the online dating service was hacked a few minutes beforehand, the infiltrators gained access to the password, and matched it to the employee. The managing director is confused—the employee training provided explicitly stated that the password for the company services should be unique, so why did this happen?

While technological devices and programs form the bulk of the defense mechanisms against malicious attacks and infiltrations, the human element in cloud security must also be factored into any protection strategy. The use of weak passwords and other aspects of poor security hygiene can dramatically reduce the efficacy of technological protective measures. While users may be aware of the best methods of ensuring increased security, they are not always inclined to follow these directions, particularly where they perceive the methods involved as being difficult, inconvenient, or ineffective, or if they feel that they do not have the skills required to implement the measures. This chapter examines how various theories and research in communication and psychology can help management to understand why users may not follow best practice in cloud security, and how they can encourage users to change such behaviors. The chapter describes theories such as Communication Privacy Management (CPM) Theory, Protection Motivation Theory, and Social

Learning Theory, as well as various cognitive biases and distortions, particularly in relation to decision making. For each theory and concept, the applicability to cloud security behaviors is considered, illustrating how such phenomena may manifest in inappropriate security behaviors. The chapter continues with insights on how behaviors can be changed, based on the theories described. Specific approaches for the development of intervention strategies are proposed which may encourage staff and individual users to more actively engage in safer cloud security behaviors. The chapter concludes with suggestions for further reading regarding several of the theories and phenomena discussed.

2 COMMUNICATION THEORIES

Communication is an important part of our daily lives, and it is an area that has been extensively researched—in terms of both online and offline communications. Certain aspects of communication theories are applicable to online security promotion, and in particular, these include CPM and Hyperpersonal Communication.

2.1 CPM THEORY

CPM Theory was outlined by Petronio (2002) and has been applied to many aspects of online communication (see, e.g., Child et al., 2012; Jin, 2012; Kisekka et al., 2013). CPM Theory comprises several basic principles, including that individuals or groups believe that they own their private information, and have the right to control how and where this information is disseminated. The user(s) also presume that anyone else who holds this private information will follow the rules that they dictate regarding the sharing of that information. And so, trust is a key element of how we share information.

From a company's perspective, CPM is important as it partially describes the relationship that the end user has with the organization. The user may be comfortable sharing certain information with the company, such as spending habits and preferences, home address, telephone number, e-mail addresses, and other personal information. But such information has become valuable in modern society and has often been sold or shared with other organizations. In other cases, the information has been shared due to legal requirements to provide data to investigative organizations or through the breach of security by cybercriminals. While such data losses may not be the fault of the organization, the users may still perceive it as a breach of trust and may be hesitant to share information with the organization at all. Should enough instances of such sharing of information occur, it may have a negative effect overall, as individuals become wary of disclosing their details online.

An awareness of CPM can help organizations to understand the trust that users place in them and the importance of not breaking that trust. Should private information be unintentionally disclosed then the organization needs to take care to build the trust relationship again, both for their own benefit, and to contribute to the continued future of online interactions as a method of communication and commerce. Basically, the more we trust an individual or organization, the more likely we are to disclose private information to them—high trust compensates for low privacy (Joinson et al., 2010).

2.2 HYPERPERSONAL COMMUNICATION

Sometimes it is easier to disclose personal or private information when you do not see the other person face-to-face, or if you think that it is a once-off meeting and you will never meet them again (Rubin, 1974, 1975). Certain aspects of Computer-Mediated Communication (CMC) can also result in higher perceived levels of affection and emotion, a phenomenon which Walther (1996, 2007) referred to as Hyperpersonal Communication. This can result in increased levels of personal disclosures online (Jiang et al., 2011).

Walther (1996) suggested that different elements of online communication influence hyperpersonal CMC—most notably the receiver, sender, feedback, and asynchronous channels of communication. In short, he suggests that it is possible that the lack of face-to-face social cues can result in communicators exaggerating the more subtle cues available in the messages, and this may result in stereotyped and possibly idealized impressions of the other person. This is exaggerated by the potential selective self-presentation that may be conducted by the sender—when communicating online we can choose to edit or omit information that might be obvious in a face-to-face discussion. For example, if a speaker makes a point that we disagree with, we may unintentionally show this disagreement in our facial expression. In a face-to-face meeting, the speaker may notice this, but if our communication is a text-only online interaction then we have the opportunity to hide our reaction. We can tailor the information that we present to the situation, putting our best selves forward, in a similar way that individuals might do when preparing a job application or curriculum vitae.

Similarly, when communicating online, we can develop an overly positive opinion of our communication partner, be they an individual, a group, or an organization. It is therefore a risk that we trust them more than we should, given our knowledge of the entity. We may offer more private information than we would otherwise do, at a much earlier stage. The submission of this private information may result in disclosure of details that might put an individual's or an organization's security at risk.

3 COGNITIVE PSYCHOLOGY

Imagine that you are responsible for the security of 600 files. You have been given the choice between two security programs, but you must choose one of them. The first guarantees protection, but only of the first 200 files. The second offers to protect all files, but with only a one-in-three chance of not being compromised. Which would you choose?

Later you are asked to make another decision regarding the files. This time you are required to choose between a program that admits that 400 files will be vulnerable and a program that has a two-in-three chance of being compromised. Which would you choose?

Chances are that, should you be required to make this decision in real life, you would probably choose the first program in the first scenario, and the second program in the second scenario (having both presented here in close succession means that you may have realized the similarity in the questions, which may affect your answer). The difference between the choices is based on how they were framed—specifically if they were given a positive spin (in the first scenario) or a negative spin (in the second scenario). This *framing effect*, described by Tversky and Kahneman (1981), is one of many different cognitive biases that we can be susceptible to (see also Tversky and Kahneman, 1974). In practice, when we think about the possible risks of sharing information online, how the risks are presented to us may have an impact on the decisions that we make—when a positive frame is presented we are more likely to try to avoid risk. If a negative frame is presented, then we will tend to choose risks. Being aware of this bias can help us to make more informed decisions.

However, there are many other biases. For example, confirmation bias (Einhorn and Hogarth, 1978) suggests that once we have a tentative hypothesis, then we are more likely to seek information that will confirm this, possibly avoiding or ignoring information that conflicts with it. So we may be aware that there are risks when we are not careful with our online security, but we are also aware that many users who are not careful have not been victimized. We also know (or think that we know!) that despite behaviors in the past that were not ideal, our data appears to be safe, and we have not experienced any negative consequences as a result. Based on this information, we might feel that we do not need to worry—our tentatively held belief that extensive security procedures are unnecessary is "confirmed," and we do not alter our behaviors. The employee in the case study at the start of this chapter has probably used the same password for multiple accounts in the past and has not noted any security problems emerging. For this reason, he feels that it is acceptable to use the same password for his company access and online dating account, despite it being against policy.

A third important bias is the availability heuristic (Tversky and Kahneman, 1973). This refers to our bias to lend more weight to information that we are presented with, or think about, the most often. For example, immediately following news reports of a crash of a passenger jet, individuals may become more wary of traveling by air, despite the relative safety of air transportation compared to many other modes of transportation. Similarly, immediately following news reports of successful infiltrations, or on hearing about a friend or colleague who has been recently victimized, we may be more conscious of the risks, and hence more likely to engage in security focused behaviors. For a while, we will remember this news report, or our victimized acquaintance, and will be more careful and security conscious. However, over time, the memory of the event will fade, and become less "available" to us. As this happens, it is possible that we will become more relaxed about the measures that we are taking, and hence more vulnerable to attack. A similar concept is salience—how much a particular item in our environment grabs our attention. This can have an important impact on our decision making (see, e.g., Payne, 1980). It is important to note that cues can have more salience because of the availability of the information in our thoughts (so that we might be more likely to remember a person's name because they share it with our sibling), or a cue can become more available because of its salience (the more eye-catching that a logo is, the more likely we are to remember it later on). So the more that we hear about security issues, the more available the information will be to us, and hence we might be more likely to engage in better preventative measures.

Optimism bias refers to a cognitive bias where we are more likely to believe that good things will happen to us, and negative events will not happen to us, when compared to the average (Weinstein, 1980). For example, people tend to believe that they are less likely to become divorced than the average person, while they might put their odds of winning the lottery at higher than they really are. Interestingly, even when informed of the actual odds of a given event occurring, individuals still demonstrate optimism bias, often only incorporating this new information if it indicates that the odds were better than they originally expected (Sharot et al., 2011). Such "unrealistic optimism" can also extend to our online activities (Campbell et al., 2007)—we may tend to believe that our data is more secure than that of others, and that we are less likely to have our information compromised than most individuals. This may result in more risky behaviors online, as we perceive ourselves to be relatively safe. The employee in the case study has possibly heard of cases where passwords had been compromised, but optimism bias prevents him from considering that he is at substantial risk of such an incident himself.

Many of the biases identified in cognitive psychology, including the ones described above, can be a little disquieting. We may like to think of ourselves as being careful decision makers, while we are in actuality vulnerable to many biases and problems in our decision making. Kahneman (2011) describes two types of thinking—System 1 and 2. System 1 is a "fast" system—it is instinctive, and emotional, and it makes many of the decisions that occur on a daily basis—from what words to use in a relaxed conversation with a friend, to which of the many identical cereal boxes to pick up in a supermarket. System 2 is the "slow" system that manages the decisions and tasks that require a great deal of effort, such as developing an acceptable use policy for an organization's technologies. We need both Systems in our daily lives—putting too much time and energy into simple and risk-free decisions would prevent us from appropriate productivity (and cause a huge bottleneck in the cereal aisle of the supermarket!). But using System 1 to make decisions that are complicated and important will result in poorly thought out policies and multiple errors.

It is helpful if we think about our online security decisions in terms of System 1 and 2. When choosing a service provider, we will possibly use System 2, particularly if trying to weigh up the potential risks and benefits of each. But when choosing a password, it is tempting to use System 1, especially if we are in a hurry or have other things on our minds. The employee in the case study outlined above used System 1 when choosing the same password for both accounts—the password was easily available to him, easy to remember, and appeared to do an adequate job of ensuring his security. Engaging System 2 requires more effort—finding inspiration, creating an appropriate password, and developing a way of remembering that password—but it does result in a more secure system. Using technological aids to turn the task of creating a new password into a System 1 decision will therefore result in more compliance with policies, and greater security. Password management tools provide such a mechanism. If users can be helped so that the System 2 password development becomes as instinctive and easy as a System 1 decision via the use of such password management tools, then compliance with policies should become more widespread. An alternative to this is to attempt to activate System 2 when it is the more appropriate means of making a decision. Kahneman indicates that one method of doing this is to frown—it reduces overconfidence and increases analytical thinking. Asking users to frown every time that they need to generate a new password may not be appropriate or realistic, but there are other mechanisms of encouraging use of System 2. For example, systems which refuse to accept weak passwords can force users into integrating more complexity in the form of including numerals, symbols, and mixed-case letters. Similarly, systems which require users to change passwords regularly and that do not permit reuse of previous passwords are also more likely to engage the System 2 decision-making process.

Overall, decision making and risk are intertwined, and some researchers, such as Chen et al. (2011), have considered how these influence online communication and behaviors. It is helpful to consider the biases that users and employees may be unconsciously experiencing when online and to draw their attention to these biases if appropriate. Ideally, a system should either divert a user into critically considering what they are about to do if it might compromise the situation, or encourage the automated "System 1" to always ensure that the safest response is followed. Unfortunately, the opposite is generally the case—current technologies and interfaces tend to encourage the user to follow System 1 when the most crucial decisions need to be made—for example, we are excited by the prospect of using a new application when we are asked to indicate that we have read the terms and conditions—at such a time, System 1 might be more likely to take over, deciding to tick the relevant box to provide our consent, without allowing System 2 to review the details. Such responses have resulted in many users being surprised by the stipulations that they have agreed to when using particular applications and feeling that the developer has deceived them by including unexpected terms and conditions. In truth, the user has almost always agreed to these terms and conditions by ticking a checkbox or a button which says "I Agree"— they simply have not read the actual policy and so are unaware of what they have agreed to.

4 OTHER RELEVANT THEORIES

In this section, we will consider some other theories that have relevance to online security behaviors. First, we will consider learning theories, and the concept of reward and punishment. Finally, Rogers' (1975, 1983) Protection Motivation Theory will be described.

4.1 **LEARNING THEORIES**

Psychology has developed many theories for how we learn, and many of these theories are primarily based on the learner seeking a reward, and trying to avoid a punishment (or at least, a lack of reward for our efforts). A key example of such a theory is *operant conditioning,* proposed by B.F. Skinner (see, e.g., Skinner, 1938). In short, we are likely to continue to exhibit behaviors that we are rewarded for and avoid behaviors that we are punished for. When considering whether or not to engage in a particular behavior, we may consider the possibility of being rewarded versus being punished and then make our choice (in criminology, and other disciplines, this is sometimes referred to as *Rational Choice Theory*). In practice, this has important consequences for security measures taken by individuals. Setting an appropriately strong password, and using different passwords for each account, is both difficult and frustrating. It can result in many attempts to gain access to an account without success and the inconvenience of resetting passwords following too many failed attempts or if the password is completely forgotten. It is far easier to choose a simple password and use it for every account, thus resulting in unsafe behaviors (and situations similar to that outlined in the case study). This was noted by Tam et al. (2009), who referred to it as the *convenience-security trade-off*. In short, for as long as setting difficult passwords is an option rather than a requirement, and the user does not see any risk in using (and reusing) a simple password, then they are unlikely to choose the more difficult, but more secure, option.

However, we do not have to previously experience reward or punishment personally in order to learn a behavior—we can learn by watching others. If we see someone steal an item, and then be arrested and imprisoned, we learn that it is better if we do not follow their example. On the other hand, if we see a person work hard and be rewarded with a pay rise, promotion, or appropriate praise and recognition, then we may be encouraged to work harder ourselves, in order to gain the same rewards. These are examples of *Social Learning Theory* or *observational learning*, most famously researched by Albert Bandura (1965) in an experiment involving children observing adults be rewarded or punished for violence toward a toy called a Bobo doll. With regard to security procedures, this means that people may look to the individuals around them to determine whether or not to engage in safer behaviors. If they see colleagues leave passwords written beside their computer, or upload confidential documents for convenience rather than out of necessity, they may be encouraged to do the same, especially if there are no obvious repercussions for the behavior. Research has already found a link between social learning and other types of negative online behaviors, such as copyright infringement (see, e.g., Morris and Higgins, 2010), and it is possible that social learning may play an important role in adoption of security measures.

4.2 **PROTECTION MOTIVATION THEORY**

Nobody wants things to go wrong in their lives, and they will make many efforts to protect the people and things that are important to them. For example, they may have a house alarm installed, or take self-defense classes, or ensure that appropriate medical care is sought if there is a possibility of illness. What they do, and when, is often driven by several factors, and many of these have been outlined by Rogers (1975; 1983) in *Protection Motivation Theory*. Specifically, these include:

1. Perceived severity of the threatened event (how bad will the consequences be if the event occurs);
2. Perceived probability of the threatened event (how likely is it that the event will occur);
3. Perceived response efficacy of the preventative measures (will the preventative measures actually work for this threat);
4. Perceived self-efficacy in using preventative measures (does the user believe that they can successfully implement the preventative measures);
5. Potential rewards (what are the expectations if avoidance of the threat is successful);
6. Potential costs (what are the sacrifices that the user must make to take the preventative measures).

Many studies have found that perceived self-efficacy is very important in determining what measures individuals will take with regard to online security (see, e.g., Lee et al., 2008; Johnston and Warkentin, 2010; Ng et al., 2009; Ng and Rahim, 2005). As noted by Power and Kirwan (2015), the importance of the self-efficacy factor may pose a problem in light of recent developments regarding international surveillance. As it has emerged that some organizations may be forced by government-run agencies to disclose user information and communications which they have collected, many users may feel that it is impossible to make their data fully secure, regardless of what preventative measures they take. A similar threat is posed by online criminals, who are constantly evolving their techniques to stay ahead of computer security (see Schneier, 2012).

5 OVERCOMING INHIBITIONS TO SAFER SECURITY BEHAVIORS

The theories above describe some of the reasons why employees and users may not engage in the safest behaviors when online. They indicate why individuals might choose weak passwords, reuse passwords, share information without fully considering whether the other party is really trustworthy and overestimate their safety and security online. In some cases, users may be aware of these biases and distortions, but in others, they are unaware of the psychological and communication theories that may explain these behaviors.

Based on the theories outlined, we can develop some specific suggestions for how to overcome inhibitors to safer security behaviors.

1. Based on CPM, it may be helpful to include cues for users before they share any information. For example, before a file with customer data is shared with a

third party, the employee could be prompted to answer a number of questions to ensure that such sharing is appropriate. These could include questions about if the potential recipient of this information is trustworthy; what we might expect the recipient to do with the data; does the recipient need all of the data that the employee is about to send; and, if the employee was the third party, would they reasonably expect the data provided to be shared. Such an approach might be effective, but would not be suitable for routine cases, partially because completing these questions may become very irritating and time-consuming, and partially because if this approach is used too frequently the employees may develop shortcuts to completing the questions, without actually considering the individual case.

2. Hyperpersonal Communication Theory could be utilized in aiding users and employees to think twice about the individuals that they are communicating with before sharing information with them. The user could be prompted to review their communications with an individual before deciding whether or not to share information with them. They could also be prompted to consider if it is appropriate to share personal information with an individual who they have not previously met, and also if it is necessary to share this information with them.

3. Given the known tendency for individuals to be risk-averse when decisions are presented in a positive frame, it could be helpful to utilize this bias when presenting the prompts described above. The language used in the prompts is important, as is the perceived source of the prompts (e.g., if the perceived source of the prompts is a trusted colleague or manager, then they may be adhered to more than if the perceived source is an impersonal computer program).

4. Be aware of confirmation bias—use mandatory checklists to demonstrate the appropriate security requirements, hence reducing the likelihood that individual users can avoid or ignore contradictory evidence. By ensuring that all information is clearly visible it can reduce the possibility that only confirmatory evidence is attended to. Such checklists may also help to overcome optimism bias by including details on the risks involved should any item be neglected. However, as with item 1 above, care must be taken to ensure that the completion of these checklists does not become so routine that they are not thoroughly read and understood each time.

5. Organizations can take advantage of salience and the availability heuristic by making the risks of poor security behaviors more visible. Use case studies and visual cues to remind employees and users about the consequences of poor security, and ensure that these include tangible and vivid examples of the potential repercussions. If the user can easily visualize the potential harms, they are more likely to remember them.

6. Where possible, try to make decision making about online security risks use System 2, to ensure that users deliberate about their actions appropriately. Do not allow shortcuts to be taken, and ensure that full risk-benefit analysis is completed before a decision can be confirmed. If situations occur where users will be tempted to use System 1, ensure that such use is "failsafe"—meaning that their

automatic response is the one which will result in higher security. For example, when prompted to create a password the easiest option should be the development of a strong password via an automated generator.

7. Bear in mind the research regarding learning when trying to encourage safer behaviors. Provide appropriate rewards for following security guidelines (while also considering that not following the guidelines, or seeking shortcuts, is a reward in itself due to the reduced effort required). The rewards offered for following security guidelines should be sufficiently desirable and visible that they are more tempting to employees than the avoidance of the effort required to obtain them. When a behavior is rewarded it is more likely to be repeated.

8. Similarly, ensure that a security-conscious organizational culture is developed where employees learn from watching others be rewarded for such safe behaviors. This could be linked to an already existing bonus system, or small, ad hoc incentives such as spot prizes or recognition awards could be utilized. Social Learning Theory and employee motivation can be combined to ensure that security is enhanced.

9. Consider the elements of Protection Motivation Theory, and in particular, consider the role of perceived self-efficacy. Give users and employees the training and tools that they require to fully protect themselves and the data that they are responsible for, and provide them with the confidence that they can manage their online security appropriately. Giving individuals ownership of their own security measures may also help, as they feel that they have some control over what happens to the data. This might include the opportunity to make decisions regarding what information they provide and under what circumstances it is shared with others.

It must also be remembered that many users do know what they should do to increase security, but fail to implement these strategies, in a discrepancy sometimes called the *knowing-doing gap* (see, e.g., Workman et al., 2008; Cox, 2012). A number of the suggestions above are developed with this gap in mind, attempting to find ways to encourage users to engage in behaviors that they are aware are appropriate, although they may prefer to choose an alternative course of action. However, individuals exhibit the knowing-doing gap for many reasons, and not all users might be persuaded by the above strategies. It may be helpful to consider the users individually, determining what their particular reasons for such behaviors are, and attempting to develop a personalized strategy if appropriate and permissible under company policy. In the case study at the start of the chapter, the employee had been given training on security, and had been advised not to use their company password for other activities, but they failed to comply. There may be many reasons for this behavior, such as lack of ability, low motivation, high stress or utilization of poor decision-making techniques. Preventing such behavior in the future requires the determination of the primary reasons why the training was not adhered to. It may be necessary to employ multiple techniques across the organization to increase security behaviors, so as to reach and influence the entire workforce. As an example, an employee with low technical skills may not be motivated by an organizational strategy that offers incentives for the use of security behaviors that require advanced skills. However, they may feel relief if the stress of developing and memorizing complex passwords is reduced because their organization provides training in the use of password management tools.

6 CONCLUSION

By necessity, this chapter has only been able to consider a small subset of the relevant psychological theories, and the interested reader is directed toward some of the texts and readings listed below, where they will find more detail on the theories outlined here, as well as many further theories that are relevant to online security. It is evident that theories taken from psychology and communication studies have relevance to the development of effective online security procedures, and specific practical recommendations can be developed. It should be noted that the relative effectiveness of many of these recommendations have yet to be tested, and future research should aim to empirically assess their benefits. Nevertheless, they provide direction for users, employees, and managers when considering potential methods of increasing adherence to security protocols.

SUGGESTED FURTHER READINGS

- Child, J.T., Haridakis, P.M., Petronio, S., 2012. Blogging privacy rule orientations, privacy management and content deletion practices: the variability of online privacy management activity at different stages of social media use. Comput. Hum. Behav. 28, 1859-1872.
    - This article examines how Communication Privacy Management Theory can be applied to online privacy.
- Cox, J., 2012. Information systems user security: a structured model of the knowing-doing gap. Comput. Hum. Behav. 28, 1849-1858.
    - This paper gives an excellent overview of the knowing-doing gap, and demonstrates why it might occur. It includes focus on the role of the organisation and perceived threat.
- Kahneman, D., 2011. Thinking, Fast and Slow. Penguin, London.
    - Daniel Kahneman is a winner of the Nobel prize in economics (2002), and has led a long and distinguished career in cognitive psychology. This book describes the System 1 and 2 classifications outlined in this chapter, along with an overview of much of his other work.
- Schneier, B., 2012. Liars and Outliers: Enabling the Trust that Society Needs to Thrive. John Wiley & Sons Inc., Indianapolis, IN.
    - In this very readable book, Bruce Schneier describes how traditional trust mechanisms need to adapt in modern society, with some specific references to technological advances.

REFERENCES

Bandura, A., 1965. Influence of models' reinforcement contingencies on the acquisition of imitative behaviours. J. Pers. Soc. Psychol. 1, 589–595.

Campbell, J., Greenauer, N., Macaluso, K., End, C., 2007. Unrealistic optimism in internet events. Comput. Hum. Behav. 23, 1273–1284. http://dx.doi.org/10.1016/j.chb.2004.12.005.

Chen, R., Wang, J., Herath, T., Raghav Rao, H., 2011. An investigation of email processing from a risky decision making perspective. Decis. Support. Syst. 52 (1), 73–81. http://dx.doi.org/10.1016/j.dss.2011.05.005.

Child, J.T., Haridakis, P.M., Petronio, S., 2012. Blogging privacy rule orientations, privacy management and content deletion practices: the variability of online privacy management activity at different stages of social media use. Comput. Hum. Behav. 28, 1859–1872.

Cox, J., 2012. Information systems user security: a structured model of the knowing-doing gap. Comput. Hum. Behav. 28, 1849–1858.

Einhorn, H.J., Hogarth, R.M., 1978. Confidence in judgement: persistence of the illusion of validity. Psychol. Rev. 85, 395–416.

Jiang, C.L., Bazarova, N.N., Hancock, J.T., 2011. The disclosure-intimacy link in computer-mediated communication: an attributional extension of the hyperpersonal model. Hum. Commun. Res. 37, 58–77.

Jin, S.-A.A., 2012. To disclose or not to disclose, that is the question: a structural equation modelling approach to communication privacy management in e-health. Comput. Hum. Behav. 28, 69–77.

Johnston, A.C., Warkentin, M., 2010. Fear appeals and information security behaviours: an empirical study. MIS Q. 34 (3), 549–566.

Joinson, A.N., Reips, U.-D., Buchanan, T., Paine-Schofield, C.B., 2010. Privacy, trust and self-disclosure online. Hum. Comput. Interact. 25, 1–24.

Kahneman, D., 2011. Thinking, Fast and Slow. Penguin, London.

Kisekka, V., Bagchi-Sen, S., Rao, H.R., 2013. Extent of private information disclosure on online social networks: an exploration of Facebook mobile phone users. Comput. Hum. Behav. 29, 2722–2729.

Lee, D., Larose, R., Rifon, N., 2008. Keeping our network safe: a model of online protection behaviour. Behav. Inform. Technol. 27, 445–454.

Morris, R.G., Higgins, G.E., 2010. Criminological theory in the digital age: the case of social learning theory and digital piracy. J. Criminal Justice 38, 470–480. Retrieved from, http://dx.doi.org/10.1016/j.jcrimjus.2010.04.016.

Ng, B.Y., Rahim, M.A., 2005. A socio-behavioral study of home computer users' intention to practice security. In: The Ninth Pacific Asia Conference on Information Systems, Bangkok, Thailand, 7-10 July.

Ng, B.Y., Kankanhalli, A., Xu, Y.C., 2009. Studying users' computer security behaviour: a health belief perspective. Decis. Support. Syst. 46, 815–825.

Payne, J.W., 1980. Information processing theory: some concepts and methods applied to decision research. In: Wallsten, T.S. (Ed.), Cognitive Processes in Choice and Decision Behaviour. Erlbaum, Hillsdale, NJ.

Petronio, S., 2002. Boundaries of Privacy: Dialectics of Disclosure. SUNY Press, Albany, NY.

Power, A., Kirwan, G., 2015. Privacy and security risks online. In: Attrill, A. (Ed.), Cyberpsychology. Oxford University Press, Oxford, pp. 233–248.

Rogers, R.W., 1975. A protection motivation theory of fear appeals and attitude change. J. Psychol. 91, 93–114.

Rogers, R.W., 1983. Cognitive and physiological processes in fear appeals and attitude change: a revised theory of protection motivation. In: Cacioppo, J., Petty, R. (Eds.), Social Psychophysiology. Guildford Press, New York, pp. 153–176.

Rubin, Z., 1974. Lovers and other strangers: the development of intimacy in encounters and relationships. Am. Sci. 62, 182–190.

Rubin, Z., 1975. Disclosing oneself to a stranger: reciprocity and its limits. J. Exp. Soc. Psychol. 11, 233–260.

Schneier, B., 2012. Liars and Outliers: Enabling the Trust that Society Needs to Thrive. John Wiley & Sons Inc., Indianapolis, IN.

Sharot, T., Korn, C.W., Dolan, R.J., 2011. How unrealistic optimism is maintained in the face of reality. Nat. Neurosci. 14, 1475–1479. http://dx.doi.org/10.1038/nn.2949.

Skinner, B.F., 1938. The Behaviour of Organisms: An Experimental Analysis. Appleton Century, Oxford.

Tam, L., Glassman, M., Vandenwauver, M., 2009. The psychology of password management: a tradeoff between security and convenience. Behav. Inform. Technol. 29, 233–244. http://dx.doi.org/10.1080/01449290903121386.

Tversky, A., Kahneman, D., 1973. Availability: a heuristic for judging frequency and probability. Cogn. Psychol. 5 (1), 207–233.

Tversky, A., Kahneman, D., 1974. Judgement under uncertainty: heuristics and biases. Science 185 (4157), 1124–1131.

Tversky, A., Kahneman, D., 1981. The framing of decisions and the psychology of choice. Science 211 (4481), 453–458.

Walther, J.B., 1996. Computer-mediated communication: impersonal, interpersonal and hyperpersonal interaction. Commun. Res. 23, 3–43.

Walther, J.B., 2007. Selective self-presentation in computer-mediated communication: hyperpersonal dimensions of technology, language and cognition. Comput. Hum. Behav. 23, 2538–2557.

Weinstein, N.D., 1980. Unrealistic optimism about future life events. J. Pers. Soc. Psychol. 39, 806–820.

Workman, M., Bommer, W.H., Straub, D., 2008. Security lapses and the omission of information security measures: a threat control model and empirical test. Comput. Hum. Behav. 24, 2799–2816.

Check: Forensics and incident response

Conceptual evidence collection and analysis methodology for Android devices

14

Ben Martini, Quang Do, Kim-Kwang Raymond Choo

*Information Assurance Research Group, School of Information Technology and
Mathematical Sciences, University of South Australia, Adelaide, Australia*

1 INTRODUCTION

The Android operating system (OS), released to the public by Google in 2008 (Morrill, 2008), is currently the most widely used smartphone OS, with a market share of 44% as of the first quarter of 2014 (Lomas, 2014). As the number of Android users rises, the potential for evidence of crimes (both cyber and traditional) to be stored on Android devices increases. This results in the need for a forensically sound methodology for extracting and analyzing evidential data from Android devices. Digital forensics is concerned with identifying, preserving, analyzing, and ultimately presenting digital evidence to a court (McKemmish, 1999). For Android data collection techniques to be considered forensically sound, they must follow the digital forensics principals of upholding data integrity, correctness, and preservation. However, much of the existing research in this field (see Section 2.2) has made compromises in these respects with the aim of acquiring all possible data on the device.

Many types of potential evidential information can be extracted from a mobile device including SMS messages, phone call logs, photos, and location data. While extraction of these types of data has been commonplace for some time, more recently a focus has been placed upon collecting data from third-party apps that users install on their mobile devices. Within the many categories of popular apps (e.g., games, shopping, finance), cloud computing apps seem some of the most likely to store data which could be of potential evidential interest in a criminal investigation or a civil litigation. Of the cloud computing apps on the Google Play Store, cloud storage, and note-taking apps are some of the most downloaded. However, there has not been a commensurate level of research conducted on the most effective method of collecting and analyzing evidence from cloud apps on Android mobile devices. Much of the research which has been conducted in this area has also aged, as Android continues to advance and change with new versions being released on a regular basis. As such, we chose to focus on cloud apps installed on contemporary versions of Android as a case study for our methodology for collecting and analyzing app data for forensic purposes (Martini et al., 2015).

The structure of the remainder of this chapter is as follows: Section 2 discusses related work in this field, in particular, looking at existing techniques for the collection and analysis of forensic artifacts on Android devices. Section 3 describes our methodology for collection and analysis of evidential data on Android mobile devices. The methodology focuses on adherence to forensic soundness principles and aims to be as device agnostic as possible. Martini and Choo (2012)'s published cloud forensics framework is used as the underlying guiding context for this research and as such the process stages are represented within the four stages of this framework (also see Figure 1). Finally in Section 4, we conclude our work with a summary of our findings.

2 RELATED WORK

2.1 BACKGROUND

The Android OS runs as middleware on top of a Linux kernel (Enck et al., 2009) meaning many Linux-specific security features are used by Android. These security features include assigning each installed app a unique user ID and running each app within its own virtual machine (Wook et al., 2009), effectively sandboxing them. Android also implements a permission-based system to further enhance security on the device.

When an Android app is to be installed, it first requests a list of permissions that it requires, which the user must then accept in order to install the app. These permissions include access to device resources such as Internet, Bluetooth, and External Storage. If an app requires access to these resources, the developer must state so in the app's "AndroidManifest.xml" file located within the Application Package (APK) for the app. Android apps are generally written in the Java programming language and converted into a format (DEX) compatible with the virtual machine used in the Android OS, known as the Dalvik Virtual Machine (Dalvik). In addition to permissions that normal apps (apps that are installed into the "/data/app" directory) may use, there are system level permissions that may only be used by apps which are installed in the "/system/app" directory and signed with the developer key that was used to sign the device's OS. These apps are known as system apps. The "data" and "system" directories, along with several others, are mountpoints for partitions that Android uses in order to further compartmentalize the system.

A typical Android device has the following partitions:

- *system*—Contains system files, system apps, device frameworks
- *data*—Contains user installed apps, user data, and Dalvik cache
- *cache*—Stores temporary system data (such as when installing apps)
- *boot*—Boot partition, used for normal booting of the Android device
- *recovery*—Recovery mode partition which the device can alternatively boot to

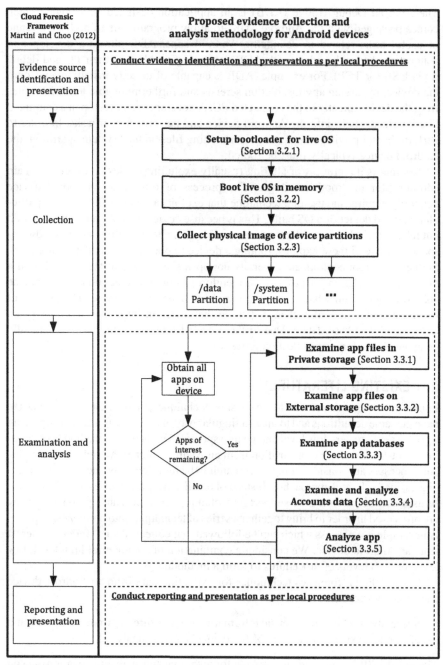

FIGURE 1

Evidence collection and analysis methodology for Android devices.

The Android Debug Bridge (ADB) is an application designed by Google, which comes packaged with the Android SDK, to allow programmers to perform a range of useful tasks related to debugging Android apps. ADB allows a developer to connect an Android device (with ADB debugging enabled) to their PC and debug it via USB (or TCP). For example, ADB is capable of directly installing apps onto the device, bypassing any installation screens and furthermore able to retrieve files from the device directly to the connected PC. A developer can even open a command line interface (shell) into the Android device and perform further tasks. In order to perform higher privileged tasks such as rewriting files on the "system" partition, the Android device typically must be rooted.

Rooting is the process of altering (usually exploiting) a device in order to gain administrator or "root" privileges. The process of rooting an un-rooted device generally requires the use of a technique that exploits a security flaw on that particular Android device and OS build. This is because device manufacturers typically do not release their devices with root access enabled. Due to the software- and hardware-specific nature of these exploits, rooting a device to obtain forensic data is not ideal. Furthermore, root exploits are generally not open source (due to the possibility of a manufacturer releasing a patch) and, therefore, a forensic practitioner may not be able to fully explain what the exploit may have done to the device. The process of rooting a device may also change data on the device in important partitions (such as "system" and "userdata"). Due to these considerations, rooting should generally be avoided in a forensic collection process.

2.2 EXISTING LITERATURE

For the purposes of this research, we consider techniques, methods, and approaches to have the same definitions and to mean a singular way of performing a task or achieving a goal. These are very low level and go into specific details (e.g., a method for obtaining a "bit-for-bit" copy of a partition from an Android phone). Models, frameworks, and processes are considered in this research to be high-level abstract forms of techniques, methods, and approaches. Instead of details, these are a series of operations to be used as the backbone or as support for techniques, methods, and approaches. They are often used in order to bring together a series of techniques into one cohesive piece. An example is a process which can be followed that collects data of forensic interest from an Android device. We consider a combination of a number of high level, low level, or both levels of procedures to form a methodology.

Current digital forensics techniques for extracting data from an Android device can be categorized into:

- live analysis where the forensic information is taken directly from the device, and
- offline analysis where a copy of the device's data is analyzed.

Maus et al. (2011) proposed an approach for obtaining and analyzing location data on Android devices. The authors performed an extraction of all the data on a rooted Android device and then analyzed the resulting data for databases containing certain attributes (such as "longitude") and photos with EXIF geo-data. The location information obtained is then plotted onto a map with timestamps and the estimated routes. Similarly, Spreitzenbarth et al. (2012) investigated the sources for location data on Android devices and found that many system apps stored a large amount of location data within their caches. The methods utilized by the authors in order to obtain the user data required for analysis once again required the device to have root access.

Al Mutawa et al. (2012) proposed a method to analyze several smartphones for evidentiary data in the form of social networking app artifacts. Once again, the authors were required to root the phone in order to access the user data needed to create a logical copy of the phone. The authors were able to recover information such as usernames, passwords, profile pictures, and chat messages.

Kim et al. (2012) proposed a technique to analyze a user's smartphone usage behavior by taking advantage of ext4 journal logs used by the Android OS to provide fault tolerance. They obtained a logical copy of the data partition of the Android device by rooting it and running the "dd" command. By using the journal logs, the authors were able to find out what actions a user performed (such as accessing or deleting a file) and recover certain deleted files.

Meanwhile, research by Barghouthy et al. (2013) attempted to retrieve private browsing session information from an Android device. Without rooting the device, the researchers found that no private Web browsing history was accessible. After rooting the device, the researchers were able to find the user's browsing history and login names.

Research by Andriotis et al. (2012) shows that while it is possible to obtain information such as files transferred via Bluetooth and visited wireless networks, this information is stored in a very small buffer. This means that the information obtained depends heavily on the time of the seizure of the device. To access this information (and to obtain a logical copy of it) also requires the device be rooted.

Finally, Chung et al. (2012) focused on extracting useful information off smartphones pertaining to apps and app data. They found that in order to access useful information such as app access keys and secret keys, the device was required to be rooted. Files such as those downloaded by cloud apps were generally kept on the external SD card and could be accessed without rooting the device.

It is clear from the literature review that existing research does not use a forensic framework as the basis of their evidence collection and/or analysis techniques. To contribute toward filling the literature gap, we will describe our proposed evidence collection and analysis methodology for Android devices in the next section.

3 AN EVIDENCE COLLECTION AND ANALYSIS METHODOLOGY FOR ANDROID DEVICES

This section outlines the methodology that we have developed for collection and analysis of evidential data from modern Android mobile devices. The methodology is constructed using the principles of Martini and Choo's cloud forensics framework (Martini and Choo, 2012) to ensure forensic soundness.

Mobile devices (*vis-à-vis* "traditional" mobile phones), having relatively recently gained maturity as a technology, tend to natively employ security features that standard PC OSs are only now beginning to introduce. Android devices are no exception to this with advanced app sandboxing to ensure that user privacy is preserved, device encryption and increasingly advanced login systems based on a range of technologies varying from simple and complex passcodes through to biometrics. This presents a far greater challenge to a forensic practitioner in comparison to traditional PC-based forensics.

When designing the evidence collection and analysis methodology, we sought to implement two key characteristics:

- *Adherence to forensic soundness principles*—One of the key characteristics of the process was to maintain forensic soundness especially in terms of data handling. The first two "rules" which McKemmish (1999, p.3) notes in his seminal paper on digital forensics are "Minimal Handling of the Original" and "Account for Any Change." In the context of contemporary smart mobile devices, this can be interpreted as ensuring that the absolute minimum changes required are made to the mobile device to collect its evidence.

  In most cases, it would be unrealistic to assume that it is possible to collect all potential evidence from a mobile device in a timely and accessible manner without at least minor modifications (e.g., bypassing security features on the device). However, adherence to McKemmish's second rule means that any operation that a practitioner undertakes on a mobile device must be fully understood by the practitioner. This is to ensure that the minimum number of changes are being made to the device, that the integrity of the evidence on the device remains intact, and that the precise steps undertaken on the device can be explained to a court as part of the reporting and presentation process.

  To date, a number of the published digital forensic processes for Android devices use methods that involve unknown instructions being executed on the device (as discussed in Section 2.1). This is most commonly part of the 'rooting' process or flashing a third-party (unverified) "recovery OS." A number of authors (Maus et al., 2011; Al Mutawa et al., 2012; Kim et al., 2012; Barghouthy et al., 2013; Andriotis et al., 2012; Sylve et al., 2012; Lessard and Kessler, 2010) use tools developed by third parties that are generally not designed for forensic collection purposes and, as such, may result in the integrity of the evidence collected being questioned as part of legal processes (e.g., changes to the user data partition without the forensic practitioner's knowledge).

- *Ensure the process is device agnostic as far as practical*—Another characteristic we sought to implement when designing the process was to ensure that the process was as device agnostic as possible. This is not a straightforward aim as the Android OS is known for the fact that it runs on many different devices manufactured by different organizations. Each of these parties almost always customizes the OS resulting in what is known as "fragmentation" or "fracturing."

From a research perspective, this means that all processes designed for Android forensics generally apply only to specific devices and particular OS versions. Our process does not aim to resolve this issue entirely; due to the customization available to OEMs and carriers, this may be an impractical aim. However, we aimed to document methods (wherever possible) that operate on the underlying Android OS and APIs rather than relying on, for example, exploits in particular customized OS libraries or utilities. This characteristic must be rationalized against our requirement for forensic soundness which is the overriding factor in the design of any digital forensic process.

Our proposed collection methodology comprises eight steps, as outlined (in bolded boxes) in Figure 1, which we discuss in the context of the cloud forensic framework (Martini and Choo, 2012) to provide background.

The methodology includes techniques to bypass device/OS security features, collect a forensic "bit-for-bit" image of the device's data partition, analyze the collected image, and where necessary inject the OS libraries with code to retrieve securely stored data and/or credentials.

3.1 IDENTIFY DEVICE AND PRESERVE EVIDENCE

The first step in our methodology for evidence collection is to identify the device and approximate the Android version so that we can use device or OS version specific methods, where necessary, for the remaining stages of the technique. This assumes that the practitioner has already placed the device in a forensic Faraday bag. Otherwise, this should be completed as a first step when the device is seized.

It is important that the device remains in a radio suppressed environment (e.g., the use of a forensic Faraday bag) while it is powered on. This is necessary as it is common for devices to have the ability to be "remotely wiped" when sent a signal over a mobile or Wi-Fi network. If this occurs, it will result in the device erasing its internal (and, potentially, SD card) memory. In many cases, this will prevent any further forensic analysis and, as such, should be avoided at all costs. If it is not possible for the device to remain in a radio suppressed physical environment and the device is unlocked, practitioners may choose to place the device in "Airplane Mode" which is designed to disable the device's radios (for use on airplanes). While this is advisable in comparison to leaving the device powered on with access to a mobile network, it introduces unnecessary risk in contrast to using a physically radio suppressed environment. Practitioners should also follow standard practices in terms of physical evidence preservation, particularly in terms of ensuring that they take appropriate photographs of the device and any attachments when it is seized.

If the device is unlocked when initially seized, the practitioner should confirm if device encryption is enabled and/or if a lock code is enabled. If device encryption is enabled, then the device should not be powered off as this will require the encryption password to be entered before the data on the phone can be accessed. At the time of research, there is no supported method for disabling device encryption without wiping the contents of the phone's data partition. As such, if device encryption has been enabled, the practitioner should consider conducting a logical acquisition using methods such as Android device backup. This may also be a prudent step (if the device is unlocked) regardless as additional evidence collection methods should be used where feasible. Although a logical collection will not be able to provide all the data possible via physical collection, it does offer a useful backup. Practitioners may also consider taking screenshots of the state of the device (including any virtual connections, e.g., to wireless networks) when the device is seized, if it is unlocked. However, the benefits of this approach must be balanced against the risk of the screenshots overwriting potential evidence that has been deleted and is located in unallocated space.

If a practitioner finds that a lock code is enabled on an unlocked device, the practitioner should consider disabling the lock code (a change which can be accounted for). While the device is powered on, the practitioner should attempt to determine the version of Android that the device is running. If the device is unlocked, this information can be gathered from the "About Phone" section of the Settings app, and the device model can also be obtained from this section. If the device is locked, the practitioner may be able to use visual artifacts on the lock screen such as the user interface style to provide an indication of the approximate Android version.

Recently, there have been a number of publications on the topic of forensic collection of volatile memory in Android devices (see Sylve et al., 2012; Stirparo et al., 2013; Thing et al., 2010). It may be necessary to collect the volatile memory of the device, as a form of preservation, before the primary evidence collection stage to ensure that potential evidence is not lost when the device is powered off. This is particularly pertinent when the device is encrypted as the encryption key may be stored in volatile memory. Unfortunately, all of the techniques that we reviewed (for modern versions of Android) required that the device be rooted. This is due to Android's sandboxing model preventing apps from reading the memory space (or heap) of another app. If the device is already rooted and unlocked, then this collection method may be an acceptable forensic procedure. However, the vast majority of Android devices will not be rooted. Many authors do not mention the requirement to root the device for forensic collection and those who do generally do not discuss the forensic implications of running code that executes unknown instructions on a device undergoing forensic analysis. As rooting relies on exploits which are generally patched in future versions of Android, its success cannot be guaranteed. Many (if not most) root exploits for modern Android mobile devices also require that the device be rebooted, which negates their use for volatile memory collection.

Once these steps have been completed the device can be powered off. After the device has been powered off, the next step is to identify the device, which is generally achieved by looking for manufacturer, model and other device-specific markings or labels on the device (generally on the back cover).

3.2 COLLECT EVIDENCE

Once the device has been identified and preserved, the next step is to collect a physical forensic image of the device's "userdata" partition. This partition is generally nonvolatile, as such practitioners should have preserved (and collected) all volatile data by this point (as discussed in Section 3.1). Under normal circumstances (as enforced by Android security), the "userdata" partition is the only internal partition to which a user can directly write data and, as such, is the most likely location for evidence to be stored. However, if the practitioner has any doubts as to the integrity of the Android security on the device (e.g., if the device is suspected of being rooted or is running a custom OS), they may choose to also collect physical images of the other partitions on the device (see Section 2.1 for a list of common Android partitions).

Physical collection is preferable to the more common logical collection (via the stock OS) for a number of reasons. Physical collection allows for a more thorough analysis of the data stored on the device's flash memory by ensuring that we collect all of the files on the partition. In comparison, a logical collection using a tool such as Android backup will only return the files that the OS provides as part of a backup (this tends to be somewhat vendor specific, but is generally a subset of the available data). The collection of a physical image also allows for the potential recovery of deleted files from unallocated space, file signature verification and header/keyword search using existing forensic tools that are able to read the ext4 partition format used by modern versions of Android.

Another major advantage of physical collection is that it will circumvent passcode lock controls on the device by bypassing the stock OS, something that will generally thwart a collection process that requires the device to be rooted and uses the stock OS.

When conducting forensic analysis on a traditional PC, a common technique for physical collection is to boot the PC using a triage live OS (which runs in RAM) or to remove the disk(s) from the PC and use a write blocker in a second PC to collect an unmodified physical image. These techniques have parallels in collection of evidence from Android mobile devices. The physical disk collection method is analogous to the "chip-off" (i.e., physically removing the NAND flash from a device) technique used in mobile forensics. While this method has proved useful, it is very time consuming and the technique may not be perfected for the flash storage used in each type of Android mobile device. The live OS collection method is used for physical collection of other mobile devices (e.g., the custom ramdisk approach used in "iphone-dataprotection" (Bédrune et al., 2011. iPhone data protection in depth, July 18 2014. http://esec-lab.sogeti.com/dotclear/public/publications/11-hitbamsterdam-iphonedataprotection.pdf.)) and can be applied on any Android device that is capable of booting from a PC via USB or external media (e.g., SD card). This method has many advantages including the speed and effort required for the collection and the relatively device agnostic process in comparison to chip-off analysis.

The selection of live OS to run on the device is integral. Wherever possible, practitioners should build an appropriate live OS using the AOSP and vendor supplied source code/drivers. Where this is not feasible the practitioner should only use a prebuilt live OS when it was designed for forensic extraction and the source of the OS is trusted.

Our technique for booting the OS into RAM on the mobile device is discussed in Sections 3.2.1–3.2.2.

3.2.1 Setup bootloader for live OS

The first step in the collection stage of our technique is to modify the bootloader so that it will allow us to boot a live OS. While in some cases this may be possible with the default factory configuration, most devices will have some security applied to the bootloader preventing the loading of custom OSs. One prominent reason for this is that manufacturers generally terminate support and warranty arrangements when a user installs a custom OS, as such they configure their devices to warn users of this and may require that they retrieve a device-specific "key" from the manufacturer's Web site. Some manufacturers also note the security flaw we are seeking to exploit, in this case, for forensic collection. By running a custom OS, we can bypass the security enforced by the stock Android OS (e.g., sandboxing and file system/device permissions) and read from the flash memory/secure storage/etc. directly.

The process for reconfiguring the bootloader to allow us to boot a live OS is commonly known as "unlocking" a bootloader. This process is device-specific (hence the requirement to gather device information as part of the first stage of this technique) although a number of manufactures use similar processes that make use of the "fastboot" tool. Many modern Android devices can be placed in "fastboot mode" (via a key combination while the device is powered off) that will allow us to provide instructions to the bootloader using the fastboot tool. Once the device is in fastboot mode, unlocking the device may be as simple as passing the "oem unlock" command via the fastboot tool. The device may respond advising that the unlock procedure has been successful or may require (as discussed above) that a unique string (displayed at this point) be provided to the manufacturer to retrieve an unlock key which will need to be provided at this point. Generally, the practitioner will be able to retrieve this key via the standard Web form used by customers for this purpose.

Some manufactures may choose to wipe the Android device's data partition as part of the unlock process. If allowed, this will prevent us from accessing the data on the mobile device and potentially destroy it, as such the wiping process (if it exists) must be bypassed or disabled. This will require research on the part of the practitioner to determine an appropriate exploit to bypass this process. This may be somewhat time consuming unless this research has already been completed and published by a trusted source. Where wiping (or any destructive operation) is involved, a practitioner is strongly advised to obtain an identical device to that which is being analyzed, which they may test the technique on before attempting to apply it in the investigation.

3.2.2 Boot the live OS in memory

Once the bootloader has been unlocked, we can commence booting the custom live OS (i.e., the custom image). In the majority of cases, a practitioner or their organization should develop their own live OS based on the Android core (kernel and low-level services).

Votipka et al. (2013) described a method for creating recovery images for forensic collection purposes. This method can be adapted to create the live OS image that is similar to a minimalist recovery image. Creating a live OS image is advantageous in a number of ways but primarily it provides the practitioner (or organization) with a higher level of confidence that the processes being run on the device are forensically sound (e.g., ensuring that partitions on the device are not mounted until an image has been collected). Creating the OS also ensures that the practitioner is aware of, and, as such, can account in their reporting for, any changes that are required to load the live OS on a particular device.

Each device will require a specific kernel and/or drivers and, as a result, each live OS image will require customization on a per device basis. However, once it is developed, it should not need to be updated for each individual device. Where it is infeasible for the organization or practitioner to create the live OS, it may be acceptable for the practitioner to use a prebuilt live OS designed for forensic collection (assuming the practitioner trusts the source of the OS). It is strongly recommended that live OS images that are not specifically designed for forensic collection not be used for this purpose. Apart from the potential for malicious intent, images may unintentionally erase or modify data that may be integral to a forensic case and in a manner that is unpredictable.

Once the image has been built, the next step is to boot the image into the volatile memory of the device. Notably, this ensures that no data needs to be wiped on the device as would be required if an OS image was flashed onto the device. A number of existing Android forensic processes flash the "recovery" partition on the basis that user data cannot be stored there (see Votipka et al., 2013; Son et al., 2013; Vidas et al., 2011). However, this is not universally true. If this becomes a common procedure for forensic collection, then suspects can begin hiding data in this partition that will implicitly be erased when the forensic collection image is written to the partition. This is analogous to writing a triage OS partition to the disk of a PC so that we can boot the forensic tool, which, will implicitly delete any data (presently allocated or unallocated) that was previously written to that location on disk.

Again using the popular fastboot system as an example, once the OS image has been created, booting the image into memory is as simple as issuing the "fastboot boot liveos.img" command from the PC to which the mobile device is attached. The live OS image file will be transferred to the mobile device memory and the device will attempt to boot it. Once the OS has completed booting and the ADB daemon has started, we can commence the final stage of image collection.

3.2.3 Collect the physical image of the device partitions

The forensic copy technique used for physical collection of the partitions and transfer of the "bit-for-bit" images to the PC will depend on the method the practitioner has chosen to implement in their live OS. The practitioner can set up this process to suit their organizational/legislative requirements. We propose using a generic process for physical collection that makes use of a common Android toolset while ensuring forensic soundness, such as the following:

ADB supports forwarding of various sockets/devices to a PC via USB. We use the "adb forward" command to forward the mobile device flash block devices to the PC via USB for collection. This is achieved by using the ADB application on the pc running a command such as "adb forward tcp:7000 dev:/dev/block/platform/[flash memory name, e.g., "msm_sdcc.1"]/by-name/userdata" which would allow the practitioner to access a "bit-for-bit" stream of the "userdata" partition on the phone by connecting to TCP port 7000 on the host PC. In practice this is achieved by having an application read from port 7000 until the end of stream and writing the received bytes to a binary file. The collection of the "userdata" partition will also result in the collection of all data on an emulated SD card (located at "/data/media/0" within the "userdata" partition). In the case of a physical SD card, the practitioner will need to undertake a separate physical collection. If they choose to do so via the live OS, it can be accessed at the "/dev/block/platform/[SD card memory name, e.g., "s3c-**sdhci**.2"]/mmcblk1" path and collected using a similar technique to that used to collect the "userdata" partition.

Once the collection has been completed, the practitioner should use one or more hashing algorithms to verify the integrity of the collected image. Using the "md5sum" and "sha1sum" tools on the mobile device's flash block device file and on the collected image files stored on the PC should result in identical hash values. These hash values should be recorded for later use as part of the reporting stage.

3.3 EXAMINATION AND ANALYSIS

Using the physical images collected from the mobile device, we can now begin examination in order to extract any potential evidential data. We will also use the information gathered from the examination stage to guide the types of analysis that will need to be conducted on the physical images and, potentially, the mobile device to retrieve further evidential data.

The first step of examination begins with determining the installed apps and which apps are of particular interest to this examination. While this stage does not prevent the practitioner from using standard forensic techniques on the physical image, such as a tool to conduct a raw keyword search for known keywords of interest, it allows us to focus the examination on and deliver in-depth results for particular apps. The apps of interest may be of a particular category (e.g., cloud apps or communication apps) or may be individual apps depending on the nature of the case.

There are a number of methods for determining the apps that have been installed on an Android device. However, once a physical image has been collected, one of the most straightforward methods is simply to list the subdirectories in the "data" directory of the "userdata" partition. Each of these subdirectories will have an app "package name" (e.g., "com.example.appname"), notably this name is not the friendly name which is used to display the app in the OS, but rather it is a unique name selected by the developer conforming to a certain standard. Generally the app friendly name will be part of this app name. This subdirectory is known as its data directory or private app storage area.

Private storage is commonly the main focus for a forensic investigation on a particular app, as Android uses sandboxing to prevent apps from interfering with each other and the OS. This also means that apps are restricted to writing files to their private app directory (and selected other places such as external storage). An app can write almost any type of file to its private storage, although it is generally preferable to write large files to "external storage" (often a physical or emulated SD card), as private storage is often limited. Private storage commonly stores the following types of files:

- "webview" data (such as cache and cookies),
- databases (generally SQLite),
- files (can be any type of file),
- cache (app cache data),
- lib (app software library files) and
- shared_prefs (preference files in a common Android XML based format).

Once the available data has been examined (and if necessary analyzed) from both private and external app storage, we may need to conduct further analysis operations on the mobile device to collect any other potential evidential data or data required to further the collection with other evidence sources beyond the individual mobile device being analyzed. This would be conducted as a separate iteration of the forensic framework (as outlined in Martini and Choo, 2012).

Our technique for examining the available evidence stored by apps and conducting further analysis on an Android device is discussed in the following five sections.

3.3.1 Examine app files in private storage

Starting the examination with each app's private storage directory seems to be the logical choice as the majority of app specific data is likely to be stored there. There are no mandatory items that need to be stored in private app storage and, as such, the exact data that will be extracted will be app dependent. However, we aim in this section to provide an overview of the types of data that would be commonly found in private app storage.

Configuration files known as "shared_prefs" are commonly used in Android apps. Access to these shared_prefs files is abstracted in the Android API, simplifying configuration directive storage and making it easily accessible to every app developer. Developers can store a wide range of data in shared_prefs files that are located in the "shared_prefs" subdirectory of the app's private storage directory.

Practitioners should ensure that they examine the contents of these shared_prefs configuration files to not only locate potential items of evidential interest (e.g., app event timestamps, credentials, user identification information, recent items, etc.) but also information which may aid in the further examination and analysis of the seized device (e.g., encryption keys, database locations) and of the user's other devices (e.g., remote server/cloud information).

Two formats are commonly found in shared_prefs files: An XML structure for standard objects such as strings, integers and Booleans and, within the XML, JSON encoding is commonly used to represent arrays of objects that have been serialized from the app. While the meaning of configuration directives in these files is not always obvious, it is generally in plain text and a meaning can often be inferred. Where there is ambiguity over the meaning of the configuration directive, a practitioner can use analysis techniques to attempt to determine a certain meaning; this is discussed further in Section 3.3.5.

Following on from the analysis of the app's shared_prefs, the practitioner should examine the other files stored by the app for evidential value. Application libraries (stored in lib) are unlikely to be of value to most forensic investigations. Cache files, if present, may expose evidential data that was temporarily stored by the app; however, nonstandard binary formats are commonly used. Unless the format can be decoded, binary analysis of the strings may be the only straightforward means for analysis. Other files, including those stored in the "files" subdirectory, may be in any format of the app developer's choosing. Standard forensic techniques, such as header analysis, can be used to determine the file type and potentially decode the file.

Web view data (cache, cookies, etc.) is stored in the "webview" subdirectory when Web views are used in the app. Analysis of this information, in a similar manner to traditional browser analysis, may provide evidence of interest.

Databases are commonly used by apps to store a range of potential evidential data including configuration information entered by the user, metadata stored by the app (especially reflecting app usage) and even the data stored by the user (depending on the nature of the app). App databases are discussed further in Section 3.3.3.

3.3.2 Examine app files on external storage

Following the examination of the files stored by particular apps within their private storage directory, a practitioner should examine files on the device's external storage. The name "external storage" is somewhat ambiguous; but for the purpose of this research, generally refers to storage on the device either provided via a physical SD card inserted into the device, emulated SD card (where data is stored on the phone's internal flash) or a combination of both. Regardless of the type, external storage is one location on the device where Android's sandboxing rules are significantly relaxed.

Generally, any app that has been granted the read and/or write external storage permission can read and/or write to any part of the external storage (unless a third-party solution, such as the one described by Do et al., 2014, is protecting the storage). This means that an app can write data to any location on external storage. However, there is a special directory on external storage specifically structured for individual app storage. It is similar to private storage but does not have the sandboxing protection available in private storage. Apps that make use of this facility will have a directory with their app name (identical to their subdirectory within the "userdata" partition's "data" directory) in the "Android/data/" directory of the external storage. Depending on directory permissions, it may be reasonable to presume that data stored in these directories was created by the app in the directory name.

The external storage should be examined in a similar fashion to the private app storage with a similar range of files being potentially stored on external storage. As noted, larger files are likely to be stored on external storage; however, any type of file can potentially be stored on external storage. Due to the lack of security controls, some apps may opt to encrypt their files which are stored on external storage.

3.3.3 Examine app databases

As both private and external storage are being examined (particularly the private app storage databases directory, but potentially in any app-writable directory on the device), a practitioner will likely locate and collect various databases of interest. SQLite is natively supported by the Android API and as such is commonly used. However, this does not prevent apps from using other database formats. For example, apps may choose to store data in a proprietary format and/or a format more suitable to their data (e.g., a key-value pair database for efficiency).

Header analysis can generally be used to identify the type of database and allow the practitioner to locate tools suitable for decoding the database. This may not be the case if the entire database file is encrypted by the app, in which case the practitioner will need to locate the database and key based on configuration file data (see Section 3.3.1) or further app analysis (see Section 3.3.5).

Similar to shared_prefs or other configuration files, the meaning of the columns and tables in a RDBMS type database, for example, should be somewhat self-explanatory as the original descriptive strings should still be available. However, in the case of ambiguity, further app-based analysis can be completed as discussed in Section 3.3.5.

3.3.4 Examine and analyze accounts data

For apps that use online services requiring authentication, the next stage is to examine and, if necessary, use analysis techniques to collect the accounts data stored by Android. Apps may choose to store their accounts (mostly credentials) data in a secure database provided by the OS AccountManager service. The AccountManager API has been designed to ensure that only the app that stored a particular set of credentials is able to retrieve them. In our experiments using seven popular cloud apps described in Martini et al. (2015), we found that there are at least two ways for this accounts data to be stored on the device. The data can be stored in an SQLite format database located at "system/users/[device user id, generally 0]/accounts.db" on the "userdata" partition. Alternatively, if implemented by the device manufacturer, accounts data can be stored in a physical secure store on the device SoC.

In the former case, analysis of the SQLite database (which was collected as part of the physical image of the "userdata" partition) is quite straightforward. In our experiments described in Martini et al. (2015), we found that the tables of particular interest were "accounts," "authtokens," and "extras," although the practitioner should examine all tables for potential evidence.

The accounts table is used to store account records including their "name," "type," and a "password" which may contain a password, a string other than a password (e.g., an authtoken), or be blank.

The authtokens records contain an "accounts_id" (to link the authtoken to their account record), a "type" and the "authtoken" (a string defined by the app or authentication service provider).

The extras table stores data added to secure storage using a key-value system which requires that the calling app not only be the app which created the associated account but also that it has the relevant key to retrieve the value (retrieval requests with unused keys return null). This table could store a range of data but commonly includes refresh tokens, account IDs, etc. The fields in the table include "account_id," "key," and "value."

If the device does not use this SQLite database and instead chooses to store the credentials in physical secure storage, this complicates collection of these credentials. However, in cases where evidence collected from remote services is integral (such as those involving cloud computing or social networking), we may need to conduct further analysis to retrieve these credentials from the device.

The analysis technique that we propose requires changes to be made to the device's software that would require "handling the original." We believe that this discrete change, which the practitioner will be able to account for, should not be able to cause modification to the evidence. As with any change, a practitioner or researcher should weigh the cost of making the change against the potential to collect further evidence and make a decision on whether to proceed on a case-by-case basis.

To proceed with the necessary changes, the practitioner will need to once again boot the phone into the live OS (as discussed in Section 3.2). They will then need to mount the "system" partition and extract the "services.jar" (and potentially "services.odex") file from the "framework" directory. If the "services.jar" which is included on the device does not contain a "classes.dex" file when decompressed from the ZIP format, then the practitioner will need to extract and deodex the "services.odex" file, otherwise they will need to "baksmali" the "classes.dex" file. In either event, the practitioner will generate a set of SMALI source files for the Android services framework.

"smali" and "baksmali" (see https://code.google.com/p/smali/) are an assembler and disassembler (respectively) for Android apps.

- baksmali is used to convert an Android app's "classes.dex" file into human readable SMALI code.
- smali is used to convert these SMALI files back into a DEX format file that is compatible with the Android Dalvik virtual machine.

The practitioner should locate the "com/android/server/pm/PackageManagerService.smali" file within this source tree and then modify and inject the "compareSignatures" method (which returns a Boolean) such that it always returns "true" when receiving the practitioner's package signing key. Injecting the "compareSignatures" method such that it always returns "true" is a known technique discussed in the Android development community (XDA Developers, 2012).

The SMALI source tree should then be recompiled (using the "smali" application), the "classes.dex" file should be replaced in the "services.jar" compressed file and the updated jar file should be uploaded via the live OS to replace the original on the device's system partition. The original "services.odex" file on the device is deleted in order to trigger the OS to rebuild its system packages.

If the practitioner was required to deodex the "services.odex" file to obtain the SMALI code, other system packages may require de-odexing as the Android OS detects all changes in system files and attempts to rebuild the package and ones it is dependent on. As the other JAR files do not contain a "classes.dex" file for Android to turn into an "odex" file, the OS may not boot.

We developed a script to automatically rebuild system JAR packages with their respective "classes.dex" files by monitoring the "logcat" output (the development log which is visible from a connected PC). Any dependencies that cannot be rebuilt are logged in the "logcat" output as a "StaleDexCacheError" type message containing the required package's name. This script simply parses the output for these strings (which contains the system package required to be de-odexed). This process is outlined in Figure 2.

Once this replacement is completed, a practitioner can develop and sign an APK which requests the relevant account credentials from the device's secure storage at boot and outputs the credentials to "logcat." This is achieved using the methods that are available when instantiating the AccountManager class. For example, an array containing all accounts on the device can be obtained with the AccountManager "getAccounts" method. Using this, the AccountManager "getPassword" method can be passed an "Account," which will return the "password" (plaintext password, authentication token, etc., depending on what the app stores) for that particular account. The "getPassword" method ordinarily requires the signature of the caller to match that of the account being obtained but the method described above gives this APK effectively system level permissions and, therefore, permission to read all data from all accounts stored upon the device.

Notably, this technique will work on devices with secure storage and, with some modification, devices where the user has enabled encryption. This is possible as Android does not encrypt the system partition when device encryption is enabled.

3.3.5 Analyze apps

Once all of the above data has been examined, and analyzed where necessary, the practitioner will have collected the majority of the body of potential evidence on the device. However, there may be some remaining ambiguity at this stage as to the exact meaning or source of some of the evidence. Before reporting and presentation commences, the methodology aims to reduce, as far as practicable, any ambiguity as to the provenance or meaning of the collected data. As such, the final stage of analysis and examination is to analyze the underlying code of the apps being examined.

There are a number of approaches to this stage of the technique which, when combined, can assist a practitioner in efficiently gathering the background information on the located evidential data. The approaches selected will vary depending on the case and apps being analyzed. Broadly speaking, most authors refer to two types of app

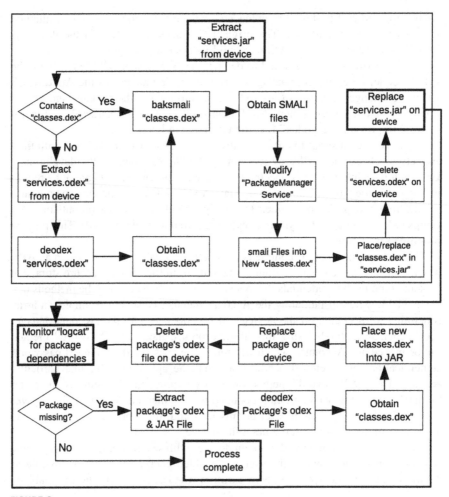

FIGURE 2

Modifying the "services.jar" file (top) and package monitoring (bottom).

analysis: static analysis where the app code/binaries are analyzed to determine app operation and dynamic analysis where the app is run to understand its operation. We propose a combination of both static and dynamic analysis approaches. This allows a practitioner to gain a complete understanding of the app while avoiding the short-comings of the individual approaches (e.g., in the case of code obfuscation).

For most apps, it will not be necessary to analyze the original instance of the app on the evidence source device to determine its operation. The APK files for apps requiring further analysis can be copied from the "/data/app" directory on the "user-data" partition (or "/system/app" on the "system" partition in the case of system apps). Once collected, these APKs can then be installed on a development device or emulator that will allow the practitioner to have a greater level of visibility into the app's operations without requiring modifications to the original evidence source device.

Most approaches for analysis of Android apps are designed from the perspective of security researchers rather than forensic practitioners. Practitioners should investigate the contemporary analysis approaches available at the time of their investigation. However, as part of our proof of concept discussed in Martini et al. (2015) we found the following techniques to be most useful for a forensic investigation.

One approach that we made extensive use of was analysis of app memory "heaps." These memory dumps represent the majority of objects that an app has currently provisioned in memory. Use of this technique on publically released apps (i.e., without a "debuggable" flag in their manifest) requires a development or engineering build of Android. We recommend that this build be installed in an emulator or virtual machine. Debugging will need to be enabled in the virtual Android device. Once debugging is enabled, the practitioner can attach the mobile device to a PC via the ADB program and use the DDMS (Dalvik Debug Monitor Server) tool available from the Google Android SDK. DDMS supports the collection of app memory heaps in the HPROF (Heap PROFile) format to collect the current memory state of running apps.

We were able to develop an application for execution on the PC that will collect the memory heap of a particular app at regular time intervals (as set by the user). This allows a practitioner to examine the changes in the app's memory as it progresses through a procedure (e.g., during a login process). We used Eclipse Memory Analyzer to analyze the "HPROF" files, which requires that the Android "HPROF" file be converted to a generic Java HPROF format. This can be achieved using the "hprof-conv" tool available with the Android SDK. Eclipse Memory Analyzer initially loads a converted HPROF file into a view known as the Dominator Tree. In this view, one is able to sort all objects within memory by shallow heap (or retained heap). This is useful as larger objects contain more data which may be of use. The Dominator List can be further defined by filtering it to only show objects part of a certain class path (e.g., "com.dropbox.android"). In order to further analyze the memory heap, we must use Object Query Language.

Object Query Language or OQL is a query language designed for databases containing objects (i.e., object-oriented databases). The syntax of OQL is very similar to SQL with keywords such as "SELECT," "FROM," and "WHERE." Examples of tasks we can accomplish by executing OQL on the memory heap include:

- Obtaining a list of all Strings in the memory heap containing the word "authentication"
- Finding all instances of the "org.apache.http.client" class.

Decompiling the app and conducting static analysis of the source code also provided a useful approach to understanding the data stored by particular apps. A number of authors describe this approach (see Zheng et al., 2013; Zhou et al., 2012; Xu et al., 2012;

Backes et al., 2013). The feasibility of this approach will be significantly reduced if the app code has been obfuscated (i.e., all identifying strings and notations—e.g., variable and method names—have been removed from the app). We found that obfuscation had been used in a number of the contemporary apps that we analyzed in Martini et al. (2015). While it is still possible to gain an understanding from code in this state, it becomes more difficult.

Analyzing the app's code is useful to determine how configuration entries are created, how the app databases are populated and read, and how security (such as tokens and encryption) is implemented and used.

3.4 REPORTING AND PRESENTATION

After the practitioner has completed examination and analysis of the relevant apps and their constituent data, they will need to produce reports and ultimately present their findings.

To demonstrate the integrity of the evidence that has been collected, cryptographic hashes (e.g., MD5 and/or SHA1) of the physical partitions (as taken from the block devices) and of the forensic images should match and be reported. This is standard practice for forensic image collection of PC hard disks and other traditional media; however, it has often been lacking in forensic analysis of mobile devices to date. This is presumably due to the difficulty in collecting this information and/or the difficulty in collecting a "bit-for-bit" image of the device's flash memory. This integrity verification process cannot be undertaken until the live OS has been booted, which demonstrates the necessity for the practitioner to completely understand the operation of the OS that they use. This is particularly notable as any minor change to the file system, which could be as simple as the live OS auto-mounting the device partitions and updating the journal, will change the file system hash.

In addition to standard reporting requirements, as defined by the practitioner's organization, Android forensic investigations should include information on the changes that were made to the original evidence item (mobile device) and any changes that were made should be fully accounted for. This may mean that a practitioner provides details of the technique that was used to collect, examine, and analyze the evidence. Practitioners may also include data that they derived from app analysis to remove any ambiguity in the terms they are reporting from app data files and databases.

---

4 CONCLUSION

In this chapter, we proposed a methodology for collection of evidential data from Android devices. To ensure forensic soundness, the methodology was designed to make as few changes to the evidence source device as possible, and when changes were made, they were discrete and, as such, could be easily accounted for by the investigating forensic practitioner. After device identification and preservation techniques (such as ensuring the device was radio suppressed to prevent remote wiping) were undertaken, the first technique in our methodology is to setup the device so that we can boot a live collection OS from the devices volatile memory (RAM).

The live OS is used for collection purposes to ensure that a copy of the device's partitions can be obtained without modifying the contents of the flash memory. Often to collect an image using the device's stock OS requires the device to be rooted, which generally has unknown consequences from a forensic soundness point of view. The live OS may also be used separately, if necessary, to modify the system partition and gain access to any protected data (such as accounts information).

In this sense, the Android live OS is similar to live OS's used on PCs for forensic triage. We recommend that practitioners design their own live OS where possible, to ensure that its operation on the device can be entirely accounted for, or use a live OS from a trusted source (such as from the law enforcement community) where this is not feasible. The practitioner should consider an appropriate method for transport of the physical forensic image collected from the mobile device to an investigation PC when designing their live collection OS. We propose the use of an ADB forwarding function that appears (based on cryptographic hashes matching) to result in a bit-for-bit copy of the device flash partitions being transferred between the mobile device and a PC attached via USB.

Once a physical image of the relevant device partitions has been obtained, a practitioner can commence analysis of the data stored, particularly within the "userdata" partition. Practitioners should commence by examining the files stored by the app in their private storage directories. Once these files have been examined and their type, format and purpose is known, the practitioner should commence examining the files stored, by apps of interest, on external storage. If databases were located as part of file examination, then the next step would be for the practitioner to analyze the databases. Databases often contain metadata that can be of particular interest in forensic investigations. Once all of the apps' files and databases have been explicated, the practitioner can undertake techniques (if necessary) to extract protected AccountManager data from the device. This is achieved by modifying the "system" partition to grant APK packages, signed by a key held by the practitioner, the ability to impersonate other apps on the device to access their secure accounts storage.

Finally, after the practitioner has collected, examined, and analyzed all of the data on the device, the majority of evidential data should be available for reporting and presentation. However, if any doubts remain as to the provenience or meaning of the data examined, the practitioner may need to undertake further app analysis. This involves analyzing the memory heaps and APKs for the relevant apps of interest to understand how they operate and ultimately under what circumstances the data located by a practitioner is created. For example, a practitioner may wish to determine how timestamps are updated in the apps databases or how the app authenticates with its hosting service.

We demonstrate the utility of this methodology using seven popular cloud apps in Chapter 15 (Martini et al., 2015).

REFERENCES

Al Mutawa, N., Baggili, I., Marrington, A., 2012. Forensic analysis of social networking applications on mobile devices. Digit. Investig. 9, 24–33.

Andriotis, P., Oikonomou, G.C., Tryfonas, T., 2012. Forensic analysis of wireless networking evidence of Android smartphones. In: IEEE International Workshop on Information Forensics and Security, pp. 109–114.

Backes, M., Gerling, S., Hammer, C., Maffei, M., von Styp-Rekowsky, P., 2013. AppGuard–enforcing user requirements on Android apps. In: Tools and Algorithms for the Construction and Analysis of Systems. Springer-Verlag, Berlin, Heidelberg, pp. 543–548.

Barghouthy, N.A., Marrington, A., Baggili, I., 2013. The forensic investigation of Android private browsing sessions using or web. In: 5th International Conference on Computer Science and Information Technology, pp. 33–37.

Bédrune, J.-B., Sigwald, J., 2011. iPhone data protection in depth, July 18, 2014. http://eseclab.sogeti.com/dotclear/public/publications/11-hitbamsterdam-iphonedataprotection.pdf.

Chung, H., Park, J., Lee, S., Kang, C., 2012. Digital forensic investigation of cloud storage services. Digit. Investig. 9 (2), 81–95.

Do, Q., Martini, B., Choo, K.-K.R., 2014. Enforcing file system permissions on Android external storage. In: 13th IEEE International Conference on Trust, Security and Privacy in Computing and Communications (TrustCom 2014), Beijing, China, .

Enck, W., Ongtang, M., McDaniel, P.D., 2009. Understanding Android security. IEEE Secur. Privacy 7 (1), 50–57.

Kim, D., Park, J., Lee, K.-g., Lee, S., 2012. Forensic analysis of Android phone using Ext4 file system journal log. In: Park, J.J., Leung, V.C.M., Wang, C.-L., Shon, T. (Eds.), Future Information Technology, Application, and Service. In: Lecture Notes in Electrical Engineering, Vol. 164. Springer, Netherlands, pp. 435–446.

Lessard, J., Kessler, G., 2010. Android forensics: simplifying cell phone examinations. Digit. Device Forensics J. 4 (1), 1–12.

Lomas, N., 2014. Android Still Growing Market Share By Winning First Time Smartphone Users, July 18, 2014. http://techcrunch.com/2014/05/06/android-still-growing-market-share-by-winning-first-time-smartphone-users/.

Martini, B., Choo, K.-K.R., 2012. An integrated conceptual digital forensic framework for cloud computing. Digit. Investig. 9 (2), 71–80.

Martini, B., Do, Q., Choo, K.-K.R., 2015. Mobile cloud forensics: An analysis of seven popular Android apps. In: Ko, R., Choo, K.-K.R. (Eds.), Cloud Security Ecosystem. Syngress Publishing, Waltham, MA.

Maus, S., Höfken, H., Schuba, M., 2011. Forensic analysis of geodata in Android smartphones. In: International Conference on Cybercrime, Security and Digital Forensics, .

McKemmish, R., 1999. What is forensic computing? Trends Issues Crime Crim. Justice 118, 1–6.

Morrill, D., 2008. Announcing the Android 1.0 SDK, release 1, July 18, 2014. http://android-developers.blogspot.com.au/2008/09/announcing-android-10-sdk-release-1.html.

Son, N., Lee, Y., Kim, D., James, J.I., Lee, S., Lee, K., 2013. A study of user data integrity during acquisition of Android devices. Digit. Investig. 10, 3–11.

Spreitzenbarth, M., Schmitt, S., Freiling, F., 2012. Comparing sources of location data from Android smartphones. In: Peterson, G., Shenoi, S. (Eds.), Advances in Digital Forensics VIII: IFIP Advances in Information and Communication Technology. Springer, Berlin Heidelberg, pp. 143–157.

Stirparo, P., Fovino, I.N., Taddeo, M., Kounelis, I., 2013. In-memory credentials robbery on Android phones. In: 2013 World Congress on Internet Security, pp. 88–93.

Sylve, J., Case, A., Marziale, L., Richard, G.G., 2012. Acquisition and analysis of volatile memory from Android devices. Digit. Investig. 8 (3), 175–184.

Thing, V.L., Ng, K.-Y., Chang, E.-C., 2010. Live memory forensics of mobile phones. Digit. Investig. 7, 74–82.

Vidas, T., Zhang, C., Christin, N., 2011. Toward a general collection methodology for Android devices. Digit. Investig. 8, 14–24.

Votipka, D., Vidas, T., Christin, N., 2013. Passe-partout: a general collection methodology for Android devices. IEEE Trans. Inf. Forensics Secur. 8 (12), 1937–1946.

Wook, S., Kiyomoto, S., Fukushima, K., Tanaka, T., 2009. Towards formal analysis of the permission-based security model for Android. In: Proceedings of the 5th International Conference on Wireless and Mobile Communications (ICWMC '09), pp. 87–92.

XDA Developers, 2012. [MOD][HOW-TO]To disable signature checks, May 29, 2014. http://forum.xda-developers.com/showthread.php?t=1698352.

Xu, R., Saïdi, H., Anderson, R., 2012. Aurasium: practical policy enforcement for Android applications. In: USENIX Security Symposium, pp. 539–552.

Zheng, M., Sun, M., Lui, J., 2013. Droid analytics: a signature based analytic system to collect, extract, analyze and associate Android malware. In: Proceedings of the 12th IEEE International Conference on Trust, Security and Privacy in Computing and Communications (TrustCom '13), July 2013, pp. 163–171.

Zhou, W., Zhou, Y., Jiang, X., Ning, P., 2012. Detecting repackaged smartphone applications in third-party Android marketplaces. In: Proceedings of the 2nd ACM Conference on Data and Application Security and Privacy (CODASPY 2012), pp. 317–326.

Mobile cloud forensics: An analysis of seven popular Android apps

15

Ben Martini, Quang Do, Kim-Kwang Raymond Choo

*Information Assurance Research Group, School of Information Technology and
Mathematical Sciences, University of South Australia, Adelaide, Australia*

1 INTRODUCTION

This chapter provides a number of proof-of-concept implementations of the collection and analysis methodology described in Chapter 14 (see Martini et al., 2015).

We implemented the methodology using a selection of popular free cloud apps. We selected apps in the categories of storage, note taking, and password sync. For the storage category, we selected Dropbox (version 2.4.1), OneDrive (version 2.5.1), Box (version 3.0.2), and ownCloud (version 1.5.5). We also investigated UPM (Universal Password Manger version 1.15) to understand the collection requirements for a third-party app which uses a cloud storage product. For the note taking category, we selected Evernote (version 5.8.1) and OneNote (version 15.0.2727.2300).

The research was conducted between April and July 2014. At the time of this research, findings are accurate to the best of the authors' knowledge. However, new releases of mobile apps and operating systems may change the way the data is collected and analyzed in the future.

2 ANDROID CLOUD APPS

2.1 DROPBOX

Dropbox is one of the top downloaded Android apps with over 100 million downloads on the Google Play store at the time of research. Dropbox provides cloud-based storage services compatible with a range of devices including PCs and mobile devices.

The following sections describe our findings for the examination and analysis stages of the collection and analysis methodology described in Martini et al. (2015). Further analysis of this app is discussed in Section 2.8.1. For Dropbox:

- The private app storage path is "/data/data/com.dropbox.android"
- The external storage data path is "/sdcard/Android/data/com.dropbox.android"

2.1.1 Examine app files in private storage (Dropbox)

Using the methodology described in Martini et al. (2015), we located and analyzed the miscellaneous files contained within the app's private directory on the Android device's internal storage. It should be noted that this section does not aim to provide an exhaustive listing of all of the files/directories located in the apps private storage, rather it only discusses items which we believe would be of particular interest to forensic practitioners.

Dropbox stores a number of items of interest in its "dropbox-credentials.xml" shared preferences file stored at "[private app storage path]/shared_prefs/dropbox-credentials.xml." The file is encoded in a standard plain text XML format. The following directives of interest were located within this file:

- *app_key*—The app_key is a necessary component of the token used to authenticate the user to the Dropbox servers. It is represented using an XML String tag. The app key is the OAuth 1.0 consumer key which represents the app (rather than the user) to the Dropbox authentication system. This is discussed further in Section 2.8.1.
- *accounts*—The accounts string contains a JSON formatted value which encloses the following values of interest.
  - *userToken*—The userToken value contains two strings delimited by a pipe, both of which form part of the authentication headers used by Dropbox.
    1. The first string is the "oauth_token" which as the name suggests is the user's token. The token is updated by the app when the user initially authenticates (using a username and password) and when the previous token expires.
    2. The second string forms the second half of the "oauth_signature," which is also used as part of the authentication header in the format "[String]&[String]." This is discussed further in Section 2.8.1.
  - *userId*—This string stores the user's numerical ID, which is used in databases and the Android file system.

2.1.2 Examine app files on external storage (Dropbox)

After examining the miscellaneous files contained within the app's private directory, we examined the collected files from the external storage. In the case of Dropbox, we found that the following paths were populated.

[external storage data path]/cache/[User ID]/miscthumbs
- This directory is populated with a "journal" file containing (mostly numerical) data, which appears to relate to the layout of the thumbnail cache.

[external storage data path]/cache/[UserID]/thumbs/[subdirectories if any]/
- This directory contains subdirectories named for the path of the image files stored in the user's Dropbox, e.g., "thumbs/My Pictures/san francisco.jpg."

[external storage data path]/cache/[User ID]/thumbs/[subdirectories]/[image name].[extension]
- The directory, named after the user's image, contains a number of sizing variations of the image presumably for display in different parts of the app.
- An interesting anomaly we noted during our research was that when images are moved on the mobile device between directories in the user's Dropbox app, the previous thumbs path and images remain. The thumbnails at the original path were not deleted even when the image was deleted from Dropbox; however, the thumbnails were deleted for the new path.

[external storage data path]/cache/[User ID]/tmp
- During our experiments, we noted that this directory is used to store temporary files (of the filename format "file0.tmp") as they are being downloaded. Once the download is completed, the file is moved to the scratch directory and the tmp file is deleted.

[external storage data path]/files/[User ID]/scratch
- This directory contains the local cache of files that have been downloaded by a user via Dropbox. These files are stored unmodified in this directory with their original filenames intact.

2.1.3 Examine app databases (Dropbox)

While there are a number of possible database formats, apps generally store data in the SQLite format (presumably due to Android's native support for the format). Dropbox stores a number of SQLite databases in its private storage "[private app storage path]/databases/" directory. This directory contained two database files of particular interest as well as two others of lesser interest. The latter were ("[User ID]-prefs.db" and "prefs.db") and the values of interest within them (such as "Account") were encoded or encrypted. The two databases of interest were "prefs-shared.db" and "[User ID]-db.db" and are described further in Tables 1 and 2. In addition to these database files, Dropbox stores another cache database in the "[private app storage path]/app_DropboxSyncCache/[app_key]" location. This database file is described in Table 3.

Table 1 "prefs-shared.db" Database File

[private app storage path]/databases/prefs-shared.db "DropboxAccountPrefs" Table	
Attribute	**Description**
LAST_REPORT_HOST_TIME	A millisecond resolution timestamp (in UTC) for the last report between the Dropbox app and server. This attribute appears to use the device clock rather than remote time

Table 2 "[user-id].db" Database File

[private app storage path]/databases/[user-id].db "dropbox" Table (describes the files stored in Dropbox)	
Attribute	**Description**
modified_millis	The timestamp in millisecond resolution of the last modification to the file on the Dropbox server
bytes	The size of the file in bytes
revision	An encoding presumably of the file revision for sync purposes. The first digit increments when the file is modified on the client or server. The last eight characters of the string match other files in the same directory
hash	Only folders had a "hash" in our experiments. While it appears to be an MD5 hash, it did not match the folder path string or other similar permutations
is_dir	This field is 1 if the entry is a directory and 0 if is not (i.e., Boolean representation)
path & canon_path	The path (including the name) to the file/directory from the root directory; path maintains capitalization whereas canon_path is lowercase
mime_type	The MIME type of the file
thumb_exists	This field indicates if a thumbnail has been cached in a Boolean representation
Parent_path & canon_parent_path	The parent path for the item with similar representation to path & canon_path
_display_name	The file/directory name and extension
ls_favorite	If the item is marked as a "favorite" in Dropbox, a 1 will be entered in this field (Boolean representation)
local_modified	A timestamp with millisecond resolution will be entered in this field representing the modified time for the file on the local file system (field is blank if not cached)
local_revision	The revision code (as discussed above) for the cached copy of the file
local_hash	An MD5 hash of the cached copy of the file
"albums" Table (describes the image albums created by the user)	
col_id	The album's unique identifier (22 characters)
name	The album's friendly name (as entered by the user)
count	The number of items in the album
cover_image_canon_path	The path to file for the image used as album cover
share_link	The full URL for public sharing link for the album (if user enabled)
creation_time	A timestamp with millisecond resolution representing the time the album was created
update_time	A timestamp with millisecond resolution representing the time the album was last updated

Table 2 "[user-id].db" Database File—cont'd

[private app storage path]/databases/[user-id].db **"dropbox" Table (describes the files stored in Dropbox)**	
Attribute	**Description**
"album_item" Table (describes the album items)	
col_id	The album identifier to which the item belongs as recorded in "albums" table
item_id	The item's unique identifier (22 characters)
canon_path	The path from the root directory to the file (including the item filename and extension)
"camera_upload" Table (describes the camera upload operations)	
local_hash	This "hash" is a concatenation of the file size in bytes, a "/" and the filename including extension
server_hash	Presumably an MD5 hash of the file which is uploaded to the server. We checked this hash against the file in our DCIM directory and found that it did not match
uploaded	A Boolean representation of whether the file has been uploaded
"pending_upload" Table (describes the pending upload operations)	
class	This field describes the type of upload which is pending (e.g., UploadTask for files or CameraUploadTask for DCIM images)
data	JSON encoded key-value pairs describing the items waiting to be uploaded. The values vary depending on the class. For example, CameraUploadTask keys include mImportTimeoffset, mMimeType, mFilePath, and mImportTime; and UploadTask keys include mLocalUri, mDropboxDir, and mDestinationFilename
"photos" Table (describes the photos in the user's Dropbox)	
item_id	The item's unique identifier (22 characters)
canon_path	The path from the root directory to the file (including the item filename and extension)
time_taken	A timestamp with millisecond resolution representing the time the image was taken
"thumbnail_info" Table (describes the thumbnails cached by Dropbox)	
dropbox_canon_path	The path from the root directory to the file (including the item filename and extension)
thumb_size	A human readable description of the thumbnail size (e.g., "1024x768_bestfit")
revision	Presumably a record of the revision of the original file from which the thumbnail was taken

Table 3 "[User ID]-notifications" Databases File

[private app storage path]/app_DropboxSyncCache/[app_key]/ [User ID]-notifications "kv" Table	
Attribute	**Description**
app_key	The static app key used by Dropbox as the "oauth_consumer_key" in the header of the URL request when authenticating the user. It represents the app that is communicating with the Dropbox servers rather than the user

2.1.4 Examine and analyze accounts data (Dropbox)

As Dropbox stores the majority of its authentication information within the Dropbox app's private directory, it does not store significant data within the device's Account-Manager API. After replacing the services.jar file as per the Android data collection process described in Martini et al. (2015), we were able to obtain (via our appropriately signed app) the user's e-mail address from within the AccountManager API. The password field for the Dropbox account, in our case, was empty.

2.2 BOX

Box is a popular file-syncing storage service with over 5 million downloads on the Google Play Store. Features of Box include the ability to share links to synced files to others and clients for devices such as PCs and mobile devices.

Readers should note that we did not investigate the "OneCloud" feature of Box as its app store-like functionality was not within the scope of our research.

For Box:
- The *private app storage path* is "/data/data/com.box.android"
- The *external storage data path* is "/sdcard/Android/data/com.box.android"

2.2.1 Examine app files in private storage (Box)

Box stores a range of files in its private app directory including configuration files, user file previews/thumbnails, and a specialized key-value pair database. These artifacts are discussed in detail below.

[private app storage path]/files/leveldb[User ID]/
- This directory contains the constituent files which describe the levelDB key-value pair database. This database is used heavily by Box to store data and metadata, and it is discussed further in the database examination section below.

[private app storage path]/files/previews/
- This directory contains "previews" of the files which have been cached by the Box app. These files can be thumbnails (for videos and images) or the actual files (e.g., PDFs). The files stored in this directory are unencrypted.

- Filenames in this directory generally use the format: preview_[file_ID]_1_[int]_.
  [file_extension].

[private app storage path]/files/thumbnails/
- This directory contains the cache of generated thumbnails used in Box. The
  files are stored in standard image file formats (e.g., PNG and JPEG). The
  filenames contain a range of information including the timestamp of thumbnail
  generation with millisecond resolution in UTC, the file ID, and dimension
  information (where applicable).
- In our experiments, we found thumbnails generated in this directory from
  internal app facilities (such as "OneCloud" which include "onecloudapp" in the
  filename), files uploaded by the user which include "file" in the filename, and the
  user's avatar which includes "avatar" and the user's ID in the filename.
- The files in this directory directly relate to the entries in the "imagecachedb"
  databases as discussed further below.

[private app storage path]/shared_prefs/GLOBAL.xml
- This XML formatted file contains a number of directives relating to app
  configuration.
- One directive is of particular interest; "storedLoggedInUsers" is a string value
  which stores a JSON formatted string containing:
  - id—The user's numerical ID.
  - userAuthToken—The current access token cached for the user.
  - userRefreshToken—The user's refresh token.
  - userName—The user's e-mail address (used as a username for Box).

[private app storage path]/shared_prefs/myPreference[User ID].xml
- This XML formatted file contains a number of configuration directives
  for individual Box users.
- The first directive of interest is "com.box.android.encryptionKey," which is
  a string containing the 512-bit encryption key used by Box to encrypt files
  stored on external storage.
- The next directive of interest is "com.box.android.MoCoBoxUsers.userInfo,"
  which is a JSON encoded string that contains:
  - "login" and "name"—The user's e-mail address (used as a username for Box).
  - id—The user's numerical ID.
  - avatar_url—The unauthenticated URL used to retrieve the user's avatar image.
  - max_upload_size—The maximum permitted upload size represented in
    bytes in exponential notation
  - space_amount—The total quota available to the user represented in bytes
    in exponential notation.
  - space_used—The total space consumed by the user represented in bytes
    in exponential notation.

[private app storage path]/shared_prefs/PREVIEW_SALTS [USER ID].xml
- This XML formatted file contains the salts of each encrypted preview file stored on external storage. These salts are generated when the preview is stored.
  - Salts are stored as strings with the file ID (of the source file of the preview) as the "name" and the salt as the value.

[private app storage path]/shared_prefs/DOWNLOAD_SALTS[USER ID].xml
- This XML formatted file contains the salts of each encrypted file cached on external storage. These salts are generated when the file is downloaded to external storage.
  - Salts are stored as strings with the file ID as the "name" and the salt as the value.

2.2.2 Examine app files on external storage (Box)

Box uses external storage to maintain a cache of various previews and downloaded files.

The majority of files which Box stores on the external storage are encrypted using a format known as "Box Crypto." In order to decrypt these files, the appropriate salt must be found (based on the file's ID) in the "DOWNLOAD_SALTS[USER ID]. xml" or the "PREVIEW_SALTS[USER ID].xml" files depending on whether a full file or a preview is being decrypted, respectively. The encryption key is obtained from the "myPreference[USER ID].xml" file. By utilizing both of these sets of data, the cached file can then be decrypted by following these steps:

1. First, the app's encryption key is appended with a "_" followed by the file's ID.
2. This concatenated string is then passed through the SHA1 algorithm a total of 10 times to produce a new string.
3. The file can then be decrypted by passing the file, the newly generated string (as the key) and the salt obtained above into Bouncy Castle's AES CBC cipher (using PKCS5Padding) for decryption.

In addition, Box stores the following files which are of forensic interest:

[external storage data path]/[User ID]/cache/dl_cache
- This directory contains the cache of files which have been downloaded by the user in Box Crypto format.
- Files in this directory have a filename format of: [File ID]_[SHA1 of the original file] with no file extension.

[external storage data path]/[User ID]/cache/dl_offline
- Contained within this directory are files that the user has specifically chosen to have offline access to. These files are also stored in the Box Crypto format.
- Similarly, files in this directory have a filename format of: [File ID]_[SHA1 of the original file] with no file extension.

[external storage data path]/[User ID]/cache/previews

- This directory contains the previews of files which have been viewed by the user in the Box Crypto format. Depending on the format of the original file, these files may be the entire original file or scaled thumbnails (in the case of images).
- The files in this directory have a filename in the following format: preview_[File ID]_[int]_[int].[file extension].

2.2.3 Examine app databases (Box)

The Box app utilizes SQLite databases located within the "[private app storage path]/databases" directory. It also makes use of a key-value pair database format known as levelDB, used by Box to store data and metadata. The databases (and items within these databases) of interest are presented in Tables 4 and 5 (both SQLite databases), and Table 6 (a levelDB format database).

Table 4 "BoxSQLiteDB_[User ID]" Database File

private app storage path]/databases/BoxSQLiteDB_[User ID] "BoxEvent" Table (records of all actions performed by the app on the user's files)	
Attribute	**Description**
source_item_type	The item type of the source of the event (e.g., "file" or "folder")
event_owner_id	The user ID of the user which triggered the event
event_type	The type of action being triggered on the source item. Examples include: • ITEM_COPY • ITEM_PREVIEW • ITEM_SHARED • ITEM_CREATE • ITEM_MOVE • ITEM_DOWNLOAD • ITEM_UPLOAD
source_item_id	The ID for the item which is being affected by the event
created_at	A millisecond resolution timestamp representing the time at which the event was initiated
user_dismissed	A Boolean value representing if the user has dismissed the notification in the Box UI
parent_id	This field was blank in our experiments
name	The event's name comprising the string "event_" and the event's ID
modified_at	An integer which was 0 for all entries in our experiments
size	A double which was 0.0 for all entries in our experiments
id	The event's unique identifier
"BoxFile" Table (metadata for files stored in Box)	
parent_id	The ID of the parent directory, 0 if root of the directory structure
name	The filename as entered by the user including any extensions

(Continued)

Table 4 "BoxSQLiteDB_[User ID]" Database File—cont'd

private app storage path]/databases/BoxSQLiteDB_[User ID] **"BoxEvent" Table (records of all actions performed by the app on the user's files)**	
Attribute	**Description**
modified_at	A timestamp with millisecond resolution which represents the last modification to the file
size	The file's size in bytes
id	The file's ID
"BoxFolder" Table (metadata for folders created in Box)	
parent_id	The ID of the parent directory, blank for the root of the directory structure
name	The folder name as entered by the user
modified_at	A timestamp with millisecond resolution which represents the last modification to the contents of the folder
size	The size in bytes of all contents of the folder combined
id	The folder ID, 0 for the root of the directory structure
"BoxRecentFile" Table (metadata for recent files accessed in Box)	
item_id	The ID of the recently accessed file
item_type	The item type, "file" in our experiments
recent_item_id	The ID of the recently accessed file, identical to "item_id" in our experiments
user_dismissed	A Boolean presumably representing if the user has dismissed the recent file from the list, "0" in our experiments
timestamp	A millisecond resolution timestamp representing the time at which the file was accessed
id	An ID consisting of the "item_type" and "recent_item_id" concatenated with an underscore
"BoxComment" Table (metadata for comments made on files in Box)	
created_at	A human readable timestamp representing when the comment was made
item_id	The item on which the comment was made
item_type	The type of item on which the comment was made
id	The comment ID as referenced in levelDB

2.2.4 Examine and analyze accounts data (Box)

After replacing the services.jar file within the "/system" partition and running our signed app, we found that Box does not store data using the AccountManager API on Android devices. This means that a Box account (pertaining to the currently logged in user) does not appear in the system Settings app under the list of accounts currently on the device and, therefore, no data relating to Box or the Box app was located using AccountManager.

Table 5 "imagecachedb" Database File

[private app storage path]/databases/imagecachedb. "files" Table (stores thumbnail information for media)	
Attribute	**Description**
_id	The ID of this particular record in the table
timestamp	A millisecond resolution timestamp representing when the image was first cached
url	The "url" for this particular item in the format [object type]_[item id]_[int] _[dimension]
image_filename	The filename of the thumbnail as stored within the "[private app storage path]/files/thumbnails" directory

Table 6 LevelDB File

[private app storage path]/files/leveldb[User ID]/ boxitem://comment/[comment ID]	
Attribute	**Description**
type	The type of entry, i.e., "comment"
item	An array which contains the values "type" and "id." In our case, "type" was "file" and "id" was the file ID of the file to which the comment was added
message	The comment text as entered by the user
id	The comment ID
created_by	An array which contains information about the user who created the comment. It comprises the values "type," "login," "name," and "id." In our case, the "type" was "user," the "login" and "name" were the user's e-mail address and the "id" is the user's ID
is_reply_comment	A Boolean representing if the comment is a reply
created_at	A human readable timestamp representing when the comment was made
boxitem://file/[file ID]	
type	The type of entry, i.e., "file"
parent	An array which contains information about the parent folder of this file. This array contains the "type" (folder), the name (folder's name), and folder id
permissions	An array containing an assortment of Boolean values relating to what actions the user is able to perform on this file. These values are: • can_comment • can_delete • can_download

(Continued)

Table 6 LevelDB File—cont'd

[private app storage path]/files/leveldb[User ID]/ boxitem://comment/[comment ID]	
Attribute	**Description**
	• can_preview
	• can_rename
	• can_set_share_access
	• can_share
	• can_upload
sha1	The SHA1 hash of the file
name	The full filename for this file including any extensions
size	The size of the file in bytes (in exponent form)
id	The file's unique identifier
path_collection	An array containing the folders which make up the path to this particular file. For example, files located in the root directory have a single folder's (root) information listed within this array. See "parent" for this folder information
shared_link	This is an (optional, depending on whether the file has been shared) array containing information about this file's link sharing. Included within this array is another array called "permissions" (Booleans listing whether the shared file can be downloaded/previewed). Other values include:
	• access—"open" if available to the public
	• url—the URL to the shared file
	• download_count—Integer value representing how many times the file has been downloaded
	• download_url—A static URL for the file
	• preview_count—Integer value representing how many times the shared file has been previewed
	• is_password_enabled—Boolean representing if the file has been password protected
comment_count	An integer representing the number of comments made on this file
content_created_at	A human readable timestamp representing when the file was created
content_modified_at	A human readable timestamp representing when the file was last modified
modified_by	An array containing information on the user who last modified the file (see "created_by" in boxitem://comment)
owned_by	An array containing information on the owner of the file (see "created_by" in boxitem://comment)
boxitem://folder/[folder ID]	
type	The type of entry, i.e., "folder"
permissions	(see "permissions" in boxitem://file)
name	The folder's name

Table 6 LevelDB File—cont'd

[private app storage path]/files/leveldb[User ID]/ **boxitem://comment/[comment ID]**	
Attribute	**Description**
size	The size of all the combined contents of the folder, represented in exponent form, in bytes
id	The folder's unique identifier
path_collection	(see "path_collection" in boxitem://file)
has_collaborations	A Boolean value representing if the folder has any collaborators
modified_by	(see "modified_by" in boxitem://file)
owned_by	(see "owned_by" in boxitem://file)
boxitem://event/[event ID]	
type	The type of entry, i.e., "event"
source	The source file of the event. This is a "boxitem://item"
event_type	The type of event that is being recorded. See "event_type" in Table 4
event_id	The unique identifier for the event
created_by	(see "modified_by" in boxitem://file)
created_at	A human readable timestamp representing when the event was triggered

2.3 ONEDRIVE

OneDrive (formerly known as SkyDrive) is another popular file-syncing storage service created by Microsoft. It has over 5 million downloads on the Google Play Store and is capable of interacting with the Microsoft Office suite of products.

Our findings are described in detail below. For OneDrive:

- The *private app storage path* is "/data/data/com.microsoft.skydrive"
- The *external storage data path* is "/sdcard/Android/data/com.microsoft.skydrive"

2.3.1 Examine app files in private storage (OneDrive)

In our experiments, we found five XML format files within the "shared_prefs" directory inside the private app storage directory of the OneDrive app. The configuration directives in these files (approximately eight in total) all relate to the app configuration. These files contained no data which we considered to be of general interest to a forensic practitioner.

2.3.2 Examine app files on external storage (OneDrive)

OneDrive stores a cache of files downloaded by the user on the device's external storage. Cached files are located at the "[external storage data path]/cache" location. They

Table 7 "cached_files_md.db" Database File

[private app storage path]/databases/cached_files_md.db "cached_files_metadata" Table (stores metadata for cached files)	
Attribute	**Description**
id	An integer identifier for the record
cache_id	The item's "resourceId" from the metadata database concatenated with "_Download"
skydrive_url	The item's "downloadUrl" from the metadata database
etag	The item's "eTag" from the metadata database
last_access_time	The timestamp representing the last time the cached item was accessed
file_size_bytes	The size of the cached item in bytes
is_at_internal_storage	Blank in our experiments as files are stored on the external storage. Presumably 1 where files are stored on internal storage

follow the "SkyDriveCacheFile_[integer].cachedata" filename convention, where the integer identifies the file based upon its "id" in the "cached_files_metadata" table of the "cached_files_md.db" database—see Table 7. Cached files are stored on the external storage unmodified (hashes match for original files uploaded and files cached).

2.3.3 Examine app databases (OneDrive)

OneDrive stores five SQLite format databases in its *[private app storage path]/databases* directory. We consider two of these databases, "cached_files_md.db" and "metadata" (see Table 8), to be of particular forensic interest and outline the contents of "auto_upload.db" and "manual_upload_db" in Tables 9 and 10, respectively.

Table 8 OneDrive "metadata" Database

[private app storage path]/databases/metadata "items" Table (stores metadata for items in the user's OneDrive)	
Attribute	**Description**
_id	An integer identifier for the record
parentRid	The resource ID of the parent folder of this file/folder if applicable. For example, root does not have a parentRid, and items stored in the root have the parentRid "root"
ownerCid	The client ID of the owner of the file/folder as stored in account manager extras
resourceId	The unique (string based) identifier for this resource
parentId	The parent "_id" for this item
downloadUrl	The URL used to download the item, where applicable. This URL requires authentication
extension	The file extension where applicable

Table 8 OneDrive "metadata" Database—cont'd

[private app storage path]/databases/metadata "items" Table (stores metadata for items in the user's OneDrive)	
Attribute	**Description**
lastAccess	Some items store a last accessed timestamp in millisecond resolution
modifiedDateOnClient	A millisecond resolution timestamp representing the last modified date as reported in the OneDrive app
creationDate	A millisecond resolution timestamp representing the date the item was added to OneDrive
name	The friendly name of the item as set by the user
ownerName	The first name and last name as entered by the user for their account
sharingLevel	A string representation of the sharing enabled on this item (e.g., "Just Me" and "Public")
size	The size of the item in bytes; in the case of a folder, the size of the sum of its contents
size_text	A human readable representation of the size field (e.g., "100 KB")
totalCount	The number of child items inside this item
mimeType	The mime type of the item
eTag	The eTag is a concatenation of "[resourceId].[version number]." We presume the final integer after the decimal is a version number as it is generally 0 for items which have not been modified and greater than 0 for those which have

Table 9 "auto_upload.db" Database File

[private app storage path]/databases/auto_upload.db "queue" Table (queuing information for files waiting to be uploaded)	
Attribute	**Description**
_id	An integer identifier for the record
creationDate	A timestamp representing the date the file was added to the queue for uploading
fileName	A concatenation of the date (in YYYYMMDD format), time (in 24-h time HHMMSS) and "Android.jpg"
fileNameOriginal	The original filename set by the user/camera app
filePath	The path on the device to the file to be uploaded
fileSize	The file size in bytes
loadingProgress	Presumably the number of bytes which have been transferred (0 in our experiments)

Table 10 "manual_upload_db" Databases File

[private app storage path]/databases/manual_upload_db "queue" Table (contains information about the user's files which were manually uploaded)	
Attribute	**Description**
_id	An integer identifier for the record
fileName	A concatenation of the date (in YYYYMMDD format), time (in 24-h time HHMMSS) and Android.jpg.
filePath	The path on the device to the file which is to be uploaded
fileSize	The file size in bytes
folderOwnerCid	The client ID of the owner of the folder the file is being uploaded to
folderResourceId	The "resourceId" of the folder the item is being uploaded to
loadingProgress	Presumably the number of bytes which have been transferred (the size of the file in bytes in our experiments)

In our experiment environment, "auto_uploaded_files_md.db" did not contain any data of general forensic interest.

2.3.4 Examine and analyze accounts data (OneDrive)

We installed our appropriately signed APK into an Android system that had been updated with our modified services.jar file and found that OneDrive stores a significant amount of data within the AccountManager service on the Android device. This may explain the lack of accounts data which was of interest within the OneDrive app's private directory. Several items of interest were found within the AccountManager API (see Table 11).

2.4 OWNCLOUD

ownCloud is a popular open source alternative to the above file-syncing apps. Users are able to freely host their own private ownCloud servers and set up a private file sync service. The Android app itself is a paid app on the Google Play Store but as the app is open source, it can simply be built from the publicly available code.

Table 11 AccountManager (OneDrive)

AccountManager API Calls	
Method	**Description**
getPassword()	Returns the OneDrive app's current refresh token
getAuthToken()	Returns a large amount of data including the current refresh token, access token, scope, account type, user ID, and access token expiry timestamp

ownCloud utilizes the following paths:

- The *private app storage path* is "/data/data/com.owncloud.android"
- The *external storage data path* is "/sdcard/owncloud"

2.4.1 Examine app files in private storage (ownCloud)

ownCloud stores its configuration in a single shared_prefs XML file named "com.owncloud.android_preferences.xml," the configuration directives in this file are discussed below:

[private app storage path]/shared_prefs/com.owncloud.android_preferences.xml

- "instant_upload_on_wifi"—This Boolean value specifies whether instant upload for pictures only occurs when connected to Wi-Fi.
- "instant_uploading"—This Boolean value specifies whether instant upload for pictures is enabled.
- "select_oc_account"—This string value represents the ownCloud account (username@server) which should be selected by the app upon launch.
- "set_pincode"—This Boolean value specifies whether an "app PIN" (a four-digit PIN which must be entered to use the app on launch) is enabled.
- "PrefPinCode[1-4]"—These string values represent the individual integers of the four-digit PIN code if enabled.

Excluding the database files discussed below, no other files of interest were found in this app's private storage directories.

2.4.2 Examine app files on external storage (ownCloud)

ownCloud stores cached and downloaded (favorite) files in a mirror of the server directory structure (for the parents of downloaded files) on external storage at the following path [*external storage data path*]/[username@server]. Files are stored in this directory structure unmodified.

2.4.3 Examine app databases (ownCloud)

The ownCloud Android app stores two SQLite format database files within its [*private app storage path*]/databases directory. Both of these files contain data that may be of general forensic interest and as such are outlined in Tables 12 and 13.

2.4.4 Examine and analyze accounts data (ownCloud)

By utilizing our installed app that is able to bypass system signature checking, we were able to obtain the data that ownCloud stored within the AccountManager API. We found that ownCloud stores the user's password in plaintext when using the "getPassword()" method of the AccountManager API.

Table 12 "filelist" Database File

[private app storage path]/databases/filelist **"filelist" Table (contains information about all of the files/folders of all the users that have authenticated in the ownCloud app)**	
Attribute	**Description**
_id	An integer identifier for the record
filename	The filename of the file including any extensions
path	The path to the file from the root directory of the ownCloud server
parent	The "_id" of the parent directory to this file/folder
modified	A millisecond resolution timestamp representing when the cached file was last modified
content_type	The mime type of a file or "DIR" for a folder
Media_path	The full path to the file on the Android device's external storage
File_owner	The owner of the file in the format of "username@server"
Last_sync_date	A millisecond resolution timestamp representing when the file was lasted synced with the ownCloud server
keep_in_sync	A Boolean value representing whether a file should be kept in sync. This function is manually enabled by the user
last_sync_date_for_data	A millisecond resolution timestamp representing the last time a file was downloaded by the user
modified_at_last_sync_date_for_data	A millisecond resolution timestamp representing the file modified date on the ownCloud server at last sync
share_by_link	A Boolean value representing if a file has been shared
etag	A unique identifier (on a per account basis) for each item used for caching purposes. Only folders had an "etag" recorded in our experiments. It is generated from the server's "eTag" database record
"ocshares" Table (metadata for the shared files supported by the ownCloud mobile app)	
_id	An integer identifier for the record
file_source & item_source	The "_id" from the filelist table for the file being shared
shate_with *[sic]*	The password required to access the share URL (blank if not set). This password is stored as a Blowfish hash
path	The path to the file from the ownCloud root directory for the user
shared_date	A second resolution timestamp indicating when the share was created

Table 12 "filelist" Database File—cont'd

[private app storage path]/databases/filelist **"filelist" Table (contains information about all of the files/folders of all the users that have authenticated in the ownCloud app)**	
Attribute	**Description**
expiration_date	A second resolution timestamp indicating when the share will/has expired
token	The token used to access the file in the share URL, e.g., "http://[ocserver]/owncloud/public.php?service = files&t = [token]"
is_directory	A Boolean value representing whether the item is a directory
owner_share	The owner of the shared item in the format of "username@server"

Table 13 "ownCloud" Database File

[private app storage path]/databases/ownCloud **"instant_upload" Table (contains information about pictures selected for auto upload, if this feature is enabled. Records are deleted once the upload is successful)**	
Attribute	**Description**
_id	An integer identifier for the record
path	The path on local storage to the file which is to be uploaded
account	The ownCloud account for the user the images will be uploaded to in the format of "username@server"

2.5 EVERNOTE

Evernote is one of the most popular note-taking apps in the Google Play Store, with over 50 million downloads. Its features include the ability to recognize text from handwritten notes (OCR) and cross-platform note syncing capabilities.

For Evernote:

- The *private app storage path* is "/data/data/com.evernote"
- The *external storage data path* is "/sdcard/Android/data/com.evernote"

2.5.1 Examine app files in private storage (Evernote)

Evernote creates a number of files in its private storage directories. Within the "shared_prefs" directory Evernote stores approximately 17 XML configuration files, of which we have selected four which we found to be of forensic interest.

[private app storage path]/shared_prefs/[User ID].pref.xml
- "userid"—The unique identifier for the user (an integer in our case).
- "username"—The user's Evernote username.
- "encrypted_authtoken"—A Base64 encoded string. Presumably an encrypted copy of the authentication token. This token can be decrypted using Evernote's "com.evernote.util" classes. These classes are heavily obfuscated.
- "default_notebook"—The GUID of the default notebook.
- "AcctInfoWebPrefixUrl"—The URL used as part of account authentication.
- "e-mail"—The user's e-mail address.
- "LAST_USER_OBJECT_SYNC_TIME"—A millisecond resolution timestamp which represents the last sync time.
- "LAST_DB_FILEPATH"—A string listing the file path to the Evernote database. Notably, this database was stored on external storage in our experiments.
- "Last_server_acc_info_timestamp"—Timestamp of last successful login to the Evernote servers (i.e., last online session).
- "AcctInfoNoteStoreUrl"—The URL used by the app for x-thrift communication.

[private app storage path]/shared_prefs/[User ID]_counts.pref.xml
- The counts configuration file maintains a listing of the number of objects in seven categories, namely, "places," "notes," "skitches," "tags," "notebooks," "snotes," and "linked notebooks."

[private app storage path]/shared_prefs/[User ID]_sync_state.pref.xml
- The sync state preference file stores a number of directives. We found the "SYNC_STATUS_MSG" to be of use as it describes the last sync information in a human readable format (e.g., "Last sync: 1 Jan 12:00 pm").

[private app storage path]/shared_prefs/com.evernote_preferences.xml
- "PREF_USERID_LIST"—The user ID of the logged in user. Presumably, if more than one user could be logged in on the device, they would be listed here.
- "PREF_ACTIVE_USERID"—The user ID of the currently active user.
- "last_viewed_notes"—The GUID of the note last viewed by the user.

[private app storage path]/files/.logs/log_file.txt
- This is a time-stamped log file generated by the Evernote app that contains events. The events recorded include files being opened, stored, and user login events. The log contains the user ID of the user to which the recorded event pertains.
- This is a serialized file created by the Evernote app.

2.5.2 Examine app files on external storage (Evernote)
Evernote stores a number of items on the device's external storage. These files are:

**[external storage data path]/files/user-[User ID]/mapthumbdb/
thumbnails_data_1.dat**
- This file contains a cache of thumbnails generated in the Evernote app. We
  were able to recover a JPEG format image from this file using header analysis.

**[external storage data path]/files/notes/[first three characters of GUID]/[note
GUID]/**
- This directory contains a note as identified by the GUID and the constituent files
  (where relevant) such as image files.
  - The main content of the note is stored in a "content.enml" file, which is a
    form of human readable XML encoding used by Evernote.
  - The content of the note may also be represented in HTML with a filename
    starting with "note" with the "html" extension.
  - Images and other file content are represented using GUIDs with the "dat"
    extension. Metadata for each of these files is available in the "resources"
    table of the Evernote database.

Evernote also stores its database files on external storage, this is discussed
further below.

2.5.3 Examine app databases (Evernote)

In our experiments, we found that Evernote does not utilize the databases folder
within its private app storage to store its app's databases. Instead Evernote stores
its database in an unencrypted file on the device's external storage. The database
and its contents are described in Table 14.

Table 14 "user-[User ID]" Database File

[external storage data path]/files/user-[User ID] "guid_updates" Table (presumably a list of GUIDs which have been updated)	
Attribute	**Description**
new_guid	The newly generated globally unique identifier (GUID)
old_guid	The previous GUID
"note_tag" Table (a relationship table between tags and notes)	
note_guid	The note's GUID from the "notes" table
tag_guid	The tag's GUID from the "tags_table" table
"notebooks" Table (a table containing metadata relating to the user's notebooks)	
guid	The GUID of the notebook
name	The friendly name of the notebook as set by the user
published	A Boolean value representing if the notebook has been shared

(Continued)

Table 14 "user-[User ID]" Database File—cont'd

[external storage data path]/files/user-[User ID] "guid_updates" Table (presumably a list of GUIDs which have been updated)	
Attribute	**Description**
"notes" Table (a table containing metadata relating to the user's notes)	
guid	The GUID of the note
notebook_guid	The GUID of the notebook parent for this note
title	The title of the note
content_length	The size of the note content (not including resources such as images) in bytes
content_hash	A binary hash of unknown type
created	A timestamp with millisecond resolution representing when the note was created
updated	A timestamp with millisecond resolution representing when the note was last modified
deleted	A timestamp with millisecond resolution representing when the note was deleted (where applicable otherwise 0)
is_active	A Boolean value representing the file's deleted state
cached	A Boolean value representing whether the file has been cached on the device
"city," "state," "country," "latitude," "longitude," "altitude"	The location data for the note, if enabled
source	The source of the note (e.g., "mobile.android")
source_url	The source URL for the note where applicable (e.g., "http://evernote.com/")
note_share_date	A timestamp with millisecond resolution representing when note sharing was enabled
note_share_key	The key component of the sharing URL which follows the following format: "[AcctInfoWebPrefixUrl]/sh/[note GUID]/[note_share_key]"
task_date	A timestamp with millisecond resolution representing when the note was created for some notes
task_complete_date	A timestamp with millisecond resolution representing when the note was marked as "Done"
task_due_date	A timestamp with millisecond resolution representing when the task is set to be due by the user
"resources" Table (a table containing metadata relating to resource objects used in notes)	
guid	The resource GUID
note_guid	The GUID of the parent note of the resource
mime	The mime type of the resource
width	The width of an image
height	The height of an image

Table 14 "user-[User ID]" Database File—cont'd

[external storage data path]/files/user-[User ID] "guid_updates" Table (presumably a list of GUIDs which have been updated)	
Attribute	**Description**
hash	A binary hash of unknown type. Used as the filename of the resource image on the file system (the binary hash is converted to hexadecimal)
cached	A Boolean value representing whether the resource has been cached on the device
length	The size of the resource in bytes
has_recognition	A Boolean value presumably representing whether the resource has undergone character recognition
timestamp	A timestamp with millisecond resolution for the resource (e.g., when the image was taken)
filename	The resource filename (where applicable)
reco_cached	A Boolean value presumably representing whether the resource character recognition is cached
ink_signature	A JSON encoded string which presumably includes ink related metadata including height, width, and a GUID
"search_history" Table (a table containing metadata relating to search history)	
query	The search queries entered by the user in the Evernote app
updated	A timestamp with millisecond resolution representing when the search using the keywords in "query" was last performed
"search_index_content" Table (a table containing metadata relating to searches)	
c0note_guid	The GUID of the note which will be returned from matching searches
c1content_id	The resource GUID (for images) or the file type
c3keywords	A string of searchable content derived from the note and resources
"snippets_table" Table (a table containing "snippets" of information about each note)	
note_guid	The GUID of the note to which the snippet relates
mime_type	The mime type of the snippet where relevant
res_count	Presumably the number of resources used in the note
snippet	The first 193 characters of the note text, where applicable
"tags_table" Table (a table containing metadata relating to tags)	
guid	The GUID of the tag
name	The name of the tag as entered by the user

2.5.4 Examine and analyze accounts data (Evernote)

The Evernote Android app utilizes the AccountManager API to store some account-related data. However, we found that Evernote does not store a "password" for the logged in account as accessible via the AccountManager API's "getPassword()" method. AccountManager's "getAuthTokens()" method also did not return any data.

2.6 ONENOTE

Microsoft's OneNote is a note-taking app with cloud syncing capabilities. It is also (like Evernote) a cross-platform app. As OneNote is a Microsoft app, it utilizes package names similar to OneDrive. OneNote has the following paths:

- The *private app storage path* is "/data/data/com.microsoft.office.onenote"
- The *external storage data path* is "/sdcard/Android/data/com.microsoft.office.onenote"

Our findings for OneNote are described in the following sections.

2.6.1 Examine app files in private storage (OneNote)

OneNote has two configuration files in its "shared_prefs" directory, "com.microsoft.office.onenote.eula2.xml" and "com.microsoft.office.onenote_preferences.xml." The former file stores EULA information which we do not consider to be of forensic interest, and the latter file stores general configuration for the OneNote app. We highlight the directives of interest in this file below.

[private app storage path]/shared_prefs/com.microsoft.office.onenote_preferences.xml
- "KEY_RESUME_VIEW_ID"—This string stores the GUID of the last notebook viewed by the user.
- "DEFAULT_LIVE_ID"—This string is used as the identifier for the user's Live ID.

Within its "files" subdirectory, OneNote stores a number of files. Within the root of this directory is a "registry.xml" which stores an XML encoded registry file.

[private app storage path]/files/registry.xml
- "SQL DB Path"—The value of this key represents the path on the local device to the SQL database directory for OneNote's file store.

If a practitioner navigates to the path listed in the file, they should locate a "File Store" directory with a number of subdirectories uniquely identifying the OneNote user. An example of the path and files stored in this location is as follows:

[private app storage path]/files/Microsoft/Office Mobile/SPM Data/File Store/1000/https:/d.docs.live.net/[DEFAULT_LIVE_ID]
- "{[section GUID]}.one"—Cached versions of the OneNote sections which have been accessed/created by the user. A notebook comprises a collection of

sections (as defined in the OneNote database). The files are in the standard "one" OneNote format and can be read using the OneNote PC application.

2.6.2 Examine app files on external storage (OneNote)

OneNote creates the "[external storage data path]/files" path on the device's external storage. However, in our experiments, we were unable to locate any files in this directory.

2.6.3 Examine app databases (OneNote)

OneNote does not create a "databases" directory within the private app storage path, but rather stores databases in various locations throughout private app storage subdirectories. In total, we located two "sdf" format databases of interest, namely, "[private app storage path]/files/Microsoft/Office Mobile/SPM Data/SPSQLStore. sdf" and "[private app storage path]/files/OneNote/hierarchy.sdf." The former file contains metadata relating to OneNote's constituent files, and the latter contains metadata relating to the notes stored in the app. The SDF format file headers identify the files as "SQLite format 3." These databases are outlined in Tables 15 and 16.

Table 15 "SPSQLStore.sdf" Database File

[private app storage path]/files/Microsoft/Office Mobile/SPM Data/ SPSQLStore.sdf **"SPMCConfigData" Table (contains general information about the account)**	
Attribute	**Description**
FieldName	This includes fields such as: • NewDefaultNotebookName • SkyDriveRootDavUrl • SkyDriveSignedInUser
FieldValue	This contains the values for the above "FieldName" fields
"SPMCItems" Table (metadata regarding the notebooks and section files)	
ObjectID	The item's GUID
ListID	The GUID of the list relating to the item (relates to the SPMCLists table)
FolderID	The GUID of the parent folder (where applicable)
SiteID	The GUID of the related site (relates to the SPMCLists table)
ContentType	The item type (e.g., "Folder" or "Document")
Created	A human readable creation time of the object, in the format YYYYMMDD HH:MM:SS
Modified	A human readable modified time for the object, in the format YYYYMMDD HH:MM:SS
FileDirRef	The parent directory path on the server for the object
ProgId	The ID of the program used to open the file (e.g., "OneNote. Notebook")

(Continued)

Table 15 "SPSQLStore.sdf" Database File—cont'd

[private app storage path]/files/Microsoft/Office Mobile/SPM Data/ SPSQLStore.sdf **"SPMCConfigData" Table (contains general information about the account)**	
Attribute	**Description**
ServerUrl	The URL (when appended to the "SkyDriveRootDavUrl") which is used to access the item
LinkFileName	The item name including extension (where applicable)
EncodedAbsUrl	A "URL Encoded" completes URL for accessing the item
FileType	The file extension (where applicable)
Etag	This field mirrors the modified date for documents, presumably used for cache management
FileSize	The item size in bytes (where applicable)
LevelDescription	The item's sharing information (e.g., "Shared with: Just me"— where applicable)
"SPMCObjects" Table (sync information for the items in OneNote)	
ObjectID	The object's GUID
LastSyncTime	A human readable timestamp representing the time of last attempted object sync, in the format YYYYMMDD HH:MM:SS
Deleted	A Boolean representing if the object has been deleted
IsOnServer	A Boolean representing if the object is located on the server
LastSuccessSyncTime	A human readable timestamp representing the time of last successful object sync, in the format YYYYMMDD HH:MM:SS
DisplayTitle	The objects name (e.g., "Quick Notes.one")
UrlString	A serialized string containing parts of the information in this record
ResId	The GUID or OneDrive File ID depending on the type of object
CreatedTime	A human readable timestamp representing the time of creation of the object, in the format YYYYMMDD HH:MM:SS

2.6.4 Examine and analyze accounts data (OneNote)

Unlike many Android apps, Microsoft's OneNote stores a significant amount of information within the AccountManager API. Using AccountManager's "getPassword()" method, we found that OneNote stores a string that was not the user's login password. This "password" is used as part of an encryption cipher for which it is the encryption key. This is used in conjunction with the additional information that OneNote stores (accessible via AccountManager's "getUserData()" method).

Within the AccountManager "UserData" key-value store, OneNote stores two values of interest. First, it stores the Live ID identifier of the logged in user.

Table 16 "hierarchy.sdf" Database File

[private app storage path]/files/OneNote/hierarchy.sdf "OnmConfigData" Table (contains information about the configuration of notebooks)	
Attribute	**Description**
FieldName	This includes fields such as: • UnfiledSectionID • SkyDriveDefaultNotebookID • LastSuccessfulUpdateNBListTime
FieldValue	This field contains the values for the above "FieldName" fields.
"OnmNotebookContent" Table (metadata for each of the users notebooks)	
ObjectID	The content's GUID.
ParentID	The GUID of the parent of this content. If this content is a notebook, then its "ParentID" is itself. If it is a section, then its "ParentID" is the notebook in which it resides
ParentNoteBookID	This field mirrors "ParentID" in our experiments
Name	The name of the content (e.g., "Quick Notes," "First Name's Notebook")
DisplayName	This field mirrors "Name" in our experiments
LastAccessTime	A human readable timestamps that was always "19000101 12:00:00" in our experiments
LastModifiedTime	A human readable timestamp representing when the content was last modified, in the format YYYYMMDD HH:MM:SS
"OnmSectionContent" Table (metadata for section content, i.e., notes)	
ObjectID	The section content's GUID
JotID	A GUID which was not found in other sections of the database or configuration
ParentID	The ID of the parent object, and in our records these IDs represented sections (see OnmNotebookContent table)
Name	The name of the content (e.g., the note name set by the user)
LastAccessTime	A human readable timestamp representing when the content was last accessed, in the format YYYYMMDD HH:MM:SS
LastModifiedTime	A human readable timestamp representing when the content was last modified, in the format YYYYMMDD HH:MM:SS
Viewed	A Boolean value representing if the note has been viewed
CreationTime	A human readable timestamp representing when the content was created, in the format YYYYMMDD HH:MM:SS

It also stores a string that contains an XML file. The contents of this string include:

- "_SEED"—The seed used to decrypt the refresh token.
- "LIVE_ID_FRIENDLY_NAME"—The user's full name (i.e., first name and last name).

- "_PASSWORD"—The user's encrypted refresh token.
- "_ID"—The user's Live ID identifier.
- "_LAST_MODIFIED"—A millisecond resolution timestamp representing when the XML string was last modified.

By using the above "_SEED" and "_PASSWORD" (decoded from Base64) and the "password" from the AccountManager "getPassword()" method, the unencrypted refresh token can be obtained. OneNote uses the AES standard for encryption and decryption, and, as such, the above values can simply be placed into an AES decryption method without any further modifications.

This concludes our analysis of the six cloud apps, which directly communicate with servers.

For completeness, we chose to perform evidence collection and analysis on an app which utilizes other (cloud) apps in order to sync its files.

2.7 UNIVERSAL PASSWORD MANAGER

Universal Password Manager or "UPM" is a password manager for Android devices with over 100,000 downloads. It does not store any details (such as usernames and passwords) on its own servers but rather in an encrypted database file stored on the user's Android device. It can utilize cloud storage services such as Dropbox, in order to allow the user to sync and backup the encrypted database among all their devices.

We chose an app that does not directly utilize its own cloud servers in order to demonstrate that our technique is applicable to more than just cloud-based apps. In principle, our process is capable of acquiring data from most Android apps.

Apart from the encrypted database, which is stored on the external storage at the appropriate location if the user opts to use a cloud syncing service, UPM does not store any additional files on external storage. This file should be stored in the cloud cache location such as within the external storage path of Dropbox, if cloud storage was utilized.

- UPM's *private app storage path* is: "/data/data/com.u17od.upm"

2.7.1 Examine app files in private storage (UPM)

UPM stores several files of interest inside its private app storage path. Within the "shared_prefs" directory are two XML files of interest.

[private app storage path]/shared_prefs/UPMPrefs.xml
- "sync.method"—The value of this string represents the method of syncing the user has chosen for the UPM encrypted database. In our case, as we had chosen Dropbox as the syncing method, the value was "dropbox."

[private app storage path]/shared_prefs/DROPBOX_PREFS.xml
- "DROPBOX_SECRET" and "DROPBOX_KEY"—The values of these strings are used by Dropbox to authenticate the UPM app to allow it to sync

the user's encrypted database. These strings are assigned by Dropbox to UPM when the user selects the sync method as Dropbox.

[private app storage path]/files/upm.db
- This file is the entirety of the encrypted UPM database containing all data the user has written into the UPM app. It is encrypted with a cipher known as "PBEWithSHA256And256BitAES-CBC-BC" and uses the user's selected password as a key. The salt for this cipher is stored in the encrypted database at positions 3 (with 0 being the first value) to 10 inclusively when read with a hex editor, for a total of eight characters. With this knowledge in mind, it is possible to decrypt the database via brute-force methods.

2.7.2 Examine app files on external storage (UPM)
UPM does not ordinarily utilize the device's external storage. However, if the user were to link the encrypted UPM database with a cloud storage syncing service (such as Dropbox), then the UPM encrypted database will be stored in that app's storage location for uploaded files.

2.7.3 Examine app databases (UPM)
The UPM Android app does not use SQLite databases in order to store metadata as other apps have. This means the app does not create a "[private app storage path]/ databases" directory.

2.7.4 Examine and analyze accounts data (UPM)
UPM does not create an account in the AccountManager API for its Android app. As such, there is no UPM "account" on the device.

Based on these results, we moved to further analyze the seven apps we selected in order to determine if additional information could be obtained from them.

2.8 FURTHER APP ANALYSIS
The apps were further analyzed below in order to understand the underlying structure of the app, and to allow a forensic practitioner to use the information obtained in order to access a suspect user's files (which may not be stored on the device). At the end of each app's section, we give a verdict on whether (based on our findings) the practitioner would have enough information in order to fully authenticate as the user and access all files on the service's servers.

2.8.1 Dropbox analysis
We collected a HPROF memory heap for the Android Dropbox app from our Android x86 virtual machine and then proceeded to analyze it using the Eclipse Memory Analyzer application.

Initial analysis of the Dominator Tree (sorted by Shallow Heap size) did not result in any significant findings. As such, we moved onto analysis using Object Query

Language (OQL) statements. OQL searches were undertaken to locate URLs (querying for String objects which contain "https" or "dropbox.com"), authentication headers (querying for String objects which contain "Authorization") and user identification information (querying for String objects which contain e-mail address attributes such as "@" as well as for strings such as username and password).

Using the OQL method, we were successful in locating the URLs that the Dropbox app uses for authentication and file retrieval. We were also successful in locating the authentication parameters required to use token authentication with Dropbox. The username of the logged in user was also located by searching for e-mail addresses.

From the memory analysis of the Dropbox app alone, we were able to locate almost all of the information we propose would be required in order to authenticate as the user. This includes the authentication URL and the format of the header parameters for this URL. The initial analysis of the Dropbox app in Section 2.1 gave us the OAuth consumer key, the OAuth token and the second half of the OAuth signature (see Section 2.1.1). We were able to discern the missing string by referring to the Dropbox developer's guide (Goundan, 2014).

As the value for the first half of the OAuth signature was not stored on the device (in our experiments), we concluded that this string must be statically assigned in the Dropbox app. Dropbox heavily obfuscates its code in order to discourage reverse engineering of its app. This means merely searching the decompiled source code for another static string used by Dropbox would not return any results (e.g., the OAuth consumer key is also generated statically). Certain strings cannot be fully obfuscated in the source code, such as URLs. Dropbox attempts to obscure these strings by building the URL as segments (e.g., "https://" + "dropbox.com") instead of having a single string object containing this information. By following these function calls through the code, we were able to locate a function that, using a static array of integers and a static seemingly random string of characters and integers, generated the OAuth consumer key and first half of the OAuth signature.

By collating all of the above information, a practitioner should be capable of authenticating as the user and accessing all files that the user had stored on the Dropbox servers.

2.8.2 Box analysis

We were able to obtain a HPROF memory dump for the Box app. A cursory analysis of the Dominator Tree did not reveal any information of interest and so we proceeded to filter the Tree.

By narrowing down the memory data to only the data within the class path of the Box app (com.box.android), we were successful in locating two key pieces of information, namely, the "mClientId" used to identify the user of the app on the Box server and the "mClientSecret" which was used to verify this particular client (app) on the server. These were both stored as strings in an instance of the "com.box.android.boxclient.BoxSdkClient" class. These strings are important as they are part of the URL used to obtain a new OAuth access token. In order to further our analysis, we utilized OQL.

We used OQL statements to obtain all URLs contained within the memory of the Box app. This resulted in two URLs of interest, namely, a URL for displaying all items located within the user's root directory and a URL for generating a new access token for the user which requires the client id, client secret, and refresh token to be transmitted as a POST request method. We were then able to determine that the client id and client secret must, therefore, be statically defined by Box. We decompiled the app and were able to locate these strings within the app's string resources file.

Our initial analysis of the Box app above (see Section 2.2) showed that the refresh token, the final piece of information we required to generate a valid access token, was stored in the Box app's private storage. We noted that access tokens expire after 60 min, making it unlikely that the access token stored within the app's private storage would be valid upon examination of the device by a practitioner. This meant that the refresh token and its URL found above would be useful in practice. We found that the refresh token expires after 60 days, and to generate a new access token, we only required a valid refresh token and the statically defined client id and client secret. Our analysis shows that we already have all of this information and, thus, should be able to obtain a valid access token given that the refresh token is still valid.

This access token could then be used with the URLs located for accessing all of a user's files. The same access token could be used (in the authorization header) to download any of the user's files. We do not believe that any additional information is required to access the user's files. Once again, we propose that access to all of the user's files would be attainable, following our analysis of the app.

2.8.3 OneDrive analysis

Using the Eclipse Memory Analyzer tool, we were able to narrow down the entirety of the memory data (which includes Java and Android class objects) to only those within the app's class path (com.microsoft.skydrive). A simple search of this data resulted in the retrieval of the static "PRODUCT_ID" value in both integer and hexadecimal formats stored within an instance of the "com.microsoft.live.authorization. TokenRequest" class. This value (in hexadecimal format) is used by OneDrive to identify the app that is communicating with the server (known as the "client_id"). We did not find any other data of interest in the sorted and filtered Dominator Tree. As a result, we continued onto analysis using OQL statements.

Searching for all "https" URLs within the memory heap resulted in several key fragments of information. We were able to identify the URLs used by OneDrive to authenticate the user and obtain a new refresh token as well as the URLs to view all user files/folders and the URL to obtain a specific item within the user's synced storage. More importantly, we found the authentication header format used to authenticate the above URLs.

By searching the heap for terms such as "refresh" and "token," we were also able to obtain the JSON encoded replies from the server for the URLs used to obtain a new access token and refresh token. Contained within these JSON encoded replies were:

- *expires_at*—The timestamp in millisecond resolution of when the refresh/access token expires.
- *user_id*—A string generated when the OneDrive account was first created by the Microsoft Live server. It is used to identify the user on the server side.
- *refresh_token*—A new refresh token which can be used to obtain a new refresh and access token.
- *scope*—The scope (limitations) of the access token received, which is also used when obtaining refresh tokens and access tokens.
- *access_token*—A new valid access token which can be used to authorize the user to access their files and folders (with one of the above obtained URLs).

Based on this information, we now knew what data was required to authenticate as the user. The URL to obtain a new access token required a valid refresh token, a client id, and a scope. From the memory heap, we already had the static client id of the OneDrive app. From the initial analysis of OneDrive in Section 2.3, we also had the refresh token and scope (both contained within the AccountManager API, see Section 2.3.4). Our analysis suggests that this is all the information required to obtain a new valid refresh token and an access token valid for 24 hours.

By utilizing this access token via the URLs used to list all user items, and then selecting an item from there to use the file downloading URL, we propose that a user's files could be obtained. The only parameter required in these URLs is the valid access token. It is, therefore, possible (with OneDrive) to obtain a user's files using only a valid refresh token (and, in turn, using the returned access token). All other values were static in our experiments.

2.8.4 ownCloud analysis

After obtaining the HPROF memory heaps, we proceeded to analyze the Dominator Tree. The tree was filtered to exclude all references to non-ownCloud related classes. We noted that ownCloud keeps all user files that have been cached within the memory, including full paths to these files on the external storage. This information was stored under the class "OwnCloudFileObserver." Another class, "AccountUtils" stored the CARDDAV, ODAV, STATUS, and WEBDAV paths on the ownCloud server.

We then proceeded to execute OQL queries on ownCloud's memory heap in order to further our examination of the app. By searching for all URLs within the memory heap, we were able to quickly locate the URLs used for authenticating with the ownCloud server, along with instances when the ownCloud app had accessed various locations within the server. Surprisingly, we were able to locate and obtain the user's username and password in plain text, which was used to authenticate the user into the ownCloud server. These details were stored in the Apache Commons "httpclient" class as opposed to residing within ownCloud's package. Unlike the previously analyzed apps, ownCloud does not appear to use access and refresh tokens to authenticate the user but rather relies on sending the server the username and password each time authentication is required.

Based on the above memory analysis, we ascertained that ownCloud must store information such as the user's username and password on the device as it does not seem to utilize security tokens. We had found in Section 2.4.4 that ownCloud stores this information in the AccountManager API. By using the server authentication URL obtained as part of ownCloud's shared preferences file (see Section 2.4.1), it was possible to log in as the user (using their username and password) and gain access to all of their files.

2.8.5 Evernote analysis

We obtained the HPROF memory heap of the Evernote Android app from our Android virtual machine. First, we inspected the Dominator Tree of the memory heap in order to find artifacts of interest. By filtering the tree to show objects associated with the Evernote app (com.evernote), we were able to locate the (heavily obfuscated) URLs for authentication and for accessing user files. This was stored in the "com.evernote.client.w" class. Furthermore, this instance of the above class also contained the user's numerical ID, Web browser agent and the parameters of the x-thrift format binary file that Evernote uses for authentication. These parameters include the user's authentication token.

In order to further our research, we proceeded to execute some OQL queries. First, we searched for all URLs stored within the memory heap. The resulting URLs of interest were once again the URLs for authentication and accessing user notes. By searching for e-mail addresses in the memory, we were able to obtain the e-mail address of the Google account on the device, the e-mail address the user used to sign up and log into Evernote and the Evernote-specific e-mail address.

We noted that the authentication URL and URLs for accessing files required an "x-thrift" format binary file to be sent in the body of the HTTP request. The contents of this binary file included the authentication token, although a significant amount of this file is in a binary format. As Evernote was heavily obfuscated, a decompilation of the code did not reveal data of significant interest.

Further analysis would be required in order to understand the inner workings of the Evernote app, to decrypt the encrypted token found in Section 2.5.1 and to understand the "x-thrift" format used by Evernote's server authentication.

2.8.6 OneNote analysis

A cursory analysis of OneNote's HPROF file revealed that OneNote stores within its memory the full URL for authenticating with the Microsoft Live servers. Included within this URL was the user's access token and client ID. Also of interest in the filtered Dominator Tree was the URL for accessing the user's notebooks and the GUID of the user's parent notebook.

By executing an OQL query to find all URLs within the memory, we were able to locate URLs to notebooks and notebook sections that had been stored in memory and, thus, likely to have been most recently accessed by the user. OneNote does not seem to store user information, such as the user's e-mail address or username, directly within the memory.

As mentioned in Section 2.6.4, the refresh token is stored more securely than that of Microsoft OneDrive's, but it is merely encrypted with data residing upon the device. The authentication scheme appears identical to that of OneDrive's in that the refresh token must first be used to generate an access token from the Microsoft Live servers before using this received token to authenticate.

2.8.7 Universal password manager analysis

A HPROF memory heap was obtained from the UPM app. The file was analyzed with Eclipse Memory Analyzer and filtered to show only objects that were within UPM's package name (com.u17od.upm).

First, we were able to locate instances of UPM's crypto classes. Within these classes we located the eight-character salt used by UPM to encrypt and decrypt the database containing the user's entries. Furthermore, we were able to locate the cipher used by UPM (PBEWithSHA256And256BitAES-CBC-BC). We proceeded to search the entirety of the memory and located an instance of the "javax.crypto.spec.PBEKeySpec" class. This Java class contained the user's password in plaintext. The use of OQL queries further strengthened the results we found via filtering of the Dominator Tree.

As previously discussed in Section 2.7.4, UPM does not communicate directly with a server. As such, the only methods to obtain the data within the UPM database are brute-force techniques based on the findings above and in Section 2.7, and obtaining the user's password via other means.

2.9 OUR RESEARCH ENVIRONMENT

In our experiments, we used several physical Android devices and an Android virtual machine. We used two popular Android phones: the Nexus 4 (E960) and Samsung Galaxy S3 (i9300). During our experiments, the Nexus 4 was running both Android 4.2.2 and Android 4.4. The Galaxy S3 was running Android 4.0.4 and the virtual machine ran a version of Android 4.4.

The following describes the device-specific procedures we performed with the above devices.

2.9.1 Nexus 4

The Nexus 4 was used as our primary device for validating our proposed evidence collection and analysis methodology (Martini et al., 2015). The following describes the process we undertook in order to prepare the device for the evidence collection, and examination and analysis.

When we first obtained the device, the Nexus 4 was running Android 4.2.2. This version of Android was released in early 2013, with many high-end phones being released toward the end of 2013 still running this version of Android. Using Android 4.2.2 on the Nexus 4 device, we proceeded to unlock the bootloader (see Martini et al., 2015 for further details), causing Android to display a warning indicating that all data on the device would be wiped upon unlocking of the bootloader. We proceeded with unlocking the bootloader and continued to load, within the device's RAM, a custom recovery image designed specifically for the Nexus 4.

The recovery mode successfully booted, allowing us to access the device (with full read and write privileges) via the ADB application over a USB cable. Navigating into the device's "userdata" partition showed that no files had yet been wiped; all user files were intact. Rebooting the device at this stage causes the Android device to wipe this partition. Using the ADB application, we successfully performed a "bit-for-bit" copy of all the device's partitions. We proceeded to modify the "services.jar" file to allow for our specially signed app to access user account information.

The Nexus 4 stores all "classes.dex" files for its system package's JAR files within the JAR file. This made it much easier for us to perform the required code injection on this file (as opposed to the Galaxy S3, see Section 2.9.3). We retrieved the "services.jar" file from the "/system" partition while in the custom recovery mode, injected our code to allow APKs containing our signature to bypass signature checks, and then replaced it on the device. Deleting the "services.odex" file on the device then prompts the device to rebuild all system packages upon next startup. No further change was necessary to allow our signature to have system-level privileges on the device. Following this, we analyzed the apps (via their forensic images). In order to read the accounts data, we copied our APK file into the "/system/app" location and rebooted the device. As our APK was signed such that it could imitate any package on the device, we were able to retrieve all accounts data from the Nexus 4's secure credentials storage.

Following our evidence collection and analysis methodology, we noted that upon encryption of the device, the "userdata" partition is encrypted but the "system" partition is not. This means that our above methodology could be utilized to inject code into any system package even on an encrypted device. We also note that Android versions after 4.2.2 erase the "userdata" partition upon unlocking of the bootloader. This means a different method would be required in order to unlock the bootloader to run the custom live OS.

2.9.2 Android VM

Our Android (user debug build) virtual machine was used primarily for the app analysis stage of our evidence collection and analysis methodology. By using a user debug build of the Android OS, we were able to obtain memory heaps (HPROF files) of all apps running regardless of whether they explicitly allow or disallow this action. To a forensic practitioner, this is an immensely useful tool to have as by default, Android apps do not allow the OS to obtain memory heaps of their data unless the app's "AndroidManifest.xml" file contains the "android:debuggable='true'" directive.

By utilizing the Android virtual machine, we were able to conduct in-depth analysis of the apps which were examined in Sections 2.1–2.7. By employing the aforementioned HPROF memory heaps, we obtained the methods in which the data collected in the initial analysis of the apps could be used in order to authenticate as the user (see Section 2.8). Without the information from each app's memory, it would be unlikely a practitioner could succeed in authenticating as these apps.

2.9.3 Samsung Galaxy S3

In our experiments, the Samsung Galaxy S3 was utilized as a secondary device used mainly for device-specific sections of our research. Most notably, when we extracted the "services.jar" file from its "system/framework" directory, we found that system packages on the Galaxy S3 do not contain a "classes.dex" file. This means we were required to go through an alternate route of repackaging each dependent JAR and APK file in the "system/framework" and "system/app" directories respectively such that the respective "odex" files were deodexed and placed as "classes.dex" files within the APK or JAR. After the JAR and APK files were replaced, we deleted their matching "odex" files in order to trigger the Android OS to rebuild the "odex" files from each app or framework's package.

The reason this process is required is due to Samsung electing to store only each system framework or app's source code within the optimized "odex" form of each framework or app. By default, the Android OS keeps all "classes.dex" files within the main package. The method Samsung employed reduces the amount of space that the "system" partition takes up significantly. In our experiments, in order to replace the "services.jar" file with our own modified version, we were required to replace a total of 175 items, with 56 of those belonging in the "system/framework" directory, and the remaining 119 in the "system/app" directory. We accomplished this using a script that monitored "logcat" output for occurrences of "StaleDexCacheError." This resulted in a successful implementation of our methodology, giving us access to the entire AccountManager API.

3 CONCLUSION

In this chapter, we implemented the methodology proposed in Martini et al. (2015) using six popular cloud apps and one password sync app as a case study to determine the types of forensic artifacts that can be collected from Android devices.

We found that all four cloud storage apps saved cached or offline files on the device's external storage. While some of the apps deleted the files after a period of time (once they were no longer being used) when the files were allocated, the majority of files were not protected. One exception to this was Box, which encrypted the files, requiring an encryption key and salt kept in the app's private storage directory to decrypt. Cloud storage apps also commonly kept thumbnails and other preview files on the device external storage. On internal storage, these apps generally stored file metadata (both for files cached on the device and files stored on the server) in an SQLite database. The usefulness of this metadata for forensic purposes varied between apps. A large amount of metadata was found, which could be of use in forensic investigations (including timestamp and file hash information). Cloud apps generally use tokens to authenticate the connection with their remote cloud servers. We found that these tokens were stored in a varied number of formats (although most of the authentication schemes were based on OAuth 1.0 or 2.0), which often required further analysis to decode or decrypt. App configuration files were also shown to contain some data of forensic interest, often this was related to authentication or encryption; however, user metadata (e.g., account names, e-mails) was also commonly found.

The two note-taking apps shared many similarities with the cloud storage apps, leading us to the conclusion that most cloud-based file-focused apps store similar types of data. However, the format and structure of the data is generally different. Microsoft's OneNote, for example, did not store any files on external storage, instead storing our test note files only on private internal storage. Generally, the note-taking apps often treated (and stored) notes as individual files or in combined files (such as Notebooks). The formats of these files were not particularly complex with Evernote using an XML based format, which made examination straightforward and OneNote using the standard OneNote file format suitable for opening in the PC version of the app.

We found that using the information obtained from both the initial and further analysis sections, a practitioner could potentially access the cloud service's servers as the user (and access their files) on the device for five of the six apps we tested that communicated and authenticated directly with cloud services. These apps were Dropbox, Box, OneDrive, ownCloud, and OneNote.

Future work includes advanced analysis of device bootloaders to determine techniques of booting live operating systems, where this is not supported by manufacturers by default, to facilitate forensic collection.

REFERENCES

Martini, B., Do, Q., Choo, K.-K.R., 2015. Conceptual evidence collection and analysis methodology for android devices. In: Ko, R., Choo, K.-K.R. (Eds.), Cloud Security Ecosystem. Syngress, an Imprint of Elsevier, Waltham, MA.

K. Goundan. Using OAuth in "PLAINTEXT" mode, July 25, 2014. https://www.dropbox.com/developers/blog/20/using-oauth-in-plaintext-mode.

Recovering residual forensic data from smartphone interactions with cloud storage providers

16

George Grispos[a], William Bradley Glisson[b], Tim Storer[a]

[a]School of Computing Science, University of Glasgow, Glasgow, United Kingdom
[b]School of Computing, University of South Alabama, Mobile, Alabama, USA

1 INTRODUCTION

An increase in demand for information technology (IT) resources has prompted many organizations to turn their attention to cloud computing. This technology has significant potential to reduce costs and increase efficiency in the workplace (Armbrust et al., 2009). Migrating to a cloud computing environment means an organization can replace much of its traditional IT hardware with virtualized, remote, and on-demand infrastructure services such as storage space, processing power, and network bandwidth (Grispos et al., 2012).

Storing corporate data online using cloud-based storage services such as Amazon S3, Google Docs, and Dropbox has become an effective solution for the business needs of a growing number of organizations (Mager et al., 2012). Cloud storage services can offer an organization greater flexibility and availability, with virtually unlimited storage space, as well as the ability to synchronize data between multiple devices. Typically, cloud storage providers will operate on the "freemium" financial model, offering customers free storage space with an option to purchase further unlimited storage space as they require (Mulazzani et al., 2011; Hunsinger and Corley, 2012). This business model has demonstrated to be successful, as the popularity of cloud storage services has soared in recent years. For example, Dropbox has seen its customer-base surpass 300 million users and now claim that over 1 billion files are saved every 3 days using its services (Hong, 2014; Constine, 2012). Mozy claim that more than six million individual users and 100,000 businesses are using their services, while Box has reported that implementation of its mobile device application increased 140% monthly in 2011 (MarketWire, 2012a; Mozy, 2014). Forrester Research has predicted that approximately two-thirds of adults who use the Internet in the United States are using some form of personal cloud storage service, often combining cloud services for both work and personal use (Forrester Research, 2012). Cloud storage services are also increasingly integrating into the retail, financial, legal, and healthcare enterprise markets (CRN, 2012; MarketWire, 2012b).

Although the benefits of using cloud storage services are attractive, a major concern is the security and privacy of data in these environments (Subashini and Kavitha, 2011; Ibrahim et al., 2010; Jansen and Grance, 2011; Grispos et al., 2014). For many organizations, there are several reasons to decline adoption of cloud storage services, including a necessity to protect mission-critical information, legal and regulatory obligations, and concerns regarding the confidentiality and integrity of their information (Grispos et al., 2013a; Zissis and Lekkas, 2012; Kaufman, 2009; Hay et al., 2011, 2012). These reservations are being validated as TrendMicro has reported that cloud adopters have witnessed an increase in the number of cloud security incidents as compared to traditional IT infrastructure security events (TrendMicro, 2011). Further complicating matters, researchers have demonstrated how cloud storage services, such as Dropbox, can be hijacked and exploited to gain access to an unsuspecting user's account (Mulazzani et al., 2011; Kholia and Wegrzyn, 2013). There is no practical barrier preventing further exploitation of cloud storage services by users to access and retrieve files. Security incidents and criminal activity involving cloud storage services could require a subsequent forensic investigation to be undertaken.

There is a general consensus from both industry and academia that it may be difficult to investigate inappropriate or illegal activity involving cloud computing environments (Grispos et al., 2012; Reilly et al., 2010; Ruan et al., 2011; Taylor et al., 2010; Brodkin, 2008). One of the biggest challenges for forensic investigators examining cloud-based services is the ability to identify and recover digital evidence in a forensically sound manner (Grispos et al., 2012; Taylor et al., 2010). This problem is magnified in public cloud environments, such as those used by cloud storage providers. The remote, distributed, and virtualized nature of a public cloud environment means that the conventional, offline approach to forensic evidence acquisition is largely invalidated (Grispos et al., 2012). The tools and methods used to preserve and acquire a forensic copy of data stored on a traditional storage device are unlikely to transfer to a public cloud environment (Grispos et al., 2012). The remote and distributed nature of public cloud architectures can also make the identification of a single storage device containing relevant data impractical and even impossible. This means that an investigator cannot directly obtain a copy of the evidence required for analysis. An alternative approach is for the investigator to request the cloud storage provider to obtain a forensic copy of the storage device. However, this approach can take a significant amount of time, or be obstructed by cross-border jurisdictional disputes (Hay et al., 2011; Jansen and Ayers, 2007).

This research investigates a practical solution to problems related to investigating cloud storage environments using practitioner-accepted forensic tools. This study extends the results from an initial investigation, which examined the feasibility of an end-device, providing a proxy view of the evidence in a cloud forensics investigation (Grispos et al., 2013b). Relevant information and data from that conference publication have been included in this chapter for completeness. The contribution of this chapter is threefold. First, the findings from this research further supports the idea that end-devices which have been used to access cloud storage services can be used to provide a partial or snapshot view of the evidence stored in the cloud service. Second, the chapter provides a comparison of the files which can be recovered from different versions of cloud storage applications. The chapter also supports the idea that amalgamating the files recovered from more than one device can result in an investigator recovering a more complete "dataset" of files stored in the cloud service. Third, the chapter contributes to the documentation and evidentiary discussion of the artifacts created from specific cloud storage applications and different versions of these applications on iOS and Android smartphones.

The chapter is structured as follows: Section 2 discusses the challenges of conducting digital forensic investigations in a cloud computing environment and examines what work has been done in relation to cloud storage forensics, as well as presenting an overview of smartphone forensics. Section 3 proposes the hypotheses and research questions which guided this research and describes the experimental design undertaken to address the research questions. Section 4 reports the findings, and Section 5 is used to discuss the results and their impact on forensic investigations. Finally, Section 6 draws conclusions from the work conducted and presents future work.

2 RELATED WORK

A growing number of researchers have argued that cloud computing environments are inherently more difficult to investigate than conventional environments (Grispos et al., 2012; Reilly et al., 2010; Ruan et al., 2011; Taylor et al., 2010; Biggs and Vidalis, 2009). Ruan et al. (Ruan et al., 2011) defined the term "cloud forensics" as a "cross discipline of cloud computing and digital forensics" and described cloud forensics as a subset of network forensics. However, this definition does not take into consideration the virtualization aspect of the cloud (Grispos et al., 2012). Ruan et al. (Ruan et al., 2011) also noted that an investigation involving cloud computing would include technical, organizational, and legal aspects. Grispos et al. (Grispos et al., 2012) described how traditional digital forensic models and techniques used for investigating computer systems could prove to be ineffective in a cloud computing environment. Furthermore, Grispos et al. (Grispos et al., 2012) identified several challenges for forensic investigators, including creating adequate forensic images, the recovery of segregated evidence, and large data storage management. Taylor et al (Taylor et al., 2010) raised the concern that potential important evidence could be lost in a cloud environment. Registry entries in Microsoft Windows platforms, temporary files, and metadata could all be lost if the user leaves the cloud (Taylor et al., 2010). Reilly et al. (Reilly et al., 2010) speculated that one potential benefit of investigating a public cloud environment is that the data being investigated will be located in a central location, which means that incidents can, potentially, be investigated quicker. This is unlikely to be the case as the very nature of a public cloud service theoretically means that even evidence related to individuals within the same organization could be segregated in different physical locations and stored alongside data belonging to other organizations and the general public (Google, 2011).

To enable a forensic investigation to be conducted, evidence needs to be collected from cloud computing environments, thus introducing a unique set of challenges for forensic investigators (Dykstra and Sherman, 2012). Researchers have begun proposing methods of acquiring evidence from a variety of cloud providers and services (Dykstra and Sherman, 2012; Delport et al., 2011). Delport et al. (Delport et al., 2011) proposed the idea of isolating a cloud instance for further investigation; however, it is not clear how a forensic image of the instance under investigation is obtained after it has been isolated from the rest of the cloud environment. Dykstra and Sherman (Dykstra and Sherman, 2012) proposed three methods of evidence collection from Infrastructure-as-a-Service (IaaS) instances stored in the Amazon EC2 Cloud. The first method evaluated the performance of several forensic tools including FTK Imager and Encase Enterprise, which were used to extract evidence directly from the cloud instance in the Amazon Cloud. An issue with this method is that the investigator must be in possession of Amazon EC2 key pairs used to connect to the instance. The purpose of the key pairs is to ensure that only the instance's owner has access to the instance (Amazon Web Services, 2011). These public/private keys are created by the owner when the instance is first created using the Amazon Web Services Management Console (Amazon Web Services, 2014). Unless the investigator can recover these keys, this method of acquisition cannot be used. The second proposed method involved acquiring evidence from the virtualization layer of a cloud by injecting a remote agent into the hypervisor of the cloud environment. This approach was evaluated in a private cloud environment, where the investigator had the ability to write into memory the guest virtual instance. However, this is unlikely to be the case in a public cloud environment, where the cloud provider will control access to the hypervisor and virtualization layer of a cloud (Grispos et al., 2013a). The final method proposed by Dykstra and Sherman involves requesting Amazon EC2 to collect the required evidence from the host on behalf of the investigator. Dykstra and Sherman note that the limitation of this method is that Amazon does not provide checksums to verify the integrity of the forensic image; therefore, the investigator cannot be certain that the data supplied by Amazon and the data stored in the cloud are identical (Dykstra and Sherman, 2012).

Researchers have also attempted to define investigative frameworks specifically addressing cloud storage providers (Chung et al., 2012; Lee et al., 2012; Quick and Choo, 2013a,b, 2014). Lee et al. (Lee et al., 2012) presented a framework for investigating incidents involving the Apple iCloud environment. The framework proposes the idea that the forensic investigator can examine Windows and Apple OSX-based systems, as well as Apple mobile devices to recover traces of data stored in the iCloud service. The research focused on the recovery of e-mail messages, memos, contacts, calendar information, and bookmarks. The limitation of this research is that Lee et al. (Lee et al., 2012) did not examine or discuss if the artifacts recovered from the end-devices were representative of the data stored in the cloud. There is the possibility that evidence still stored in the iCloud service was not recovered from the end-devices. Chung et al. (Chung et al., 2012) have also proposed a framework for investigating cloud storage services including Amazon S3, Google Docs, Dropbox, and Evernote.

Quick and Choo (Quick and Choo, 2013a,b, 2014) have undertaken three separate case studies to investigate the data remnants from Dropbox, Google Drive, and SkyDrive (now called OneDrive). In all three case studies, a Windows 7 personal computer and an Apple 3G iPhone were used to access and view a dataset stored in the cloud storage service. A Windows 7 personal computer was emulated using virtual machines. A variety of Web browsers were used in conjunction with the virtual machine and the specified cloud storage client application to collect data (Quick and Choo, 2013a,b, 2014). The findings from the personal computer analysis revealed that usernames, passwords, filename listings, file content, as well as dates and times that files were accessed are recoverable from a personal computer which has interacted with the above cloud storage services (Quick and Choo, 2013a,b, 2014). An iPhone device was used to access the dataset through the "on-device" Web browser in order to interact with the specified iOS cloud storage application. A logical extraction using MicroSystemation's XRY was then performed. Their analysis of the logical extraction revealed that a number of artifacts can be recovered from various locations on the device which included the account services' username, as well as the filenames of viewed files (Quick and Choo, 2013a,b, 2014). However, it is worth noting that the content of the files stored in the cloud storage services were not recovered from the iPhone. Quick and Choo noted that future work should examine the physical acquisition of iPhone devices to determine if this method of acquisition can be used to recover the files stored in the cloud storage services (Quick and Choo, 2013a,b, 2014; Quick et al., 2013).

Separately, Quick and Choo (Quick and Choo, 2013c) investigated the modification of file content and metadata when potential evidence is downloaded and collected from a cloud storage account. Quick and Choo (Quick and Choo, 2013c) reported that the cryptographic hashes calculated from file manipulations, like uploading, storing, and downloading, using Dropbox, SkyDrive (now called OneDrive), and Google Drive reveal that no changes were made to the files' content. Quick and Choo (Quick and Choo, 2013c) also state that after further analysing the downloaded files, notable changes were visible in the timestamp metadata. This was particularly evident in the "last accessed" and "file creation" time-stamps which indicated the last interaction with the cloud storage client software (Quick and Choo, 2013c).

Martini and Choo (Martini and Choo, 2013) focused on client and server-side forensic investigations involving the "ownCloud" service. Martini and Choo reported that forensic artifacts found on the client machine can link a user to a particular "ownCloud" instance (Martini and Choo, 2013). Furthermore, Martini and Choo recovered authentication and file metadata from the client, which were then used to decrypt files stored on the server (Martini and Choo, 2013). Martini and Choo (Martini and Choo, 2014) have also examined XtreemFS, a distributed filesystem commonly used in cloud computing environments, and documented both client and server-side artifacts which may be relevant to forensic investigations.

As part of the "Cloud Computing and The Impact on Digital Forensic Investigations" project, Biggs and Vidalis (Biggs and Vidalis, 2010) reported that very few High Tech Crime Units in the United Kingdom were prepared to deal with crimes involving cloud computing. As a result, Biggs and Vidalis believe a "cloud storm" will create difficulties and challenges for law enforcement investigators charged with investigating such environments (Biggs and Vidalis, 2010). Taylor et al. (Taylor et al., 2010) have extensively examined the legal issues surrounding cloud computing and comment that any evidence gathered from the cloud should be conducted within local laws and legislation. Phillips (Phillips, 2011) discussed the issue of keeping a chain of custody for such an investigation and has argued that the cloud is a dynamic paradigm and physically isolating it to conduct an investigation could be a daunting task for the investigator.

When multiple devices are used to access data in the cloud, the issues with the dynamic paradigm are exacerbated. A prime example of this impediment is the increasing use of mobile devices such as smartphones to access data stored in a cloud (Forrester Research, 2012; Chung et al., 2012). A smartphone device is distinguishable from a traditional mobile phone by its superior processing capabilities, a larger storage capacity, as well as its ability to run complex operating systems and applications (Grispos et al., 2011). From an evidentiary perspective, the smartphone potentially contains a considerable amount of forensic evidence. This potential is demonstrated in a study where researchers recovered more than 11,000 data artifacts from 49 predominately low-end devices (Glisson et al., 2011). As with a traditional mobile phone, the smartphone not only stores call logs, text messages, and personal contacts, but it also has the ability to store Web-browsing artifacts, e-mail messages, GPS coordinates, as well as third-party application related data (Hoog, 2011; Levinson et al., 2011; Morrissey, 2010). There are a number of tools that can be used to perform a data acquisition from a smartphone. Examples of these tools include Cellebrite's Universal Forensic Extraction Device (UFED) (Cellebrite, n.d.); Micro-Systemation's XRY tools (Micro Systemation, n.d.); The Mobile Internal Acquisition Tool (Distefano and Me, 2008); Paraben's Device Seizure (Paraben, n.d.) and RAPI Tools (Hengeveld, 2003). These forensic toolkits make it possible to investigate mobile devices that have been used to access cloud storage providers and extract evidence without directly accessing the cloud storage provider's service. However, there is currently a lack of research as to the relationship between the residual data retained on multiple mobile devices subsequent to cloud interaction. There is also a lack of research into the impact that cloud storage applications have on mobile device residual data.

3 EXPERIMENT DESIGN

The lack of research examining the gap between device residual data and existing cloud data prompted research into the following hypothesis:

H1: Smartphone devices present a partial view of the data held in cloud storage services, which can be used as a proxy for evidence held on the cloud storage service itself.

H2: The manipulation of different cloud storage applications influences the results of data collection from a smartphone device.

H3: Different versions of cloud storage applications implemented on diverse operating systems retain varying amounts of residual data.

To address the hypotheses, the following questions were proposed:

1. To what extent can data stored in a cloud storage provider be recovered from a smartphone device that has accessed the service?
2. What features of the cloud application influence the ability to recover data stored in a cloud storage service from a smartphone device?
3. Do different versions of a cloud application used on the smartphone devices affect the ability to recover data stored in a cloud storage service from a smartphone device?
4. What metadata concerning the cloud storage service can be recovered from a smartphone device and what does the metadata data, recovered from a smartphone device, reveal about further files stored in the cloud service?
5. Does the amalgamation of files recovered from two or more versions of a specific cloud storage application provide a more complete dataset of files stored in the cloud service?

An experiment was devised to support the hypotheses and research questions proposed above. The experiment was broken into six stages. The six stages included (1) preparing the smartphone device and installing the cloud application; (2) loading a dataset to a cloud storage provider; (3) connect to the data through the application on the smartphone; (4) performing various file manipulations to the dataset and smartphone device; (5) processing the device using the UFED; and (6) using a number of forensic tools to extract the files and artifacts from the resulting memory dumps.

The forensic tools used in this experiment were the Cellebrite UFED version 1.8.5.0 and its associated application the "Physical Analyzer" version 3.7.0.352; FTK Imager, and FTK Toolkit version 4.0. The smartphone devices were processed with the UFED tools. The memory card used in the HTC Desire was processed using FTK Imager. The memory dumps were examined using a combination of Physical Analyzer and the FTK toolkit. Three smartphone devices were selected for use in this experiment: an Apple iPhone 3G and two HTC Desire devices. Table 1 highlights the

Table 1 Smartphone Device Features

Feature	iPhone 3G	HTC Desire	HTC Desire
Operating system	iOS v. 3	Android v. 2.1	Android v. 2.3
Internal memory	8 GB storage	576 MB RAM	576 MB RAM
Memory card	No	Yes (4 GB)	Yes (4 GB)

notable features of these devices. These devices were selected for two reasons. First, they are compatible with the choice of forensic toolkit (UFED) used to perform a physical dump of the internal memory. Second, the operating systems used on these devices represent the two most popular smartphone operating systems in use (Gartner, 2012). Although more recent devices with newer versions of both the Android and iOS operating system exist, a lack of support from the forensic tools to perform a physical acquisition meant that these newer devices could not be included in the experiment. The decision to use these specific devices and tools was a pragmatic decision based on practicality and availability to the authors.

The selection criteria for the smartphone devices limited the number of cloud storage applications available to only the applications compatible with both operating systems. The scope of the experiment was limited in the following ways:

- This experiment was conducted in the United Kingdom, where Global System of Mobile (GSM) is the predominant mobile phone type, therefore non-GSM mobile devices were not considered;
- a number of smartphone devices which run either iOS or Android were not considered due to compatibility issues with the toolkit; and
- various cloud storage applications were not considered because they do not support either or both of the chosen operating system platforms.

The original implementation of this experiment used an iPhone 3G running iOS version 3.0 and an HTC Desire running Android version 2.1. The cloud storage applications for iOS included Dropbox v. 1.4.7, Box v. 2.7.1, SugarSync v. 3.0, and Syncplicity v. 1.6. The cloud storage applications for the Android device included Dropbox v. 2.1.3, Box v. 1.6.7, SugarSync v. 3.6, and Syncplicity v. 1.7. The experiment was then extended and repeated using an HTC Desire running Android version 2.3. Newer versions of the Android cloud storage applications implemented in this portion of the experiment included Dropbox v. 2.2.2, Box v. 2.0.2, SugarSync v. 3.6.2, and Syncplicity v. 2.1.1. Extending the experiment provides the opportunity to compare the results obtained between different versions of specific cloud storage applications. Updating the operating system and applications used on the iPhone device was considered. However, based on discontinued application support for iPhone 3G, a lack of support, at the time of the experiment, from the forensic tools for newer versions of the iPhone, as well as device availability, a pragmatic decision was made not to include an iOS device in the extended experiment.

Table 2 Experimental Dataset

Filename	Size (bytes)	Manipulation
01.jpg	43183	File viewed/played
02.jpg	6265	File viewed/played and saved for offline access
03.jpg	102448	No manipulation
04.jpg	5548	File viewed/played and then deleted
05.mp3	3997696	File viewed/played
06.mp3	2703360	File viewed/played and saved for offline access
07.mp3	3512009	No manipulation
08.mp3	4266779	File viewed/played and then deleted
09.mp4	831687	File viewed/played
10.mp4	245779	File viewed/played and saved for offline access
11.mp4	11986533	No manipulation
12.mp4	21258947	File viewed/played and then deleted
13.pdf	1695706	File viewed/played
14.pdf	471999	File viewed/played and saved for offline access
15.pdf	2371383	No manipulation
16.pdf	1688736	File viewed/played and then deleted
17.docx	84272	File viewed/played
18.docx	85091	File viewed/played and saved for offline access
19.docx	14860	No manipulation
20.docx	20994	File viewed/played and then deleted

A predefined dataset was created, which comprised 20 files, made up of image (JPEG), audio (MP3), video (MP4), and document (DOCX and PDF) file types. Table 2 defines the files used in this dataset. The same dataset was used in both the original and extended experiments. The following steps were used in both the original and extended experiments. These steps were repeated every time the experiment was reset for a different cloud storage application.

1. The smartphone was "hard reset," which involved restoring the default factory settings on the device. In the case of the HTC Desire, the Secure Digital (SD) memory card was forensically wiped using The Department of Defence Computer Forensics Lab tool—*dcfldd* (Department of Defense Computer Forensics Lab, 2006). These steps were done to remove any previous data stored on the devices and the memory card.
2. The device was then connected to a wireless network which was used to gain access to the Internet. The cloud storage application was downloaded and installed either via the Android or Apple "app market," depending on the device used. The default installation and security parameters were used during the installation of the application.

3. The cloud storage application was executed, and a new user account was created using a predefined e-mail address and a common password for that cloud storage application.

4. After the test account was created, the application was "connected" to the cloud storage provider's services, which meant the device was now ready to receive the dataset.

5. A personal computer running Windows 7 was used to access the test account created in Step 4 and the dataset was then uploaded to the cloud storage provider using a Web browser. The date and time the files were uploaded to the cloud storage provider was noted. The smartphone was synchronized with the cloud storage provider to ensure the dataset was visible via the smartphone application.

6. When the entire dataset was visible on the smartphone, a number of manipulations were made to files in the dataset. Table 2 summarizes these manipulations. These included:
   - a file being viewed or played;
   - a file viewed or played then saved for offline access;
   - a file viewed or played then deleted from the cloud storage provider; and
   - some files were neither opened/played nor deleted (no manipulation).

7. The smartphone and cloud storage application were also manipulated in one of the following ways:
   - *Active power state*—the smartphone was not powered down and the application's cache was not cleared;
   - *Cache cleared*—the applications cache was cleared;
   - *Powered off*—the smartphone was powered down; and
   - *Cache cleared and powered off*—the applications' cache was cleared and the smartphone was powered off.

   These manipulations were done to mimic various scenarios a forensic investigator could encounter during an investigation. The smartphone was then removed from the wireless network to prevent any accidental modification to the dataset.

8. After the above manipulations, the smartphone device was processed to create a forensic dump of its internal memory. In the case of the HTC Desire, the SD memory card was processed separately from the smartphone. The HTC Desire was processed directly using the UFED, while a binary image of the SD card was created using FTK Imager. Before the HTC Desire was processed, the USB debugging option was enabled on the smartphone. This is required by the UFED to create the binary images from the device. The default parameters for a Physical Extraction on the UFED were selected, and the make and model of the device were provided. In the case of the SD card, the default parameters were used to create a binary image of the storage card. The resulting binary images were saved to a forensically wiped 16 GB USB flash drive. The extraction process for the iPhone differed from that of the HTC Desire as the device was processed using the Physical Analyzer "add-on," which is designed to extract binary images from

the iPhone. A step-by-step wizard provided instructions on how to prepare the device for the extraction. From the selection menu, the User partition was selected for extraction from the device, and the resulting memory dump was saved to a 16 GB USB flash drive.

9. The images extracted from the smartphone device were then loaded into Physical Analyzer, where the iOS and Android file systems were reconstructed. FTK 4 was used as the primary tool for analysis. This involved extracting the partitions from the dumps in Physical Analyzer and then examining them using FTK. Analysis techniques used included: string searching for the password, filtering by file types and browsing the iOS and Android file systems.

4 FINDINGS

A summary of files recovered from the devices is shown in Tables 3-6. Several observations can be drawn from these results. Smartphone devices can be used to recover artifacts related to cloud storage services. These artifacts can include the files stored in the cloud storage service which have been accessed using the smartphone device and metadata associated to user and service activity. The exception to this was the recovery of a thumbnail of the JPEG image file not viewed on the device (03.jpg), which was recovered from 10 of the 12 applications examined.

The chances of recovering a file increase if the file has been saved for offline viewing. Files which were marked for offline viewing were recovered from all the applications except from version 2.0.2 of the Box Android application. The results also indicate that different versions of the Android applications can result in different files being recovered from a smartphone device. This finding was particularly evident for the Box and Syncplicity applications. The two different versions of these applications resulted in different files from the dataset being recovered. The metadata recovered from the devices included SQLite databases, text-based transaction logs, JavaScript Object Notation (JSON), and XML files. These metadata artifacts contained information related to user activity, account-specific information such as e-mail addresses, and described which files are stored in the cloud storage service.

An analysis of the memory dumps revealed that forensic artifacts can be recovered from the smartphone devices and in the case of the Android devices, the SD memory card. The Android operating system allows files to be stored in either the device's internal storage memory or on an external memory card (Hoog, 2011). The iPhone does not have an external storage device and all artifacts recovered from the device were from the internal storage memory. The SD memory card used with the Android devices contained files which were either deleted by the user or deleted as a result of the cache being cleared. Clearing the application's cache has an adverse effect on the recovery of files. This is more evident on the iPhone, which does not contain an SD card. Powering down the smartphone devices did

Table 3 Dropbox Files Recovered

Filename	Android Application Version 2.1.3				Android Application Version 2.2.2				iOS Application Version 1.4.7			
	APS	CC	PWD	CC & PWD	APS	CC	PWD	CC & PWD	APS	CC	PWD	CC & PWD
01	T	T	T	T	T	T	T	T	T	✓	T	✓
02	✓	✓	✓	✓	✓	✓	✓	✓	✓		✓	
03	T	T	T	T	T	T	T	T	T		T	
04	T	T	T	T	T	T	T	T				
05												
06	✓	✓	✓	✓	✓	✓	✓	✓	✓	✓	✓	✓
07												
08												
09												
10	✓	✓	✓	✓	✓	✓	✓	✓	✓	✓	✓	✓
11												
12												
13	✓	D	✓	D	✓	D	✓	D	✓		✓	
14	✓	✓	✓	✓	✓	✓	✓	✓	✓		✓	
15												
16	D	D	D	D	D	D	D	D	✓	✓	✓	✓
17	✓	D	✓	D	✓	D	✓	D	✓		✓	✓
18	✓	✓	✓	✓	✓	✓	✓	✓	✓		✓	✓
19												
20	D	D	D	D	D	D	D	D				

APS, active power state; PWD, powered down; CC, cache cleared; CC & PWD, cache cleared and powered down; ✓, file recovered; D, deleted file recovered; T, thumbnail recovered.

Table 4 Box Files Recovered

Filename	Android Application Version 1.6.7				Android Application Version 2.0.2				iOS Application Version 2.7.1			
	APS	CC	PWD	CC & PWD	APS	CC	PWD	CC & PWD	APS	CC	PWD	CC & PWD
01	✓	D	✓	D	T	T	T	T	T	T	T	T
02	✓	D	✓	D	T	T	T	T	✓	✓	✓	✓
03	T	T	T	T	T	T	T	T	T	T	T	T
04	✓	D	✓	D	T	T	T	T	T	T	T	T
05	✓	D	✓	D	✓		✓		✓	✓	✓	✓
06	✓	D	✓	D	✓		✓					
07												
08	✓	D	✓	D	✓	D	✓	D	✓	✓	✓	✓
09	✓	D	✓	D	✓	D	✓	D				
10	✓	D	✓	D	✓	D	✓	D				
11												
12	✓	D	✓	D	✓	D	✓	D	✓	✓	✓	✓
13	✓	D	✓	D								
14	✓	D	✓	D								
15												
16	✓	D	✓	D					✓	✓	✓	✓
17	✓	D	✓	D								
18	✓	D	✓	D								
19												
20	✓	D	✓	✓								

APS, active power state; PWD, powered down; CC, cache cleared; CC & PWD, cache cleared and powered down; ✓, file recovered; D, deleted file recovered; T, thumbnail recovered.

Table 5 SugarSync Files Recovered

Filename	Android Application Version 3.6				Android Application Version 3.6.2				iOS Application Version 3.0			
	APS	CC	PWD	CC & PWD	APS	CC	PWD	CC & PWD	APS	CC	PWD	CC & PWD
01	✓	D	✓	D	✓	D	✓	D	✓	✓	✓	✓
02	✓	✓	✓	✓	✓	✓	✓	✓	✓	✓	✓	✓
03	T	T	T	T	T	T	T	T	✓	✓	✓	✓
04	✓	D	✓	D	✓	D	✓	D	✓	✓	✓	✓
05									✓	✓	✓	✓
06	✓	✓	✓	✓	✓	✓	✓	✓	✓	✓	✓	✓
07									✓		✓	
08									✓	✓	✓	✓
09									✓		✓	
10	✓	✓	✓	✓	✓	✓	✓	✓	✓	✓	✓	✓
11									✓		✓	
12	✓	✓	✓	✓	✓	✓	✓	✓	✓	✓	✓	✓
13	✓	✓	✓	✓	✓	✓	✓	✓	✓	✓	✓	✓
14	✓	✓	✓	✓	✓	✓	✓	✓	✓		✓	
15	✓	✓	✓	✓	✓	✓	✓	✓	✓	✓	✓	
16	✓	✓	✓	✓	✓	✓	✓	✓	✓		✓	
17	✓	D	✓	D	✓	D	✓	D	✓	✓	✓	✓
18	✓	✓	✓	✓	✓	✓	✓	✓	✓		✓	
19									✓		✓	
20	✓	D	✓	D	✓	D	✓	D	✓	✓	✓	✓

APS, active power state; PWD, powered down; CC, cache cleared; CC & PWD, cache cleared and powered down; ✓, file recovered; D, deleted file recovered; T, thumbnail recovered.

Table 6 Syncplicity Files Recovered

Filename	Android Application Version 1.7				Android Application Version 2.1.1				iOS Application Version 1.6			
	APS	CC	PWD	CC & PWD	APS	CC	PWD	CC & PWD	APS	CC	PWD	CC & PWD
01	D	D	D	D	✓	D	✓	D	✓		✓	
02	✓	✓	✓	✓	✓	✓	✓	✓	✓		✓	
03	T	T	T	T	T	T	T	T				
04	D	D	D	D	✓	D	✓	D	✓		✓	
05					✓	D	✓	D	✓		✓	
06	✓	✓	✓	✓	✓	✓	✓	✓	✓		✓	
07												
08					✓	D	✓	D			✓	
09	✓	✓	✓	✓	✓	D	✓	D	✓		✓	
10					✓	✓	✓	✓	✓		✓	
11												
12					✓	D	✓	D			✓	
13	✓	✓	✓	✓	✓	D	✓	D	✓		✓	
14					✓	✓	✓	✓	✓		✓	
15												
16	D	D	D	D	✓	D	✓	D			✓	
17	✓	✓	✓	✓	✓	D	✓	D	✓		✓	
18					✓	✓	✓	✓	✓		✓	
19	D	D	D	D								
20	D	D	D	D	✓	D	✓	D	✓		✓	

APS = active power state; PWD, powered down; CC, cache cleared; CC & PWD, cache cleared and powered down; ✓, file recovered; D, deleted file recovered; T, thumbnail recovered.

not have an effect on the recovery of data. As a result, the files recovered were identical to that of the active power state scenario.

Artifacts stored in the internal memory of the Android devices can be recovered from a subfolder named after the application name. This subfolder can be recovered from the path `/data/data` (Hoog, 2011). Unlike the internal storage device, applications can store data in any location on the SD memory card (Lessard and Kessler, 2010). Therefore, the location of evidence on the SD card varies, depending on the application being investigated. The iOS file system creates a subfolder for each installed application under the directory `/private/var/mobile/Applications` in the User partition (Levinson et al., 2011). The name of the application directory installed under this location is assigned a unique 32-character alphanumeric folder name (Zdziarski, 2008). The folder name is different for each application installed on the device. Artifacts related to the iOS applications were stored under this folder location.

4.1 DETAILED DROPBOX FINDINGS

On the HTC Desire, the forensic toolkits recovered nine files from both Android versions of Dropbox. Depending on application and device manipulation, either five or seven files were recovered from the iOS version of Dropbox. The results of which files were recovered from the Dropbox application are shown in Table 3.

4.1.1 Android applications

Files stored in the Dropbox service can be recovered from two locations on the SD card. These locations and their contents are valid for both versions of the Android Dropbox application. First, thumbnails of the JPEG images were recovered from the path `/Android/data/ com.dropbox.android/cache/thumbs/`. Second, files which were saved for offline viewing and the document files which were viewed and not deleted on the device were recovered from the path `/Android/data/com.dropbox.android/files/scratch`. Analyses of the "unallocated space" for both Android applications revealed that the two document files which were deleted (16.pdf and 20.docx) were still physically stored on the SD card. These two document files were recovered by FTK.

Metadata related to both versions of the Dropbox application were recovered from the internal memory of the smartphone. The metadata recovered were valid for both versions of the Android application. This metadata consisted of two SQLite databases and a transaction log. The two databases were recovered from the path `/data/data/com.dropbox.android/databases/`. The first database, `db.db`, has a table called `dropbox`, which contains metadata related to the files currently stored in the service, i.e., files which have not been deleted from the Dropbox service. Fields identified from this table are shown in Appendix A.

The second database, `prefs.db`, has a table called `DropboxAccountPrefs` which contains metadata related to the end-user. Information which can be recovered includes the user's name and e-mail address used to register for the Dropbox service.

A transactional log called `log.txt` is created by the Dropbox application to record service and user-related events including the creation of a new user account; successful and unsuccessful login attempts; as well as which files are synchronized to the Dropbox service. A UNIX epoch timestamp accompanies the documented event. This log can be recovered from the path `data/data/com.dropbox.android/files`.

Clearing the cache of both versions of the Dropbox Android application, removes the documents viewed and not deleted using the smartphone device (13.pdf and 17.docx), which are stored in the `com.dropbox.android/files/scratch` directory. These files were still physically stored on the SD card and are recovered by FTK. The files saved for offline access, JPEG thumbnails, and metadata remain unaltered.

4.1.2 iOS application

On the iOS device, a number of files stored in the Dropbox service were recovered from a subfolder called `Dropbox`, which can be found in the path `/Library/Caches`. The following files were recovered from this location: thumbnails of three JPEG images (01.jpg, 02.jpg, and 03.jpg); five files saved for offline access; and PDF and DOCX files, viewed but not deleted from the device (13.pdf and 17.docx). No other files stored in the Dropbox service were recovered from the iOS device.

The metadata artifacts recovered include an SQLite database, property list (plist) files, and text-based logs. These metadata artifacts described user activity and the files stored in the service. The main metadata repository is an SQLite database called `Dropbox.sqlite` which contains metadata about the files stored in the Dropbox service. This database can be recovered from a subfolder called `/Documents` from the application's root directory. The `ZCACHEDFILE` table within this database contains metadata related to the files recovered from the directory located at `/Library/Caches/Dropbox`. Fields identified from the `ZCACHEDFILE` are shown in Appendix A.

Additional metadata related to the files which were saved as "favorite" and user-specific information can be recovered from two property list (plist) files. The first plist file located from the path `/Library/Preferences/com.getdropbox.Dropbox.plist` contains the e-mail address used for the Dropbox account and information related to files which were saved as "favorite." The second plist file called `FavoriteFiles.plist` located from the path `/Library/Caches/` contains further information about files which were downloaded and saved as "favorite." Metadata which can be recovered from the `FavoriteFiles.plist` file includes the size of the file in bytes, the last modified time, the filename, and if the file has been deleted.

Two transaction logs were also recovered from the iOS device. The first log called `Analytics.log` records user-related activity and can be recovered from the path `/Library/Caches`. Each entry in the log is accompanied by a UNIX epoch timestamp. Figure 1 shows an example record from the `Analytics.log` file, which describes a PDF file which was viewed and then saved for offline access. The second log, `run.log`, which can be recovered from the path `/tmp/` contains additional information about service-related transactions performed by Dropbox. When the Dropbox iOS application cache is cleared on the device, the only files which remain are those five files saved for offline access. This action also affects the `Dropbox.sqlite`

{"retry":0,"favorite":false,"extension":"pdf","id":23,"cached":false,"ts":"1335445641.29","event":"file.view.start","size":1695706}
{"id":23,"ts":"1335445641.31","size":1695706,"event":"download.start","extension":"pdf","connection":"wifi"}
{"ts":"1335445641.84","screen":"DocumentViewController","event":"screen.view"}
{"id":23,"ts":"1335445657.75","size":1695706,"event":"download.success","extension":"pdf"}
{"id":23,"event":"file.view.success","ts":"1335445659.92"}
{"ts":"1335445669.71","screen":"SearchableFolderListController","event":"screen.view"}
{"ts":"1335445670.04","cached":true,"path_hash":912,"event":"metadata.load.start"}
{"path_hash":912,"event":"metadata.load.unchanged","ts":"1335445673.07"}

FIGURE 1

Analytics.log file describing a PDF file which was viewed and then saved for offline access using the Dropbox iOS application.

database. When the application's cache is cleared, the database only contains metadata for the five files which remain on the device. All other metadata artifacts remain unchanged.

4.2 DETAILED BOX FINDINGS

From the Android applications, the forensic toolkits recovered 15 files from version 1.6.7 and between four and six from version 2.0.2, depending on application and device manipulation. Five files were recovered from the iOS version of the Box application. The files which were recovered from the Box application are summarized in Table 4.

4.2.1 Android applications

On the Android devices, Box-related artifacts varied between the two versions of the application. Artifacts related to version 1.6.7 of the Box application were recovered from three locations on the SD card. The files saved for offline access (02.jpg, 06. mp3, 10.mp4, 14.pdf, and18.docx) were recovered from the path /Box/email_ address/, where email_address is the e-mail address used to register for the service. This version of the application caches any files which have been viewed on the device. These can be recovered from the directory /Android/data/com.box. android/cache/filecache. Fifteen files from the dataset were found in this directory. The files missing are those which are marked as "no manipulation" in Table 2. Thumbnails of all four JPEG images (01-04.jpg) can be recovered from a subfolder of the above location called /tempfiles/box_tmp_images.

Artifacts related to version 2.0.2 of the Box application were recovered from four locations on the SD card. This version of the Box application encrypts the cache folders used by the service. Three encrypted folders called dl_cache, dl_offline, and previews were recovered from the path /Android/data/com.box.android/ cache. No files from the dataset were recovered from these three folders. Thumbnails of all four JPEG images can be recovered from the path /data/data/com.box. android/cache/tempfiles/box_tmp_images. The six MP3 (05.mp3, 06.mp3, and 08.mp3) and MP4 (09.mp4, 10.mp4, and 12.mp4) files viewed on the device can be recovered from a subfolder called `working` located under the path `/data/data/com.box.android/cache`. This version of the Box application creates an additional folder of interest called `previews` which can be recovered from the path `/data/data/com.box.android/files/`. The `previews` folder contains PNG image files of "snapshots" of the text-based documents (DOCX and PDF) and JPEG images from the dataset which have been viewed using the device.

The metadata artifacts for both versions of the Box application can be recovered from the smartphone, which unless stated were the same for both versions of the application. The Box application creates a JSON file called `json_static_model_emailaddress_0`, where `emailaddress` is the e-mail address used to sign-up to the Box service. This file can be recovered from the path `/data/data/com.box.android/files/`. This JSON file contains property metadata about the files stored in this Box service. Fields identified from the JSON file are described in Appendix B.

A second location containing metadata related to the Box application can be found under the path `/data/data/com.box.android/shared_prefs`. This location contains a number of XML files which contain user and service-specific information. The files created in this location vary between the two versions of the application. The files recovered from this path include:

- *myPreference.xml*—which contains the authentication token associated with this particular account and the e-mail address used to register for the Box service. This can be recovered from both versions of the application.
- *Preview_Num_Pages.xml*—this file is related to the folder recovered from the path `/data/data/com.box.android/files/previews` and contains metadata such as the `mId` of the file whose "preview" is stored in the folder as well as the number of "preview" pages. This file can only be recovered from version 2.0.2 of the application.
- *Downloaded_Files.xml*—contains metadata about the files downloaded to the SD card from the Box service. `Long name` is the ID number assigned to that particular file and `value` is the date and time the file was deleted. The data and time is stored as a UNIX epoch timestamp. This filename is only valid for version 1.6.7 of the Box application. The file is renamed to `offlineFileSharedPreferences.xml` for version 2.0.2 but contains the same metadata related to files saved for offline viewing.

When the cache is cleared on the version 1.6.7 of the Box application, the contents of the `Android/data/com.box.android/cache/filecache` and the `/Box/email_address/` directories are deleted and recovered by FTK. All other files and metadata related to the Box service are not affected. When the cache is cleared on version 2.0.2 of the application, the three encrypted folders, the files stored in the `/data/data/com.box.android/cache` and `working` folders as well as the PNG "snapshot" files stored on the device are deleted but can be recovered using FTK. All other files and metadata related to the Box service are not affected.

4.2.2 iOS application

On the iOS device, the files and metadata related to the Box service can be recovered from three main locations under the application's root directory. The files saved for offline viewing (02.jpg, 06.mp3, 10.mp4, 14.pdf, and 18.docx) can be recovered from a subfolder located under the path /Documents/SavedFiles. The thumbnails of the four JPEG images stored in the Box service can be found in the subfolder /Library/Caches/Thumbnails. No other files from the dataset were recovered from the Box service. Metadata related to files stored in the service can be recovered from a SQLite database called BoxCoreDataStore.sqlite found under the subfolder /Documents/. This database contains a table called ZBOXBASECOREDATA, which includes property metadata for all 20 files in the dataset. The metadata which can be recovered from this database is described in more detail in Appendix B. Additional information which can be recovered from this database includes the username and e-mail address used to create the Box account and a unique authentication token assigned to the user account. Clearing the cache of the iOS Box application has no effect on the data or metadata stored on the device.

4.3 DETAILED SugarSync FINDINGS

On the HTC Desire, the forensic toolkits recovered 11 files from both Android versions of SugarSync and, depending on application and device manipulation, either 7 or 15 were recovered from the iOS version of the application. The results of which files were recovered from the SugarSync application are shown in Table 5.

4.3.1 Android applications

Files stored in the SugarSync service can be recovered from three locations on the SD card. These locations and their contents are valid for both versions of the Android SugarSync application. First, the three PDF files viewed on the smartphone (13. pdf, 14.pdf, and 16.pdf) can be recovered from a folder called /.sugarsync located in the root directory of the application. Second, the thumbnails of all four JPEG images, the three JPEG images viewed on the device (01.jpg, 02.jpg, and 04.jpg), and four document files viewed on the device (13.pdf, 16.pdf, 17.docx, and 20.docx) can be recovered from a subfolder called /.httpfilecache found in the above location. The third location is a folder called /MySugarSyncFolders located in the root directory of the application where the five files saved for offline viewing (02.jpg, 06. mp3, 10.mp4, 14.pdf, and 18.docx) can be found.

Metadata related to the SugarSync service can be recovered from two text-based transaction logs and an SQLite database. The metadata artifacts recovered from the device are valid for both versions of the Android application. The first transaction log is called sc_appdata and is recovered from the path /data/data/com.sharpcast. sugarsync/app_SugarSync/SugarSync/. This log contains the user's e-mail address used to register for the service, the unique ID assigned to the user, and a hash of the user's password.

The second transaction log is called sugarsync.log and is recovered from the path /data/data/com.sharpcast.sugarsync/app_SugarSync/SugarSync/log. This log contains events related to the SugarSync service. For example, entries in this log include the user authenticating with the service, the user downloading files on the device, and an MP4 file being "synced" from the service and then played on the device.

The SQLite database relevant to this application is called SugarSyncDB and can be recovered from the path /com.sharpcast.sugarsync/databases. This database has a table called rec_to_offline_file_XYZ, where *XYZ* is the unique ID number assigned to the user. This table contains metadata related to files saved for offline viewing and a UNIX epoch timestamp of when the file was saved for offline viewing.

When the cache is cleared on both versions of the Android application, the files affected are those stored under the location /.sugarsync/.httpfilecache, which are deleted from the SD card and recovered by FTK. All other files and metadata artifacts are not affected.

4.3.2 iOS application

Files and metadata related to the iOS version of the SugarSync application can be recovered from four locations on the device under the application's root directory. The SugarSync service caches the files viewed on the device in a folder called /tmp. Files from the dataset can be recovered in two subfolders within this location. The JPEG, MP4, DOCX, and PDF files viewed on the device can be recovered from a subfolder from the path /tmp/http_cache. The three MP3 files (05.mp3, 06.mp3, and 08.mp3) viewed on the device were recovered from the path /tmp/cache. The files which were saved for offline viewing (02.jpg, 06.mp3, 10.mp4, 14.pdf, and18.docx) can be recovered from a subfolder called /MyiPhone located under the /Documents directory.

The SugarSync service creates two main artifacts containing metadata related to the user and files stored in the service. These two artifacts can be recovered from the /Documents subfolder. Account-specific information such as the e-mail address used to register for the service can be recovered from a file called ringo.appdata. An SQLite database called Ringo.sqlite, contains a table called ZSYNCOBJECT. This table can be used to recover metadata related to the files saved for offline access. When the SugarSync application cache is cleared, the contents of the /http_cache folder are deleted. No other files and artifacts are affected when the cache is cleared.

4.4 DETAILED SYNCPLICITY FINDINGS

From the Android Syncplicity applications, the forensic toolkits recovered 9 files from version 1.7 and 15 from version 2.1.1. Depending on application and device manipulation, either 0 or 14 were recovered from the iOS version of the application. The results of which files were recovered from the Syncplicity application are shown in Table 6.

4.4.1 Android applications

On the Android devices, Syncplicity-related artifacts varied between the two versions of the application. For version 1.7 of the application, files were recovered from three locations on the SD card. Thumbnails of all four JPEG images can be recovered in the path `Android/data/ com.syncplicity.android/cache/cachefu/image_cache`. The files which were saved for offline viewing (02.jpg, 06.mp3, 10.mp4, 14.pdf, and 18.docx) can be recovered from a folder called `/Syncplicity`, which is stored in the root directory of the application. Version 1.7 of the application encrypts the cache folder used by the application. This folder can be recovered from the path `/Android/data/com.syncplicity.android/cache/private_syncp_file_cache_v3/encrypted/XYZ`, where *XYZ* is the unique ID assigned to the user. No files from the dataset were recovered from this location.

Further, files and metadata related to version 1.7 were recovered from four locations on the smartphone device. Files from the dataset can be recovered from the device in a directory located at the path `/data/data/com.syncplicity.android/files`. The files recovered from this location have been deleted; however, FTK was used to recover specific files from the dataset. The files recovered were the three JPEG files (01.jpg, 02.jpg, and 04.jpg) and the three DOCX files (17.docx, 18.docx, and 20.docx) viewed and not deleted on the smartphone device. No other files were recovered from this location.

Metadata artifacts related to version 1.7 which were recovered from the device included a text-based log, XML files, and an SQLite database. These artifacts contained metadata related to both user activity and the files stored in the service. A text-based transaction log called `0000000000000000000.log.gz.tmp` contains metadata about the application and its interaction with the cloud service. This log can be recovered from the path `/data/data/com.syncplicity.android/app_log_syncplicity`. An SQLite database called `CacheDatabase` can be recovered from the path `/data/data/com.syncplicity.android/databases`. This database contains a table called `Files`, which can be used to recover property metadata for all 20 files stored in the Syncplicity service. The information which can be recovered from the `Files` table can be seen in Appendix C.

A final source of metadata related to version 1.7 can be recovered from the path `/data/data/com.syncplicity/shared_prefs`. This folder contains the following XML files created by the application:

- *auth_prefs.xml*—this file contains the e-mail address used to register for the Syncplicity service;
- *file_cache_preferences(XYZ).deleted.xml*—XYZ is a number and 25 different files can be found with such a naming convention. The format of the file is shown in Figure 2 below. These XML files can be used as a mapping for the encrypted directory found on the SD memory card.

When the cache is cleared on version 1.7 of the application, the contents of the `cache/cachefu/image_cache` and encrypted folders are both deleted and recovered by FTK. No other files or artifacts are affected by the cache being cleared.

```
<?xml version="1.0" encoding="utf-8" standalone="yes" ?>
- <map>
    <long name="FILE_CACHE_PREFERENCES_LAST_DECRYPTED_FILE_VERSION_ID" value="145789448" />
    <string name="FILE_CACHE_PREFERENCES_LAST_DECRYPTED_FILE_NAME">016.pdf</string>
  </map>
```

FIGURE 2

Example of file_cache_preferences(XYZ).deleted.xml file mapping retrieved from the Syncplicity Android application.

For version 2.1.1 of the application, files from the dataset were again recovered from both the SD card. Thumbnails of all four JPEG images can be recovered from the directory /Android/data/ com.syncplicity.android/cache/cachefu/ image_cache. As with the previous version, version 2.1.1 of the application also encrypts the cache folder used by the Syncplicity service. This folder can be recovered from the path /Android/data/com.syncplicity.android/encrypted_storage. No files from the dataset were recovered from this location. This version of the Syncplicity application also contains a "decrypted" cache folder where 15 files from the dataset which were viewed on the device can be found. This folder can be recovered from the path /Android/data/com.syncplicity.android/temporary_decrypted_ storage.

The metadata artifacts recovered from version 2.1.1 of the application included an SQLite database, a text-based transaction log and XML files. These artifacts were recovered from the internal memory of the device. A text transaction log called 0000000000000000000.log.gz.tmp contains metadata about the application and its interaction with the cloud service. This log can be recovered from the path /data/data/com.syncplicity.android/app_log_syncplicity. An SQLite database called VIRTUAL_FILE_SYSTEM.db was recovered from the path /data/data/ com.syncplicity.android/databases. This database contains two tables of interest. The first table is called Files and contains metadata about all 20 files stored in the Syncplicity service. Appendix C shows the metadata which can be extracted from this table. The second table of interest is called Files_and_Folders_to_ Synchronize which contains the names of the files saved for offline viewing. The XML files recovered from version 2.1.1 of the application can be found in the same location as the files in version 1.7: /data/data/com.syncplicity/shared_prefs. The contents of the XML files recovered from this location are the same for those recovered from version 1.7.

When the cache is cleared on version 2.1.1 of the application, the contents of the /cache/cachefu/image_cache and encrypted folders are both deleted and recovered by FTK. The files recovered from the temporary_decrypted_storage folder are also affected when the cache is cleared. This folder now contains only the files which were saved for offline access. All other files have been deleted and recovered by FTK. The VIRTUAL_FILE_SYSTEM database is also affected when the cache is cleared. No other files and artifacts are affected by the cache being cleared.

4.4.2 iOS application

Files and metadata related to the iOS version of the Syncplicity application can be recovered from four locations on the device under the application's root directory. The only location where files from the dataset can be recovered from the iOS device is a cache folder created by the application under the path /Documents. Fourteen out of the fifteen files viewed on the device can be recovered from this folder. The MP4 file viewed and then deleted (12.mp4) was the only file viewed on the device and not recovered from this location.

Metadata related to the iOS application consists of an SQLite database, a plist file, and a text-based log. The SQLite database is called syncplicity.sqlite and can be recovered from the path /Documents/. This database contains a table called ZFILES which contains metadata about 18 files from the dataset; the entries which are missing from this table are related to files 04.jpg and 08.mp3. The property metadata, which can be recovered from this table, is shown in Appendix C. Metadata related to the user account can be recovered from a plist file called syncplicity.plist, which can be found in the path /library/preferences/com.syncplicity.ios. This plist file can be used to recover information such as the type of account used in the service (free or paid) along with the first and last name of the user who registered for the account. The final location of metadata related to the iOS Syncplicity application is a transaction log called syncplicity_0.log, which can be found in the location /library/caches. This log contains user and service-related transactions including files that were downloaded to the device and authentication token synchronization between the device and the Syncplicity service.

When the Syncplicity iOS application cache is cleared, the contents of the /Documents folder are deleted and no files are recovered from this location. No other files and artifacts are affected when the cache is cleared.

5 DISCUSSION

The results described in the previous section can be used to provide answers to the research questions proposed in Section 1. Forensic toolkits, including the Cellebrite UFED, can be used to recover data from a smartphone device that has accessed a cloud storage service. The proposed use of forensic and analysis toolkits currently available to the forensic community provides a practical solution for investigating cloud computing environments. The lack of forensic tools is commonly cited as a mainstream challenge for investigating cloud environments (Grispos et al., 2012; Taylor et al., 2010; Dykstra and Sherman, 2012). The results from this research suggest that end-devices, such as a smartphone, may contain evidence in relation to cloud storage services which may be important in an investigation, and that this resource should be considered and examined. Furthermore, the tools and methods used in the experiment to recover data from the smartphone device are widely used and accepted by the forensic community. It must be acknowledged that the files recovered from the smartphone devices present a "snapshot in time" of the dataset stored in the cloud storage service. A file which is recovered from a smartphone does not mean that the file still exists in the cloud storage service, but provides an indication that at a point in time this file was stored in the service.

The results indicate that it is possible to recover files, providing a snapshot in time, that indicates the existence of potential data that is stored in cloud services like Dropbox, Box, SugarSync, and Syncplicity. On the HTC Desire, both deleted and available files were recovered. No deleted files were recovered from the iPhone. Certain file types were recovered more than other types. For example, the results show that JPEG thumbnail images were produced on all the devices running the Android applications. Thumbnail images were also recovered from the Dropbox and Box applications on the iOS device. In general, very few MP3 and MP4 files were recovered from all three devices. It is also interesting to note that more deleted files were recovered from the Box and Syncplicity applications than Dropbox or SugarSync applications on the HTC Desire.

The recovery of files from a smartphone device is affected by the user's manipulation of the device and the cloud storage application. The Box iOS application and version 1.7 of the Android Syncplicity application were the only applications where there was no difference in the number of files recovered from the "active power state" and the "cache cleared state." The results also show that when the cache was cleared in all other instances, fewer files were recovered than from the "active power state." In the case of the iOS Syncplicity application, no files were recovered when the application's cache was cleared. User actions on specific files have shown to influence the recovery of these files. For example, if a file has been viewed using the smartphone there is the opportunity for it to be recovered using forensic toolkits. This is provided that the user has not deleted the file or cleared the application's cache. Files saved for offline access by the user can be recovered from the Android and iOS applications. There were two exceptions to recovering these files. The first is when the cache was cleared for the Syncplicity iOS application, none of the files saved for offline viewing were recovered. The second is when the cache was cleared for version 2.0.2 of the Android Box application, none of the files for offline viewing were recovered from any of the states. Deleted files were recovered from the Android devices. The recovery of these files is dependent upon them not being overwritten by new data on the SD memory card. No deleted files were recovered from the iOS device.

It is interesting to note that there are discrepancies in the number of files recovered depending on the version of the cloud storage service implemented on different mobile platforms and operating systems. While the versions of Dropbox produced the same number of files, there were vast differences between specific versions of Box, SugarSync, and Syncplicity. A summary of the total number of active power state files recovered from the Android and iOS devices by cloud application is shown in Figure 3. This table presents the files recovered from the active power state excluding thumbnails and deleted files.

Metadata was recovered from all the applications on all three devices. The metadata recovered included text-based transaction logs containing user and service activity, SQLite databases, and JSON files containing property metadata data related

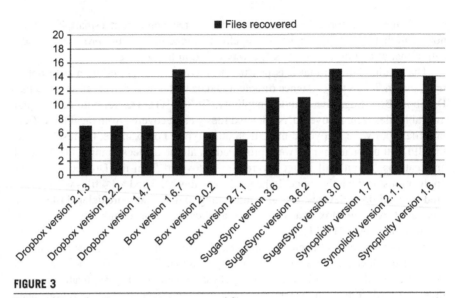

FIGURE 3

Total number of active power state recovered files.

to the files in the service, as well as XML files containing user-specific metadata such as login credentials. The metadata recovered from the devices can also present the investigator with a greater representation of the dataset stored in the cloud. For example, depending on the operating system platform, device and application manipulation, between 4 and 15 files were recovered from the iOS and Android Box applications. However, the metadata artifacts recovered from these applications run on the Android and iOS devices revealed information about files stored in the Box service which were not recovered from the device. The JSON files and SQLite databases recovered from the internal memory of these devices contained records for all 20 files stored in the Box service. The information which can be recovered includes the filenames and unique identification number assigned to each file as well as user-specific identification numbers and e-mail addresses used to register for the storage services. This metadata could help an investigator justify requesting a court order or warrant for a cloud storage provider to recover further files from the account being investigated (Chung et al., 2012).

Furthermore, using metadata artifacts recovered from the Box application, it is possible to download further files from the Box service. This can include files which were not recovered from the smartphone device itself. This information can be recovered from all three versions of the Box application which were included in this experiment. This is possible by constructing a direct link to the file stored in the Box service using the Box API (Box Platform Developer Documentation, n.d.). This direct link requires three pieces of information from the smartphone device, for example, from an Android device:

1. The authentication token, which can be recovered from the `myPreference.xml` file found in the path `/data/data/com.box.android/shared_prefs`. For

example, in Figure 4, the authentication token is shown as `<string name="authToken">u5es7xli4xejrh89kr6xu14tks6grjn3</string>`;

2. The unique file ID number called `mId`, which is the ID number assigned to each file stored in the service. This information can be recovered from the `json_static_model_ emailaddress_0` file stored in the directory `/data/data/com.box.android/files/`. The investigator requires the ID number for each file they wish to download from the Box service (Figure 5); and

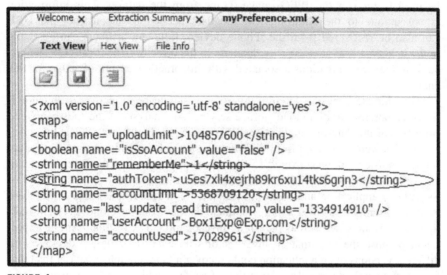

FIGURE 4

Metadata artifact containing the authentication token from Box Service.

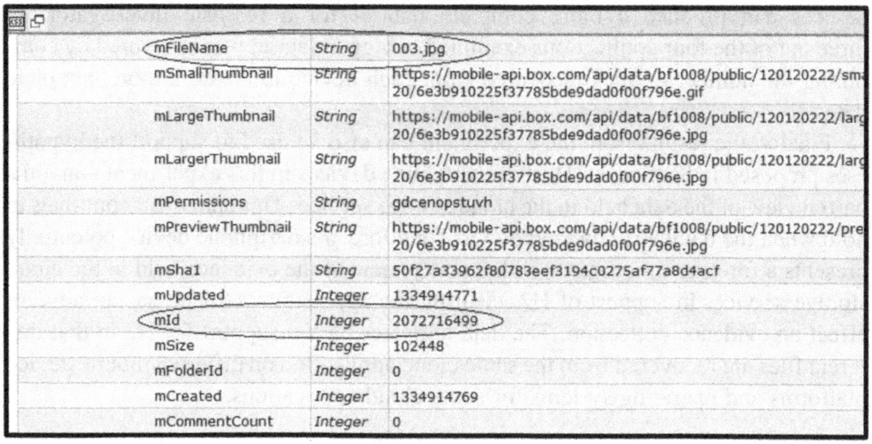

FIGURE 5

mID value for file 03.jpg.

3. A URL from the Box API (Box Platform Developer Documentation, n.d.): `https://www.box.net/api/1.0/download/auth_token/file_id`, where auth_token is the authentication token for the account and file_id is the `mId` number of the file to be downloaded.

This information can be combined to reconstruct a direct link, which will result in the file associated with the `mId` being downloaded. For example, the URL: https://mobile-api.box.com/api/1.0/download/u5es7xli4xejrh89kr6xu14tks6grjn3/2072716499 can be used to recover the JPEG image 03.jpg from the dataset. This information is not unique to the Android, and the data needed to reconstruct the URL can also be recovered from the iPhone device. Relevant artifacts can be found in the `BoxCoreDataStore.sqlite` database in the directory `/Documents/`. The privacy and legal implications associated with this practice are out of scope for this chapter.

The ultimate goal of a forensic investigator should be to recover as much evidence as possible from a cloud storage service. An analysis of the files recovered from two of the Android applications (Box and Syncplicity) has revealed that different files were recovered from different versions of these cloud storage applications. Forensic toolkits recovered 15 files from version 1.6.7 of the Box application and only 6 from version 2.0.2, while 5 files were recovered from version 1.7 of Syncplicity application and 15 from version 2.1.1. These results suggest that there is an opportunity to recover a more complete dataset from the cloud service if multiple devices are examined as part of an investigation. The results from the experiment propose the idea that an investigator who analyzes multiple devices with different versions of an application could recover a more complete dataset than that from just a single device. The proportion of artifacts which can be recovered from two or more devices are calculated as $|m_1 \cup m_2 \cup m_3|$, where m_n, are the devices which are being analyzed as part of a forensic investigation of cloud storage services. Preliminary data demonstrated in Table 7 supports the idea that multiple devices can produce a more complete dataset for a forensic investigator. In three out of the four applications examined, a bigger dataset was recovered by combining the number of files recovered from each device to create a more complete dataset.

Finally, the results from the experiment can also be used to support the hypotheses proposed in Section 1. H1, the smartphone devices in this experiment contain a partial view of the data held in the cloud storage service. This statement continues to hold when the device is powered down. Therefore, a smartphone device potentially presents a forensic investigator with a proxy view of the evidence held in the cloud storage service. In support of H2, clearing the application's cache has an adverse effect on evidence collection. The data indicates partial support for H3 in that different files are recovered from the same cloud application on different mobile device platforms and operating systems for some cloud applications.

Table 7 Total Files Recovered from Multiple Devices

Cloud Storage Service	m_1 {files recovered}	m_2 {files recovered}	m_3 {files recovered}	$|m_1 \cup m_2 \cup m_3|$ {total files recovered}
Dropbox	{2,6,10,13,14,16,17,18,20}	{2,6,10,13,14,16,17,18,20}	{2,6,10,13,14,17,18}	{2,6,10,13,14,16,17,18,20} = 9
Box	{1,2,4,5,6,8,9,10,12,13,14, 16,17,18,20}	{5,6,8,9,10,12}	{2,6,10,14,18}	{1,2,4,5,6,8,9,10,12,13,14, 16,17,18,20}=15
SugarSync	{1,2,4,6,10,13,14,16, 17,18,20}	{1,2,4,6,10,13,14,16,17, 18,20}	{1,2,4,5,6,8,9,10,12, 13,14,16,17,18,20}	{1,2,4,5,6,8,9,10,12,13,14,16, 17,18,20} = 15
Syncplicity	{2,6,10,14,17,18,20}	{1,2,4,5,6,8,9,10,12,13, 14,16,17,18}	{1,2,4,5,6,8,9,10,13, 14,16,17,18,20}	{1,2,4,5,6,8,9,10,12,13,14, 16, 17,18,20} = 15

6 CONCLUSIONS AND FUTURE WORK

The attractiveness of cloud computing is impacting where individuals and organizations store their data. The growing popularity of cloud storage services means that such environments will become an attractive proposition for cybercrime. This could result in an increase in demand for investigations of cloud storage services. However, the issue of conducting digital forensic investigations of cloud computing environments is an increasingly challenging and complex task. One of the biggest challenges facing investigators is the ability to identify and recover digital evidence from the cloud in a forensically sound manner. The remote and distributed nature of cloud computing environments means that the traditional offline approach to forensic evidence acquisition is invalidated. As a result, both industry and academia are beginning to examine different methods and techniques to investigate cloud computing environments.

This work presents the examination of end-devices such as smartphones, which have been used to access cloud storage services. The data recovered from these devices can be used by investigators as a proxy for potential evidence stored in cloud storage services. The effectiveness of this method is dependent on the operating system, specific cloud storage application implementation, and usage patterns. In other words, the potential recovery of data increases if a device has been used to view the files through a cloud storage application and the user has not attempted to clear the cache of recently viewed files.

Two advantages become apparent to using this investigative approach. First, the investigator can begin the chain of custody process when the device is seized and does not need to rely on the cloud provider to begin this process. Second, the tools and methods which have been used to recover data stored in cloud storage services are widely used by the forensic community. The recovery of metadata artifacts from the smartphone device can, in some scenarios, provide the investigator with insight into further data stored in a cloud service. The information recovered can also help justify a court order requesting assistance from the cloud storage provider to recover further files from the specific account.

Future research needs to be conducted to extend the analysis of smartphone hardware and operating systems, to increase the size and file types of the dataset and conduct research into other cloud storage services. The methodology proposed in this chapter can be extended to other smartphone devices and operating systems such as Windows Mobile and Blackberry devices. In addition, research can also be conducted to investigate other cloud storage services such as Google Drive, OneDrive, and CloudMe. The dataset used in future experiments can also be extended to include additional data types as well increasing the overall number of files and files of varied sizes.

The analytical findings from this research indicated that examining multiple devices and multiple versions of cloud storage applications can result in a more complete dataset being recovered. This experiment can be extended to examine a number of mobile devices such as tablets, iPads, iPods, and eBook readers. Other research questions that warrant investigating include the examination of usage patterns along with the construction of relevant timelines across multiple devices and cloud applications.

From a corporate security perspective, future work needs to examine the risk of data leakage that cloud storage applications can introduce to an organization. This research identifies the implications from a corporate policy perspective and determines if cloud applications introduce opportunities for data leakage in organizations. If so, what is the most effective way to minimize risk and maximize employee productivity? The results from this research provide the foundation for further development of security measures and policies for both cloud providers and smartphone users that mitigate the potential risk of data leakage.

APPENDIX A METADATA ARTIFACTS RECOVERED DROPBOX SERVICE

OS	Filename	Fields
Android	db.db	_data:_ path gives the location of where the file can be recovered from the device _modified:_ date and time file was uploaded to Dropbox service _is_favorite:_ boolean field which indicates if file has been saved as a "favorite," i.e., offline viewing _parent_path:_ parent directory for the file, root directory is the default _last_modified:_ last date and time the file was open/modified on the device, stored as a UNIX epoch timestamp _display_name:_ contains the name of the file as stored in the storage service _local_hash:_ MD5 hash of file
iOS	Dropbox.sqlite	_ZFAVORITE:_ boolean field which indicates if file has been saved as a "favorite" _ZSIZE:_ size of the file in bytes _ZVIEWCOUNT:_ number of times file has been viewed using the device _ZISTHUMBNAIL:_ boolean field which indicates if a thumbnail exists for the file _ZLASTVIEWEDDATE:_ date and time file was last viewed stored in MAC Absolute time _ZPATH:_ path and filename for particular file

APPENDIX B **METADATA ARTIFACTS RECOVERED BOX SERVICE**

OS	Filename	Fields
Android	json_static_model_emailaddress_0	*mThumbnail:* The URL of the thumbnail image of the file *mFileName:* Name of the file as stored in the Box service *mSha1:* SHA1 hash of the file *mUpdated:* UNIX epoch timestamp which states the last time the file was updated, in this experiment it is the last time the file was last viewed on the device *mId:* Unique ID number assigned to each file *mSize:* Size of the file in bytes *mCreated:* UNIX epoch timestamp which states when the file was created, in this experiment this is the time when the file was uploaded and stored in the Box service *mShared:* Boolean (True/False) filed which indicates if file has been shared.
iOS	BoxCoreDataStore.sqlite	*ZBOXID:* unique ID number assigned to each file stored in the Box service account *ZSIZE:* size of the file in bytes *ZFAVORITEOBJECT:* boolean field which indicates if file has been saved as a "favorite," i.e., offline viewing *ZUPDATED:* absolute timestamp showing when file was last updated *ZLASTDOWNLOADDATE:* absolute timestamp showing when file was last downloaded to device *ZCREATIONTIME:* absolute timestamp showing when file was stored in Box service *ZNAME:* name of file *ZSHA1:* SHA1 hash of file in Box service *ZLOCALURLSTRING:* directory location for file stored on the device *ZSTREAMINGURLSTRING:* URL location for file which can be accessed from Box service *ZLOCALSHA1:* SHA1 hash of file on device

APPENDIX C METADATA ARTIFACTS RECOVERED SYNCPLICITY SERVICE

OS	Filename	Fields
Android	CacheDatabase. sqlite Virtual_File_System. db	*fileId:* unique ID number assigned to each file stored in the service *name:* name of file *length:* size of the file in bytes *fileStatus:* boolean value which indicates if file is still stored in the service, if the value is 1 then file is still stored in service, if value is 0 then file has been deleted *thumbnailURL:* if file has a thumbnail, this is a working URL to the thumbnail stored in the service *File_ID:* unique ID number assigned to each file stored in the service *File_Name:* name of file *Is_Favorite:* boolean field which indicates if file has been saved as a "favorite," i.e., offline viewing *Server_Length:* size of file stored in service, presented in bytes *Local_Length:* size of file stored in device, presented in bytes *Is_Deleted:* boolean field which indicates if file has been deleted. *Thumbnail_URL:* if file has a thumbnail, this is a working URL to the thumbnail stored in the service
iOS	syncplicity.sqlite	*ZLENGTH:* size of file in bytes *ZFILEID:* unique ID number assigned to each file stored in the service *ZDELETED:* boolean field which indicates if file has been deleted *ZFILENAME:* name of file *ZEXT:* file type *ZTHUMBNAILURL:* if file has a thumbnail, this is a working URL to the thumbnail stored in the service

REFERENCES

Armbrust, M., Fox, A., Griffith, R., Joseph, A.D., Katz, R., Konwinski, A., Lee, G., Patterson, D., Rabkin, A., Stoica, I., Zaharia, M., 2009. Above the clouds: a Berkeley view of cloud computing. Technical report no. UCB/EECS-2009-28, University of California, Berkeley.

Grispos, G., Storer, T., Glisson, W.B., 2012. Calm before the storm: the challenges of cloud computing in digital forensics. Int. J. Digit. Crime Forensics 4 (2), 28–48.

Mager, T., Biersack, E., Michiardi, P., 2012. A measurement study of the Wuala on-line storage service. In: 2012 IEEE 12th International Conference on Peer-to-Peer Computing (P2P).

Mulazzani, M., Schrittwieser, S., Leithner, M., Huber, M., Weippl, E., 2011. Dark clouds on the horizon: using cloud storage as attack vector and online slack space. In: USENIX Security.

Hunsinger, D.S., Corley, J.K., 2012. An examination of the factors influencing student usage of Dropbox, a file hosting service. In: Proceedings of the Conference on Information Systems Applied Research, (CONISAR 2012), New Orleans, Louisiana, USA.

Hong, K., 2014. Dropbox reaches 300m users, adding on 100m users in just six months. Available from: http://thenextweb.com/insider/2014/05/29/dropbox-reaches-300m-users-adding-100m-users-just-six-months/.

Constine, J., 2012. Dropbox is now the data fabric tying together devices for 100M registered users who save 1B files a Day. Available from: http://techcrunch.com/2012/11/13/dropbox-100-million/.

MarketWire, 2012a. Box Triples Enterprise Revenue in 2011. Available from: Box Triples Enterprise Revenue in 2011, http://www.marketwire.com/press-release/box-triples-enterprise-revenue-in-2011-1605187.htm.

Mozy, 2014. Mozy—About Us. Available from, http://mozy.com/about/about-mozy.

Forrester Consulting, 2012. Personal Cloud Services Emerge to Orchestrate Our Mobile Computing Lives. A Forrester Consulting Thought Leadership Paper Commissioned By SugarSync. https://www.sugarsync.com/media/sugarsync-forrester-report.pdf.

CRN, 2012. Box Triples Enterprise Cloud Storage Revenue. Available from: Box Triples Enterprise Cloud Storage Revenue, http://www.crn.com/news/cloud/232400190/box-triples-enterprise-cloud-storage-revenue.htm.

MarketWire, 2012b. Box Sees 70 percent growth in legal services cloud adoption. Available from: http://www.marketwire.com/press-release/Box-Sees-70-Percent-Growth-in-Legal-Services-Cloud-Adoption-1749461.htm.

Subashini, S., Kavitha, V., 2011. A survey on security issues in service delivery models of cloud computing. J. Netw. Comput. Appl. 34 (1), 1–11.

Ibrahim, A.S., Hamlyn-Harris, J.H., Grundy, J., 2010. Emerging security challenges of cloud virtual infrastructure. In: APSEC 2010 Cloud Workshop, Sydney, Australia.

Jansen, W., Grance, T., 2011. Guidelines on Security and Privacy in Public Cloud Computing. NIST Special Publication 800-144. National Institute of Standards and Technology, Gaithersburg, Maryland, USA.

Grispos, G., Glisson, W.B., Pardue, J.H., Dickson, M., 2014. Identifying user behavior from residual data in cloud-based synchronized apps. In: Conference on Information Systems Applied Research (CONISAR 2014), Baltimore, Maryland, USA.

Grispos, G., Glisson, W.B., Storer, T., 2013a. Cloud security challenges: investigating policies, standards, and guidelines in a fortune 500 organization. In: European Conference on Information Systems 2013, Utrecht, Netherlands.

Zissis, D., Lekkas, D., 2012. Addressing cloud computing security issues. Futur. Gener. Comput. Syst. 28 (3), 583–592.

Kaufman, L.M., 2009. Data security in the world of cloud computing. IEEE Secur. Priv. 7 (4), 61–64.

Hay, B., Nance, K., Bishop, M., et al., 2011. Storm clouds rising: security challenges for IaaS cloud computing. In: 2011 44th Hawaii International Conference on System Sciences (HICSS), pp. 1–7.

Hay, B., Nance, K., Bishop, M., McDaniel, L., 2012. Are your papers in order? Developing and enforcing multi-tenancy and migration policies in the cloud. In: 2012 45th Hawaii International Conference on System Science (HICSS), pp. 5473–5479.

TrendMicro, 2011. Cloud Security Survey Global Executive Summary. http://www.tre ndmicro.com/cloud-content/us/pdfs/about/presentation-global-cloud-survey_exec-sum mary.pdf.

Kholia, D., Wegrzyn, P., 2013. Looking inside the (Drop) box. In: 2013 USENIX Annual Technical Conference, San Jose, CA, USA.

Reilly, D., Wren, C., Berry, T., 2010. Cloud computing: forensic challenges for law enforcement. In: International Conference for Internet Technology and Secured Transactions (ICITST), pp. 1–7.

Ruan, K., Carthy, J., Kechadi, T., Crosbie, M., 2011. Cloud forensics. In: Peterson, G., Shenoi, S. (Eds.), Advances in Digital Forensics VII. Springer, Boston, pp. 35–46.

Taylor, M., Haggerty, J., Gresty, D., Hegarty, R., 2010. Digital evidence in cloud computing systems. Comput. Law Secur. Rev. 26 (3), 304–308.

Brodkin, J., 2008. Gartner—Seven Cloud-Computing Security Risks. Available from: Gartner: Seven cloud-computing security risks, http://www.infoworld.com/d/security-cen tral/gartner-seven-cloud-computing-security-risks-853.

Jansen, W., Ayers, R., 2007. Guidelines on Cell Phone Forensics. NIST Special Publication 800-101. National Institute of Standards and Technology, Gaithersburg, Maryland, USA.

Grispos, G., Glisson, W.B., Storer, T., 2013b. Using smartphones as a proxy for forensic evidence contained in cloud storage services. In: Hawaii International Conference on System Sciences (HICSS-46) Grand Wailea, Maui, Hawaii, USA.

Biggs, S., Vidalis, S., 2009. Cloud computing: the impact on digital forensic investigations. In: International Conference for Internet Technology and Secured Transactions, ICITST 2009.

Google, 2011. Security Whitepaper: Google Apps Messaging and Collaboration Products. https://www.google.co.uk/work/apps/business/resources/docs/security-whitepaper.html. Available from: Google. "Google Security Whitepaper: Google Apps Messaging and Collaboration Products".

Dykstra, J., Sherman, A.T., 2012. Acquiring forensic evidence from infrastructure-as-a-service cloud computing: exploring and evaluating tools, trust, and techniques. In: Digital Forensic Research Workshop (DFRWS), Washington, DC, pp. S90–S98.

Delport, W., Olivier, M.S., Kohn, M., 2011. Isolating a cloud instance for a digital forensic investigation. In: Venter, H.S., Coetzee, M., Loock, M. (Eds.), 2011. Information Security for South Africa, Johannesburg, South Africa.

Amazon Web Services, 2011. About AWS Security Credentials. Available from: Amazon Web Services. "About AWS Security Credentials". http://docs.aws.amazon.com/ AWSSecurityCredentials/1.0/AboutAWSCredentials.html.

Amazon Web Services, 2014. Amazon Elastic Compute Cloud Microsoft Windows Guide. http://awsdocs.s3.amazonaws.com/EC2/2014-05-01/ec2-wg-2014-05-01.pdf.

Chung, H., Park, J., Lee, S., Kang, C., 2012. Digital forensic investigation of cloud storage services. Digit. Investig. 9 (2), 81–95.

Lee, J., Chung, H., Lee, C., Lee, S., 2012. Methodology for digital forensic investigation of iCloud. In: Park, J.H. et al., (Ed.), Information Technology Convergence, Secure and Trust Computing, and Data Management. Springer, Netherlands, pp. 197–206.

Quick, D., Choo, K.-K.R., 2013a. Dropbox analysis: data remnants on user machines. Digit. Investig. 10 (1), 3–18.

Quick, D., Choo, K.-K.R., 2013b. Digital droplets: Microsoft SkyDrive forensic data remnants. Futur. Gener. Comput. Syst. 29 (6), 1378–1394.

Quick, D., Choo, K.-K.R., 2014. Google drive: forensic analysis of data remnants. J. Netw. Comput. Appl. 40, 179–193.

Quick, D., Martini, B., Choo, R., 2013. Cloud Storage Forensics. Syngress, Amsterdam, the Netherlands.

Quick, D., Choo, K.-K.R., 2013c. Forensic collection of cloud storage data: does the act of collection result in changes to the data or its metadata? Digit. Investig. 10 (3), 266–277.

Martini, B., Choo, K.-K.R., 2013. Cloud storage forensics: ownCloud as a case study. Digit. Investig. 10 (4), 287–299.

Martini, B., Choo, K.-K.R., 2014. Distributed filesystem forensics: XtreemFS as a case study. Digit. Investig. 11 (4), 295–313.

Biggs, S., Vidalis, S., 2010. Cloud computing storms. Int. J. Intell. Comput. Res. 1 (1/2), 61–68.

Phillips, A., 2011. E-evidence and international jurisdictions: creating laws for the 21st century. In: 2011 44th Hawaii International Conference on System Sciences (HICSS), pp. 1–5.

Grispos, G., Storer, T., Glisson, W.B., 2011. A comparison of forensic evidence recovery techniques for a windows mobile smart phone. Digit. Investig. 8 (1), 23–36.

Glisson, W., Storer, T., Mayall, G., Moug, I., Grispos, G., 2011. Electronic retention: what does your mobile phone reveal about you? Int. J. Inf. Secur. 10 (6), 337–349.

Hoog, A., 2011. Android Forensics—Investigation, Analysis and Mobile Security for Google Android. Syngress, Waltham, MA.

Levinson, A., Stackpole, B., Johnson, D., 2011. Third party application forensics on apple mobile devices. In: 2011 44th Hawaii International Conference on System Sciences (HICSS), pp. 1–9.

Morrissey, S., 2010. iOS Forensic Analysis: for iPhone, iPad, and iPod Touch. Apress, New York.

Cellebrite. Cellebrite UFED. Available from: Cellebrite UFED, http://www.cellebrite.com/mobile-forensics-products/forensics-products.html.

Micro Systemation. What is XRY?. Available from: What is XRY?, http://www.msab.com/xry/what-is-xry.

Distefano, A., Me, G., 2008. An overall assessment of mobile internal acquisition tool. Digit. Investig. 5 (Suppl.), S121–S127.

Paraben, n.d. Device Seizure. Available from: Device Seizure, http://www.paraben.com/device-seizure.html.

Hengeveld, W.J., 2011. RAPI Tools. Available from: RAPI Tools, http://itsme.home.xs4all.nl/projects/xda/tools.html.

Gartner, 2012. Gartner says worldwide sales of mobile phones declined 2 percent in first quarter of 2012; previous year-over-year decline occurred in second quarter of 2009. Available from: Gartner Says Worldwide Sales of Mobile Phones Declined 2 Percent in First Quarter of 2012; Previous Year-over-Year Decline Occurred in Second Quarter of 2009, http://www.gartner.com/it/page.jsp?id=2017015.

Department of Defense Computer Forensics Lab. dcfldd. 2006; Available from: http://dcfldd.sourceforge.net/.

Lessard, J., Kessler, G., 2010. Android forensics: simplifying cell phone examinations. Small Scale Digit. Dev. Forensics J. 4 (1), 1–12.

Zdziarski, J., 2008. iPhone Forensics: Recovering Evidence, Personal Data, and Corporate Assets. O'Reilly Media, Incorporated, Sebastopol, California, USA.

Box Developer Documentation, 2015. Get Started with the Box API. Available from: https://developers.box.com/get-started/.

Integrating digital forensic practices in cloud incident handling: A conceptual Cloud Incident Handling Model

Nurul Hidayah Ab Rahman[a,b], Kim-Kwang Raymond Choo[a]

*Information Assurance Research Group, School of Information Technology and Mathematical Sciences, University of South Australia, Adelaide, Australia[a]
Information Security Department, Faculty of Computer Science and Information Technology, University of Tun Hussein Onn Malaysia, Batu Pahat, Johor, Malaysia[b]*

1 INTRODUCTION

The trend of organizations moving sensitive data to the cloud infrastructure has resulted in an urgent need to ensure that security and privacy safeguards are in place, as cloud services are potential criminal targets due to the amount of sensitive organization data stored in the cloud. A successful security incident occurrence or breach can cause direct (e.g., theft of intellectual property and customer data) and/or indirect losses (e.g., reputational and legal) (Böhme, 2010; Tsalis et al., 2013) to organization assets, and can have significant financial implications.

A proactive incident handling strategy is one key approach to mitigate risks to the confidentiality, integrity and availability of assets, as well as minimizing loss (e.g., financial, reputational, and legal) in a dynamic cloud environment. This is consistent with the Cloud Security Alliance (CSA) report entitled "Security Guidance for Critical Areas of Focus in Cloud Computing," which highlights three critical focus areas, namely, incident response, notification, and remediation (Cloud Security Alliance, 2011). The National Institute and Standards Technology (NIST) defines incident handling as a lifecycle consisting of four phases as follows: (1) preparation; (2) detection and analysis; (3) containment, eradication, and recovery; and (4) post-incident activity (Cichonski and Scarfone, 2012).

In investigating and responding to computer security incident, digital forensics can play a crucial role (Cichonski and Scarfone, 2012; Freiling and Schwittay, 2007; Gurkok, 2013). The collection, analysis, and interpretation of digital data associated with a computer security incident during an incident handling process, for example, overlap with the collection, analysis, and presentation of evidential data in a digital forensic process (Freiling and Schwittay, 2007). In addition, ensuring that a system is in a state of forensic readiness (i.e., capable of determining in advance what evidence is required when an incident occurs, Pangalos et al., 2010) will expedite incident handling as the incident responder would know where evidential data exists and how to go about collecting the required data. Forensic readiness also aligns with the proactive element of incident handling in the Preparation phase.

In this chapter, we propose a Cloud Incident Handling Model that integrates digital forensic practices into incident handling strategies, which would allow cloud service providers (CSPs) and organization cloud service users (CSUs) to respond to incidents more effectively. We then demonstrate the utility of the model using an ownCloud (an open-source private Storage as a Service solution) simulation (similar to the approach of Monfared and Jaatun, 2012).

In the following section, we will outline the background which includes challenges of incident handling in the cloud computing environment, as well as related work. We then present our proposed model in Section 3, before describing our case study in Section 4. The last section concludes this chapter.

2 BACKGROUND
2.1 CLOUD COMPUTING INFRASTRUCTURE

In cloud computing, there are four deployment models (i.e., private cloud, public cloud, community cloud, and hybrid cloud) and three architectures (i.e., Software as a Service (SaaS), Platform as a Service (PaaS), and Infrastructure as a Service (IaaS)) (Mell and Grance, 2011).

Buyya et al. (2013) explained that the underlying cloud computing infrastructure consists of several cloud stacks (see Figure 1). The lowest stack or system infrastructure, Cloud Resources, consists of hundreds to thousands of nodes to form a datacentre. Virtualization technology is deployed in the core middleware to create the distributed infrastructure, and the Cloud Hosting Platform supports main functions of infrastructure management such as usage metering, billing, and accounting. IaaS is formed from the underlying system infrastructure and core middleware. In user-level middleware, cloud service is offered as a development platform, referred to PaaS, and CSU develops applications to run on the core middleware infrastructure. The top stack represents user applications, or referred to SaaS, that deliver cloud applications to CSU.

One of the key differences between cloud and "traditional" (or in-house) infrastructure is the scope of user control as the roles and responsibility over cloud resources are segregated between the CSP and CSU (Pearson, 2013; Jansen and Grance, 2011). In Figure 1, we adopted the cloud stack architecture from Buyya et al. (2013) and the scope of control from Jansen and Grance (2011) to explain the control scope between the CSP and CSU, for each stack of the cloud architecture.

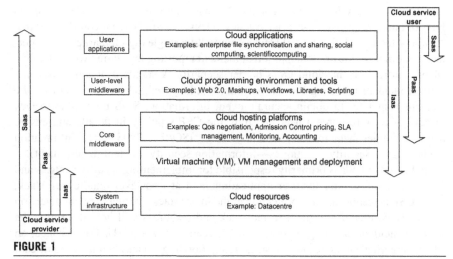

FIGURE 1

The scope of control between CSP and CSU on cloud computing architecture.

Adopted from Buyya et al. (2013) and Jansen and Grance (2011).

The range of scope and control over the stack of resources is represented by the arrows. The CSU will have more control over the resources as the stack gets lower. For example, the CSU will have less control over the resources in SaaS but more control in IaaS; and conversely the CSP will have more control in SaaS but less control in IaaS. The control over resources determines the scope of the capability of the entity (CSU or CSP) to implement and manage security mechanisms. In PaaS, for example, the CSU is responsible for their application security protection (e.g., secure coding, and encryption) while the CSP is responsible for hypervisor protection (e.g., hypervisor vulnerability management). The shared responsibility of security control implementation and management needs to be taken into consideration in planning cloud incident handling strategies.

2.2 INCIDENT HANDLING IN CLOUD COMPUTING

A notable challenge between traditional incident response and cloud incident response is that different cloud architectures require different strategies. As highlighted in the report by CSA (Cloud Security Alliance, 2011), the identification control scope on cloud architecture can facilitate a mapping of roles and responsibilities of incident handling for both CSP and CSU.

As CSP has more control of cloud stacks in SaaS, CSU relies on the CSP to provide proactive mechanisms such as log and monitoring, vulnerability scanning, patch management, forensic readiness plan, and incident detection/prevention tool. As pointed out by Grobauer and Schreck (2010), CSU, particularly small-to-medium sized organizations, may have limited knowledge of the underlying infrastructure, thus it is not likely for them to conduct forensic analysis in-house. The European Network and Information Security Agency (Dekker et al., 2013) recommended that "to allow for a level playing field and a competitive single digital market it is important to harmonize the implementation of incident reporting legislation whenever possible," particularly in cloud cross-border scenario. A standard or guidelines that include incident reporting format, terminology, knowledge-base, can facilitate the incident responder to obtain accurate event information. SaaS users (due to lack of control over resources) need to study the CSP's policy in details and ensure that it complies with industry standards (e.g., ISO/IEC 27035:2011 Information Technology—Security techniques—Information security incident management).

In PaaS, the CSU is primarily responsible for implementing security controls and forensic readiness plan for user applications and at user-level middleware stack, while CSP is responsible for protection at the lower stack. During incident detection and analysis, identifying the affected stack and resources will help determine the scale of incident handling involvement between CSP and CSU. For instance, an attack targeting cloud resources stack (e.g., flooding attack) requires significant involvement from the CSP. Although the CSU has more control at user-level middleware stack and, most probably, can conduct client-side forensics (Zimmerman and Glavach, 2011), assistance from CSP, for example, to acquire the relevant log files from the server, is still required. For example, Amazon CloudWatch, a cloud application that can be deployed by the CSU to collect and track metrics, collect and monitor log files, and set event alarms (Amazon Web Services, 2014), but it would have added cost for the CSU.

IaaS most closely resembles the "traditional" in-house computing infrastructure. Generally, CSU can undertake forensic examination at their end using existing procedures and best practices such as those described in Martini and Choo (2014) and Quick et al. (2014). A virtual machine (VM) snapshot, for example, can serve as an acquisition image (Grobauer and Schreck, 2010; Zimmerman and Glavach, 2011). CSP incident handling responsibilities such as vulnerability and patch management rely on the system infrastructure stack.

When formulating incident handling strategy, one also needs to take into consideration the cloud deployment model. In a public cloud model, for instance, undertaking incident response and forensic examination will be most challenging due to geographical constraints.

2.3 RELATED WORK

Other studies focus on specific incident handling theme(s) such as incident detection and prevention (Modi et al., 2013; Patel et al., 2013; Khorshed et al., 2012), monitoring and vulnerability management (Kozlovszky et al., 2013; Monfared and Jaatun, 2011), and risk management (Aleem and Sprott, 2013; Albakri et al., 2014). Only a few studies, however, discuss cloud incident handling from a technical perspective. Grobauer and Schreck (Grobauer and Schreck, 2010) pointed out various cloud-specific challenges and suggested suitable approaches from both CSP and CSU perspectives. Monfared and Jaatun (2012) demonstrated that NIST incident handling guidelines can be adapted for cloud incident handling, in their case study. In the latter, the authors simulated an OpenStack environment (IaaS) and introduce cloud-specific strategies. Both studies (Pangalos et al., 2010; Monfared and Jaatun, 2012) adapt existing incident handling phases by introducing cloud-specific strategies in each phase.

In the automated cloud incident management system of Gupta et al. (2009), multi-dimensional knowledge is the key component while the system of Sarkar et al. (2011) designed for a PaaS environment used a finite state-based machine to deliver an integrated monitoring and event correlation system.

Cloud forensics research has received considerable attention in recent years (Quick et al., 2014; Ruan et al., 2011; Quick and Choo, 2013; Birk and Wegener, 2011; Martini and Choo, 2012), and a small number of studies have highlighted the need to integrate incident handling and digital forensics due to overlapping tools and processes (Freiling and Schwittay, 2007; Mell and Grance, 2011; Buyya et al., 2013). Although there have been attempts to integrate both incident response and digital forensics (Kohn et al., 2013; Mitropoulos et al., 2006; Pilli et al., 2010), there has been no published cloud incident handling strategy that integrates digital forensics practices. This is the gap we attempt to fill in this chapter. We also explained how the Situational Crime Prevention Theory (Clarke, 1997) can be used in our model to design mitigation strategies.

3 CLOUD INCIDENT HANDLING MODEL: A SNAPSHOT

In our design of the proposed model (see Figure 2), we draw upon principles and practices from incident handling and digital forensics. The proposed model consists of six phases, namely, Preparation (integrated with forensic readiness principles), Identification, Assessment (integrated with forensic collection and analysis practices), Action and Monitoring, Recovery, and Evaluation (integrated with forensic presentation practices). This model is an extension of our recently published conceptual Cloud Incident Handling Model in Rahman and Choo (2015). The earlier work discussed the model in four major phases, namely, preparation, detection and analysis, incident response, and postincident, as well as the involved costs at each phase. In this study, the Detection and Analysis and the Incident Response phases are expanded to include Identification and Assessment, and Action and Monitoring, and Recovery, respectively.

Preparation phase integrates forensic readiness requirements. The phase has a proactive element such as understanding and preparing the necessary tools or resources required to protect and secure a cloud's systems or networks. Activities associated with forensic readiness include the identification of potential sources of evidential data (e.g., log files, network traffic records, CSU devices, off-site data centers, continually tracking authentication) in a cloud environment (e.g., CSPs,

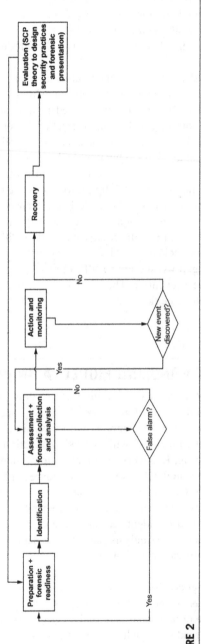

FIGURE 2

Our proposed cloud incident handling model.

internet service providers, and third parties) and deciding where identified potential evidence sources should be stored.

Identification phase begins immediately after an incident or vulnerability is detected and reported, either by human (cloud users or CSP's personnel) or automated tool. Unlike Preparation, this phase consists of reactive incident handling strategies.

In the Assessment phase, information from the received reports will be assessed to determine if the incident is a false alarm, and the potential impact(s) to the cloud's core services and assets. If it is determined to be a false alarm, the process will be terminated. The integrated conceptual cloud forensic framework from Martini and Choo (2013) is implemented to enable forensic investigations. Forensic examiners will undertake the evidence collection process from the potential sources identified in the Preparation phase. Once the evidence has been preserved and collected, the forensic analysis process will then commence.

Action and monitoring phase involves the execution and monitoring of the appropriate response strategy in an effective and timely manner as determined in the incident escalation strategy. It is important to note that the response strategy (i.e., action) may vary between incidents and incidents assigned to different priority levels.

Recovery phase involves the restoration of system operation back to normal at both logical and physical levels. Evaluation phase involves a formal evaluation (e.g., postmortem meeting) where issues such as the nature of the incidents, a review of what had occurred, the intervention techniques, and the (in) effectiveness and lessons learnt are examined.

4 CASE STUDY SIMULATION: ownCloud

ownCloud allows users to deploy their own storage service in a private cloud environment (Saha, 2012). Users of ownCloud can access their account and data using the following options:

(i) Web-based front end application with username and password;
(ii) Client-based application such as a mobile application that allows files to be synchronized between the server and the client devices; and
(iii) WebDAV via Web browser.

In our case study, we deploy the Security Information and Event Management (SIEM) system that allows us the capability to have real-time monitoring, correlation of events, issuing of alert notification, and historical reporting of security events (e.g., by gathering data from many sources such as network, system, and appliances) (Suarez-Tangil et al., 2014). The cloud's VM instances and internal network environment are simulated using Oracle VirtualBox.

For attack setting, we consider a malicious insider as an insider compromise usually has the greatest impact due to the likelihood of them circumventing existing controls (e.g., the incident involving Edward Snowden, a former US National

Security Agency contractor). In 2013, for example, CSA identified the malicious insider as one of the top threats to cloud computing (Cloud Security Alliance, 2013). The simulation of an insider attack includes the following steps:

- Step 1: Reconnaissance—This is typically the first step in an attack lifecycle, which involves scanning activities such as port scanning of networks and machines to map the target network (Trček et al., 2010). An insider will be in an advantageous position due to his/her understanding of the system as well as having the appropriate credentials and rights to the internal system.
- Step 2: Define the target—Based on information from reconnaissance, the attacker will then select and define the target. For this study, the target will be the ownCloud server.
- Step 3: Discovery—Involves the identification of hardware and software vulnerabilities on the server that can be exploited.
- Step 4: Escalate privileges to conduct the attack—For this study, we will simulate an offline password attack.
- Step 5: Establish foothold by using tool(s) or other techniques to launch the password attack to gain unauthorized remote access.
- Step 6: Capture and exfiltration—The attacker will then capture username and password, and exfiltrate sensitive information from the ownCloud server. This results in the violation of data confidentiality and integrity.
- Step 7: Delete audit trails.

The findings of each phase of our proposed model are discussed in the next section.

4.1 PREPARATION AND FORENSIC READINESS

Risk assessment is the key task in the Preparation phase and includes classifying assets, vulnerabilities, and threats. The first step is to identify important assets connected to the organization network and incorporate them into the SIEM database. The assets can be automatically discovered through network address range and classified into host, host group, network, and network group. Value of each asset must then be defined according to the asset criticality, for instance, ranging between 0 (not important) and 5 (very important). For this case study, the value of the ownCloud server is the highest due to the amount of sensitive data stored on the server as well as its role in ensuring service availability. The asset value of the Head of Department's workstation (in an organization) is another example asset that should be set higher than the subordinates' workstation due to the data confidentiality concern.

Vulnerability assessment process commences as soon as asset inventory tasks are completed. The Common Vulnerability Scoring System (CVSS) is one example approach to define vulnerability severity and determine urgency. From the identified vulnerabilities, we can attempt to address potential threats using appropriate mitigation strategies (e.g., system patching and installing security update). For instance, as ownCloud is a Web-based technology, existing Web vulnerabilities might expose the Web server to Cross-Site Scripting, a common Web attack.

Risk assessment outcomes facilitate forensic readiness decision in determining the required digital forensic practices and tools. For example, the assets' architecture specifies potential location of evidential data at the server and client devices (e.g., mobile devices used to access cloud services). Based on the findings from the first academic in-depth server and client forensic investigations of an ownCloud installation in Grobauer and Schreck (2010), for example, potential evidential data on client devices include sync and file management metadata, cache files, cloud service and authentication data, encryption metadata, browser artifacts, and mobile client artifacts. Identified potential evidential data on the ownCloud server include administrative and file management metadata, stored files uploaded by the user, encryption metadata, and cloud logging and authentication data.

Monitoring at both host-based and network-based levels must be proactive and continuous (e.g., by using Intrusion Detection and Prevention System) to minimize risk to data at-rest and in-transit. The identification of data at-rest and in-transit flow is essential to determine the required data protection mechanisms. For our case study, an open source of host-based intrusion detection system (i.e., OSSEC) is deployed at the host-based level, and an open-source network-based intrusion detection and prevention system (i.e., Snort) for network monitoring. Events generated by OSSEC and Snort are displayed on event logs in a real-time environment, which facilitate the detection of an attack or security breach.

4.2 IDENTIFICATION

During the reconnaissance stage (from attack simulation) in our case study, the OSSEC agent detected network scanning activities, originating from an internal IP address (see Table 1). This typically requires further investigation as the user is an internal employee.

To proceed to the next phase in our case study, we assume that no further action was undertaken to investigate the detected network scanning activities. Subsequently, Snort detected a "HTTP Password detected unencrypted" event targeting the ownCloud server (see Figure 3). Both events originated from the same legitimate

Table 1 An Example of Insecure SSH Connection Attempt Event

Signature	Date GMT+9:30	Sensor	Source	Destination
ossec: SSH insecure connection attempt (scan)	2014-08-18 05:40:55	alienvault	Host-192-168-0-3	alienvault

	Signature	Date GMT+9:30 ▲	Sensor	Source	Destination	Asset S → D	Risk
	snort: "ET POLICY Outgoing Basic Auth Base64 HTTP Password detected unencrypted"	2014-08-18 06:28:50	alienvault	Host-192-168-0-3:44855	Nurul-PC:80	3→2	0

FIGURE 3

An event of password detected unencrypted.

user. An incident alarm should be created by generating the ticketing system that may include person in charge, status, priority, actions, and incident workflow tracking. Further investigation will be undertaken in the next phase, Assessment.

4.3 ASSESSMENT, FORENSIC COLLECTION, AND ANALYSIS

In this phase, the assigned personnel will conduct preliminary investigation of the reported incident. Activities in this phase diligently incorporate forensic collection and analysis processes. SIEM tools, such as OSSIM, can be used to facilitate incident investigations, for example, flagging known vulnerabilities and the associated patches. This is consistent with findings from Kohn et al. (2013) and Freiling and Schwittay (2007) which further support the suggestion that there are overlaps between incident handling and digital forensic practices.

In our case study using OSSIM, we were able to gather information relating to the host such as Asset Report, Traffic, and All Events from the Host. Further event information such as event detail, snort rule detection, Knowledge Database (KDB), and captured packet in *pcap* format can be viewed on OSSIM's Forensic Console. From the captured packet (see Figure 4), it is determined that the attacker uses Hydra (an open-source tool to perform brute force on a remote authentication service). This suggests a deliberate attack by a malicious insider. Cloud logging and authentication data should be collected as they may offer further insights into the incident.

At this stage, management would need to decide whether to lodge a police report or proceed to internal disciplinary committee and (close the loophole), if the decision is to:

- lodge a police report—forensic investigation would likely be undertaken by law enforcement agencies and findings will be used in judicial proceedings, or
- internal disciplinary action—forensic investigation will be undertaken by an in-house forensic team or a third-party forensic organization. Results will be presented during the postmortem (or incident closure) meeting and may be used to dismiss the employee.

An overview of Assessment analysis and tasks is illustrated in Figure 5. The attack actor in our case study is a malicious insider who exploits technology as the attack

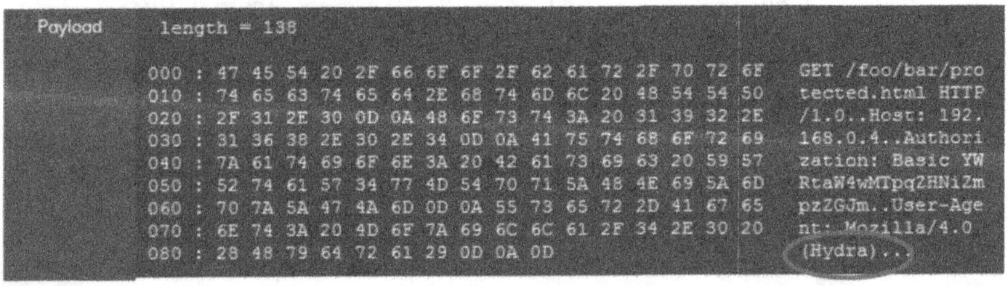

FIGURE 4

Suspicious network packet.

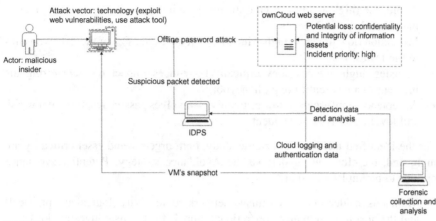

FIGURE 5

An overview of the assessment phase.

vector to launch an offline password attack against the ownCloud Web server. Confidentiality and integrity of information assets are the potential consequences and this is considered a high priority incident. The compromised Web server, analysis data from IDPS (e.g., log capturing, event correlation), and the malicious VM are three potential evidential data sources in the forensic collection and analysis tasks. Findings from the investigation and the gathered evidence need to be updated into the ticket detail, and the ticket must now be assigned to the responsible team in the next phase, Action and Monitoring.

4.4 ACTION AND MONITORING

The Action phase is designed to contain the incident in a timely and effective manner. Cloud settings are able to facilitate response strategies (Grobauer and Schreck, 2010). For example, pause and snapshot, two VM features can facilitate the execution of strategies to prevent further exploitation in both the attacker's VM (e.g., pause current activities for forensic analysis) and the compromised VM (e.g., block malicious activities).

As the incident identified in the previous phase was classified high priority, the response strategies must be undertaken immediately. It is important to note that new security incident might be discovered in this phase; thus, the flow will return to the Assessment phase (i.e., an iterative process). In our case study, however, no new event is detected.

Adopting the response strategy model of Anuar et al. (2012), we select the appropriate strategy based on the incident's urgency and asset criticality level. The four response options are as follows:

- Avoidance (high urgency, high criticality)—eliminates risk by reducing factors that have direct influences.
- Mitigation (low urgency, high criticality)—reduces the size of the risk exposures to the lowest risk.
- Transfer (high urgency, low criticality)—reduces impact by transferring the incident to a new entity (e.g., honeypot).
- Acceptance (low urgency, low criticality)—involves passive response to low risk and low impact type of incident.

For the identified incident in our case study, both urgency and asset criticality are high, and, therefore, we undertake the Avoidance strategy. Potential avoidance options to be implemented are:

- Malicious insider's host—terminate network connectivity (logical and physical) and the host must remain in operational model (for forensic investigation), pause or snapshot the VM image.
- Server—investigates the server instance for other malicious activities (e.g., file deletion). Based on the outcome of the investigation, actions such as termination or limiting network connectivity, and shutting down the compromised server may need to be undertaken.

4.5 RECOVERY

During the Recovery phase, we need to restore normal cloud service and avoid disrupting existing security protection mechanisms. Cloud infrastructures can facilitate recovery strategy. For example, having multiple server instances (particularly in Infrastructure as a Service) can minimize downtime impact if the compromised instance needs to be shut off.

In the context of our case study, one may undertake the following actions to avoid further compromise:

- Other server instances need to operate normally to ensure service availability and the cloud service needs to be monitored for any performance issue (e.g., due to the security breach or identified incident).
- Require users to change their ownCloud account password.
- Implement two-factor authentication.
- Install software and hardware patches.
- Deploy security mechanisms such as Secure Socket Layer to reduce attacks such as man-in-the-middle.
- Review priority and reliability value of events.

4.6 EVALUATION AND FORENSIC PRESENTATION

A postmortem meeting will be held to discuss the chain of events and present outcomes from the disciplinary committee (if required to deal with a malicious insider). The meeting may encompass various cloud stakeholders depending on the particular cloud ecosystem. In the case of private cloud, for instance, external parties may not be involved as it is managed internally. Findings will need to be written up as a report according to the requirements of the jurisdiction that the organization operates in.

"Lesson-learnt" can be explained from the perspectives of People, Process, and Technology, for example:

- People—enforce separation of duties, organize information security awareness workshop (specifically in cloud computing as employees may lack of understanding of risks and threats in cloud-based workflow)
- Process—review and update policies of Human Resources, and Bring Your Own Device.
- Technologies—enforce better security mechanisms to internal and external networks.

In this phase, criminological theory such as the Situational Crime Prevention Theory (Clarke, 1997) can also be used to create conditions unfavorable to crime with the aim of deterring future incidents or breaches. Findings from the "Lesson-learnt" can then be integrated into the following five broad categories (comprising 25 techniques) of the Situational Crime Prevention Theory:

(1) Increasing perceived effort: Target hardening, controlling access to facilities, screen exits, deflecting offenders, and controlling tools/weapons;
(2) Increasing perceived risks: Extending guardianship, assisting natural surveillance, reducing anonymity, utilizing place managers, and strengthening formal surveillance;
(3) Reducing rewards: Concealing targets, removing targets, identifying properties, disrupting markets, and denying benefits;
(4) Removing excuses: Reducing frustrations and stress, avoiding disputes, reducing emotional arousal, neutralizing peer pressure, and discouraging imitation; and
(5) Reducing provocations: Setting rules, posting instructions, alert conscience, assisting compliance, and controlling drugs and alcohol (which we will replace with "provocation factors").

Measures that organizations can undertake to ensure a secure cloud environment are outlined in Table 2.

5 CONCLUDING REMARKS

One may say with confidence that our increasing reliance on cloud services means that the cloud infrastructure will continue to be exploited for criminal purposes by malicious actors, both terrestrial and cyber. Although both CSP and CSU need to take cyber threats seriously, it would be unrealistic to expect an incident-proof cloud computing environment or infinite resources to action upon all potential threats and risks identified. One key measure that CSP and CSU can adopt is having in place an

Table 2 Security Practices Based on Situational Crime Prevention Theory

Increase the Perceived Effort	Increase the Perceived Risks	Reduce the Rewards	Remove Excuses	Reduce Provocations
Target hardening such as installing antivirus software and software updates on corporate devices regularly (e.g., daily)	*Extending guardianship* by not collecting personal information not related to the functions or activities of the device or users of the cloud service	*Concealing targets* by securing corporate devices when not in use, using a different e-mail address for suspicious account sign-up, etc.	*Reducing frustrations and stress* by providing a transparent online reporting system where users can report malicious activities including those of their colleagues for remediation action, etc.	*Setting rules* such as best practices to ensure the security and privacy of organizational data
Access control such as securing corporate devices when not in use	*Assisting natural surveillance* such as reporting lost or stolen devices and cyber victimization to appropriate authorities	*Removing targets* such as avoiding visiting Web sites of dubious repute or downloading apps from third-party app stores	*Avoiding disputes* between employees by allowing users to opt in or out to the collection or use of their personal information, and identifying third parties and including links to information in the privacy policy about how employees can modify or delete the data used by those parties, etc.	*Posting instructions* such as limiting dissemination of sensitive and personally identifiable information on public forums such as enterprise or social networking sites
Screen exits such as deleting personal information from corporate devices before disposing of the devices	*Reducing anonymity* by registering employees or vendors who access the organization network (e.g., no guest account)	*Identifying properties* such as physical marking of corporate devices or use of remote wiping and locating apps	*Reducing emotional arousal* by banning or removal of programs that encourage violence or facilitate criminal behavior	*Alert conscience* by providing regular user education to train them to be vigilant and for managers to conduct due diligence on their employees

Deflecting offenders by reducing their possibility or incentive to commit a crime such as prompt installation of patches to software and hardware	*Utilizing place managers* that will be responsible for vetting corporate devices and apps before they are approved for use within the organization (e.g., Bring your Own Device (BYOD)/Apps), secure the data collected from users, etc.	*Disrupting markets* by reporting the lost or stolen devices to authorities and wiping lost or stolen devices with remote wiping apps	*Neutralizing peer pressure* such as avoid creating situations that could lead to collusion between malicious employees and vendors or external parties to target the organization	*Assisting compliance* by encouraging users to report cyber victimization, and discouraging employees to collect and store personal information unnecessarily
Controlling tools such as using privacy enhancing tools or opt out of sharing personal information with third parties	*Strengthening formal surveillance* such as monitoring of network activities (e.g., is a user's movements and activities collected through the use of integrated location and movement sensors without informed consent?)	*Denying benefits* such as using encryption and alphanumeric and nonguessable password, and prosecution of offenders	*Discouraging imitation*	*Controlling provocation factors* using measures such as setting of rules to discourage noncompliant behaviors

effective incident handling strategy that provides guidance on what to do when incidents occur, the actions that need to be undertaken when incidents are detected, how can the identified incidents be mitigated, what evidential data should be collected, etc.

In this chapter, we proposed a Cloud Incident Handling Model that incorporates incident handling, digital forensic practices, and the Situational Crime Prevention Theory (Clarke, 1997). We then explained how the proposed model can be implemented using a case study in the private IaaS cloud environment. Cloud attributes of relevance to the formulation of an incident handling response that were identified included (i) how cloud-based workflow affects risk assessment, (ii) the need to identify the flow of data at-rest and in-transit required in proactive security controls and forensic acquisition, and (ii) potential attack vectors which are also sources of evidential data (e.g., desktop, laptop, tablet, smartphone). Further research includes further validation and refinement of the proposed model in different context, particularly in a real-world deployment.

REFERENCES

Albakri, S.H., Shanmugam, B., Samy, G.N., Idris, N.B., Ahmed, A., 2014. Security risk assessment framework for cloud computing environments. Secur. Commun. Networks 7 (11), 2114–2124.

Aleem, A., Sprott, C.R., 2013. Let me in the cloud: analysis of the benefit and risk assessment of cloud platform. J. Financ. Crime 20 (1), 6–24.

Amazon Web Services, 2014. Amazon CloudWatch [Online]. Available: http://aws.amazon.com/cloudwatch/ [Accessed: 28-Oct-2014].

Anuar, N.B., Papadaki, M., Furnell, S., Clarke, N., 2012. A response strategy model for intrusion response systems. In: Information Security and Privacy Research. Springer, Berlin Heidelberg, pp. 573–578.

Birk, D., Wegener, C., 2011. Technical issues of forensic investigations in cloud computing environments. In: 2011 Sixth IEEE International Workshop on Systematic Approaches to Digital Forensic Engineering, pp. 1–10.

Böhme, R., 2010. Security metrics and security investment models. In: Advances in Information and Computer Security. Springer, Berlin Heidelberg, pp. 10–24.

Buyya, R., Vecchiola, C., Selvi, S.T., 2013. Cloud Computing Architecture. In: Mastering Cloud Computing:Technologies and Applications Programming. Morgan Kaufmann, pp. 111–140.

Cichonski, P., Scarfone, K., 2012. Computer Security Incident Handling Guide Recommendations of the National Institute of Standards and Technology (NIST). NIST, Gaithersburg.

Clarke, R.V., 1997. Situational Crime Prevention: Successful Case Studies, second ed. Harrow and Heston, New York.

Cloud Security Alliance, 2011. Security Guidance for Critical Areas of Focus in Cloud Computing, CSA [Online]. Available: https://cloudsecurityalliance.org/guidance/csaguide.v3.0.pdf [Accessed: 01-Aug-2014].

Cloud Security Alliance, 2013. The Notorious Nine Cloud Computing Top Threats in 2013, CSA [Online]. Available: http://www.cloudsecurityalliance.org/topthreats/ [Accessed: 12-Jul-2013].

Dekker, M., Liveri, D., Lakka, M., 2013. Cloud Security Incident Reporting Framework for Reporting About Major Cloud Security Incidents. ENISA, Athens.

Freiling, F.C., Schwittay, B., 2007. A common process model for incident response and computer forensics. In: Proceedings of the 2007 IT Incident Management & IT Forensics (IMF 2007), vol. 7, pp. 19–40.

Grobauer, B., Schreck, T., 2010. Towards incident handling in the cloud. In: Proceedings of the 2010 ACM Workshop on Cloud Computing Security Workshop (CCSW'10), pp. 77–85.

Gupta, R., Prasad, K.H., Luan, L., Rosu, D., Ward, C., 2009. Multi-dimensional knowledge integration for efficient incident management in a services cloud. In: 2009 IEEE International Conference on Services Computing, pp. 57–64.

Gurkok, C., 2013. Cyber forensics and incident response. In: Computer and Information Security Handbook, second ed. Elsevier, pp. 601–622.

Jansen, W., Grance, T., 2011. Guidelines on Security and Privacy in Public Cloud Computing. National Institute of Standards and Technology, Gaithersburg.

Khorshed, T., Ali, A.B.M.S., Wasimi, S.A., 2012. A survey on gaps, threat remediation challenges and some thoughts for proactive attack detection in cloud computing. Futur. Gener. Comput. Syst. 28 (6), 833–851.

Kohn, M.D., Eloff, M.M., Eloff, J.H.P., 2013. Integrated digital forensic process model. Comput. Secur. 38 (2013), 103–115.

Kozlovszky, M., Kovacs, L., Torocsik, M., Windisch, G., Acs, S., Prem, D., Eigner, G., Sas, P., Schubert, T., Póserné, V., 2013. Cloud security monitoring and vulnerability management. In: IEEE 17th International Conference on Intelligent Engineering Systems, pp. 265–269, no. 70.

Martini, B., Choo, K.-K.R., 2012. An integrated conceptual digital forensic framework for cloud computing. Digit. Investig. 9 (2), 71–80.

Martini, B., Choo, K.-K.R., 2013. Cloud storage forensics: ownCloud as a case study. Digit. Investig. 10 (4), 1–13.

Martini, B., Choo, K.-K.R., 2014. Remote programmatic vCloud forensics: a six-step collection process and a proof of concept. In: Proceedings of 13th IEEE International Conference on Trust, Security and Privacy in Computing and Communications (TrustCom 2014), pp. 935–942.

Mell, P., Grance, T., 2011. The NIST Definition of Cloud Computing Recommendations. National Institute of Standard and Technology, Gaithersburg.

Mitropoulos, S., Patsos, D., Douligeris, C., 2006. On incident handling and response: a state-of-the-art approach. Comput. Secur. 25 (5), 351–370.

Modi, C., Patel, D., Borisaniya, B., Patel, H., Patel, A., Rajarajan, M., Jan. 2013. A survey of intrusion detection techniques in cloud. J. Netw. Comput. Appl. 36 (1), 42–57.

Monfared, A.T., Jaatun, M.G., 2011. Monitoring intrusions and security breaches in highly distributed cloud environments. In: 2011 IEEE Third International Conference on Cloud Computing Technology and Science, pp. 772–777.

Monfared, A., Jaatun, M.G., 2012. Handling compromised components in an IaaS cloud installation. J. Cloud Comput. Adv. Syst. Appl. 1 (1), 1–21.

Pangalos, G., Ilioudis, C., Pagkalos, I., 2010. The importance of corporate forensic readiness in the information security framework. In: 2010 19th IEEE International Workshops on Enabling Technologies: Infrastructures for Collaborative Enterprises, pp. 12–16.

Patel, A., Taghavi, M., Bakhtiyari, K., Celestino Júnior, J., Jan. 2013. An intrusion detection and prevention system in cloud computing: a systematic review. J. Netw. Comput. Appl. 36 (1), 25–41.

Pearson, S., 2013. Privacy, security and trust in cloud computing. In: Pearson, S., Yee, G. (Eds.), Privacy and Security for Cloud Computing. Springer, London, pp. 3–42.

Pilli, E.S., Joshi, R.C., Niyogi, R., 2010. A generic framework for network forensics. Int. J. Comput. Appl. 1 (11), 1–6.

Quick, D., Choo, K.-K.R., 2013. Digital droplets: microsoft SkyDrive forensic data remnants. Futur. Gener. Comput. Syst. 29 (6), 1378–1394.

Quick, D., Martini, B., Choo, K.-K.R., 2014. Cloud Storage Forensics. Syngress Publishing, Waltham, MA.

Rahman, N.H.A., Choo, K.-K.R., 2015. A survey of information security incident handling in the cloud. Comput. Secur. 49, 45–69. http://dx.doi.org/10.1016/j.cose.2014.11.006.

Ruan, K., Carthy, J., Kechadi, T., Crosbie, M., 2011. Cloud forensics. In: Advances in Digital Forensic VII. Springer, Berlin Heidelberg, pp. 35–46.

Saha, A., 2012. A look at ownCloud. Linux J. 2012 (218), 64–75.

Sarkar, S.R., Mahindru, R., Hosn, R.A., Vogl, N., Ramasamy, H.V., 2011. Automated incident management for a platform-as-a-service cloud. In: Proceedings of the 11th USENIX Conference on Hot Topics in Management of Internet, Cloud, and Enterprise Network and Services, pp. 5–11.

Suarez-Tangil, G., Palomar, E., Ribagorda, A., Zhang, Y., 2014. Towards an Intelligent Security Event Information Management System [Online]. Available: www.seg.inf. uc3m.es/papers/2013nova-AIS-SIEM.pd [Accessed: 05-May-2014].

Trček, D., Abie, H., Skomedal, A., Starc, I., 2010. Advanced framework for digital forensic technologies and procedures. J. Forensic Sci. 55 (6), 1471–1480.

Tsalis, N., Theoharidou, M., Gritzalis, D., 2013. Return on security investment for cloud platforms. In: 2013 IEEE 5th International Conference on Cloud Computing Technology and Science, pp. 132–137.

Zimmerman, S., Glavach, D., 2011. Cyber forensics in the cloud. IA Newsletter 14 (1), 4–7.

Cloud security and forensic readiness: The current state of an IaaS provider

18

Chaz Vidal, Kim-Kwang Raymond Choo

Information Assurance Research Group, School of Information Technology and Mathematical Sciences, University of South Australia, Adelaide, Australia

1 INTRODUCTION

The use of cloud computing has gained momentum over the past few years. What, arguably, began as a marketing buzzword used by information technology companies, cloud computing is now an entrenched part of the consumer world. With a wide-ranging set of applications and various entities and organizations touting so-called cloud services, attempts have been made to define what cloud computing should be. The definition by National Institute of Standards and Technology (NIST) is what many have considered the de-factor industry standard, which defines cloud computing as a model for enabling network access to configurable computing resources quickly with minimal interaction from service providers (Mell and Grance, 2011).

NIST ascribes five characteristics of a cloud service model: on-demand self-service, seamless network access, resource pooling, rapid elasticity, and measured services. There are also various service models used by consumers, namely, Software as a Service (SaaS), Platform as a Service (PaaS), and Infrastructure as a Service (IaaS). NIST further defines how these service models are deployed such as a through a private cloud, a community cloud, a public cloud, or a hybrid cloud.

Of the three cloud computing service models, IaaS is said to be the foundation of cloud services (Choo, 2010). In the IaaS model, users have access to fundamental computing resources such as CPU processing and memory and storage resources. This provides them with the building blocks for the users own applications available for use in SaaS or PaaS models. IaaS is made possible because of virtualization, which can be used to segregate and provision these computing resources quickly and efficiently (Antonopoulos and Gillam, 2010).

Virtualization is the ability to abstract physical computing resources into segregated objects called virtual machines (VMs). The latter represents the division of physical infrastructure into multiple, separate and distinct chunks of CPU, Memory, and Storage space which can then be rapidly provisioned for cloud computing consumers (Beek, 2010, p. 5). VMs are then allocated to users when requested through online means. These users effectively share the physical resources of the underlying physical infrastructure.

There are a few components to these virtualization technologies that a Cloud Service Provider (CSP) must be able to implement. Foremost to these components are the physical resources required in the form of computer servers and storage devices that are housed in large datacenters (Khan et al., 2012). These datacenters can contain hundreds, if not thousands, of physical servers whose computing resources are then aggregated through the use of Virtualization software (also known as hypervisors). Hypervisors control the segregation and allocation of the servers' collected physical hardware resources, and run the different VMs that the consumers access.

Despite the availability and maturity of the Cloud, there are other difficulties that have been recognized as barriers to its wider acceptance. Information security has emerged as a great concern because of the shared nature of cloud computing and this aspect raises questions on the confidentiality, integrity, and availability of data stored by cloud computing users within this infrastructure (Grobauer et al., 2011). Research suggests that addressing information security is a key challenge in the ongoing use of cloud computing platforms.

Cloud computing, like any new technology, also has the potential to be abused or used for illegal or illegitimate means. Cloud resources can be compromised and used to house malware botnets (Choo, 2010) or illegal and contraband files (Rogers, 2012) (Julidotter and Choo, 2015). These illegal activities within the cloud computing platforms then introduce the prospect of digital investigations to determine the extent of this activity and to identify and prosecute the perpetrators. Damaging attacks on major organizations are often not being publicly reported but these incidents require investigations by both internal and external security and incident response teams in order to determine the source of the attacks, determine what the attackers did, and how to recover from the incident(s). In recent times, there has been a noted increase in a demand for forensic investigation. A number of recent studies provided greater insight into the challenges of such investigations when cloud based services are involved (Martini et al., 2015a,b; Quick and Choo, 2013a,b,c, 2014; Quick et al., 2013).

Digital forensics involves the identifying, preserving, analyzing, and presentation of digital data for use in legal proceedings (McKemmish, 1999). This is often difficult in a cloud computing scenario primarily because the ability to preserve data and ensure its integrity is not guaranteed (Simou et al., 2014). Possibly evidence data would generally reside in the cloud computing infrastructure and not on the locally secured desktops or devices involved in the criminal activity (Pearson et al., 2013) (Martini and Choo, 2014b). Access to this data is more than likely controlled by the CSP and research shows that the ability to investigate data in the cloud relies on having the CSP cooperate with the ongoing investigations (Barrett and Kipper, 2010) (Martini and Choo, 2013, 2014a).

Because of the importance of the involvement of CSP in digital forensic investigations, it is imperative for them to understand how as an organization they can be ready to respond to requests for evidentiary data and their role in the forensics process. This concept of forensic readiness is important because not only does it facilitate digital investigations but it allows these activities to proceed with minimal interruption or cost to the business (Pangalos et al., 2010) (Rahman and Choo, 2015b). In a cloud computing environment, this is especially critical because of the many other consumers using the service and the potential for service disruptions during a digital investigation can be detrimental to viability of the business itself.

With all these challenges around CSP's security and forensic readiness, a number of conceptual solutions have been proposed to address these weaknesses, for example, in the establishment of security policies to improve security of an IaaS provider (Karadsheh, 2012), proposal of specific solutions to particular technological security problems such as vulnerabilities in the underlying Web interfaces (Angadi et al., 2013) and constant monitoring of VM communication to ensure operational integrity (Dawoud et al., 2010). To improve digital forensic readiness, processes have been suggested that can be implemented across entire organizations (Rowlingson, 2004). These policy-based solutions could be evolved into a model for forensic readiness that may be applied to the cloud computing scenarios (Sibiya et al., 2013).

This chapter takes into account the research available and focuses on the practical experience of an existing organization in incorporating information security processes and mitigating security threats as well as evaluating digital forensic readiness into their cloud service offering. This chapter then provides a high-level review of the case study organization's information security as well as its implementation of forensic readiness steps based on prevailing standards in relation to its IaaS service.

Using observations of the organization's information security policies and forensic readiness, this chapter then analyzes how this organization utilizes their existing technologies and information security policies to their cloud computing offerings and where the security gaps may be and what improvements can be made.

2 REVIEW OF THE PRIVATE IaaS PROVIDER

With a wide variety of security challenges to cloud computing, it is important to understand where to begin analyzing security threats faced by an IaaS provider. The global standard for information security management was used as a starting off point because this provided a consistent and globally accepted set of techniques for developing information security controls and implementing them in an organization (AS/NZS, 2006).

Using these security standards (described in this section), an existing organization was assessed to see if it has implemented some of the controls and objectives set out by the standard on the cloud service it provided. Observations were then recorded as to the extent of the use of these controls and how the organization was utilizing them or not.

Reviewing the organization's infrastructure through information security management standards was important because these standards have been established specifically as a guide for other organizations to implement their own information security strategies. Some research has already looked into the effectiveness of applying security policies to specific cloud services to show their contributions to the service's overall security (Karadsheh, 2012).

The ISO 27002 standard itself is a comprehensive piece of standard, which consists of several security controls placed on an organization and their objectives and guidelines to their implementation. Because of these standards, organizational stakeholders, including users of the organization's services, can be assured of compliance to certain security controls that enhance the organization's information security profile.

The second part of the assessment methodology was to gather information on the top threats that CSP faces and then try to observe if the organization has mitigated these threats (Cloud Security Alliance, 2013). These top threats compiled by the Cloud Security Alliance (CSA) represented specific security issues that may compromise the security of a cloud service; therefore, it is also important to understand if the CSP had a plan for mitigating these threats to their IaaS platform.

The third part of the assessment involved utilizing a 10-step process for forensic readiness (Rowlingson, 2004). The intent of this forensic readiness process is to increase an organization's use of digital evidence but at the same time, minimize the cost of utilizing the data during a digital forensic investigation. This process generally suggests improvements to system monitoring; technical, procedural, and policy improvements to securing possible digital evidence; staff training; and improvements of the interfaces with law enforcement. Using this process, the case study organization's IaaS service was assessed and observations were made against each of these steps to determine the state of the forensics readiness.

The observations of security controls, cloud security threats, and forensic readiness serve a high-level overview of how the organization establishes and maintains the security of the cloud service it provides. The resulting analysis is made with a view toward identifying specific remediation items that could be implemented by the organization to improve its cloud security and forensic readiness posture.

2.1 OVERVIEW OF THE CASE STUDY ORGANIZATION

This security analysis was performed on an existing organization that services the higher education sector. To ensure anonymity, the organization will be referred to as Company A in the remainder of this chapter.

Company A is a medium- to large-sized organization competing and operating in Australia and New Zealand region. It has an annual budget in excess of $A400M and provides services in different locations within Australia and Asia.

Company A's primary business is not cloud services but rather a part of their ongoing IT support work involves the provisioning of VMs for different business groups within the organization. In a way, Company A has established a private IaaS cloud specifically for use by internal business units.

Company A's internal IT group receive requests for new computer servers from internal groups and following a VM requisitioning process, these groups then receive their requested virtual servers with the required CPU, memory, and storage amounts to use for whatever purpose they may have. These VMs are automatically connected to Company A's network with access to the Internet as required.

Company A's physical IaaS resources comprised multiple modular hardware servers called Blade servers. Such servers share a common back-end Ethernet network and Fiber-Channel connections to a Storage Array Network (SAN) that enable rapid expansion of the physical resources as required. These physical servers are all located in physical datacenters within Australia with no data being stored offshore.

2.2 SECURITY ANALYSIS METHODOLOGY

Using the ISO 27002 security standard, a method was developed to analyze Company A's IaaS environment. This involved breaking down the different security categories specified in the standard and observing whether Company A has implemented specific activities or controls that have been outlined to support the security categories of the standard.

The ISO 27002 standard is comprised of over 100 different security controls that identify specific activities that organizations can perform to counter threats to information system security (René, 2005). Because information and data are important business assets, they should be protected to maintain the organization's long-term viability in terms of competitiveness and profitability. These global standards have, therefore, been established to guide businesses in formulating information security strategies to ensure their success.

Not all security controls need to be implemented, however. An organization has to identify the security requirements and risks that would necessitate the application of such controls (Horvath and Jakub, 2009). These security requirements can be derived from three sources, namely:

1. Organizational risks;
2. Legal, statutory, regulatory, or contractual requirements; and
3. Any principles or objectives that the organization has developed and must adhere to in processing information.

Once these requirements have been identified and risks assessed, then the appropriate security controls as suggested by the standard can be employed. A balance must also be made between the costs of implementation of these controls against the cost of the risk involved.

The 27002 security standard defines different groups, or clauses, for different security categories:

- Establishment of security policy;
- Organization of information security;

- Asset management;
- Human resources security management;
- Physical and environmental security;
- Communications and operations management;
- Access control;
- Information systems acquisition, development, and maintenance;
- Information security incident management;
- Business continuity management; and
- Compliance.

The analysis of these categories against the implementation of Company A's IaaS service was done with observations as how far the controls in each category have or have not been implemented.

The following sections will go through each clause and attempt to document the observed security controls implemented in relation to the IaaS service. This security assessment is not in-depth but rather just documentation of observable characteristics that the case study organization's IaaS platform has with regard to the standard.

2.2.1 Establishment of a security policy

A security policy is one important business document of an organization, as it not only describes the organization's security goals but also what the role's responsibilities toward security of each member of the organization will have. A good security policy protects the organization's asset (e.g., intellectual property), minimizes business risks, and helps track compliance to ongoing regulations.

Company A has an established security policy available to all internal staff as well as external customers with references to Acceptable Computer Use policies as well as documenting specific responsibilities for security and security incidents. What has been observed is there are no specific policies around the private cloud infrastructure provided by Company A to its users and it appears that the generalized information security policy is intended to apply to all usage of information technology within the organization.

2.2.2 Organization of information security

This clause determines the commitment and responsibilities of the case study organization's management in relation to information security. This involves the establishment of a security culture within the organization (e.g., the establishment of a dedicated information security division) as well as controlling external third-party access and customer risks.

Company A has an information security division with various roles and responsibilities. They are mostly doing coordination of security-related work such as authorisation and security assessments of new and existing IT infrastructure and risk assessment toward new application or patch implementations and third-party and customer access.

The IaaS infrastructure appears to be considered as part of the overall IT infrastructure without any specific or separate security organization scrutiny. With regard to third-party and customer access to the IaaS infrastructure, there are some risk assessment processes to be followed prior to establishing new access requests. These risk assessment processes are, however, not documented and are performed on an *ad-hoc* basis.

2.2.3 Asset management

This asset management clause relates to the assignment of ownership to the organization's major assets. This allows asset owners to become largely responsible for the maintenance and updates of each asset such that vulnerabilities can be mitigated and or fixed.

This clause also focuses on the proper identification and handling of information within an organization. Different information may have different security requirements such as personal information or business information or confidential information. As such, there could be potentially different rules regarding the handling of each type of information such as where it can be stored or who should have access to it.

Its been observed that the organization's IaaS infrastructure has clearly marked asset owners and responsibilities for updates are assigned. In some cases, hosted VMs have different ownership and will have different responsibilities as to ongoing support and maintenance based on internal hosting agreements between the business unit and the case study organization's IaaS service.

VMs and the data they store do not have observable information classifications and Company A does not have quite a clear information classification policy but are working toward improving this.

2.2.4 Human resources security management

This clause deals with the main phases of employment for a company. The importance of security is emphasized during a new employee's induction, tenure, and after the employee leaves. Because people have been determined as the organization's greatest security risks, this clause assists in ensuring security is foremost in employee's day-to-day activities.

Company A provides specific activities performed generally across all employees such as ensuring compliance to security responsibilities as well as established steps toward account deactivation after employee termination. There is no specific employee security training prior or during employment with regard to securing the IaaS environment.

It is observed that the IaaS infrastructure is treated as part of the overall IT infrastructure and the employment policies are generalized. Systems administrators working on the IaaS infrastructure receive no specific security training; however, when they do work on the IaaS systems, they are expected to learn the security best practices as provided by the software vendors.

2.2.5 Physical and environmental security

This clause relates to the controlling of manual access to the physical IT resources. This clause highlights the implementation of secure areas and ensuring authorized entry to these areas as well as the physical security of equipment identifying that it operates according to recommended environmental conditions and protected from accidental damage. This clause also applies to equipment that has reached its end-of-life and should be disposed of appropriately.

It has been observed that Company A does maintain secure and environmentally controlled datacenters that only allow access only by properly authorized personnel. These datacenters house the IaaS infrastructure, and access to the physical resources of the IaaS service involves access to the entire datacenter itself.

There is an existing security policy governing access to the entire datacenter, but there is no specific control observed for the IaaS resources. The blade servers that provide the physical resources for the IaaS infrastructure do not have separate secure areas within the datacenters. These blade servers are housed in computer racks accessible to anyone with previous access to the datacenters. Access to the datacenters is logged and video recording is enabled for activities within these datacenters.

VMs that are no longer required go through a decommissioning process that also includes appropriate deletions of these VM's disks and configurations within the IaaS system. Any physical servers within the environment (including the IaaS hardware) go through the same decommissioning process when they reach end-of-life.

2.2.6 Communications and operations management

This part of the security standard contains the most number of security controls. Because of the operational nature of managing information security, it is understandable that the bulk of the work of securing this information comes under this clause. Because of the importance operations management has to ongoing IT support and maintenance, the observations have been made for each category in this security clause.

Establish operational procedures and responsibilities

This category defines controls used to secure day-to-day IT operations. This category outlines the need of documented operating procedures, appropriate change management processes are identified, different operational duties are segregated, and different environments are separated.

Company A has been observed as having operational documentation for a number of different systems including that for the running and maintenance of the IaaS infrastructure. There are also observable IT service management processes including change control processes as well as established roles and responsibilities within the IT support team that manages the IaaS environment. Production and nonproduction environments are separated within the VM environments, but there is no physical equivalent to a nonproduction IaaS infrastructure, i.e., there is only one production environment for the IaaS physical systems.

Third-party service delivery management

This category is used to manage any activities that any enterprise needs to coordinate with third-party companies related to the delivery of IT services. This involves establishment of Service Level Agreements, monitoring and reviewing of third-party services, and management of changes toward third-party services.

Although there are other organizations involved with Company A including the vendors of the virtualization software, there is no observed specific service-level agreement with these vendors outside standard end user license and support agreements.

Malicious/mobile code

This set of controls relates to the management or containment of malicious software (e.g., viruses, Trojan code), and vulnerabilities in software and hardware, a well as ensuring the correct processing of legitimate network connected software. The controls set out in this category highlight the need for organizations to have policies or controls to manage the deployment or proliferation of malicious software.

It is observed that Company A has established a number of operational processes and tools to ensure management of malicious software. Some observed processes include a regular patching and maintenance cycle for all systems, the deployment of anti-virus software as well as multiple firewall deployments. There is no observed white-listing process where the company only allows approved software to run on IT systems.

Although there is a regular patching window for operating systems (including operating systems on VMs), there is no regular and scheduled patching window for the IaaS platform itself and that this is often an *ad-hoc* schedule based on fixing of identified critical vulnerabilities.

Backup

This category relates to the availability of a backup strategy or policy for IT information and resources. Company A has a backup strategy utilizing a number of backup and recovery tools. For the IaaS infrastructure in particular, the VM backup process is performed on a regular basis. There is, however, no observed backup process specifically for the IaaS operating environment or hypervisor and that utilizing a rapid deployment method is the assumed manner for recovering a single host system. There is also no observed process for testing restores on a regular basis and only *ad-hoc* requests for restores are observed.

Network security management

Networking components are critical in the deployment of IT services. This category defines the controls required to protect networking equipment and to ensure this infrastructure remains operational and operationally available.

It is observed that Company A has networking systems that are managed separately from systems and application management platforms. It is also observed that the IaaS infrastructure itself does not deploy networking changes but rather rely on a separate set of systems and processes to be available prior to deployment of VMs. Company A's networking environment has a built-in redundant infrastructure that supports a variety of segregated virtual local area networks (VLANs) from which the VMs operate. These VLANs serve as a means to protect and separate network traffic based on access controls and firewall rules.

Media handling

Media refers to all data storage devices in use within the organization. Handling of this media to ensure protection from unauthorized removal or disclosure, destruction, or tampering is what this category seeks to enforce.

Although Company A's IaaS infrastructure does not utilize removable media during day-to-day processing, ongoing backups tend to use tape storage for long-term archiving. There is an observed process for handling these backup tapes both for archiving and daily backup purposes. For other types of media, there is no observed process for their use especially the use of removable storage within the datacenter in general or the physical IaaS components in particular.

Information exchange

This set of controls is designed to ensure compliance with exchanging of information between organizations and external parties. This could mean an electronic exchange via the network such as via e-mail or application communications, or physical exchange via removable media.

Although Company A has observed policies for communication especially around e-mail communications and management, there is no observed policy in place for such exchange of information specifically for the IaaS infrastructure. Any communication to and from IaaS infrastructure follows the general organization's policies.

Electronic commerce services

Aside from regular communication and information exchange, this set of controls concern electronic commerce information specifically. Information for financial transactions and banking communication are treated differently under the security standards.

Company A operates a number of electronic commerce activities and processes. Because the organization's IaaS service is an internal private IaaS, activities for resource, or VM provisioning do not require financial transaction processing and, therefore, there is no observed ecommerce activity for the IaaS. However, the VM's provisioned under the IaaS service may be involved with electronic commerce depending on the applications they host and there is no observed documented process or procedure specifically to secure VM operating an ecommerce or financial activity and these VMs are managed on a case-by-case basis.

Monitoring

Monitoring of critical systems is an effective information security process. It is important to identify the ongoing health and performance of IT infrastructure to ensure their availability. This set of controls ensures that adequate monitoring is available to those key applications and systems.

It is observed that Company A utilizes a number of monitoring systems to detect anomalies or threshold conditions within the environment. There are IaaS infrastructure specific monitoring systems in use, which include the keeping of audit trails and logs for further analysis as required.

One specific control in this category involves ensuring accurate clock synchronization across the organization to ensure the accuracy of log analysis. It is observed that Company A utilizes an organization-wide time synchronization system that ensures compliance to this control.

2.2.7 Access control

This clause refers to the logical access of IT resources in the organization. This clause deals with controls to user management, their responsibilities, password management, network and operating system, and application access control.

Company A is observed to have a documented acceptable use policy for overall usage of IT assets that also defined good access practices for users. There is an observed password policy and workstation lockout policy that is enforced through automated tools. These policies apply to administrator workstations and accounts that are used to manage the IaaS infrastructure. Access to the IaaS management systems and hosted VMs are provided on a role-based mechanism. Members of the IT Systems Administrators unit have access to these systems by default, but other users can get access to perform administration of the hosted VMs through a request mechanism and if they are approved accordingly.

2.2.8 Information systems acquisition, development, and maintenance

This clause is primarily to push the importance of including information security as part of making business decisions. This is to ensure security is included in the design and acquisition of any project enacted by the business. These set of controls describe how security should be part of the requirements and to identify where security techniques should be utilized.

During new application or solution implementations, it has been observed that input from the security team was required as part of starting up phases. There is no observed specific security requirement and input when developing enhancements to the IaaS infrastructure and again, a generalized view of the IaaS infrastructure as part of overall IT has been taken. Any changes to the IaaS infrastructure are expected to conform to best practices as suggested by product or vendor advice and documentation.

2.2.9 Information security incident management

This clause involves ensuring the lifecycle of security management is intact. Any changes or incidents related to security should be reported through the proper chain and changes to security profiles must be addressed in the correct manner.

Company A has a documented security incident reporting process that the Information Security team manages. This process involves all of Company A's stakeholders including clients and customers. It has been observed that the information security team handle the generalized management of security incidents from collection of evidence or incident information to coordination of changes required to remediate any vulnerabilities that the incident has uncovered. There is no observed incident management process specifically related to the IaaS infrastructure and it is again treated as part of the general IT systems.

2.2.10 Business continuity management

This security clause ensures that businesses can still operate in a safe and secure manner even after being interrupted for whatever reason. The controls in this clause involve the implementation of business continuity plans to ensure the business can still process information securely.

It has been observed that Company A has a wide range of disaster recovery plans for major systems including the IaaS infrastructure. These disaster recovery plans are developed, maintained, and tested on an annual basis. It has been observed that the disaster recovery plans of most systems that are hosted in the IaaS environment do not have specific IaaS steps and features that can be taken advantage of such as snapshot technology or replication processes. The IaaS infrastructure has been observed to have disaster recovery plans that do not appear to be regularly maintained.

2.2.11 Compliance management

Ensuring that the organization adheres to all applicable laws and regulations is what this clause pertains to. The organization opens itself up to unwanted legal issues or liabilities if it does not comply with their legal responsibilities.

Company A operates within a legal and legislative framework around the industry it is in; however, there is no observed policy used specifically for compliance for the IaaS infrastructure and service.

2.2.12 Summary of observations

It was observed that a number of security controls already existed and implemented within Company A's environment. It is noted that there was no control for the IaaS infrastructure directly and that generalized security controls were expected to be applied to the entire enterprise including the IaaS service.

Table 1 shows a summary of security controls observed within Company A.

There is no direct measurement as to the effectiveness of some of the controls and there does not appear to be a rigorous and regular review of these controls. Measuring the effectiveness of these controls such as the testing of backups for restoration or the

Table 1 Summary of Security Controls

Security Clause	Availability of IaaS Security Controls
Security policy available	Partial. Policy available for all of IT but nothing specific for the IaaS infrastructure
Information security organization	Yes. IT security organization established
Asset management	Partial. IaaS infrastructure and VM asset ownership defined but security classifications not available
Human resources security	Partial. Security training not available specifically for the handling of the IaaS infrastructure
Physical and environmental security	Yes. IaaS infrastructure is housed in managed datacenters
Operational procedures and responsibilities	Yes. Processes and procedures for IaaS support and maintenance are documented and available
Third-party service management	Yes. Third-party relationships with the IaaS infrastructure vendors are governed by existing license and support agreements
Malicious code	Yes. Maintenance work of applying patches to the IaaS infrastructure to counter security vulnerabilities has been observed
Backup	Yes. Backups are available but not tested on a regular basis
Network security	Yes. Network equipment and traffic are protected through available redundancy and access control lists and firewalls
Media handling	Partial. No specific policies for removable storage within the datacenter or IaaS use
Information exchange	Partial. No specific policies for IaaS network communication and only generalized information rules apply
Electronic commerce services	Partial. VMs that manage financial transactions are not covered by any specific policy but on a case-by-case basis
Monitoring	Yes. Monitoring on all levels of the IaaS infrastructure is available and in use
Access control	Yes. There are well-defined access control processes to the IaaS infrastructure
Information systems acquisition	Partial. The security team has inputs into generalized IT infrastructure but no specific IaaS policies are in place
Incident management	Partial. There are no specific policies in place for security incident management involving IaaS infrastructure or VMs
Business continuity	Yes. IaaS disaster recovery plans are available
Compliance management	Partial. There are generalized policies that apply to the entire organization but nothing specific observed for the IaaS infrastructure

availability of operational documentation for certain aspects of IT security should be employed to ensure improvements where necessary.

In addition to the effectiveness of existing controls, there is a lack of controls for the availability of information security classifications on VMs or a risk assessment methodology for new or existing IT activities. Because these controls have not been observed does not mean that the organization does not require them. Therefore, a review of Company A's security requirements and policies should be performed *vis-à-vis* the IaaS infrastructure such that the expected and required security controls can be implemented.

2.3 CLOUD VULNERABILITIES AND THREAT ASSESSMENT

Aside from challenges with developing an information security process, it is also established that there are numerous security threats being faced by the infrastructure for cloud computing services (Bhadauria and Sanyal, 2012). These threats compromise basic information security of a CSP by affecting the confidentiality, integrity and availability of the information kept in the cloud service.

In this section, Company A's IaaS service was evaluated against these threats and observations made on whether mitigation activities have been implemented to counter these threats.

Researchers and security vendors have attempted to put together various lists of cloud computing threats, such as threats exploiting vulnerabilities in the underlying cloud infrastructure (Grobauer et al., 2011), and Web platforms used to drive access to cloud services. There is also the possibility of data exposure because of the multi-tenanted nature of Cloud Services where physical resources are shared across different VMs and their owners (Hay et al., 2011).

Threats can be nontechnical. The latter includes uncertain security management responsibilities between VM owners and CSPs (Pearson and Benameur, 2010). There also the operational issues and threats that emanate from inadequate monitoring and auditing of cloud services both by CSPs and the consumers (Vaquero et al., 2011).

Given the wide definition of different threats to cloud computing, it was necessary for this chapter to utilize a single source to evaluate Company A's IaaS service. CSA's list of relevant threats is used as the primary source for this chapter (Cloud Security Alliance, 2013), and the nine identified threats are as follow:

1. Data breaches;
2. Data loss;
3. Account hijacking;
4. Insecure interfaces and APIs;
5. Denial-of-service;
6. Malicious insiders;
7. Abuse of cloud services;
8. Insufficient due diligence; and
9. Shared technology issues.

We will now briefly review each threat and attempt to document the observed remediation or actions raised by Company A to ensure the threat is minimized.

2.3.1 Data breaches

In a multi-tenanted environment, such as in typical IaaS scenarios, the potential exists for VMs to view information from other parts of the infrastructure. This has been demonstrated in attacks involving separate VM's on the same infrastructure and the ability to extract crucial information such as cryptographic private keys (Zhang et al., 2012). There is also the possibility that disks can be reused and as such, unwanted users may inadvertently see existing data.

Mitigation steps such as timely virtual infrastructure updates to patch known vulnerabilities are currently present within Company A. It has been observed that these updates do not have a set schedule and are performed on an *ad-hoc* basis to counter critical vulnerabilities as deemed by the organization.

Another way to prevent such data leakage is to ensure that data disks are properly erased prior to allocation to different VMs. This activity is not observed in Company A's environment as disk storage is often allocated in an as-needed basis. However, during a physical decommissioning (i.e., when storage arrays are physically removed from the datacenter), disk scrubbing occurs prior to the disks being removed from the premises.

2.3.2 Data loss

Cloud computing enables rapid data movements between platforms but can also have the potential for data loss be it due to environmental factors such as catastrophic failure to the physical infrastructure or accidental and malicious data deletion.

Company A has a backup and recovery solution in place that maintains backups of the environment. It is observed that these backups are managed operationally. Processes are also in place to ensure availability of VM snapshots, which preserve the data state of VM at a point in time, when requested by users especially prior to potential changes to the VMs that may require a rollback. There is, however, inadequate testing of these backups via regular test restores and as such restores are mostly performed when they are actually operationally required.

2.3.3 Account or service hijacking

Service accounts used to access cloud computing services can be compromised and used to access cloud resources without authorization. This happens when generic system administrator accounts are shared across many individuals and attackers gain access to these powerful accounts.

It has been observed that Company A utilizes individual system administrators' accounts and policies are observed against sharing of these same accounts. Audit logs are also maintained within the IaaS environment although there is no observed monitoring process that looks into unusual usage patterns in real-time.

2.3.4 Insecure interfaces and APIs

Remote management of Cloud Services infrastructure is typically done over secure Web services but there may be inherent vulnerabilities in these interfaces that may be exploited by would-be attackers. These vulnerabilities are usually reported on and addressed by vendor-released patches to that are then implemented on the IaaS platform.

It has been observed that Company A has strong authentication mechanisms for management access to the IaaS platform using SSL-encrypted Web management front ends. Access to hosted VMs utilizes standard operating system connectivity such as the Remote Desktop Protocol and SSH.

There is an established patching and remediation process for the IaaS platform but there is no observed regular schedule for this patching process. The patching and remediation of the IaaS service are performed on an *ad-hoc* basis if and when vulnerabilities are discovered and patches released.

There are also regular security scans of the overall IT environment and not just the IaaS hosted VMs. These scans would sometimes reveal vulnerabilities in running applications that would then be remediated by regular VM operating system patching or *ad-hoc* application patching as the need and criticality arises.

2.3.5 Denial-of-service

IaaS infrastructure provides some sort of protection from denial-of-service attacks by the nature of its ability to spread the application serving across many VMs (Angadi et al., 2013). However, this does not help if there is no ability for applications to spread the load of incoming attacks.

There is no observed ongoing monitoring of unusual network traffic patterns in Company A's IaaS infrastructure that would signal a distributed Denial-of-service (DDOS) attack. Additionally, there is no consideration for such attacks on specific applications hosted on the infrastructure so there is no observed mitigation step when such attacks occur.

2.3.6 Malicious insiders

System administrators now have a greater scope to affect change on numerous VMs or platforms hosted in a single cloud service and present a risk if access to these administrative powers is granted to unauthorized users.

In Company A's IaaS environment, the system administrators are guided by processes and the organization-wide policy of acceptable computer usage. There is no documented policy specifically for the use of management systems of the IaaS environment (or for management of any other IT system). The acceptable use policy is also expected to be followed by users of the VMs hosted in the IaaS environment.

There is no enforcement of this policy from a management perspective and it is observed that these administrators and users are then expected to use personal ethical judgements when performing their management and operational tasks. Occasionally there may be reviews of the policies as part of responding to service delivery issues but this process is not a regular one.

2.3.7 Abuse of cloud computing

This threat is brought about when cloud computing resources can be used to host malware sites or servers with malicious content such as spam bots (Choo, 2010).

Because of the private cloud nature of Company A's services, it will be a breach of Company A's documented acceptable use policy to perform such activities within the organization's virtual infrastructure. However, it has been observed that there is no ongoing monitoring or introspection of network traffic coming out of the VMs but only on a case-by-case basis as required to support issue identification or application problem resolution.

2.3.8 Insufficient due diligence

This involves the ability of CSPs and consumers to understand the increasing risk profile of interconnected cloud services and outlining of security responsibilities and compliance. As new VMs and new connections are provisioned within the environment, it is important for the IaaS provider to understand the changing risks of the entire environment. New VMs and new functions bring with them new risks to the business in the form of increased scrutiny of applications or increased value of the information.

Some security evaluation and risk assessments are performed on a case-by-case basis. However, Company A is observed as not having an established process to determine and evaluate security risks when provisioning different type of VMs in the environment.

2.3.9 Shared technology issues

Because of the multi-tenanted characteristic of cloud computing, vulnerabilities exist that may allow attackers access to different VMs within the same infrastructure or to virtualization infrastructure. Shared resources could also mean customers have the ability to inadvertently use up all other computing resources meant for other VMs in the shared infrastructure.

The Cloud Software Alliance recommends a defense-in-depth approach toward securing issues with shared technology. This is where the different layers of virtualization (e.g., operating system, virtualization, network, and storage layers) are protected to prevent an attacker from unauthorized access between layers (Byres, 2012). Recommendations are in place to ensure regular patching and maintenance of the IaaS platform is performed in order to remediate vulnerabilities that could expose systems to such issues.

Company A's IaaS implementations follow security best practices through the use of vendor-documented and tested procedures. VM implementations ensure that latest patches are tested automatically installed on provisioned VM's. It is also observed that there is regular and *ad-hoc* scanning of the overall enterprise environment to discover any discoverable vulnerability. These scans sometimes involve the entire network including the IaaS platform or targeted scans involving particular systems. Numerous layers of firewalls (network and local host) have been observed as being deployed throughout the organization's network and not just for the IaaS environment.

2.3.10 Summary of observations

The CSA provided a good overview of baseline security threats to cloud computing infrastructure. This approach can be used to develop possible solutions to mitigate such threats.

Within Company A, it has been observed that these top threats have been mitigated to some degree. Several suggested steps by the CSA have already been implemented within the case study organization but it has been observed that there are areas that need to be strengthened.

Table 2 summarizes existing threats and controls available within the organization.

Overall, there is room for improvement in the mitigation of both cloud computing-specific and general information security threats. In the case of abuse, more regular process for VM traffic inspection can be made to ensure that the acceptable use policies of hosted VMs is monitored. Instead of relying on issues or incidents to trigger investigative activities, ongoing or regular packet inspection of the applications hosted on VMs can be performed.

Table 2 Cloud Threat Summary

Cloud Threats	IaaS Controls Available
Data breaches	Partial. Regular patching is used to remediate known vulnerabilities but additional technical steps such as securely deleting virtual disks prior to allocations are not observed
Data loss	Yes. Comprehensive backup policy available
Account hijacking	Yes. Administrative accounts to the IaaS infrastructure are separated from normal user logons and there is no shared account for IaaS administration
Insecure interfaces	Yes. Encryption is available when accessing the IaaS infrastructure and regular security scans of applications running on VMs are performed
Denial-of-service (DoS)	No. There is no mechanism within the IaaS infrastructure to automatically overcome DOS attacks
Malicious insiders	Yes. Internal acceptable use policies are available and are expected to be adhered to, but there is no enforcement of the policy nor there is any regular check to ensure compliance such as application or traffic inspection
Abuse of cloud computing	Partial. There is no ongoing procedure to investigate VM traffic but consumers of the IaaS service are expected to adhere to acceptable use policies
Insufficient due diligence	Partial. Security risk assessments are performed *ad hoc* when required but no established risk assessment process is available
Shared technology issues	Yes. A combination of defense-in-depth techniques and regular vulnerability scanning and patching of the IaaS infrastructure is available

A more rigid operating system and hypervisor maintenance schedule as well as an emergency or critical patching schedule should be implemented to ensure technological vulnerabilities are dealt with in a timely manner.

Having a policy of effective disk wiping of secure VMs could be implemented to ensure that the possibility of data leakage can be minimized.

A risk assessment methodology should also be employed to recognize changes in the risk profile in the IT environment. This is critical for the IaaS infrastructure because of the number of systems in such an environment. Single changes to the IaaS environment can lead to many affected VMs and applications. Therefore, having a consistent risk assessment methodology that takes into account the varying uses of the VMs hosted in the IaaS service will create measurable and documented responses by IT support in dealing with changes to the environment.

2.4 DIGITAL FORENSIC READINESS ASSESSMENT

Digital forensics readiness is the ability of organizations to respond quickly and collect digital evidence related to a security incident with minimal cost or interruption to the ongoing business. This involves being able to define digital evidence required so that security aspects in an organization such as programs or teams and infrastructure can be adapted and modified to provide this evidence in a timely manner (Trenwith and Venter, 2013).

There are several global standards to aid organizations in the processing of digital evidence. The International Standards Organization proposes a standard for the processing of digital evidence in a consistent manner (Standardization and Technical Committee ISO/IEC JTC1, 2012). NIST also describes a process for the integration of digital forensics during the management of IT incidents (Kent et al., 2006). Both standards provide a good starting point for organizations to understand the processes involved with collecting digital evidence. For example, the ISO standard goes through defined phases in digital evidence collection: identification, collection, and preservation. The NIST standard includes recommendations that involve the establishment of a forensic capability within the organization to better respond to security incidents requiring digital evidence.

In 2004, Rowlingson proposed a 10-step process that could be used by organizations as a means to improving their forensic readiness (Rowlingson, 2004). The intent of this forensic readiness process is to increase an organization's use of digital evidence but at the same time, minimize the cost of utilizing the data during a digital forensics investigation. This process generally includes improvements to system monitoring, technical and procedural and policy improvements to securing possible digital evidence, staff training and improvements of the interfaces with law enforcement.

Implementing digital forensics readiness should be incorporated as part of overall information security within an organization, and provides many benefits (Pangalos et al., 2010) (Rahman and Choo, 2015a). IaaS providers should have the capability to conduct forensic investigations with minimal impact to the running of the service and to be able to respond quickly to requests for digital forensic evidence from law enforcement agencies or internal security teams.

Implementing forensic readiness may come at a cost, but for an existing organization which has already implemented a basic information security mechanism, the costs of extending existing information security mechanism to include forensic readiness activities are less expensive (Rowlingson, 2004).

The methodology used for judging forensic readiness is as follows:

1. Define the business scenarios that require digital evidence.
2. Identify available sources and different types of potential evidence.
3. Determine the evidence collection requirements.
4. Establish a capability for securely gathering legally admissible evidence to meet the requirement.
5. Establish a policy for secure storage and handling of potential evidence.
6. Ensure that monitoring is targeted to detect and deter major incidents.
7. Specify circumstances when escalation to a full formal investigation should be launched
8. Train staff in incident awareness.
9. Document an evidence-based case describing the incident and its impact.
10. Ensure legal review to facilitate action in response to the incident (Rowlingson, 2004).

Utilizing the above process, Company A was assessed and observations were made against each of these steps to determine the state of the organization's forensics readiness.

2.4.1 Define business scenarios that require digital evidence

This step focuses on the purpose of digital evidence collection in the organization. The organization should know under what circumstances in the running of its business such data should be collected. In other words, this is a risk assessment activity to understand whether or not collecting digital evidence should be done and what costs and benefits it could bring.

Within Company A, there is already a mechanism in place for digital evidence collection in the IaaS service. Default logging configurations have been implemented on hypervisor systems and individual VMs. However, it is not clear on how logging data are chosen and whether the data currently collected are useful for digital investigations.

2.4.2 Identify available sources and different types of potential evidence

This step is to enable organizations to recognize the sources of potential evidence within the organization. Primary sources of evidence in an IaaS infrastructure include:

1. Hypervisor access and audit logs
2. VVM logs within the hypervisor

3. VM OS logs or logs generated by the virtualized operating systems
4. Firewall logs
5. Application and server monitoring logs
6. Storage area network logs
7. Virtualized disks and memory snapshots
8. VM backups

The above is not an exhaustive list of all the available data sources in Company A as there are other systems that contribute to the IaaS infrastructure such as e-mail systems, third-party vendor connections, and internal system administrator desktops.

2.4.3 Determining the evidence collection requirement

This step focuses on the identification of the evidence collection requirement within the organization collect needed to support digital investigations set out in Step 1.

In Company A, there is no observed documented security requirement for evidence collection from the IaaS infrastructure. IaaS systems administrators have configured data and log file storage utilizing default vendor parameters or previous institutional knowledge.

2.4.4 Establish a capability securely gathering legally admissible evidence to meet the requirement

After the establishment of the data collection requirement, this step is to understand how the required data can be collected without interfering with ongoing business processes and to ensure that collection of the required data is compliant with existing laws and regulations. Methods of securely gathering data include remote logging wherein systems that generate log data send this data to servers for storage rather than keeping logs local to the system (Ghorbani et al., 2010).

Within Company A, the IaaS infrastructure sends certain log data remotely to established servers within the organization's network. System events for hypervisors are remotely logged but only for administration purposes in case of technical troubleshooting with no observed consideration for forensic uses. It is observed that majority, if not all, of these log files are not encrypted and no increased security is put on these log files with access controlled to standard organization means. There is also no observed log archiving to secure and encrypted media.

2.4.5 Establish a policy for secure storage and handling of potential evidence

This step takes into account that once data has been collected, it should be protected to ensure that it could be retrieved in a safe and secure manner which ensures the integrity of the data. This step is also concerned with ensuring the longer term availability of this information should it be needed for investigations at a later time.

Within Company A, there are facilities available for long-term data storage. Company A utilizes storage area networks that can be used for online data storage but also have the ability to send data to tapes for offline and longer term storage. There is, however, no observed policy on evidence handling for IaaS data.

2.4.6 Ensure monitoring and auditing is targeted to detect and deter major incidents

Aside from collecting data to support postincident investigations, it should be noted that monitoring plays a vital role in preventing or detecting security incidents that may be in progress. Establishing a monitoring and auditing facility such as an intrusion detection system would allow organizations to respond to and minimize the consequences of security threats and incidents (Bolt and Ficher, 2012).

Company A utilizes various monitoring tools that target parts of the IaaS infrastructure. There is hardware infrastructure monitoring that looks for errors and failures within the hardware housing the IaaS systems. There is operating system monitoring to alert on errors of the VM guest OS or threshold conditions such as disk space and CPU usage. There is also application-level monitoring for critical business applications performance. However, there is neither a monitoring and auditing mechanism to log and alert on suspicious access events nor an intrusion detection policy within the organization.

2.4.7 Specify circumstances when escalation to a full formal investigation is required

If a suspicious event is triggered or manually detected, such as detected intrusion or failed access events, the event needs to be reviewed and a process has to be established to decide which of the detected events need to be followed up with formal investigations and escalated to management for further action. This will involve an impact assessment of the event and the cost of investigation. If it is determined that further action is required, formal investigations involving the organization's security teams and even law enforcement agencies should be considered (Grobler et al., 2010).

Within Company A, there does not appear to be a set policy dictating the escalation of security incidents that involve IaaS data, as there are existing policies for reporting all information security-related incidents. There is no observed policy or process for escalation of security incidents and this appears to be within the discretion of the case study organization's security team and management on a case-by-case basis.

2.4.8 Train staff, so that all those involved understand their role in the digital evidence process and the legal sensitivies of evidence

For organization personnel who may subsequently be involved with digital investigations, it is important that they are adequately trained to understand on digital forensics and digital investigation best practices (Grobler and Louwrens, 2006; Hooper et al., 2013). This is important in order to preserve the integrity of the evidence being used as well as ensuring compliance with the applicable laws and regulations.

Company A does not have an observed training plan for the handling of digital evidence and digital investigations. It is observed that systems administrators within the case study organization are expected to have prior knowledge to ensure the integrity of evidence during the collection process.

2.4.9 Present an evidence-based case describing the incident and its impact

This step establishes the output of digital investigations in a readily available report or case file. This case file may be referenced by law enforcement agencies for further investigations or prosecutions of individuals responsible or to ensure that similar security incidents are avoided in the future (Casey, 2011, p. 508). Such a case file could include the facts of the incident and findings from the analysis of the digital evidence.

Within Company A, there is no observed policy on the production of case files or security incident information. There are observed incident report mechanisms that provide details on specific IT issues or incidents. However, there is no established reporting mechanism for digital investigations within the case study organization.

2.4.10 Ensure legal review to facilitate action in response to the incident

During a digital investigation, it is important to obtain legal advice to ensure that the evidence collection process is forensically and legally sound and whether sufficient evidence has been collected to identify and prosecute the offenders. The legal team may also assist with assessing whether the cost of the investigation and prosecution is too high.

Within Company A, incidents involving other parts of the IT infrastructure (including IaaS service) require management review that may include legal advice. However, there is no formal process to seek legal review of security incidents and legal advice is sought on an as-needed basis.

2.4.11 Summary of observations

Our observations of Company A's forensic readiness is summarized in Table 3.

In the first instance, there is no documented scenario for incidents that would require a digital forensic investigation. In some cases where digital evidence is required from the IaaS infrastructure, it is to support technical troubleshooting or application issues rather than supporting investigations of criminal or malicious activity. Possible criminal or illegal scenarios have not been documented and made available to the IaaS support staff such that there is minimal comprehension of what risks to the IaaS infrastructure should be considered critical enough to warrant active management of possible evidentiary data.

Although the IaaS systems administrators are knowledgeable and maintain an understanding of all the possible sources of evidence within the IaaS infrastructure, there is no prioritization of which sources should be considered critical for evidence gathering purposes. This is a function of not understanding the scenarios required for possible investigation; therefore, only default configurations for logging have been enabled within the IaaS infrastructure which includes the hypervisor systems (VMware), the hardware elements (Blade servers and Blade enclosures), and SAN systems.

Because of the lack of requirements for gathering data for these sources of evidence, there is no established policy for gathering this data. Despite the capability

Table 3 Forensic Readiness Summary

Forensic Readiness Step	IaaS Implemented
Define business scenarios for evidence gathering	Partial. Logging is performed largely to support operational activities with no specific business scenarios in mind
Identify available sources	Partial. There are well-established sources for digital evidence but these are utilized primarily for support operations and not digital investigations
Determining evidence collection requirement	Partial. Although audit logs and similar information are used and collected, there is no evidence requirement
Establish evidence handling capability	Partial. Some log data is collected remotely but there is no observed capability and training to ensure forensically sound evidence collection
Storage of potential evidence	Yes. System logging is available to be stored on secure media
Monitoring policies	Partial. No monitoring for intrusions or anomalous network behavior
Escalation processes	Partial. There is no observed escalation process and escalation is undertaken on a case-by-case basis
Training for staff	No. There is no digital forensic or digital investigation training for staff
Evidence-based case	No
Legal review	Partial. Although not documented in policies, legal assistance and advice are sought on a case-by-base basis

within Company A's for secure evidence collection and storage, without any guiding policies there is no proactive storage and collection of possible evidentiary data. Within the case study organization, backup and restore policies are in effect to store certain aspects of this data, and not all logs emanating from the hypervisors and IaaS infrastructure are saved for long-term retention and a rotating logging facility is in effect for many of these IaaS infrastructure logs.

Despite availability of monitoring for the IaaS infrastructure and associated services, there is no targeted monitoring for potential suspicious activity. Company A does not have production intrusion detection systems that could assist with identifying possible security breaches or provide automated monitoring of suspect activity. Most security incidents are reported manually through a security incident reporting process. Company A has extensive monitoring tools and capabilities from built-in IaaS-based monitoring and alerting to third-party element monitoring applications. If scenarios that require digital evidence can be established, then these monitoring tools can be configured appropriately to monitor these scenarios.

There is no specific training for IaaS personnel to prepare them for working with digital evidence and forensic investigations. This stems from the nonavailability of digital forensic requirements and, therefore, there is a lack of clarification of the roles and responsibilities of Company A's employees during a digital forensic investigation. If evidence collection requirements are defined as part of the forensic readiness process, then it is expected that IaaS personnel should be trained for their roles within this process.

3 CONCLUSIONS

In this chapter, a general overview of the security posture of an existing organization has been shown through an employee's observations of the various security controls and technological solutions deployed by the organization.

The observations suggested that while there is a security culture and security measures are implemented within the organization, these initiatives are inadequate to deal with cloud-specific threats. For example, various IT security and related policies and controls are in place to mitigate existing security threats including cloud computing-specific threats. However, there is no IaaS-specific policy as existing security and related policies apply generally to all use of information technologies within the organization. It is also observed that mitigation solutions for IaaS security threats are not regularly monitored or reviewed for effectiveness. There is no review structure set up to ensure that existing mitigation solutions continue to be effective, particularly against emerging and new threats. This suggested the need for an ongoing risk assessment methodology or plan for both the IaaS infrastructure and the general IT infrastructure.

As more of Company A's business units decide to utilize the IaaS infrastructure for different purposes, there is an urgent need for IaaS-specific policies particularly those relating to evidence collection and forensic readiness. Without established digital forensics and forensic readiness policies and best practices, it would have been costly and in some cases impossible to collect adequate evidence to identify and prosecute offenders involved in security incidents such as

- Inappropriate use of VMs to host unwanted software (Choo, 2010).
- Use of VMs to store inappropriate or illegal data or files (Archer and Boehm, 2009).
- Unauthorized access to management interface (Grobauer et al., 2011).
- DDoS attacks and various network based attacks (Dawoud et al., 2010).

Considerations should be made toward gathering data such as e-mail entries or remote monitoring events and alerts for correlation toward the security incidents or scenarios, and storing such data securely (Dykstra and Riehl, 2012) as well as having an established procedure for digital investigations and responding to law enforcement requests.

In conclusion, there appears to be a lack of clarity with regard to the requirements for specific IaaS security, digital evidence collection, and digital investigation. Having IaaS-specific controls and steps in place for security, digital forensics and forensic readiness will provide a more focused approach to security which could make better use of the finite amount of resources the organization may have.

It is, therefore, suggested that the various stakeholders within the organization review and put forward definitive requirements for the implementation of the IaaS-specific security, digital forensics, and forensic readiness policies within Company A.

One potential future work is to develop and validate a cloud incident handling and forensic readiness model such as the model of Ab Rahman and Choo (Rahman and Choo, 2015b).

REFERENCES

Angadi, A.B., Angadi, A.B., Gull, K.C., 2013. Security issues with possible solutions in cloud computing—a survey. Int. J. Adv. Res. Comput. Eng. Technol. (IJARCET) 2, 652.

Antonopoulos, N., Gillam, L., 2010. Cloud Computing: Principles, Systems and Applications. Springer.

Archer, J., BOEHM, A., 2009. Security guidance for critical areas of focus in cloud computing. Cloud Security Alliance.

AS/NZS, 2006. ISO/IEC 27002:2006—Information Technology—Security Techniques—Code of Practice for Information Security Management.

Barrett, D., Kipper, G., 2010. Virtualization and forensics: a digital forensic investigator's guide to virtual environments.

Beek, C., 2010. Virtual forensics. Ten ICT Professionals, Paper.

Bhadauria, R., Sanyal, S., 2012. Survey on security issues in cloud computing and associated mitigation techniques. Int. J. Comput. Appl. 47, 47.

Bolt, S., Ficher, J., 2012. Network Intrusion Analysis. Syngress, Waltham, MA.

Byres, E.J., 2012. Defense in Depth. INTECH 59, 38.

Casey, E., 2011. Digital Evidence and Computer Crime: Forensic Science, Computers and the Internet. Academic Press.

Choo, K.-K.R., 2010. Cloud Computing Challenges and Future Directions. Australian Institute of Criminology, Canberra.

Cloud Security Alliance, 2013. The Notorious nine: cloud computing top threats in 2013. Cloud Security Alliance.

Dawoud, W., Takouna, I., Meinel, C., 2010. Infrastructure as a service security: challenges and solutions. In: Informatics and Systems (INFOS), 2010 The 7th International Conference on, 2010. IEEE, pp. 1–8.

Dykstra, J., Riehl, D., 2012. Forensic collection of electronic evidence from infrastructure-as-a-service cloud computing. Rich. J. Law Tech. 19, 1.

Ghorbani, A.A., Lu, W., Tavallaee, M., 2010. Network Attacks. Springer US, Boston, MA.

Grobauer, B., Walloschek, T., Stocker, E., 2011. Understanding cloud computing vulnerabilities. Security Privacy IEEE 9, 50–57.

Grobler, C., Louwrens, B., 2006. Digital forensics: a multi-dimensional discipline. Information Security South Africa 2006. http://icsa.cs.up.ac.za/issa/2006/Proceedings/Research/62_Paper.pdf

Grobler, C.P., Louwrens, C.P., Von Solms, S.H., 2010. A framework to guide the implementation of proactive digital forensics in organisations.

Hay, B., Nance, K., Bishop, M., 2011. Storm clouds rising: security challenges for IaaS cloud computing. System Sciences (HICSS). In: 44th Hawaii International Conference on, 2011. IEEEpp. 1–7.

Hooper, C., Martini, B., Choo, K.-K.R., 2013. Cloud computing and its implications for cyber-crime investigations in Australia. Comput. Law Security Rev. 29, 152–163.

Horvath, M., Jakub, M., 2009. Implementation of security controls according to ISO/IEC 27002 in a small organisation. Qual. Innovation Prosperity 13, 48–54.

Julidotter, N., Choo, K.-K.R., 2015. CATRA: conceptual cloud attack taxonomy and risk assessment framework. In: Ko, R., Choo, K.-K.R. (Eds.), Cloud Security Ecosystem. Syngress, and Imprint of Elsevier.

Karadsheh, L., 2012. Applying security policies and service level agreement to IaaS service model to enhance security and transition. Comput. Security 31, 315–326.

Kent, K., Chevalier, S., Grance, T., Dang, H., 2006. Guide to integrating forensic techniques into incident response. NIST Spl. Public.. 800–86.

Khan, M.F., Ullah, M.A., Aziz-Ur-Rehman, 2012. An approach towards customized multi-tenancy. Int. J. Modern Educ. Comput. Sci. 4, 39.

Martini, B., Choo, K.-K.R., 2013. Cloud storage forensics: ownCloud as a case study. Digit. Investig. 10, 287–299.

Martini, B., Choo, K.-K.R., 2014a. Distributed filesystem forensics: XtreemFS as a case study. Digit. Investig. 11, 295–313.

Martini, B., Choo, K.-K.R., 2014b. Remote programmatic vCloud forensics. In: Proceedings of 13th IEEE International Conference on Trust, Security and Privacy in Computing and Communications (TrustCom 2014).

Martini, B., Do, Q., Choo, K.-K.R., 2015a. Conceptual evidence collection and analysis methodology for Android devices. In: Ko, R., Choo, K.-K.R. (Eds.), Cloud Security Ecosystem. Syngress, and Imprint of Elsevier.

Martini, B., Do, Q., Choo, K.-K.R., 2015b. Mobile cloud forensics: An analysis of seven popular Android apps. In: Ko, R., Choo, K.-K.R. (Eds.), Cloud Security Ecosystem. Syngress, and Imprint of Elsevier.

Mckemmish, R., 1999. What is forensic computing?

Mell, P., Grance, T., 2011. The NIST definition of cloud computing.

Pangalos, G., Ilioudis, C., Pagkalos, I., 2010. The importance of corporate forensic readiness in the information security framework.

Pearson, S., Benameur, A., 2010. Privacy, security and trust issues arising from cloud computing. In: IEEE Second International Conference on Cloud Computing Technology and Science (CloudCom). IEEE, pp. 693–702.

Pearson, S., Yee, G., Springerlink, 2013. Privacy and Security for Cloud Computing. Springer, London.

Quick, D., Choo, K.-K.R., 2013a. Digital droplets: microsoft SkyDrive forensic data remnants. Futur. Gener. Comput. Syst. 29, 1378–1394.

Quick, D., Choo, K.-K.R., 2013b. Dropbox analysis: data remnants on user machines. Digit. Investig. 10, 3–18.

Quick, D., Choo, K.-K.R., 2013c. Forensic collection of cloud storage data: does the act of collection result in changes to the data or its metadata? Digit. Investig. 10, 266–277.

Quick, D., Choo, K.-K.R., 2014. Google drive: forensic analysis of data remnants. J. Netw. Comput. Appl. 40, 179–193.

Quick, D., Martini, B., Choo, R., 2013. Cloud Storage Forensics. Syngress.

Rahman, A., Choo, K.-K.R., 2015a. A survey of information security incident handling in the cloud. Comput. Security 49, 45–69.

Rahman, A., Choo, K.-K.R., 2015b. Integrating digital forensic practices in cloud incident handling: a conceptual cloud incident handling model. In: Ko, R., Choo, K.-K.R. (Eds.), Cloud Security Ecosystem. Syngress, and Imprint of Elsevier.

René, S.-G., 2005. Information security management best practice based on ISO/IEC 17799. Inf. Manage. J. 39, 60.

Rogers, A. 2012. From Peer-to-Peer Networks to Cloud Computing: How Technology Is Redefining Child Pornography Laws. Available at SSRN 2006664.

Rowlingson, R., 2004. A ten step process for forensic readiness. Int. J. Dig. Evid. 2, 1–28.

Sibiya, G., Fogwill, T., Venter, H.S., Ngobeni, S., 2013. Digital forensic readiness in a cloud environment. In: AFRICON. IEEE, pp. 1–5.

Simou, S., Kalloniatis, C., Kavakli, E., Gritzalis, S., 2014. Cloud forensics: identifying the major issues and challenges. In: Advanced Information Systems Engineering. Springer, pp. 271–284.

Standardization, I. O. F. & Technical Committee ISO/IEC JTC1, I. T. S. S., IT Security Techniques 2012. Information technology: security techiques: guidelines for identification, collection, acquisition and preservation of digital evidence = Technologies de l'information: techniques de securite: lignes directrices pour l'dentification, la collecte, l'acquisition et la preservation de preuves numeriques, Geneva, Switzerland, ISO.

Trenwith, P.M., Venter, H.S., 2013. Digital forensic readiness in the cloud. In: Information Security for South Africa. IEEE, pp. 1–5.

Vaquero, L.M., Rodero-Merino, L., Morán, D., 2011. Locking the sky: a survey on IaaS cloud security. Computing 91, 93–118.

Zhang, Y., Juels, A., Reiter, M.K., Ristenpart, T., 2012. Cross-VM side channels and their use to extract private keys. In: Proceedings of the 2012 ACM Conference on Computer and Communications Security. ACM, pp. 305–316.

Ubuntu One investigation: Detecting evidences on client machines

19

Mohammad Shariati[a], Ali Dehghantanha[a], Ben Martini[b]
Kim-Kwang Raymond Choo[b]

School of Computing, Science and Engineering, University of Salford, Greater Manchester, UK[a]
Information Assurance Research Group, School of Information Technology and Mathematical
Sciences, University of South Australia, Adelaide, Australia[b]

1 INTRODUCTION

The term cloud computing refers to a model whereby a user can access computing resources via a network on an on-demand basis (Mell and Grance, 2011). Various types of resources can be shared between users and in a way that remote clients can utilize them, e.g., processing, volatile and persistent storage, and so on. This pool of resources is commonly available as a service via an internal network (private cloud) or publically via the Internet (public cloud). In addition to providing the *de facto* definition of cloud computing the National Institute of Standards and Technology (NIST) also defined a number of service models including: Software as a Service (SaaS), Platform as a Service (PaaS), and Infrastructure as a Service (IaaS) (Mell and Grance, 2011). Storage as a Service (STaaS) is an addition to these traditional service models. STaaS technologies enable users to store, download, and share their data in a very accessible manner. There are a number of STaaS service providers including Dropbox, Microsoft OneDrive, Google Drive, and Ubuntu One. These service providers commonly provide personal accounts for minimal or no cost. Cloud Service Providers (CSPs) have made significant efforts to attract customers by supporting various types of devices ranging from traditional PC platforms such as Windows, Mac OS X, and Linux to more recent smart phone operating systems such as iOS and Android. Also, CSPs generally offer access to their services via standards compliant Web browsers including Internet Explorer, Google Chrome, Mozilla Firefox, and Apple Safari. These features allow users to access their data via the majority of Internet connected devices.

However, while STaaS services provide legitimate users with significant utility and convenience, they are equally useful to criminals who utilize them for storing and sharing illicit materials. The global nature of cloud computing infrastructure contributes to the numerous technical and jurisdictional challenges in the identification and acquisition of evidential data by law enforcement and national security agencies.

Digital forensics is the process of identifying, preserving, analyzing, and presenting evidence for use in legal proceedings (McKemmish, 1999). The process of traditional forensic investigation is often impeded by some of the key characteristics of the cloud environment such as multitenancy and global data distribution. Taylor et al. (2011) highlighted that with the advent of cloud computing acquiring and analyzing digital evidence from cloud services using traditional processes is generally infeasible. One key area of difficulty is in identifying the particular service utilized by suspects and then extracting potential remnants of user activities involving that service.

In this chapter, we seek to assist forensic investigators and practitioners to detect possible evidential remnants derived from the Ubuntu One cloud storage service. The artifacts discussed in this chapter should assist in detecting the use of Ubuntu One and the associated evidential remnants stored on client devices. The focus of this study is to detect file system, RAM, and network artifacts present after utilizing Ubuntu One on the Windows 8.1, Mac OS X 10.9, and iOS 7.0.4 platforms.

In this chapter, we intend to address the following research questions:

1. What data can be found on a device's persistent storage after using the Ubuntu One client software and the location of data remnants within Windows, Mac OS X, and iOS devices?
2. What data can be found in a device's persistent storage after using Ubuntu One via a Web browser?
3. What data can be extracted from volatile memory on Windows and Mac OS X devices when utilizing Ubuntu One?
4. What data can be extracted from collected network traffic after Ubuntu One has been accessed on Windows, Mac OS X, and iOS devices?

The remainder of this chapter is organized as follows; in the next section, we provide a brief review of related work in the field of cloud forensics. In Sections 3 and 4, we outline both the methodology and experiment setup utilized in our experiments, respectively. In Section 5, we present our research findings, and finally in Section 6, we conclude the chapter.

2 RELATED WORK

Grispos et al. (2012) discussed a number of challenges for forensic investigations in the cloud, namely, creating valid forensic images, recovery of distributed evidence, and management of large data sources. There are a number of other research studies that highlight a number of the major issues of cloud forensics (Biggs and Vidalis, 2009; Birk and Wegener, 2011; Martini and Choo, 2012; Damshenas et al., 2012; Daryabar et al., 2013; Aminnezhad et al., 2013).

In the case of STaaS forensic research, the majority of existing research has been conducted on STaaS clients, with a smaller subset of the published materials focusing on server side STaaS investigation. Quick and Choo (2013a,b,c, 2014) have developed a forensic framework to identify, acquire, and present evidential data remnants of Dropbox, Google Drive, and Microsoft SkyDrive on the Windows 7 and iPhone platforms. Hale (2013) published a similar investigation on the Amazon Cloud Drive client on Windows XP and 7. In addition, Chung et al. (2012) analyzed Amazon S3, Google Docs, and Evernote and outlined a technique to collect data from personal computers and mobile devices. Federici (2014) described the concepts and internals of the Cloud Data Imager tool which he developed to provide read-only access to files and metadata of selected remote folders on STaaS services and currently provides access to the Dropbox, Google Drive, and Microsoft SkyDrive services. In terms of server STaaS analysis, Martini and Choo (2013) focused upon the client and server artifacts created with use of ownCloud. The analysis of the ownCloud server component, after analysis of the client component, allows the practitioner to obtain a wider range of evidential data (e.g., previous versions of files).

The numerous publications that investigate STaaS products demonstrate the need for researchers to undertake detailed analysis to guide practitioners in collecting all available evidence from cloud storage products.

3 METHODOLOGY

Using Ubuntu One as a case study, artifacts were identified that are likely to remain after the use of cloud storage, in the context of several experiments conducted on Windows, Mac OS X, and Apple iPhone 3G clients. As Ubuntu One supports accessing, uploading, and sharing data using both client software and a browser, we have undertaken experiments across multiple platforms to locate evidential data sources on different client devices.

In each experiment, the investigator first determines whether it is possible to collect volatile data on the platform being investigated. If so, the investigator acquires the contents of physical memory and captures the network traffic. Next, if nonvolatile data can be obtained, the investigator gathers data from the file system such as log files, configuration files, internet history data, databases, and directories. For the Windows and Mac operating systems, we were able to collect volatile and nonvolatile data, but in the case of iOS only network traffic was collected. This was due to the lack of opportunities for forensically sound physical memory acquisition on iOS devices. After collection, the investigator searches for traces of the Ubuntu One cloud storage service in the collected images.

4 EXPERIMENT SETUP

The research experiment was broken into six stages, namely, (1) preparing the Virtual Machines and iPhone, including installing the cloud applications; (2) uploading a dataset to the cloud storage provider; (3) accessing the data through the client application/Web browser on the VMs and iPhone; (4) perform various file manipulations to the dataset on both the VMs and iPhone; (5) process the VMs and iPhone to extract volatile and nonvolatile data; and (6) use numerous forensic tools to analyze the collected forensic images and present the final result.

We undertook experiments within the following four usage environments:

(1) Windows browser-based (see Section 5.1);
(2) Windows app-based (see Section 5.2);
(3) Mac OS X app-based (see Section 5.3); and
(4) iOS app-based (see Section 5.4).

We have used Ubuntu One 4.0.2 which provides users with 5 GB of free space and utilized the following three files from the Enron e-mail dataset, downloaded from the project Web site (http://bailando.sims.berkeley.edu/enron_email.html) on 15 April 2014, to conduct our experiments:

1. AQUA-OS2.BMP (151 kB),
2. HANGING.DOC (22 kB),
3. HANGING.txt (2 kB)

Different file types were utilized in the experiments to determine whether any discrepancies in forensic collection were observable for the different file types.

Windows 8.1 and Mac OS X 10.9 experiments were conducted on virtualized environments utilizing VMware Player 6.0.2. An iPhone 4S with iOS 7.0.6 was used to undertake iOS investigation experiments. Each VM was configured with one CPU, 2 GB of RAM, and 20 GB of hard disk space.

Our experiments were designed to simulate common user activities on cloud platforms, namely, uploading, downloading, opening, and deleting files. For the purposes of this research, one set of credentials were used in all experiments to simplify the location of the credentials as part of forensic image examination.

Web Browser Investigation Experiments Setup: To commence our environment setup for Web browser analysis, we installed the four most popular browsers at the time of research, namely, Microsoft Internet Explorer (version 10.0.9200.16384), Mozilla Firefox (version 25.0.1), Google Chrome (version 31.0.1650.63), and Apple Safari (version 5.1.7), on four VMs. We then performed a series of upload, open, download, and delete operations with one VM for each type of operation. Table 1 outlines the list of tools that were copied to each VM for monitoring changes and detecting possible evidential data.

Figure 1 shows the VM hierarchy for our browser-based experiments.

Table 1 Software Used on VMs for Analysis

Software	Version	Purpose
Regshot	1.9.0	Registry monitor
Process Monitor	3.05	Process, registry, and file activity monitor
Nirsoft Web browser passview	1.43	Saved password retrieval
Digital detective net analysis	1.5	Browser cache retrieval

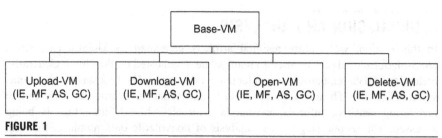

FIGURE 1

VMs created for Web browser usage investigation.

Windows App-Based Investigation Experiment Setup: In addition to the series of upload, download, open, and delete operations, we also experimented installing and uninstalling the Ubuntu One app to determine the artifacts that could be detected after such activities on client devices, as outlined in Figure 2.

Mac OS X App-Based Investigation Experiment Setup: Similar experiments to Windows platform were conducted on Mac OS X 10.9 Mavericks. However, the process for uninstalling applications on Mac OS X is different in comparison to uninstalling an app in the Windows environment. While most Windows programs include an uninstaller that can be run using the Add/Remove Programs tool available in Control Panel, no such feature exists in Mac OS X and therefore, most users simply move application bundles to the Trash. Assuming that the trash is not emptied, we should be able to locate significant application artifacts after an uninstallation of the Ubuntu One client on OS X client machines.

iOS App-Based Investigation Experiment Setup: For our iOS experiment, we used a jailbroken iPhone 4S running iOS 7.0.6 to conduct our experiments. iFile 2.0.1-1 was installed from Cydia to browse iOS storage directories. The directory holds the associated files and folders of apps from the Apple Store is/private/var/mobile/Applications, with each app being assigned a subdirectory name by universally unique identifier (UUID). Activating the "Applications Names" option under iFile's Preferences (File Manager section) translates the UUIDs to the human readable names of all the subdirectories. Mobile Terminal was another application installed from Cydia enabling execution of UNIX commands in the iOS environment.

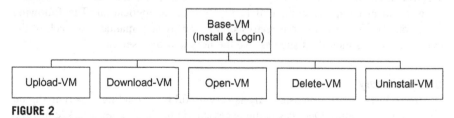

FIGURE 2

VMs created for Windows and Mac OS X platforms investigation.

5 DISCUSSION AND ANALYSIS

In this section, we explore residual artifacts generated by Ubuntu One when cross-platform methods are used to manipulate data hosted on the cloud. Generally, collection of data remnants was conducted in two stages. The first stage is the acquisition of live data. The analysis of this live (volatile) data is regarded as significant in recovering sensitive information that is available while Ubuntu One is being accessed. The second stage is the analysis of nonvolatile data remnants that can be located on the local system. These two methods complement each other to maximize the amount of available evidential data during an investigation. In our research, forensic analysis of live data encompasses analysis of live memory and network traffic, while data remnants analysis involves the persistent files such as log files, databases, and the registry (for Windows platforms).

In all versions of the client applications, after lunching Ubuntu One, the user must enter a device name and their authentication credentials. At next launch, Ubuntu One logs-in automatically unless the user unlinks the device.

For this research, virtual hard disks, virtual memory, and forensic images of real memory and network traffic were examined using multiple forensic tools. We analyzed the VM's VMEM file as a memory dump file and the VMDK file as an image of the hard disk using AccessData FTK (version 1.86.1). We also used Hex Workshop (version 6.7) for analysis of memory and hard disk images, which enabled searching for keywords such as the Ubuntu One credentials, files being accessed, and words such as "Ubuntu One," "Ubuntu," and "UbuntuOne," The network traffic was captured and analyzed using Wireshark (version 1.10.2) and further analysis was conducted using NetworkMiner (version 1.5). SQLite DB Browser under OSForensics (version 2), PList Explorer (version 1.0), and Notepad++ (version 6.4) were employed to access and retrieve evidential data from the Ubuntu One databases and log files. AccessData Registry Viewer (version 1.7.4.2) and Regripper (version 2.8) were utilized to analyze Windows registry and NTUSER.dat files.

5.1 WINDOWS BROWSER BASED

Ubuntu One allows users to access and manipulate their data on the cloud without installing the client application, via a Web browser. From an evidence collection perspective, it can be presumed that the browser-based application leaves fewer remnants on local computer compared to the full client application. The following stages outline the results of our analysis, in a step-by-step manner, for each of the evidence sources identified such as live memory and browser cache.

5.1.1 Memory

We found live memory forensic analysis very useful for extracting important digital artifacts when Ubuntu One was being accessed via the Web interface. We utilized two methods to detect Ubuntu One user identity information in the live memory:

Method 1—Searching for the string "login&password=" to retrieve the user's credentials in plain text (see Figure 3).

Method 2—Searching for the string "openid.ax.value.email" to retrieve the users e-mail address (see Figure 4).

We also noted that it was possible to extract the names of files that had been accessed or manipulated depending on the specific operation used. A selection of operations and the associated artifacts are outlined in Figures 5–7.

```
.y...csrfmiddlewaretoken=uV
N9hjU1F3G0IZHtcbt6UcRo6d97d
5ND&email=▬▬▬▬▬▬▬▬▬▬▬
%40gmail.com&user-intention
s=login&password=▬▬▬▬▬▬▬▬▬
▬.....................
```

FIGURE 3

User credentials located in live memory.

```
name="openid.ax.value.email
.1" value="▬▬▬▬▬▬▬▬▬▬▬▬
t@gmail.com"/><input type="
```

FIGURE 4

Username located in live memory.

```
.    .    <li>.        <a ti
tle="Delete File" alt="Dele
te File".          id="fus
uENo_p5wTZCKgkT9NNi2YQ-dele
te".            class="ul-fi
les-delete-link delete-butt
on">Delete file</a>.    </l
i>.      </ul>.      </td>.</tr
>...        .        .<
tr id="fusWbdqbNWeQnu8YNOUG
bheow".      class="file".
 title="File">.      <td clas
s="files-td-name" id="HANGI
NG.txt">.        .        .
  <a title="HANGING.txt"hre
f="https://files.one.ubuntu
.com/WbdqbNWeQnu8YNOUGbheow
" target="_blank">HANGING.t
```

FIGURE 5

Filename located after delete operation.

```
......?.....Content-Length:
 0..Content-Disposition: at
tachment; filename=HANGING.
txt..Vary: Accept-Encoding,
```

FIGURE 6

Filename located after open/download operation.

```
ata; name="file"; filename=
"HANGING.txt"..Content-Type
```

FIGURE 7

Filename in upload operation.

5.1.2 Browser cache and history

When a user has accessed Ubuntu One via the online interface the Web browsers cache and history may contain evidential data and should be extracted. Although it will not generally be possible to extract the Ubuntu One user credentials from the browser cache and history, numerous other evidential artifacts can often be retrieved. While we were not able to extract credentials from the cache directly, in the case of the Chrome and Internet Explorer browsers, the Nirsoft Web Browser Pass View was able to extract the stored password which we saved using the browser.

For an investigator, the first step in a cloud investigation is often to determine which cloud storage services have been used by the suspect, and URL addresses are one source of evidential data useful in determining this. In our experiments, we noted a number of Web addresses in the cache and history that relate to Ubuntu One. These addresses are listed below:

https://media.one.ubuntu.com
https://one.ubuntu.com
https://login.ubuntu.com/
https://files.one.ubuntu.com/

From our analysis of the cache data, we determined that there were three Web pages that we considered to be of particular importance, namely, "dashboard.htm," "files.htm," and "+opened.htm."

The dashboard.htm file contains the first name and last name that has been entered by the Ubuntu One user. In our case, "Test" and "Project" were the first name and last name, respectively (see Figure 8).

The opened.htm file stores the username as well as the full name of the Ubuntu One user (see Figure 9).

```
<span>Welcome Test Project</span>
<a href="/account/" class="account">My Account</a> |
<a href="/auth/logout/">logout</a>
```

FIGURE 8

The user's full name in dashboard.htm.

FIGURE 9

The user's username and full name in opened.htm.

```
<td class="files-td-name" id="AQUA-OS2.BMP">

    <a title="AQUA-OS2.BMP" href="https://files.one.ubuntu.com/YUS8opQZQSOCavYpI-3sDQ" target="_blank">AQUA-OS2.BMP</a>

</td>
<td class="files-td-size">

        150.1 KB

</td>
<td class="files-td-date">

        <span title="2014-04-22 03:15:30">2014-04-22</span>

</td>
```

FIGURE 10

Filename and associated timestamp in files.htm.

Finally, files.htm cache files often contain filenames, file size, and the date and time that an operation on the file was carried out (see Figure 10).

5.1.3 Registry

There was no information regarding Ubuntu One credentials and usage located in the registry except for a "TypedURL" entry from Internet Explorer (see Figure 11). As the name suggests, these registry entries are stored when a user types a URL in Internet Explorer (Mee et al., 2006).

5.1.4 Network traffic

Wireshark was used for collecting the network traffic from Ubuntu One usage, which was then analyzed using NetworkMiner. We found that all of the collected traffic was encrypted due to the use of SSL/TLS when communicating with the Ubuntu One servers. For this reason, we were unable to extract any data of significant evidential value. However, a number of common IP addresses were used for Ubuntu One communications,

```
TypedURLsTime
Software\Microsoft\Internet Explorer\TypedURLsTime
LastWrite Time Tue Apr 22 03:48:04 2014 (UTC)
  url1 -> Tue Apr 22 03:48:04 2014 Z (http://one.ubuntu.com/)
```

FIGURE 11

"TypedURL" in the Windows registry.

Table 2 List of IP Addresses and Hostnames Extracted from Network Traffic

IP Address	Hostname
91.189.89.77−91.189.89.78	one.ubuntu.com
91.189.89.182−91.189.89.183	media.one.ubuntu.com
91.189.89.206−91.189.89.207	login.one.ubuntu.com

which resolve to Ubuntu.com subdomains. Table 2 shows the IP addresses and associated hostnames that were extracted from the network traffic capture file after a login to Ubuntu One and contents of the user's account had been accessed/manipulated.

5.2 WINDOWS APP-BASED

Upon installation the Ubuntu One client software creates a folder named Ubuntu One stored in the "\Users\<user>\Ubuntu One" directory, by default. The folder only appears to be utilized while the Ubuntu One client is running, during which content can be found in the directory as discussed below. By default, this folder is used by Ubuntu One for automatic synchronization of files. In addition to this directory, the installation of Ubuntu One creates some folders on the local computer to store persistent data including log files, databases, and other related files. Utilizing Process Monitor, we detected the following folders that were used by Ubuntu One:

1) C:\ProgramData\Microsoft\Windows\Start Menu\Programs\Ubuntu One
2) C:\Program Files (x86)\ubuntuone\
3) C:\Users\[user]\AppData\Local\ubuntuone
4) C:\Users\[user]\AppData\Local\xdg\cache
5) C:\Users\[user]\AppData\Local\xdg\ubuntuone
6) C:\ProgramData\ubuntuone
7) C:\Users\[user]\Ubuntu One

We also noted three processes related to the use of the Ubuntu One client, namely, *ubuntu-sso-login.exe, ubuntuone-control-panel-qt.exe, ubuntuonesyncdaemon.exe*.

5.2.1 Memory

Unlike our browser-based experiments discussed above, analysis of live memory for the Windows client did not result in the location of the user's password in plaintext. However the username was located by searching for the string "https://login.ubuntu.com/+id" (see Figure 12).

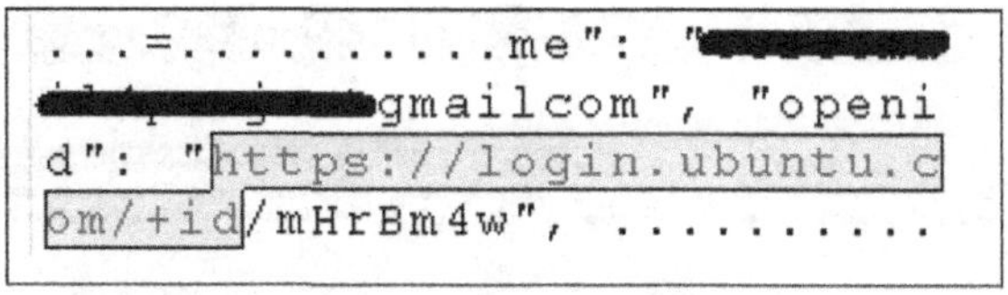

```
...=.........me":  "
         gmailcom",  "openi
d":  "https://login.ubuntu.c
om/+id/mHrBm4w",  .........
```

FIGURE 12

Located username in client memory.

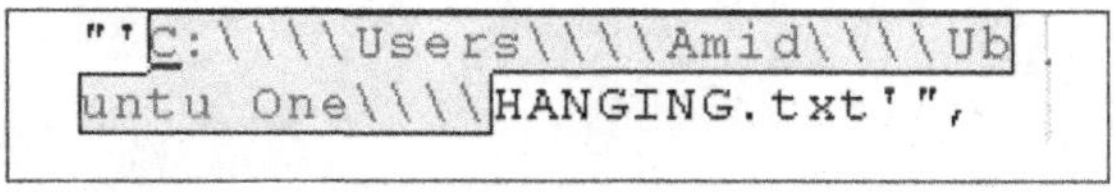

```
"'C:\\\\Users\\\\Amid\\\\Ub
untu One\\\\HANGING.txt'",
```

FIGURE 13

Located filenames in client memory.

We were also able to locate filenames for files being accessed from the Ubuntu One default folder; however, this required the use of double escaped backslashes. For example, when the default path is C:\Users\username\Ubuntu One, the term to search for in the image of live memory is "C:\\\\Users\\\\username\\\\Ubuntu One\\\\" (see Figure 13).

5.2.2 File system

The Ubuntu One folder in Program Files contains many files including .pem and .conf files. The .pem files are certificate files in the PEM encoding format and .conf files contain configuration values for the Ubuntu One client. There is only one log file in the folder, namely, install.log, which holds information regarding Ubuntu One's installation process.

The Ubuntu One folder in ProgramData also stores configuration files as well log files in .xdg format. We determined that information of importance can be recovered from the "xdg" log files, including the username used for logging into Ubuntu One and the name and path of the files listed below:

C:\Users\[user]\AppData\Local\xdg\cache\sso\sso-client.log
C:\Users\[user]\AppData\Local\xdg\cache\sso\sso-client-gui.log

Surprisingly, no database files were located in Ubuntu One's folders.

5.2.3 Event logs

Windows event logs store useful and valuable information about a system and its users (Do et al., 2014). Depending on the enabled logging level and the installed version of Windows, event logs may provide investigators with valuable data about application operations, login timestamps for users, and other system events of interest.

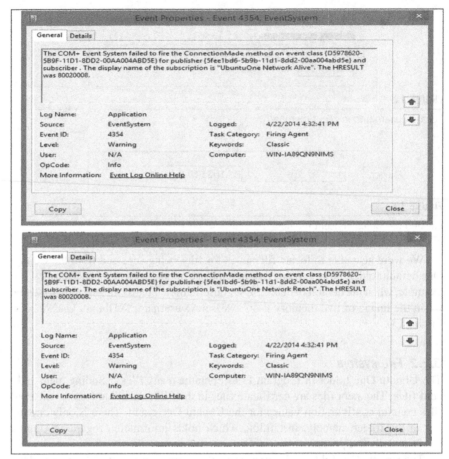

FIGURE 14

Evidence located in the Windows Event Log.

In our research, we located several logs associated with Ubuntu One within the application and services log. Searching for the keyword "Ubuntu" in the Windows event log leads to several hits as shown in Figure 14.

5.2.4 Registry

We noted the creation of the following keys in the registry after installation of the Ubuntu One client:

HKEY_LOCAL_MACHINE\SOFTWARE\Wow6432Node\Ubuntu One
HKEY_CURRENT_USER\Software\Ubuntu One

Also, searching for the keyword "Ubuntu One" located the following results in the registry:

HK_Current_User/Software/Microsoft/Windows/Run:
C:\Program Files (x86)\ubuntu one\dist\ubuntuone-syncdaemon.exe
HK_Current_User/Software/Microsoft/Windows/Current version/UFH/SHC:
HKEY_LOCAL_MACHINE\SOFTWARE\Wow6432Node\Microsoft
\Windows\CurrentVersion\Uninstall\Ubuntu One 4.2

Opening files synced via the Ubuntu One, client leads to addition of entries in the RecentDocs registry subkey as expected (see Figure 15).

We did not locate any data regarding the files that had been uploaded or downloaded or Ubuntu One credentials in the registry.

5.2.5 Network traffic

Our results for network traffic capture when using the Ubuntu One client was similar to our findings for browser-based access as all network data is encrypted using SSL. As such, plaintext data of value could not be found. However, the captured network traffic shows some differences compared to the network capture acquired using the Ubuntu One online interface. Quick and Choo (2013a,b, 2014) observed Online Certificate Status Protocol traffic relating to the presented SSL certificate in their captured network traffic. We did not note an OSCP query in our network capture. In addition, there were no connections recorded associated with the "media. ubuntu.com" subdomain. The list of IP addresses and associated hostnames extracted from the network traffic collected is listed in Table 3.

5.2.6 Uninstallation

The uninstallation process for Ubuntu One removes all of the files located in the Ubuntu One folder in "Program Files" except for the "dist" folder. All other folders associated with Ubuntu One remain on the client machine after uninstallation, including the Ubuntu One default folder and its contents.

Uninstallation also only removes Ubuntu One artifacts from the "HKEY_CURRENT_USER\Software" key, while the remaining registry artifacts are left intact.

```
recentdocs v.20100405
(NTUSER.DAT) Gets contents of user's RecentDocs key

RecentDocs
**All values printed in MRUList\MRUListEx order.
Software\Microsoft\Windows\CurrentVersion\Explorer\RecentDocs
LastWrite Time Tue Apr 22 11:10:53 2014 (UTC)
    1 = Ubuntu One
    3 = HANGING.txt
    2 = HANGING.DOC
    0 = AQUA-OS2.BMP
```

FIGURE 15

Recently opening files located in the Windows registry.

Table 3 List of IP Addresses and Hostnames Extracted from the Ubuntu One Windows Client Network Traffic

IP Address	Hostname
91.189.89.77–91.189.89.78 91.189.89.206–91.189.89.207	one.ubuntu.com login.one.ubuntu.com

5.3 MAC OS X APP-BASED

After installation of the Ubuntu One client on Mac OS X 10.9, we located the following directories created by the installation process:

/Applications/Ubuntu One.app
/Users/<user>/Ubuntu One (default Ubuntu One directory)
/Users/<user>/Library/Application Support/Ubuntuone
/Users/<user>/Library/Caches/ubuntuone
/Users/<user>/Library/Caches/sso

Uninstallation of the Ubuntu One client only removes the first directory while the rest remain intact. Some of these directories contained information related to Ubuntu One credentials and sync files such as the following:

~/Library/Caches/sso/sso-client.log
~/Library/Caches/sso/sso-client-gui.log
~/Library/Caches/ubuntuone/syncdaemon.log

The username of the Ubuntu One user can be located within the first two log files as shown in Figure 16.

Files which have been synced can be found in the syncdaemon.log log file as can be seen in Figure 17.

5.3.1 Memory

We were unable to locate plaintext credentials in our memory capture file (.vmem) of the Ubuntu One client on the Mac OS X platform. However, searching for the Ubuntu One default directory string in memory led to a number of filenames when we conducted upload, download, and delete operations (see Figure 18).

From the other keywords present in the memory capture, we were able to determine the operation that was being undertaken on the file. For example, "*ubuntuone. SyncDaemon.EQ—DEBUG—push_event: FS_FILE_CREATE, kwargs: {'path':*" and "*EVENT: FS_FILE_DELETE:{} with ARGS*" represent upload and delete operations, respectively.

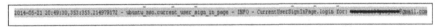

FIGURE 16

Username located in OS X Ubuntu One log file.

```
2014-05-22 20:24:41,213 - ubuntuone.SyncDaemon.sync - DEBUG - -:-:- - ['-'::'-'] ''/Users/Test/Ubuntu One/AQUA-OS2.BMP'' | EVENT: SV_FILE_NEW:{} with ARGS:{'',
2014-05-22 20:24:41,213 - ubuntuone.SyncDaemon.sync - INFO - -:-:- - ['-'::'-'] ''/Users/Test/Ubuntu One/AQUA-OS2.BMP'' | Calling new_file (got SV_FILE_NEW:{})
2014-05-22 20:24:41,214 - ubuntuone.SyncDaemon.fsm - DEBUG - set_node_id: path='/Users/Test/Ubuntu One/AQUA-OS2.BMP' mdid='37a3fd60-3281-4871-acce-2ba4137ea007
2014-05-22 20:24:41,214 - ubuntuone.SyncDaemon.fsm - DEBUG - create: path='/Users/Test/Ubuntu One/AQUA-OS2.BMP' mdid='37a3fd60-3281-4871-acce-2ba4137ea007' sha
```

FIGURE 17

Synced Filenames located in OS X Ubuntu One log file.

```
...../Users/Test/Ubuntu One
/AQUA-OS2.BMP..............
```

FIGURE 18

Filenames of synced files located in Mac OS X Memory.

Table 4 List of IP Addresses and Hostnames Extracted from OS X Client Network Traffic

IP Address	Hostname
91.189.89.77–91.189.89.78	one.ubuntu.com
91.189.89.206–91.189.89.207	login.one.ubuntu.com

5.3.2 Network traffic

The results of our network traffic capture is similar to that of the Windows client application discussed above, where we did not note any OCSP queries. Table 4 outlines the list of IP addresses (and associated hostnames) extracted from the network traffic capture file.

5.4 iOS APP-BASED

There does not appear to be an official Ubuntu One app available for iOS in the Apple App Store. We selected the "U1Files" (version 0.5) unofficial Ubuntu One client app for analysis on iOS. We installed the app on a jailbroken device running iOS 7.0.4. Application data for apps installed from the App Store is stored in/var/mobile/Applications on iOS. The iFile app (version 2.0.1-1) was also installed from Cydia to locate the directories created by U1Files. The directory name for U1Files in our case was EDF4B87E-CBC0-466C-2377A089DB10. The U1Files directory had five sub directories named Documents, Library, StoreKit, tmp, and U1Files.app. Ubuntu One's default directory was located at the following path:

/var/mobile/Applications/EDF4B87E-CBC0-466C-2377A089DB10/Documents/Ubuntu One

We determined that all synced files were stored in that directory. The "Documents" directory contained the "u1.db" database, which we found contains the three tables provided in Figures 19–21:

Table Contents					
id	consumer_key	consumer_secret	token		token_secret
1	mHi8m4w	wYFitYcQSIdFytMSNGfEeQmUSEWUEP	kdEYALSLiecaiKWMufBnYJcpNDsWSbZHYvPQvNiVFiFdnDRkJ		ERYAtMidazPTMHyikfYNbooOJmstAsniTmPeQhBkNkQRtaL...

FIGURE 19

u1.db login_info_table.

Table Contents									
parent_path	type	path	content_path	name	is_public	public_url	size	last_modified	hash
/~/	1	/~/Ubuntu One	/content/~/Ubu...	Ubuntu One	0		-1		
/~/Ubuntu One	2	/~/Ubuntu One...	/content/~/Ubu...	AQUA-OS2.BMP	0		153674	2014-05-29T03...	sha1:93e06221...
/~/Ubuntu One	2	/~/Ubuntu One...	/content/~/Ubu...	HANGING.DOC	0		22016	2014-05-29T03...	sha1:706504l2f...
/~/Ubuntu One	2	/~/Ubuntu One...	/content/~/Ubu...	HANGING.txt	0		2019	2014-05-29T03...	sha1:6a1583fe2...

FIGURE 20

u1.db nodes_table information.

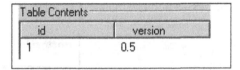

Table Contents	
id	version
1	0.5

FIGURE 21

version_table.

1—login_info_table (see Figure 19): These appear to be the authentication token components stored by the mobile app for authenticating to Ubuntu One services. The topic of authentication token use in mobile apps is discussed further in Martini et al. (2015a,b).

2—nodes_table (see Figure 20): Filenames, last modified date, size, and hash values are the notable values we located in this table.

3—version_table (see Figure 21): The currently installed version of the U1Files app can be retrieved from this table. We also located a file named "iTunesMetadata. plist" which contained information including the date that we purchased the U1Files app and the Apple ID that was associated with the purchase.

The results of our network traffic capture analysis on iOS did not differ significantly from our findings for Mac OS X.

6 CONCLUSION

Cloud storage has attracted many individuals and business users by offering cost-effective storage and services across a variety of devices. However, the prevalence of cloud storage has provided criminals with opportunities, including the ability to organize their activities in a distributed, scalable, and somewhat anonymous way. The nature of the cloud environment imposes several challenges to the traditional process of digital forensic investigation. Data of interest may be segregated on shared storage in different physical locations, where such data is subject to foreign laws and regulations (Hooper et al., 2013).

One area of difficulty in cloud forensics is in identifying the use of cloud services by suspects and, then determining the particular cloud service used and acquiring the account credentials for the service (Quick et al., 2014). The evidence sources in a digital investigation vary and may include computer hard disks and live memory, network traffic captures, and mobile devices such as the Apple iPhone and Android mobile devices. The identification and collection of suspect's data must be carried out in timely fashion before the data can be moved to another unknown location or even permanently deleted. The legislative process for seizing data also differs between jurisdictions. Hence, forensic investigators and practitioners need to preserve suspects' data as soon as possible after identification.

In this chapter, we carried out a number of experiments on Ubuntu One to examine the artifacts that may be left behind on client devices after use of this cloud service. First, Windows 8.1 was utilized to access Ubuntu One via its online interface using four major browsers (Internet Explorer, Mozilla Firefox, Apple Safari, and Google Chrome). We then deployed Ubuntu One's client application to Windows 8.1, Apple Mac OS X 10.9, and an unofficial Ubuntu One client on iOS 7.0.4. During our experiments on these platforms, we simulated a user carrying out common operations on cloud storage, such as uploading, downloading, and deleting files, with a standard dataset. The evidence sources under investigation varied between on operating systems, but included sources such as the Windows registry, event logs, network traffic captures, live memory captures, and persistent file system changes. We found that it was likely that practitioners would be able to locate a range of distinct remnants in relation to Ubuntu One usage, but access to valuable evidential artifacts (such as authentication and user action logs) varied between platforms. The artifacts described in this chapter may assist forensic practitioners in detecting Ubuntu One use and hopefully assist in acquiring data of potential evidential value.

Cloud storage is likely to remain popular and even grow in usage as the dominant technology used in file hosting and transmission of files among individuals and organizations. As a result, it is recommended that those undertaking future work in this area continue to examine cloud storage including investigation of other cloud storage applications using various devices and operating systems. Future work also includes further analysis of the authentication token system used by the Ubuntu One client, which may allow for the location of authentication credentials on the PC operating systems, in addition to the token credentials located on the mobile client.

REFERENCES

Aminnezhad, A., Dehghantanha, A., Abdullah, M., Damshenas, M., 2013. Cloud forensics issues and oppurtunities. Int. J. Inf. Process. Manage. 4 (4), 76–85.

Biggs, S., Vidalis, S., 2009. Cloud computing: the impact on digital forensic investigations. In: International Conference for Internet Technology and Secured Transactions.

Birk, D., Wegener, C., 2011. Technical issues of forensic investigations in cloud computing environments. In: 6th International Workshop on Systematic Approaches to Digital Forensic Engineering—IEEE/SADFE 2011, pp. 1–10.

Chung, H., Park, J., Lee, S., Kang, C., 2012. Digital forensic investigation of cloud storage services. Digit. Investig. 9 (2), 81–95.

Damshenas, M., Dehghantanha, A., Mahmoud, R., bin Shamsuddin, S., 2012. Forensics investigation challenges in cloud computing environments. In: Cyber Security, Cyber Warfare and Digital Forensic (CyberSec), 2012 International Conference, IEEE, pp. 190–194.

Daryabar, F., Dehghantanha, A., Udzir, N.I., 2013. A review on impacts of cloud computing on digital forensics. Int. J. Cyber-Security Digital Forensics (IJCSDF) 2 (2), 77–94.

Do, Q., Martini, B., Looi, J., Wang, Y., Choo, K.-K.R., 2014. Windows event forensic process. IFIP Int. Federation Inf. Process. 433, 87–100.

Federici, C., 2014. Cloud data imager: a unified answer to remote acquisition of cloud storage areas. Digit. Investig. 11 (1), 30–42.

Grispos, G., Storer, T., Glisson, W., 2012. Calm before the storm: the challenges of cloud computing in digital forensics. Int. J. Digital Crime Forensics 4 (2), 28–48.

Hale, J.S., 2013. Amazon cloud drive forensic analysis. Digit. Investig. 10 (3), 259–265.

Hooper, C., Martini, B., Choo, K.K.R., 2013. Cloud computing and its implications for cybercrime. Comput Law Security Rep. 29 (2), 152–163.

Martini, B., Choo, K.-K.R., 2012. An integrated conceptual digital forensic framework for cloud computing. Digit. Investig. 9 (2), 71–80.

Martini, B., Choo, K.K.R., 2013. Cloud storage forensics: ownCloud as a case study. Digit. Investig. 10 (4), 287–299.

Martini, B., Do, Q., Choo, K.-K.R., 2015a. Conceptual evidence collection and analysis methodology for Android devices. In: Ko, R., Choo, K.-K.R. (Eds.), Cloud Security Ecosystem. Syngress, an Imprint of Elsevier.

Martini, B., Do, Q., Choo, K.-K.R., 2015b. Mobile cloud forensics: an analysis of seven popular Android apps. In: Ko, R., Choo, K.-K.R. (Eds.), Cloud Security Ecosystem. Syngress, an Imprint of Elsevier.

McKemmish, R., 1999. What is forensic computing? Trends Issues Crime Crim. Justice 118, 1–6.

Mee, V., Tryfonas, T., Sutherland, I., 2006. The Windows Registry as a forensic artefact: illustrating evidence collection for Internet usage. Digit. Investig. 3 (3), 166–173.

Mell, P., Grance, T., 2011. The NIST definition of cloud computing-recommendations of the National Institute of Standards and Technology. NIST. NIST Special Publication.

Quick, D., Choo, K.-K.R., 2013a. Digital droplets: Microsoft SkyDrive forensic data remnants. Futur. Gener. Comput. Syst. 29 (6), 1378–1394.

Quick, D., Choo, K.-K.R., 2013b. Dropbox analysis: data remnants on user machines. Digit. Investig. 10 (1), 3–18.

Quick, D., Choo, K.-K.R., 2013c. Forensic collection of cloud storage data: does the act of collection result in changes to the data or its metadata? Digit. Investig. 10 (3), 266–277.

Quick, D., Choo, K.-K.R., 2014. Google Drive: forensic analysis of data remnants. J. Netw. Comput. Appl. 40, 179–193.

Quick, D., Martini, B., Choo, K.-K.R., 2014. Cloud Storage Forensics. Syngress Publishing/Elsevier.

Taylor, M., Haggerty, J., Gresty, D., Lamb, D., 2011. Forensic investigation of cloud computing systems. Netw. Secur. 2011 (3), 4–10.

Act: Governance and Auditing

Governance in the Cloud

20

Sai Honig

Waikato District Health Board, Hamilton, New Zealand

1 WHY IS GOVERNANCE IMPORTANT?

The mission of the Organisation for Economic Co-operation and Development (OECD) is to promote policies that will improve the economic and social well-being of people around the world. The OECD works to advance these causes, throughout its 34 member nations, through various means including corporate governance. To this end, the OECD has produced guidelines for and reporting of corporate governance.[1]

The OECD defines corporate governance as "Procedures and processes according to which an organization is directed and controlled. The corporate governance structure specifies the distribution of rights and responsibilities among the different participants in the organization—such as the board, managers, shareholders and other stakeholders— and lays down the rules and procedures for decision-making."[2]

So why is governance important? As the OECD has stated, governance defines the rules and procedures for decision making and ensuring oversight of operations. As business operations are moved to cloud service providers (CSPs), the decision-making process can become (for lack of a better word) cloudy. Oversight of operations can become difficult. How do customers, their boards, managers, shareholders, and other stakeholders ensure that their business requirements and interests are adequately met? Unless the risk is also outsourced (e.g., insurance), the responsibility still remains with the customer.

Boards are hearing much about the benefits of cloud computing—lower cost, higher efficiency, faster innovation, and implementation. These are some of the potential benefits depending on strategy and implementation. A full discussion of these potential benefits will not be included in this chapter. For the purpose of this chapter, it is assumed that the enterprise is considering an *external* cloud provider. Also, for the purpose of this chapter, the word "enterprise" will refer to the organization, or customer, seeking services from a CSP.

---

[1]Guidelines for multinational enterprises (http://www.oecd.org/corporate/mne/).
[2]OECD Glossary of Statistical Terms (http://stats.oecd.org/glossary/detail.asp?ID=6778).

2 WHAT ARE THE QUESTIONS THAT BOARDS SHOULD BE ASKING?

There are questions that boards, to whom the responsibility for the overall governance falls, as well as managers, shareholders, and other stakeholders should be asking. These questions apply to both for-profit and non-profit enterprises. Ideally, these questions should be asked before the transition of operations to cloud services. With the exuberance of something new and exciting, these questions may be ignored or set aside. The answers can determine the readiness of an enterprise in implementing a cloud technology solution and whether that enterprise can be comfortable with the governance and operations of the cloud provider.

These questions may be simple but do require an extensive review of the internal structure of an enterprise.[3] Here is a brief discussion of some of these questions:

- *Is there a plan for cloud computing and does that plan include benefits as well as risks?*

There are potential benefits to implementing a cloud technology solution. These include competitive advantage by bringing new or improved products faster to market (faster development to deployment time), increasing productivity, containing costs. All of these should not be overlooked. If effectively implemented, cloud technology adoption may be worth the risks when compared to opportunity costs of transforming the customer's enterprise.

What operations will be transitioned to a CSP? Is there an opportunity cost to outsourcing critical operations? An enterprise should consider the potential loss of knowledge (technical and business) if moving to a CSP. Is there a business continuity plan in case of disruption?

- *Does these plans support the enterprise's strategy?*

It is not enough to implement cloud technology. How will the solution support the enterprise? What objectives are to be achieved by implementing a cloud technology solution? Careful consideration should be given to tie the objectives of cloud technology implementation to specific goals of the enterprise's strategy.

- *Is the enterprise ready for such a transition?*

Does the enterprise have the appropriate staffing to develop and manage cloud services? The expectation will be that the CSP will be hosting services. However, those services will need to be managed. Contracts and service level agreements (SLAs) will have to be negotiated. Terms and conditions will have to be understood and

---

[3]ISACA, 2013. Cloud Governance: Questions Boards of Directors Need to Ask, USA (http://www.isaca.org/Knowledge-Center/Research/ResearchDeliverables/Pages/Cloud-Governance-Questions-Boards-of-Directors-Need-to-Ask.aspx).

adhered to by the enterprise. If the CSP does not meet the enterprise's needs, the remaining needs will have to be undertaken by the enterprise.

Does the enterprise understand the effort to transition to a cloud technology? Cloud technology has the potential to disrupt an enterprise's operations and culture. An enterprise with a centralized structure may not be adequately ready for potentially decentralizing their operations and functions. Also, an enterprise may have to consider adapting their change management or sourcing functions. In addition, the enterprise may have to undertake a review of their staffing skills in order to determine if they can support their own users of cloud services (e.g., access management, help desk support).

What about the enterprise's regulatory and compliance requirements? The CSP's data center may not be physically located in the same legal jurisdiction. They may not even be located in the same country. Several nations have their own regulations about the movement of data within and outside their borders. What are the enterprise's responsibilities regarding compliance? What is the enterprise's responsibility in case of a breach?

One area that is not often fully defined within organizations prior to migrating to a cloud infrastructure is data management. The issues encountered here include[4]:

- Unclear ownership—ownership is dispersed among various groups within the organization
- Undefined data meaning—incomplete or nonexistent data dictionaries which may lead to data obtained for one purpose but used for another purpose which may not be captured when loading data into a warehouse
- Inflexible data structures or legacy systems
- Ever increasing amounts of data—potential for metadata-related risk, where various sources are correlated to obtain confidential information, or data loss due to incomplete, invalid, or inconsistent practices
- Access controls—acquiring more privileges due to limited access review

What about the enterprise's existing investments or commitments (e.g., technology, procurement, financial, etc.)?

A cloud technology solution may not be easily or immediately adopted. Current technologies or contracts may be in place with a pre-determined end date (e.g., software or services that are still supported or under contract). If it is determined that adopting a cloud technology solution is in the best interest of the enterprise, the costs of continuing existing technology may have to be included in the cost of implementation.

In addition to staffing skills that may need to be updated, the enterprise may need to consider if there are additional technology investments that need to be made (e.g., data centers, software applications, network infrastructure).

---

[4]Gelbstein, Ed, Polic, V., 2014. Data owners' responsibilities when migrating to the cloud. ISACA J. 6.

- *How will the enterprise measure benefit or risk after implementing cloud technology solution?*

As with any new investment and implementation, it is best to measure the value obtained or risk introduced. It is advisable to determine how the value or risk is to be measured before implementation. This is to better understand the position of the enterprise after potentially strategic changes are implemented. These measurements should be shared with the board in order to assess determine if further implementations are warranted.

One commonly used measurement is return on investment (ROI). Such calculations need not be complicated. The next section discusses one methodology.

Cloud services and providers are increasing their abilities to service their customers and many providing niche services such as storage, backup, security, and customer relations management. Therefore, more enterprises will find that cloud technology solutions will become more available. Enterprises will need their boards to provide governance in managing cloud technology solutions and realizing potential benefits while reducing risk and cost.

In order for the board to provide governance, expectations of the cloud technology solution must be aligned with the strategic initiatives of the enterprise. These expectations should also be aligned with guiding principles for using the cloud: enablement, cost benefit, enterprise risk, capability, accountability, and trust.[5]

The process of implementing a cloud technology solution will not be discussed in this chapter. However, a basic process could be defined in four steps[6]:

1. Preparation of the internal environment—principles, policies, frameworks, processes, organization structure, etc.
2. Selection of the cloud *service* model—determine if migration to cloud model is best solution for the enterprise and, if so, what service (e.g., SaaS, PaaS, IaaS, some combination or subset)
3. Selection of cloud *deployment* model—determine if a private, public, hybrid, or community cloud model is the best solution for the enterprise
4. Selection of the CSP

This chapter will not discuss in detail the various service or deployment models. For a more detailed review, the reader is urged to consult "The NIST Definition of Cloud Computing."[7]

---

[5]ISACA, 2012. Guiding Principles for Cloud Computing Adoption and Use, USA (http://www.isaca. org/Knowledge-Center/Research/ResearchDeliverables/Pages/Guiding-Principles-for-Cloud-Comput ing-Adoption-and-Use.aspx).
[6]ISACA, 2012. Security Considerations for Cloud Computing, USA, pp. 35-52. (http://www.isaca.org/ Knowledge-Center/Research/ResearchDeliverables/Pages/Security-Considerations-for-Cloud-Com puting.aspx).
[7]NIST, 2011. The NIST Definition of Cloud Computing, Special Publication 800-145, USA, September 2011 (http://csrc.nist.gov/publications/nistpubs/800-145/SP800-145.pdf).

3 CALCULATING ROI

The ROI is one of several methods of *estimating* potential financial outcome of an investment. To calculate (simple) ROI, the investment cost is subtracted from the investment gain; the result is then divided by the investment gain and expressed as a percentage[8]:

$$ROI = \frac{\text{Gain from Investment} - \text{Cost of Investment}}{\text{Cost of Investment}}$$

It must be understood that this calculation does not factor in cost of funding (e.g., interest) or time value of money (e.g., the value of money in the future is less than the value of money today). An enterprise needs to define what financial calculations it would use to determine if an investment is worthy of its efforts. Also, an enterprise needs to define what is its investment timeframe horizon (e.g., 1 year, 5 years, etc.). Doing so will indicate what costs and well as gains are to be included in the financial calculations.

Despite its simplicity, the ROI calculation is a good starting point for those investments where the benefits and costs can be quantified. In implementing a cloud technology solution, there are both tangible (which can be quantified) benefits and costs and intangible (could be considered as strategic) benefits and costs. CSPs and other providers would gladly calculate these benefits and costs. The true calculation must be considered from the perspective of the enterprise.[9]

It may be easy to list the tangible benefits of a cloud implementation. There are potential benefits to be gained by cost reductions (e.g., physical hosting, labor, licensing, support, maintenance), increased productivity, scalability, and reliability. What may not be easy is defining the metrics in order to quantify these benefits.

For example, an enterprise may consider greater customer satisfaction as a benefit. This may be defined as reduced time in collaborative efforts with or reduced response time to customer inquires. After consideration, an enterprise may consider this to be an intangible benefit. As an enterprise details their cloud technology solution, addition benefits may be evident.[10]

Intangible benefits are those that may not be quantifiable and, therefore, may not be included in financial calculations. However, they should be considered as part of the proposal to consider a cloud technology solution. These benefits may not initially have quantitative value but may produce such values as the enterprise moves through its implementation phase and conducts business. For example, increased business

---

[8]Investopedia (http://www.investopedia.com/terms/r/returnoninvestment.asp).

[9]ISACA, 2012. Calculating Cloud ROI: From the Customer Perspective, USA (http://www.isaca.org/Knowledge-Center/Research/ResearchDeliverables/Pages/Calculating-Cloud-ROI-From-the-Customer-Perspective.aspx).

[10]ISACA, 2012. Calculating Cloud ROI: From the Customer Perspective, USA (http://www.isaca.org/Knowledge-Center/Research/ResearchDeliverables/Pages/Calculating-Cloud-ROI-From-the-Customer-Perspective.aspx).

opportunities (or avoidance of missed business opportunities) may not be evident initially.[11]

One potential intangible benefit that an enterprise may consider is security risk transfer. CSP's may be better able to prevent or mitigate security breaches or loss of data. They may also be partners in disaster recovery. However, the customer must understand that ultimate responsibility for their assets (including data), regardless of their location, rests with the customer. The enterprise is ultimately responsible for security and compliance.[12]

The ROI includes not only benefits but costs as well. These costs can be broken down into upfront, recurring, and termination costs. As with benefits, the costs must be considered over the timeframe of the investment. These costs also need to be considered from the enterprise's perspective.[13]

It may be easier to consider the upfront or initial costs. As with implementing any new technology, there are costs for configuration and integration. As mentioned in the previous section, there are costs to be considered regarding the enterprise's readiness. These could include training and process reevaluation.[14]

Recurring costs include those items that the enterprise pays on a periodic basis. These include subscription and support fees, which are usually defined in the contract and may be incurred on a per user basis. However, there are costs in monitoring the CSP's activities and verifying that they are meeting the enterprise's mutually agreed contract, SLAs, and other operating procedures.[15] This is where the governance of the enterprise can dictate the level of review.

The costs due to termination of a contract may not always be considered as part of the cost of investment. These costs are incurred when services are either transferred to another provider or reverted into the enterprise's internal operations. In some cases, this transition may be due to changes in regulations or economics. It may also be due to changes in the enterprise's business operations.[16]

---

[11]ISACA, 2012. Calculating Cloud ROI: From the Customer Perspective", USA (http://www.isaca.org/Knowledge-Center/Research/ResearchDeliverables/Pages/Calculating-Cloud-ROI-From-the-Customer-Perspective.aspx).

[12]ISACA, 2013. Security as a Service: Business Benefits with Security, Governance and Assurance Perspectives, USA (http://www.isaca.org/Knowledge-Center/Research/ResearchDeliverables/Pages/Security-As-A-Service.aspx).

[13]ISACA, 2012. Calculating Cloud ROI: From the Customer Perspective, USA (http://www.isaca.org/Knowledge-Center/Research/ResearchDeliverables/Pages/Calculating-Cloud-ROI-From-the-Customer-Perspective.aspx).

[14]ISACA, 2012. Calculating Cloud ROI: From the Customer Perspective, USA (http://www.isaca.org/Knowledge-Center/Research/ResearchDeliverables/Pages/Calculating-Cloud-ROI-From-the-Customer-Perspective.aspx).

[15]ISACA, 2012. Calculating Cloud ROI: From the Customer Perspective, USA (http://www.isaca.org/Knowledge-Center/Research/ResearchDeliverables/Pages/Calculating-Cloud-ROI-From-the-Customer-Perspective.aspx).

[16]ISACA, 2012. Calculating Cloud ROI: From the Customer Perspective, USA (http://www.isaca.org/Knowledge-Center/Research/ResearchDeliverables/Pages/Calculating-Cloud-ROI-From-the-Customer-Perspective.aspx).

Regardless of the causes, considerations should be given for these costs. Once assets are placed in the cloud, extraction and validation from cloud storage or processing hardware will be necessary. This may also require reconfiguration or reprovisioning of systems, recruitment of staff resources, and early termination fees. A customer may consider including costs due to running dual processes as data and systems are being transferred and confirmed.[17]

Once an enterprise has determined that the investment is necessary, the need to verify operations in a cloud technology solution may be required. There are a number of regulations, such as Sarbanes-Oxley in the United States, that require enterprises to verify controls are in place and working effectively. The following section describes a methodology to audit a cloud technology solution.

4 AUDITING THE CLOUD
4.1 PLANNING AND SCOPING THE AUDIT

Planning an audit of the cloud will require understanding of information governance, IT management, as well as network, data, disaster recovery, and encryption controls used by the enterprise. An understanding of the cloud technology solution used by the enterprise is also necessary. It is also helpful to have an understanding of the regulatory and compliance requirements of the enterprise. Therefore, staff performing this audit will need to a wide variety of skills. The audit scope may need to be tailored to match the skills of the enterprise's staff or external resources may be necessary for a more complete review.

It also necessary to understand what the objective of such an audit will provide to the enterprise. ISACA® has published an audit program that intends to provide[18]:

- An assessment of the internal controls of a CSP.
- Identify internal control deficiencies within the *enterprise*.
- An assessment of the ability to rely on the CSP's attestations regarding internal controls.

This audit program has included in its scope[19]:

- Governance affecting cloud computing
- Contractual compliance between the CSP and the enterprise

---

[17]ISACA, 2012. Calculating Cloud ROI: From the Customer Perspective, USA (http://www.isaca.org/Knowledge-Center/Research/ResearchDeliverables/Pages/Calculating-Cloud-ROI-From-the-Customer-Perspective.aspx).

[18]ISACA, 2010. Cloud Computing Management Audit/Assurance Program, USA (http://www.isaca.org/Knowledge-Center/Research/ResearchDeliverables/Pages/Cloud-Computing-Management-Audit-Assurance-Program.aspx).

[19]ISACA, 2010. Cloud Computing Management Audit/Assurance Program, USA (http://www.isaca.org/Knowledge-Center/Research/ResearchDeliverables/Pages/Cloud-Computing-Management-Audit-Assurance-Program.aspx).

It should be noted that the identification of internal controls deficiencies is of the *enterprise* and not the CSP. This is due to the fact that, unless negotiated prior to service, most CSPs will not allow their customers to review their internal controls. However, there are some methods, including external reporting, which will provide an assessment of the CSP's internal controls. A brief review of elements of such an audit is included here.

4.2 GOVERNANCE AND ENTERPRISE RISK MANAGEMENT

An initial review should include an assessment of governance functions within the enterprise. This is to determine if there are effective processes in place with clear lines of responsibility and is in alignment with the enterprise's regulatory requirements and policies. This would include the enterprise's governance model, information security collaboration with CSPs and performance metrics.[20]

Since the use of a cloud technology solution can be done quickly and easily, the enterprise should have mechanisms to identify all CSPs and all deployments. This is to ensure that all business activities, including those of the CSPs, are aligned with the enterprise's policies and procedures. It would be helpful if the enterprise has a method of inventorying all services provided via CSPs or if services can be procured without the involvement of the enterprise's information technology and security staff and key business units.[21]

An example of the lack of governance of cloud deployment can be observed when such deployments are procured outside of the organization's procurement processes. In one such case, staff at a Fortune 1000 company, with a large development group, found it easier and faster to purchase instances from a CSP, using corporate-issued credit cards. (Such purchases generally do not require management pre-approval or procurement review.) The results may have achieved faster development but also failed the procurement process:

- Failure to identify all services provided by CSPs and confirming such services comply with organization's requirements.
- Increased operational costs due to instances being purchased but not monitored and closed after use.
- Failure to manage organization's intellectual property.

Collaboration between the enterprise and the CSP may be inherent. However, such collaboration should have the responsibilities and reporting relationships defined.

---

[20]ISACA, 2010. Cloud Computing Management Audit/Assurance Program, USA (http://www.isaca.org/Knowledge-Center/Research/ResearchDeliverables/Pages/Cloud-Computing-Management-Audit-Assurance-Program.aspx), p. 16.
[21]ISACA, 2010. Cloud Computing Management Audit/Assurance Program, USA (http://www.isaca.org/Knowledge-Center/Research/ResearchDeliverables/Pages/Cloud-Computing-Management-Audit-Assurance-Program.aspx), p. 16.

Often, key contacts within the enterprise and the CSP are assigned. In addition, metrics, SLAs, and contract terms are defined to indicate to all parties what is considered acceptable performance. This facilitates the governance processes of both the enterprise and the CSP.[22]

It is also worth noting that contracts between organizations' and CSP are often dependent up the number of instances or licenses. Careful consideration should be given for such quantities. CSPs may give a specific rate for up to a specified number of instances or licenses. Exceeding the specified number may require additional unplanned costs. A Fortune 50 company implemented a SaaS solution with a specified number of licenses. This number was quickly used and each additional license added an unexpected higher per license cost. These additional higher per license costs canceled any savings in using the SaaS solution.

It is easy to dismiss operational risks if an external entity is providing services. However, the enterprise's risk management processes may need to be updated to evaluate any inherent risks in using a cloud technology solution. An enterprise should consider information usage, access controls, security controls, location management, privacy controls. Depending on the service (e.g., SasS, PaaS, IaaS), the enterprise needs to determine what analytical information it will need to verify contractual obligations are met. For example[23]:

- For SaaS—analytical data relating to performance and security
- For PaaS—control practices relating to availability, confidentiality, data ownership, privacy
- For IaaS—controls for a secure operating environment

The depth of a review of the CSP's operations will be determined by mutually agreed contract. The CSP may provide policies regarding incident management, business continuity, and disaster recovery. If so, these policies should be in alignment with the enterprise's policies.

4.3 LEGAL AND ELECTRONIC DISCOVERY

It would benefit the enterprise to take a detailed review of the contract terms and establish an understanding of those terms. If possible, a due diligence of the CSP's security governance, risk management, and compliance should also be conducted. The enterprise would also find that developing business continuity and disaster

---

[22]ISACA, 2010. Cloud Computing Management Audit/Assurance Program, USA (http://www.isaca. org/Knowledge-Center/Research/ResearchDeliverables/Pages/Cloud-Computing-Management-Audit-Assurance-Program.aspx), p. 17.

[23]ISACA, 2010. Cloud Computing Management Audit/Assurance Program, USA (http://www.isaca. org/Knowledge-Center/Research/ResearchDeliverables/Pages/Cloud-Computing-Management-Audit-Assurance-Program.aspx), pp. 19-20.

recovery plans, in case of the loss of services by the CSP, useful. These plans should be evaluated for adequacy.[24]

The contract terms should also be reviewed to ensure that they address the compliance requirements of both the enterprise and the CSP. Since there may be more than one set of jurisdictional oversight (e.g., across national borders) or regulatory requirements (e.g., US HIPAA, PCI DSS, etc.), it is important to identify responsibilities of all parties. Procedures on data retention, security practices, and geographic location of data should be made available to the enterprise. With regard to electronic discovery (e-Discovery), there may be circumstances in which data could be legally obtained by law enforcement authorities and notification of such events should be delineated.[25]

4.4 COMPLIANCE AND AUDIT

The "right to audit" is a broad term. Often when it is used in contracts, it gives the customer of a service provider some availability to review the service provider's operations. Generally, the availability is limited. In the case of a CSP, third-party reviews may be conducted and the results may be shared with external parties upon request. Such third-party reviews may be conducted by external auditing assurance and advisory services.

One such report is the "Service Organization Control" (SOC) reports. The SOC reports (Type 1 and Type 2) are prepared under the guidance of the American Institute of CPAs® (AICPA). The use of these reports is intended for stakeholders of the service organization. The SOC Type 2 reports on the "suitability of the design and operating effectiveness of controls." These reports are intended to provide[26]:

- Oversight of the organization
- Vendor management program
- Internal corporate governance and risk management processes
- Regulatory oversight

The Cloud Security Alliance® (CSA) is also working to provide further assurance of CSPs. The CSA Security, Trust, and Assurance Registry (STAR) Program is multiple reporting mechanisms for cloud provider trust and assurance through a publicly accessible registry. Currently, CSPs can conduct a self-assessment (level 1) based on

---

[24]ISACA, 2010. Cloud Computing Management Audit/Assurance Program, USA (http://www.isaca.org/Knowledge-Center/Research/ResearchDeliverables/Pages/Cloud-Computing-Management-Audit-Assurance-Program.aspx), p. 22.

[25]ISACA, 2010. Cloud Computing Management Audit/Assurance Program, USA (http://www.isaca.org/Knowledge-Center/Research/ResearchDeliverables/Pages/Cloud-Computing-Management-Audit-Assurance-Program.aspx), p. 23.

[26]American Institute of Certified Professional Accountants (AICPA), (http://www.aicpa.org/InterestAreas/FRC/AssuranceAdvisoryServices/Pages/AICPASOC2Report.aspx).

the CSA's Cloud Controls Matrix (CCM). The CSA CCM is a controls framework intended to provide structure, detail, and clarity relating to information security tailored to cloud computing.[27]

Currently, there is also an external attestation (level 2) and an external certification (level 2) that CSPs can have conducted[28]:

- CSA STAR Attestation provides guidelines for conducting SOC Type 2 engagements using criteria from the AICPA (Trust Service Principles, AT 101) and the CSA CCM. The CSA has recently published "Guidelines for CPAs Providing CSA STAR Attestation."[29]
- The CSA STAR Certification is a third-party independent assessment of the security of a CSP. The technology-neutral certification leverages the requirements of the ISO/IEC 27001:2005 management system standard together with the CSA CCM.

It must be understood that these reports are intended for those who are familiar with the controls of the service provider. These reports may not provide complete assurance of the service provider's controls. The controls described in these reports may also not match controls of the customer. Some evaluation of these reports will have to be conducted by the customer to determine if:[30]

- Report addresses control environment used by customer
- Descriptions and processes are relevant to customer
- Testing satisfies customer's regulatory and compliance objectives including any trans-border requirements

4.5 PORTABILITY AND INTEROPERABILITY

Although planning to transition into a cloud technology platform is conducted, planning to transition from that platform is often overlooked. Such planning should include not only data but also formats. Portability testing should include procedures and alternatives to prove a state of readiness exists should the need to be transfer cloud computing operations. This could prevent unnecessary delays if an event occurs that requires disaster recovery or business continuity plans to be implemented.[31]

---

[27]Cloud Security Alliance (CSA Security, Trust and Assurance Registry (STAR), (https://cloudsecurityalliance.org/star/).
[28]Cloud Security Alliance (CSA Security, Trust and Assurance Registry (STAR), (https://cloudsecurityalliance.org/star/).
[29]Cloud Security Alliance, Guidelines for CPAs Providing CSA STAR Attestation (https://cloudsecurityalliance.org/download/guidelines-for-cpas-providing-csa-star-attestation/).
[30]ISACA, 2010. Cloud Computing Management Audit/Assurance Program, USA (http://www.isaca.org/Knowledge-Center/Research/ResearchDeliverables/Pages/Cloud-Computing-Management-Audit-Assurance-Program.aspx), pp. 25-26.
[31]ISACA, 2010. Cloud Computing Management Audit/Assurance Program, USA (http://www.isaca.org/Knowledge-Center/Research/ResearchDeliverables/Pages/Cloud-Computing-Management-Audit-Assurance-Program.aspx), pp. 27-28.

A number of testing steps could be done validate a state of readiness in the event a transition occurs. For each cloud initiative, a portability analysis should be conducted to[32]:

- Determine hardware and software requirements.
- Validate procedures and time estimates to move large volumes of data, applications, and infrastructure (as needed).
- Identify proprietary functions, processes, applications modules that may require customized programming and could delay transfer.
- Determine if backup data and applications are routinely stored in a format that is usable by other systems.

4.6 OPERATING IN THE CLOUD

A strong partnership is necessary between the CSP and the customer when operating in a cloud technology platform. Therefore, incident notification, responses, and remediation should be timely and addresses the risk that caused the incident. It is necessary to have such procedures documented as to the notification timeliness and process. Issue monitoring should be conducted on both the customer side and on the provider's side.[33]

Faster innovation and implementation are consistently touted as part of the development processes in a cloud technology environment. However, such fast changes could introduce unintended and unwanted security risks. As part of the design process, the customer should consider including security reviews as part of the change management process. This may require the use of subject matter experts.[34]

Maintaining data security and integrity is a consideration for data in transit as well as data at rest and data backup. If encryption is used, key management processes should be reviewed. The customer should review if the level of encryption is appropriate.[35]

Because of the multi-tenancy nature of many cloud technology environments, there is a potential for cross-contamination. Virtualized operating systems should be hardened with isolation and security controls implemented by the CSP. Additional

---

[32]ISACA, 2010. Cloud Computing Management Audit/Assurance Program, USA (http://www.isaca. org/Knowledge-Center/Research/ResearchDeliverables/Pages/Cloud-Computing-Management-Audit-Assurance-Program.aspx), pp. 28-29.

[33]ISACA, 2010. Cloud Computing Management Audit/Assurance Program, USA (http://www.isaca. org/Knowledge-Center/Research/ResearchDeliverables/Pages/Cloud-Computing-Management-Audit-Assurance-Program.aspx), p. 30.

[34]ISACA, 2010. Cloud Computing Management Audit/Assurance Program, USA (http://www.isaca. org/Knowledge-Center/Research/ResearchDeliverables/Pages/Cloud-Computing-Management-Audit-Assurance-Program.aspx), p. 31.

[35]ISACA, 2010. Cloud Computing Management Audit/Assurance Program, USA (http://www.isaca. org/Knowledge-Center/Research/ResearchDeliverables/Pages/Cloud-Computing-Management-Audit-Assurance-Program.aspx), pp. 33-35.

controls may also be considered and incidents should be reported through incident monitoring process:[36]

- Intrusion detection
- Vulnerability scanning
- Security-related APIs
- Virtual machine validation
- Separate production and testing/development environments

4.7 IDENTITY AND ACCESS MANAGEMENT

A strong identity and access management process should ensure that only authorized users have access to resources and users activities can be reviewed. In a cloud technology environment, the customer should have control over user provisioning, user deprovisioning, and access changes. The controls should allow for management of user access, including authentication, according to the customer's user access policies.[37]

Authentication is dependent upon the service that an enterprise chooses. For SaaS and PaaS, the enterprise may want to verify that a trust relationship exists between the enterprise's internal authentication system and the cloud system. For IaaS, the enterprise may want to employ dedicated VPNs between enterprise's systems and the cloud system. Where possible, standard authentication formats, such as SAML or WS-Federation, should be considered.[38]

5 CONCLUSION

A successful implementation of cloud technology depends upon the relationship between the enterprise and the CSP. That relationship starts with an understanding of the governance structures of both parties. This understanding can start with the enterprise asking questions of how the cloud technology solution is to benefit the enterprise's strategic goals and how the enterprise is ready for such a transition. A calculation of the investment from the enterprise's perspective can provide a starting point of the benefits as well as the costs of a cloud technology implementation.

Even prior to an implementation, an enterprise could consider reviewing the operations of a potential CSP. Such a review could include available policies and

---

[36]ISACA, 2010. Cloud Computing Management Audit/Assurance Program, USA (http://www.isaca. org/Knowledge-Center/Research/ResearchDeliverables/Pages/Cloud-Computing-Management-Audit-Assurance-Program.aspx), p. 37-38.

[37]ISACA, 2010. Cloud Computing Management Audit/Assurance Program, USA (http://www.isaca. org/Knowledge-Center/Research/ResearchDeliverables/Pages/Cloud-Computing-Management-Audit-Assurance-Program.aspx), p. 36.

[38]ISACA, 2010. Cloud Computing Management Audit/Assurance Program, USA (http://www.isaca. org/Knowledge-Center/Research/ResearchDeliverables/Pages/Cloud-Computing-Management-Audit-Assurance-Program.aspx), p. 37.

procedures as well as third-party reports. Regulatory and compliance requirements of both parties should be understood prior to services being conducted. This is particularly important in industries with multiple regulatory bodies or where there is a potential for trans-border data flows. It is important to note that cloud technology development should be integrated into the enterprise's change management process. Monitoring and incident reporting should also be integrated into an enterprise's processes.

Finally, the breadth and depth of a review of the implementation of a cloud technology can be broad. The level of review needs to be defined by the enterprise's governance requirements and agreements with the CSP.

Computational trust methods for security quantification in the cloud ecosystem

21

Sheikh Mahbub Habib, Florian Volk, Sascha Hauke, Max Mühlhäuser
Telecooperation Lab, Technische Universität Darmstadt/CASED, Darmstadt, Germany

1 INTRODUCTION

According to the 2014 Gartner hype cycle for emerging technologies report (LeHong et al., 2014), cloud computing technology is moving toward maturity. However, the main barrier for business users' adoption of cloud services is still the lack of security assurance from cloud providers. Another barrier for users is the growing number of cloud outages (Tsidulko, 2014) either due to the network failures, software updates, or security breaches. These barriers along with users' inability to measure the security services erode their confidence in cloud providers' overall security capabilities (Intel, 2012).

Security assurance in the cloud computing ecosystem has gone some promising steps forward since the introduction of the Security, Assurance and Trust Registry (STAR) (CSA, 2012) by the Cloud Security Alliance (CSA) in 2011. A growing number of cloud providers are sharing their service-specific security capabilities in a public repository, e.g., the CSA STAR. Potential users are able to browse this public repository in order to reason about the capabilities of different cloud providers. In order to provide users with security assurance, technical methods are required to quantify the security capabilities of cloud providers. The methods for quantification, aggregation as well as visual communication in an automated manner are necessary to achieve the goal of effective security assurance.

In this chapter, computational trust methods are leveraged to quantitatively assess the security capabilities of cloud providers. As underlying information of those capabilities is based on the cloud providers' self-assessments, such information might contain inconsistencies. Moreover, when several sources such as experts or auditors assess that inconsistent information in different manner, conflicting assessment results might appear. The trust methods described in this chapter are able to quantify the level of security capabilities in presence of inconsistent and conflicting information. These methods also provide means to visually communicate the quantitative assessment to users based on their requirements.

2 COMPUTATIONAL TRUST: PRELIMINARIES

Computational trust provides means to support entities to make informed decisions in electronic environments, where decisions are often subject to risk and uncertainty. Research in computational trust addresses the formal modeling, assessment, and management of the social notion of trust for use in risky electronic environments. Examples of such risky environments span from social networks over e-marketplaces to cloud computing service ecosystems. In theory, trust is usually reasoned in terms of the relationship within a specific context between a *trustor* and a *trustee*, where the trustor is a subject that trusts a target entity, which is referred to as trustee. Mathematically, trust is an estimate by the trustor of the inherent trustworthiness of the trustee, i.e., the quality of another party to act beneficially or at least nondetrimentally to the relying party.

In order to estimate trustworthiness of a trustee, a trustor requires evidence about the trustee's behavior in the past. Evidence about a trustee can be derived from *direct experience* or asking other trustor about their own experiences, i.e., *indirect experience*. This is termed as social concept of *trust* and has been widely used in the field of computer science (Jøsang et al., 2007). For detailed discussion on the definitions in the field of philosophy, sociology, psychology, and economics, we refer the readers to McKnight and Chervany (1996) and Grandison (2007).

Although researchers agree on the social concept of trust, it is not easy to get a single definition of trust based on the universal consensus. A definition that is adopted by many researchers in the field of computer science is the definition provided by the sociologist Gambetta (1990, 2000):

Definition 1. *Trust (or, symmetrically, distrust) is a particular level of the subjective probability with which an agent assesses that another agent or group of agents will perform a particular action, both before he can monitor such action (or independently of his capacity ever to be able to monitor it) and in a context in which it affects his own action.*

In the context of this chapter, *an agent* or *a group of agents* refers to service providers, who provide the requested service by contemporaneously meeting a service-specific requirement *r*, e.g., confidentiality, availability, etc. In another setting, a service provider may publish *r* by means of service capabilities, e.g., compliance, information security (IS), data governance. The assurance of *r* corresponds to what is referred to as *perform a particular action*.

3 STATE-OF-THE-ART APPROACHES TACKLING CLOUD SECURITY

In this section, we provide a number of approaches that aim to tackle the cloud security issues from the perspective of computational trust, trusted computing, security transparency, and security quantification.

3.1 COMPUTATIONAL TRUST MODELS AND MECHANISMS

Computational trust mechanisms are useful for trustworthiness evaluation in various service environments (Jøsang et al., 2007) such as in e-commerce and P2P networks. These mechanisms have also been adapted in grid computing by Lin et al. (2004) and Haq et al. (2010), in cloud computing by Pawar et al. (2012), as well as in the context of web service selection by Wang et al. (2010). Haq et al. proposed a trust model based on certificates (i.e., PKI-based) and a reputation-based trust system as a part of an Service Level Agreement (SLA) validation framework. Wang et al. proposed a trust model, which takes multiple factors (reputation, trustworthiness, and risk) into account when evaluating web services. Both approaches consider SLA validation as the main factor for establishing trust on the grid service and web service providers. An SLA validation framework can help to identify the compliance of SLA parameters agreed between a user and a cloud provider. Pawar et al. (2012) proposed a trust model to evaluate trustworthiness of cloud infrastructure providers based on SLA compliance.

In order to serve the customers best, a trust mechanism should take multiple available sources of information into account, such as past experience of the users as well as third-party certificates. The past experience about the capabilities and competency of the service providers might be based on the insufficient information or extracted from unreliable sources. Moreover, certificates issued by incompetent and unreliable certificate authorities (CAs) might render the trust evaluation process useless. Thus, trust mechanisms in Habib et al. (2013) considered these issues important and trust is modeled under uncertain conditions such as insufficient information and unreliable CAs or trust sources. Furthermore, trust mechanisms also need to consider service-specific capabilities that are relevant when selecting service providers in cloud marketplaces.

Trust operators. Non application-specific computational trust models usually provide mathematical operators for trustworthiness assessment. One of such operators is *consensus*, which combines evidence from different sources about the same target. Another operator is *discounting*, which weights recommendation based on the trustworthiness of the sources. These two operators are important when deriving trustworthiness based on direct experience and recommendation. In the cloud computing ecosystem, services are hosted in complex distributed systems. In order to assess the trustworthiness of cloud providers regarding different capabilities such as security and compliance, we additionally need operators; logic-based approaches that can provide such operators are *Subjective Logic* (SL) (Jøsang, 2001), *Certain-Logic* (Ries et al., 2011), and *CertainTrust* (Ries, 2009a).

3.2 TRUSTED COMPUTING TECHNOLOGIES

Apart from the field of computational trust mechanisms, a number of approaches from the field of trusted computing are proposed to ensure trustworthy cloud infrastructures. Krautheim (2009) proposed a private virtual infrastructure; this is a security architecture for cloud computing and uses a trust model to share the responsibility of security between the service provider and client. Schiffman et al. (2010) proposed a hardware-based attestation mechanism to provide assurance of data processing protection in the cloud for customers. There are further approaches like property-based Trusted Platform Module (TPM) virtualization (Sadeghi et al., 2008), which can be used in the cloud scenario to assure users about the fulfillment of security properties or attributes in cloud platforms using attestation concepts. However, in general, attestation concepts based on trusted computing (e.g., Sadeghi and Stüble, 2004) focus on the evaluation of single platforms. while services in the web are often hosted in composite platforms. Moreover, uncertainty arises due to the nature of the property-based attestation mechanism, which requires dynamic trust-based models such as the one addressed in Nagarajan (2010). This approach also considered composite service platforms while designing the trust model.

3.3 CLOUD SECURITY TRANSPARENCY MECHANISMS

The CSA launched the STAR in order to promote transparency in cloud ecosystems. Cloud providers answer the Consensus Assessment Initiative Questionnaire (CAIQ) (CSA, 2011) and make the completed CAIQ available through the CSA STAR. The CAIQ profiles of cloud providers are useful for potential cloud users in order to assess the security capabilities, e.g., compliance, IS, governance, of cloud services before signing up contracts. Although the CAIQ profiles are based on the cloud providers' self-assessments, the CSA make sure that cloud providers publish their information truthfully and update them regularly in the STAR. One of the major drawbacks of the completed CAIQ profiles is that the information underlying the profiles is informally formatted, e.g., by means of free form text spreadsheets. This drawback limits human users to quantify security capabilities based on the information provided in those profiles.

3.4 CLOUD SECURITY QUANTIFICATION METHODS

Security quantification is essential and useful for cloud users in order to compare the cloud providers based on the level of their security capabilities. In order to address the STAR's drawback, Luna Garcia et al. (2012) proposed an approach to quantify Security Level Agreements, i.e., the CAIQ profiles. The proposed approach leverages Quantitative Policy Trees (QPTs) to model security capabilities underlying the CAIQ. Related AND/OR-based aggregation methods are used to aggregate the qualitative or quantitative values (i.e., answers provided in the CAIQ profiles) associated with different nodes of QPTs. Aggregated values represent the security capability level of cloud providers. However, those security quantification and aggregation methods are not able to deal with uncertainty and inconsistencies associated with answers provided by cloud providers.

4 COMPUTATIONAL TRUST METHODS FOR QUANTIFYING SECURITY CAPABILITIES

In cloud computing ecosystems, computing resources such as computing power, data storage, and software are modeled as services. A number of cloud providers offer those services with similar functionality. However, there can be huge differences regarding the published security capabilities of those service providers. Therefore, security capabilities need to be quantified in order to support users to compare the cloud providers.

Computational trust methods are useful tools to assess the quality of a trustee based on the available evidence that is subject to uncertainty. When evidence is derived from multiple sources, there might be conflicting evidence due to the nature of information sources. Those trust methods are able to deal with conflicting evidence while assessing the quality of that trustee. Such methods can be used to assess and quantify security capabilities as underlying evidence of those capabilities is often conflicting and uncertain. Furthermore, trust methods provide visual aids to communicate the quality of a trustee (e.g., cloud provider) to the trustor. This can be a useful technique to communicate the security levels of cloud providers to users in order to support them in making informed decisions.

4.1 FORMAL ANALYSIS OF SECURITY CAPABILITIES

In a cloud ecosystem, service providers may publish service-specific security capabilities using a self-assessment framework such as the CSA CAIQ. Users can make use of these capabilities, publicly available from the STAR, to get a better handle on the security attributes that cloud providers claimed to have. In the CAIQ, fulfillment of capabilities can be reasoned in a composite manner, for instance, a cloud provider is considered to fulfill the IS capability given that the constituent attributes (IS-01– IS-34) are also fulfilled. However, the CAIQ framework as it stands does not provide a solution on analyzing such a *composition* in the context of security quantification.

Each of the security capabilities has underlying attributes that are, again, composed of several other attributes. If capabilities are associated with attributes that cannot be split further, they are denoted as "atomic attributes." If capabilities are associated with attributes that are composed of further attributes, these are denoted as "nonatomic attributes." In the context of service-specific capabilities, a consumer's requirement(s) is denoted as R, where consumers might prefer to personalize a set of requirements.

4.1.1 Transforming security attributes into formal security terms

The definition of formal "security terms" in the context of published security attributes follows a similar syntax and semantics of the definitions presented in Schryen et al. (2011). Therefore, formal definitions were proposed to analyze composite distributed services. Here, similar definitions are formulated to analyze composite service attributes, i.e., a service attribute may consist of subattributes. Regarding service-specific composite attributes, the definitions are as follows.

Let S be a service with atomic attributes, $P = \{P_i\}_{i=1}^{n}$. Assume that the user requirements, $R = \{R_1, \ldots, R_n\}$, are a subset of published attributes, $R \subseteq P$. A single requirement is denoted by $r \subseteq P$. Every attribute P_i is assumed to have subattributes, $|N|$.

Definition 2. *An atomic attribute P_i of a service S can be described by the security term (k "out-of" N), $k \in \{1, \ldots, |N|\}$, $N \subseteq P_i$, wrt r*

$$:\Leftrightarrow \begin{cases} \textit{At least } k \textit{ subattributes "out-of"} \\ N \textit{ need to be satisfied so that } S \\ \textit{meets requirement } r. \end{cases}$$

In order to describe atomic attributes of a service that satisfies more than one requirement, we define the following security terms:

Definition 3. *Different atomic attributes P of a service S can be described by the security term* $((k_1 \oslash \cdots \oslash k_m)$ *"out-of"* $(N_1, \cdots, N_m)); \forall ik_i \in \{1,\ldots,|N_i|\}, N_i \subseteq P, \textit{wrt } R$

$$:\Leftrightarrow \begin{cases} \textit{For each } i \in \{1,\ldots,m\} \textit{ at least} \\ k_i \textit{ subattributes "out-of" } N_i \textit{ need} \\ \textit{to be satisfied so that } S \textit{ meets} \\ \textit{requirements } R. \end{cases}$$

In order to represent nonatomic security attributes of a service by means of security terms we define the following two definitions. Let $\{P_i\}_{i=1}^n$ be subattributes of a system S, and let property P_i of the system be described by the following security term $l_i, \forall i \in \{1,\ldots,n\}$. Assuming that user requirements, $R = \{R_1,\ldots,R_n\}$, are a subset of published attributes, $R \subseteq P_i$. In the case of a single requirement, $r \subseteq P_i$.

Definition 4. *A nonatomic attribute* P_i *of a service S can be described by the security term* $(k \textit{ "out-of" } \{l_{i_1},\ldots,l_{i_m}\}), k \in \{1,\ldots,m\}, \{i_1,\ldots,i_m\} \subseteq \{1,\ldots,n\}, \textit{wrt } r$

$$:\Leftrightarrow \begin{cases} \textit{At least } k \textit{ attributes "out-of"} \\ \{P_{i_1},\ldots,P_{i_m}\} \textit{ need to be satisfied} \\ \textit{so that } S \textit{ meets requirement } r. \end{cases}$$

Definition 5. *Different nonatomic attributes P of a system S can be described by the security term* $((k_1 \oslash \cdots \oslash k_m)$ *"out-of"* $(Q_1, \cdots, Q_m)); \forall ik_i \in \{1,\ldots,|Q_i|\}, Q_i \subseteq \{l_1,\ldots,l_n\}, \textit{wrt } R$

$$:\Leftrightarrow \begin{cases} \textit{For each } i \in \{1,\ldots,m\} \textit{ at least} \\ k_i \textit{ attributes "out-of" the set of} \\ \textit{attributes for which } Q_i \textit{ contains} \\ \textit{security terms need to be satisfied} \\ \textit{so that } S \textit{ meets requirements } R. \end{cases}$$

We demonstrate the analysis and determination of security terms with the following example.

4.1.1.1 Example

Assume that a cloud provider publishes service-specific capabilities regarding a set of attributes like security, compliance, data governance, etc. Those capabilities and attributes are published through a public repository named STAR following the CSA CAIQ framework. A user wants to assess the security level of a cloud provider wrt. the following requirements: security and compliance. We assume that a static mapping between the user requirements and published capabilities of cloud providers is already available. In order to satisfy the user's *security* requirement, a cloud provider has to possess capabilities regarding following three attributes: Facility Security (FS), Human Resources Security (HS), and IS. Additionally, in order to satisfy user's *compliance* requirement, a cloud provider has to possess capabilities regarding following two attributes: technical compliance (CO) and legal compliance (LG). The above definitions are used to convert the service-specific attributes into security terms. Applying Definitions 2 and 4, the following security terms are obtained according to the given requirements of the user, i.e., *security* and *compliance*.

- *Security*: $\underbrace{(3 \text{ "out-of" } \{FS, HS, IS\})}_{=:l_1}$ (Definition 2)

- *Compliance*: $\underbrace{(2 \text{ "out-of" } \{CO, LG\})}_{=:l_2}$ (Definition 2)

- *{Security, Compliance}*: $(2 \text{ "out-of"}(\{l_1, l_2\}))$ (Definition 4)

4.1.2 Mapping security terms to PLTs

The example shows that the representation of composite service attributes by means of *security terms* can become complex even for a simple set of attributes. In order to represent security terms in a simple format to allow easy interpretation and evaluation, security terms are transformed into *Propositional Logic Terms* (PLTs). The following theorem is required for this purpose.

Theorem 1. *Let the attributes P of system S consist of subattributes $P = \{P_1, \ldots, P_n\}$ and let $\{X_{P_1}, \ldots, X_{P_n}\}$ be literals with $\forall i: X_{P_i} = true$, if $R \subseteq P$ and $r \subseteq P_i$. Then, the security term l can be mapped to a propositional logic formula f(l) such that S is trustworthy wrt r or R if and only if f(l) is satisfied.*

The proof regarding Theorem 1 is provided in Appendix.

We use the above-mentioned example to illustrate how to determine the propositional logic formula of particular security terms, namely l_1, l_2, and l.

4.1.2.1 Example
- $l_1 = (3 \text{ "out-of" } (\{FS, HS, IS\}))$

$$\Rightarrow f(l_1) \overset{(A.1)}{=} (FS) \wedge (HS) \wedge (IS)$$
$$= FS \wedge HS \wedge IS =: f_{security}$$

- $l_2 = 2 \text{ "out-of" } (\{CO, LG\})$

$$\Rightarrow f(l_2) \overset{(A.1)}{=} (CO) \wedge (LG)$$
$$= CO \wedge LG =: f_{compliance}$$

- $l = 2$ "out-of" $(\{l_1, l_2\})$

$$\Rightarrow f(l) \overset{(A.3)}{=} (f(l_1)) \wedge (f(l_2))$$
$$= (f_{\text{security}}) \wedge (f_{\text{compliance}})$$
$$= (\text{FS} \wedge \text{HS} \wedge \text{IS}) \wedge (\text{CO} \wedge \text{LG}) \tag{1}$$

4.2 EVALUATING SECURITY CAPABLITIES

The framework discussed in the previous section provides means to model the security capabilities of cloud providers considering different security attributes. Particularly, the framework formally analyzes the dependencies underlying those attributes and represents the dependencies by means of PLTs. However, PLTs do not serve the purpose of quantifying the security capabilities of service providers. Security quantification is essential to compare cloud services as well as cloud providers that have similar capabilities. In order to quantify security levels of cloud providers, there is a need to associate values with the PLTs. This means that capabilities of a service should be associated with a *value* that represents the existence of underlying attributes and subattributes. The values should be *aggregated* according to the derived attribute specification, i.e., PLTs.

According to Ries et al. (2011), such a *value* can appear in the form of an *opinion*, which is based on the available pieces of evidence. Derived pieces of evidence can be incomplete, unreliable, or indeterminable due to the type of measuring methods. Thus, opinions derived from this evidence are subject to *uncertainty*. Moreover, the opinions derived from different sources might be *conflicting* either due to the method they use for assessing evidence, or simply because the sources are unreliable. The mechanism should also be able to aggregate opinions in *compositions* as represented in PLTs. The propositions in the PLTs are combined with a logical AND ($\wedge$) operator and this operator should be able to combine opinions derived from uncertain and conflicting evidence. Therefore, novel *CertainLogic* logical operators and nonstandard operators (i.e., FUSION) are leveraged to quantify the security capabilities of cloud providers. The *CertainLogic* operators are defined to deal with uncertain and conflicting opinions associated with propositions.

In the following section, the *CertainLogic* AND ($\wedge$) and FUSION operators are defined. The definitions are based on an established model, CertainTrust, which serves as a representational model to represent opinions under uncertain probabilities.

4.2.1 CertainLogic operators

As *CertainLogic* operators are based on the CertainTrust representational model, we start this section with a brief overview on that model.

4.2.1.1 CertainTrust

Ries proposed the *CertainTrust* model (Ries, 2009b) in order to represent trust under uncertain probabilities. With this model, the truth of a statement or proposition can also be expressed by a construct called *opinion*. By design, this opinion construction addresses evidence under uncertainty and a user's initial expectation about the truth of a proposition. The definition of CertainTrust is as follows.

Definition 6 (CertainTrust Representation). *An opinion o_A about the truth of a proposition A is given as $o_A = (t, c, f)$ where the parameters are called average rating $t \in [0,1]$, certainty $c \in [0,1]$, and initial expectation value $f \in [0,1]$. If $c = 0$ holds (complete uncertainty), the expectation value (cf. Definition 7) depends only on f, however, for soundness, $t = 0.5$ is defined in this case.*

Here, the *average rating t* indicates the degree to which past pieces of evidence support the truth of a proposition. It depends on the relative frequency of observations or pieces of evidence supporting the truth of a proposition. The *certainty c* indicates the degree to which the average rating is assumed to be representative for the future. It depends on the number of past observations (or collected pieces of evidence). The higher the certainty of an opinion is, the higher is the influence of the average rating on the expectation value (cf. Definition 7) in relation to the initial expectation. When the maximum level of certainty ($c = 1$) is reached, the average rating is assumed to be representative for future outcomes. The *initial expectation f* expresses the assumption about the truth of a proposition in absence of evidence.

Definition 7 (Expectation value of CT). *The expectation value of an opinion $E(t, c, f) \in [0,1]$ is defined as $E(t, c, f) = t \cdot c + (1 - c) \cdot f$.*

It expresses the expectation about the truth of a proposition taking into account the initial expectation, the average rating and the certainty. In other words, the expectation value shifts from the initial expectation value (f) to the average rating (t) with increasing certainty (c). The expectation value, E, expresses trustworthiness of the trustor on the trustee and is referred to as *trustworthiness value* in CertainTrust model.

4.2.1.2 CertainLogic AND ($\land$) Operator

The operator $\land$ is applicable when opinions about two-independent propositions need to be combined in order to produce a new opinion reflecting the degree of truth of both propositions simultaneously. Note that the opinions (cf. Definition 6) are represented using the CertainTrust model. The rationale behind the definitions of the logical operators of CertainTrust (e.g., AND ($\land$)) demands an analytical discussion.

In standard binary logic, logical operators operate on propositions that only consider the values "TRUE" or "FALSE" (i.e., 1 or 0, respectively) as input arguments. In standard probabilistic logic, the logical operators operates on propositions that consider values in the range of [0,1] (i.e., probabilities) as input arguments. However, logical operators in the standard probabilistic approach are not able to consider *uncertainty* about the probability values. SL's logical operators are able to operate on opinions that consider uncertain probabilities as input arguments. Additionally, SL's logical operators are a generalized version of standard logic operators and probabilistic logic operators.

Table 1 Definition of the Operators

AND

$$c_{A\land B} = \begin{cases} c_A + c_B - c_A c_B - \dfrac{(1-c_A)c_B(1-f_A)t_B + c_A(1-c_B)(1-f_B)t_A}{1-f_A f_B} & \text{if } f_A f_B \neq 1, \\ \text{"undefined"} & \text{else} \end{cases}$$

$$t_{A\land B} = \begin{cases} \dfrac{1}{c_{A\land B}}\left(c_A c_B t_A t_B + \dfrac{c_A(1-c_B)(1-f_A)f_B t_A + (1-c_A)c_B f_A(1-f_B)t_B}{1-f_A f_B}\right) & \text{if } c_{A\land B} \neq 0, \text{if } f_A f_B \neq 1, \\ 0.5 & \text{else} \end{cases}$$

$$f_{A\land B} = f_A f_B$$

CertainLogic's logical operators operate on CertainTrust's opinions, which represent uncertain probabilities in a more flexible and simpler manner than the opinion representation in SL. Note that both CertainTrust's representation and SL's representation of opinions are *isomorphic* with the mapping provided in Ries (2009b). For a detailed discussion on the representational model of SL's opinions and CertainTrust's opinions, we refer the readers to Chapter 2 of Habib (2014). The definitions of CertainLogic's logical operators are formulated in a way so that they are equivalent to the definitions of logical operators in SL. This equivalence serves as an argument for the *justification* and *mathematical validity* of CertainLogic logical operators' definitions. Moreover, these operators are generalization of binary logic and probabilistic logic operators.

Definition 8 (Operator AND). *Let A and B be two independent propositions and the opinions about the truth of these propositions be given as $o_A = (t_A, c_A, f_A)$ and $o_B = (t_B, c_B, f_B)$, respectively. Then, the resulting opinion is denoted as $o_{A\land B} = (t_{A\land B}, c_{A\land B}, f_{A\land B})$ where $t_{A\land B}$, $c_{A\land B}$, and $f_{A\land B}$ are defined in Table 1 (AND). We use the symbol " $\land$" to designate the operator AND and we define $o_{A\land B} \equiv o_A \land o_B$.*

The aggregation (using the *AND* operator) of opinions about independent propositions A and B are formulated in a way that the resulting initial expectation (*f*) is dependent on the initial expectation values, f_A and f_B assigned to A and B, respectively. Following the equivalent definitions of SL's normal conjunction operator and basic characteristics of the same operator ($\land$) in standard probabilistic logic, we define $f_{A\land B} = f_A f_B$. The definitions for $c_{A\land B}$ and $t_{A\land B}$ are formulated in similar manner and the corresponding adjustments in the definitions are made to maintain the equivalence between the operators of SL and CertainLogic. The *AND* ($\land$) operator of CertainLogic is associative and commutative; both properties are desirable for the evaluation of PLTs.

4.2.1.3 CertainLogic FUSION operator
Assume that one wants to fuse conflicting opinions (about a proposition) derived from multiple sources. In this case, one should use the conflict-aware fusion (C. FUSION) operator as defined in Habib (2014). This operator operates on dependent

conflicting opinions and reflects the calculated degree of conflict (DoC) in the resulting fused opinion. Note that the C.FUSION operator is also able to deal with preferential weights associated with opinions.

Definition 9 (C.FUSION). *Let A be a proposition and let $o_{A_1} = (t_{A_1}, c_{A_1}, f_{A_1})$, $o_{A_2} = (t_{A_2}, c_{A_2}, f_{A_2}), ..., o_{A_n} = (t_{A_n}, c_{A_n}, f_{A_n})$ be n opinions associated to A. Furthermore, the weights $w_1, w_2, ..., w_n$ (with $w_1, w_2, ..., w_n \in \mathbb{R}_0^+$ and $w_1 + w_2 + \cdots + w_n \neq 0$) are assigned to the opinions $o_{A_1}, o_{A_2}, ..., o_{A_n}$, respectively. The C.FUSION is denoted as*

$$o_{\hat{\oplus}_c(A_1, A_2, ..., A_n)} = ((t_{\hat{\oplus}_c(A_1, A_2, ..., A_n)}, c_{\hat{\oplus}_c(A_1, A_2, ..., A_n)}, f_{\hat{\oplus}_c(A_1, A_2, ..., A_n)}), DoC)$$

where $t_{\hat{\oplus}_c(A_1, A_2, ..., A_n)}$, $c_{\hat{\oplus}_c(A_1, A_2, ..., A_n)}$, $f_{\hat{\oplus}_c(A_1, A_2, ..., A_n)}$, the DoC are defined in Table 2. We use the symbol $(\hat{\oplus}_c)$ to designate the operator C.FUSION and we define $o_{\hat{\oplus}_c(A_1, A_2, ..., A_n)} \equiv \hat{\oplus}_c((o_{A_1}, w_1), (o_{A_2}, w_2), ..., (o_{A_n}, w_n))$.

Table 2 Definition of the C.FUSION Operator

$$t_{\hat{\oplus}_c(A_1, A_2, ..., A_n)} = \begin{cases} \dfrac{\sum\limits_{i=1}^{n} w_i t_{A_i}}{\sum\limits_{i=1}^{n} w_i} & \text{if } c_{A_1} = c_{A_2} = \cdots = c_{A_n} = 1, \\ 0.5 & \text{if } c_{A_1} = c_{A_2} = \cdots = c_{A_n} = 0, \\ \dfrac{\sum\limits_{i=1}^{n} (c_{A_i} t_{A_i} w_i \prod\limits_{j=1, \ j \neq i}^{n} (1 - c_{A_j}))}{\sum\limits_{i=1}^{n} (c_{A_i} w_i \prod\limits_{j=1, \ j \neq i}^{n} (1 - c_{A_j}))} & \text{if } \{c_{A_i}, c_{A_j}\} \neq 1 \end{cases}$$

$$c_{\hat{\oplus}_c(A_1, A_2, ..., A_n)} = \begin{cases} 1 \cdot (1 - DoC) & \text{if } c_{A_1} = c_{A_2} = \cdots = c_{A_n} = 1, \\ \dfrac{\sum\limits_{i=1}^{n} (c_{A_i} w_i \prod\limits_{j=1, \ j \neq i}^{n} (1 - c_{A_j}))}{\sum\limits_{i=1}^{n} (w_i \prod\limits_{j=1, \ j \neq i}^{n} (1 - c_{A_j}))} \cdot (1 - DoC) & \text{if } \{c_{A_i}, c_{A_j}\} \neq 1 \end{cases}$$

$$f_{\hat{\oplus}_c(A_1, A_2, ..., A_n)} = \dfrac{\sum\limits_{i=1}^{n} w_i f_{A_i}}{\sum\limits_{i=1}^{n} w_i}$$

$$DoC = \dfrac{\sum\limits_{i=1}^{n} \sum\limits_{j=1, j \neq i}^{n} DoC_{A_i, A_j}}{\dfrac{n(n-1)}{2}}$$

$$DoC_{A_i, A_j} = |t_{A_i} - t_{A_j}| \cdot c_{A_i} \cdot c_{A_j} \cdot \left(1 - \left|\frac{w_i - w_j}{w_i + w_j}\right|\right)$$

The C.FUSION operator is commutative and idempotent, but not associative.

The rationale behind the definition of the C.FUSION demands an extensive discussion. The basic concept of this operator is that the operator extends the Certain-Logic's *Weighted fusion* (Habib et al., 2012) operator by calculating the DoC between a pair of opinions. Then, the value of $(1-\text{DoC})$ is multiplied with the certainty (c) that would be calculated by the weighted fusion (the parameters for t and f are the same as in the weighted fusion).

Now, we discuss the calculation of the DoC for two opinions. For the parameter, it holds $\text{DoC} \in [0,1]$. This parameter depends on the average ratings (t), the certainty values (c), and the weights (w). The weights are assumed to be selected by the trustors (consumers) and the purpose of the weights is to model the preferences of the trustor when aggregating opinions from different sources. We assume that the compliance of their preferences are ensured under a policy negotiation phase. For example, users might be given three choices: high (2), low (1), and no preference (0, i.e., opinion from a particular source is not considered), to express their preferences on selecting the sources that provide the opinions. Note that the weights are not introduced to model the reliability of sources. In this case, it would be appropriate to use the discounting operator (Ries, 2009b; Jøsang, 2001) to explicitly consider reliability of sources and apply the fusion operator on the results to influence users' preferences. The values of DoC can be interpreted as follows:

- **No conflict (DoC=0):** For DoC=0, it holds that there is *no conflict* between the two opinions. This is true if both opinions agree on the average rating, i.e., $t_{A_1} = t_{A_2}$ or in case that at least one opinion has a certainty $c = 0$ (for completeness we have to state that it is also true if one of the weights is equal to 0, which means the opinion is not considered).
- **Total conflict (DoC=1):** For DoC=1, it holds that the two opinions are weighted equally $(w_1 = w_2)$ and contradicts each other to a maximum. This means, that both opinions have a maximum certainty $(c_{A_1} = c_{A_2} = 1)$ and maximum divergence in the average ratings, i.e., $t_{A_1} = 0$ and $t_{A_2} = 1$ (or $t_{A_1} = 1$ and $t_{A_2} = 0$).
- **Conflict (DoC∈]0,1[):** For DoC∈]0,1[, it holds that there are two opinions contradict each other to a certain degree. This means that the both opinions does not agree on the average ratings, i.e., $t_{A_1} \neq t_{A_2}$, having certainty values other than 0 and 1. The weights can be any real number other than 0.

Next, we argue for integrating the DoC into the resulting opinion by multiplying the certainty with $(1-\text{DoC})$. The argument is, in case that there are two (equally weighted) conflicting opinions, then this indicates that the information which these opinions are based on is not representative for the outcome of the assessment or experiment. Thus, for the sake of representativeness, in the case of total conflict (i.e., DoC=1), we reduce the certainty $(c_{(o_{A_1}, w_1) \oplus (o_{A_2}, w_2)})$ of the resulting opinion by a multiplicative factor, $(1-\text{DoC})$. The certainty value is 0 in this case.

For n opinions, (i.e., DoC_{A_i, A_j}) in Table 2 is calculated for each opinion pairs. For instance, if there are n opinions there can be at most $\frac{n(n-1)}{2}$ pairs and is calculated for each of those pairs individually. Then, all the pairwise *DoC* values are averaged, i.e., averaging $\frac{n(n-1)}{2}$ pairs of DoC_{A_i, A_j}. Finally, the certainty (i.e., $c_{\hat{\oplus}_c(A_1, A_2, \ldots, A_n)}$) parameter of the resulting opinion (cf. Table 2) is adjusted with the resulting *DoC* value.

In Table 2, for all opinions if it holds $c_{A_i} = 0$ (complete uncertainty), the expectation values (cf. Definition 7) depends only on *f*. However, for soundness we define $t_{A_i} = 0.5$ in this case.

4.2.2 Security capability assessment using certainLogic operators

We consider the CSA STAR as an information repository of security capabilities that are published by cloud providers. In the CSA STAR, cloud providers publish one set of valid answers in response to the CAIQ regarding each of the services they offer. The answers are evidence of corresponding capabilities that cloud providers claimed to have. Here, the CSA is assumed responsible for checking the authenticity and the basic accuracy of the answered questionnaires as mentioned in CSA (2013).

In order to assess security capabilities as published in the CSA STAR, we follow a two-step approach:

1. First, PLTs are constructed from the given CAIQ domains by means of formal analysis (cf. Section 4.1). The CAIQ domains are termed as security capabilities in this chapter. In the context of the CAIQ, a PLT configuration consists of 11 operands (i.e., capabilities) combined with 10 AND ($\wedge$) operators. Conceptually, a PLT configuration is constructed as follows:

$$\text{CO} \wedge \text{DG} \wedge \text{FS} \wedge \text{HR} \wedge \text{IS} \wedge \text{LG} \wedge \text{OP} \wedge \text{RI} \wedge \text{RM} \wedge \text{RS} \wedge \text{SA}$$

   where, CO, DG, FS, HR, IS, LG, OP, RI, RM, RS, and SA are the acronyms for Compliance, Data Governance, Facility Security, Human Resources Security, Information Security, Legal, Operations Management, Risk Management, Release Management, Resiliency and Security Architecture, respectively.

2. Second, for each of the propositions (security capabilities), an associated opinion (t, c, f) is required to evaluate the PLTs. The opinions need to be extracted from cloud providers' answers to the CAIQ domains. The answers are usually in the form of "yes" or "no", which upon analysis can be classified to *positive* and *negative* pieces of evidence. These evidence units demonstrate the level of security capabilities a cloud provider has regarding the services it offers in cloud ecosystems. In Ries (2009b), a mapping is proposed to map the collected pieces of evidence to the opinion space. The mapping (cf. Equation 2) has been proposed in the context of ubiquitous computing environments, where evidence units are collected based on a trustor's interaction experience with a trustee. In this context, positive (*r*) and negative (*s*) pieces of evidence are mapped to the CertainTrust opinion space. In the context of CAIQ, evidence units are based on the cloud providers' self-assessment of security capabilities regarding each of the services they offer. As the existence of the capabilities are reasoned based on the given assertions, the same mapping function is used to derive opinions from those assertions, i.e., positive and negative pieces of evidence, under each of the

capabilities. The mapping between the evidence space and the CertainTrust opinion space is as follows:

$$t = \begin{cases} 0 & \text{if } r+s=0, \\ \dfrac{r}{r+s} & \text{else.} \end{cases}$$

$$c = \frac{N \cdot (r+s)}{2 \cdot (N - (r+s)) + N \cdot (r+s)} \qquad (2)$$

$$f = 0.99$$

The definitions regarding the parameters are as follows:

- Average rating, t, is calculated based on the number of *positive* assertions (r) and the number of *negative* assertions (s) under each domain. If there are no questions answered, t is 0. Otherwise, t is the relative frequency of *positive* and *negative* assertions.
- Certainty, c, is calculated based on the total number of questions, N and the number of positive (r) and negative (s) assertions under each domain. c is 1 when all questions under each domain are answered with *positive* or *negative* assertions and 0 if none are answered.

   The definition of N is adjusted according to the context of CAIQ assessment. The total number of questions, N, not only considers *positive* and *negative* assertions but also the unanswered questions under each domain. The unanswered questions can be of two types:

   (a) Questions that cloud providers left out for *unknown* reasons or an answer to a question is indeterminable to classify as "yes" or "no".

   (b) Questions that do not fit the scope of the services (i.e., *Not Applicable*) offered by the respective cloud providers.

   In order to deal with the above-mentioned types of questions, we define N as following:

   - For type (a), the *unknown* (to which we refer as "u") marked answer(s) to the corresponding question(s) under each domain are taken into account. That means, $N = r + s + u$.
   - For type (b), the *Not Applicable* (to which we refer as "NA") marked answers under each domain are not included in the calculation of N. That means, $N = (r + s + u) - NA$.

- Initial expectation, f, is set very high (i.e., 0.99) for every single domain assuming that cloud providers publish information regarding their capabilities in the STAR repository truthfully and that the accuracy of this information is validated using the CloudAudit (CSA, 2012a) framework.

   In the CertainTrust model, the expectation value (E) is calculated based on Definition 7. E is computed based on t, c, and f. Herein, with increasing certainty (which means that a large amount of evidence is available), the influence of the f ceases. In the context of security capability assessment, the E represents the level of security capability that a cloud provider possess.

4.3 VISUALLY COMMUNICATING MULTIPLE SECURITY CAPABILITIES

When communicating the results of a security capability evaluation to human users, a set of numerical expectation values or opinion tuples is usually inferior to a visual representation. The latter one is intended to be understood easier and faster by humans in comparison with textual descriptions that include numerical values only.

The *Human Trust Interface* (cf. Figure 1 (c)) in Ries and Schreiber (2008) is used to visualize a single CertainTrust opinion. It can be used to display the overall result of trust assessments of cloud providers. However, it is often more suitable to convey detailed information to potential customers.

The *Star-Interface* is one of the most popular visualizations for trustworthiness. The more stars a product is given, the higher its rating and thus, its trustworthiness. However, the Star-Interface lacks two important features to be used in communicating multicriterial trust: (i) it lacks a certainty measure, i.e., how much evidence a rating is based on and (ii) only one rating is shown at a time. Nurse et al. present a multicriterial trust visualization using radar charts in Nurse et al. (2013) (cf. Figure 1 (a)). Five *trust factors*—namely recency, competence, corroboration, popularity, and

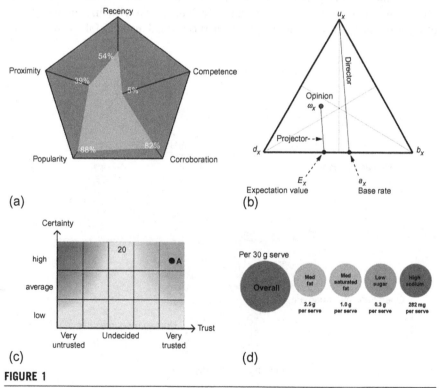

FIGURE 1

Trust visualizations from Nurse et al. (2013) (a), Jøsang et al. (2012) (b), Ries and Schreiber (2008) (c), and Kelly et al. (2009) (d). (a) and (d) have been altered for better display.

proximity—are shown within one graph. The score for each trust factor is ploted on one of the axis of the pentagon-shaped graph. Aside being limited to these five fixed trust factors, the graph does not denote certainty at all. The *Opinion Triangle* by Jøsang et al. (2012) (cf. Figure 1 (b)) enriches the display of a trust value with an uncertainty measure. Similar to the Star-Interface, the Opinion Triangle displays only one opinion at a time. The Opinion Triangle is very well suited for analysis done by experts. However, it is not readily accessible on an intuitive level. The expressive power of Ries et al.'s *Human Trust Interface* (Ries and Schreiber, 2008) (cf. Figure 1 (c)) is similar to the Opinion Triangle. The introduction of a color-gradient trades off quantitative-analytical capabilities for a more intuitive display of the given trust value. Kelly et al. (2009) evaluate the expressive power of a Traffic Light scheme, enriched with an overall rating, to communicate food trustworthiness (cf. Figure 1 (d)). On the one hand, this visualization combines an intuitive color-coded interface and the display of multiple criteria. On the other hand, this visualization lacks the display of certainty values.

Inspired by the four visualizations from Figure 1, the *T-Viz* chart was designed with three features in mind: intuitive readability, presentation of multiple trust values, and conveying certainty values alongside the trust values (Volk et al., 2014). An exemplary *T-Viz* is shown in Figure 2. In order to visualize multiple levels of security capabilities, the circular *T-Viz* chart is divided into multiple segments, one

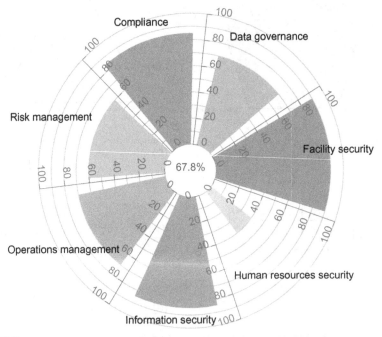

FIGURE 2

T-Viz chart showing the evaluation results of an exemplary cloud service provider.

per criterion. Within each segment, a colored slice's height denotes average rating (t) while its width denotes certainty (c). Moreover, the color of the slice denotes the expectation value (E) calculated based on trust, certainty, and initial expectation value. Thereby, the selection of colors is the same as in the Human Trust Interface. In the middle of the *T-Viz* graph, an overall score is shown.

The *T-Viz* visualization was evaluated in a user study with 229 participants. Thereby, two hypothesis have been tested based on the product ratings. We believe that the study results also apply to cloud service provider ratings.

H1: Decisions regarding quality made using the *T-Viz* chart are at least as good as decisions made using multiple Star-Interfaces (one per criterion).

H2: Decisions made using *T-Viz* are faster than decisions made using multiple Star-Interfaces.

The results of the study show a nonsignificant advantage of *T-Viz* over the Star-Interface regarding H1: when using multiple Star-Interfaces, participants decide correctly in 89.2% of the cases. When using *T-Viz*, 92% correct decisions are made. Therefore, H1 cannot be rejected. Regarding H2, a Wilcoxon-Mann-Whitney test confirms ($p < 0.001$) that decisions made using *T-Viz* are significantly faster than those made by using multiple Star-Interfaces.

Moreover, the study yielded two noteworthy qualitative results. Participants generally favor *T-Viz* over multiple Star-Interfaces when there are more than four categories taken into account. Several participants reported an "unexpected ease-of-use" regarding *T-Viz*, although they considered *T-Viz* to be less intuitive on first sight.

5 CASE STUDIES

In this section, we demonstrate the practicality of computational trust methods, described in Section 4, in quantifying security capabilities of cloud providers. A Java-based automated tool, Cloud Computing Assessment (CCA), was used to conduct the experiments in this section.

5.1 CASE STUDY 1: QUANTIFYING AND VISUALLY COMMUNICATING SECURITY CAPABILITIES

In the first case study, we demonstrate how to quantify the level of security capabilities that are published by the cloud providers in the CSA STAR. In order to do so, the *CertainLogic* AND ($\wedge$) operator is applied into the CSA CAIQ datasets published in the STAR. For brevity, only two CAIQ datasets of cloud storage providers are considered for experimental analysis. Our experiments are centered around two cases:

Practical. In this case, all relevant assertions derived from the STAR datasets are considered for the experiments. The idea is to demonstrate the result of security quantification when *all* security capabilities are considered by a cloud user. Naturally, the *CertainLogic* AND ($\wedge$) operator is applied in this case.

Customized. This case considers personal preferences of a user on selecting capabilities, e.g., CO, DG, FS, and IS in the context of CAIQ. This particular case demonstrates the result of security quantification when a subset of security capabilities is specified by a user.

In order to visually communicate the level of security capabilities to potential cloud service users, *T-Viz* (cf. Section 4.3) is used for representing multicriterial values regarding those capabilities.

5.1.1 Experiments: practical case

We choose two *CAIQ* profiles of Cloud storage providers, "D" and "M." The identities of the cloud providers are *anonymized* due to usage restrictions of the STAR.

Tables 3 and 4 present a summary of the assertions. Corresponding resulting opinions are calculated using Equation 2 to map the given assertions to opinions. According to the final assessment, given in Tables 3 and 4, cloud consumers are able to identify a potential cloud provider based on the computed expectation value, i.e., the quantified security level. The security level of Cloud provider "D" is higher than that of Cloud provider "M." It means that the level of security capabilities claimed by provider "D" is better than that of provider "M" based on the detailed assessment of underlying attributes of those capabilities. Hence, the expectation value is a reasonable indicator for users to compare cloud providers. Note that in addition to the expectation value, the certainty (c) value is a good indicator of whether the aggregated rating (t) is representative or further analysis is required.

5.1.2 Experiments: customized case

Tables 5 and 6 reflect a user's preference while quantifying security levels of cloud providers. A user might require cloud providers to possess security capabilities regarding CO, DG, FS, and IS as a part of their service provisioning policy. We demonstrate experiments on the CAIQs submitted by Cloud "D" and Cloud "M" in the STAR. By enabling the *customization* feature of the CCA tool on the completed CAIQs, we observe notable changes in opinion values as well as in expectation values (security levels) calculated for both providers in comparison to the results given in Tables 3 and 4. Moreover, the customization feature enables the customers to get a personalized assessment of a cloud providers' security capabilities in contrast to the fixed Excel-based CAIQ assessment available in the CSA website. In our case study, we mimicked user preferences by randomly selecting security capabilities from the given list using our tool.

In continuation, now we analyze the documented results in Tables 5 and 6. The security levels, calculated based on the customization of the capabilities, are significantly higher than the values calculated in Tables 3 and 4. The reason behind the deviation of the security levels is that the underlying assertions of required capabilities are more "positive" than those of Tables 3 and 4. It means that the cloud providers in Table 5 and 6 have a higher security level in the customized case than in the practical case. Based on the results of the final assessment in the customized case, we conclude that cloud provider "D" has a better security level than cloud provider "M."

Table 3 Practical Case: Quantified Security Capabilities of Cloud "D" (Anonymized)

Domains	r	s	u	NA	N	Resulting Opinion (t,c,f)	Final Assessment (t,c,f);E
CO	16	0	0	0	16	(1,1,0.99)	(0.3085,0.9978,0.8953);E = 0.3098
DG	13	2	1	0	16	(0.8667,0.9917,0.99)	
FS	8	1	0	0	9	(0.8889,1,0.99)	
HS	4	0	0	0	4	(1,1,0.99)	
IS	64	3	5	3	72	(0.9552,0.9979,0.99)	
LG	2	0	0	2	2	(1,1,0.99)	
OM	5	0	1	3	6	(1,0.9375,0.99)	
RI	10	4	0	0	14	(0.7143,1,0.99)	
RM	4	1	0	1	5	(0.8,1,0.99)	
RS	10	1	0	1	11	(0.8182,1,0.99)	
SA	27	3	0	2	30	(0.9,1,0.99)	

Table 4 Practical Case: Quantified Security Capabilities of **Cloud "M"** (Anonymized)

Domains	r	s	u	NA	N	Resulting Opinion (t,c,f)	Final Assessment (t,c,f);E
CO	13	1	0	2	16	(0.9286,1,0.99)	(0.1998,1,0.8953);E = 0.1998
DG	14	2	0	0	16	(0.875,1,0.99)	
FS	8	1	0	0	9	(0.8889,1,0.99)	
HS	4	0	0	0	4	(1,1,0.99)	
IS	64	8	0	3	72	(0.8889,1,0.99)	
LG	2	0	0	2	2	(1,1,0.99)	
OM	4	1	0	4	5	(0.8,1,0.99)	
RI	12	1	1	1	13	(0.9231,1,0.99)	
RM	3	2	0	1	5	(0.6,1,0.99)	
RS	9	2	0	1	11	(0.9091,1,0.99)	
SA	17	5	0	10	22	(0.7727,1,0.99)	

Table 5 Customized Case: Quantified Security Capabilities of Cloud "D" (Anonymized)

Domains	r	s	u	NA	N	Resulting Opinion (t,c,f)	Final Assessment (t,c,f);E
CO	16	0	0	0	16	(1,1,0.99)	(0.7363,0.9978,0.9606);E = 0.7368
DG	13	2	1	0	16	(0.8667,0.9917,0.99)	
FS	8	1	0	0	9	(0.8889,1,0.99)	
IS	64	3	5	3	72	(0.9552,0.9979,0.99)	

Table 6 Customized Case: Quantified Security Capabilities of Cloud "M" (Anonymized)

Domains	r	s	u	NA	N	Resulting Opinion (t,c,f)	Final Assessment (t,c,f);E
CO	13	1	0	2	14	(0.9286,1,0.99)	(0.642,1,0.9606);E = 0.642
DG	14	2	0	0	16	(0.875,1,0.99)	
FS	8	1	0	0	9	(0.8889,1,0.99)	
IS	64	8	0	3	72	(0.8889,1,0.99)	

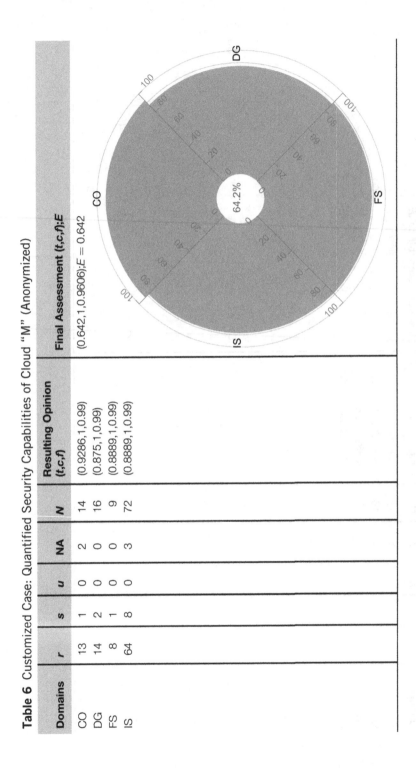

The reason here is that "D" posseses *all* the attributes under CO capability as well as a *lower* number of missing attributes under IS capability compare to "M."

In this section, we have demonstrated the applicability of the formal framework (cf. Section 4.1) and the *CertainLogic* AND ($\land$) operator for combining opinions on independent propositions. The propositions are constructed according to the independent *domains* given in the CSA CAIQ. Opinions on the propositions are derived from the assertions given by the cloud providers in the STAR. Considering the *CertainLogic* AND ($\land$) operator for quantifying security capabilities in this context demonstrates the operator's applicability in real world settings.

5.2 CASE STUDY 2: QUANTIFYING AND COMMUNICATING SECURITY CAPABILITIES IN PRESENCE OF MULTIPLE SOURCES

In this section, we assume that the security capabilities of Cloud "D" and Cloud "M" are assessed by multiple sources. Along with the default CAIQ assessment, discussed in the previous section, two other sources are considered for our case study. In the following, we provide a brief overview of those sources and their opinion generation process.

The resulting three opinions are extracted in the following manner:

1. CAIQ *assessment*: The resulting opinion (o_Q) on the trustworthiness of Cloud "D" and "M" is generated from their completed CAIQ published by the CSA STAR.
2. *Accreditors:* Accreditors use the CCA tool to assess the capabilities of Cloud "D" and "M." The resulting opinion (o_A) is then extracted based on the assessment. The opinion is represented using the CertainTrust model.
3. *Expert assessment:* The capabilities of Cloud "D" and "M" are assessed by experts using our CCA tool. The resulting opinion (o_E) is then derived by the experts using the CCA tool. The opinion is represented using the CertainTrust model.

5.2.1 Experiments

In order to derive the opinion o_Q, the published CAIQs in the STAR are considered. Hence, we use the resulting opinions (derived from CAIQs) documented in Tables 5 and 6 for the experiments conducted in this section. The accreditors and experts may analyze the assertions of CAIQs in a different manner which results in four different outcomes: Tables 7–10. Thus, the resulting opinions (o_A and o_E), derived from the CAIQ profiles of Cloud provider "D" and "M," are different than the opinion o_Q in Tables 5 and 6.

In a real world setting, one would assume that a user can choose between a couple of cloud providers, e.g., Cloud provider "D" and "M." In this case, we propose to sort the cloud providers based on their expectation value E and using the DoC as a second criteria if necessary. The opinions considered to calculate the fused opinions of Cloud provider "D" and Cloud provider "M" are given in Tables 5, 7, 8 and Tables 6, 9, and 10 respectively.

Table 7 Quantified Security Capabilities of **Cloud "D"** (Anonymized): *Accreditor* Perspective (o_A)

Domains	r	s	u	NA	N	Resulting Opinion (t,c,f)	Final Assessment o_A;E
CO	16	0	0	0	16	(1,1,0.99)	(0.8994,0.9938,0.9606);E = 0.8998
DG	15	1	0	0	16	(0.9375,1,0.99)	
FS	8	0	1	0	9	(1,0.973,0.99)	
IS	72	3	0	1	75	(0.96,1,0.99)	

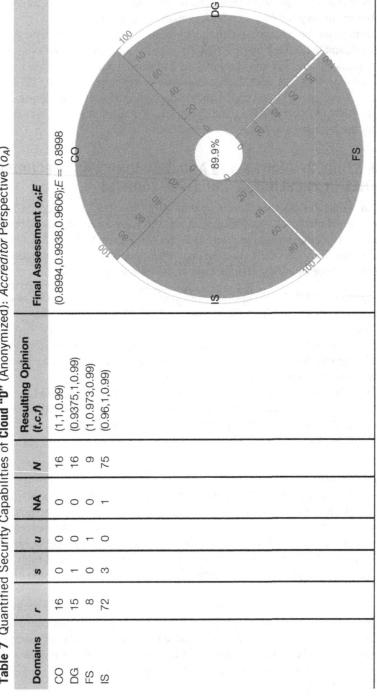

Table 8 Quantified Security Capabilities of **Cloud "D"** (Anonymized): *Expert* Perspective (o_E)

Domains	r	s	u	NA	N	Resulting Opinion (t,c,f)	Final Assessment $o_E;E$
CO	16	0	0	0	16	(1,1,0.99)	(0.8003,0.9937,0.9606);E = 0.8013
DG	15	1	0	0	16	(0.9375,1,0.99)	
FS	7	1	1	0	9	(0.875,0.973,0.99)	
IS	73	2	0	0	75	(0.9733,1,0.99)	

Table 9 Quantified Security Capabilities of **Cloud "M"** (Anonymized): *Accreditor* Perspective (o_A)

Domains	r	s	u	NA	N	Resulting Opinion (t,c,f)	Final Assessment o_A;E
CO	11	1	2	2	14	(0.9167,0.9767,0.99)	(0.6277,0.9957,0.9606);E = 0.6291
DG	15	1	0	0	16	(0.9375,1,0.99)	
FS	7	2	0	0	9	(0.7778,1,0.99)	
IS	62	4	4	5	70	(0.9394,0.9983,0.99)	

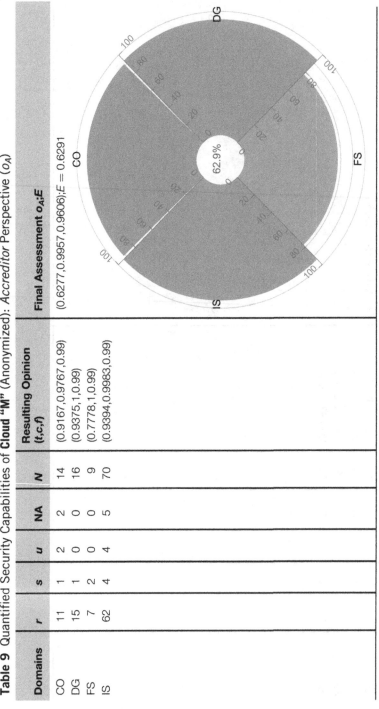

Table 10 Quantified Security Capabilities of **Cloud "M"** (Anonymized): *Expert* Perspective (o_E)

Domains	r	s	u	NA	N	Resulting Opinion (t,c,f)	Final Assessment $o_E;E$
CO	11	3	0	2	14	(0.7857,1,0.99)	(0.6894,0.9893,0.9606);$E = 0.6923$
DG	15	1	0	0	16	(0.9375,1,0.99)	
FS	7	0	2	0	9	(1,0.9403,0.99)	
IS	63	4	3	5	75	(0.9403,0.9987,0.99)	

Table 11 Cloud "D" vs. Cloud "M"

Cloud provider "D": $o_{\hat{\oplus}_c(Q,A,E,F)}$	Cloud provider "M": o_Q; o_E
(0.7832,0.8888,0.9606)	(0.642,1,0.9606); (0.6894,0.9893,0.9606)
$E = 0.8029$	$E = 0.642$; $E = 0.6923$
DoC= 0.1076	DoC=N/A

In Table 11, C.FUSION (cf. Table 2) is applied to aggregate the opinions, derived from multiple sources, on security capabilities of Cloud provider "D" and "M." Here, we found a special case while fusing the opinions regarding security capabilities of Cloud provider "M." The default opinion (o_Q) regarding the security capabilities of Cloud provider "M" has absolute certainty (i.e., $c = 1$); according to the definition of C.FUSION, fusion is only possible if and only if none of the opinions have absolute certainty. Therefore, for comparing security capability levels between Cloud "D" and "M," users might either choose the resulting opinion that calculates the highest expectation value or choose the opinion that has absolute certainty regarding the security capabilities of Cloud "M."

According to the calculated expectation values, Cloud provider "D" has a better security level than Cloud provider "M" considering either of the two potential opinions. This comes from the fact that the given assertions by provider "D" are more *positive* ($t = 0.7832$) than those of provider "M" ($t = 0.6894$ or $t = 0.642$) regarding the required capabilities, CO, DG, FS, and IS. Even though the certainty values (0.9604 and 1) indicate better representativeness of the average rating of Cloud "M," it is not enough for provider "M" to receive a better expectation value E than provider "D." In this special case, the DoC value is not a deciding factor because of the special case of Cloud "M."

6 CONCLUSION

Computational trust methods support cloud users to quantitatively reason the security capabilities of cloud providers in presence of uncertain and conflicting information. This is a significant step forward in the research context of security quantification. Automated security quantification techniques (formal framework along with *CertainLogic* operators and multicriterial visualization), as described in this chapter, remove the burden of the users in assessing the security capabilities *manually* using the STAR platform. By using the automated techniques, users in cloud ecosystems will be able to assess the overall security capabilities of cloud providers. Hence, they will feel more confident in adopting cloud services for their business.

In this chapter, the computational trust methods provide means to compare cloud providers in a qualitative manner. It would be interesting to investigate quantitative benchmarking methods to rank cloud providers based on their security capabilities.

These methods should not only consider user requirements but also consider the correlation of underlying attribute assertions of security capabilities under specific service types.

ACKNOWLEDGMENT

This work has been (co)funded by the DFG as part of project S1 (Scalable Trust Infrastructures) within the CRC 1119 CROSSING.

APPENDIX. PROOF FOR THEOREM 1

We prove the theorem along the inductive definition of security terms, and we provide the corresponding propositional logic formula for each definition of security terms. The principal idea of the proof is that we reformulate the expression "k out of a set L" by explicitly considering all combinations of elements of L, where L can be either a set of properties or of trustworthiness terms of sub-properties. The provision of such a mapping f (of trustworthiness terms on propositional logic terms) proves the theorem.

Proof 1

- If $l = (k$ "out-of" $N)$, $k \in \{1, ..., |N|\}$, $N \subseteq A$ (Definition 2), then

$$f(l) := \bigvee_{\substack{\{A_{i_1}, ..., A_{i_k}\} \subseteq A \\ |\{A_{i_1}, ..., A_{i_k}\}| = k}} \left(\bigwedge_{j=i_1}^{i_k} A_j \right) \tag{A.1}$$

- If $l = ((k_1 \oslash \cdots \oslash k_m)$ "out-of" $(N_1, \cdots, N_m))$, $N_i \subseteq A \ \forall i$ (Definition 3), then

$$f(l) := \bigwedge_{i=1}^{m} (f((k_i \text{ "out-of" } N_i))) \tag{A.2}$$

- If $l = (k$ "out-of" $\{l_{i_1}, ..., l_{i_m}\})$, l_{i_j} trustworthiness terms, $\{i_1, ..., i_m\} \subseteq \{1, ..., n\}$ (Definition 4), then

$$f(l) := \bigvee_{\substack{\{j_1, ..., j_k\} \subseteq \{i_1, ..., i_m\} \\ |\{j_1, ..., j_k\}| = k}} \left(\bigwedge_{j=j_1}^{j_k} (f(l_j)) \right) \tag{A.3}$$

- If $l = ((k_1 \oslash \cdots \oslash k_m)$ "out-of" $(Q_1, \cdots, Q_m))$, Q_i set of trustworthiness terms (Definition 5), then

$$f(l) := \bigwedge_{i=1}^{m} (f((k_i \text{ "out-of" } Q_i))) \tag{A.4}$$

REFERENCES

CSA, 2012a. Cloud Audit, https://cloudsecurityalliance.org/research/cloudaudit/ (accessed 15.09.14).

CSA, 2011. Consensus Assessments Initiative (CAI) Questionnaire, https://cloudsecurityalliance. org/research/cai/ (accessed 15.09.14).

CSA, 2012b. Security, Assurance & Trust Registry (STAR), https://cloudsecurityalliance.org/ star/ (accessed 15.09.2014).

CSA, 2013. Security, Assurance & Trust Registry (STAR) FAQ, https://cloudsecurityalliance. org/star/faq/ (accessed 15.09.14).

Gambetta, D., 1990. Can we trust trust? In: Gambetta, D. (Ed.), In: Trust: Making and Breaking Cooperative RelationsBasil Blackwell, New York, pp. 213–237.

Gambetta, D., 2000. Can we trust trust? In: Gambetta, D. (Ed.), In: Trust: Making and Breaking Cooperative Relations, Electronic Edition (Chapter 13), pp. 213–237.

Grandison, T., 2007. Conceptions of Trust: Definition, Constructs, and Models, Trust in E-Services: Technologies, Practices and Challenges. IGI Global, Hershey, PA (Chapter 1), pp. 1–28.

Habib, S.M., 2014. Trust Establishment Mechanisms for Distributed Service Environments. Ph.D. thesis. Technische Universität Darmstadt.

Habib, S.M., Ries, S., Hauke, S., Mühlhäuser, M., 2012. Fusion of opinions under uncertainty and conflict—application to trust assessment for cloud marketplaces. In: IEEE 11th International Conference on Trust, Security and Privacy in Computing and Communications (TrustCom), 2012, pp. 109–118.

Habib, S.M., Varadharajan, V., Mühlhäuser, M., 2013. A trust-aware framework for evaluating security controls of service providers in cloud marketplaces. In: IEEE 11th International Conference on Trust, Security and Privacy in Computing and Communications (TrustCom), 2013, pp. 459–468.

Haq, I.U., Alnemr, R., Paschke, A., Schikuta, E., Boley, H., Meinel, C., 2010. Distributed trust management for validating sla choreographies. In: Grids and Service-Oriented Architectures for Service Level AgreementsSpringer, US, New York, pp. 45–55.

Intel, 2012. What's Holding Back the Cloud, http://www.intel.de/content/dam/www/public/ us/en/documents/reports/whats-holding-back-the-cloud-peer-research-report2.pdf Technical Report. Intel IT Center.

Jøsang, A., 2001. A logic for uncertain probabilities. Int. J. Uncertainty Fuzziness Knowledge Based Syst. 9, 279–311.

Jøsang, A., Azderska, T., Marsh, S., 2012. Trust transitivity and conditional belief reasoning. In: IFIPTM. Springer, New York, pp. 68–83.

Jøsang, A., Ismail, R., Boyd, C., 2007. A survey of trust and reputation systems for online service provision. Decis. Support Syst. 43 (2), 618–644.

Kelly, B., Hughes, C., Chapman, K., Louie, J.C.Y., Dixon, H., Crawford, J., King, L., Daube, M., Slevin, T., 2009. Consumer testing of the acceptability and effectiveness of front-of-pack food labelling systems for the Australian grocery market. Health Promot. Int. 24, 120–129.

Krautheim, F.J., 2009. Private virtual infrastructure for cloud computing. In: Proceedings of the HotCloud'09. USENIX Association, Berkeley, CA, USA, p. 5.

LeHong, H., Fenn, J., Toit, R.L.-d., 2014. Hype Cycle for Emerging Technologies, https:// www.gartner.com/doc/2809728 (accessed 15.09.14).

Lin, C., Varadharajan, V., Wang, Y., Pruthi, V., 2004. Enhancing grid security with trust management. In: Proceedings of the 2004 IEEE International Conference on Services Computing, SCC'2004. IEEE Computer Society Press, New York, pp. 303–310.

Luna Garcia, J., Langenberg, R., Suri, N., 2012. Benchmarking cloud security level agreements using quantitative policy trees. In: Proceedings of the 2012 ACM Workshop on Cloud Computing Security Workshop. ACM, New York, NY, pp. 103–112.

McKnight, D.H., Chervany, N.L., 1996. The Meanings of Trust, Technical Report. Management Information Systems Research Center, University of Minnesota, USA.

Nagarajan, A., 2010. Techniques for trust enhanced distributed authorisation using trusted platforms. Ph.D. thesis. Macquarie Universtiy.

Nurse, J.R., Agrafiotis, I., Creese, S., Goldsmith, M., Lamberts, K., 2013. Communicating trustworthiness using radar graphs: a detailed look. In: The 11th International Conference on Privacy, Security and Trust (PST). IEEE, New York, pp. 333–339.

Pawar, P., Rajarajan, M., Nair, S., Zisman, A., 2012. Trust model for optimized cloud services. In: Trust Management VI. IFIP Advances in Information and Communication Technology. 374, Springer, Berlin, pp. 97–112.

Ries, S., 2009a. Extending bayesian trust models regarding context-dependence and user friendly representation. In: Proceedings of the ACM SAC. ACM, New York, NY, pp. 1294–1301.

Ries, S., 2009b. Trust in Ubiquitous Computing. Doctoral thesis. Technische Universität Darmstadt.

Ries, S., Habib, S., Mühlhäuser, M., Varadharajan, V., 2011. Certainlogic: a logic for modeling trust and uncertainty. In: Trust and Trustworthy Computing, 6740. Springer, Berlin/Heidelberg, pp. 254–261.

Ries, S., Schreiber, D., 2008. Evaluating user representations for the trustworthiness of interaction partners. In: International Workshop on Recommendation and Collaboration (ReColl '08) in Conjunction with the International Conference on Intelligent User Interfaces (IUI'08). ACM, New York, NY.

Sadeghi, A.R., Stüble, C., 2004. Property-based attestation for computing platforms: caring about properties, not mechanisms. In: Proceedings of the NSPW'04. ACM, New York, NY, pp. 67–77.

Sadeghi, A.R., Stüble, C., Winandy, M., 2008. Property-based TPM virtualization. In: Information Security. Lecture Notes in Computer Science, 5222. Springer, Berlin/Heidelberg, pp. 1–16.

Schiffman, J., Moyer, T., Vijayakumar, H., Jaeger, T., McDaniel, P., 2010. Seeding clouds with trust anchors. In: Proceedings of the ACM CCSW'10. ACM, New York, NY, pp. 43–46.

Schryen, G., Volkamer, M., Ries, S., Habib, S.M., 2011. A formal approach towards measuring trust in distributed systems. In: Proceedings of the 2011 ACM Symposium on Applied Computing. ACM, New York, NY, pp. 1739–1745.

Tsidulko, J., 2014. The 10 biggest cloud outages of 2014 (so far). http://www.crn.com/slide-shows/cloud/300073433/the-10-biggest-cloud-outages-of-2014-so-far.htm (accessed 15.09.14).

Volk, F., Hauke, S., Dieth, D., Mühlhäuser, M., 2014. Communicating and visualising multi-criterial trustworthiness under uncertainty. In: 12th Annual Conference on Privacy, Security and Trust (PST 2014). IEEE, New York, pp. 391–397.

Wang, S.X., Zhang, L., Wang, S., Qiu, X., 2010. A cloud-based trust model for evaluating quality of web services. J. Comput. Sci. Technol. 25, 1130–1142.

Tool-based risk assessment of cloud infrastructures as socio-technical systems

22

Michael Nidd[a], Marieta Georgieva Ivanova[b], Christian W. Probst[b], Axel Tanner[a]

IBM Research, Zürich, Switzerland[a]
Technical University of Denmark, Kongens Lyngby, Denmark[b]

1 INTRODUCTION

Assessing risk in cloud infrastructures is difficult. While a singular node is not so difficult to configure and analyze, a typical cloud infrastructure contains potentially thousands of nodes that are highly interconnected and dynamic. Studies by ENISA (2009) as well as CSA (2010) highlight the risks and threats in such environments.

In this chapter, we present a modeling exercise of a process developed in the TRE$_S$PASS project. The model captures details of cloud infrastructures at several levels—from the overall structure over network communications to services running on a single node—and can represent typical artifacts. Using this model, one can perform security analyzes of the modeled infrastructure to then deliver an assessment of risk.

A typical cloud environment comprises multiple access domains, including systems that share a host, wired network connections, and physical proximity. While simple cloud infrastructures may be limited to one such host and a few virtual systems, a complex infrastructure often incorporates myriad virtual systems running on many different, often widely spread physical servers with a complex mix of real and virtual networking, routing, and control points between them. This dynamic and flexible structure is one of the major success criteria for cloud infrastructures. At the same time the flexible interconnections between virtual and real machines make risk assessment in cloud infrastructures so difficult.

If risk assessment in complex technical infrastructures already is difficult, it is even more complicated when adding human factors and physical infrastructure into the setup, which therefore often are ignored (Probst and Hunker, 2009). The goal of the TRE$_S$PASS project is to develop models and processes that support risk assessment in complex organizations *including* human factors and physical infrastructure.

The goal of this support is to simplify the identification of possible attacks and to provide qualified assessment and ranking of attacks based on factors such as the expected impact.

For cloud infrastructures, the TRE$_S$PASS model distinguishes components at a level of abstraction that corresponds well to security-relevant control points in these domains, enabling the discovery and analysis of potential attacks that exploit their connectivity. Using the model, one can formalize typical components in cloud infrastructures and their interrelationships. These include network components like switches, routers, firewalls; virtual and physical servers; actors, including administrators, users, and attackers; location details that represent rooms, doors, and other physical consideration. Because these component models show how actions on one element influence other elements, they can be combined with the connectivity relations to form an implicit search-space of all possible activity paths in the system. Based on the formal model, the TRE$_S$PASS analyzes then identify interesting action sequences by walking through this search-space and intelligently pruning paths as they are constructed.

The attacks identified on a modeled infrastructure then form the basis for risk assessment, including the overall likelihood of certain actions to occur, the skills, resource, and abilities of attackers, and the structure of the underlying infrastructure.

The rest of this chapter is structured as follows. We start by setting the scene in Section 2 with a more detailed description of the structure of a typical cloud environment as outlined above. After introducing the TRE$_S$PASS project and the TRE$_S$PASS model in Section 3, we demonstrate the development of a formalization of the cloud infrastructure in Section 4, including human factors and physical infrastructure. Using this model, we then outline how to identify attacks in Section 5 and discuss its application to risk assessment in Section 6. Finally, Section 7 concludes the chapter with an outlook on future work.

2 STRUCTURE OF A TYPICAL CLOUD INFRASTRUCTURE SCENARIO

Cloud infrastructures are potentially complex and span many different layers of an organization. The first layer is obviously the technical infrastructure and relevant data, applications, and services; these constitute the actual computing infrastructure. Closely related to the actual machines connected through the technical infrastructure is the physical environment, which represents the second layer; on this layer we consider buildings, rooms, and ways of controlling access to them. Finally, to obtain a complete view of the infrastructure, and especially for performing a complete risk analysis, it is also important to capture and model both social/human and organizational/procedural aspects of running a cloud environment. This results in a third layer, which models risk stemming from elements such as human factors, social engineering, and insider attacks, to name a few.

2.1 LEVELS OF ABSTRACTION

In the *technical infrastructure layer*, a cloud environment consists of the physical compute hardware, which includes servers, storage, and internal and external network connections. This infrastructure enables the virtualization infrastructure, consisting of concepts such as hypervisors, virtual machines, network and storage components together with their configurations and management applications, and the software layers of operating systems, middleware, applications, and services.

The second layer, the *physical environment layer*, consists of the building infrastructure that contains the hardware portion of the first layer, including server rooms and the buildings they are contained in.

On the third layer we then consider the *social and human side*, where we have to capture the different roles of the actors involved in providing the services of the cloud environment, such as system administrators and support staff with their respective access to the computing system (first layer) or the physical environment (second layer). This layer should ideally include profiles of (potential) behavior.

Also on the third layer we consider *organizational/procedural* aspects of the modeled infrastructure. This is an important component of the model because aspects such as typical workflows in the organization often can be exploited in attacks will influence the usefulness of many attack components.

2.2 ATTACKER GOALS

The goals of adversaries are difficult to identify beforehand, and the more complex an environment, the more difficult this goal identification becomes. In an environment as complex and dynamic as a cloud environment, adversaries can have many different goals, such as to steal sensitive data, corrupt business operations, or achieve financial gains. Each of these goals coincides with one or numerous possible paths of attacks within or across the different layers identified above.

In the following, we list some examples for elements of attack paths on the layers:

- On the technical infrastructure layer:
  - Physical attacks (e.g., to steal harddisk, get logical access through placing a device, dump of memory);
  - Access data on compute nodes (e.g., hypervisor, VM dumps), storage (e.g., VM data at rest), network (e.g., migration attacks);
  - Use of software bugs (e.g., hypervisor software exploitation and break-out);
  - Side-channel attacks due to colocation and data-processing in virtual machines;
  - Backdoors in software or virtual machine images; or
  - Changing configuration (e.g., access control settings).
- On the physical environment layer:
  - Get access to a server room;
  - Place wiretap on internal network connections; or
  - Get access to backup or boot media.

- On the social/human and organizational/procedural layer:
  - With social engineering, bribing or through targeted attack (e.g., of system administrators);
  - Convince other users to use a backdoored image (VM image security);
  - Change of procedures; or
  - Changes of compliance legislation on a political or organizational level.

Most often, attacks will involve a combination of these different possibilities. For example, normal operating procedures may be exploited, possibly through social engineering, to get access to stepping stones in terms of physical or technical infrastructure, to finally use technical means to gain illegitimate access. It should also be noted that the goal of attack steps on the second and third layer is usually to facilitate an access on the first layer.

2.3 A CLOUD SCENARIO

As a scenario for demonstration, we focus for simplicity on the goal of gaining access to a confidential document *fileX* in a highly simplified private cloud environment, as shown in Figure 1.

On the physical layer, this scenario is comprised of two rooms, *RoomInternal* and *RoomDatacenter*, and a *Hallway*, where controlled access is possible from the outside to the *Hallway* and from the hallway to *RoomInternal* and from there to

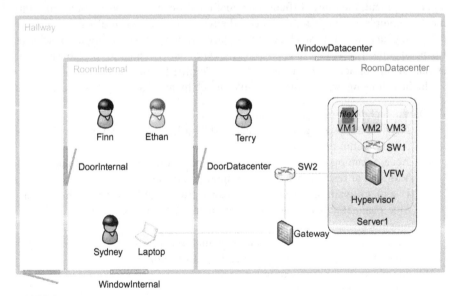

FIGURE 1

Highly simplified scenario of a private cloud environment with various actors.

RoomDatacenter. Both rooms have a window each, *WindowInternal* and *Window-Datacenter*, which are usually closed and locked.

On the technical infrastructure layer, the actual cloud infrastructure is exemplified by a physical server *Server1*, on which three virtual machines *VM1*, *VM2*, *VM3*, a virtual switch *SW1*, and a virtual firewall *VFW* are running on top of a *Hypervisor*. These virtual components are connected to physical network components, namely another switch *SW2* and a *Gateway*. Through this connection it is possible to reach the physical and virtual infrastructure from the *Laptop*.

The confidential document *fileX* is located in the storage of *VM1*. Its rightful owner is *Ethan*, working in the organized crime department. Other actors include *Finn*, a member of the finance department, using *VM2* for their work, *Terry*, a technician of the IT support group, and *Sydney*, a system administrator in IT support. Terry has physical access to the datacenter, whereas Sydney has full logical access to all elements of the cloud infrastructure.

Additional details like power supply, cooling, and so on have been omitted in order to keep the scenario simple, but could be modeled as resources in a real environment, as they may facilitate alternative attack scenarios.

3 THE TRE$_S$PASS PROJECT

Current risk management methods provide descriptive tools for assessing threats by systematic brainstorming. Identifying and consequently preventing attack opportunities in this approach is heavily based on the defenders being able to conceive those opportunities. In a not too volatile world, this reactive approach has proven to work.

However, in today's dynamic attack landscape, this process is often too slow and exceeds the limits of human imaginative capabilities. Emerging security risks demand tool support to predict, prioritize, and prevent complex attacks systematically.

The TRE$_S$PASS project (TRE$_S$PASS, 2012) aims at supporting the identification of attack opportunities by building an "attack navigator." Like a navigator in the real world, an attack navigator works on a map (of an organization) and computes a route (an attack) for reaching a goal (an asset), taking the mode of transportation (the attacker) and the road network (the infrastructure) into account.

Such a navigator would indicate which attack opportunities are possible, which of them are the most threatening, and which countermeasures are most appropriate. To this end, the project combines knowledge from technical sciences, for example, how vulnerable are protocols and software, social sciences, for example, how likely are people to succumb to social engineering, and state-of-the-art industry processes and tools.

One of the goals in TRE$_S$PASS is to develop models that capture the essentials of an organization and its structure, namely the map for the attack navigator. This map represents an organization on three core levels: the physical, digital, and social domains. The model thus contains entities, attributes, and relations that are relevant for analyzing the organization's security. For validating the results from the TRE$_S$PASS project, one of the case studies used is based on a cloud environment similar to the one described in this chapter.

The layers described in Section 2 map to the domains just mentioned. The physical and digital domain represent the technical infrastructure (first layer) and the physical environment (second layer), and the social domain represents the third layer.

The socio-technical security models are at the heart of the technical part of TRE$_S$PASS, and constitute the interface between the organization being modeled and the processes and tools developed in other parts of the project, such as the analysis tools, and the visualization tools. For the integration into risk assessment frameworks, the models developed in TRE$_S$PASS are the entry point into the TRE$_S$PASS process.

Models of organizational infrastructures have been used before, for example, for identifying insider threats and attacks on organizations (Probst and Hansen, 2008; Dimkov et al., 2010; Pieters, 2011). An important aspect of these models is modularity, not only to support modular model development and maintenance, but also to support compositional analysis of the models being developed. The modularity of the TRE$_S$PASS socio-technical security models allows features to be added on demand; features such as detective components, for example, are optional and only added when needed for modeling the organization.

4 MODELING THE SCENARIO FOR ANALYSIS

In this section, we give an introduction to how to model organizational infrastructures in the TRE$_S$PASS model. For space reasons we only cover the example introduced in Section 2 and discuss some of its peculiarities; more general discussions can be found in related work (Dimkov et al., 2010; Probst and Hansen, 2008).

Modeling the scenario from Section 2 and Figure 1 turns all infrastructure locations, independent of their kind, into nodes in a graph. For the physical infrastructure, this results in the graph shown in Figure 2.

As is usual in modeling, the TRE$_S$PASS model offers multiple dimensions along which granularity can be adjusted. For example, dealing with virtual connectivity versus physical connectivity quickly leads to difficult questions with respect to the modeling of intermediate nodes and steps in establishing a connection. If connectivity was to be modeled as end-to-end, then every computer would be a room with a door for every other computer in the system. Apart from the obvious connectivity problem, it would be prohibitively difficult to discover vulnerabilities that involve a compromised intermediate node.

Also, different classes of vulnerabilities require different levels of detail in modeling; if redundant paths between two components are available then all nodes on either path are potential sources of data leaks, but denial-of-service attacks will need to involve some combination.

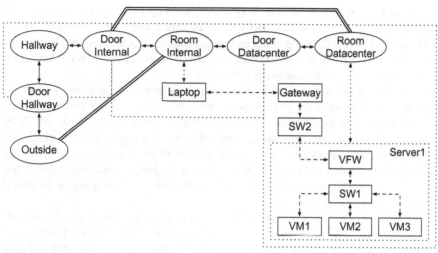

FIGURE 2

The model for the physical infrastructure of the scenario shown in Figure 1. The different kinds of boxes and edges show different kinds of elements and connections; ellipses represent elements in the building infrastructure and boxes represent elements in the (real or virtual) computing infrastructure. The solid and dashed edges represent connectivity between these kinds of nodes, and the dotted edges represent access from the one part to the other. The double lines represent that the windows may permit observation of what is happening on either end of the edge.

The TRE$_S$PASS model unifies the representation of building infrastructure and compute infrastructure. Nodes in the model of a building represent rooms or control points such as card readers; nodes in the model of a computer network represent computers, firewalls, switches; edges in both models represent connectivity; actors in the model of a building represent employees; actors in the model of a network represent programs; nodes can be annotated with policies that limit accessibility based on credentials that an actor provides.

When modeling cloud infrastructures these considerations lead to models that represent Layer 2 connections as "doors"; in this view, connections between computers are abstracted as connections between nodes with communicating processes, with access on each door controlled with checks on the identity and/or actions of the actor. There is an important difference between a person in a building and the way we model network connections: the person is free to make decisions in the rooms, while the connection is not. In the model this means that the person is "just" a node, while the connections are a predetermined process that realizes the functionality in question.

The model of a physical environment might permit an actor to pass a door if the actor is in possession of the necessary credentials, but it would not restrict the actions of that actor once access has been granted.

A firewall, on the other hand, may allow incoming connections from any user over port 80 on a web server, and also from authorized users to port 21 on an FTP server. However, after gaining entrance, a web connection cannot change into an FTP connection to a different server; the actions permitted for an actor depend on how that actor gained access to the room.

Modeling network connectivity requires further modeling artifacts; the routing and automatic forwarding of packets as encountered in network communication can be represented by processes in the TRE$_S$PASS model (Probst et al., 2007). In the most simplistic case in a physical model, processes trigger direct actions; for example, an actor who knows a password and has physical access to the computer can access a file that is known on the computer. In general, and especially when modeling network connectivity, we use a more complex configuration in which actions trigger other processes.

Consider the case of two systems, A and B, connected through a firewall router R. If A sends a message to B then the message passes through R without A being aware of that. When A's message to B is received by R, the processes implemented in R may decide to send a message to B that contains the request from A. By implementing this in processes, the contents of the message sent to B depends completely on the actual message for which R allowed A to have access.

Compare this approach to modeling the firewall by granting A access to R, and then allowing a new process to start from location R. Such a model would find false positives (i.e., attacks that are consistent with the model, but not actually possible) in which a stream arrives at the router as "https" but continues as "ssh." Attacks where traffic is admitted with one destination address but then continues with a different destination would also be possible within the constraints of such a model, although these would not normally be practical on an actual router.

While the automated processes avoid false positives in which a network device becomes a staging point for a two-phase attack, they do still permit the detection of attacks in which a device is controlled by the remote attacker. In the cloud model, R might allow any "ssh" traffic destined for B. If the user U at A knows an ssh password for B, then the processes would respond with success, adding an attribute to A that from this location user U can control B via "ssh." If another server, C, allowed anonymous HTTP connections from internal servers only (i.e., any user with control access to B can retrieve some file from C) then an attack would exist in which a user with physical access to A could get the credentials and could access the content on C although A would not have been able to connect with C directly.

In the TRE$_S$PASS model, state information can be retained for actors and locations. In the example above, access permission for U from location A to location C is stored at A. Alternatively (or additionally) it could have been stored at U that access is available to C from A. By convention, we store location-bound information in the location, even if it is also bound to an actor.

On a technical level, the TRE$_S$PASS model stores state information and access policies in tuple spaces (Probst and Hansen, 2008), which are part of the underlying process calculus Klaim (de Nicola et al., 1998), as are the process components mentioned above.

4.1 HIGH-LEVEL MODEL

When modeling the cloud scenario as shown in Figure 1, we need to represent the different entities from the layers introduced above.

4.1.1 Infrastructure

As discussed above, infrastructure is essential to both the model and identifying attack vectors; it represents both physical locations and network locations; the actual hardware enabling data connections can reasonably be modeled in the same way as a host, that is, as a location, but with fewer actor-initiated processes. The virtual equivalents to physical routers, switches, firewalls, and so on are also modeled as locations that are co-located with a host.

A server (virtual or otherwise) is therefore modeled as a location object. In the case of a virtual machine, it is co-located with a host that is also a location. In the example in Figure 2, *Server1* is an example for a host that serves three virtual machines.

In practice, many infrastructure devices are extremely sophisticated and flexible. An actor with access to the console and with knowledge of the administrative password could easily use such a device as an entry-point to an attack.

4.1.2 Actors

Actors represent attackers, defenders, victims, collaborators, and any other human factor relevant to the scenario modeled. The concept of actor in the TRE$_S$PASS model is however quite general, in that it also represents processes such as an ssh service as an actor; this is natural since processes perform actions in the model and can roam the model.

4.2 MIDDLE-LEVEL MODEL

In the high-level model many internal details are hidden from the modeler. For example, the handling of network packets is implicit; a process at a location only sends a packet with a destination address, and as in real life does need to consider the connection with that destination. The middle-level model realizes the sending and actual routing of packets.

The benefit of hiding this from the high-level model is two-fold. On the one hand, the actor does not have the possibility to access and change packets, so on this level a man-in-the-middle attack that changes packet contents cannot be crafted. On the other hand, this attack is of course still possible and can be identified in this middle-level model.

It is important to notice that many of the functionalities modeled in the middle-level model can be extracted from the actual network and cloud infrastructure, or from access-control configurations in the infrastructure.

4.2.1 Routing

The routing processes model and reproduce IP forwarding by automatically generating the outgoing action when the incoming action is accepted. These processes are instantiated based on network masks, and cannot be changed by actors in the network.

For modeling network connection in a general model, IP is an appropriate choice not only because it is a good solution for carrying out hierarchical routing, but also because it is the protocol actually in use in cloud infrastructures and networking in general.

4.2.2 Network traffic set-up

By implementing network access as a chain of processes, and by using pessimistic routing of the traffic (c.f. Section 4.4.3), any side effects of network access will be detectible as a side effect of incorporating it in an attack path.

If in the example shown in Figure 1 a goal of the system is that the user at *Laptop* should have access to *VM1*, then the attack generator, trying to invalidate this goal, will be able to identify processes that disable intermediate nodes (such as the firewall *VFW*) as an attack. Similarly, if another goal is that this access must be private, then other systems to which the network traffic of that access may be visible will be able to use it to trigger interception processes that would qualify as an attack.

4.2.3 Flow-based access control

Routing connections through intermediate nodes allows flow-based access control, such as may be provided by firewalls, to be implemented with rules that correspond to the actual configuration of the corresponding physical devices. The data in and out of a model component that represents a firewall can be altered, redirected, or dropped without explicitly incorporating these possibilities in how the endpoints are modeled.

As mentioned above, the initial configuration of flow-based access control will usually be extracted from the actual devices in the network or cloud infrastructure.

4.3 LOW-LEVEL MODEL

Finally, at the lowest layer we need to model the actual services running on nodes in the network. This can for example be used to link services to vulnerability databases.

As outlined at the beginning of this section, and detailed below in Section 4.4, network traffic is modeled by triggering processes on the various nodes along a route. The service at the destination is again represented as a process that triggers some computation and the return message.

For example, an SSH connection request from the *Laptop* to *VM1* in Figure 1 will trigger a series of repetitions along the chain of intermediate nodes between the source and the destination. If permitted by the intermediate nodes, eventually this will trigger a process at the destination node *VM1* that triggers a connection acceptance message. That result is then returned to *Laptop* by a series of triggered processes back to the initiator. The process that will be waiting to be triggered at the initiator upon receipt of the acceptance message will register the connection.

4.4 MODELING TYPICAL NETWORK COMPONENTS

Using the different modeling levels just introduced, we will now show how typical components found in networks can be represented.

4.4.1 Routers and routing

Data routing follows the same general method as IP routing, matching destination networks and replicating traffic to the next hop. Where more than one path would be possible, traffic will be sent over all available (acyclic) paths. Although the routing uses IP addresses, it is implemented on a Layer 2 network topology. This will ignore potential data leaks via ARP broadcasts, but is generally a sound model for how the packet will travel.

For example, assume *VM1* and *VM2* in Figure 1 to have IP addresses `192.167.1.1` and `192.167.1.2`, respectively. Both nodes are part of network `192.167.1.0/24`, and are connected by switch *SW1* with a default gateway on *VFW*. The resulting basic model is part of Figure 2 and the textual representation of the involved processes and policies is shown in Listing 22.1.

Each node is annotated with its kind and its domain, and has a policy and processes. The policies specify which other nodes are allowed to communicate with this node, and which form of messages are allowed to be sent; policies basically realize the network infrastructure and the kind of protocol supported. For example, *SW1* accepts packages from *VM1*, *VM2*, or *VFW* in the form of IP packages. Policies thus specify the trigger points introduced above, through which communication can happen.

The processes specify how the node reacts to triggers, basically by describing how to react to different kinds of messages received. This is similar to pattern matching. For example, the node *SW1* defines three processes that are all triggered by receiving an *IP* message. For the sake of simplicity we assume that all packets have the form of 7 tuples consisting of the tag "IP," the source address and source port, the destination address and destination port, the request, and a user name. Depending on the scenario in question this can be adjusted. Each routing process consists of inputting a tuple based on a pattern, and routing the tuple to the correct next hop. Processes use the exclamation mark for binding variables to values and the $\sim$ operator for matching addresses. Processes are ordered by mask size, so the first match is the route taken. Empty tuple elements are wildcards, so (`"TAG"`, `192.167.1.1`, `"Content1"`, `"Content2"`) would match (`"TAG"`, `!addr~192.167.0.0/16`,,) while binding the variable `addr` to the address `192.167.1.1`.

```
1  locations
2    VM1 kind = host domain = network
3      policies = { [SW1] : {out("IP",,,,,,) } };
4      processes = {
5        in("IP", !dstAddr, !dstPort, !srcAddr, !srcPort, !req, !usr)
6          .out("IP", dstAddr, dstPort, srcAddr, srcPort, req, usr)@SW1
7      };
8    VM2 kind = host domain = network
9      policies = { [SW1] : {out("IP",,,,,,) } };
10     processes = {
11       in("IP", !dstAddr, !dstPort, !srcAddr, !srcPort, !req, !usr)
12         .out("IP", dstAddr, dstPort, srcAddr, srcPort, req, usr)@SW1
13     };
14   SW1 kind = host domain = network
15     policies = { [VM1 | VM2 | VFW] : {out("IP",,,,,) } };
16     processes = {
17       in("IP", !srcAddr, !srcPort, 192.167.1.1, !dstPort, !req, !usr)
18         .out("IP", srcAddr, srcPort, 192.167.1.1, dstPort, req, usr)@VM1
19       in("IP", !srcAddr, !srcPort, 192.167.1.2, !dstPort, !req, !usr)
20         .out("IP", srcAddr, srcPort, 192.167.1.2, dstPort, req, usr)@VM2
21       in("IP", !srcAddr, !srcPort, !dstAddr~0.0.0.0/0, !dstPort, !req, !usr)
22         .out("IP", srcAddr, srcPort, dstAddr, dstPort, req, usr)@VFW
23     };
24 edges
25     VM1 -> SW1;
26     VM2 -> SW1;
27     SW1 -> VM1, VM2, VFW;
28     VFW -> SW1;
```

LISTING 22.1

Example model for a part of the scenario from Figure 1 with the two virtual machines *VM1* and *VM2*, the switch *SW1* and the firewall *VFW*. The policies at the nodes specify, which nodes are allowed to send data, and which format the data is required to have. The processes describe how the data is handled.

For the specification in Listing 22.1 the switch *SW1* sends packets for *VM1* and *VM2* directly to them, and packets for any other address to *VFW*.

4.4.2 Defining a service

Once we can route packets to the correct location, we need to be able to consume (or refuse) the operation. As mentioned before, the constant "IP" in the first parameter of the routing processes is used to differentiate the events in transit from services. When a packet reaches its end destination and if that particular location has a service listening on the destination port, then the packet is consumed. Whether the service is available to a specific user can then be determined with a policy for that service. In this way, the access control for the network is separated from the access control for services.

For example, if *VM1* is running an FTP daemon on port 20, then we can define a receiver as shown in Listing 22.2. These processes describe terminating the request to port 20 by passing it to an FTP process, retrieving the file, and giving it to the requesting user. Access to that service can then be controlled with the policy for in("FTP",,,,).

```
1  in("IP", !srcAddr, !srcPort, 192.167.1.1, 20, !request, !user)
2    .out("FTP", srcAddr, srcPort, 192.167.1.1, 20, request, user)
3  in("FTP", !srcAddr, !srcPort, 192.167.1.1, 20, !filename, !user)
4    .read("FileSystem", filename, !content)
5    .out("IP", 192.167.1.1, 20, srcAddr, srcPort, content, "REPLY")
```

LISTING 22.2

Modeling of FTP daemon on port 20.

The user is changed to the constant value `"REPLY"` for the return traffic. This allows firewall rules to emulate normal firewall behavior, allowing return traffic for existing connections.

In this case, if anonymous FTP is available on *VM1* for the asset *fileX*, the policy on *VM1* would look like this

```
{ [ VM1 ] : { out("FTP", , , , , "fileX", ) } }
```

If the asset *fileX* was protected by a password *secret*, then this could be modeled as:

```
{ [ VM1, has(USER, "secret") ] : { out("FTP", , , , ,"fileY", USER) } }
```

where USER is a free variable that is bound when evaluating policies and secret is the password of the file being protected.

4.4.2.1 Generic Service Access

Adding a generic IP process to each host allows IP traffic that reaches the host to be identified even if it does not reach any specific service. For example, host 192.167.1.1 might have policies as shown in Listing 22.3.

This additional process does not need any additional policies, as it matches the normal IP tuples. It returns a constant value `"CONNECT"`, which can be used to model basic connectivity.

4.4.2.2 Administrator Access

Differentiation of access rights based on knowledge of passwords can be modeled through policies, granting the actor the ability to directly access data stored on the machine. Note that this does not interfere with the defined services, but covers direct physical access or from a login shell; therefore the policy for this access does not use the `"IP"` tuples. A policy line with the following form is added to all servers:

```
1  //
2  // ftp service process definition here
3  //
4  in("IP", 192.167.1.1, !dstPort, !srcAddr, !srcPort, !request, !user)
5    .out("IP", srcAddr, srcPort, 192.167.1.1, dstPort, "CONNECT", "REPLY"),
```

LISTING 22.3

Generic service process for a host 192.167.1.1.

```
policies = { [has(ACTOR, "admin_password")] : {read}}
```

where `ACTOR` is a free variable that is bound when evaluating the policy and `admin_password` represents the actual administrator's password. This allows requests for any non-destructive read from the server location itself that are initiated by an actor who knows `admin_password`.

4.4.3 Switch versus hub

Technically, a switch does normally behave as described in Section 4.4.1. Once it sees IP traffic to a particular address being accepted by a directly-connected device, further traffic to that address is sent to that device only. In practice, however, it is possible for devices to alter their own IP address to conflict with another device on the same subnet, and generally to interfere with the normal flow of data.

Although hubs, which repeat all incoming traffic to all other interfaces, are not used much in the 21st century, modeling their behavior allows for a more conservative security assessment. This is achieved by changing processes implementing the switch shown above to the ones shown in Listing 22.4.

Another approximation of reality is that switches (and hubs) are not specifically aware of their subnet mask so, by the argument above, they should echo all packets to all neighbors. In our actual modeling, they echo to all neighbors for local traffic only. This is meant to reflect the relative difficulty of intercepting traffic from a server to a router, or between two routers.

If we classify an attack that is able to intercept traffic to a router as a compromise of the router, then attacks on this traffic are staged attacks that first require the router to be compromised, and then intercept the traffic to that router.

4.4.4 Firewalls

Firewalls play an integral role in network security. Normal best-practices deployment of firewalls separates not only inside from outside, but also separates sections of an internal network. This deployment philosophy is very similar to the use of their original namesake in building design, limiting the scope of damage likely to result from a single incident.

```
1  processes = {
2    in("IP", !srcAddr, !srcPort, !dstAddr~192.167.1.0/24, !dstPort, !req, !usr)
3    . out("IP", srcAddr, srcPort, dstAddr, dstPort, req, usr)@VM1
4    | out("IP", srcAddr, srcPort, dstAddr, dstPort, req, usr)@VM2
5    | out("IP", srcAddr, srcPort, dstAddr, dstPort, req, usr)@VFW,
6    in("IP", !srcAddr, !srcPort, !dstAddr~0.0.0.0/0, !dstPort, !req, !usr)
7    . out("IP", srcAddr, srcPort, dstAddr, dstPort, req, usr)@VFW
8  };
```

LISTING 22.4

Modeling of a hub. Compare this with the switch processes introduced in Listing 22.1.

In modern network appliances, a firewall is just one aspect of a "Unified Threat Management" appliance that offers various services, including NAT, load balancing, and routing. The functionality of the actual firewall goes beyond simple allow/deny rules based on protocol, address, and port; deep-packet inspection, protocol validation, external black-lists, and HTTP header filtering are all useful and common firewall services. While these other services have implications on network security, the present analysis focuses on the traditional allow/deny for a given protocol on a given source and destination address and port. Adding more extensive checking can be modeled by processes in a way similar to routing described above.

As mentioned above, routing is implemented on a worst-case assumption that any acyclic path might be used. This can be determined from the network topology without internal configuration details of the routers. The firewall behavior cannot be guessed in this way, since its behavior even in the simplest case goes beyond routes. The analysis therefore requires a read-only interface to the extract the configuration from whatever firewall model is in use. In the current tools, we are supporting Cisco ASA firewalls, both physical and virtual.

After parsing, the firewall model is an extension of a basic router. For example, Listing 22.5 shows a Layer-3 switch. In this example, all traffic received for either of the attached networks will be repeated to the destination network. If this appliance were acting as a firewall that allows no incoming connections to 10.0.1.0/24, this could be built as in Listing 22.6. Notice that returning traffic, which will have the user set to the constant "REPLY" is still routed, but new connections will be ignored.

One approach to modeling firewall behavior would be to build what amounts to a custom routing table for every permitted flow. In a normal firewall with one interface on each connected network, this would build a correct model, but tying the routing to the flow rules will make it difficult for a human to read, especially if some subnets are connected to more than one interface.

In order to separate routing from flow rules, we have introduced a layer of indirection in the firewall processes relating to IP traffic, as shown in Listing 22.7.

```
1  fwExample kind = host domain = network
2     policies = {
3        { [ Sys1, Sys2, Sys3, Sys4 ] : { out("IP",,,,,,) } },
4        { [ has(ACTOR, AdminAccess_fwExample) ] : { read(,,) } }
5     }
6     processes = {
7        in("IP", !dstAddr~10.0.0.0/24, !dstPort, !srcAddr, !srcPort, ↩
                !request, !user)
8        . out("IP", dstAddr, dstPort, srcAddr, srcPort, request, user)@Sys1
9        | out("IP", dstAddr, dstPort, srcAddr, srcPort, request, user)@Sys2,
10       in("IP", !dstAddr~10.0.1.0/24, !dstPort, !srcAddr, !srcPort, ↩
                !request, !user)
11       . out("IP", dstAddr, dstPort, srcAddr, srcPort, request, user)@Sys3
12       | out("IP", dstAddr, dstPort, srcAddr, srcPort, request, user)@Sys4
13    };
```

LISTING 22.5

Layer-3 switch on 10.0.0.0/24 (Sys1 and Sys2) and 10.0.1.0/24 (Sys3 and Sys4).

```
1   fwExample kind = host domain = network
2       policies = {
3           { [ Sys1, Sys2, Sys3, Sys4 ] : { out("IP",,,,,,) } },
4           { [ has(ACTOR, AdminAccess_fwExample) ] : { read(,,) } }
5       }
6       processes = {
7           in("IP", !dstAddr~10.0.0.0/24, !dstPort, !srcAddr, !srcPort, ↩
                !request, !user)
8           . out("IP", dstAddr, dstPort, srcAddr, srcPort, request, user)@Sys1
9           | out("IP", dstAddr, dstPort, srcAddr, srcPort, request, user)@Sys2,
10          in("IP", !dstAddr~10.0.1.0/24, !dstPort, !srcAddr, !srcPort, ↩
                !request, "REPLY")
11          . out("IP", dstAddr, dstPort, srcAddr, srcPort, request, "REPLY")@Sys3
12          | out("IP", dstAddr, dstPort, srcAddr, srcPort, request, "REPLY")@Sys4
13      };
```

LISTING 22.6

The switch from Listing 22.5 blocking incoming connections to 10.0.1.0/24. Differences to Listing 22.5 have been highlighted by underlining.

```
1   fwExample kind = host domain = network
2       policies = {
3           { [ Sys1, Sys2, Sys3, Sys4 ] : { out("IP",,,,,,) } },
4           { [ has(ACTOR, AdminAccess_fwExample) ] : { read(,,) } }
5       }
6       processes = {
7           in("IP", !dstAddr, !dstPort, !srcAddr, !srcPort, !request, "REPLY")
8           .out("APPROVED", dstAddr, dstPort, srcAddr, srcPort, request, "REPLY"),
9           in("IP", !dstAddr, !dstPort, !srcAddr 10.0.0.0/24, !srcPort, !request, !user)
10          .out("APPROVED", dstAddr, dstPort, srcAddr, srcPort, request, user),
11          in("APPROVED", !dstAddr~10.0.0.0/24, !dstPort, !srcAddr, !srcPort, ↩
                !request, !user)
12          . out("IP", dstAddr, dstPort, srcAddr, srcPort, request, user)@Sys1
13          | out("IP", dstAddr, dstPort, srcAddr, srcPort, request, user)@Sys2,
14          in("APPROVED", !dstAddr~10.0.1.0/24, !dstPort, !srcAddr, !srcPort, ↩
                !request, !user)
15          . out("IP", dstAddr, dstPort, srcAddr, srcPort, request, user)@Sys3
16          | out("IP", dstAddr, dstPort, srcAddr, srcPort, request, user)@Sys4
17      };
```

LISTING 22.7

Two-phase flow approval and routing to forward all reply traffic, and any traffic originating from 10.0.1.0/24. Differences to Listing 22.5 have been highlighted by underlining.

4.4.5 VPNs

Not every switch is a router, and not all traffic arriving at a Layer-3 switch is routed. If half of the ports on a particular Layer-3 switch are assigned to VLAN 10, and the other half to VLAN 20, then that switch represents two broadcast domains. If it also defines an interface in each of these domains, then it may route traffic between them, but it does not need to.

VLANs are assigned to ports, which correspond in this model to the identity of the device being communicated with. This is difficult to model because the identity of the partner is referenced in the policies section, but not where routing is implemented in the processes section. At least two solutions are available: anti-spoofing and greater partitioning.

Anti-spoofing can be implemented by including a source address mask in the policy for each partner system in a particular VLAN. Messages can be accepted if and only if their source address is from an address known to be local to (or reachable from) that VLAN. If this is in place, then the source addresses can be used to filter traffic in the policy, preventing communication to leak between VLANs.

The problem with the anti-spoofing solution is that it may not be how the actual device is implemented. If the device itself does not have an anti-spoofing service, then including it in the model of that device may be trading potential false positives for potential false negatives. For example, the example in Listing 22.7 would allow a device in 10.0.0.0/24 to spoof a source address in 10.0.1.0/24 to successfully send a packet to 10.0.1.0/24. It would not receive the reply, but some attacks do not need to receive a reply.

An alternative to including anti-spoofing in the policies would be to implement each VLAN on a switch as a separate device. Logically, this is close to an accurate representation of the topology, but it may make it difficult to place firewall rules, and will certainly make it difficult to model trunking.

The best solution for modeling any particular topology will depend on how the switch is being used in that installation.

4.5 MODELING ACTORS

Like locations, actors have knowledge stored in tuple spaces and defined processes that may be triggered when operations are performed on those tuplespaces. Actions will most often be associated with the transfer of knowledge or physical objects, but the tuplespace itself will also hold information about the actor.

4.5.1 Actor processes

One of the most basic actions for an actor would be to transfer knowledge to another actor. This action needs an initiator, and there is no strong argument for which party (the giver or the receiver) that should be, so let us arbitrarily decide that the action is initiated by the receiver making a request. In Listing 22.8, Sydney is capable of telling his password to others.

The "initialize" block in Listing 22.8 initializes the contents of the tuplespaces of Sydney and Terry (discussed more below in Section 4.5.2). The assets block also implicitly populates the initial tuplespace of Sydney with a tuple of the form (`"knows"`, `SydneyPassword`, `"SydneyPasswordValue"`).

4.5.2 Non-process attributes

In the example of Listing 22.8, the tuplespaces of actors Sydney and Terry hold the information that these two actors are mutual friends. This information does not directly affect any processes, but can be used during the attack generation to annotate attack scenarios. In this case, it may be that the action of transferring a knowledge asset from one actor to another is more likely if those two actors are friends.

```
1  actors
2     Sydney
3        policies = {
4           { [ ANY ] : { out("Request",) } },
5        };
6        processes = {
7           in("Request", !object)
8           . read("knows", object, !value).
9           . out("knows", object, value)@ACTOR
10       };
11       initialize = {
12          ("friends", Terry)
13       };
14    Terry
15       initialize = {
16          ("friends", Sydney)
17       };
18 assets
19    SydneyPassword kind = know at = Sydney;
```

LISTING 22.8

If Sydney knows a password, he is able to tell it to other actors.

4.6 PROCESS LIBRARY

The possibility of transferring a knowledge asset from one actor to another (people telling other people things that they know) is generally present. It may be more difficult for some assets (knowledge of a floor plan is harder to communicate than knowledge of a password), and more likely for some actors (depending on security training level, relationship status, etc.), but the basic operation is generally possible. Technically, repeating the definition for every actor is a possible solution, but it would clutter the model and greatly reduce the model's readability and auditability.

To circumvent this, a process library of standard processes and policies is therefore used to capture common standard behavior. This standard behavior is applied wherever relevant.

5 IDENTIFYING ATTACKS

The goal of formalizing the model of an organization and its IT infrastructure as shown above is to guide attack generation and, based on those attacks and their impact, risk assessment (c.f. Section 6). From the viewpoint of this chapter, attack identification is a black box; we briefly discuss its working for completeness (for alternative approaches, see e.g., Sommestad et al., 2013 or Kriaa et al., 2012).

Based on the model of the organization, we use "policy invalidation" (Kammüller and Probst, 2013) to identify paths by which a system-wide policy can be broken in the modeled organization. An important property of the attacks we want to find is that they span the social, physical, and virtual domain; an attacker can use actions in all three domains to reach their goal, and the attack generation should be able to identify and generate these steps.

Policies have surfaced several times before; in our model they are either associated with the overall system or with individual nodes. Policies at a node in the graph represent access control points; they are also used to trigger processes as described in the previous section.

The policy to invalidate can be specified as part of the model, or we can try to invalidate *all* policies in the model. The former approach results in a relatively targeted set of attacks, while the latter, though exhaustive, may contain many attacks that are not of interest. In parallel with the invalidation, one can also generate attack trees (Schneier, 1999) for the identified attacks.

In the example from Figure 1, the attack considered is that an adversary is able to access the confidential file *fileX*. A typical organizational policy could be that confidential files are not allowed to leave the organization's perimeter, here identified by the organization's building infrastructure. In the model of the scenario shown in Figure 2, the area outside of the organization's perimeter is represented by the node *Outside*. The goal policy would then be translated to

```
goal = not fileX@Outside
```

Goal policies can be more complex; they can contain first order logical formulae with predicates, but for space reasons we limit ourselves to this rather simple example. Therefore the goal function above abstracts from reality; it can be seen as a representative for policies such as that non-employees are not allowed to know the file contents. This would require a more detailed model containing employees and non-employees, as well as the actual content of the file. The latter would also support modeling encrypted files.

On a high level, the attack generation performs four major steps:

- First, identify a policy to invalidate; this results in actors who might perform the attack, along with a series of pairs that identify actions to perform and locations at which to do so;
- Next, identify the required assets to perform this action; and
- Generate attacks for obtaining these assets.
- Finally, the attacker moves to the location identified for the first step and performs the action.

This attack generation starts from a goal policy and works iteratively until the prohibited action can be performed. For the organizational policy in the example scenario described above, the attack generation identifies a number of possible attacks:

- The rightful owner Ethan takes the file outside.
- The system administrator Sydney uses his access rights to make a copy of the file.
- The technician Terry removes the server from the server room.[1]
- The financial accountant Finn accesses the file from *VM2*.
- Sydney or Terry place a wire tap on the network to observe the traffic.

---

[1] In practice he could remove the hard disk, which is not part of the current model.

- Ethan, Sydney, or Terry are social engineered to perform any of the above actions.
- Terry is being social engineered to let an adversary into the server room. This requires that somebody let the adversary into the building and into the internal room.
- An adversary observes Sydney's password being typed into the laptop and uses it to get access.
- An adversary breaks a combination of the doors and the windows to get physical access to the server room.

The attack generation will result in an attack tree representing all these attacks as options in the tree. In the TRE$_S$PASS project we are currently developing techniques for generating attacks for socio-technical systems. For technical systems similar approaches exist (Vigo et al., 2014).

6 RISK ASSESSMENT

The previous sections have introduced a model for cloud infrastructures as socio-technical systems and a process for identifying attacks in those systems. The attacks identified on the model together with the model form the basis for risk assessment of the system. Being based on both the model and the attacks, the risk assessment can take a number of factors into account. These factors can originate from either the model or the attacks, or from a combination of both (Probst and Hunker, 2009; Probst and Hansen, 2013).

All the approaches to risk assessment presented here benefit from the automatic extraction of the cloud infrastructure part of the model, which makes dynamic updates of the risk assessment straight forward and easy to automate. This automatic extraction and auditing of infrastructure information from cloud infrastructures will become increasingly important in risk assessment (Bleikertz et al., 2010; Probst et al., 2012).

Besides the model and the attacks, the risk assessment is based on additional information similar to traditional risk assessment approaches; for example, it requires a valuation of assets and an estimate of the likelihood that certain events occur. The valuation is used in computing the potential impact of an identified attack. The estimated likelihood can be used for sanity checking of results of the risk assessment and the attack generation. If the predicted numbers differ significantly from the observed numbers this difference should trigger an examination.

6.1 MODEL-BASED RISK ASSESSMENT

When taking only the model into account, risk assessment can be based on the reachability of assets that should be protected or that occur in organizational policies such as the one presented in the previous section. On this level, the risk assessment is mostly based on paths through the system graph as shown in Figure 2 for the example scenario.

Being graph based, identifying paths and computing metrics on them is straightforward (Probst and Hansen, 2013). Basing the risk assessment exclusively on the model will result in imprecise results at best; nevertheless the results will support a very quick identification of problematic or areas at risk in an organization to pinpoint further, more detailed investigations.

6.2 ATTACK-BASED RISK ASSESSMENT

Risk assessment can also be based exclusively on the identified attacks. Similarly like the model-based risk assessment the results will only be indicative; they do not relate an attack and its impact to infrastructure, actors, and assets, nor to policies.

Attack-based risk assessments computes likelihood and impact for the identified attacks, taking the valuations of assets and the estimated likelihoods for events into account. Other properties of attacks that can be of interest include minimum and maximum time to perform an attack, required resources or skill level, or likelihood of detection. The result of this assessment is a list of attacks ranked on any of the computed properties of the attack.

The attack-based risk assessment supports identification of endangered assets and policies that are likely to be violated; it also provides additional metrics as described above. Since the attack tree will be based on actors in the model, their actions, and locations in the model, the attacks can also be combined with the model; this approach results in the third kind of risk assessment.

6.3 COMBINED RISK ASSESSMENT

The attacks described in Section 5 consist of sub-attacks by actors that obtain necessary assets such as keys to perform actions, and of these actions being performed. Consequently there is a direct relation between the model, providing the actors, locations, and assets, and the generated attacks plus their computed properties as described above.

The combined approach to risk assessment utilizes the model-based evaluations (Probst and Hansen, 2013) and extends them with the computed attack properties. This approach provides a more detailed insight into the contribution of parts of the model to different attacks, and thus supports a better understanding of the risk that areas of the modeled organization either are exposed to or pose by contributing to attacks.

Mapping the attack properties to the model often results in common areas of a model to have a very high risk of contributing to attacks; in the model shown in Figure 2, the hallway will contribute to all attacks that require physical access. This kind of result will often represent unwanted artifacts that can be ignored.

On the other hand, most attacks identified in Section 5 involve network-based access through at least the switch *SW1* or also other nodes in the network infrastructure. This will result in *SW1* getting a high contribution to potential attacks; this node or the traffic through it might be subjected to additional logging. The only attacks not involving the network infrastructure are the ones where the hardware storing the file is physically removed.

7 CONCLUSION

Assessing risk in cloud infrastructures is difficult. Cloud infrastructures can be very big, are highly interconnected, and very dynamic. They contain network infrastructure nodes and computing nodes, and they also are integrated in some way into organizations; this integration can be directly, that is, the cloud being operated by the organization and being accessed through the local network, or indirectly, that is, the cloud being operated by a cloud provider and being accessed remotely. In either of these scenarios human actors become an essential part of the whole system.

In this chapter, we have presented a modeling exercise for socio-technical systems, introducing a process developed in the TRE$_S$PASS project. The model for the cloud infrastructure captures details at several levels and can represent typical artifacts. Using this model, we have discussed how to identify potential attacks and how to integrate them into risk assessment.

One attack possibility that is not covered in our approach yet are attacks on policies or processes, where an actor with administrator rights maliciously or by accident changes parts of the system to give access to adversaries. We are currently working on extending our system with such meta-rules.

If risk assessment in complex technical infrastructures already is difficult, it is even more complicated when adding human factors and physical infrastructure into the setup, which therefore often are ignored (Probst and Hunker, 2009). Using automated extraction of network infrastructure configurations, our approach not only supports on-the-fly risk assessment of cloud infrastructures; it also supports analyzing the combined soco-technical system consisting of the organization, its employees, and assets, including for example staff at a remote cloud operator.

ACKNOWLEDGMENTS

Part of the research leading to these results has received funding from the European Union Seventh Framework Programme (FP7/2007-2013) under grant agreement no. 318003 (TRE$_S$-PASS). This publication reflects only the authors' views and the Union is not liable for any use that may be made of the information contained herein.

REFERENCES

Bleikertz, S., Schunter, M., Probst, C.W., Pendarakis, D., Eriksson, K., 2010. Security audits of multi-tier virtual infrastructures in public infrastructure clouds. In: Perrig, A., Sion, R. (Eds.), Proceedings of the 2010 ACM Workshop on Cloud Computing Security Workshop (CCSW 2010). ACM, New York, pp. 93–102.

Cloud Security Alliance, 2010. Top threats to cloud computing v1.0, https://cloudsecurityalliance.org/topthreats/csathreats.v1.0.pdf.

de Nicola, R., Ferrari, G.L., Pugliese, R., 1998. Klaim: a kernel language for agents interaction and mobility. IEEE Trans. Softw. Eng. 24 (5), 315–330. http://dx.doi.org/10.1109/32.685256.

Dimkov, T., Pieters, W., Hartel, P.H., 2010. Portunes: representing attack scenarios spanning through the physical, digital and social domain. In: Proceedings of the Joint Workshop on Automated Reasoning for Security Protocol Analysis and Issues in the Theory of Security (ARSPA-WITS'10). In: Lecture Notes in Computer Science, vol. 6186. Springer-Verlag, Berlin, pp. 112–129.

ENISA, 2009. Cloud Computing Risk Assessment, Tech. rep., ENISA.

Kammüller, F., Probst, C.W., 2013. Invalidating policies using structural information. In: 2nd International IEEE Workshop on Research on Insider Threats (WRIT'13). IEEE, Washington, DC, USA.

Kriaa, S., Bouissou, M., Pietre-Cambacedes, L., 2012. Modeling the Stuxnet attack with BDMP: towards more formal risk assessments. In: 2012 7th International Conference on Risks and Security of Internet and Systems (CRiSIS), pp. 1–8. http://dx.doi.org/10.1109/CRISIS.2012.6378942. URL, http://ieeexplore.ieee.org/lpdocs/epic03/wrapper.htm?arnumber=6378942.

Pieters, W., 2011. Representing humans in system security models: an actor-network approach. J. Wireless Mobile Netw. Ubiquitous Comput. Dependable Appl. 2 (1), 75–92.

Probst, C.W., Hansen, R.R., 2013. Reachability-based impact as a measure for insiderness. J. Wireless Mobile Netw. Ubiquitous Comput. Dependable Appl. 4 (4), 38–48.

Probst, C.W., Hansen, R.R., 2008. An extensible analysable system model. Inform. Secur. Tech. Rep. 13 (4), 235–246. http://dx.doi.org/10.1016/j.istr.2008.10.012.

Probst, C.W., Hansen, R.R., Nielson, F., 2007. Where can an insider attack? In: Proceedings of the 4th International Conference on Formal Aspects in Security and Trust, FAST'06. Springer-Verlag, Berlin/Heidelberg, pp. 127–142. URL, http://dl.acm.org/citation.cfm?id=1777688.1777697.

Probst, C.W., Hunker, J., 2009. The risk of risk analysis—and its relation to the economics of insider threats. In: Proceedings of the 8th Annual Workshop on the Economics of Information Security (WEIS 2009).

Probst, C.W., Sasse, M.A., Pieters, W., Dimkov, T., Luysterborg, E., Arnaud, M., 2012. Privacy penetration testing: how to establish trust in your cloud provider. In: Gutwirth, S., Leenes, R., De Hert, P., Poullet, Y. (Eds.), In: European Data Protection, Springer, Berlin/Heidelberg, pp. 251–265.

Schneier, B., 1999. Attack trees: modeling security threats. Dr. Dobb's J. Softw. Tools 24 (12), 21–29. URL, http://www.ddj.com/security/184414879.

Sommestad, T., Ekstedt, M., Holm, H., 2013. The Cyber Security Modeling Language: A Tool for Assessing the Vulnerability of Enterprise System Architectures. Systems Journal, IEEE 7 (3):363–373. ISSN: 1932-8184. http://dx.doi.org/10.1109/JSYST.2012.2221853.

TREsPASS, 2012. TREsPASS project, http://www.http://trespass-project.eu/ (accessed 18.09.14) [Online].

Vigo, R., Nielson, F., Nielson, H.R., 2014. Automated generation of attack trees. In: IEEE 27th Computer Security Foundations Symposium, CSF 2014, Vienna, Austria, 19-22 July, 2014, pp. 337–350.

Index

Note: Page numbers followed by *b* indicate boxes, *f* indicate figures, *t* indicate tables and *np* indicate footnotes.

A

Access control, 411
Account hijacking
  defenses, 70–71
  impacts, 71
  risk rating, 71, 73*t*
  source, 70
  targets, 71
  vectors, 70
  vulnerabilities, 70
AccountManager class, 300–301
Account/service hijacking, 415
Action phase, 389, 393–394
Amazon Elastic Compute Cloud (Amazon EC2), 47, 49, 70
Amazon Web Services, 350
American Institute of CPAs® (AICPA), 458
Android Debug Bridge (ADB), 288
Android devices
  ADB, 288
  analysis methodology (*see* Evidence collection)
  AndroidManifest.xml file, 286
  app access and secret keys, 289
  digital forensics, 285, 288
  evidentiary data, 289
  Linux-specific security features, 286
  location information, 288–289
  mobile device, 285–286
  partitions, 286–288
  private browsing session information, 289
  rooting, 288
  smartphone usage behavior, 289
Android virtual machine, 343–344
Application integration, 222
Application service provider (ASP) model, 191
Approximate eigenvector algorithm, 114–115, 118–122
  decryption, 117*b*
  encryption, 116*b*
  Flatten function, 120–121
  homomorphic addition and multiplication operations, 117
  MPDec function, 116–117, 117*b*, 121–122
  public key generation, 116, 116*b*
  secret key generation, 115–116, 116*b*
  security parameters, 115*b*
Artifact, 178, 314–316
ASP model. *See* Application service provider (ASP) model
Assessment phase, 389
Asset management, 407
Attack-based risk assessment, 515
Attack taxonomies
  attack-centric taxonomies, 45
  botnets and malware taxonomies, 47
  CATRA (*see* Conceptual cloud attack taxonomy and risk assessment framework (CATRA))
  classifiers, 38–39
  cloud security challenges, 47
  countermeasure tools taxonomy, 45
  cyber attack taxonomies, 40–44, 41*t*
  DDoS attacks, 45–46, 49
  defense-centric taxonomies, 45
  network attacks, 41*t*, 45
  proactive measures, 45
  protocol vulnerability taxonomies, 46
  reactive measures, 45
  survey of, 41*t*
  Web Service attacks, 47
Auditing, 227–228
  compliance and, 458–459
  planning and scoping, 455–456
Australian government, e-Paper, 152
Australian Individual Healthcare Identifier (IHI), 152*np*
Australian Law Reform Commission (ALRC), 166*np*, 167–168
"Australian Privacy Principles" (APPs), 166–167
Authenticated authorization, 234
  actors, 238
  constrained level, 238–239
  less-constrained level, 239–240
  managers' selection (*see* Authorization Managers)
  principal level, 239
Authentication, 234, 372, 373*f*
Authorization granting ticket (AGT), 244, 244*f*
Authorization Managers
  amount of control, 241–242

Authorization Managers *(Continued)*
  CAM and SAM, 241
  implementation, 244–245, 245*f*
  key management, 242–243, 243*f*
Authorization ticket, 244, 245*f*

B

Backup strategy, 409
Binary translation, 131
Biometrics, 155
Bitcoin theft, 52–53
Box services, 357, 359*t*
  accounts data, 318–320
  analysis, 338–339, 374, 375*t*
  Android applications, 364–365
  authentication token, 372, 373*f*
  BoxSQLiteDB_[User ID], 317, 317*t*
  cache cleared state, 371
  external storage, 316–317
  imagecachedb, 317, 319*t*
  iOS application, 366
  LevelDB File, 317, 319*t*
  metadata artifacts, 378
  mID value, 373, 373*f*
  private storage, 314–316
  URL, 374
Bring your own device (BYOD), 58
British Broadcasting Corporation (BBC), 26–27
BSI-Standard100-3, 2008, 207
Business continuity management, 412

C

CATRA. *See* Conceptual cloud attack taxonomy
    and risk assessment framework (CATRA)
CertainLogic operators
  CertainTrust model, 470–471
  CSA STAR, 475–476
  FUSION operator, 472–475, 473*t*
  AND (∧) Operator, 471–472
CertainTrust model, 470–471
Client Authorization Manager (CAM), 240
Closest vector problem (CVP), 112–113
Cloud attacks
  broken authentication and session management, 50
  CATRA (*see* Conceptual cloud attack taxonomy
      and risk assessment framework (CATRA))
  cross-site request forgery, 51
  cross-site scripting, 50
  cross-VM attacks, 49
  cryptography, 51
  DDoS attacks, 49
  impact of, 59

injection flaws, 50
insecure direct object references, 50
malware vector and virtualization vulnerabilities,
    49–50
management console, 51
missing function level access control, 51
network attack surface, 51–52
network protocols, 51
nonvalidated redirects and forwards, 51
people, process and physical vulnerabilities,
    48–49
phishing, 50
security misconfiguration, 50
sensitive data exposure, 50
target, 58
taxonomies (*see* Attack taxonomies;
    Countermeasures)
threats (*see* Threats)
Web Services, 50
Cloud computing
  advantages and disadvantages, 450, 452
  Article 29 Working Party, 160
  auditing, 455–456, 458–459
  control and lack of transparency, 160
  data transfers, 163
  definition, 17–18
  definition by NIST, 401, 429
  digital forensics, 402, 403 (*see also* Digital
      forensics readiness)
  disadvantages, 402
  enterprise's investments/commitments, 451
  enterprise staffing, 450–451
  EU citizens' data, 165
  FHE (*see* Fully homomorphic encryption (FHE))
  France's data protection laws, 164
  goals of enterprise's strategy, 450
  Hong Kong (*see* Hong Kong, cybercrime)
  hypervisor isolation (*see* Hypervisors)
  identity and access management, 461
  implementation process, 452
  individual identity, 160–161, 161*f*
  information security, 402
  internet-based computing, 158–159
  network-based services, 158–159
  "one-stop-shop" enforcement system, 164
  online privacy rights, 163–164
  operation, 460–461
  PHE (*see* Partially homomorphic encryption
      (PHE))
  portability and interoperability, 459–460
  Privacy Act, 166
  regulatory and compliance requirements, 451
  service models, 401

Singapore (*see* Singapore, cybercrime)
streamlining and extending, 164
taxonomies (*see* Taxonomies)
threats, 414, 414–415 (*see also* Cloud
    vulnerabilities and threat assessment)
transition, 451
Cloud Computing Assessment (CCA).
    See Quantified security capabilities
Cloud consumer, 206
Cloud Controls Matrix (CCM), 458–459
Cloud data accountability
  data-generating tools, 172
  DPA, 171
  HIPAA, 171
  inhibitors, 171
  provenance (*see* Data provenance model;
    Provenance reconstruction)
Cloud infrastructures
  attacker goals, 497–498
  organizational/procedural aspects, 497
  physical environment layer, 497
  private cloud environment, 498, 498f
  social and human side, 497
  technical infrastructure layer, 497
Cloud integration, 221–222
Cloud migration
  auditing, 227–228
  cloud consumer, 206
  cloud integration, 221–222, 221f
  confidentiality, 218
  contract type, 216
  control and visibility, 211–212
  costs, 212, 213f
  CSP, 205
  data protection, 217
  detecting and preventing sensitive data, 210–211
  internet speed, 221
  interoperability, 220, 220t
  interoperability and portability, 212
  IT-Knowledge, 211
  IT-Systems and IT-Applications, 207
  latency, 219
  migration phase, 223f, 225–226
  operations phase, 223f, 226
  ownership, 216–217
  performance, 212–214
  planning phase, 223f, 224
  policy development, 209
  private files, 217
  protecting data, 211
  security, 219–220
  security and privacy, 210, 210f
  security policy, 208–209

small law office, 206–208, 207f
  territoriality principle, 218
  vendor lock-in, 214–215
Cloud Security Alliance® (CSA), 86, 383, 458–459,
  463, 466–467, 475, 479
Cloud service model characteristics, 401
Cloud Service Provider (CSP), 205, 384–387,
  402–403
  CSA, 86
  ENISA, 86
  FSI, 84
  MTCS, 88–89
  policy and regulatory framework, 85
  SME, 84
Cloud service users (CSUs), 384–387
Cloud storage services
  benefits, 348
  Box files (*see* Box services)
  business model, 347–348
  cloud computing environments (*see* Digital
    forensic models)
  Dropbox files (*see* Dropbox services)
  experiment design (*see* Smartphone devices)
  industry and academia, 348
  iOS file system, 362
  metadata, 371–372
  offline viewing, 357
  practitioner-accepted forensic tools,
    348–349
  SD memory card, 357–362
  SugarSync files (*see* SugarSync services)
  Syncplicity files (*see* Syncplicity services)
Cloud Track Back (CTB), 57
Cloud vulnerabilities and threat assessment
  abuse of cloud computing, 417
  account/service hijacking, 415
  data breaches, 415
  data loss, 415
  denial-of-service attacks, 416
  information confidentiality, integrity and
    availability, 414
  insecure interfaces and APIs, 416
  insufficient due diligence, 417
  malicious insiders, 416
  nontechnical threats, 414
  observation of Company A, 418–419, 418t
  shared technology issues, 417
Cloudy Internet of Things
  authenticated authorization (*see* Authenticated
    authorization)
  authentication-related tasks, 235–236
  authorization-related tasks, 236–237
  device constraints, 237–238

Cloudy Internet of Things *(Continued)*
  local *vs.* cloud-based systems, 232
  physical limitations, 233–234
  security objectives, 234–235
  usage scenario, 245–246
  web-of-things approach, 232
Cognitive psychology
  availability heuristic, 272–273, 277
  confirmation bias, 272, 277
  decision making and risks, 274, 277
  fast and slow systems, 273
  framing effect, 272
  optimism bias, 273
  password management tools, 273–274
Combined risk assessment, 515
Common Vulnerability Scoring System
    (CVSS), 390
Communication Privacy Management (CPM)
    Theory, 270–271
Communications and operations management,
    408–411
Compliance management, 412
Computational trust methods
  definition, 464
  security (*see* Security capabilities)
  tackle (*see* Tackling cloud security)
Computer emergency response teams, 40
Computer-Mediated Communication (CMC), 271
Computer Misuse Act, 28
Conceptual cloud attack taxonomy and risk
    assessment framework (CATRA)
  color coding, 60, 61*f*
  DDoS and account hijacking, 66–71
  defense dimension, 65–66, 66*f*
  impact dimension, 63–65, 65*f*
  source dimension, 60, 61*f*
  target dimension, 63, 64*f*
  vector dimension, 60–62, 62*f*
  vulnerability dimension, 62, 63*f*
Consensus Assessment Initiative Questionnaire
    (CAIQ)
  certainLogic operators, 475–476
  cloud security transparency mechanisms, 466
  formal analysis, 467
  quantified security capabilities, 480–485,
    481–484*t*
Constrained devices, 233
Countermeasures
  add-on mitigation, 143–144, 143*t*
  attack-centric taxonomies, 45
  backups, 58
  bandwidth assignment, 143, 143*t*
  cloud intrusion detection systems, 56
  cross-VM attacks, 55

  cryptography and network protocols, 56
  DDoS defense mechanisms, 57
  defense centric taxonomies, 45
  HVM malware, 57
  management console, 56
  network attack surface, 58
  people, process, and physical vulnerabilities, 55
  phishing, 57
  proactive measures, 45
  randomization, 143, 143*t*
  reactive measures, 45
  user/provider security responsibility, 54, 55*f*
  utilizing virtualization, 58
  Web services and applications, 55–56
Cross-border data disclosure, 151
Cryptography, 51
  and network protocols, 56
  vulnerabilities in, 51
Cyber attack taxonomies, 40–44, 41*t*

D

Dalvik Debug Monitor Server (DDMS)
    tool, 303
Dalvik Virtual Machine (Dalvik), 286
Data breaches, 415
Data integration, 222
Data loss, 415
Data Protection Act (DPA), 171
Data Protection Directive 95/46 EU, 162
Data provenance model, 182
  actions, 178–179
  artifact, 178–180
  context, 178–179
  entity, 178–179
  OPM, 180
  PROV-DM, 180
  SRE, 177
  time, 179
Data security, 199–200
Denial-of-service attacks, 416
Digital citizenship, 152
Digital forensic models
  Amazon Web Services, 350
  Apple iCloud environment, 350–351
  Biggs and Vidalis report, 352
  FTK Imager and Encase Enterprise, 350
  iPhone, 351
  MicroSystemation's XRY, 351–352
  Paraben's Device Seizure, 352
  pro-posing methods, 350
  RAPI tools, 352
  registry entries, 349–350
  Windows 7 personal computer, 351

Digital forensics, 285, 288, 290, 430.
  See also Mobile cloud forensics
Digital forensics readiness, 403
  data collection requirement, 421
  digital evidence collection, 420
  evidence-based case description, 423
  evidence collection requirement, 421
  evidence handling policy, 421
  formal investigation, 422
  implementation cost, 420
  ISO and NIST standards, 419
  legal review, evidence collection process, 423
  monitoring and auditing, 422
  observation of Company A, 423–425, 424*t*
  secure storage policy, 421
  sources of potential evidence, 420–421
  staff training, 422
Digital identity. *See also* Transaction identity
  APP 8 and 8.1, 167–169
  APPs, 166–167
  definition, 150
  Estonia, 153
  identification *vs.* identity, 156–157
  identifying information, 155
  internet-based computing (*see* Cloud computing)
  Privacy Act, 166–169
  Senate Report, 167–168
  transaction identity and other information,
      153, 154*f*
Distributed denial-of-service (DDOS) attack,
      60–62, 416
  countermeasure taxonomy, 45–46
  defense mechanisms, 57, 70–71
  Git revision control system, 49
  impacts, 71
  risk rating, 71, 72*t*
  source, 70
  targets, 71
  taxonomy, 45–46
  tool taxonomy, 45–46
  vectors, 70
  vulnerabilities, 70
Distributed Network Protocol (DNP3), 46
Dropbox services, 103, 357, 358*t*
  accounts data, 314
  analysis, 337–338, 374, 375*t*
  Android applications, 362–363
  external storage, 310–311
  iOS device, 363–364
  metadata artifacts, 377
  prefs-shared.db, 311, 311*t*
  private storage, 310
  [User ID]-db.db, 311, 312*t*
  [User ID]-notifications, 311, 314*t*

E

Eclipse Memory Analyzer tool, 339
Electronic commerce services, 410
El Gamal scheme, 107–109
Electronic Transactions Act (ETA) of Singapore,
      152–153
Enterprise risk management, 456–457
Entity, 178
Entrepot, 22, 22*np*
e-privacy Directive 2002/58/EC, 162*np*
Estonia, 153
European Data Protection Directive, 218
European Economic Area (EEA), 162–163
European Union (EU), 151, 162
Evernote
  accounts data, 332
  analysis, 341
  external storage, 328–329
  Google Play Store, 327
  private storage, 327–328
  user-[User ID] database, 329, 329*t*
Evidence collection
  accounts data, 299–301, 302*f*
  ADB application, 295–296
  APK files, 302–303
  bit-for-bit image, 291, 295
  chip-off technique, 293
  databases, 299
  DDMS tool, 303
  decompiling, 303–304
  device agnostic, 290
  external storage, 298–299
  forensic soundness principles, 290
  HPROF file, 303
  identify device and preserve evidence, 291–292
  live OS (*see* Live OS)
  mobile devices, 290
  OQL, 303
  physical collection, 293
  private storage, 296–298
  reporting and presentation, 304
  static and dynamic analysis, 301–302
  userdata partition, 292–293
External Authorization Manager (EAM), 244
External Client Authorization Manager (ECAM),
      242–243
External Server Authorization Manager (ESAM),
      242–243

F

Federal Information Security Management Act
      (FISMA), 86
Federal Risk and Authorization Management
      Program (FedRAMP), 86

FHE. *See* Fully homomorphic encryption (FHE)
Financial services industry (FSI), 84
Firewall, 502
Five-Phase-Model, 222, 223*f*
Flow-based access control, 504
Formal analysis, security capabilities
    PLTs, 469–470
    transforming security attributes, 467–469
Fully homomorphic encryption (FHE)
    approximate eigenvector algorithm, 114–122
    basic 2D lattice, 112*f*
    basic 3D lattice, 112*f*
    CVP, 112–113
    LWE problem, 113–114
    protection, utility and performance, 102, 102*f*
    SVP, 112–113

G

German Federal Association, 189
Git revision control system, 49
Google's ex-Site Reliability Engineer (SRE), 177
Governance
    and enterprise risk management, 456–457
    identity and access management, 461
    legal and electronic discovery, 457–458
    OECD (*see* Organisation for Economic Co-
        operation and Development (OECD))
    portability and interoperability, 459–460
    ROI (*see* Return on investment (ROI))
Gross Domestic Product (GDP), 22

H

Hardware-assisted virtualization, 131
Hardware-based virtual machine (HVM), 49–50, 57
Health Insurance Portability and Accountability
    Act (HIPAA), 171
Hex Workshop, 434
Homomorphic encryption, 122–124
    CryptDB, 122
    database encryption scheme, 104
    Dropbox, 103
    FHE (*see* Fully homomorphic encryption (FHE))
    Helios, 122
    history, 104–105, 105*t*
    Mega Limited, 103
    PHE (*see* Partially homomorphic encryption
        (PHE))
    protection, utility and performance, 102, 102*f*
    RSA encryption scheme, 104
Hong Kong, cybercrime
    business, 29
    computer-related crime, 18

criminal justice and legal systems, 24
cultural factors, 23
economy, 22–23
fighting technology-related crimes, 34
government recognization, 31
Internetwork, 18–19
investigating officer's jurisdiction, 33
KPMG International report, 20
Legislative Council, 30
mobile apps, 20–21
Nielsen smart phone report, 20
political structure, 23–24
UNITU 2012 report, 19
victims, 22
virtualization, 19–20
"Hotel-California" syndrome, 214–215
Human resources security management, 407
Human Trust Interface, 477–478
Hyperpersonal communication theory, 271, 277
Hypertext Transfer Protocol Secure (HTTPS), 106
Hypervisors. *See also* Virtualization
    cloud providers, 132*t*
    Domain0, 131–132, 135, 141, 144
    events, 133
    hypercalls, 133
    isolation-based attack surface, 138–140
    KVM (*see* Kernel-based Virtual Machine
        (KVM))
    Linux kernel module, 133–134, 133*f*
    memory-mapped I/O (MMIO), 134
    network-based attacks, in clouds (*see* Network-
        based attacks)
    networking in clouds (*see* Networking)
    programmed I/O (PIO), 134
    vCloud (*see* vCloud)
    Xen (*see* Xen)

I

IaaS. *See* Infrastructure-as-a-Service (IaaS)
Identification phase, 156–157, 389, 391–392, 391*t*
Identity, 156–157. *See also* Digital identity
Identity management, 222
Incident handling model
    cloud computing, 384–386
    CSA report, 383
    CSP and CSU, 386–387
    NIST, 383
    ownCloud (*see* ownCloud server)
    snapshot, 387–389, 388*f*
Infocomm Development Authority (IDA), 25–26
Information exchange, 410
Information security incident management, 412

Information security management system
(ISMS), 209
Infrastructure-as-a-Service (IaaS), 17, 54, 386,
401, 429
International Organization for Standardization
(ISO), 207
Interoperability, 220, 220*t*
Intrusion detection/prevention systems (IDS/IPS/
IDPS), 56, 195–196
iOS app-based environments, 432
network traffic, 444
u1.db login_info_table, 443–444, 444*f*
u1.db nodes_table information, 443–444, 444*f*
U1Files unofficial Ubuntu One client app, 443
version_table, 443–444, 444*f*
ISO 27002 security standard, 404–406

K

Kerckhoffs's principle, 242
Kernel-based Virtual Machine (KVM), 131, 132*t*,
133–135, 133*f*, 136*f*, 138–139, 144
KM as a service (KMaaS), 254–255
Knowledge as a service (KaaS), 254–255, 254*f*
Knowledge management (KM)
activities and allocations, 257*f*, 258–259, 260*b*
business environment, 251
cloud computing, 250*f*, 252–253, 255–256
definitions, 250
KaaS and KMaaS, 254–255, 254*f*
organizations and groups, 254*f*, 256–258, 260*b*
processes, 250, 250*f*
scalability and privacy (*see* Scalability and
privacy modeling)
security and privacy, 252
technology, 251–252
Knowledge organization (KO), 256–258

L

Latency, 219
Law office, 206, 207*f*
Learning with errors (LWE) problem, 113–114
Lightweight security, 238
Live OS
ADB application, 295–296
bit-for-bit images, 295
bootloader, setup, 294
collection method, 293
"md5sum" and "sha1sum" tools, 296
in memory, 294–295
selection, 293
Living systems theory (LST), 256

M

Mac OS X app-based environments, 432
directories, 442
memory, 442, 443*f*
network traffic, 443, 443*t*
synced filenames, 442, 443*f*
username, 442, 442*f*
Malicious insiders, 416
Malicious/mobile code, 409
Managed security monitoring (MSM), 193
Managed security service provider (MSSP), 193
Managed security services (MSS), 188
Media handling, 410
Mega Limited, 103, 123
Migration phase, 223*f*, 225–226
Migration security concept (MSC), 225
Mobile cloud forensics
Android apps (*see* Box; Dropbox services;
Evernote; OneDrive; OneNote; ownCloud;
Universal password manager (UPM))
Android virtual machine, 343–344
Nexus 4, 342–343
Model-based risk assessment, 501*f*, 514–515
Monitoring phase, 389, 393–394
MTCS model. *See* Multitiered cloud security
(MTCS) model
Multitiered cloud security (MTCS) model
awareness, 84
benefits, 88–89
certification, 85, 92
classification, 84
CSA, 86
CSP, 83–84, 86
deployment, 94, 96
design considerations, 87–88
FedRAMP, 86
harmonization, 94–95, 94–96*f*
hypervisors and virtual machines, 83
ISO27001, 87
Launchpad Europe, 83–84
multi-pronged holistic approach, 84, 85*f*
policy and regulatory framework, 85
SAS70, 86
self-disclosure, 92, 93*f*
Service Level Agreement, 96
standards, 85–86, 89–92, 89–91*f*
status, 92–93
technology, 85

N

National Institute of Standards and Technology
(NIST), 383, 401, 429

Network-based attacks, 41t, 45
  address deanonymization, 140t, 142
  coresidence detection, 140t, 141
  covert channels, 140t, 141
  performance attacks, 140t
  sequence of, 142f
  side channels, 140t
Network components
  administrator access, 507–508
  firewalls, 508–509, 509–510f
  FTP daemon on port 20, 506, 507f
  generic service access, 507, 507f
  routers and routing, 498f, 501f, 505–506, 506f
  switch $vs.$ hub, 508, 508f
  VPNs, 510–511, 510f
Networking
  capabilities, 129
  packet scheduling, 135
  social, 300
  traffic shaping, 136–138
Network integration, 222
Network intrusion detection (IDS), 197
Network intrusion prevention systems
    (IPS), 197
Network security, 196–197
Network security management, 409–410
Network service scanning, 197
Nexus 4, 342–343
Nontechnical threats, 414

O

OAuth, 338
Object Query Language (OQL), 303
OneDrive
  accounts data, 324, 324t
  analysis, 339–340
  auto_upload.db, 322–324, 323t
  external storage, 321–322, 322t
  manual_upload_db, 322–324, 324t
  metadata, 322–324, 322t
  private storage, 321
OneNote
  accounts data, 334–336
  analysis, 341–342
  external storage, 333
  hierarchy.sdf, 333, 335t
  private storage, 332–333
  SPSQLStore.sdf, 333, 333t
"One-stop-shop" enforcement system, 164
On-premise security systems, 189–191
Open Provenance Model (OPM), 180
Operations phase, 223f, 226

Organisation for Economic Co-operation and
    Development (OECD)
  boards questions, 450–452
  corporate governance, 449
  decision-making process, 449
OWASP risk rating, 195
ownCloud server
  action phase, 393–394
  analysis, 340–341
  assessment, forensic collection, and analysis,
    392–393, 392–393f
  attack setting, 389–390
  evaluation phase, 394–395
  external storage, 325
  filelist database, 325, 326t
  forensic presentation, 394–395
  forensic readiness, 390–391
  Google Play Store, 324
  identification, 391–392, 391t
  instant_upload, 325, 327t
  monitoring, 393–394
  options, 389
  preparation phase, 390–391
  private storage, 325
  recovery phase, 394
  SIEM system, 389
Owner Client Authorization Manager
    (OCAM), 243
Owner Key (OK), 243
Owner Server Authorization Manager
    (OSAM), 243

P

PaaS. See Platform as a Service (PaaS)
Packet scheduling, 135
Paillier cryptosystem, 109–110
Paravirtualization, 131–133
Partially homomorphic encryption (PHE)
  El Gamal decryption algorithm, 107b
  El Gamal encryption algorithm, 107b
  El Gamal key generation algorithm, 107b
  Paillier cryptosystem decryption
      algorithm, 110b
  Paillier cryptosystem encryption algorithm, 110b
  Paillier cryptosystem key generation
      algorithm, 109b
  protection, utility and performance,
      102, 102f
  public key encryption, 106
People Action Party (PAP), 27
People's Republic of China (PRC), 22
Phishing, 50, 57

Physical and environmental security, 408
Planning phase, 223f, 224
Platform as a Service (PaaS), 17, 54, 386, 401, 429
Preparation phase, 390–391
The Privacy Amendment (Enhancing Privacy
  Protection) Act 2012, 166, 166np
Privacy homomorphisms, 104
Private IaaS provider
  case study organization, 404–405
  cloud security threats, 404, 404 (see also Cloud
    vulnerabilities and threat assessment)
  forensic readiness process, 404 (see also Digital
    forensics readiness)
  information security management standards,
    403–404
  security controls, 404, 404 (see also Security
    analysis methodology)
Propositional Logic Terms (PLTs), 469–470
Protection motivation theory, 275–276, 278
PROV Data Model (PROV-DM), 180
Provenance reconstruction, 172–173, 180, 181f
  active monitoring strategies, 176
  AI planning techniques, 180, 183
  cloud data accountability, 174
  content similarity analysis, 174
  domain-specific rules, 181
  element miner, 180–181
  hypothesis generation phase, 174, 175f
  jigsaw puzzle analogy, 176
  logging mechanisms, 182
  model-specific rules, 181
  Python script, 175
  rule engine, 181
  semantic similarity, 175
  UUID, 176
  workflow/process driven environment, 175
Psychology
  cognitive (see Cognitive psychology)
  CPM theory, 270–271, 276
  knowing-doing gap, 278–279
  protection motivation theory, 275–276, 278
  social learning theory, 275, 278

Q

Quantified security capabilities
  accreditors, 485, 488t
  CAIQ assessment, 485–490, 486t
  Cloud "D" vs. Cloud "M,", 490, 490t
  customized case, 480–485, 483–484t
  expert assessment, 485, 487t, 489t
  practical case, 480, 481–482t
Quantitative Policy Trees (QPTs), 466

R

Rate limiting, 143t, 144
Rational choice theory, 275
Real-time configuration and alerting, 197
Recovery phase, 389, 394
Recurring costs, 454
RESeED, 124
Return on investment (ROI), 452
  calculation, 453
  intangible benefit, 453–454
  reconfiguration/reprovisioning, 455
  recurring costs, 454
  tangible benefits, 453
  termination costs, 454
  upfront/initial costs, 454
Risk assessment
  attack-based, 515
  combined, 515
  model-based, 501f, 514–515
RoomDatacenter, 498–499
RoomInternal, 498–499

S

SaaS. See Software-as-a-Service (SaaS)
Samsung Galaxy S3, 344
SCADA systems, 59, 65
Scalability and privacy modeling, 263f
  hospital and bags factory, 259f, 264b
  In-Business and Out-Business, 260
  In-KO and Out-KO, 260, 261f
  mechanisms, 263
  options, 262
  public and private cloud, 262f, 263
Script kiddies, 54
Security, 219–220. See also Psychology
  assurance, 463
  policy, 208–209
Security analysis methodology
  access control, 411
  acquisition, development, and maintenance, 411
  asset management, 407
  business continuity management, 412
  communications and operations management,
    408–411
  compliance management, 412
  human resources security management, 407
  information and data, business assets, 405
  information security incident management, 412
  information security organization, 406–407
  observation of Company A, 412–414, 413t
  physical and environmental security, 408
  security policy establishment, 406

Security analysis methodology *(Continued)*
  security requirements, 405
  27002 security standard, 405–406
Security as a service (SecaaS)
  ASP model, 191
  business model, 189
  categories, 194*t*
  classification of, 190*t*, 200–201
  data security, 199–200
  definition, 188
  German Federal Association, 189
  managed security services, 192–193
  market-oriented taxonomy, 189
  network security, 196–197
  vs. on-premises, 192*t*
  on-premise security, 189–192
  outsourcing models, 191
  security service delivery models, 190*f*
  system security, 194–196, 195*t*
  web security, 197–199, 199*f*
Security, Assurance and Trust Registry (STAR)
  certainLogic operators, 475
  cloud security transparency mechanisms, 466
  formal analysis, 467
  quantified security capabilities, 480–485,
    483–484*t*
  security assurance, 463, 466
Security capabilities
  CCA (*see* Cloud Computing Assessment (CCA))
  CertainLogic operators (*see* CertainLogic
    operators)
  formal analysis (*see* Formal analysis, security
    capabilities)
  quantified (*see* Quantified security capabilities)
  visualizations, 477–479, 477–478*f*
Security Information and Event Management
  (SIEM) system, 389
Security service delivery models, 190*f*
Self-efficacy factor, 276
Semantic similarity, 175
Server Authorization Manager (SAM), 240
Service Level Agreement (SLA), 189–191, 215
Service Level Agreement (SLA) validation
  framework, 465
Service Organization Control (SOC) reports, 458
Service Oriented Architecture, 47
Shortest vector problem (SVP), 112–113
Simple Object Access Protocol (SOAP) attacks,
  47, 50
Singapore, cybercrime
  ATM, 21
  business, 29
  computer-related crime, 18

criminal justice and legal systems, 28
cultural factors, 26–27
democratic process, 31–32
economy, 25–26
fighting technology-related crimes, 34
Internetwork, 18–19
investigating officer's jurisdiction, 33
KPMG International report, 20
mobile data and Wi-Fi, 32
Nielsen smart phone report, 20
PAP, 32
political structure, 27
Smart Nation plan, 31–32
UNITU 2012 report, 19
victims, 22
virtualization, 19–20
WebSynergies, 21
WhatsApp, 21
Singapore Electronic Transactions Act (ETA),
  152–153
Situational Crime Prevention Theory, 395
SkyDrive. *See* OneDrive
SMALI source files, 300
Small/medium-sized enterprises (SME), 84, 205
Smartphone devices
  Apple iPhone 3G, 353–354
  cloud storage application, 355–357
  dataset, 355–357, 355*t*
  features, 353–354, 354*t*
  HTC Desire, 353–354, 354*t*, 356
  hypothesis, 353, 374
  stages, 353
  UFED, 353–354
Social learning theory, 275, 278
Socio-technical system. *See* TRE$_S$PASS project
Software-as-a-Service (SaaS), 17, 50–51, 54, 58,
  385–386, 401, 429
Star-Interface, 477–478
Storage as a Service (STaaS)
  forensic research (*see* Ubuntu One, STaaS
    forensic research)
  service providers, 429
Structured query language (SQL) injection, 39, 50, 62
SugarSync services, 357, 360*t*
  analysis, 374, 375*t*
  Android applications, 366–367
  iOS application, 367
Syncplicity services, 357, 361*t*
  active power state, 371, 372*f*
  analysis, 374, 375*t*
  Android applications, 368–369
  iOS applications, 370
  metadata artifacts, 379

Syrian Electronic Army (SEA), 53
System monitoring, 411
System security, 194–196, 195*t*

T

Tackling cloud security
    cloud security quantification methods, 466
    cloud security transparency mechanisms, 466
    e-commerce and P2P networks, 465
    operators, 465
    private virtual infrastructure, 465–466
    SLA validation framework, 465
    TPM, 465–466
Taxonomies
    attack taxonomies (*see* Attack taxonomies)
    characteristics, 38
Termination costs, 454
Third-party service delivery management, 409
Threats, 52*t*
    corporate and political espionage, 53
    financial motivation, 52–53
    of insiders, 53–54
    script kiddies, 54
    SEA, 53
Traffic shaping, 136–138
Transaction identity
    authentication of, 154
    identifying information, 153–155
    individual and digital identity relationship, 155*f*
    matching information, 156
    matching process, 156*f*
    verification of, 154
TRE_SPASS project
    access policies, tuple spaces, 502–503
    actor processes, 511, 512*f*
    attack identification, 512–514
    attack navigator, 499
    building infrastructure, 501
    cloud infrastructures (*see* Cloud infrastructures)
    firewall, 502
    goal, 495–496, 499–500
    high-level model, 498*f*, 501*f*, 503
    infrastructure locations, 498*f*, 500
    location-bound information, 502
    low-level model, 498*f*, 504–505
    middle-level model, 503–504
    network communication, 502
    network components (*see* Network components)
    non-process attributes, 511, 512*f*
    physical infrastructure, 500, 501*f*
    process library, 512
    risk assessment (*see* Risk assessment)
    risk assessment frameworks, 500
    security-relevant control points, 496
    stores state information, 502–503
    virtual connectivity *vs.* physical connectivity, 500
Trusted Platform Module (TPM) virtualization,
        465–466
T-Viz visualization, 478–479, 478*f*

U

Ubuntu One, STaaS forensic research
    experiment environments, 432
    experiment stages, 431–432
    forensic framework, 430–431
    iOS app-based investigation experiment setup,
        432–433, 443–444
    live data acquisition, 434
    Mac OS X app-based investigation experiment
        setup, 432–433, 442–443
    method, 431
    nonvolatile data remnants analysis, 434
    web browser investigation experiments setup,
        433*f*, 432 (*see also* Windows browser based
        environments)
    Windows app-based investigation experiment
        setup, 432–433, 433*f*
    Windows browser based environments, 432
United Nation Telecommunication Union (UNITU)
    report, 19
United States and Asia Pacific Economic
    Cooperation (APEC), 151
United States' Federal Trade Commission, 165*np*
Universal Forensic Extraction Device (UFED), 352
Universally unique identifier (UUID), 176
Universal Password Manager (UPM)
    accounts data, 337
    analysis, 342
    databases, 337
    external storage, 337
    private storage, 336–337
Upfront/initial costs, 454

V

vCloud, 131, 132*t*
Virtualization, 401–402
Virtual machine monitors (VMMs).
    see Hypervisors
Virtual machines (VMs), 49, 55, 401–402
Virtual private networks (VPNs), 45, 56
VLANs, 510–511, 510*f*
VMDK file, 434
VM's VMEM file, 434
VMware, 131

W

Web browser, 50–51, 57
Web security, 197–199, 199*f*
Web Services, 47, 50, 55–56
Windows app-based environments, 432
    event logs, 439–440, 440*f*
    file system, 439
    memory, 438–439, 439*f*
    network traffic, 441, 442*t*
    registry, 440–441, 441*f*

Windows browser based environments, 432
    browser cache and history, 436–437, 437*f*
    memory, 434–435, 435–436*f*
    network traffic, 437–438, 438*t*
    registry, 437, 438*f*

X

Xen, 130–131, 132*f*, 132*t*, 133–135, 137–139, 137*f*,
    143–144
XML Signature Element Wrapping attack, 50

Printed in the United States
By Bookmasters